Romantic Texts and Contexts

Romantic Texts and Contexts

Donald H. Reiman

University of Missouri Press
Columbia, 1987

Copyright © 1987 by
The Curators of the University of Missouri
University of Missouri Press, Columbia, Missouri 65211
Printed and bound in the United States of America
All rights reserved

Library of Congress Cataloging-in-Publication Data

Reiman, Donald H.

Romantic texts and contexts.

Includes index.
1. English literature—19th century—History and
criticism. 2. Romanticism—England. 3. Poetry—
Editing. I. Title.
PR457.R45   1987   820'.9'145   87-6030
ISBN 0-8262-0649-2 (alk. paper)

∞™ This paper meets the minimum requirements of
the American National Standard for Permanence of Paper
for Printed Library Materials, Z39.48, 1984.

For Jan

My dear, dear Sister! . . .
              thy mind
Shall be a mansion for all lovely forms,
Thy memory be as a dwelling-place
For all sweet sounds and harmonies.

and Hal

—He who, though thus endued as with a sense
And faculty for storm and turbulence,
Is yet a Soul whose master-bias leans
To homefelt pleasures and to gentle scenes.

In our day the literary researcher may try to make his material seem as remote from the layman as are the arcana of the physicist. If a poem can be read by any educated man, what sort of scholarship does it require?

—Allan H. Gilbert,
Dante and His Comedy

I am persuaded that the only kind of education that endures is self-education and that the function of the teacher is to invite—or better yet, to incite—students to address themselves to questions.

—Royal A. Gettmann,
The Rime of the Ancient Mariner: A Handbook

Preface

Henry W. Reiman and Mildred A. Pearce Reiman, my parents, were both students and high-school teachers of history, and history was my first love. That interest was stimulated during my early years by Franklin D. Roosevelt's third-term presidential campaign against Wendell Willkie and by America's entry into the Second World War. As a schoolboy, my avocations were following the progress of that war and reading the military history of the American Civil War. These formative influences unquestionably helped to shape the way I approach any intellectual problem. I believe that to understand an idea—or to understand any *advocate* of an idea—one must trace its history, or his or her biography, back to the roots. (Should those who disagree with my conclusions attempt to discredit them by pointing to the historical bias that grows out of my particular, delimiting experience, they would merely be supporting the validity of my premise.)

The biographical facts revealed and the biases confessed in the course of this volume are not meant to be merely personal, but to exemplify the way that particular circumstances shape the attitudes and perspectives of any critic—or any artist. My scholarly and critical writings on the English Romantics have subjected the lives and backgrounds of the writers to such scrutiny, and I see no reason why my own standpoint—or those of other critics—should be exempt from it. There are, doubtless, many relevant facts and attitudes not mentioned in the Introduction, headnotes, or Afterword. (This work is, after all, literary scholarship and criticism—not autobiography.) This survey of vital issues involving the study and teaching of the British Romantics during the past quarter-century adumbrates a program of scholarly criticism that is practical, accessible, and democratic as an alternative to systems that are theoretical, esoteric, and elitist.

For help in formulating ideals of scholarly criticism, I am grateful not only to my parents but also to my teachers, from Miss Hoon—who in her second-grade class recited Shelley's image of the moon from "The Cloud" ("That orbed maiden, with white fire laden / Whom mortals call the moon") so memorably that her recitation remains with me to this day—through my high-school and college English teachers, who nurtured my love for literature (but only one of whom, Lowell W. Coolidge, is alive to receive my thanks), to Royal A. Gettmann, Gwynne Blakemore Evans,

Robert W. Rogers, Jack Stillinger, and others at Illinois who polished my skills and fostered my academic career.

For love, comfort, and assistance of all possible kinds with the various parts of this work, I am grateful to Mary Warner Reiman, Sharon B. Powers, and Hélène Dworzan (Reiman), and for emotional support of a unique kind, to Laurel E. Reiman.

For direct help with the scholarly criticism republished in this volume, thanks are due to those whose names are mentioned in the headnotes and footnotes and to colleagues in English departments and libraries all over this country, Canada, the United Kingdom, and Italy who have aided me with various specific problems since the late 1950s. Most recently, for advice in selecting, arranging, and introducing these papers for republication, I am grateful to Hélène Dworzan (Reiman), Doucet Devin Fischer, David C. Greetham, Paul Magnuson, William Keach, and E. B. Murray. For permission to reprint the following copyrighted material, I thank the editors and the holders of copyrights where the following publications first appeared: "Editing Shelley," in *Editing Texts of the Romantic Period* (Toronto: A. M. Hakkert, 1972); review of L. J. Zillman, *Shelley's "Prometheus Unbound": The Text and the Drafts,* in *JEGP* 68 (1969): 539–43; review of *The Complete Poetical Works of Percy Bysshe Shelley,* ed. Neville Rogers, vol. 1, in *JEGP* 73 (1974): 250–60; review of Robert Browning, *Complete Poetical Works,* ed. Roma A. King, Jr., vols. 3–4, in *Victorian Poetry* 12 (1974): 86–96; "Coleridge as Prophet of Property," in *SiR* 18 (1979): 141–50; review of Coleridge, *Biographia Literaria,* ed. J. Engell and W. J. Bate, in *RPP* 8 (1984): 39–44; "The Four Ages of Editing and the English Romantics," in *TEXT* 1 (1984): 231–55; "Romantic Bards and Historical Editors," in *SiR* 21 (1982): 477–96; review of Wordsworth, *Benjamin the Waggoner,* ed. Paul Betz, and *The Prelude,* ed. J. Wordsworth, M. H. Abrams, and S. Gill, in *SiR* 21 (1982): 502–9; review of Byron, *Complete Poetical Works,* ed. Jerome J. McGann, vols. 1–3, in *KSMB* 34 (1983): 66–72; "Poetry of Familiarity: Wordsworth, Dorothy, and Mary Hutchinson," in *The Evidence of the Imagination,* ed. Donald H. Reiman, Michael C. Jaye, and Betty T. Bennett (New York: New York University Press, 1978), pp. 142–77; "The Beauty of Buttermere as Fact and Romantic Symbol," in *Criticism* 26 (1984): 139–70; "Thematic Unity in Lamb's Familiar Essays," in *JEGP* 64 (1965): 470–78; "Shelley as Agrarian Reactionary," in *KSMB* 30 (1979): 5–15; "Roman Scenes in *Prometheus Unbound,* III.iv," in *PQ* 46 (1967): 69–78; "Shelley's 'The Triumph of Life': The Biographical Problem," in *PMLA* 78 (1963): 536–50; "Keats and the Humanistic Paradox: Mythological History in *Lamia,*" in *SEL* 11 (1971): 659–69; "*Don Juan* in Epic

Context," in *SiR* 16 (1977): 587–94; "Wordsworth, Shelley, and the Romantic Inheritance," in *RPP* 5, 1 (December 1981): 1–22.

This book is dedicated to Janet Ruth Reiman Laise and William Harold Laise, just for being a wonderful sister and brother and exemplary human beings.

D. H. R.
Bronx, N.Y.
June 1987

Abbreviations

BJ	*Byron Journal*
BNYPL	*Bulletin of the New York Public Library*
CE	*College English*
CLB	*Charles Lamb Bulletin*
DNB	*Dictionary of National Biography*
ELH	*ELH: A Journal of English Literary History*
ELN	*English Language Notes*
JEGP	*Journal of English and Germanic Philology*
K-SJ	*Keats-Shelley Journal*
KSMB	*Keats-Shelley Memorial Bulletin*
MLA	*Modern Language Association of America*
MLN	*Modern Language Notes*
MLQ	*Modern Language Quarterly*
MLR	*Modern Language Review*
MP	*Modern Philology*
PMLA	*PMLA: Publications of the Modern Language Association of America*
PQ	*Philological Quarterly*
RES	*Review of English Studies*
RPP	*Romanticism Past and Present*
SAQ	*South Atlantic Quarterly*
SB	*Studies in Bibliography*
SEL	*Studies in English Literature*
SiR	*Studies in Romanticism*
SP	*Studies in Philology*
WC	*The Wordsworth Circle*

Contents

Preface, vii
List of Abbreviations, x
Introduction, 1

Part One: Romantic Texts
1. Editing Shelley, 17
2. Zillman's *Prometheus Unbound*, 33
3. Rogers's Oxford Shelley, 41
4. The Ohio Browning, 55
5. The Bollingen Coleridge, 69
6. The Four Ages of Editing and the English Romantics, 85
7. Romantic Bards and Historical Editors, 109
8. The Cornell Wordsworth and the Norton *Prelude*, 130
9. The Oxford Byron, 156
10. "Versioning": The Presentation of Multiple Texts, 167

Part Two: Romantic Contexts
11. Poetry of Familiarity: Wordsworth, Dorothy, and Mary Hutchinson, 183
12. The Beauty of Buttermere as Fact and Romantic Symbol, 216
13. Thematic Unity in Lamb's Familiar Essays, 248
14. Shelley as Agrarian Reactionary, 260
15. Roman Scenes in *Prometheus Unbound* III.iv., 275
16. Shelley's "The Triumph of Life": The Biographical Problem, 289
17. Keats and the Humanistic Paradox: Mythological History in *Lamia*, 321
18. *Don Juan* in Epic Context, 334
19. Wordsworth, Shelley, and the Romantic Inheritance, 344

Afterword, 368
Index, 377

Introduction

Collections of scholarly and critical essays on literature have at best a mixed record, and anyone who brings together a selection of earlier publications (with a few new ones) should tell librarians and teachers why such a volume deserves shelf-room. From my hundred-odd articles, reviews, and lectures of the past twenty-five years, I have selected those that my colleagues have found particularly useful—that made a distinctive contribution to their subjects at the time of their first publication in specialized journals or collective volumes of limited circulation and that, after due reflection, seem to merit the attention of new generations of students and teachers. To these I have added an expanded version of a short paper delivered at a recent convention of the Modern Language Association of America and two reports written for the Center for Scholarly Editions (heretofore circulated only among textual scholars involved in CSE and the project under review) that clarify my ideas on editing.

These studies have a collective value exceeding their individual merits. Representing a wide range of techniques and approaches to common textual and contextual problems, they show students and younger scholar-critics how to grapple with complex research situations and critical cruxes; their very diversity suggests that scholar-critics who focus their attention on the authors and works being studied, rather than on an ideology or methodology, can write about a variety of literary works without homogenizing them to the point where it is difficult to tell whether the work being examined is a seventeenth-century epic, a nineteenth-century lyric, or a twentieth-century anti-fiction. All these papers do, however, share one perspective: that of a scholar-critic involved in analyzing literature through the use of primary sources, who tries to take into account the textual and biographical documents that reveal the author's intention, not just at some single point (when the first edition appeared, or when the author last revised the work), but throughout the course of its conception, birth, and development. Thus, the clarification—or, sometimes, the growing ambiguity—of the author's intention provides one of the contexts that I take into consideration while unveiling the meaning of the work of art and, sometimes, the psyche of its author.

Beyond trying to include only materials of lasting value that illustrate a variety of problems and solutions, I have selected papers that cohere around a unified period—English Romantic literature—and those that grapple with major figures and pervasive issues. Among my essays *not* reprinted here are contributions to *Shelley and his Circle,* which accompany the detailed discussions of the manuscripts in The Carl H. Pforzheimer Library—now The Carl H. Pforzheimer Shelley and His Circle Collection of The New York Public Library—to which the essays pertain. I omitted "Structure, Symbol, and Theme in 'Lines written among the Euganean Hills,'" originally published in *PMLA* (1961), because it has been reprinted in the widely available student's edition *Shelley's Poetry and Prose,* which I edited with the help of Sharon B. Powers.[1] Excluded also are all critical essays on subjects outside the Romantic period, among them papers on Chaucer, Shakespeare, Cowper, Henry James, and A. R. Ammons, and studies of such lesser figures as Leigh Hunt and Edward John Trelawny that might otherwise merit reissue. In short, I have included only those items for which the reprinting can be justified by standards of general utility that I would gladly see other scholars and critics apply to the republication of their writings.

Finally, I have refrained from reissuing, or publishing for the first time, my lectures, reviews, and controversial letters that center on the merits of poststructuralist criticism. Now that those on all sides have stated their cases, I shall heed the counsel of Gamaliel: insofar as this teaching "be of men," deriving its popularity simply from novelty or from its advocates' political power in the academy, "it will come to nought"; but whatever has the higher sanctions of good sense and usefulness for the study of literature cannot be overthrown. So I shall merely state the best case I can for the textual and historical scholarship that I have found congenial.

I

The title *Romantic Texts and Contexts* pinpoints the subjects of the two main sections of the volume. Since I include no examples of my editing, the first part inevitably seems more theoretical than the second. But my penchant has always been to study the particular case and extrapolate from that, not a generalization applicable to all literary works, but a conclusion or lesson to be considered in relation to other specific situations where it may apply. The papers on both editorial and literary matters move from ascertainable facts to a wider understanding of the significance of those facts, initially ferreting out new evidence about a work or a situation and then integrating the new material with what had previously been known, under a more substantially supported hypothesis.

1. A Norton Critical Edition (New York and London: W. W. Norton, 1977).

Introduction

The subject of originality has been crudely bludgeoned in recent years both by those whose claim to have it exhibits a fear of deprivation and by those who deny its existence because it exceeds their personal expectations. I have never been troubled about this particular matter; I would no more expect to create a civilization de novo than I would fear being unable to see and say something new on almost any subject to which I decided to give diligent attention. By "new," I do *not* mean something that nobody else ever thought of, but something that is not in the discussions of the subject to which I have access. Most people cannot aspire to be a Copernicus, Newton, Marx, Freud, or Einstein and provide a whole society with new ways of evaluating their place in the universe. Yet many lesser thinkers are original in articulating and bringing forward concepts and taxonomies relevant to the cultural and intellectual developments of their times. Many more who can claim no originality in relation to the age can contribute or revive concepts needed at a particular time in their nations, disciplines, institutions, or classrooms, thereby exhibiting the originality of students who struggle through to personal epiphanies, guided by earlier mastery of a portion of their subject, or of teachers who, in similar moments of éclaircissement, discover how to reach whole classes at once. For a specialist who has mastered the primary texts and the secondary commentaries in his field—the manuscripts and the first editions, as well as principal secondary discussions of those texts—slightly larger claims to originality may be possible. When such a scholar-critic has an idea, he or she, aware of what has previously been said on the subject, is able to recognize whether the thought is both sound (i.e., in accord with the overall evidence) and novel, so far as the secondary studies of the time and place are concerned. The originality claimed for the papers here collected is of this last type. They provide sound and unhackneyed ideas and facts and illustrate how these can be developed and evaluated by students, teachers, and scholars who study a particular period of English literature in the late twentieth century.

II

To illustrate fully the principles underlying this book, "Part One: Romantic Texts" ought to contain a major example of my own editing to show a positive ideal against which I developed my critical reviews and papers on the history of editing. But none of my editorial work has appeared in periodicals, and it seemed wasteful to reprint the material (already most easily available to scholars and students of the period) in the Shelley section of *The Norton Anthology of English Literature*, the Norton Critical Edition of

Shelley's Poetry and Prose, *Shelley's "The Triumph of Life": A Critical Study, Based on a Text Newly Edited from the Bodleian Manuscript*, volumes 5–8 of *Shelley and his Circle*, the Shelley volumes in *Manuscripts of the Younger Romantics*, and the first volume of *The Bodleian Shelley Manuscripts*. Many of these editions are addressed to special audiences or edit particular documents, and are not critical editions comparable to those that have been the subjects of most of the reviews I reprint. Too many "critical editions" have been attempted, I believe—and have even been billed as "definitive" editions—before the basic groundwork had been established by locating and studying in detail all the underlying authorities. Much of my editorial work has involved the study of primary documents that will serve the editors of standard editions in the future. Had this basic research been done earlier by someone else, I might have been able to undertake the kinds of critical editions that I have, instead, reviewed with less than unqualified enthusiasm. This scholarly reality explains why, in at least two reviews, I praise the capabilities of the editors more highly than I do their editions: the materials that would have made possible the kind of definitive editions for which they strove were just not available to them. Another reason may be that I have developed my own professional deformation, from which I argue in the final paper in Part One that the presentation of multiple texts through "versioning" instead of "editing," as that enterprise has come to be defined, may prove to be the most useful fruit of textual criticism in our time.

The reviews and essays reprinted in Part One are arranged *almost* in the chronological order in which they were written; I place "Editing Shelley" first, however, because it provides an overview of the work I've been doing seven hours a day for over twenty-one years at The Carl H. Pforzheimer Library (and am now continuing, under the same auspices, at The New York Public Library). It thus tells readers who I am and—to use a colloquialism that is too useful not to survive in standard English—where I'm coming from. "Romantic Texts" takes readers on a historical tour of the issues and some of the personalities in textual scholarship over the past half-century. Since all scholarship is cumulative, with new work gradually absorbing the contributions of past scholars and going beyond them, the continuing interest in some of these pieces will, inevitably, be primarily historical. The first three, on the editing of Shelley and other Romantics in the 1960s, will (I devoutly hope) seem to readers two decades hence like reports of imaginary monsters or accounts of nightmares. The situations they describe were, however, too true when I began "editing Shelley." Due, in part, to reviews that candidly exposed the shortcomings of some egregious editions of Shelley, editors of the Romantics have been encouraged to study the issues of modern textual criticism and to discover the values, as well as the pitfalls, of the several competing schools of editing that I discuss in "The Four Ages of Editing and the English Romantics" and "Romantic Bards and Historical Editors."

Mirroring the progress in the overall standards of editing the Romantics, the textual reviews shift from critiques of editions based on erroneous principles (Rogers and Zillman) to the analysis of an edition with sound editorial premises that began publication before anyone had given sufficient thought to its plan of presentation ("The Oxford Byron"). Typographical and factual errors are always with us, as I know to my own chagrin, but spending enough time to perfect *most* of the details—or, lacking that, dividing the work and then carefully monitoring the quality of the contributions by various sub-editors, as the general editors of The Collected Coleridge and The Cornell Wordsworth are doing—may ultimately prove to be the better part of hubris. My critiques of some details and emphases in the latter two editions and in the Norton edition of *The Prelude* merely suggest how far their editors have gone toward performing their tasks to the present satisfaction of most of us.

The two-part survey published as "The Four Ages of Editing and the English Romantics" and "Romantic Bards and Historical Editors" presents the historical overview that puts into perspective the editorial efforts evaluated in the more specific reviews. The review-essay entitled "The Ohio Browning" examines fundamental editorial problems different from those arising in any of the Romantics' texts and also shows how details of orthography can contribute to the textual analysis of nineteenth-century poetry in ways that have not yet been widely adopted by textual critics working on the Romantics and Victorians.

Progress in textual criticism remains slower than it need be simply because many textual scholars seem to protect as trade secrets their methods of analyzing texts. To read most textual introductions and notes, one would think that, after an editor collated all the available manuscripts and editions, their relationships to one another and to the author's intention would leap out at the casual observer. Most of the detailed methods of analyzing evidence used by knowledgeable textual critics have been passed on in a kind of Masonic initiation rite under the direct tutelage of more experienced textual scholars at the Huntington, Newberry, Folger, Library of Congress, Pierpont Morgan, New York Public, Beinecke, Houghton, Trinity, Dove Cottage, Bodleian, Cambridge, or British libraries—or at a restaurant near one of them. Those who happen to study or teach at universities where they lack textual scholars as teachers or colleagues (and who don't receive grants to travel to one of these centers) are doomed, therefore, to mature in their ignorance until they advance too far in the profession to ask basic questions without embarrassment. In self-defense, these individuals then often perpetuate the fashionable show (or reality) of indifference to textual criticism.

The most useful book hitherto available to students of the English Romantics who wished to learn the methods of textual criticism is Jack Stillinger's *The Texts of Keats's Poems*,[2] which discusses problems of transmission and editorial treatment, while teaching a variant of the Lachmann method of evaluating the relative authority of nineteenth-century manuscripts and editions through analyses of particular textual cruxes. Now in process are several new series of facsimiles (with transcriptions, textual notes, and other helps) of primary textual materials: *The Manuscripts of the Younger Romantics*, *The Bodleian Shelley Manuscripts*, and *The Tennyson Archive*, for example, will provide students of nineteenth-century poetry with a wealth of examples of different kinds of textual witnesses—first drafts, fair copies (both holographs and transcriptions, some done under the author's supervision), corrected proofsheets, and contemporary editions annotated by the authors or their friends.[3] Accompanying these primary materials are specialists' analyses of the textual authorities and the relationships among them, as well as textual notes that point out how the editor can recognize these relationships and the limits of authority in each document or edition. Soon, students and critics may not need travel to the world's few great repositories of such materials in order to learn the fundamentals of the craft. But until enough specialists who study the Romantics and Victorians take an interest in the issues of textual criticism to master these basic skills and to pass them on to all students who enter the field, the textual discussions in this volume—both in "Romantic Texts" and in the explicatory essays in "Romantic Contexts"—should help stimulate an awareness of the basic issues of textual criticism among those who study nineteenth-century poetry, providing the perspective, terminology, and techniques that they will need to free themselves from blind slavery to the textual philosophy—or the carelessness—of the latest editors of the works they study.

2. Cambridge, Mass.: Harvard University Press, 1974.
3. All three of these series are published at New York and London by Garland Publishing, Inc. Donald H. Reiman is the general editor of *The Bodleian Shelley Manuscripts* (1986–) and *The Manuscripts of the Younger Romantics* (1985–), and Jack Stillinger is the area editor for Keats in the latter series. *The Tennyson Archive* (1987–) is edited by Christopher Ricks and Aidan Day.

III

"Part Two: Romantic Contexts" follows roughly the chronology of the subjects discussed, rather than the dates when my essays were written. There are two reasons for thus departing from the arrangement of Part One. First, Part Two centers attention on the Romantic authors and their writings, rather than on the theories and (mal)practice of modern scholar-critics; therefore, the chronology moves through the sequence of these writers' historical, emotional, and intellectual contexts and their interactions with one another, rather than through my colleagues' and my growth in understanding them. Second, the ideas and methods that underlie the research in Part Two are not of such recent development that they show any particular progress during the past quarter-century. Whether or not there is anything new under the sun of English Romantics studies, the methods here illustrated (as distinguished from the particular information and conclusions that have been educed) depend on techniques and traditions of scholarship that I learned from my teachers and they from theirs.

These papers involve the analysis of textual evidence, detailed biographical research, psychological inference, historical study, sociological theorizing, definitions of literary genres, and analyses of the structures, symbolic patterns, and thematic implications of discrete literary artifacts. Though I've certainly learned a good deal about the implementation of these methodologies from colleagues, editors, family, and friends with whom I've discussed my ideas or who read and reacted to my work, and though I've garnered much specific information from publications issued as recently as 1986, each of these approaches antedates 1960. My basic principles of literary scholarship appeared in a credo I published in *College English* for October 1961, entitled "Research Revisited: Scholarship and the Fine Art of Teaching." Those ideas, articulated during my first year of teaching freshmen and sophomores at Duke, ran counter to the doctrines of the "New Criticism," then in the saddle in English departments, just as my ideas are out of step with recent poststructuralist doctrines. But my principles (unlike those of inveterate fad-followers) show considerable continuity. In 1961 I wrote:

> . . . teachers of the humanities, who must encounter great-souled works of art produced by intellectual and spiritual giants and who must somehow capture enough of this genius to plant, in the minds of the young, seeds of intellectual maturity, may be excused for hunting in packs, for tying down the living masterpieces with threads of criticism as the Lilliputians secured Gulliver. Some teachers

may indeed rise to the height of the great arguments unaided, but most of us require the discoveries and insights of dozens of our colleagues before we can hope to do justice to the twenty-five or more achievements of genius with which we contend in the classroom each year—or each semester. This much agreed upon, the crux of the matter would seem to be a clear-cut delineation of what constitutes useful scholarship and criticism: how can an article justify space in the professional journals?

Literary *scholarship* should aid the teacher and student in understanding what a work of art did mean or should have meant to the sensitive reader at the time of its composition. To reconstruct this potential effect, one must establish an accurate text of the work; define its words and terms; elucidate its allusions, literary or topical; explain the intellectual milieu in which the work of art grew (survey the world-view of the age together with the world-view of the author); and implicate any historical or biographical information that contributes to the above ends. . . .

Criticism, on the other hand, should aid the teacher and student in ascertaining what the work of art amounts to in the present tense. Criticism must always be in the first-person singular or the imperative. It is a normative act in which the critic witnesses to the value of a work of literature that he fully understands after a careful application of scholarship. Explication, which is simply the inevitable last step of scholarship, can never be divorced from less glamorous scholarly activities (such as textual and historical study) and forced to cohabit in isolation with criticism. Only bastard offspring can result from such a union, for no critic, new or old, can render normative judgments worth printing unless his evaluation is based upon a sound text of the work and upon a thorough knowledge of the language and ideas of the author and his times. . . . Once the objective creation has been identified through careful analysis of its words, structure, and ideas, the critic must then determine the value of the experience captured in the work of art for the living man who re-experiences it. . . .

Although criticism thus involves the so-called "affective fallacy," just as scholarship does the "intentional fallacy," neither violates the genuine autonomy of the work of art, which rests not on the omission of such pertinent considerations as the author's aims and the effects upon a reading public, but on a comprehensive view of all stages of the author-to-reader communication that is a literary work. Literature is a human product, having relevance only to human beings: without the author and his imaginative soul, the work of art cannot exist at all, for although we can read *The Iliad* in complete ignorance of Homer as an individual man, we cannot remain ignorant of a human consciousness with particular ideals and aspirations that lies behind that magnificent achievement; without the reader, on the other hand, the poem is uncreated, becoming mere marks on paper or stone that await reanimation by a sensitive human soul.[4]

Were I to restate my beliefs today, I would emphasize even more strongly the distinction between *scholarship* as the identification and explication (within our all-too-human limitations) of the work as the author wished to present it to its original intended audience and *criticism* as the

4. *College English* 23 (October 1961): 10–12.

evaluation of that work's relevance and value to another audience. Confusion between the roles of scholar and critic often leads to evasion of questions fundamental to the study of any literary work. *Scholars* too often fail to integrate their discoveries into the larger contexts that demonstrate the significance of their new information to an overall understanding of the author's relevant works; while *critics* too often write subjective, evaluative explications that may be successful appraisals of a poem's significance for modern readers, but then try to palm off these modern renditions as the original poems that Shelley or Keats thought *he* had written. If scholars and critics considered their two distinct functions, they could abandon many defensive games: scholars could present discoveries about the author's original intention and the occasion of a poem's composition without claiming that this discovery changes the present significance of the poem, while critics could discuss its meaning and value for themselves and their contemporaries without trying to rewrite the past.

In the Introduction to *The Evidence of the Imagination* (1978), I restated some of my basic perspectives in terms of the poststructuralist wave then sweeping over the profession:

Whatever linguistic, semantic, or aesthetic theories may be current, such doctrines cannot change the basic facts of the literary venture. First, a human being living in a particular place and time, stimulated by individual circumstances, puts words together in an order determined in part by that artist's experience, in part by the supposed expectations of the specific audience he/she is addressing (whether that audience be one friend, all fellow poets, or an entire nation), in part by the denotations, connotations, past associations (public and private), sounds, and appearance of the words themselves, in part by grammatical, syntactical, and rhetorical concerns, and in part by the requirements of the form (tragedy or sonnet) in which he/she chooses to embody these ordered words. Second, the words are transmitted from the form in which the author (or a scribe) first committed them to paper (or tape recorder or the memory of an auditor); they are transcribed by others, printed or engraved or recorded, reprinted, possibly miscopied, and eventually read and/or heard by human beings living in a variety of times and places and with their own personal experiences. The words (and the punctuation marks and spacing—or the pauses and intonations) read and/or heard by this audience may differ somewhat from those the writer first wrote or uttered; certainly the significance and associations of individual words, phrases, or even subjects will differ vastly from one reader or hearer to another. The communication of a literary work thus embodies three distinct elements—an elusive author, a mutable text, and an ever-changing audience.

Whatever one's epistemology, psychology, or semiotics may be, three separate functions must be performed by students of literature. The first is to ascertain, by a study of the transmission of the text, what words—in what order and with what emphasis—the poet approved as his poem. This is the task of the textual critic. Second, the specialist literary historian, beginning with this authoritative text, examines the life and works of the author and the history and culture of his/her times to determine what forces shaped the creation of the particular literary work, at what audience it was directed, and what the work should have meant to that intended audience. The final task of the specialist scholar is thus to provide a detailed explication of the literary work in the light of the author's life, his other works, his times, and all of the past that was alive for him. Third, the general critic—beginning, ideally, with the authoritative text of the work of art and a full understanding of its probable intended meaning, as provided by specialized literary researchers— reacts to the literary work in the present tense, elucidating it for modern readers and evaluating its continuing relevance.[5]

This 1978 redaction of the basic ideas I expressed in 1961 was describing the function of specialized historical and biographical scholarship, such as that represented in *The Evidence of the Imagination*, the subtitle of which was *Studies of Interactions between Life and Art in English Romantic Literature*. Though I believe in a clear delineation of the separate functions of scholarship and criticism, so that the successes of one activity do not become the contaminants that sour the other, there can be no total separation of powers among the textual critic, the historical scholar, and the literary critic. Rather, I believe, "one man in his time plays many parts"—each significant contributor to literary understanding must be three in one and one in three. I thus agreed beforehand with Jerome J. McGann's observation that any aspect of scholarly criticism is impoverished that does not unite all three functions and relate the implications of each to the other two.[6] Without understanding textual criticism, specialist historical scholars cannot select the best text (and correct it, if necessary, from the primary witnesses) to explicate the work in the final stages of their prescribed sphere. Without a thorough knowledge of the methods of both textual criticism and contextual scholarship, the general critic cannot fully judge the textual and contextual origins of the work of art and, thus, cannot meaningfully mediate between the poet and his modern readers. Unless modern critics comprehend thoroughly the elements present in the literary text—its actual words and its intended structure and significations—they will be unable to determine what it has of value to communicate to them and their contemporaries. Without comprehending the situation of mod-

---

5. *The Evidence of the Imagination*, ed. Donald H. Reiman, Michael C. Jaye, and Betty T. Bennett (New York: New York University Press, 1978), pp. xiii-xiv. My contribution to the volume appears below as item 11.
6. "The Monks and the Giants: Textual and Bibliographical Studies and the Interpretation of Literary Works," in McGann's *The Beauty of Inflections: Literary Investigations in Historical Method and Theory* (Oxford: Clarendon Press, 1985), pp. 69-89.

ern critics vis-à-vis contemporary social and cultural conditions, textual and contextual scholars cannot compensate for the inevitable distortions of the past that otherwise result from limitations inherent in their own historical perspectives as they work to unearth the situation in the author's age.

I deny, however, McGann's inference that there have been no such scholar-critics for all seasons since the nineteenth-century Germans. Among those whom I know to combine the qualities necessary for textual and historical scholarship and evaluative criticism and to whom my own work is especially indebted are (in alphabetical order) M. H. Abrams, W. Jackson Bate, Kenneth Neill Cameron, Kathleen Coburn, David V. Erdman, Royal A. Gettmann, Leslie A. Marchand, Morse Peckham, Jack Stillinger, and Carl Woodring. Certainly McGann's own work is indebted to many of these people, as well as to such others as Cecil Y. Lang.

Almost any "scholar" or "critic" whose work contributes meaningfully to the progress of knowledge possesses the essential qualities of both scholar *and* critic. But the value of scholarly work may be vitiated if textual or historical scholars allow their sifting of the evidence to be distorted by what they first conceive to be the present needs of society, or if the critic tries to impose, without change, a vision from one age on a different cultural scene. To avoid such "contamination," it is useful for textual critics to work through the evidence of the textual witnesses as impartially as possible, before formulating detailed views about what the poem means; that is, they should identify, from the weight of the textual evidence, which words and punctuation probably belong to the poem *before* beginning to explicate it; they should then explicate it on its own terms (that is, as nearly as can be determined on its author's terms) before trying to translate its significance for modern readers.

One crude but effective way to prevent such contamination is to divide the labor on each poet, or for scholar-critics to allow time to pass between completing one task and undertaking another, in order to gain perspective on their work: one person may establish Shelley's text and then go on to unearth the historical context and to interpret poems by Wordsworth, Byron, or Ammons from texts that others have established. Or, one person can establish the texts of Shelley's poems at one time and then go back a few years later, after others have responded to the new textual evidence, to write critical essays on those texts for modern readers. In this way, no editor-critic becomes the judge in his own case, either establishing a text to prove his predetermined critical theory (e.g., that Shelley's poems are incoherent, or mystical) or imposing his authority as editor to establish a critical viewpoint in the editions where readers must first encounter the works. (It seems to me fortunate, for example, that the critical notes to new texts of Wordsworth and Shelley in *The Norton Anthology of English Literature* were written, not by their editors, but by M. H. Abrams.)

In most of the papers in "Romantic Contexts," the function of the historical scholar is primary. But they also provide evaluative judgments, most of which are positive. One reason is simply that I have not spent time on authors or works that seem to lack modern relevance. Conversely, looked into deeply enough, every human product has its connections with the lives of all other human beings. One of my aims as a scholar-critic has been to bridge the gap between the Romantic period and our time by pointing out some of those relationships.

IV

Because I do not believe in perpetuating errors, I have not included papers that seem in the light of subsequent research to have been substantially flawed. But it would be dishonest to rewrite my previously published essays to benefit from hindsight or from recent discoveries by others. Besides correcting typographical errors and factual slips that were (or should have been) noted soon after each paper appeared, I have eliminated a few awkward verbal repetitions and other minor stylistic infelicities. Otherwise, the texts of the pieces represent the state of my knowledge and reflect that of the scholarly community at the times they first appeared. The headnotes update the essays and reviews by locating each within the context of its composition, telling briefly what has been learned about the subject since I wrote the paper and providing bibliographical information on important subsequent treatments of the topic. The headnotes also suggest some personal and situational factors that governed the approach or even the tone in each particular instance. Recent criticism, influenced by deconstructionism, has called for an awareness of subtexts and hidden motives; though I applaud this emphasis in literary studies, with the laws of libel being what they are and most of us living in glass houses, very few scholar-critics are willing to probe in print their own or their colleagues' motivations below those at the ideological or sociological level. We scholars and critics, I believe, write when and as we do for far deeper reasons. Without getting very psychoanalytical, we can often recognize motive forces that make one critic praise, attack, or ignore another if we know enough about the personal interactions between the two or among their friends. After the gossip has passed away, most of this information is burned or buried with us. Yet these nonintellectual, deeply personal feelings—admiration, gratitude, love, jealousy, hurt pride, and the like—actually foster some aspects of what and how we write more than do purely professional or intellectual concerns (as the writings of Wordsworth, Coleridge, Byron, and Shelley clearly illustrate). Such private ties and antipathies neither validate nor discredit our ideas, but an awareness of them will help the reader to recognize and compensate for some biases and subtexts in our work, without wasting years on our lives and letters, rather than on those of the important authors whom we study.

The headnotes, then, without being confessional, attempt to sketch circumstances and personal relationships that, I am sure, influenced my stance in various reviews and essays. At Columbia, I once taught a master's candidate fresh out of Haverford who had decided to become an academic so that he could get away from the kind of politics his father faced in the business world. If my comments on some of the quotidian realities that affected my own writings can disillusion such idealists, I will probably have done them a favor in the long run. I consider myself an idealist, too: I believe that those in academe who become as wise as serpents can enjoy the luxury of being as harmless as doves.

Wherever I have been in the academic world, there have been men and women of great intelligence, professional skills, dedication, and moral awareness who have navigated carefully to positions of power in their institutions and their disciplines in order to battle those of equal political finesse who are crass, ignorant, intellectually lazy, and self-serving. These heroes of the profession are senior professors who protect graduate students from exploitation or vendettas by senior colleagues; the chairs, deans, and those who sit on hiring, tenure, promotion, and grants committees who reward true merit in teaching and publication, rather than subservience, benign mediocrity, or flash and glitter; the readers for scholarly journals and publishers who insist that good work be published, even if it is not fashionable or commercial at the moment. If meritorious students learn from the headnotes to navigate more skillfully among the shoals of the academic bayous, that benefit—in part my inheritance from such wise mentors as Royal Gettmann, Robert W. Rogers, George Sherburn, and Jack Stillinger—will usefully supplement the positive scholarly attitudes and intellectual substance that are the primary goals of this volume.

Part One

Romantic Texts

1

Editing Shelley

Like most textual scholars, I entered the world of editing and textual criticism through the back door, urged by my need to cope with problems in the text of "The Triumph of Life," a poem that I wanted to understand and explicate. Once I realized that it had to be reedited from the draft manuscript that provided the only authorial witness to the text, I sought models and guidelines that would bring my work into conformity with the highest standards of editing in English literature.

At Illinois, G. Blakemore Evans, Royal A. Gettmann, Jack Stillinger, and Bruce Harkness warned me about the pitfalls of working from microfilms and of depending on secondary sources, as well as shared with me their personal experiences of editing from both printed and manuscript sources. Though I did not know it at the time, most of the editorial ideas at Illinois in my student days exemplified or paralleled what in "Romantic Bards and Historical Editors" I designate as the "Harvard School" of editing, deriving from Hyder E. Rollins and William A. Jackson. (Bruce Harkness, who had studied at Chicago, brought a slightly different perspective.) After I began teaching at Duke in 1960, I first encountered the work of W. W. Greg, Fredson Bowers, and William B. Todd, partly through reading reviews and articles in current periodicals and partly through interchanges with colleagues who had studied under or been influenced by them. (George Walton Williams, a student of Bowers, and S. K. Heninger, Jr., were most helpful in educating me.)

By this time, I was also working with Neville Rogers, who intended that young scholars should become contributing editors to his Oxford English Texts edition of Shelley by first publishing editorial work under our own names and then turning it over to him for use in the Oxford Shelley. Though I had not found this suggestion entirely satisfactory, the question remained moot until the editorial work on "The Triumph of Life" was completed. Rogers, in the meantime, asked Mary W. Reiman and me to help with his edition of The Esdaile Poems by serving as "younger eyes" to check his typescript for typographical errors in his texts and collations. We devoted a month or so in the summer of 1962 to this task, but at the end of that time—and after a long correspondence between Rogers and me—I realized that, though my own philosophy of editing was still developing, I totally disagreed with Rogers's practice; he seemed to emend Shelley's text—particularly the punctuation *and orthography—where Mary Reiman and I could see little or no reason for doing so. By the time that Rogers and I had made our respective sentiments clear, we had reached a parting of the ways. The next time that Mary and I saw Rogers (at Brandeis University, where he was then teaching), he literally read us a paper on his theory of editing Shelley—a paper that took issue with all my nascent ideas on the subject. And, unbeknownst to me, he published that paper, in a form containing echoes of and allusions to our private correspondence, in two essays on Shelley's spelling and punctuation in* Keats-Shelley Memorial Bulletin *(16 [1965] and 17 [1966]).*

While breaking with Rogers and what might be called, in honor of Frederick Gard Fleay, the schoolmaster tradition of editing (see pages 88–89), I was still testing my ideas and looking for ways to integrate the advances made by Bowers and his colleagues in the theory of editing Renaissance plays and American novels with the problems encountered in work with Shelley's texts. My ideas became more ordered as I worked for a month or more in the spring of 1969 on a review for JEGP *of L. J. Zillman's latest edition of* Prometheus Unbound. *Robert K. Turner, Jr., my former colleague at Milwaukee, put me on the program of the Bibliographical Evidence section at the Modern Language Association convention in December 1969 (Denver), where the other speaker on the program was a man exactly my age— G. Thomas Tanselle of the University of Wisconsin–Madison. Tom Tanselle and I supported the same position from opposite perspectives: I argued that editing, while necessarily partly subjective, should follow principles more objective than those advocated by Rogers and Zillman—that editing was a science as well as an art; Tanselle argued that editing could not be done by formulas, but required an element of informed subjective judgment—that it was an art as well as a science. Each paper ended with a quotation from the same essay by A. E. Housman to nail home its point. Tom Tanselle and I (who had never met or corresponded before) knew that our papers had not been planned to complement one another so neatly, but we both felt strongly that they did so.*

At the end of the review of Zillman (item 2 below), I called for meetings like the Toronto Conference on Editorial Problems to help develop standards and principles of editing Romantic poetry. After the review appeared, I was invited to participate in just such a conference at Toronto in 1971. The result was "Editing Shelley," originally published in Editing Texts of the Romantic Period, *edited by John D. Baird (Toronto: A. M. Hakkert, Ltd., 1972; now issued by AMS Publishing, New York). Besides its discussion of the rationale for* Shelley and his Circle, *as those principles had been worked out by Kenneth Neill Cameron, it included a call for more uniformly high standards in editorial matters, even at the price of a fair amount of coercion. Given the chaos then regnant, my tone was, perhaps, justified. (At the conference, that tone was approached, if not matched, in W. J. B.*

Owen's fine paper entitled "Annotating Wordsworth.") But now I would agree with Kathleen Coburn, the featured speaker there, who afterwards remarked to me in private that I was "very fierce." This paper can now be considered an artifact representative of the tone and issues in the wars over editorial standards during their early, anarchic phase, when the field did not even have an orthodoxy to rebel against and all the discussants tended to appear a bit red in tooth and claw. Although I do not take back any of the paper's normative judgments, it would be possible, given today's climate, to rephrase them in less stringent terms without losing the point.

Shelley and his Circle is an unusual publication that does not attempt to be a complete edition of the letters or writings of any single author; it is a catalogue-edition of one library's collection of manuscripts centering on William Godwin, Shelley, Lord Byron, Leigh Hunt, and their friends and correspondents.[1] For those not familiar with our editorial procedures, let me outline them briefly. The manuscripts—the great majority of them holograph letters—appear in chronological order, as nearly as that can be determined. Each manuscript is introduced by a bibliographical description, which first describes the literary and the physical aspects in general terms—the number of pages of writing and the size of the pages—and then enumerates the kind of paper (and its watermark and countermark, if any), the seal, the postal fee(s), the postmark(s), any dockets, notations, or additions (such as spindle holes or adhering pieces of paper or tape), and the provenance of the manuscript. Next there is a diplomatic transcription of the text of the manuscript, with textual notes keyed to the transcription by line number. There may be collations of other authoritative manuscripts or of printed texts. Finally, there is a commentary that attempts to elucidate all factual problems and literary and biographical implications of the letter, document, or literary text that are not discussed in another commentary—its date, its biographical significance, the background of its references and allusions.

To provide broader contexts for these specific commentaries, each major figure whose manuscripts appear in the series is introduced by a general essay on his life and works. Various other topics—biographical, bibli-

1. *Shelley and his Circle*, published by Harvard University Press and Oxford University Press: vols. 1-2 by Kenneth Neill Cameron, editor, with contributing editors Eleanor L. Nicholes and Frederick L. Jones, 1961; vols. 3-4 by Kenneth Neill Cameron, editor, with contributing editors Sir Gavin De Beer, David V. Erdman, Eleanor Flexner, Frederick L. Jones, and Sylva Norman, 1970; vols. 5-6 by Donald H. Reiman, editor, with coordinating editor Doucet D. Fischer and contributing editors David V. Erdman, R. Glynn Grylls (Lady Mander), Sylva Norman, and Marion Kingston Stocking, 1973.

ographical, and critical—are also given extended treatment in essays. The essays in volumes 5-6, for example, are "Edward John Trelawny (Life and Works)"; "Trelawny to Augusta White: Introduction to a Correspondence"; "The Composition and Publication of *The Revolt of Islam*"; "Keats and Shelley: Personal and Literary Relations"; "Claire Clairmont's Journal"; "Peacock in Leadenhall Street"; and "Shelley's Treatise on Political Economy." The late Carl H. Pforzheimer and Kenneth Neill Cameron conceived of the entire catalogue-edition as comprising an interlocking collective biography of William Godwin, Mary Wollstonecraft, Percy Bysshe Shelley, Mary W. Shelley, Thomas Love Peacock, Leigh Hunt, and Lord Byron, up to the time of Shelley's death. This general aim continues (though we have extended the terminal date from 1822 to include the important Byron manuscripts that postdate Shelley's death). The volumes are focused to include an audience composed not only of literary scholars but of literate general readers as well. With this broader audience in mind, we avoid coding our footnote references by initials and in-group abbreviations, a practice that we hope will also help to keep the work readable after some of the currently fashionable abbreviations are passé.

Because all of the edited materials are taken directly from manuscripts that are on the premises, the editor and staff enjoy repeated opportunities to collate the typescript or the proofs of a text with the manuscript to ascertain the most probable readings and to comment on difficulties in textual notes. Having a large group of interrelated manuscripts greatly aids us also in dating letters and establishing their sequence. A letter, otherwise undatable, may be put within certain limits because the paper on which it is written is from the stock used by the writer only during a short period of time. We can more accurately date some letters because we have the dated postmarks on the letters to which they are answers, and we can date others because we know the post days in Italy and how long it took letters to travel from Italy to England, where they received a date-stamp from the Foreign Post Office. In the commentaries, we attempt to extend the available information on such minor figures as Shelley's publisher Charles Ollier by drawing together references from manuscripts and from obscure books that more general libraries, or more specialized scholars who devote themselves entirely to Shelley or one major figure, might not be aware of.

Sometimes we are enabled to correct the text of Shelley's letters simply because we repeatedly encounter similar small problems. In three cases, for example, we found notations written on letters that were apparently in handwriting other than that of the author and that were difficult to connect with the context of their respective letters. One was a letter from Peacock to Charles Ollier, one from Shelley to Ollier, and one written by Mary Shelley in Shelley's name to Ollier. In the case of the two Shelley items, previous editors had included the notations as postscripts or notes in the texts of the letters themselves. We finally concluded, however, after considering the position of the words, the similarity of the scrawled handwriting, and the common destination of the three letters, that the notations had been random notes jotted down by Charles or James Ollier while the letters in question were spindled on the desk in front of him. We were thus able to remove these irrelevant notes from the texts of the letters.

In addition to the opportunities afforded by the concentration of manuscripts in The Carl H. Pforzheimer Library, the format of *Shelley and his Circle* provides the editor with scope to pursue in detail topics that would necessarily be scanted in an edition that confined annotation to laconic footnotes. On a few topics at least, *Shelley and his Circle* may serve as a textbook for novice scholars. When we redate a letter, we outline the evidence on which we do so, providing other scholars not only with the material to judge the validity of the individual decision, but also with paradigms of arguments and types of evidence that they can apply to similar problems. Besides noting such customary details as literary and historical allusions, we delve into publishing and printing techniques, the operation of the postal system, banking and business practices, relevant medical and legal information, and, in general, the web of daily affairs in the early nineteenth century that underlay the lives and literary works of the major figures.

For example, when analyzing the textual changes that Shelley made in December 1817 while transforming *Laon and Cythna* into *The Revolt of Islam*, I found it useful to discover that incest was not a civil crime in England in Shelley's day—and therefore Shelley's depiction of incest in *Laon and Cythna* did not render the poem liable to prosecution on that account, although *Blackwood's Edinburgh Magazine* for November 1817 contained a fierce attack on Leigh Hunt's use of incest in *The Story of Rimini*. On the other hand, the uncomplimentary references to Christianity were *legally* dangerous, since a bookseller named James Williams of Portsea had just been convicted, fined, and imprisoned for republishing two relatively innocent political tracts cast in the form of religious parodies. Study of a tradesman's bill for Russia oil has enabled us to elucidate the point of a contemporary joke in *Peter Bell the Third*. And for writers of more frequent contemporary allusiveness—Byron in *Don Juan*, or Leigh Hunt and Thomas Moore in their journalistic poetry and prose—such commentary on the methods and manners of Regency England should prove useful not only because of specific information that we provide but also because we point other scholars toward particular books and methods of research.

As an astute reviewer of volumes 3 and 4 of *Shelley and his Circle* pointed out, one characteristic of the research in the edition is that it raises almost as many scholarly questions as are answered. Indeed, I think that it is an important duty of any scholar not only to track down particular information that has eluded his predecessors, but also to raise new questions and problems that, if solved by researchers in the future, will result in fuller knowledge not only of the *actions* of poets but of their unstated reasonings as well. The commentaries in the forthcoming volumes of *Shelley and his Circle* probe into Shelley's motivations, for example, in the dates he assigned to the composition of his poems. Using varied evidence, I reject the date conventionally agreed upon for the composition of *Julian and Maddalo*. I argue that Shelley, for quite cogent and intelligible reasons, purposely misled Leigh Hunt and Mary Shelley about the period in which the poem was composed.

In short, though we begin with the physical evidence of the manuscripts, leading to verbal and syntactical evidence of the texts, our aims are larger. From the unvarnished facts, we move first to biographical or bibliographical evidence and finally to literary implications. By analyzing closely three leaves of the holograph fair copy of *Laon and Cythna* in the Pforzheimer Library and using evidence from their provenance and from the other scattered leaves of fair copy, I was able to determine that the surviving portion of fair copy of Canto IX actually contains the final text and served as press copy, whereas the surviving fair copy of Canto I (which previous commentators have assumed to be part of the same continuous manuscript) was actually an *intermediate* fair copy, which did *not* go to press. This conclusion, on the one hand, refutes those who have used the state of the fair copy of Canto I as evidence that Shelley did not take great pains in preparing his poem for the press; on the other hand, coupled with analysis of the rough-draft manuscripts in the Bodleian, it suggests that parts of Canto I were written either after or at the same time as the end of Canto XII. This inference, in turn, has critical implications by pointing up hitherto unnoted parallels between the symbolic voyages at the end of the first and twelfth cantos.

A cardinal principle that has guided us in editing *Shelley and his Circle* is the assumption that the author of the manuscript before us is correct until he has been proved to be in error. By searching diligently for first-class confirmatory evidence to document a reference or assertion, by checking contemporary dictionaries and rhetorics, as well as the *Oxford English Dictionary*, to vindicate an unusual spelling or use of a word, by following technical terms (*chariot* for a particular kind of coach, or *Russia oil* for a specific hairdressing) into the technical manuals and even the magazine advertisements of the period, we have learned far more and added more to the stock of knowledge than would have been possible had we simply assumed that references and usages not found in standard reference works or earlier books on Shelley were either erroneous or insignificant.

One might suppose that the principle I have just stated—that the writer being edited is presumed to be correct until he has been proved to be in error—would be accepted by most modern scholars. Unfortunately, its acceptance by Shelley scholars does not appear to be at all unanimous. One can contrast Kenneth Neill Cameron's annotation of Shelley's letters in *Shelley and his Circle* with that of Frederick L. Jones in his *Letters of Percy Bysshe Shelley*.[2] Although Jones declares that he is publishing the text of Shelley's letters as faithfully as possible, he sometimes gives way to an urge to show his intellectual superiority to Shelley—usually with disastrous results. For example, when he corrects Shelley's "agua" to "acqua" in a foreign quotation, he has failed to notice that the quotation is Spanish, not Italian (2:132). Another time he adds this note to the opening sentence of one of Shelley's letters: "The syntax of this sentence is confused: 'would have operated' appears to have no subject." In fact, the sentence—though complex—is grammatically and syntactically quite correct, the subject of the verb in question being a gerund ("your declining") that Jones must have read as a present participle (1:578–79). The sentence reads: "It is to be regretted that you did not consult your own safety and advantage, if you consider it connected with the non-publication of my book, before your declining the publication, after having accepted it, would have operated to so extensive and serious an injury to my views as now."

When Shelley twice within a month writes to two publishers about "your announce of *Frankenstein*" (1:564) and "the announce of *Laon & Cythna* in the public papers" (1:568), Jones twice adds a bracketed suffix after Shelley's word, changing "announce" to "announce[ment]." Why? A better course would have been to note that "though *announce* does not appear in the *Oxford English Dictionary*, Shelley is clearly coining the word on the analogy of the French '*annonce*' and Italian '*annuncio*.'" In fact, Shelley's usage is not wholly without contemporary parallel.[3]

2. 2 vols. Oxford: Clarendon Press, 1964.
3. While reading periodical reviews of the time for my edition of contemporary reviews of the Romantic poets (*The Romantics Reviewed*, 9 vols. [New York: Garland Publishing, Inc., 1972]), I came upon two analogous uses of the French form. Francis Jeffrey writes in his review of Wordsworth's *Poems, in Two Volumes* (1807): ". . . we read the *annonce* of Mr. Wordsworth's publications with a good deal of interest and expectation . . ." (*Edinburgh Review* 11 [October 1807]: 215), and twelve years later a reviewer writes of Wordsworth's *Peter Bell* and *The Waggoner*: ". . . the pompous *annoncé* of these tales . . . seemed like the

Using my marked copy of *The Letters of Percy Bysshe Shelley*, I could enumerate many similar instances in which Jones has provided information that is erroneous, often contradicting Shelley as he does so. But perhaps it would be more efficient to cite one epitomizing example of what happens when a scholar sets out to supplement or correct his author without devoting sufficient care or attention to his research. Jones's edition of Mary Shelley's letters contains an editorial blunder that I find dazzling. Mary Shelley, writing to Maria Gisborne, discusses Jane Williams, and adds: "but I preach in vain—J—— C—— says 'Do unto others as you would they should do unto you.'" Jones, ever mindful of the ignorant reader, identifies the source of the quotation by expanding the initials "J. C." to "J[ohn] [Wheeler] C[leveland]," Jane Williams's brother.[4]

All editors make errors, and I do not mean to imply that Jones's work is below the usual standards of editions of the letters of nineteenth-century poets. Those who have followed the reactions to the Clarendon Press editions of Thomas Moore's letters and the letters of Dante Gabriel Rossetti will be aware that not all the work in this field has met the high standards set by the editors of the letters of Blake, Keats, and Swinburne. But the standards of competence exhibited in editions of the letters, poetry, and prose of nineteenth-century authors *must* rise above their present dead level if literary scholars, students, and literate readers are to appreciate fully the intelligence, wit, wisdom, and great aesthetic power of the major figures of the period. I am not calling for new theoretical breakthroughs in the techniques of textual analysis; I am simply suggesting that, unless editors of literary texts of the nineteenth century learn the basic methods already employed in other areas of literary scholarship, the work of an entire generation of such scholars may turn out to be little more than a furious spinning of wheels.

For example, scholars of the Romantic period, in general, stand greatly in need of training in the analysis and use of manuscript evidence. No medievalist would think of editing an important text without studying paleography. No editor of Shakespeare or other Renaissance dramatists could work in ignorance of the principles of bibliographical analysis, and if he did, no respectable press would publish his efforts. Yet in nineteenth-century scholarship, edition after edition appears in which editors, apart from a general interest in writing criticism or studying the biography of a poet or novelist, demonstrate few qualifications for their principal task of

---

ushering of a washer-woman into a drawing room" (*Eclectic Review,* 2nd ser., 12 [July 1819]: 63).

4. *Letters of Mary W. Shelley* (Norman: University of Oklahoma Press, 1944), 2:107–8.

producing a text as close to the author's intention as surviving evidence and human fallibility will permit.

For one thing, the editor of a work for which a full holograph manuscript survives ought to be able to determine whether the manuscript he has before him is a rough draft, an intermediate fair copy, the copy that went to press, or an extra transcript retained by the author. Obviously, if the manuscript was the one carefully prepared by the author to send to press, the manuscript ought to be used as copy-text, especially if the author is known not to have revised proofs. Whereas, if the manuscript is either an intermediate fair copy or what we may term a "safe-keeping copy," it is not as authoritative on accidentals and may not be as authoritative on substantives as the text of the first edition. On the other hand, an intermediate fair copy often reveals much about the author's intentions when he revises, cancels, or inserts passages. These are simple truths. Yet texts of two works by the younger Romantics that have been most lavishly reedited are fundamentally flawed because the editors failed to determine the nature and the implications of the manuscripts available to them.

I have written and spoken elsewhere about the limitations of Lawrence John Zillman's two editions of Shelley's *Prometheus Unbound*.[5] Let me say here only that Zillman's recent Yale University Press edition uses Shelley's intermediate fair copy in two illegitimate and harmful ways. First, he introduces too many readings from it into the text of *Prometheus* against the authority of the first edition (which was taken directly from the lost final copy prepared for the press by Shelley and Mary Shelley). Second, Zillman uses the wide divergence in many accidental features between the first edition and the very unfinished fair copy that survives to argue for and to practice a textual relativism in which the editor's taste rather than objective evidence becomes the factor determining which readings will be given.

Truman Guy Steffan began his textual study of Byron's poetry years ago as coeditor with Willis W. Pratt of the elaborate Variorum Edition of *Don Juan*. More recently he has appeared as editor of *Lord Byron's "Cain."* Both of these editions have their useful features, but when it comes to the tech-

---

5. *Shelley's "Prometheus Unbound": A Variorum Edition* (Seattle: University of Washington Press, 1959); *Shelley's "Prometheus Unbound": The Text and the Drafts, Toward a Modern Definitive Edition* (New Haven: Yale University Press, 1968). The latter edition was reviewed by Donald H. Reiman in *JEGP* 68 (July 1969): 539–43; both editions were discussed by Reiman in "Textual and Aesthetic Problems in Shelley's *Prometheus Unbound*," a paper delivered to the Bibliographical Evidence group of the Modern Language Association of America, 28 December 1969, at Denver.

nical matter of determining textual authorities and analyzing evidence from them, Steffan throws up his hands in confusion and patches together a text as best he can. Steffan speaks at length of "the MS of *Cain*," and even asks whether this manuscript served as printer's copy. But he gives no answer, even though the unsorted facts he supplies make it evident that the manuscript is *not* the one that went to John Murray, but Byron's intermediate fair copy, kept by him in Italy. What happened to the press copy? Is it now in John Murray's files in Albemarle Street? Does Steffan know? He gives no indication of having written to ask. In any case, without seeing anything except the manuscript before him at Texas, Steffan should have known that it had not received Byron's final polishing and that it therefore has limited usefulness as a textual authority. But Steffan does not reach this logical conclusion: instead he, like Zillman, falls back on personal taste. Though properly taking the first edition as his copy-text, Steffan adds: "There are a few deviations in words from the 1821 text, and on these occasions I used the MS version, because it seemed preferable" (p. 147). All in all, *Lord Byron's "Cain"* joins Zillman's two editions of *Shelley's "Prometheus Unbound"* as an example of how the lack of a true theory of editing can vitiate years of industry and file drawers full of information.

I feel that the decision to include Steffan's edition of *Lord Byron's "Cain"* among the MLA Book Club selections was an especially unfortunate one. But because there is a lack of knowledge of editing procedures among editors of the Romantics themselves, it should not be surprising to find a similar dearth of knowledge and standards of judgment of editing in places of authority: among those who read and make editorial decisions for university presses and other scholarly publishers, among those who review such publications in learned journals, and among deans and department chairmen who provide tangible rewards for productive scholarship. In Elizabethan drama, the theoretical groundwork of bibliography laid by Pollard, Greg, and McKerrow was perhaps not as determinative in broadening the acceptance and implementation of improved textual standards as were the dedicated efforts of a handful of university teachers who sent out generations of students trained to understand, accept, inculcate, and enforce those higher standards. In the United States, those teachers have included Hyder Rollins and William A. Jackson at Harvard and Fredson Bowers at Virginia. Among their students have been many of the leading exponents of textual analysis in other literary periods. In eighteenth-century studies a similar influence has been exercised by Allen Hazen at Columbia and William B. Todd at Texas. Many of the scholars of the

Romantic period who have developed a serious interest and sound knowledge of textual analysis are students of men deriving from these traditions.

One of the greatest problems with developing a tradition of sound textual scholarship in the Romantic period is that so few of the senior scholars in the field have the interest to guide their students to sound examples and authorities, much less to enforce high standards among their colleagues. A substantive reason for this lack of enthusiasm for collating texts is that the Romantic poets are still ideologically alive. Their critics refuse to treat their works as mere artifacts, but respond fully to their thought as well as their artistry. Many of the finest scholars in the field are deeply engaged in writing close-reading explications of particular poems or surveys of epistemological, political, or moral patterns in the literature of the period. They tend to nod and mumble gratefully if someone, at no cost to them in time or effort, provides a text printed with legible type and wide margins suitable for extra-annotating. The teacher-scholars who appreciate the vitality and genius of the Romantics should recognize, however, that over the past fifty years, hundreds or even thousands of students have been driven away from the Romantics because of false impressions about them generated in part by faulty editing of their poetry. (Here I am speaking principally of Shelley's text, though the editorial annotation of all Romantic poetry has left room for considerable improvement down to the present day.) Because the Romantics use approximately the same vocabulary we do, editors have not felt it necessary to study the poets' usage and to gloss special or unusual meanings of words. Thus critics have mistaken Shelley's use of *Celtic*, which he and his contemporaries used in the Greek manner to designate barbarians from the north who threatened the classical Mediterranean civilization and cultural heritage. Critics have likewise constantly misread various writers who used *mother-in-law* and *sister-in-law* to signify *step-mother* and *step-sister*. But far more fundamental to an edition than precise annotation is an accurate text. It is time, I believe, for critics to recognize that they have said about most poems all that can be usefully said before textual analysis establishes exactly what the poets wrote.

With this thought, let us return to the main subject with a consideration of the editorial situation as it regards Shelley's poetry. What has been happening recently, and what appears to lie ahead? The reappearance in 1948 of Shelley's rough-draft notebooks, so long unavailable to scholars, has led to improved texts of a number of poems for which the sole authority is a holograph draft. "The Triumph of Life," "Charles the First," and a number of Shelley's posthumously published lyrics and translations have been brought nearer to Shelley's intention, though in several cases the unfinished state of the extant manuscripts will always leave scope for disagreement over details. Since 1964 Shelley's previously unpublished early shorter poems of the Esdaile Notebook have been published in full three times, making their substantive texts readily available. But all editing that depends on a single authoritative manuscript is child's play compared with reconstructing the author's text from a printed version through bibliographical analysis, and against this larger challenge, editors of Shelley's poetry have yet to prove themselves.

Shelleyan studies face, in fact, problems quite beyond those afflicting editing of the Romantic poets in general. I have already mentioned Lawrence John Zillman's two editions of *Prometheus Unbound*. The failures of his editorial principles are epitomized in a sentence in which he states that the editor must work to eliminate "the mannerisms to which the poet was subject."[6] Neville Rogers, editor of the forthcoming Clarendon Press edition of Shelley's poetry, has made pronouncements on editorial policy saying, in effect, that the particular words and punctuation Shelley employed are relatively unimportant because—to quote Rogers—"the words on his page are no more than drops in the cascade of ideas which poured from that furiously rapid mind" and "despite his almost miraculous power of holding long, subtle and wonderful passages of Platonic syntax in his head, Shelley had neither the temperament nor the technique to make them intelligible to his readers by punctuation."[7] Professor Rogers's most recent editorial effort—Shelley's *Selected Poetry*, published in the United States as Houghton Mifflin's Riverside Edition (1968) and in Great Britain by the Oxford University Press (1969)—does not augur well for his projected edition. It contains errors of every imaginable sort. Shelley's poems are misnamed: "Lines written among the Euganean Hills," a poem in tetrameter couplets, becomes "Stanzas Written in the Euganean Hills" (p. viii), and "Ode to Liberty" becomes "Ode of Liberty" (p. 457). Biographical dates are confused, from the birth dates of William Shelley (p. xxi) and Queen Victoria (p. 471) to the death dates of Fanny Imlay and Harriet Shelley (p. xxi). The publication date of Shelley's *Posthumous Poems* (p. 467) is given incorrectly, as is the year of the revolution in Naples to which Shelley alludes frequently in his letters and about which he wrote an important poem. Rogers confuses names of people: Rousseau's Saint-

---

6. *Shelley's "Prometheus Unbound": The Text and the Drafts*, p. 25.
7. "Shelley's Spelling: Theory and Practice," *Keats-Shelley Memorial Bulletin* 16 (1965): 21; and "The Punctuation of Shelley's Syntax," *Keats-Shelley Memorial Bulletin* 17 (1966): 23.

Preux becomes "Des Prieux" (p. xx and p. 463), Eliza O'Neill becomes Eliza "Neill." He gives Pisa rather than Venice as the setting of *Julian and Maddalo* (p. xxii). He truncates *Studia Neophilologica* to *Studia Philologica* (p. 462).

But two other limitations exhibit themselves in Rogers's recent publications that are far more significant so far as his qualifications as a textual editor are concerned. The first, paralleling his imaginative rearrangement of facts, is his imaginative reordering of words he is supposedly quoting. Second is his tendency to rationalize his limitations into critical principles. If *he* does not quote accurately, the precise words are of little concern; if *he* ignores the principles of bibliographical analysis or textual criticism, those who attempt to employ such methodologies have (and I quote) "for the devoted learning and accomplishment flowering around 1492 . . . substituted a merely professional cleverness and efficiency with small, mechanical (yclepèd 'scientific') skills."[8] And, even more disastrously, if *he* has not updated his text of one of Shelley's poems to conform with what he himself agrees is the text Shelley intended, he can write critical notes to justify the corrupted text he chooses to reprint. Let me cite one specific example: in the Riverside Shelley, Rogers begins his notes on "The Triumph of Life" by observing that (though he reprints the version edited by Thomas Hutchinson in 1904) "the text has been emended and expanded by subsequent editors." A few lines below this admission appears this note: "The blank spaces in lines 115 and 175 are examples of Shelley's unwillingness to slow down his rapid composition when he could not, momentarily, hit on the right word or syllables: his MSS frequently contain these blanks, which he intended to fill up later" (p. 460). Unfortunately for Rogers's generalization, one of the lines he cites does *not* contain blanks in Shelley's manuscript but reads (as Geoffrey Matthews's text and mine firmly agree): "And frost in these performs what fire in those." In the other instance, I at least am convinced that Shelley intended the passage to read: "When Freedom left those who upon the Free / Had bound a yoke" (115–16), leaving no blanks whatsoever in the two lines cited.[9]

Progress in editing Shelley is, however, being made and will be made. G. M. Matthews is working on the Longmans Shelley, which, whatever limitations the series imposes with regard to the critical apparatus, will undoubtedly have a text much better than any collected edition of Shelley's

---

8. "Shelley: Texts and Pretexts, The Case of First Editions," *Keats-Shelley Memorial Bulletin* 19 (1968): 46.

9. See G. M. Matthews, " 'The Triumph of Life': A New Text," *Studia Neophilologica* 32 (1960): 271–329; and Donald H. Reiman, *Shelley's "The Triumph of Life": A Critical Study, Based on a Text Newly Edited from the Bodleian Manuscript* (Urbana: University of Illinois Press, 1965).

poetry currently available. Judith Chernaik, in a critical study of Shelley's lyrics forthcoming from the Press of Case Western Reserve University, has reedited most of Shelley's best lyrics from the manuscripts and early printings. Timothy Webb of the University of Leeds has published a new text of Shelley's translation of Homer's "Hymn to Venus" and is working on an edition of all Shelley's translations from Greek and Latin. R. B. Woodings hopes to publish soon his text of "Charles the First." Irving Massey, Stuart Curran, and Joseph Raben have probed special textual problems in Shelley.

None of the above-named scholars, or anyone else that I am aware of now working in Shelley studies, has had the benefit of first-rate training in modern textual criticism. And there has been no solid attempt to apply the methods of textual criticism to the editions published during Shelley's lifetime. (It may have been partly the dearth of such studies in the primary area of need that led Fredson Bowers some years ago to hail as extremely important Charles H. Taylor's slim but sound volume entitled *The Early Collected Editions of Shelley's Poems*,[10] which analyzed the transmission of Shelley's text from the first editions through the piracies of the 1820s and 1830s to Mary Shelley's first collected edition of 1839.) In the hope, however, that scholars trained in textual analysis will soon begin to undertake systematic study of Shelley's poetry, I shall conclude this paper by suggesting how such a study might begin and proceed.

First, the volume of Shelley's poems that would provide the best opportunity for such analysis is *Hellas*. For *Hellas* the press copy—Edward Williams's fair copy with Shelley's corrections—survives in the Huntington Library. *Hellas* was printed by Samuel and Richard Bentley, who had printed *Epipsychidion* a year earlier, and a study of their press style in printing *Hellas*, in conjunction with a study of other poetic texts printed by the Bentley brothers during the early 1820s for which press copy may survive, might lead naturally into textual analysis of *Epipsychidion*. There are two rather simple ways to study the house style of C. H. Reynell, printer of *History of a Six Weeks' Tour* (1817), *Rosalind and Helen* (1819), the second edition of *The Cenci* (1821), and *Posthumous Poems* (1824). First, one can analyze the changes made in *The Cenci* from the first edition, printed by Glauco Masi of Livorno under Shelley's supervision, to the second edition, which was printed by Reynell, using the first edition as copy-text; one can also study changes made by Reynell when he reprinted *Alastor* in *Posthumous*

---

10. The book is subtitled: *A Study in the History and Transmission of the Printed Text* (New Haven: Yale University Press, 1958). Bowers's review appeared in *Keats-Shelley Journal* 9 (1960): 35-38.

Poems, using the first edition as copy-text. Second, one can study some fragments of press copy that survive for these and other volumes of poetry published by Reynell to determine what changes in orthography and punctuation would have originated in the printing house. Once Reynell's house style has been examined, bibliographers can move on to that of Marchant, the printer of *Prometheus Unbound*. One helpful place to begin might be a comparative analysis of the two volumes of Ollier's edition of *The Works of Charles Lamb* (1818), the second volume printed by Reynell and the first by Marchant.

There are available to would-be textual critics of the period at least five general printer's manuals published between 1808 and 1841;[11] there is a book on the patents taken out for various improvements in printing presses from 1617 to 1866, which outlines the technical developments available to the printer;[12] there are Howe's account(s) of *The London Compositor*[13] and Shorter's study of English paper mills.[14] The basic techniques of textual analysis have been worked out, challenged, and polished by bibliographers and textual critics working with incunabula, with books of the English Renaissance and eighteenth century, and—most recently—with major American authors of the nineteenth century. All that is needed is that someone committed to overcoming the problems connected with Shelley's texts direct his efforts to analyze the transmission of those texts of Shelley's poetry, taking the initiative away from those who cannot distinguish an accidental from a substantive feature, who do not understand the criteria for selecting and emending a copy-text, and who persist in thinking it the duty of an editor to alter features of the best authorities on the basis of their own whimsical preferences.

It ought to be possible to create, within a few years, a climate in which the influence of incompetent editors would be curtailed in Romantic studies as effectively as it has been among Shakespeareans. One of the surest ways in which the standards of scholarly editing could be improved would

---

11. Caleb Stower, *The Printer's Grammar* (London, 1808); John Johnson, *Typographia, or The Printer's Instructor* (London, 1824); Thomas C. Hansard, *Typographia* (London, 1825); Charles H. Timperley, *The Printer's Manual* (London, 1838); William Savage, *A Dictionary of the Art of Printing* (London, 1841). These titles have recently been reprinted as vols. 4–8 in Series 3: Printers' Manuals, of *English Bibliographical Sources*, ed. David F. Foxon (London: Gregg Press and Archive Press, 1965).

12. *Printing Patents: Abridgments of Patent Specifications Relating to Printing, 1617–1857 (with Supplement, 1858–1866)*, intro. James Harrison (London: Printing Historical Society, 1969).

13. Ellic Howe, ed., *The London Compositor: Documents relating to Wages, Working Conditions and Customs of the London Printing Trade, 1785–1900* (London: The Bibliographical Society, 1947).

14. Alfred H. Shorter, *Paper Mills and Paper Makers in England, 1495–1800* (Hilversum, Holland: The Paper Publications Society, 1957).

be for foundations, publishers, and librarians with significant manuscript collections to withhold their support from individuals whose only claim to edit the writings of a major figure is priority in the field. If someone has had the diligence to collect numerous photostats and make approximate transcriptions of them, but has exhibited neither editorial acumen nor enough intellectual curiosity to master the techniques and to acquire the knowledge necessary for superior editing, he should be encouraged by every positive and negative persuasion either to learn his trade or to collaborate with a scholar who has demonstrated that mastery. And if a scholarly press cannot tell whether or not a manuscript exhibits such standards until the edition is reviewed, it ought seriously to reexamine its publishing policies or its editorial personnel.

But the climate about which I am speaking that will stimulate and support editorial excellence will not initially be generated by foundation executives, publishers, or curators of rare-book and manuscript collections. It must begin among textual scholars in all periods of English literature and among scholars of the Romantic period—those who direct dissertations or serve on dissertation committees, those who review newly published editions, and those who lecture to their students and colleagues on editing the Romantics. It must begin at conferences like this and spread throughout all levels of the profession on both sides of the Atlantic. Speaking with a group of scholars who *are* interested in improving standards of editing in the period, I can articulate candidly those truths that are difficult to direct to those who need them most. Had I more—to use a fashionable word—*chutzpah*, I would say *directly* to the man who lacks the wit or who refuses to undergo the discipline necessary to edit with accuracy, knowledge, and understanding: "You may teach the unlettered; you may golf, fish, garden, and retail academic gossip. I will drink with you at MLA and invite you to my home for dinner; if you have certain other important humane virtues, I'll even approve of your marrying my daughter. But one thing I ask: Please keep your hands off my literary heritage."

2

Zillman's Prometheus Unbound

Lawrence John Zillman is one of the few Romanticists whose work I have reviewed or discussed over the past quarter-century whom I have never met and with whom I have never corresponded. "Zillman" represents to me two editions of Prometheus Unbound *on my shelf—books that seem now, even more than they did earlier, sad wastes of dedicated scholarly efforts and of the resources of two university presses.*

Working (as most scholars did in those days) with limited outside help, Zillman read almost everything that had been published on Prometheus Unbound *up through the early 1950s (as well as a few major items as late as 1956 and 1957, which appear in his bibliography). In 1959 the University of Washington Press published his eight-hundred-page* Shelley's "Prometheus Unbound": A Variorum Edition, *in which he melded partially digested facts and opinions from a few hundred scholars, critics, and amateurs, piecing together a mosaic of quotations from a representative sample of those who had written on each problem, character, and passage. The result was a series of contradictory and incompatible interpretative and evaluative statements, ripped from their original contexts. Thus far the book had its uses, for its very pedestrian arrangement permitted scholars and critics writing in the 1960s to key in their arguments to the mass of earlier research and opinion and to avoid the necessity of rediscovering the basic facts and ideas over and over again. Zillman's idea influenced me to write my dissertation on "The Triumph of Life" partly on the same pattern, though I discarded the cumbersome critical variorum section when reworking the dissertation for publication.*

In presenting the text of Shelley's poem, however, Zillman was out of his depth. He had not kept up with editorial theory and practice on Shakespeare or in Renaissance studies from the work of McKerrow, Greg, and their followers. He must not even have read reviews in the major scholarly journals that discussed editorial work going forward in other fields, and he also seemed to be unfamiliar with, or not to have learned from, the Oxford English Text editions of Wordsworth and Keats, R. W. Chapman's text of Jane Austen, or Geoffrey Keynes's Blake, any of which at least showed how the text of an author of the Romantic period could be edited eclectically, correcting a copy-text from a series of other witnesses. Instead,

Zillman "reproduced with verbal exactness" the first edition of 1820, which he knew from Shelley's own complaints to have been full of errors; then he collated variants from all other sources—Shelley's drafts and intermediate "safe-keeping" fair copy, Mary Shelley's editions, and the editions of a selection of influential later editors (some of whom never looked at any of the primary witnesses deriving from Percy Bysshe or Mary W. Shelley). The text was unsatisfactory for any purpose, untrustworthy as a facsimile of the first edition and yet not correcting the errors and other problems about which Shelley had complained.

Among the reviewers who scolded Zillman for his textual innocence, some—Carl Woodring, for one—knew what should have been done. But another reviewer was Neville Rogers, the editor-designate of the Oxford Shelley. Rogers, I believe, persuaded Zillman to try again, this time following the textual "principles" that Rogers was planning to use in his Oxford English Text edition; perhaps he arranged with Zillman, as he had done with me, to adopt his revised text as the basis of the OET text of Prometheus Unbound. *In any case, the result was the Yale University Press edition of* Shelley's "Prometheus Unbound": The Text and the Drafts, Toward a Modern Definitive Edition *(1968). My review appeared in JEGP 68 (July 1969): 539–43.*

Lawrence John Zillman has for many years been pursuing the elusive Grail of a "modern definitive edition" of *Prometheus Unbound*.[1] It is now clear, I think, that it has not been vouchsafed him to see it, except dimly and from afar off. Later questers will pay homage to his courage and perseverance, but they will be fortunate, indeed, if they do not follow his track into the wilderness.

In an earlier typescript publication, available on microfilm or in xerographic booklet from Xerox's University Microfilms division,[2] Zillman recorded for interested scholars his transcriptions of all the rough-draft material for *Prometheus Unbound* that he had been able to locate—most in the Shelley notebooks at the Bodleian and Huntington libraries. There he usefully arranged those drafts according to the act and scene divisions of the completed drama (noting the exact page or folio references to his sources) and included a list (with very brief bibliographical descriptions) of the source manuscripts.

Zillman's new complete edition of *Prometheus Unbound*, to which one can refer simply as *The Text and the Drafts* to avoid confusion with Zillman's *Shelley's "Prometheus Unbound": A Variorum Edition* (University of Wash-

---

1. *Shelley's "Prometheus Unbound": The Text and the Drafts, Toward a Modern Definitive Edition* (New Haven and London: Yale University Press, 1968).
2. *The Complete Known Drafts of Shelley's "Prometheus Unbound"* (Ann Arbor, 1967).

ington Press, 1959), incorporates most of the readings from the Xerox publication, though here Zillman neglects to give the specific page locations of the various drafts. In *The Text and the Drafts*, he presents these scattered first-draft readings prominently in the textual notes on pages facing his own text of *Prometheus*, but he relegates to an appendix the more authoritative variant readings from Shelley's intermediate fair-copy manuscript, the first edition (1820), and Mary Shelley's collected editions of Shelley's poems. The presentation of the less authoritative variants in the most convenient place is only one of a number of questionable editorial decisions made in *The Text and the Drafts* that require an examination of editorial principles and methods, rather than analysis of the accuracy of the editorial performance.

Professor Zillman's chief handicap is the lack of a clear understanding of the methods of modern textual criticism, as practiced and taught, for example, by students of Tudor and Stuart drama—the tradition of Pollard, Greg, McKerrow, and Bowers. In his first attempt to "edit" *Prometheus Unbound* (*Shelley's "Prometheus Unbound": A Variorum Edition*), he simply reproduced the error-ridden first edition of 1820 "with verbal exactness" and defended the decision on the grounds that he had found it "necessary to decide between the relatively imperfect text . . . and the [even more imperfect] manuscript left by the poet" (p. xvii). Although the thought of emending a copy-text according to clearly stated, defensible principles apparently did not occur to Zillman on that occasion, it occurred to most reviewers of *A Variorum Edition*, and the outcry about the inadequacies of that volume apparently provided the occasion for the edition now under scrutiny.

Zillman, having fallen out of the boat on the starboard side, gamely clambered back in and leaned out dangerously far on the port side. He took so much to heart the criticism that he had edited insufficiently in *A Variorum Edition* that in *The Text and the Drafts* he "edits" almost everything in sight, altering spelling and punctuation in the name of modernity, consistency, and readability, and even apologizing (pp. 26–27) for not changing Shelley's "Poeticisms" (e.g., his use of the familiar second person, singular and plural). In a characteristic statement, he declares that, in determining the punctuation of the poem, the editor must "avoid the mannerisms to which the poet was subject" (p. 25).

Zillman has not studied sufficiently the work of other modern editors of the Romantics who have grappled with similar problems of editorial policy; he indicates no awareness, for example, of the editorial policies in the texts of Blake by Keynes and Erdman, of Clare by Robinson and Summerfield, or even of most of the recent studies of Shelley's text. Nor has Zillman attempted to substantiate his generalizations by reference to the ascertainable practices of the early nineteenth-century writers themselves. He writes, for example, on the question of whether to follow Shelley's spelling *sate* or to substitute his own *sat*: "The now archaic *sate* . . . was obsolescent in the early nineteenth century and appears to have been pronounced optionally with the long or short *a*. The long *a* is suggested where Shelley, in other poems, employed *sate* as a rime (although there the possibility of approximate rime cannot be overlooked), but in the two occurrences in *Prometheus Unbound* (I.723 and II.i.134, both non-riming) modern usage seems preferable" (p. 8n). Let us examine the evidence. A glance at the available concordances to the Romantic poets (some of which are themselves based on partially modernized texts) shows that *sate*, far from being "obsolescent," was the spelling preferred by Shelley, Byron, Wordsworth, and Coleridge.[3]

When one analyzes the use of *sate* and *sat* by these poets, one discovers that *sate* is invariably rhymed with words like *hate, late, weight*, etc., whereas *sat* is rhymed with *that* and *hat*. This shows that *sate* was pronounced with a long *a* during the period these poets were writing, and that this pronunciation was the usual or preferred one. If *sate* had been commonly pronounced with a short *a*, there would have been no reason for these poets to alter their preferred spelling *sate* to *sat* when rhyming with *hat*. To change Shelley's spelling of *sate* to *sat* changes the pronunciation and thus alters the poetic effect of the line. In the two instances where Zillman changes Shelley's *sate* to his own *sat*, the poetic quality is affected slightly. In one instance (I.723) Zillman has removed assonance from a line in an important lyric; in the other (II.i.134), he has introduced nonfunctional assonance. Shelley's poem is not, certainly, ruined, but it has been hurt slightly, and as Fredson Bowers observed on the general question of whether to modernize nineteenth-century texts, "no gain results from modernizing, and much is lost that is characteristic of the author" (*SB* 17 [1964]: 223).

On at least one crucial issue, Zillman misinterprets Shelley's statements about putting his poems through the press. As evidence that Shelley cared nothing about matters of spelling and punctuation and left such details to the printer, Zillman (mis)quotes from Shelley's letters as follows: "I send

3. That *sate* was not used extensively by Blake and Keats (or, so far as I have checked, by John Clare) suggests—what historians of the language would be much better able to judge—that *sate* was an upper-class usage fostered at such schools as Eton, Harrow, and Christ's Hospital. I find Lamb also rhyming *sate* with *state* (*Works* [1818], 1:46), but lack of a concordance to Lamb makes it difficult to generalize about him.

you the Revise, which may be put to press when corrected" (*Letters*, ed. Jones, 1:532) and "I have written it so as to give very little trouble, I hope, to the printer, or to the person who revises. I would be much obliged if you could take this office on yourself" (*Letters*, 2:263). From the context (these quotations are found in a footnote to the statement that "punctuation and spelling were generally left to the discretion of the printer," pp. 11–12), it appears that Zillman interprets the word *revise* in these quotations as meaning "conventionalize spelling and punctuation," but bibliographically it meant then, as now, "a second or subsequent proof" (as a noun) and "to correct proofs" (as a verb). In the first quotation, when Shelley had marked the proofs himself, he simply instructed his publisher to check to see that the things he had marked were corrected in type before the pamphlet was "put to press"; in the second quotation, Shelley is tactfully hinting that he has prepared his copy carefully so that the printer and proofreader need not trouble themselves to change or "improve" his work. These, like other quotations from Shelley's letters in the same footnote, thus work against—not for—Zillman's thesis.

A knowledge of the printer's manuals of the period—Stower, Johnson, Timperley, etc.—would have provided Zillman with some evidence that the printers *desired* that punctuation and spelling be left to their discretion. But those same manuals also indicate that many, if not most, authors disputed them on this point. With Shelley, the evidence of his letters overwhelmingly supports the view that he wished to have the final word on all accidental, as well as substantive, textual matters. When Harry Buxton Forman examined in detail the evidence for Shelley's concern in the case of *Laon and Cythna* (*The Revolt of Islam*) he concluded that Shelley sent his manuscript to the "printer with strict instructions to 'follow copy,' that is to print it *verbatim, literatim*, and point for point, and to leave revision to the author" (*The Shelley Library*, p. 81). I accept Forman's conclusions as basically valid, and I shall present additional evidence on this question in forthcoming volumes of *Shelley and his Circle*.

Great difficulties still arise about the texts of Shelley's poems not because he was indifferent to details of spelling and punctuation, nor because he was unduly careless in preparing copy (though everyone makes mistakes), but because several of his poems were printed and revised (that is, proofread) without his supervision by people who understood and cared less about them than he did and who then proceeded to discard the manuscripts that had been carefully prepared for the printer. Zillman rightly notes that the true authoritative text of *Prometheus Unbound* is the lost manuscript sent to Ollier in 1819. But he imagines that, simply by comparing substantive features of the first edition of 1820 with the first fair copy (Bodleian MSS Shelley e. 1, e. 2, and e. 3), he can re-create that lost manuscript. Such a re-creation is impossible for anyone who begins with the assumption that both Shelley's printer and he were given carte blanche to tinker with punctuation, orthography, and (I gather from pp. 26-27) unusual or "poetic" pronouns and verb forms.

If one wishes to approach nearer to the details of Shelley's press-copy manuscript (and, hence, to his intended text), one must emulate textual scholars who study Renaissance drama: first, learn the characteristic printing practices of the day; second, study the peculiar practices of the printing houses in which Shelley's works were printed (Marchant in the case of *Prometheus Unbound*, but C. H. Reynell for several other volumes of Shelley's poetry); third, compare features of "good" texts (including manuscripts that Shelley prepared for the press and printed works that Shelley himself saw through the press) with the practice in volumes such as *Prometheus Unbound* that Shelley did not proofread. This last phase includes a systematic study of Shelley's practice in orthography and punctuation—a study that should endeavor to sort out mere errors from Shelley's preferred or characteristic spellings, use of capitals, and modes of punctuation.

In order to undertake this study, it is important to know what Shelley actually wrote in his various manuscripts and what precisely was printed when he himself revised the proofs. To ascertain the first, the textual scholar can study either facsimiles of the manuscripts or diplomatic texts based on the manuscripts (and then check his work by consulting the originals). First editions of Shelley's poetry are located in enough major research libraries to make study of those that Shelley corrected in press— *Queen Mab*, *The Revolt of Islam*, *The Cenci*, and *Adonais*—relatively easy, even though the scholar must collate several copies of each work.[4]

There survives from this period at least one complete manuscript that Shelley himself prepared for the press and sent to be published, and for which he did not intend to read proofs—the so-called Hunt manuscript of *Julian and Maddalo* (now in the Pierpont Morgan Library). There was also a "safe-keeping" copy of this poem originally in the fair-copy book now at Harvard, which was probably removed to serve as the basis for the text in *Posthumous Poems* (1824). From a detailed study of the transmission of the texts of this poem (and *The Mask of Anarchy*, for which similar evidence is available) one might begin to understand the characteristic changes in

---

4. On the value of the Hinman collator for such comparisons, see Fredson Bowers, "Old Wine in New Bottles: Problems of Machine Printing," in *Editing Nineteenth-Century Texts*, ed. John M. Robson (Toronto: University of Toronto Press, 1967), pp. 9-36.

orthography and punctuation that Shelley made between his own "safe-keeping" copies (e.g., the Esdaile copybook, the Harvard copybook, and the fair-copy notebooks containing *Prometheus Unbound*) and the manuscripts sent to the press. If characteristic patterns emerged from this analysis, one could work more intelligently from the extant "safe-keeping" copies and the first editions to approach the "ideal state" of the copy that Shelley intended to send to press. Orthography and punctuation would be altered from those in the safe-keeping text, but the alterations would follow a pattern that Shelley initiated—not simply the impressionistic guesses of a modern editor.

The above-suggested approach to the text of *Prometheus Unbound* would not apply to all of Shelley's works. For those volumes that Shelley saw through the press and for which the press copy does not survive, the copy-text would be the ideal state of the first edition. With these poems the editor would, of course, be very hesitant about making substantive emendations without strong corroborating evidence (e.g., finding a more suitable and meaningful alternative in Shelley's drafts), and he would seldom alter the accidental features, inasmuch as the drafts would be still less authoritative in those matters. On the basis of his understanding of Shelley's handwriting and the printing practices of the day, the editor should in his textual notes suggest possible misprints that Shelley could easily have overlooked while proofreading.

For poems unpublished after Shelley's death and for which the only authorities are one or more unrevised rough drafts in Shelley's notebooks, two stages are requisite. First, one must determine whether the holograph draft or drafts always provided the only authority, or whether there might have been a lost fair copy, either a holograph or a transcription done by Mary when Shelley was still alive and could have approved it, underlying the printed text. If there might have been a lost manuscript more authoritative than any now extant, then the problems become similar to those in *Prometheus Unbound*. If Shelley's holograph drafts provide the only clear indication of his intention, then they should be compared, priorities among them determined, and a text edited. This text should be one of two kinds: (1) a diplomatic text (like Hyder Rollins's edition of Keats's letters) that closely follows the copy-text, emending sparingly where necessary and then often with explanatory notes; or (2) a critical text in which the accidentals are emended either according to Shelley's common practice, as determined by study of his finished and published poems, or according to modern usage; in either case, a scholarly edition will record all departures from the copy-text and all variants in other holograph manuscripts. It is also necessary to record variants in other printed texts based directly on the manuscripts, because all editors are fallible.[5]

Because textual editors, like all other mortals, are prone to error and slothful in good, they cannot bear the additional handicap of a want of a true theory of editing. Professor Zillman came to his study of Shelley's manuscripts relatively late in his career, and he depended for some of his ideas of editing on scholars who also lack an understanding of the modern principles of textual criticism. There ought to be a series of conferences—like that held at Toronto in November 1966—so that scholars who undertake the editing of nineteenth-century poetry can exchange information and air their views openly. If such meetings could encourage the growth of a general consensus of standards in editing early nineteenth-century texts, such industrious scholars as Professor Zillman and such imaginative university presses as Yale would be spared the misdirected effort that produced this handsome volume.

5. Fredson Bowers would add that only a text that records variants from *all* historically important editions "can truly be called a 'definitive edition'" (see *Nineteenth-Century Fiction* 23 [1968]: 237).

3

Rogers's Oxford Shelley

The headnote to "Editing Shelley" (1) gives part of the background for this review. In the late 1960s, Kenneth Neill Cameron and I were reviewing the scholarly publications on Shelley for "The Romantic Movement: A Selective and Critical Bibliography" (then, as now, edited by David V. Erdman, but at that period appearing in ELN). There I reviewed Rogers's Riverside Edition of Percy Bysshe Shelley: Selected Poetry for the 1969 issue. (For some of my findings, see "Editing Shelley.") When I was asked to review the first volume of the Oxford English Text edition for JEGP, I decided not to center on my disagreements with Rogers about editorial principles; it is always difficult to convince those who are not personally familiar with the textual evidence of the best editorial method for a complex situation, and in a time of theoretical anarchy, to do so may be impossible. After stating my differences with Rogers's chosen methodology, I concentrated, therefore, on Rogers's failure to implement successfully his own principles.

Because my initial list of errors and problems with the edition was several times longer than I had room to discuss, I selected a broad sampling of different types of errors and tried to write clearly and at sufficient length about each to convince readers that my overall judgment was justified. Jack Stillinger read a draft and made several useful suggestions about condensing the review and moderating its tone. Though it was assigned to the April 1974 issue of JEGP (73:250–60), problems at the University of Illinois Press delayed the publication of that issue for several months. Finally, in October 1974, I sent for a proof copy of the review, reproduced twenty copies of it, and mailed these to Neville Rogers, leading Shelleyans, textual scholars, and officials of the Oxford University Press in England and New York.

My knowledge of Rogers's working habits had served me well, for a correspondent at Oxford who had seen the manuscript that Rogers had sent to the press informed me that, for most of the volume, it consisted of two copies of Hutchinson's text pasted up, with a few points altered in the margins—just as my collations suggested.

The reviews of the first volume of the Oxford Shelley were mixed. But by the time the second volume appeared in 1975, the users of the first had lost faith in

Rogers's capacity to edit, and the negative reviews that pursued the second volume eventually convinced the Clarendon Press (a decade later) that they were not obligated to throw good paper after bad. By that time, I was engaged in other matters and did not review volume 2 of the Oxford Shelley, first purchasing a copy in the summer of 1986.

According to Neville Rogers, the most authoritative keys to Shelley's texts are not the poet's manuscripts or first editions, but later editions of Shelley's poems—particularly that of Thomas Hutchinson (1904), which since 1905 has been available as the Oxford Standard Authors edition (OSA). In his General Introduction, for example, Rogers writes: "Out of the two accidental facts of Shelley's residence in Italy and the posthumous publication of much of his poetry has grown the bibliographical myth of a text corrupted by an incompetent publisher during his lifetime and by editors after his death, and needing to be 'corrected' by 'accurate' reproduction of his manuscripts. The truth . . . is the exact opposite—his editors have provided correction of the error of which his manuscripts are usually the source."[1]

This unusual view seems to grow out of Rogers's (demonstrably mistaken) belief that Shelley took no interest in the final presentation of his text to the public and out of a novel definition of the term *copy-text*, by which Rogers understands "the substitution for those principles of reasoned judgement known as 'textual criticism' of a Fundamentalist faith in a manuscript as something merely requiring to be copied" (p. xxx). I know of no other editor who employs the technical term *copy-text* to mean what Rogers accuses most modern editors of meaning by it. Had he read W. W. Greg, Fredson Bowers, G. Thomas Tanselle, and others in the numerous articles, textual introductions to editions of poetry and prose, and reviews in which *copy-text* is defined and employed, he could never have written under such a misapprehension.

Though Rogers throughout his General Introduction seems to think that he is attacking the methods of Greg, Bowers, and those who have profited from their ideas, the textual principles that he advocates reduce themselves to a naive version of theirs. Rogers believes that an editor must examine all available textual evidence and construct an eclectic text on the basis of his reasoned analysis of it. In this I agree with him. I differ from him, however, on two matters: (1) the appraisal of what constitutes authoritative textual evidence (that is, evidence indicative of the *author's*

1. *The Complete Poetical Works of Percy Bysshe Shelley*, ed. Neville Rogers, vol. 1: 1802–1813 (Oxford: Clarendon Press, 1972), p. xxii.

intention); and (2) the methods one should use to safeguard the author's text from contamination because of the fallibility of those through whose hands the physical record of that intention has passed—transcribers (including, of course, the author himself), compositors, proofreaders, and, especially, editors whose well-intentioned efforts to improve a text by conjectural emendation affect the music or meaning of a passage.

Specifically, on the first matter, I consider proper evidence of the author's intended text to include the following, in roughly descending order of reliability (though this relative authority must in practice be determined through analysis of each individual situation). In the highest category are: (1) holograph manuscripts prepared by the author for the press or given to friends as finished copies; (2) an edition for which the author both supplied press copy and read proofs; (3) a copy of such a published text containing corrections in the author's hand; (4) a manuscript prepared as press copy by someone close to the author (e.g., Mary Shelley, Dorothy Wordsworth, Charles Brown) and known (from holograph corrections, etc.) to have been read and approved by the author; (5) proofsheets corrected in the author's hand and written corrections given by the author to the publisher while the work was in press, or for errata lists. Authorities of the second rank include: (6) the author's desire for changes in his texts as expressed in letters to friends other than his publisher (usually less reliable evidence than instructions directed to the publisher, because the author may merely be trying to mollify the particular friend); (7) published texts for which the author supplied press copy *or* for which he corrected proof but did not do *both*; (8) the author's safekeeping manuscript copy, retained by him when 1 or 4 was sent to press; (9) another, earlier intermediate holograph fair copy; (10) the author's original holograph draft. A third category would include: (11) transcripts made by friends or relatives of the author during his lifetime; (12) editions published during the author's lifetime for which he is not known to have *either* provided press copy or corrected the proofs, but which can plausibly be supposed to have been authorized by him—that is, issued by his publisher or friends with his knowledge and consent; (13) editions published after the author's death by his publisher or friends, based on manuscripts or printed texts of uncertain authority but possibly including authoritative corrections or revisions from sources now lost, or from the author's orally expressed desires; (14) critical editions emended and normalized by editors fully familiar with the author's works and their history.

If I understand Rogers correctly, he would theoretically choose my 14 as his primary textual authority; in his practice, he certainly does so.

On the second matter of difference between us—how an editor makes sure he is keeping to the author's intended text, rather than to a coagulant of diverse bits and pieces that the author did not originate and never specifically approved—I believe that the editor of a major new collected edition should, first, collate all textual authorities described above, 1 through 14, and, second, present readers of the edition with a record of substantive variants from all extant authorities in items 1 through 10 and (depending upon the nature of that evidence) a record of accidental variants from the four or five best authorities. This practice not only forces the editor to consider all relevant evidence, but it enables readers to analyze the judiciousness of the editor's individual choices and decisions. In practice, editors who follow the two steps I have suggested usually feel the need to justify their decisions in series of textual notes that illuminate critical as well as merely textual problems.

Rogers does not specify the steps *he* has taken to eliminate mechanical errors from his text, or to allow the reader to identify and correct whatever faulty editorial decisions may have been transmitted by the "generations of accomplished workers, from Mary Shelley to Thomas Hutchinson, whom it is [his] privilege and [his] responsibility to succeed" (p. vii). Though he seems generally confident in the efficacy of his efforts, which "in terms of time and technical study have seemed infinite," he does recognize that all editors occasionally err, and he appeals to his readers to "be as patient as I believe that Shelley would have been" (pp. vii-viii). Since he thinks that Shelley had little concern with "the words on his page," as being "no more than drops in the cascade of ideas which poured from that furiously rapid mind" (Rogers in *KSMB* 16 [1965]: 21), perhaps a scholarly reviewer would do better to apply the somewhat more rigorous standards that govern Oxford English Texts editions in other periods of English literature.

The first thing that struck me after collating a number of Rogers's texts was that he had not followed his stated principles of constructing an eclectic text but had followed his "starting text" (usually Hutchinson's OSA edition) almost verbatim and literatim, in some cases retaining Shelley's own ungrammatical usages and punctuation (often usages that were unacceptable in Shelley's day and are not to be found in his own mature poetry) and at other times transmitting substantive errors introduced by Hutchinson or one of his predecessors.

Consider, for example, the texts of the two earliest volumes of Shelley's published verse, *Original Poetry* by "Victor and Cazire" (1810) and *Posthumous Fragments of Margaret Nicholson* "edited by John Fitzvictor"

(1810). Both volumes, whatever the occasions of their publication and even the authorship of their contents, are known to have been printed from press copy supplied by Shelley and seen through the press (insofar as anyone took pains with that) by him or under his direction. Rogers gives as his textual authority for *Original Poetry*, not the first edition, but "1904" (i.e., Hutchinson's edition) and "1898" (i.e., Richard Garnett's type facsimile reprint of the first edition). From T. J. Wise's *A Shelley Library* (p. 30), we know that the facsimile is imperfect because two words had been erased from the copy Garnett followed, for reasons that are clear when the provenance of that copy is compared with Jones's fourth footnote to Shelley's letter to Graham of 11 August 1810 (Shelley's *Letters*, 1:13-14). The sensible procedure—that which Rogers's own General Introduction endorses—would have been to collate Hutchinson's and Garnett's text against at least one, but, better, against both extant perfect copies of *Original Poetry*, the one at the Huntington and the other in the Ashley Collection, British Museum. Had Rogers done so, he would have found that his text (Hutchinson) differs from the first edition in 128 noteworthy instances (not counting merely formal differences such as their entirely different systems of indicating quotations), among which differences are thirteen that I regard as significant corruptions of the text. The most serious example occurs in the seventh poem (the "Song" subtitled "Hope"), line 15, where the change of "deceivers" (1810) to "deceiver," (the "deceivers" are the "flowers" of line 13) has made nonsense out of the poem. In "Revenge" (p. 54), an apostrophe has been added in the wrong place to Shelley's text, producing another serious misreading: "I must seek the drear tomb of my *ancestor's* bones, / And must dig *their* remains from beneath the cold stones."

Collation of Rogers's text of *Posthumous Fragments of Margaret Nicholson* reveals that he has followed Hutchinson, his "starting text," without change, including Hutchinson's few errors and his frequent but usually meaningless alterations of Shelley's orthography—this despite the fact that the *Margaret Nicholson* volume is one that cries out for emendation of the erratic punctuation (and lack of punctuation) at the ends of lines. It is almost as though Rogers had merely cut up copies of Hutchinson and sent them directly to the printer.

In a major section where he does not reprint OSA, Rogers reprints his own earlier editorial efforts from *The Esdaile Poems* (1966) without significant change, apparently consulting neither the photostats of the manuscript from which his original work was done nor Kenneth Neill Cameron's literal transcription of 1970. The few minor changes I have noted carry the reader farther from Shelley's manuscript without adding substantially to either clarity or consistency. In the first line of "To Harriet," Rogers lowercases *Sun*; in "Zeinab and Kathema" he does not capitalize *superstition's* in line 25 (though Shelley does), but he does follow Shelley in capitalizing *Ocean's* in line 49. Rogers has replaced Shelley's inconsistency (if the poet's capitalizations can, in fact, be shown to be illogical and nonfunctional) with the editor's inconsistency, but because Rogers takes some of his texts from Hutchinson (who took some of *his* texts from the first editions and others from heavily edited texts) and then adds other texts that he has edited on different principles, the result is not one pattern of inconsistency, based on the vagaries of Shelley's own care, or lack of it, but rather a cacophony of inconsistencies, some originating in Shelley's own manuscripts, some from a variety of compositors, others from Hutchinson and *his* sources, and a goodly number introduced by Rogers himself. It seems especially ironic that Rogers, who frequently expatiates on the distinction between "editors" and "transcribers," has, in this first volume, proved himself to be a transcriber rather than an editor; it is unfortunate that he has chosen to transcribe in bulk Hutchinson rather than Shelley.

Turning to the matter of canon, we find that the chief novelties in the edition are brief translations of four epigrams from the *Greek Anthology* and of two Latin epigrams by the English Latinist Vincent Bourne (pp. 6–8) that appeared over the signatures "S." and "Versificator" in the *Oxford University and City Herald* in January, February, and March 1811, and "Sadak the Wanderer" (pp. 20–22). All these poems had been advanced as Shelley's in the 1860s and 1870s, but had been rejected after investigation by W. M. Rossetti and H. B. Forman. As Rogers notes, it was D. F. Mac-Carthy who first championed Shelley's authorship of the translations from the *Greek Anthology* and from Bourne's Latin (along with an English "Ode: To the Death of Summer," which Mac-Carthy felt more certain was Shelley's, but which Rogers ignores). But the arguments that Mac-Carthy advanced in *Shelley's Early Life* (1872) appear much weaker now than they did at the time they left Rossetti and Forman unconvinced. Mac-Carthy himself noted that another translation from Vincent Bourne appeared in the paper signed "S. S.—Edmonton." To one familiar with the relations between reader-contributors and the weekly and monthly periodicals of the era, it seems likely that after "S." had contributed two translations from the *Greek Anthology,* another reader using the distinct name "Versificator" contributed the translation from Vincent Bourne, adding two weeks later two translations from the *Anthologia* in emulatory rivalry of the contributions by "S.," to which in turn "S.S." of Edmonton (possibly, but not necessarily, the same person as the original "S.") replied with *his* translation from Bourne. The burden of proving Shelley's authorship of these translations lies with Rogers, if he wishes to include them in a standard edition, and he provides no objective evidence linking them to Shelley.

The case against "Sadak the Wanderer" being by Shelley is clearer but more complex. Rogers follows Davidson Cook's article on "Sadak" (*TLS*, 16 May 1936), which points out that the poem, first published in *The Keepsake for 1828* (1827), was attributed to Shelley in the table of contents to the bound volume of press-copy manuscripts (then owned by Cook), from which the manuscript of "Sadak" itself had been removed. Cook did not give the provenance of this bound volume of *Keepsake* contributions; we find, however, that in June 1870 J. Dykes Campbell owned the manuscript book (with the manuscript still intact) and that Campbell told W. M. Rossetti about the poem, who in turn told Garnett and investigated the matter.[2] Campbell, a friend and scholarly correspondent of Edward Dowden, certainly would have mentioned the poem to him, had he still thought it genuine. If Mary Shelley had contributed the poem to the *Keepsake* as Shelley's (as Cook postulates), she surely would have included it among Shelley's works in 1839, as she did the poems by Shelley that she contributed to later volumes of the *Keepsake*. And a draft of the poem should appear among the Bodleian (or Huntington) Shelley notebooks, from which Mary drew all the rest of Shelley's posthumously published poems. But, if we suppose for a moment that Mary sent the only manuscript of the poem directly to the *Keepsake* and that she later forgot about it, on what basis can Rogers publish it among Shelley's *juvenile* poems, which include only poems that Shelley wrote *before* he met Mary, none of which survives in any manuscript form that Mary ever owned? If "Sadak" was contributed to the *Keepsake* by Mary Shelley, it must belong to a later period. But since Campbell, Rossetti, and Dowden never identified the poem as Shelley's when the manuscript was extant, it seems clear that whoever attributed the poem to Shelley in the handwritten list bound with the manuscripts was simply mistaken or misinformed. "Sadak the Wanderer," like the translations, is not by Shelley—at least the preponderance of evidence suggests this—but Rogers includes the poem without qualification.

Queen Mab alone of the poems in this volume is frequently read and studied. I shall, therefore, conclude this review with a detailed examination of Rogers's editing of that poem, discussing it under the following

---

2. *Letters about Shelley Interchanged by Three Friends—Edward Dowden, Richard Garnett and Wm. Michael Rossetti*, ed. R. S. Garnett (London, New York, Toronto: Hodder and Stoughton, 1917), p. 36.

three heads: (1) the text itself; (2) the collations and textual notes; (3) the critical notes.

Rogers's text is that of Thomas Hutchinson—not 1904, as Rogers claims, but the OSA edition as reset in 1933 and following (and recently corrected by G. M. Matthews). His use of OSA is obvious from errors in the paragraphing of the verse that carry over from the 1933 setting to Rogers's text but which are not present in 1904 (e.g., Rogers's lack of spaces between IV.120 and 121, and between IV.153 and 154). The OSA text is reprinted almost letter for letter and space for space; the chief differences are the correction of one typographical error in OSA (*villanous* to *villainous* in IV.184), the introduction of at least two typographical errors (omission of the indefinite article from I.165 and a change from *and* to *amd* at V.179), and the following six conjectural emendations. At I.133-34, Rogers sensibly adopts Locock's suggested punctuation. In V.34 he emends "heart impassive *by* more noble powers" to "heart impassive *to* more noble powers"; here his choice is clearly wrong, inasmuch as in the context (as several generations of editors who refrained from emending this phrase apparently recognized) *impassive* means *impassible* (*OED* 4). In VIII.26, Rogers changes a colon to a comma, obscuring the rhetoric of Shelley, whose system of punctuation required a longer pause at this position than the comma produces. At VIII.77 and VIII.81 Rogers adds two dashes to set off what he apparently regards as a parenthetical construction. At IX.130 he emends Shelley's *wreck* to *rack* (citing Shakespeare's *Tempest*, IV.i.156); he has evidently failed to consult the *OED*, which lists Shelley's use of *wreck* in *Queen Mab*, along with parallel instances (including one from Wordsworth's *An Evening Walk*) to illustrate the eighth main meaning of *wreck* as substantive. Rogers's conjectural emendation, though clearly erroneous, fulfills poetic justice by returning to a form that—through Malone's earlier conjectural emendation of *The Tempest*—had been obscured during Shelley's time. Finally, at IX.167, Rogers adds an innocuous but superfluous comma to the end of the line. The net improvement in the text of *Queen Mab* from the readily available OSA text to Rogers's text is one typo corrected, one mark of punctuation emended sensibly, and two moot changes in punctuation, as against two typos introduced, one mark of punctuation wrongly altered, and two new words introduced without authority in place of Shelley's correct diction.

The OSA text itself, however, cannot be accepted, I believe, as an appropriate copy-text (or "starting text"). Thomas Hutchinson made few positive contributions to the texts of Shelley's poetry; he chose somewhat eclectically between readings in Rossetti's and Forman's editions. Most prominent among Hutchinson's innovations was his addition of capital letters for which there is no authority, and nowhere does sprinkling Shelley's text with added capitals create as much havoc as in *Queen Mab*. Hutchinson obviously tried to uppercase common nouns when they were personified or had special religious significance—nouns and pronouns that refer to God or Christ. Shelley, who himself saw *Queen Mab* through the press, apparently used other criteria, though precisely what those criteria were and how systematically they were followed in his own manuscript and by the compositors who set the poem would require detailed textual analysis. Hutchinson added to the text of Shelley's first edition only one capital to Canto I (209), eight to Canto II, twelve each to the third and fourth, and thirteen and fifteen to Cantos V and VI respectively. (He occasionally lowercases Shelley's capitals along the way.) Then, in Canto VII, amid the all-out onslaught on Christianity, Hutchinson adds no fewer than forty-five capitals, mostly to words referring to God—including such irreverent titles as "Fiend" (VII.97), "Tyrant" (VII.199, 257), and "Foe" (VII.248). Thus the modern reader is treated to the ironic spectacle of Shelley, in the text of his most outspokenly anti-Christian poem, paying court through his reverent orthography to the god whose objective existence he denies and whose myth he is denouncing. Moreover, Hutchinson's capitalizations are also erratic—certainly as inconsistent as Shelley's own (cf. *Freedom* with *truth* and *virtue*, VII.244–47; *Man*, III.199, VIII.187, with *man*, III.225, IV.166, 167, and VIII.209; *Death*, V.156, with *lust*, equally personified, V.166). As in the cases where Hutchinson alters a number of Shelley's characteristic spellings, he has merely substituted his own erratic usage for forms that in Shelley were no more inconsistent and were equally comprehensible to the modern reader. Thus, in my opinion the OSA text is not so reliable a "starting text" as to justify Rogers's faithfulness in reproducing it.

Turning to the collations, we find that very few variants are recorded from the hundreds of differences between Rogers's text and Shelley's first edition and Mary Shelley's editions, and a considerable proportion of those few collations are either superfluous or incorrect. A large number of the variants Rogers records come from H. B. Forman's description of the manuscript revisions by Shelley in the Pforzheimer copy of *Queen Mab* (work outdated by the prior publication of the complete text of these changes in volume 4 of *Shelley and his Circle*). Since these variants (as well as those from the similar Ashley copy) represent versions, not of *Queen Mab* but "The Dæmon of the World," it is unclear why Rogers did not wait until volume 2 of the OET Shelley to include reference to them. Does their inclusion here mean that he intends to omit Shelley's "The Dæmon of the World" from his second volume? Omitting collations of "The Dæmon of the World" from the count, we find a total of twenty-six notes recording variants between Rogers's text and various other editions or texts. I shall discuss the variants that Rogers does record and mention in passing a few typical omissions. (Recording all variants is, after all, the function of the editor, not the reviewer.)

On page 231 Rogers notes that the Dedication to Harriet was "*omitted in 1839*[1]"; he does not mention that in *1813* the epigraph from Lucretius read *juratque novos* instead of *juvatque novos*, or that the first line of the Dedication *1813* has a comma after *that*, or that in line 15 Shelley used the spelling *flowret* for the word that Rogers spells *floweret* (*flow'rets* at VIII.106).

On page 236 Rogers records his alteration of the punctuation at I.133–34, but neglects to mention the *1813* variants in orthography at I.140 and in end-punctuation at I.154. At III.74, he neglects to record that the change of speakers is not found in *1813*. On page 257, he records minor punctuation differences in which he follows Hutchinson (*1904*), but ignores a variant in orthography (*Learnt/Learned*) that may change the reader's pronunciation of a word, and he skips over the most promising place in the poem for a significant verbal emendation: in IV.133, does not the context suggest that *longings* (*1813*, followed by all editors, including Rogers) may be a typo for *lodgings*?

On page 258, Rogers records two of his textual changes: in one case, his change is probably wrong and in the other his collation is erroneous; collating his correction of Hutchinson's typo (*villanous* to *villainous*), Rogers indicates that all other editions contain the error, but actually *villainous* is correct in *1813*, Forman, Herne Shepherd, Woodberry, Locock, and Julian; the word is incorrectly spelled in the editions of Mary Shelley and William Michael Rossetti (who perpetuated the error by using as press copy cut-and-pasted leaves from Moxon's 1853 one-volume reprint of Mary's edition). At IV.176, Rogers follows Hutchinson in emending *Secures* (*1813*) to *Secure*; though this change appears in Mary Shelley's editions, Charles H. Taylor, Jr., has shown that it and other deviations from Shelley's first edition can be traced, not to conscious decisions on Mary's part (much less new authoritative evidence), but to John Brooks's unauthorized reprinting of *Queen Mab* (1829) via Ascham's 1834 text, which Mary used as press copy for the poem. Whether one *should* emend the text here is at least debatable; I incline to accept Rogers's retention of *Secure*, but he should justify emending the first edition rather than simply follow the (perhaps) fortuitous appearance of the change in Mary Shelley's edition. Though on pages 259,

269, and 274, Rogers notes that portions of Cantos V and VI and all of Canto VII were omitted by Mary Shelley from her first edition of 1839, on page 279 he seems to have forgotten this, for he collates VII.180 with both the first and second editions of 1839, giving *reillumined* as the reading of *1839*[1]. On page 264, Rogers records that in V.116 *offsprings* appeared in *1813*, and *offspring's* in his text, as well as OSA and *1839*; he fails to note, however, that if an apostrophe is to be added, the passage requires the possessive *plural*, not the possessive singular. Shelley's first edition reads (italics added): "[He] ever hears his famished *offsprings* scream, / Whom *their* pale mother's uncomplaining gaze . . . ." The error apparently originated in the *1839* edition, since both Brooks and Ascham emend the text—more satisfactorily—to *offspring*, reading *scream* as a verb instead of as a singular noun and thereby eliminating *all* anomalies from the passage with the removal of a single letter from Shelley's text. But an even simpler solution is to suppose that Shelley uses *offsprings* as a plural noun (*OED* 1.b.), in which case no emendation is necessary, *offsprings* being the correct subject of the verb *scream*.

A reading for VIII.81 that Rogers says is found in all editions (*edd.*)—namely, *rang* both preceded and followed by commas—I can find in none. In *1813*, Forman, Hutchinson, and Julian, commas follow the word but none precedes; in both Mary Shelley's editions of *1839* no comma precedes *rang* and a semicolon follows it; in the editions of Rossetti (1870 and 1878), Woodberry (1892 and 1901), and Locock no comma precedes *rang* and both a comma *and* a dash follow the word.

On page 287 Rogers creates confusion in his collation for VIII.204; the reading in the *1813* text is *lore*, not *store* (the reading in the note to the line is also *lore*). On page 288, Rogers incorrectly assesses the significance of Shelley's revision of lines 232–33 in the Pforzheimer copy of *Queen Mab* (see *Shelley and his Circle*, 4:559). On page 289, Rogers is wrong in saying that in IX.27 the word *millenniums* is italicized in *1813*. This record of errors raises serious questions about the care exercised by Rogers and his editors at the Clarendon Press to ensure the accuracy of the edition.

Turning to Rogers's notes to *Queen Mab*, one finds similar errors of both omission and commission. He fails to discuss such relevant features as the background of the title character, Queen Mab, in eighteenth-century children's literature (and, hence, Shelley's probable purpose in giving his prolocutor that name), and he does not comment on many difficult words or passages that, I would judge, require annotation. What, for example, is that "rock, / The utmost verge of earth / The rival of the Andes, whose dark brow / Lowered o'er the silver sea" (I.218–21)? Rogers notes merely, for

I.200–19, "cf. Erasmus Darwin, *Loves of the Plants*, III.161–4," a reference that casts no light on the identity of the "rock." In his note to II.109 and following (which begins, "Behold . . . / Palmyra's ruined palaces!—"), Rogers fails to identify Palmyra, though he mentions "Cameron" (no title or page reference), who does discuss the matter. At V.44–45 (as elsewhere in Shelley's early poetry), there is an allusion to the legendary poisonous Upas tree, and at V.80 a more obvious reference to Adam Smith's *Wealth of Nations*; Rogers does not identify these or other such references that are important for a clear conception of Shelley's meaning and method.

But, of course, every annotator omits information that another would include. The notes on *Queen Mab* that Rogers *has* included tend to be interpretive rather than factual. Some of them seem to be apologies for Shelley's early beliefs, combined with high praise for the intimations of "natural" and "direct" Platonism that Rogers discerns amid Shelley's professed necessitarian atheism and political radicalism. But even those notes that might otherwise be merely irrelevant may be misleading to novice students. On page 385, for example, Rogers concludes a note to IV.139–53 by observing: "For all the materialism and professed atheism something in Shelley too takes flight from this point in the poem." Whether Shelley was, strictly speaking, a materialist in *Queen Mab* is at least debatable; what is clear is that Shelley (unlike Godwin, Coleridge, and others) saw no conflict between "materialism" and the doctrine of moral disinterestedness preached in Godwin's *Political Justice* (see Shelley's *Letters*, 1:315–16) and therefore that his idealistic aspirations in *Queen Mab* need not be attributed to "Platonism" or any other "ism" that Shelley may or may not have embraced in later years.

On Shelley's vegetarianism, Rogers feels that "Shelley's zeal may seem to have run away with him," but he takes comfort in the speculation that "this subject appears soon to have faded from his life and thoughts," and he adds, "I have wondered whether his vegetarianism affected his health and whether it became a source of domestic trouble. Perhaps he abandoned it when he left Harriet for Mary" (p. 398). Had Rogers wished to *know* rather than "wonder" about Shelley's vegetarianism, he could have turned to Shelley's letters, where we find that in 1817 Shelley not only was practicing vegetarianism but had converted various friends to it, including Leigh Hunt's nephew Henry L. Hunt (*Letters*, 1:543). Or he could have turned to Dowden's biography of Shelley for the same period and found that while at Marlow the vegetarian Shelley "would purchase cray-fish of the men who brought them through the street, and would order his servant to bear them back to their lurking-places in the Thames" (2:123). Or he might have turned to the widely quoted passage in Leigh Hunt's defense of Shelley's morality against the *Quarterly Review*'s attack on *Laon and Cythna*; Hunt tells that, during the time he spent with Shelley at Marlow, Shelley lived like Plato, "or rather still more like a Pythagorean" (i.e., a vegetarian) who "came home to a dinner of vegetables (for he took neither meat nor wine)" (*Examiner*, 10 October 1819, p. 653). Or he might have recalled Haydon's story of how, meeting Shelley at a dinner party, he was startled by an attack on Christianity from that "little, delicate, feeble creature . . . eating vegetables only" (Haydon's *Diary*, ed. Pope, 2:372-73). Or he might have learned from Thomas Medwin's account of Shelley in Italy in 1820 that Shelley was "most abstemious in his diet, . . . and, although he had been obliged for his health to discontinue his Pythagorean system, he still almost lived on bread, fruit, and vegetables" (Medwin, *Revised Life of Shelley*, ed. Forman, pp. 372-73). Or, if going to such first-hand authorities proved too burdensome, Rogers could have turned to Newman Ivey White's *Shelley*, which, though not recording the particular information given above, has an analytical index that would have answered the question as to whether or not Shelley abandoned vegetarianism "when he left Harriet for Mary."

Rogers, besides "wondering" about facts that he could easily verify or refute by looking into primary sources, often repeats information—and misinformation—from earlier scholars. For example, Edward Dowden pointed out in 1870—and Cameron and I have demonstrated more than once since—that Shelley's fragmentary essay "On Life" was written in 1819-1820; Rogers dates it 1812-1814 (p. 396). On the same page, Rogers declares that previous editions have misprinted as "Christiern" what should be "Christian"; in fact, King Christian II of Denmark was known as "Christiern" and Shelley used that form of the name in "A Philosophical View of Reform" as well as in the notes to *Queen Mab*. Rogers systematically emends the Latin quotations in Shelley's notes to conform to the texts in the Loeb Classical Library editions, which practice both renders it impossible for scholars to identify the texts Shelley used and distorts the meaning that Shelley attached to the texts he chose to reprint. Dr. Shackleton, Bodley's Librarian, provided Rogers with the most useful original information in the notes on *Queen Mab*—the identification of a line of French poetry (p. 394); that identification itself is modified in a corrigendum on page 400, in which Dr. Shackleton demonstrates his true scholarly spirit by looking further into the matter and suggesting a more plausible source. We can only lament that the work of Rogers himself does not evince the same spirit of intellectual curiosity that leads to continuing inquiry.

It is not enough, I think, to conclude simply by saying that scholars and students ought to ignore this volume, unless they find use for it as an egregious example of how *not* to edit poetry. If this volume had been published by a minor university press, the voices of scholarly reviewers might suffice. But it appears as the first of four massive volumes bearing the imprimatur of the English-speaking world's oldest academic press; it comes to us with the official sanction and support of one of the world's great universities and the repository of the largest collection of Shelley's literary manuscripts; it is advertised and distributed by the world's largest publishing organization, with offices from Melbourne to Nairobi and Toronto to Kuala Lumpur.

Neville Rogers has made many positive contributions to Shelley studies. He was a leading force, for example, in the formation and growth of the Keats-Shelley Memorial Association in Britain and the Keats-Shelley Association of America—and, hence, of the founding of their respective annual journals; his *Shelley at Work*, whatever its shortcomings, has been seminal for studies of Shelley's manuscripts and the revival of textual studies of Shelley's poetry and prose; he has cast original light on Shelley's interest in music, art, and certain Continental writers. But he has not demonstrated that he is capable of producing a sound new edition of Shelley's poetry. If loyalty to their long association with Rogers precludes the officials of the Clarendon Press withdrawing the first volume of the OET Shelley, they owe it to those scholars and librarians who have learned to rely on the Clarendon Press for a high degree of scholarly competence to take extraordinary steps to make sure that subsequent volumes in this edition are not as wrongly conceived and as poorly executed as this one.

4

The Ohio Browning

Fate sometimes brings a young scholar too much of a good thing. In April 1973, while I was still drafting my review of Neville Rogers's Oxford Shelley edition, I received an invitation from Victorian Poetry to contribute a review article, of whatever length and for whatever deadline I might "find convenient," on volume 3 of the Ohio Edition of The Complete Works of Robert Browning, Roma A. King, general editor, in which (it was suggested) I treat the edition "against a frame of principles of editing/textual criticism." While I was working on the review, volume 4 of the edition appeared and was added to the assignment. Roma King, like Rogers, was a professor at Ohio University in Athens, Ohio, and that connection inevitably had something to do with the tone I felt obliged to adopt in my essay on the Ohio Browning. For this work I had at my disposal, besides the fine collection of Browning editions, proofsheets, manuscripts, and holograph letters in The Carl H. Pforzheimer Library, my own nearly complete collection of the first editions of Browning's poetry. As I mention in the review, I had earlier tried to assist the editors of the Ohio Browning by sending them information on the Pforzheimer Library's important manuscripts and corrected proofs. So I undertook the review with a good deal of enthusiasm. When, however, I realized the limitations of the edition itself, I faced the decision of whether or not to publish at nearly the same time two long reviews that savaged the editorial efforts of two professors at a single institution.

Inasmuch as reviews of the first two volumes of the Ohio Browning—especially reviews by Thomas J. Collins, Rowland L. Collins, and John Pettigrew—had already called attention to many shortcomings of the edition, I was spared the duty of being the first to bring the bad news to Ghent. Instead, I decided to treat in detail a special concern of mine at the time, drawn from my awareness of how few scholars wrote to inquire whether the holdings in the Pforzheimer Library might be relevant to their researches: textual scholars sometimes expend too little effort searching, even among well-known rare book and manuscript collections, for the documents and editions basic to their projects. In the review, I also treated the question of copy-text and Robert Browning's handling in later editions of what I was still calling "accidentals."

As should be clear from the review-essay itself, my expert adviser on some Browning matters was Philip Kelley, whose subsequent career, now culminating in his and Ronald Hudson's edition of The Brownings' Correspondence *(1984–), is demonstrating to the world what I surmised soon after we met in New York in the 1960s: though he earned only a B.A. and has never held an academic appointment, Kelley is probably the most dedicated and knowledgeable person working on Browning anywhere in the world. It was my idea at the time to list in the review examples of "lost" literary manuscripts and proofsheets of Browning, identifying the then-missing items from the Pforzheimer's selection of catalogues of famous literary collections. Since then, the problem has been all but solved by Kelley and Betty A. Coley with* The Browning Collections: A Reconstruction *(1984), a unique and masterful book that gives the present location of books, manuscripts, and memorabilia from the Brownings' possessions that were sold at Sotheby's in 1913, as well as giving the whereabouts of many other manuscripts and annotated and association copies of the Brownings' own publications.*

In October 1973, having heard a rumor that Morse Peckham had resigned as an editor of the Ohio Browning, I wrote to him. He replied with characteristic directness, beginning his letter: "I have not only resigned from the edition but recommended that it be abandoned." And he concluded his detailed account of its problems thus: "In your review . . . you have my unqualified permission to use any material in this letter or quote it, if you wish, and to use my name as the author of this letter." I had always admired Peckham's scholarship; the forthrightness that he exhibited on this and other occasions is a breath of fresh air in a profession in which so many people gossip behind their colleagues' backs about their personal foibles, but refuse to stand up and record their opinions on issues of genuine intellectual substance, either in print or face to face with those holding contrary opinions.

While focusing on the limitations of the Ohio Browning, I was able to suggest some concrete and theoretical ways in which its shortcomings could be remedied, suggestions from which both editors of the later volumes of the Ohio Browning and those undertaking competing editions seem to have profited. Though I have not been able to follow all these developments in detail, the reviews, controversies in TLS *and* London Review of Books, *and conversations with students of Browning suggest that there are still problems with the editions now available and in progress. Perhaps there will have to be a redaction twenty years or so from now, building on the contributions of the three recent and current editions—the Ohio Browning, the Yale English Poets edition by John Pettigrew (who died before its completion) and Thomas J. Collins (1981), and the Oxford English Text edition, edited by Ian Jack and Margaret Smith (1983–).*

The Ohio University Press edition of *The Complete Works of Robert Browning* is, as Rowland L. Collins emphasized in his review of the first two volumes (*VP* 9 [1971]: 351–56), a handsome set of books that evinces highly skilled and motivated professionalism in every aspect of its design and production. It would be pleasant to report that the editorial efforts and talents employed in filling the pages have been of equally high quality. On the basis of the volumes before me,[1] I should say that, because the editorial principles of the edition are fundamentally sound and because individual contributors have executed their collating, selection of text, recording of variants, and annotation with reasonable though not consistent care, the edition is a significant milestone on the road to a standard text of Browning's works. But the edition has many deficiencies.

I shall discuss the edition under the following heads: (1) location of relevant authoritative materials; (2) articulation of editorial principles; (3) execution of editorial plan in regard to text, collations, and critical notes.

Near the end of the front matter (section *VIII*) the editors give the locations of Browning manuscripts known to them and another list of manuscripts "not known to be extant"; there they request "information about any of the manuscripts which are presently unknown to the scholarly world" (p. xxvi). The phrasing seems a little forbidding, suggesting as it does that anyone who knows the location of one of the missing manuscripts cannot, by definition, belong to "the scholarly world." Perhaps the thought that the entire scholarly world's knowledge would preclude discovery of new material by the individual teacher-scholar or librarian explains why no one bothered to mention to the editors that the holograph of "Cavalier Tunes" from *Dramatic Lyrics* is described in *The Tinker Library* (New Haven, 1959), pp. 85–86, and is at present in the Beinecke Library of Yale University. My personal experience suggests, moreover, that Browning's editors are not, in fact, as eager to acquire information on the available manuscripts as they might be. On 8 November 1968, soon after the announcement of the forthcoming publication of the first volume of *The Complete Works of Robert Browning* came to our attention, the librarian at The Carl H. Pforzheimer Library wrote to the general editor, Roma A. King, Jr., mentioning that "this library has a considerable number of Browning manuscripts, including poetic manuscripts" and offering to assist in any way. There was no reply to that letter. A second letter, written 13 April 1973,

---

1. *The Complete Works of Robert Browning*, Roma A. King, Jr., general editor, vols. 3 and 4 (Athens: Ohio University Press, 1971 and 1973). Vol. 3 contains *Pippa Passes*, ed. Morse Peckham; *King Victor and King Charles*, ed. Park Honan; *Essay on Chatterton*, ed. Donald Smalley; *Dramatic Lyrics*, ed. John Hulsman; and *The Return of the Druses*, ed. Morse Peckham. Vol. 4 contains *A Blot in the 'Scutcheon*, ed. Thomas F. Wilson; *Colombe's Birthday*, ed. Park Honan; *Dramatic Romances and Lyrics*, ed. Raymond Fitch; and *Luria*, ed. Morse Peckham.

the day I received the review copy of volume 3 of the edition, was sent in care of the director of the Ohio University Press, describing in detail our relevant holdings, which include the complete holograph press-copy manuscript of *Colombe's Birthday* and the author's corrected page proofs of *Jocoseria* and *La Saisiaz* and *The Two Poets of Croisic*. We finally received a reply from Professor King on 10 October 1973, thanking us and saying that the editors would be in touch with us sometime in the future. I notice that there is in the first issue of *Studies in Browning and his Circle* an appeal by Professor King for information on the location of page proofs—including those about which we informed him in April—and in volume 4 before me is the text of *Colombe's Birthday* edited without the advantage of the author's manuscript that was offered the editors five years ago.

Though it may be belaboring the obvious, I shall list some Browning manuscripts and proofs that have been sold at public auction in the twentieth century but which may not have been located by the editors. In the Spoor sale, Part I (1939), lot 85: proofsheets of "A Dream of Arcady" and "Stanzas" with 200 words in Browning's hand; lot 86: *Dramatis Personae* (1864) corrected in the author's hand for a proposed second edition; lot 90: "A Miniature," an album poem attributed to RB. In the Jerome Kern sale of 1929 we find: lot 102, a copy of *Paracelsus* (1835) with Browning's holograph corrections for a second edition; lot 103, *Sordello* (1840) with the author's corrections and additions; lot 104, *Strafford* (1837) containing numerous pencil corrections and notations in Browning's autograph; lot 105, *Bells and Pomegranates*, with alterations in *Colombe's Birthday* for a proposed stage production; lot 114, *Red Cotton Night-Cap Country*, author's corrected proofs. (This last item was later listed for sale by Charles S. Boesen of New York in the catalogue *The Samuel Wyllis Bandler Library, Part I* and in his list no. 22, "Balance of the Bandler Library.") In the *Catalogue of the Private Library of Mr. Adolph Lewisohn* (1923), we find on page 33 not only the author's corrected proofs of *Dramatis Personae* but also a copy of *Ferishtah's Fancies* containing "a page in the hand of Browning . . . giving instructions regarding the printing of the book." Similarly there are listed holographs of fugitive Browning occasional verses in the catalogue of Harry B. Smith's *Sentimental Library* (1914), pages 10–11, with facsimile plate, and the catalogue of the Marsden J. Perry sale (1936), item 56.

I am certain that a thorough search of auction and dealers' catalogues at the Grolier Club and British Museum would yield a much larger number of relevant manuscripts, proofsheets, corrected copies, and instructions to the printer. Through the record of their latest purchase the editors might be led to the present owners. I do not personally know what has happened to the items named above, but were I responsible for producing an elaborate, expensive set of the complete works of a major author, I would want on my editorial board the person who knows more than anyone else in the world about the present location of the writer's manuscripts and association copies. In the case of Browning, that person is without doubt Mr. Philip Kelley of Princeton, New Jersey, and even at this late date, securing Kelley's counsel may make the difference between an edition that will be self-corrective in its later volumes and one that may become obsolete through the rediscovery of such relevant new authoritative materials.

In discussing the editorial principles of this edition, I am employing not a standard of ideal perfection but one that takes into account the practical difficulties inherent in editing Browning's text as well as the present chaotic state of textual criticism as applied to nineteenth-century poetry. As changes in the front matter from volume to volume of the Ohio Browning make clear, the editorial principles were determined before all the relevant evidence was examined, and they have been revised as the work progressed. Yet there is virtue in the editors' very willingness to treat their work as a learning process rather than pretending that it is an incarnation of immutable, ideal principles brought down on stone tablets from the Blue Ridge near Charlottesville.

The basic question of the choice of the 1889 collected edition as the copy-text for the poems it contains is treated at length on pages xiii-xxii of volume 3. A recent article by Philip Kelley and William S. Peterson ("Browning's Final Revisions," *Browning Institute Essays* 1 [1973]: 87ff.) presents information from Browning's letters and from a copy of the 1888–1889 set in Brown University Library with corrections in Browning's hand that parallel, but do not exactly correspond with, those in the Dykes Campbell copy, including seven changes that are not available in the Campbell copy (which the Ohio Browning did use) and five cases in which Browning's corrections differ in the two sets. Kelley and Peterson suggest that "since the stereotype plates were becoming very worn by late 1889, the 1889 edition may also contain some non-authorial changes resulting from the resetting of type" (p. 98). Such a sequence seems to me unlikely, since the introduction about 1850 of reusable flong molds for casting stereotype plates made the resetting of type within a year or two to produce a second set of plates a very remote theoretical contingency (see Philip Gaskell, *A New Introduction to Bibliography*, pp. 203–4). Of course, if Kelley and Peterson have documentary or bibliographical evidence that the 1889 edition was, in fact, printed from reset type (or from plates made from reset type), their point about the greater authority of 1888–1889 is well taken, for they have shown beyond doubt that 1888–1889 was the last edition to receive Browning's personal attention. If, on the other hand, the 1889 edition contains the substantial text of the 1888–1889, and in addition corrects 90 percent of the errors marked by Browning in the Campbell and Brown University copies (as it does, according to the count of Kelley and Peterson), 1889 may have been the correct choice in the first place. In either case, in volume 4 the front matter of the Ohio Browning has been revised on pages xix-xxii to take into account the evidence of the Brown University marked copy.

On one significant theoretical question—whether to accept the "accidental" as well as the "substantive" features of the latest revision in which Browning was involved (rather than those of the poet's press-copy manuscripts or his first editions)—Kelley and Peterson agree with the Ohio editors, as do I, that Browning's clear control of and interest in all features of his final collected edition give that text unique authority, if—as in any critical edition—typographical errors and compositorial tinkering can be identified and corrected. For the latter task, the collation of all major earlier texts should provide substantial help. Browning may, like Wordsworth, have changed some passages or lines for the worse in later revisions, but it makes no sense in dealing with a nineteenth-century writer who corrected, in parts at least, all features of his work in press copy and proofs to follow the words of his latest revision and the punctuation and orthography of an earlier version. On the whole, the rationale for choosing the later collected edition is more clearly and succinctly stated by Kelley and Peterson, who have no need to adopt a defensive posture, than by the Ohio editors. But the main facts remain that the Ohio editors have chosen rightly in ignoring the McKerrow-Greg-Bowers dictum on differentiating between substantives and accidentals and that their text—subject to emendation from Browning's late holograph corrections and letters—is the most appropriate basis for a complete edition of his works.

Though the editors have, I believe, adopted a sound copy-text, they have not faced squarely the difficulties presented by the long transmission of such a text through the vagaries of its recordless history from first editions in the 1840s, through collected editions in 1849, 1863, 1868, and 1888. Obviously, though Browning corrected errors and polished individual lines as he oversaw each new edition, he could not give the same attention to all the details of punctuation and orthography that he had given to each first edition when he was concentrating on presenting it to the public for the first time. Here is where jettisoning the *experience* of McKerrow, Greg, and Bowers along with their *dogmas* proves harmful, for though the latest edition has to be used as the copy-text to incorporate Browning's final changes, there must be continual vigilance on the part of each editor of a work—and, especially, by the general editor who oversees the whole—to catch and correct the unauthorized compositorial changes that inevitably creep in. In other words, the editors must not hesitate to emend the late copy-text a hundred times in a hundred lines if a collation of various works shows them that on certain points Browning himself was probably not responsible for the changes.

For example, in the eighteenth and early nineteenth centuries, the abbreviated spellings *tho'* and *thro'* were quite acceptable alternatives in manuscript and print for *though* and *through*. Being short, they were in favor both with authors transcribing their works for the press and with compositors. By the time of Browning's death, *tho'* and *thro'* had generally fallen out of favor, but they were not regarded as errors. Here is one feature of orthography, then, that can be used to see how meticulous Browning was in regularizing the merely formal aspects of his text. When we look at a work such as *The Return of the Druses*, we find that the Ohio University text is inconsistent: Act I.84, II.199, and III.153 and 169 read *thro'* whereas Act II.2 and III.12 read *through*. Both these latter lines originally read *thro'* (which seems to have been the favored form in Browning's manuscripts), and both were changed in the 1863 edition. In volume 4 of the Ohio Browning, the same inconsistency continues; in *A Blot in the 'Scutcheon*, I.iii.133, *through* appears (having been altered from *thro'* in 1863), whereas on the next page at I.iii.166 *thro'* remains unchanged. The texts of his late first editions suggest that Browning never totally abandoned the use of the abbreviated forms *thro'* and *tho'* (see *Balaustion's Adventure* [1872], p. 20, line 6, and *Jocoseria* [1883], p. 69, line 3), but his, as well as the compositors', preference for the regular, expanded spellings seems clearly established and, unless the editors can detect a pattern in which the abbreviated form with apostrophe occurs in cases where there is elision with the initial vowel of the following word, I would suppose that the spellings ought to be regularized to *though* and *through* in the Ohio Browning.

Or, to take a similar question, while it is fairly clear that Browning originally spelled *honor* without the *u*, in later editions the spelling was gradually changed to *honour*. Again in *The Return of the Druses*, I.169–172 contains three instances in which the spelling was altered in 1863, but at II.245 the alteration was not made until 1888 (at the same time that, nearby at II.238 and II.281, *tho'* remained unaltered through all editions to emerge in the Ohio text). Or, to look at yet another random instance, in *A Blot in the 'Scutcheon*, I.i.4, the word *poursuivant* appears (and is duly defined in a note to the line), whereas the same word in *King Victor and King Charles*, First Year, Part I.109 is spelled *pursuivant* (and not defined, though this appearance is in volume 3 and the reader must await the definition in volume 4). Which way did Browning originally spell this word in his manuscripts? Was he inconsistent there? Is there an accepted English form of the word? It seems quite clear that in revising his works for later editions, Browning made no systematic effort to regularize such forms as *thro'* and *tho'* or to establish a single spelling for *pursuivant*. If Browning did not take it upon himself to eliminate these inconsistencies, he left the matter to the compositors and pressroom proofreaders and accepted their text. In this case, such merely formal features may not be as authoritative in later editions as in Browning's manuscripts and first editions, and a modern critical edition ought to attempt to determine which forms he preferred at last and then regularize his texts on the basis of that preference.

The question of the "house styling," which the editors discuss on page xvi, seems to me a complete red herring insofar as it relates to English *publishers* of the early nineteenth century. In examining press-copy manuscripts and proofsheets of a variety of writers whose works were published by such small publishers as Charles Ollier and Taylor and Hessey and by the giant John Murray, I have seen no evidence of "house styling" or copyediting as publishers now practice it. Neither, apparently, have Browning's editors, but because of the doctrines of the editors of the Center for Editions of American Authors, they are led to worry about the apparent anomaly of finding no consistency either in the styling found in books published by the same publisher but printed by different printers, or in books issued by different publishers that used the same printer. It seems clear to me that different *printers* do sometimes style the work of the same author differently, but these differences can be easily explained as normal variations occasioned by the interactions of author, compositor, and printer's proofreader, the work of the last individual being crucial. In a small pressroom, which one reader may have dominated, there was likely to be a greater degree of consistency than in a larger shop. But such matters would be subject to infinite variations and accidents—such as illnesses of the chief reader; his relations with an older or particularly strong-willed compositor; the degree of consistency in the author's press copy; or the particular prejudices of the publisher (who, though he did not style press copy, may well have complained loudly if certain typographical peculiarities, such as the possessives *its, yours, theirs, hers,* and *ours* spelled with an apostrophe, appeared in his books). As Morse Peckham rightly insists in "Reflections on the Foundations of Modern Editing"

(*Proof* 1 [1971]: 122–55), textual criticism resolves finally into a branch of history, and—I should add—a branch for which, by the nature of the interactions that produced printed books, few written records exist and, therefore, untestable hypotheses abound.

Browning did give attention to some details of orthography. It is clear, I think, that in *King Victor and King Charles* he systematically changed the spelling *Chamberri* of 1842 to *Chambery* (the spelling current in Italy) in 1849 and later editions. In the same poem, Browning's frequent revisions in the 1849 edition of many lines in which the name *D'Ormea* appears must certainly result from the discovery that the name was pronounced *D'Orméa*, not *D'Órmea*. (This explanation does not appear in the volumes under review, possibly because the apparatus provides no convenient place for discursive notes exploring the implications or significance of the textual variants.) But it is clear that Browning did not give all minor features of all poems equal attention in later editions.

In volumes 3 and 4 there are a number of instances in which palpable errors have been perpetuated because the editors were not aggressive and imaginative enough in emending their copy-text. On page 203 of volume 3, line 1 of "Count Gismond," a necessary comma after *God* was dropped in the 1868 edition and not restored by either Browning or the Ohio editors. An even more obvious error resulted from the dropping of a comma in line 45 on page 91 of volume 3, leaving "I" meaninglessly marooned between two commas. On the facing page (3:90), lines 36 and 37 are improperly arranged on the page, Polyxena's "I know" being the first foot of line 37, not the end of line 36. (The spacing is correct in the 1849 edition.) In other cases, the authority of changes is less certain, as when many words that were capitalized in the first editions and 1849 are lowercased in the 1863 or 1868 edition. Perhaps seeing the corrected copy that Browning sent to press and his corrected proofsheets of each edition would be the only certain way to know what his intentions were, but it seems to me worth an effort on the part of scholarly editors of a text of this magnitude to assemble the evidence for each edition and formulate an educated guess on which kinds of changes reflect Browning's active choice and which occurred because he overlooked or acquiesced to compositorial error or innovation.

From my own limited observations of Browning's proofsheets for first editions of two late works (1878 and 1883) in the Pforzheimer Library, I have the distinct impression that the poet was not meticulous in marking all details of the text even where errors appeared. For example, in the *Jocoseria* volume Browning had presumably sent copy that gave the title of the fourth poem as "Cristina and Monaldeschi"; when his compositors

Anglicized the title name from *CRISTINA* to *CHRISTINA,* Browning corrected the error on the contents page, marking the *H* for deletion. On the fly-title he marked through the *H* and wrote *Cr* in the margin; on page 35 he erroneously marked through the *R* and wrote *Cr* in the margin. He neglected to mark the running heads on pages 37, 39, 41, and 43 where the same error was repeated. (The name does not appear in the text of the poem itself.) The printer made the corrections as Browning obviously intended, altering *CHRISTINA* to *CRISTINA* in each place the name appears. But Browning's own carelessness in marking the change should warn his editors that they must exercise judgment similar to that of the compositor of *Jocoseria* and infer from the evidence of manuscripts and proofs what changes Browning authorized from edition to edition.

While completing this review-article, I wrote to Professor Morse Peckham, who informed me that he had resigned from the Editorial Board of the Ohio Browning because of his dissatisfaction with the overall quality and accuracy of the editing, after he had checked in detail volumes 1, 2, and 4. With Professor Peckham's permission, I quote from his letter of 12 October 1973:

In January 1972 I . . . undertook an investigation of the first two volumes with a view to publish a list of errata and emendata as an Appendix to Vol. V . . . . I interrupted that investigation in order to work on the galleys for Vol. IV . . . . Thus it was not until this past August that I returned to my examination of Vols. I and II. When I discovered errors on more than 60% of the pages of Vol. I and on at least 34% of the pages of Vol. II—a total of probably somewhere between 800 and 900 errors in text, failure to make emendations, errors and omissions from the variants, and the explanatory notes (all but three in the notes to *Sordello*, the entire responsibility of the general editor . . . .)—I decided that there was no point in further examination. . . . As soon as this became widely known, it was obvious, the credibility of the edition would be lost, and it was a matter of simple honesty to make it as widely known as possible. . . . I therefore withdrew my completed edition of *Men and Women,* together with a considerable amount of miscellaneous work I had done for Vols. V and VI, recommended that the edition be abandoned, and resigned.

. . . Browning's Final Edition, . . . even after Browning's corrections for the second impression, is the worst of his collected editions and of any single volume he published. Details on this will appear in the next issue of *Studies in Browning and his Circle.* This is the only valuable information yet to emerge from the edition, except for the explanatory notes. Even the imperfect *Sordello* [notes], marred as they are, contain useful material.

Professor Peckham, who had exerted a strong influence on shaping general editorial policy for the edition, whose own editorial work in the volumes under review is generally excellent, and who has written vigorous public rebuttals to criticisms of the early volumes, has sufficient reason to be disappointed with a cooperative effort that is not, as a whole, as good as his contribution to it. But he is being too severe in thinking that the edition should be abandoned, or that the text and apparatus are not useful. From the collation of variants I was able, in my spot-checking, to identify problems in the text and to draw critical inferences (such as Browning's reason for rewriting lines in *King Victor and King Charles* that contain D'Ormea's name). Even errors, by Peckham's count, on 60 percent of the pages is not nearly as high a proportion of deviations from an authoritative text and accurate collations as in Thomas Hutchinson's Oxford Standard Authors edition of Shelley, which has five to twenty such deviations and errors on almost every full page. Yet Hutchinson's text, having been the best available edition of Shelley's poetry for almost seventy years, is being used as "starting text" in the new Oxford English Text edition of Shelley and reproduced almost to the letter and without systematic recording of its variants from the authoritative manuscripts and editions. Or, take the classic edition of Wordsworth's *Prelude* originally done for Oxford University Press by Ernest de Selincourt, corrected twice by de Selincourt through the use of lists of addenda and corrigenda and corrective appendixes, and finally completely revised by Helen Darbishire and printed anew in 1959. Jack Stillinger noted in his review (*JEGP* 59 [1960]: 161–64) that the appearance of Darbishire's redaction "may further dispel some of the smoke from that old pipe dream, the 'definitive' work. . . . Perhaps the most interesting among what she calls 'minor corrections' is the restoration to the early text of two lines that de Selincourt had inadvertently omitted from Books VIII and IX. . . . At I, 284, de Selincourt misread or misrecorded 'foretaste' for 'knowledge' in not one but three manuscripts." And, after recording a number of new errors he had discovered in Darbishire's work, Stillinger concluded: "Lest the chagrined amateur, still in quest of the 'definitive' work, now hope that Miss Darbishire's revised edition is at last conclusive, let him take note that it begins with a corrigenda slip and ends (save for the appendix and index) with a page of 'Addenda to Notes.'"

I have not myself found anything as horrendous as the omission of full lines from poems in the third and fourth volumes of the Ohio Browning. The only dramatic typographical error I have noticed in the text itself (in Peckham's part of volume 3) is *Ture* for *True* in *The Return of the Druses* IV.5 (3:312). Doubtless Peckham in his detailed checking and Browning scholars who study and consult the volumes frequently have found others. I agree with Peckham that the explanatory notes are generally very good and probably represent a higher level of scholarship than the textual work, but a severe examination would reveal errors and omissions equally frustrating when judged by standards of *absolute* accuracy. In his notes to *King Victor and King Charles* (Part II, I.ii.8–9) Park Honan states that "in August, 1718, . . . Admiral Byng destroyed Alberoni's powerful Spanish fleet off Sicily." The *DNB* article on Admiral George Byng, Viscount Torrington (1663–1733), states, however, that the battle commenced with a chase about noon on 30 July 1718 and that "about ten o'clock the next morning (31 July 1718), being then some three leagues to the east of Cape Passaro, the leading English ships came up with the sternmost of the Spaniards." What degree of precision and accuracy is required here? Aristotle averred that "discussion will be adequate if it has as much clearness as the subject-matter admits of, for precision is not to be sought for alike in all discussions, any more than in all the products of the crafts." Though Honan did not give the first name of Admiral Byng, or the exact location of the battle, or the precise date on which it commenced, the information he gives is more than sufficient for a comprehension of the point of the lines in Browning's play; and it may (for all I know) be closer to the information Browning had at his disposal than the *DNB* account that Browning certainly could not have seen. By an absolutist standard, one could quarrel with Honan's note at 3:360 to *King Victor*, Part II, 312, where he identifies *Janus* as a "Two-faced Roman god [etc.]." This note ignores the whole tradition of *Janus Quadrifrons* in which (as Lempriere's *Classical Dictionary* in its early versions makes clear) Janus with *four* faces was worshipped as god of the four seasons and the temporal order. Here, perhaps, the note is inadequate, if Browning (who certainly encountered *Janus Quadrifrons* in Shelley's "The Triumph of Life," if nowhere else) intended D'Ormea to allude to the *Quadrifrons* tradition. And yet scholars who have not been puzzled by a Janus-visaged charioteer with four faces may feel that I am being unduly influenced by an unrelated problem and that Honan's note is adequate to the poetic passage.

To omit the reference to *Janus Quadrifrons* does *not* constitute an error in annotation, but a similar deviation from absolute accuracy would be counted as an error by Peckham if it occurred in the collations. I feel that—even if there are fairly frequent slips in the collations or even in the readings accepted for the final text—if enough accurate information is presented, the individual scholar, to whatever extent his own knowledge of editorial problems and his particular use for the text allow, can compensate for these errors. We should always bring a healthy skepticism to any secondary source; if, from the Ohio Edition, I learn that, in a passage crucial to my interpretation of a poem, Browning altered the punctuation radically in 1868, I will consult the originals to see what the effect of the changes was for the meaning. The text and collations should *ideally* provide an accurate record of the materials needed by the textual critic, but the text itself cannot have *every* choice made to suit the judgment of *every* qualified scholar who examines that evidence.

In my opinion, the level of accuracy in the Ohio Browning is high enough to raise it above the average quality of editions of nineteenth-century English poets presently available. This does not mean that there is no room for improvement. The most important need is to gather and examine all the relevant materials. Philip Kelley should be made a member of the Editorial Board and be given a specified amount of clerical assistance by the Ohio University Press to canvass *all* libraries and private collectors who may have Browning materials. Second, the Ohio Browning should appoint a noted authority on textual criticism to the Editorial Board whose sole responsibility would be to check the texts contributed by the editors of individual works. He should be empowered to send the texts back to the sub-editors for correction as often as necessary to achieve a high level of adherence to good textual principles and accuracy of execution. Third, rather than attempting to push out volumes on a precise schedule based on budgetary considerations, the Ohio University Press must be content to wait until the materials for each volume have been accurately edited and checked more than once. Fourth, if possible, Professor Peckham should be persuaded to rejoin the Editorial Board. His contributions seem to me the best parts of the two volumes under review, and to lose permanently his knowledge of the period would be a serious blow to the quality of the edition. Finally, as lists of addenda and corrigenda for the earlier volumes are published in later volumes, they should also be printed as separate lists on gummed-edge pages suitable for insertion in each volume, mentioned in advertisements for future volumes, and sent out on request to owners of the early volumes.

Some such procedures as I have suggested above would improve subsequent volumes of the Ohio Browning, go a long way toward making the edition self-correcting, and earn the renewed confidence of the scholarly community. I hope that the time, effort, and resources that have been expended in producing the first four handsome and useful volumes can be reinforced by better quality-control of the editing and by broader participation of those involved in Browning research. It behooves Professors

King and Peckham, who did so much to initiate this worthwhile undertaking, to make certain that they do not play King Victor and King Charles to the detriment of the realm of Browning's poetry.

5

The Bollingen Coleridge

The *review-essay on David V. Erdman's edition of Coleridge's* Essays on His Times *was commissioned for* Studies in Romanticism *by David Wagenknecht in the spring of 1978 and published in the spring issue of 1979 (18: 141–50). David Erdman was then and is still (as I hope is clear from "Romantic Bards and Historical Editors") one of my mentors, models, and intellectual heroes, as well as a good friend. I had no doubt, when I began to read his edition for review, that his knowledge of Coleridge's life, works, and times was far greater than mine. But I knew also that he, like the rest of us, has a few blind spots.*

Essays on His Times *impressed me with its comprehensiveness, but for that very reason, as well as because of the rarity of the ephemeral primary materials that Erdman had used in his research, few if any scholars would ever have the interest or the capacity to duplicate his efforts. That consideration made it all the more important that I not allow friendship to influence me to put the edition beyond analysis and discussion. I had already observed how scholars and critics too often fail to distinguish between primary and secondary evidence, basing their detailed theories and elaborated arguments on hints that they find in modern critical editions, instead of checking the crucial evidence against primary manuscripts and editions. Moreover, it was becoming clear that, because I enjoyed wide familiarity with the three major collections of manuscripts from the Shelley circle and had at hand, at the Pforzheimer Library and in my personal collections, most of the first editions and contemporary materials and secondary scholarship on the Romantics, I was coming to be considered an "expert" whose word would be too readily believed about Shelley and a number of other writers. At the same time, I knew both how much I did not know and how often I let silly errors slip into print—more in recent years than when I was younger and not quite so busy.*

In this review-article, therefore, I undertook to put into perspective the strengths and limitations of all critical editions by analyzing one of the best parts of the Bollingen Coleridge, which may be the most thoroughly researched and painstakingly checked collective edition in the English Romantic field. Without debunking the process of critical editing, I wished to undercut the notion that any student, critic, or scholar could safely rely on the materials contained in any secondary critical edition, rather than seek out the crucial information in the primary authorities. This cautionary reminder of what can and what cannot *legitimately be expected of a "definitive" edition was thus perpetrated on an admired friend because David Erdman had such well-deserved authority in his field that his edition was more likely than most to lull its readers into false security, as well as because nobody could suspect me of saying (as I had of Zillman and Rogers) that I could have done Erdman's work better than* he *did—however much better* he *might have done it.*

The ideas on Coleridge's political and economic acumen and consistency came to me while reading his journalism in Erdman's edition. The notion, hinted at the end of this piece, that Biographia Literaria *is a consciously Shandean work had been a bee in my bonnet for a few years, and some Coleridgean friends were rash enough to encourage me to propound it. (I have since developed it into a paper entitled "Coleridge and the Art of Equivocation," published in the "Homage to Carl Woodring" issue of* SiR *(25 [Fall 1986]: 325–50), condensed from a longer chapter on Coleridge in* Intervals of Inspiration: The Skeptical Tradition and the Psychology of Romanticism *(Greenwood, Fla.: Penkevill Publishing, 1988).*

For help with this review, which was my baptism in Coleridge studies, I wish to thank Raimonda Modiano, who at my request read it in manuscript and saved me from some errors, and David Wagenknecht and his sterling staff at Studies in Romanticism, *who caught several more things. Needless to say, we did not detect all my oversights, and I have corrected half a dozen typos and minor errors for this reprinting.*

* * *

The review of Engell's and Bate's edition of Biographia Literaria *(RP&P 8 [Summer 1984]: 39–44) is not substantial enough in itself to merit republication. But, in conjunction with the review-essay on* Essays on His Times, *it broadens the perspective on the strengths and limitations of The Collected Coleridge. Since the review appeared, I have been reliably informed that the edition's reluctance to probe Coleridge's foibles originated, in part, with Kathleen Coburn, the general editor. As I emphasize both in this review and elsewhere in the present volume, sympathy for the author, the work, and the subject being studied is a sine qua non of all good scholarship and criticism. But like all virtues, sympathy can exist in excess as well as in deficiency. Aristotle has dealt with this problem.*

Coleridge as Prophet of Property: A Review of Samuel Taylor Coleridge's *Essays on His Times in THE MORNING POST and THE COURIER,* ed. David V. Erdman.[1]

1. 3 vols., in *The Collected Works of Samuel Taylor Coleridge,* general editor Kathleen Coburn, associate editor Bart Winer (vol. 3), Bollingen Series 75 (London: Routledge & Kegan Paul; Princeton: Princeton University Press, 1978).

The first volume in this third title of the Bollingen Coleridge contains (besides a detailed list of the contents and illustrations in all three volumes) a six-page description of "Principles of Attribution"; nine pages on "Editorial Practice, Symbols, and Abbreviations"; a "Chronological Table" that records key events in STC's life (1772–1834), paralleled through the year 1818 with a list of important historical, literary, and intellectual occurrences; a 121-page "Editor's Introduction" that outlines in month-by-month detail Coleridge's "oscillations" as a political journalist and his relations with Daniel Stuart, owner of the *Morning Post* and the *Courier*; and 436 pages containing the texts of all contributions to the *Morning Post* from January 1798 through August 1803 that Erdman can firmly attribute to Coleridge, together with extensive annotation.

The second volume exhibits the firmly attributed contributions by STC to the *Courier* between February 1804 and March 1818. The third volume contains five appendixes: A. "Conjectural or Collaborative Attributions" (thirty-eight items in the *Morning Post*, including, for example, material contributed by Coleridge though originally drafted by Thomas Poole, and forty-one items from the *Courier*); B. "Related Manuscripts and Letters"; C. three "Contemporary Attacks" on STC's journalism (by the *Anti-Jacobin*, Cobbett, and Hazlitt); D. "Verse Contributions by Coleridge and Wordsworth" to the two newspapers; and E. "Puffs and Advertisements of Coleridge and His Works, with a List of Excerpts from *The Friend* and Notices of His Lectures." In short, the three volumes attempt to embody all of STC's writings and the Coleridgiana related to Coleridge's contributions to the two newspapers. The third volume and set conclude with a 200-page index (the work of Bart Winer, associate editor of the series) that, like the other indexes in the Bollingen Coleridge, is in itself an invaluable scholarly tool, recording not only names of people, places, periodicals, and political parties, but also key images from STC's writings. For example, the entry on William Pitt (two-and-a-half tightly packed columns of fine print) is followed, in the first column of 3:471, by "Pittsburgh," "pity, philanthropic cant of," "Pius VI, Pope (Giovanni Angelo Braschi) (1717–99)," "Pius VII, Pope (Luigi Barnaba Chiaramonti) (1742–1823)," "place(s)," "placemen," "Placentia," "plagiarism, and Scott," "plague(s)," "plain-dealing," "plaister, basilicon," and "planet(s)," with four of these entries further subdivided. To study this index itself, even without looking up the contexts indexed, would provide an abundance of information about the people, events, ideas, and idiom of the period.

Like the indexes and other volumes in the Bollingen Coleridge series, the text and apparatus of *Essays on His Times* are undoubtedly "definitive" for *our* times. Erdman has spent a full fifteen years on this project, with the aid and counsel of many of the most knowledgeable Coleridgeans, Romanticists, and historians of journalism in the world—especially Carl Woodring, Lucyle Werkmeister, Bart Winer, Kathleen Coburn, John Colmer, and Max F. Schulz. Erdman, in addition, brings to this effort a lifetime of research on the intellectual, literary, and political history of the period and a masterful knowledge of the secondary material about it. But the word *definitive* needs itself to be defined, in this case and in all other instances where an excellent edition of a major author has replaced a mishmash of inadequate texts done in—or according to the standards of—the later nineteenth century. The editions of major Romantic writers that set the standards for those of us who were graduate students in the 1950s and earlier have all been shown to be incomplete or inadequate to one extent or another; Lucas's Lamb letters, the Julian Shelley, the E. H. Coleridge-Prothero edition of Byron, Garrod's Keats, and even the de Selincourt-Darbishire Wordsworth texts have been, or are now in the process of being, supplemented or replaced. A few more recent major editions—such as F. L. Jones's edition of P. B. Shelley's letters, E. L. Griggs's Coleridge letters, and Neville Rogers's O.E.T. Shelley—have already been judged inadequate by the higher standards of editors now at work. Even Kathleen Coburn's magisterial edition of Coleridge's *Notebooks* has been judged flawed in details of dating and annotation, and an effort as elaborate as *Shelley and his Circle* seems, to an editor who tries to grow as he works, riddled with minor (and a few major) errors and omissions.

To call an edition "definitive," then, never means "complete" or "errorless"; it simply implies that the edition *defines, for the time in which it is produced*, the basic canon of its designated subject; presents the textual details as carefully as is humanly likely (nobody actually achieves the "possible"); and collects in its annotation much of the best factual information that the scholarly world has hitherto dug out on this text, besides whatever original information the editor himself unearths as he ponders its problems. The chief function of such an edition is to save the nonspecialist student or scholar time and effort by gathering a great deal of correct information (and a balanced, though not exhaustive, understanding of the significance of an author's writings) in one place, with a good index and with various bibliographical helps for the student who wishes to pursue further a particular aspect of the author's work. It can never be—and should never claim to be—a single sufficient source for all pertinent data even on the text, much less on the intellectual context that produced the text. And a scholar or critic who uses a "definitive" edition without consulting first editions, manuscripts, letters, and journals (of the author, his friends, and contemporaries) or other primary sources when treating cruxes that basically affect his argument is simply leaning on a straw. A few years ago I reviewed a book on Peacock in which the author showed no sign of having gone behind the Halliford Edition of Peacock's works and other secondary materials. As a result, his work—though still the most comprehensive study of Peacock's intellectual development and art—is already becoming dated by its original errors, as well as by new factual and textual discoveries. What specialist scholar-critics must always do, in approaching their subject—at least after they finish a first draft of an article or book—is to check out every statement and textual crux on which their arguments depend in the primary, as well as in relevant secondary, sources. And for texts, this means not only following the best "definitive" editions but, where the dating of a letter or the punctuation of a poetic passage really makes a difference, writing to the owner of the poetic manuscript (or consulting a facsimile of it) to ascertain the date of the postmark or the punctuation in the author's final holograph and in the editions that he saw through the press. For historical facts (dates of battles, births, and deaths), it means consulting two or three independent sources—if possible, one contemporary newspaper, the *Annual Register,* and the journal or correspondence of a participant in the event. If I'm making scholarship and scholarly criticism sound like hard work and a deadly bore, I answer that it is difficult to root out entrenched and often-repeated errors, but that the most boring thing in the world is to read essay after essay that is completely useless because it is based on a corrupt text or regurgitated misinformation.

David V. Erdman's edition is one of the best in a very good series. He is working with difficult material. Unlike most editors, he has not only had to edit known materials, but to discover and validate the full canon that he was to include. Because he is dealing with hastily written and ephemerally produced prose, the details of orthography and punctuation (over which Coleridge himself had little or no control) cannot be considered crucial. The editor, therefore, deserves only raised eyebrows—rather than a slap on the wrist—when he writes that his texts "preserve the original spelling and even the punctuation, *except when the punctuation* (which may be the compositor's) *obscures meaning* . . . . But liberties have been taken with the paragraphing and in the invention of titles . . . and in the addition of subtitles . . . [etc.]" (p. xxxiii; italics added). It is, of course, one of the editor's functions to clarify meaning, but not in such a way as to destroy some of the evidence on which he based his judgment. It would have been better in a definitive edition (especially when the primary sources are so rare) to follow the text literally except for typos (which could have been listed in an appendix) and to clarify the author's intention, in those few cases where a reader unfamiliar with the idiom of the age might be confused, with concise footnotes beginning "I.e." This method would not only reassure the reader that he was encountering the same text that faced STC's contemporaries when they opened their copies of the *Morning Post* or *Courier* (except for such unintentional variants as inevitably creep into all except facsimile reprintings), but would encourage students of the period to master the intricacies of the punctuation (quite different from ours) that was current during the Romantic period, just as students of Elizabethan and Jacobean literature have to master old-spelling texts and students of Middle English must learn to read various dialects. Editorial principles that justify tinkering of this kind invariably smack of condescension, either to the author (who is presumed not to have been knowledgeable or careful enough to spell or punctuate "correctly") or to the reader (who is assumed to be incapable of learning what the editor knows).

Other than this lame apologia for not presenting Coleridge's journalism just as the *Morning Post* and the *Courier* published it, I find nothing to object to in Erdman's front matter or editorial apparatus. His "Principles of Attribution" should be a model for other students of anonymous journalism. The only useful tests (of which I am aware) that he does not employ are that of variant grammatical forms (e.g., "has"/"hath") used by Leonidas M. Jones in distinguishing the prose of Hazlitt from that of John Hamilton Reynolds (see *SB* 29 [1976]: 342–46) and that of computerized statistical analysis of vocabulary such as Alvar Ellegård employed in seeking the identity of Junius (*A Statistical Method for Determining Authorship: The Junius Letters, 1769–1772*, Goteborg, 1962). These methods would not seem to have been useful or practical in studying years of daily newspapers to which there were many unknown, anonymous contributors for whom there could be no body of clearly identifiable prose to use as a control. The "Editor's Introduction" itself joins Woodring's *Politics in the Poetry of Coleridge* (1961) and John Colmer's *Coleridge: Critic of Society* (1959) as a major study of STC's political development, and provides as well the authoritative account of his journalistic career. The historical and interpretive annotation is of a high order, and Erdman's masterful notes on the political figures and events in England and on the Continent during the years covered by STC's journalism bring the whole period to life.

Erdman seems to me to comment insufficiently only on Coleridge's perceptive awareness of the change and development of the economic order during his time. STC—writing half a century before the Communist Manifesto—has almost a post-Marxist awareness of the transition in European society from a feudal agrarian to a bourgeois commercial-industrial society. In a real sense, Coleridge's awareness of his place within this march of historical necessity justifies his socio-political conservatism. He—with or without Daniel Stuart's pragmatic counsels—determined that the time was not ripe for the transition from an oligarchy to an egalitarian society. How far he had come from his youthful Pantisocratic idealism can be seen not only in his famous apologia "Once a Jacobin Always a Jacobin" of October 1802 (also reworked for *The Friend*) but in his first article "On the French Constitution," written in November 1799 on returning to the *Morning Post* after his sojourn in Germany:

The prejudices of superstition, birth, and hereditary right, have been gradually declining during the last four centuries, and the empire of property as gradually establishing itself in their stead. Whether or no this too will not in a distant age submit to some more powerful principle, is, indeed, a subject fruitful in *dreams* to poetic philosophers . . . ; but to all present purposes it is a useless and impertinent speculation. For the present race of men Governments must be founded on property; that *Government is good in which property is secure and circulates;* that *Government the best, which, in the exactest ratio, makes each man's power proportionate to his property.* (1:31–32; italics in original)

Coleridge goes on to say that perhaps in America, "where the great mass of the people possess property," there may be universal suffrage, but that "when the physical strength of a nation is in the poor, the Government must be in the hands of the rich" (1:32). The assumption underlying this thesis was obviously that equal distribution of political power would lead to equal distribution of wealth, which in an economy of scarcity would reduce everyone to a subsistence level and make impossible any social, economic, or intellectual growth and development. Whether this was true or not in Coleridge's time is a question for endless debate by the scholastic philosophers of economics (Marxists and their opposites), but no reader of the British press during this period or of *The Travel Diaries of T. R. Malthus* (ed. Patricia James, 1966), which documents the subsistence level maintained in parts of Norway and Sweden in 1799, can doubt that such fears by Coleridge and his contemporaries were both real and based (as they might be in Calcutta or Dacca today) on visible evidence.

When arguing political questions of war and peace—friendship or enmity—with the regimes of France, America, and Russia, one of Coleridge's primary concerns (beyond his personal admiration for or disgust with Pitt, Napoleon, Fox, Canning, Jefferson, or Czar Alexander) was the impact of such decisions on British industry, commerce, and agriculture. On 30 January 1800, for example, he writes that the Ministers, in continuing the war, are making "a complete sacrifice of the permanent and landed interest of the country to the moneyed and commercial interests" (1:139; see also the following pages). Erdman notes (1:143) that STC favored landed property over "the commercial spirit," but Coleridge's views, though consistent, are not doctrinaire. He acknowledged that "commerce is the blessing and pride of this country" (1:144), and in May 1811, he regretted the defeat by the agricultural interests of the "Distillery Bill," which would have kept down the price of grain to urban consumers and stimulated the West Indian sugar and rum trade by forbidding the sale of British grain to distillers (2:127–29). British industrialization was tipping the balance of power very rapidly during Coleridge's lifetime, but his "Cross of Gold" speeches were considerably milder and probably better informed than Bryan's.

"It is instructive," writes Erdman, "to study Coleridge's political utterances in chronological order, but we are observing a weathervane, not a magnetic needle" (1:lxxxi). Without ever accusing STC of bad faith (Erdman finds adequate reasons for most of Coleridge's shifts both in contemporary events and in the commensurate shifts of position by STC's political allies and foes), Erdman implies that Coleridge's "oscillations" represent greater changes than, I believe, they do if one centers on Coleridge's views of the economic and social-class structure that underlay political events and personalities. Once STC had come to believe that his Pantisocratic, egalitarian social ideal was visionary, or at least premature (Erdman and Woodring would be able to fix this date better than I), he seems to me to have been fairly consistent in trying to moderate the final shift of power from the landed aristocracy and gentry to the moneyed commercial and industrial interests and the urbanized professional and mercantile classes. Though less "reactionary" in this regard than Wordsworth or Shelley, Coleridge—like others of his educational and social peers—identified himself with the old aristocracy who prized a classical humanistic education as the sign of their status and whose principal life-options (besides being "gentlemen") were to enter the military, the clergy, the academy—ideally at Oxford or Cambridge—or the government (usually diplomatic or parliamentary service). By 1807 STC had tried each of these with indifferent results and (not being suited to the law or medicine, the other logical choices) had either to accept the role of professional author (with all the smell of Tom Brown's Grub Street still attached to that title) or—even lower—the title "contributor to a daily *newspaper*," the lowest species of journalism. As late as 1825 John Gibson Lockhart, a university graduate who had for years earned his living by writing for one of the less reputable monthlies, refused to lower himself to edit a daily newspaper that John Murray planned to establish (see Samuel Smiles, *A Publisher and His Friends* [1891], 2:196-97). Writing on politics for a popular daily newspaper in the 1790s, when Coleridge was forced into the profession, was socially comparable to managing a Medicare nursing home or abortion clinic today. Even in those days of duels and frequent suspension of habeas corpus, journalism was safer than dealing drugs is today—but not nearly as lucrative. Southey (who knew whereof he spoke—and may have been speaking for STC as well as himself) wrote in the *Quarterly Review* in 1817 "On the Rise and Progress of Popular Disaffection":

When literature was confined to colleges and convents . . . men of letters were at the same time the happiest and the most useful of their generation . . . . If they obtained celebrity, it was well; and if they failed, the labour had been its own reward . . . . Great as have been the advantages of printing, it was a lamentable change, when literary composition and that exercise of reason which should be . . . the noblest of human occupations and the highest of human enjoyments, became a mere trade, to be pursued . . . from necessity and for daily bread.[2]

Coleridge's changing awareness of who really wielded the power in Great Britain went a long way toward reconciling him with the landed aristocracy that he had earlier decried. The experience of working for and with Daniel Stuart, a shady journalistic entrepreneur and a fraudulent stock-manipulator, as well as the shame of *needing* to work for him in a low-prestige capacity, undoubtedly played a part in Coleridge's countervailing expressions of respect for wealthy men of leisure of the old gentry, including Sir George Beaumont, William Sotheby, and John Hookham Frere. It reinforced his valuation of the gentlemen of the established clergy and stimulated his conception of a "clerisy" who could civilize the rude lower and still ruder middle classes before they came to full power. These class feelings, combined with personal disappointment, explain in large measure—more, certainly, than any constitutional laziness or distaste for routine—Coleridge's resistance to his life as a journalist and parliamentary reporter and his eagerness to seize any opportunity to remove himself from its toils.

By thus understanding Coleridge's views on property, his class biases, and his personal sense of insecurity, as well as his humanistic moral val-

2. *Essays, Moral and Political* (London: John Murray, 1832), 2:82-83.

ues, it is possible, I believe, to find a greater stability and consistency in his day-to-day political stance than has hitherto been recognized. The word *trimmer*, after all, derives from one who helps to keep a boat stable by moving or leaning toward the lighter side; a true trimmer—and, in this sense, Coleridge was often one—takes the less popular side of an argument merely to prevent ill-considered, precipitous action on the other side. Coleridge opposed Pitt, Fox, and Napoleon each at the height of his power and praised their good qualities when each was out of office. When Napoleon's authority had been established as first consul, Coleridge praised the ideas of Benjamin Constant and Madame de Staël's circle. When the "war hawks" were in power, Coleridge presented the advantages of peace; when the peace-at-any-price Addington regime had demonstrated its general incompetence, STC recalled the superior qualities of Pitt.

Certainly Coleridge had personal favorites and bêtes noires and executed a few remarkable about-faces based on such considerations—the most notable, perhaps, being his sudden enthusiasm for the genius of George Canning after 1816, when he met and was flattered by his old scourge from *The Anti-Jacobin* at Frere's house.[3] But beyond normal human foibles of this kind, Coleridge seems to me to show remarkable consistency and understanding of the long-term implications of the events and people about whom he had to write hasty paragraphs of instant commentary on the basis of sketchy news reports and rumors. Indeed, in reading the four volumes on *The French Revolution* and *Napoleon* translated from Georges Lefebvre's general history of the period at the same time I was reading Coleridge's journalism, I was amazed at the high degree of correspondence between STC's contemporary judgments and those of a great French Marxist historian with the advantage of access to a wealth of then-secret documents and the perspective of over a century and a quarter. The mere quantity of Coleridge's contributions to the *Morning Post* and the *Courier*—now, through Erdman's assiduous researches, greatly expanded from Sara Coleridge's edition of 1850—should help put to rest forever the myth that STC's literary career was unproductive—that he wasted himself in talk and so had no time to write. But the high *quality* of this work of Coleridge's left hand should also go far toward destroying the even more insidious myth of STC as an unrealistic and ineffectual angel, lost in abstruse speculations (in Hazlitt's too-memorable words) about "Hartley's

---

3. See Donald H. Reiman's Introduction to Canning in the volume containing reprints of six titles of poetry by George Canning and William Gifford (New York: Garland Publishing, 1978) in the series entitled *The Romantic Context: Poetry*.

tribes of mind . . . and the great law of association that binds all things in its mystic chain," "Bishop Berkeley's fairy-world," Spinoza's "spectral philosophy," and "Plato's shade." Hazlitt's portrait of Coleridge in *The Spirit of the Age*—like similar portrayals in "On Going a Journey" and "My First Acquaintance with Poets"—is Hazlitt's lament for the loss of his *own* youthful hopes, which he clearly identified with his earliest encounters with Samuel Taylor Coleridge.

Coleridge was "silly like us," but, as we know by our very interest in him, his "gift survived it all." David V. Erdman's brilliant edition of *Essays on His Times* shows us that Coleridge's gifts made him not only at moments one of the great poets in the language, one of the fathers of modern English and American literary criticism, and one of the chief molders of the British liberal theological tradition, but also (would he be proud or ashamed to hear it?) the most perceptive and distinguished political journalist of his day—much greater than Hunt, Hazlitt, or Cobbett. Coleridge often seems to have been a divided man, but like Osiris, even his dismembered elements flourished in and fertilized the soil wherever they chanced to be buried.

Just as Thomas McFarland's *Coleridge and the Pantheist Tradition* gives us a classic statement of STC's deep intellectual coherence, Erdman's edition of *Essays on His Times* provides us with a basis for fully appreciating the socioeconomic and political aspects of Coleridge's thought. No teacher of the *Biographia Literaria* can afford to ignore these volumes, for they demonstrate, perhaps better than any of STC's other works, the sanity of his true genius. Coming away from *Essays on His Times*, I am more than ever convinced that *Biographia Literaria* is a cleverly rhetorical book that draws its central conception from *The Life and Opinions of Tristram Shandy, Gent.* and that the oddities, the digressions, and even the plagiarisms of that work find their raison d'être and their unity in the Shandean persona that STC artfully introduced to represent his own "*literary* life and opinions." But to pursue that thought would lead us far beyond the requirements of the present occasion.

*   *   *

Samuel Taylor Coleridge. *Biographia Literaria.* Ed. James Engell and W. Jackson Bate. 2 vols. (*The Collected Works of Samuel Taylor Coleridge*, 7). London: Routledge & Kegan Paul; Princeton: Princeton University Press, 1983.

In the third chapter of *Biographia Literaria,* Coleridge gives (amid counsel on various subjects) a piece of good advice for reviewers of poetry and other creative literature: "He who tells me that there are *defects* in a new work, tells me nothing which I should not have taken for granted without his information. But he, who points out and elucidates the *beauties* of an original work, does indeed give me interesting information . . . " (1:62). When one applies this advice to the reviewing of scholarly editions, however, the terms almost reverse themselves. A reviewer who writes that Coleridge's *Biographia Literaria* is an interesting and important work, or that the edition published as part of The Collected Coleridge, under the supervision of Kathleen Coburn and Bart Winer, is likely to be the standard edition and must be purchased by every library and consulted by every scholar with high standards, has, in fact, said nothing that most readers of *RP&P* don't already know. I shall, therefore, spend less time elucidating the beauties of this fine edition than evaluating its strengths and weaknesses in relation to both the scholarly tradition out of which it springs and the needs of the academic community it is designed to serve.

First, let me say that the work of James Engell, the junior partner in this enterprise, is up to the high scholarly standards of Bate and The Collected Coleridge. Engell's primary responsibility was the annotation of the first volume (chapters 1–13) and the second part of the Introduction, which "concentrates on problems in the intellectual content of the *Biographia*" (1:xvi), whereas Bate has annotated the second volume and written the first half of the Introduction on the biographical problems connected with the writing, publication, and reception of the work. There are clearly two minds at work, but the differences are primarily those of perspective and personality, rather than scholarly quality. James Engell will have more information when he is fifty, but he will then have no reason to be ashamed of his part in this important edition. He has done an excellent job of drawing upon the vital Coleridge scholarship of recent decades, as well as on his own researches and the help of other specialist scholars, to annotate in rich—sometimes almost overpowering—detail the sources of STC's ideas, the particular editions from which Coleridge quoted, and his use of parallel phrases and sentiments in his letters, notebooks, marginalia, and other publications. Editors of such standard editions as The Collected Coleridge must both master the relevant primary and secondary sources and compile a base of true and useful information that will serve the student and non-Coleridgean teacher-scholar as a guide to the best that has been known and thought about the work that they are editing, saving their readers from having to recapitulate the history of scholarship before attempting further advances in the understanding and appreciation of it. In most respects, the annotation by both Bate and Engell admirably fulfills this responsibility. I have not tried, while writing this review, to duplicate their research, but having studied in recent years the early chapters of *Biographia Literaria*—and the relevant scholarship—in some detail, I believe that from the point of view of factual information and the compilation of past discoveries relating to STC's reading and his use of sources, this edition will satisfy all except, perhaps, the most learned specialists. (The few oversights that I noted involve the historical, rather than the intellectual background—but that is my hobby-horse.)

Bate and Engell exhibit great sympathy for Coleridge, and whenever ethical issues arise (I speak especially of the plagiarisms), they give STC the benefit of the doubt. Their explanation—sketched in Bate's part of the Introduction—is that Coleridge's health and the circumstances of the printing and publication, which required Coleridge to expand the work at what seemed to be the last minute, left him no other choice. Bate relies largely on statements in Coleridge's letters of the period (the veracity of which he seldom questions) and letters by J. J. Morgan and the various publishers involved (which are reprinted in a valuable appendix to the second volume). Engell, while pinpointing the exact places and quantities of the plagiarized texts, accepts the defense offered by Thomas McFarland—that Coleridge merely embedded fragments of his learning in a mosaic that represents his own, intrinsically independent thought. Two sentences from Engell's discussion in the Introduction epitomize the tone: "A maximum of a quarter of the total material in the philosophical chapters is used without citing its source" (1:cxvii) and "In 1817, the *Biographia* showed more personal acquaintance with a range of German literature and philosophy than any book previously published in English" (1:cxxvii). Engell attempts to show that, since the basic assumptions underlying the unitary philosophy expounded in the work were "in Coleridge's very nature" (1:lxxiv), he was able to write an organically coherent philosophical work in spite of incorporating extensive translation, paraphrase, and summary of the words of German philosophers.

By combining a detailed presentation of the evidence of where Coleridge depended on others, and where he added to or altered their thought, with a sympathetic judgment of Coleridge's motives and achievement in the philosophical chapters, Bate and Engell perform the most important duty of scholar-critics toward the writers they serve: they present their learned friend (with a few quirks) to readers, who can thereafter develop their own relationships with him. But their very sympathy for Coleridge also leads them to neglect some recent studies that, though limited, provide a necessary corrective to uncritical acceptance of STC's every thought and word. Essays on *Biographia Literaria* by Michael G. Cooke (*PQ*, 1971), Jerome C. Christensen (*SiR*, 1978), and Lawrence Buell (*ELH*, 1979) represent the kind of informed and respectful, yet critically inquiring analysis (carried forward in books that are, perhaps, too recent to have been considered by the editors) that posits a Coleridge whose underlying motives and intentions (whether one thinks of these as being subconscious, or consciously masked) are more complex and somewhat darker than he ever admits to in his correspondence. Coleridge did not write *Biographia Literaria* simply to enlighten the British reading public from German sources, or even to defend himself from misunderstanding and abuse: he had old scores to settle. Bate alludes to the possibility of such resentments in his Introduction, where he speaks of STC as feeling toward Wordsworth "an emotion—naturally repressed—as close to anger as his inner censor could allow him to feel toward a friend" (1:l).

But surely Coleridge's letters and other overt behavior warrant us to believe that "his inner censor" often failed him, permitting him to say some devastating things about such friends, or sometime friends, as Wordsworth, Southey, and Hazlitt. In my view, Coleridge consciously constructed a case against these and other friends and rivals, at the same time that he appeared to be (and was, in a sense) confessing his own shortcomings. But even if I attribute too much Machiavellian subtlety to the construction of the work, there are certainly levels and nuances that readers will never detect unless they, guided by the editors, open their minds to the possibility that STC's language may often be, intentionally or not, evasive and equivocal. It would be merely part of the comprehensiveness of standard editions for the editors to point out that "some say . . ." and name these deconstructive critics, as well as to mention in the notes where some of these supposedly equivocal passages appear. (The editors could, of course, record their own doubts about the suppositions, or even about the approach.) As the edition stands, an entire dimension of Coleridge's most psychologically and rhetorically complex work, noted by readers from John Thelwall to the present day, has been virtually ignored in the Introduction and notes to this edition—repressed by its admiring editors.

A second area of relative weakness in an excellent edition lies in the statement of its editorial principles and, to a lesser degree, in a few textual decisions that may have been made by the general editors to uphold the uniformity of The Collected Coleridge. With this work, there is no question about the choice of the base or copy-text. In the editors' short statement entitled "Editorial Practice, Symbols, and Abbreviations," they point out that the 1817 edition "is the only authoritative text as it was the only English edition published during Coleridge's lifetime. Nor has any manuscript copy ever been discovered" (1:xix). But there is always—especially with Coleridge—another potential source of textual authority: copies of the first edition that have been corrected by the author. Bate and Engell don't mention searching for such copies, though at 1:58 they add a sentence to the text on the authority of "Gillman's 'corrected' copy" mentioned in a letter from STC to Montagu. The accompanying note indicates that H. N. Coleridge probably used Gillman's (now lost) corrected copy for his 1847 edition. That knowledge, in the absence of Gillman's copy, would give the variants in the 1847 edition at least some potential authority, but since Bate and Engell neither provide collations of that edition with 1817 nor discuss the pattern of variants between the two editions, it is difficult to determine whether any other authorial changes transmitted through Gillman's copy or other copies of 1817 emended by STC might be available in the 1847 text. In any case, this issue and the question of the search for other annotated copies ought to have been discussed in a full textual introduction. The editors do tell us that (following the policy of The Collected Coleridge) they silently correct "obvious misprints." A listing of these, presumably few, intentional editorial changes would have clarified for the later textual critic (who must, because of this editorial silence, collate the edition with 1817 to see what kinds of changes were made) which changes were intentional and which result from new typographical errors. I presume, under the circumstances, that the omission of the comma after "inwardly" at 2:110, line 18, is a typographical error, but perhaps it was omitted for some purpose. The silent corrections that my spot-collations turned up are few and minor (e.g., the insertion of the apostrophe in "critic's" at 2:112, line 5) and the number of potential places for emendation are much greater (e.g., "neither indecent or immoral" at 2:112, line 4). The few acknowledged emendations are equally trivial, sometimes simply replacing the spellings that were standard in Coleridge's time with those now in fashion (e.g., the changes of "Spencer" to "Spenser"); on the other hand, the first page of Chapter 15 (2:19) has Shakespeare's name spelled in two different contemporary ways: "Shakespeare" in the analytical chapter heading and "Shakspear" in the middle of the first paragraph. With so few significant emendations, silent or acknowledged, done without any clear statement of editorial principles, Engell and Bate might just as well have followed the 1817 text in all respects and produced an accurate diplomatic reprint, except for any corrections to be garnered from Coleridge's own marked copies. Such discrepancies as "Christ Hospital" (1:8) would then simply reinforce what the editors say about Coleridge's haste and his method of dictating to J. J. Morgan, who was obviously left to transcribe his shorthand notes without Coleridge's careful correction of the text.

In "Romantic Bards and Historical Editors" (*SiR*, 1982), I described the "Harvard School" as the most important force in editing the Romantics at the present time and pointed out its strengths and its limitations. It has always—since the days of Hyder Rollins—been best at factual annotation and at presenting the evidence of the early authorities and weakest on the philosophy and principles of editing—selecting a copy-text and stating the principles on which it is to be emended systematically from other authorities. The Collected Coleridge avoids the pitfalls of the changing fads and fashions in theories of textual criticism, but it fails to present enough evidence to obviate the need for other scholars to duplicate the work that has gone into establishing the text. It thus leaves itself open to having its textual authority challenged and to being reduced to partial obsolescence some fifty or sixty years sooner than necessary.

The Collected Coleridge now nearing completion is, though mortal, one of the great achievements of twentieth-century scholarship; it introduces one of the most complex and learned writers of the nineteenth (or any other) century and makes him accessible, intelligible, and even congenial to a generation of students—and teachers—who not only have not read the authors Coleridge read (and could not read them, as he did, in their original languages), but who have literally never previously encountered a majority of the names that they find in the text and footnotes of *Biographia Literaria*. The few shortcomings of these volumes must be measured against this achievement. James Engell and W. Jackson Bate deserve our gratitude both for what they have given us and for the useful and rewarding work that they have left for us to do.

6

The Four Ages of Editing and the English Romantics

"The Four Ages of Editing" began as the first part of the introductory essay I was writing for the section on "Romantic Texts" in a special issue of Studies in Romanticism *that Morris Eaves organized as a* Festschrift *for David V. Erdman. The essay was originally entitled "The Four Ages of Editing; or, English Bards and American Editors." But while I was outlining the paper and selecting reviewers to evaluate various current editions in the review section, David Greetham of the Society for Textual Scholarship invited me to lecture at that group's first International Conference in April 1981. Pressed by this new deadline and filled with the ideas developing for the* SiR *paper, I asked Morris Eaves and David Wagenknecht if I might expand and split my paper into two parts, giving the first, more abstract and theoretical part at the STS Conference (publishing it in* TEXT*), while reserving the second part, which dealt in more detail with the editions and editors of the Romantics, for the "Homage to David Erdman" issue of* SiR.

The two deadlines were duly met. But then a series of unforeseen circumstances delayed publication of the first volume of TEXT: Transactions of the Society for Textual Scholarship, *containing the first half of the two-part paper; it finally appeared in December 1984 (1: 231–55), two years after the second half had been published in* SiR *(21 [Fall 1982]: 477–96). Here the two parts are reunited, to be read as a continuous historical survey of—with theoretical warnings to—the two centrifugal forces in current editorial theory. "The Four Ages of Editing" warns against the extremes of "scientific" analysis and against attempts to replace actual textual authorities with imaginative reconstructions or idealizations; "Romantic Bards and Historical Editors" suggests that those whose interest centers on historical artifacts often neglect helpful textual methodologies developed by the school of Greg, Bowers, and Tanselle. I call for an eclectic and pragmatic approach that can adopt (or* adapt) *the virtues—while avoiding the excesses—of both camps.*

In the spirit of mediation, I asked several friends to read drafts of the two essays and give me their comments before I rewrote them for delivery and publication. I am especially grateful for the helpful comments of David Greetham, David Nordloh, Jack Stillinger, Tom Tanselle, and Carl Woodring.

Since these essays appeared, the most relevant new theoretical publications through the middle of 1985 have been surveyed by G. Thomas Tanselle in "Historicism and Critical Editing" (Studies in Bibliography 39 [1986]: 1–46). That analysis does not treat all of the latest work of Jerome J. McGann in his collection of essays The Beauty of Inflections *(Oxford: Clarendon Press, 1985); though Tanselle knew most of them from their earlier appearances elsewhere, he was unfamiliar, when he wrote, with McGann's "The Monks and the Giants" (pp. 69–89). My own dialogue both with Bowers and Tanselle on the Right and with Erdman and McGann on the Left continued in two papers I wrote near the end of 1985: "Gentlemen Authors and Professional Writers: Notes on the History of Editing Texts of the Eighteenth and Nineteenth Centuries" will appear in a volume collecting the lectures from the 1985 Toronto Conference on Editorial Problems; "Versioning: The Presentation of Multiple Texts," which was read at MLA in December 1985, ends Part One of this volume.*

I

As Shelley's friend Thomas Love Peacock discussed the evolution of literature from Homer into his own time under the rubric "The Four Ages of Poetry," so we can divide the texts of the English Romantics into products of Four Ages of Editing. In the first, or Golden Age of Innocence, the widow, son, daughter, son-in-law, nephew, friend, publisher, or enthusiastic disciple of the poet simply gathered whatever letters and unpublished literary manuscripts he or she could collect from other relatives and friends of the dead writer, added fugitive periodical publications, and either issued these as a supplement to the works already published during the poet's lifetime or (perhaps later) combined these with republication of the writings issued earlier. Such works include Mary Shelley's editions of Shelley's poems and essays (1824, 1839, 1840); Cadell's "Magnum Opus" edition of Scott, with Lockhart's *Life* (1829–1840); the John Murray edition of Byron's *Works* (1832–1833); editions of Coleridge by Henry Nelson Coleridge and Sara Coleridge (1835, 1836, 1840, 1849, 1850); Richard Monckton Milnes's *Life, Letters, and Literary Remains of John Keats* (1848); the Gilchrist-Rossetti *William Blake* (1863); and Moxon's and Macmillan's editions of Wordsworth's *The Prelude* and *Poetical Works* published under the supervision of Edward Quillinan and Christopher Wordsworth in the 1850s and 1860s. The prefaces and "texts" of these editions often contain apologetic biographical materials and notes, the main aim of the editors being to win for the writer the wide readership that the writer's publisher, heirs, and admirers thought he deserved. Though these editions also constituted serious attempts to expand and authenticate the canon, less effort was made to identify and follow the best textual authorities, and where the author's own publications and manuscripts seemed obscure, the editor or publisher often "clarified" the text by repunctuating it, filling in blanks, or omitting fragments of uncompleted poems. All these "improvements" were made in a spirit of affection or reverence for the author, rather than in the condescending search for superficial polish and decorum that so often characterized the subsequent Silver Age.

From the later Victorian period and into the twentieth century, there appeared a great many texts of the Romantics edited by those who thought, with Matthew Arnold, that the Romantics did not *know* enough—that (as Milton, Dryden, and their contemporaries too often thought of Shakespeare and his age) the poets of the early part of the century were untrained geniuses, warbling woodnotes wild in a rude and barbarous age. The more dedicated among these editors set about "improving" the texts of the Romantics right and left, patching and tinkering as they went.

William Michael Rossetti exemplifies the best editors of the Silver Age. On 28 March 1868 Rossetti entered a controversy in *Notes and Queries* on the text and meaning of Shelley's poems that showed him to be very knowledgeable about them. While declaring himself opposed to the "'cobbling and tinkering' of the verses of deceased poets," he argued that Shelley's poetry had suffered from numerous printers' errors in need of correction, and he followed with a series in *Notes and Queries* of proposed "Notes and Emendations on Shelley" (11, 18, and 25 April 1868) that won him the favorable attention of Moxon & Company (whom Rossetti had only two years before caught in unethical behavior connected with the suppression of Swinburne's *Poems and Ballads*).[1] By 5 November 1868, Rossetti and J. Bertrand Payne of Moxon's had agreed that Rossetti would make what he terms "editorial revisions of the text [of Shelley's poetry] to be, if practicable, such as will not render the stereotype-plates useless, but only entail alterations here and there." Payne, Rossetti continued, "concurs in my proposal of occasional notes, accompanying the actual revision of the text. For this work I proposed to charge £30, to which he at once acceded:

1. See *Rossetti Papers, 1862–1870*, ed. William Michael Rossetti (New York: Charles Scribner's Sons, 1903), pp. 197, 199–200, 206, 224, 306, 352–53.

indeed, I suspect it was sensibly less than he had expected to be asked."[2] In the same conversation, Rossetti notes, "Payne seems to have also some undefined notions as to a re-edition and Life of Coleridge; and I think it possible that he might eventually make some proposal to me on this subject also."

In carrying out his "editorial work," Rossetti relied chiefly on "editions of Shelley" sent to him by Payne on 17 November 1868. Naturally, these editions consisted primarily of texts Moxon's had published, especially multiple copies of the one-volume stereotyped edition (1866), which Rossetti cut up, marked with his insertions and changes, and eventually sent back to Moxon's as printer's copy.[3] By 4 January 1869 Rossetti had begun "a tabular compendium of the facts etc. of Shelley's life" in order to begin his introductory "Memoir" of Shelley, and thereafter he devoted most of his time to gathering material for that memoir. Much of his "editing" had been completed by this date, as emerges from his diary entry for 12 January 1869:

Swinburne came for a Shelley discussion. . . . He is strenuous for sticking to the texts revised, or which might have been revised, by Shelley himself: urges the restoration of *Laon and Cythna* bodily—but this I shan't do. On various points he convinced me that alterations which I had introduced—however plausible—had better be excluded; and this I *shall* do. Got no further than the Prometheus in reading him the principal of my notes.[4]

Swinburne's advice to let the poet have his say was, however, counteracted by other friends and correspondents of Rossetti, including Frederick Gard Fleay (1831–1904), at that time headmaster of a grammar school, with whom Rossetti exchanged a series of letters on proposed conjectural emendations of Shelley's texts in 1869–1870, and to whom Rossetti pays tribute as "the earliest & most systematic of Shelley's emendators."[5]

    2. *Rossetti Papers, 1862–1870*, pp. 331–33; ultimately Rossetti persuaded Payne to abandon the stereotyped plates (see pp. 381–82).
    3. These sheets, bound in three volumes, are now in The Carl H. Pforzheimer Library and are cited by permission of The Carl and Lily Pforzheimer Foundation, Inc.
    4. *Rossetti Papers, 1862–1870*, p. 379 (ellipsis in original). Swinburne's ideas on the subject appear in his "Notes on the Text of Shelley," *Fortnightly Review*, n.s. 5 (1 May 1869): 539–61; rpt. in *Essays and Studies* (London: Chatto and Windus, 1875), pp. 184–237.
    5. Six letters from Rossetti to Fleay, 17 October [1869]–27 February [1870], are in The Carl H. Pforzheimer Library (Rossetti, 6–11). The phrase is quoted from the letter 14 November [1869]. The Pforzheimer Library also owns the manuscript of an unpublished study by Fleay, entitled "On the received text of Shelley's poems," that occupies 52 numbered, lined half-sheets and is at the end dated "12 Sep 1894." In it, Fleay systematically proposes emendations for all of Shelley's published poetry and (on page 8) calls attention to an earlier paper by him published in *The Provincial Magazine* for February 1859, in which he had first

Though Rossetti resisted many of Fleay's more elaborate plans to emend the text to improve Shelley's rhythm and rhymes, he doubtless was encouraged by Fleay's attitude to introduce a number of his own favorite conjectures into the text. In the end, Rossetti's two-volume edition of 1870 contains more such speculative changes than any other edition of Shelley's poetry. Moreover, as can be clearly seen from Rossetti's press copy in the Pforzheimer Library, he made no systematic attempt—how could he, in the short time he devoted to the text?—to collate the Moxon editions with Shelley's original editions or with Mary Shelley's edition of Shelley's *Posthumous Poems*.

The nature of Rossetti's corruptions of Shelley's texts may be seen from the notes to Harry Buxton Forman's edition of Shelley's *Poetical Works*[6] and in the work of modern editors who have worked with the primary published and manuscript authorities.[7] Rossetti was devoted to Shelley and to the other Romantic and Victorian poets and was an industrious biographer and (in some ways) bibliographer of them. His emendations exhibit both common sense and attention to the poet's meaning. Nevertheless, he too often simply revised the poems to represent what *he* judged to be the best poetry or the most coherent meaning, rather than following the evidence of the author's intention. And he soon became too busy to concentrate on detailed collation of any poet, for he records in his diary for 3 February 1869 a discussion with J. B. Payne about what became the Moxon's Popular Poets series:

He [Payne] has an idea of bringing-out a series of English Poets, non-copyright works, very cheap; a publication similar to one by Nimmo, but in better taste. Longfellow would be first: followed by Scott, Byron, Shelley, Thomson, Keats, Selections, etc. etc. . . . For these books he wishes to obtain brief prefatory memoirs, with some critical estimate (say 18 to 20 pp. apiece); and wishes besides to have a paper selection made of the editions to be printed from. This, without any following of the text through the press, would constitute the editorial work. . . . I proposed to do it for £25 per book, excluding selections, for which I would charge higher: he replied that his calculations admitted of only £21 per book (allowing the

---

proposed a number of the same emendations that were later adopted by Rossetti and others. In the unpublished manuscript, Fleay proposes, among other emendations, changing several words in "Mont Blanc" to make sure that no lines in that poem remain rhymeless and canceling lines 95–96 of *Rosalind and Helen* because, he notes, the substance of their meaning appears in subsequent lines (p. 11).

6. 4 vols. London: Reeves and Turner, 1876–1877.

7. My own detailed analysis of Rossetti's practice comes from work on the text of "The Triumph of Life" for *Shelley's "The Triumph of Life": A Critical Study* (Urbana: University of Illinois Press, 1965; rpt. New York: Octagon, 1979) and "Athanase: A Fragment" in *Shelley and his Circle*, 7 (Cambridge, Mass.: Harvard University Press, 1986).

same exception): . . . I assented to this.[8]

The references in Rossetti's diary and letters make clear that, though he was assiduous in gathering new biographical material and some unpublished fragments for *The Complete Poetical Works of Percy Bysshe Shelley* (2 vols., 1870), he made no serious efforts to establish the authority of the texts; most of his concern in the other volumes devolved on what selections he could or could not publish without paying a copyright fee.

Even such questions as copyright seem not to have concerned American editors of the period. A letter from James Russell Lowell to "Mr. Bolles," perhaps a printer with H. O. Houghton and Company, the printers of the 1854 edition of Keats published by Little, Brown & Co., reads simply:

20th April.

Mr. Bolles

Dear Sir,

You can begin printing from any edition of Keats's poems - putting the "Endymion" first as it now stands. There is nothing to be done to it in the way of editing. Before you get through that, I will have the other poems (of Keats) arranged & prefix a sketch of his life.

Very truly Yours
J. R. Lowell[9]

Landmarks of the latter end of this Silver Age include Thomas Hutchinson's texts of Shelley and Wordsworth and the other Oxford Standard Authors editions, Macmillan's Globe Editions, and Houghton Mifflin's Cambridge Editions done around the turn of the century. Again, the aim of these editors was to gain as wide a public as possible, but, given the nature of their professional concerns and their opinions of the poets, some of them seemed to work not so much to enhance the reputation and influence of the writers as to increase the earnings of the publishers and them-

8. *Rossetti Papers, 1862–1870*, p. 381. W. M. Rossetti's editorial labors can be followed by means of the indexes to this volume and *The Diary of W. M. Rossetti, 1870–1873*, ed. Odette Bornand (Oxford: Clarendon Press, 1977); *Letters about Shelley Interchanged by . . . Edward Dowden, Richard Garnett and Wm. Michael Rossetti*, ed. R. S. Garnett (London: Hodder and Stoughton, 1917); and *Letters of William Michael Rossetti concerning Whitman, Blake and Shelley to Anne Gilchrist and . . . Herbert Gilchrist*, ed. Clarence Gohdes and Paull Franklin Baum (Durham: Duke University Press, 1934).

9. Manuscript in The Carl H. Pforzheimer Library; published by permission of The Carl and Lily Pforzheimer Foundation, Inc.

selves. The editors, who decided (after consulting the publishers) that their highest obligation was to the reading public that they hoped would buy their books, modernized and smoothed out the texts still further and in several cases observed the prudential standards of the day by softening anything overly radical or indecorous in the poetry and especially in the letters of the Romantics.[10] For example, in the Oxford Standard Authors edition of Shelley, Hutchinson (or the printer) added capital letters wherever Shelley alluded to the Supreme Being. In Canto VII of *Queen Mab*, in the midst of Shelley's most strident attack on Christianity, Hutchinson's text capitalizes such words referring to God as "Fiend" (VII.97), "Tyrant" (VII.199), and "Foe" (VII.248), thus providing an ironic spectacle in which Shelley pays court through his reverent orthography to a god whose objective existence he denies and the morality of whose myth he denounces. By the same token, in 1898 Rowland E. Prothero and the firm of John Murray produced the bowdlerized texts of Byron's *Letters and Journals* that have been corrected only now by Leslie A. Marchand and a more enlightened John Murray.

II

Developing concurrently with this Victorian compromise was another tradition of editing. When Harry Buxton Forman, whom John Carter hailed as a pioneer in descriptive bibliography,[11] undertook his editions of Shelley and Keats, there began what may be termed the Brazen Age, or the age of "scientific" editors of the Romantics. Forman respected the poets far more than he did the reading public, but he had even greater respect for his own capacity to deduce the forms that the poets intended to use. From careful collations and analysis of the works of Shelley, Forman evolved what he took to be Shelley's rules of spelling, punctuation, and usage.

Forman, who never went to college and made his career in the Post Office while developing as an amateur scholar, nevertheless managed to establish his authority as a bibliographer and editor of the Romantics both because he took more time to be meticulously accurate than his rivals did

---

10. For the bowdlerizing by W. M. Rossetti and John Camden Hotten of the first British edition of Whitman's poems, see Morton D. Paley, "John Camden Hotten and the First British Editions of Walt Whitman—'A Nice Milky Cocoa-Nut,'" *Publishing History* 6 (1979): 5–35.

11. Carter wrote: "Buxton Forman's *A Shelley Library* . . . was . . . no mere handlist but a fully annotated and richly informative study of Shelley's original editions. Published by the Shelley Society in 1886 . . . , Forman's book marked a radical advance. . . . Forman set a wholly new standard both for his readers and for subsequent bibliographers. His *Shelley Library* was a prototype as well as a portent" (*Taste and Technique in Book-Collecting* [New York: R. R. Bowker, 1948], p. 15).

and because, as a collector of books and manuscripts and a haunter of auction rooms, he eventually owned or examined many more of the original authorities than did Rossetti or any other competitor.[12] Forman was constantly correcting his own published editions in later reprintings, and if he fell short of modern standards in his work on Keats, his Shelley editions remain the most carefully proofread and accurate (according to the evidence available to him) that have ever been produced.[13] Forman's striking superiority to his contemporaries in bibliographical knowledge not only led him into the temptation of initiating and/or abetting the printing forgeries circulated by T. J. Wise,[14] but also gave him an exalted sense of his own knowledge that may have led him to trust too securely in his pet ideas: "The sense that he was greater than his kind / Had struck, methinks, his eagle spirit blind."

In his playful notes to Wise and, by the end of his career, his equally flippant remarks in his transcription of three Shelley rough-draft *Note Books of Percy Bysshe Shelley* owned by W. K. Bixby (privately printed, 1911), Forman demonstrated that even one who began as a humble student and servant of the work of a great poet is not immune to a hubris that can transform the poet's writings into a mere occasion for the editor to display his own ingenuity and taste. I choose one example at random: the page on which Shelley drafted *Prometheus Unbound* IV.495–502. There Forman quotes one rejected version of IV.500 ("The caverns of my Pride's deep Universe") that reads, "The solid heart of my glad Universe," and comments that this is "a line which no poet less opulent than Shelley could have afforded to reject. Indeed it is by no means clear that he could, for it is a nobler line than that to which it gave place, though presumably not satisfying the poet as an expression of his meaning" (Shelley, *Note Books*, 1:93).

12. The bulk of "The Library of the Late H. Buxton Forman (1842–1917)," strongly centered upon manuscripts and rare editions of nineteenth-century poetry and biographical materials relating to those poets, was auctioned at the Anderson Galleries, New York, in three parts. A total of 3,572 lots were sold in fourteen sessions on 15–17 March, 26–28 April, and 4–7 October 1920.

13. The Carl H. Pforzheimer Library has one set of Forman's eight-volume Library Edition, corrected and interleaved by Forman with new information garnered from various sources, as well as piles of clippings, once belonging to H. B. Forman, taken from book catalogues, newspapers, magazines, and journals that contain mentions of Shelley, his family, or his writings. Forman obviously subscribed to a clipping service and followed up all leads. Within this collection, for example, is a copy of W. M. Rossetti's "Shelley in 1812–13" from the *Fortnightly Review* for 1 January 1871, upon which Forman has collated Rossetti's printing of "The Devil's Walk," recording over a hundred "variations of this reprint from the original broadsheet" in the Public Record Office.

14. On this question, see *Between the Lines: Letters and Memoranda Interchanged by H. Buxton Forman and Thomas J. Wise*, ed. Fannie E. Ratchford, with a Foreword by Carl H. Pforzheimer (Austin: University of Texas Press, 1945) and *Thomas J. Wise Centenary Studies*, ed. William B. Todd (Austin: University of Texas Press, 1959).

Luckily, by this date Forman's days of editing final versions of Shelley's poems were past, and he thus was not tempted to substitute rejected "nobler" lines for the ones Shelley had finally decided upon, as his successors (such as C. D. Locock) sometimes did.

The practice of emending according to editors' conception of "nobler" lines rather than evidence of the author's intention derives, of course, from the practice of editors of classical Greek and Latin and biblical Hebrew and Greek texts. Given a transcription based on earlier manuscripts of uncertain origin or authority but in the hand of a scribe who lived many centuries after the composition of the text (in which all punctuation is known to have been later and nonauthorial), there are ample grounds for the modern editor (who has often the advantage of comparing several manuscripts of differing backgrounds) to try to reason back to the original text that had, through a series of scribal errors or attempted emendations, deteriorated into what seems to be nonsense. It is so much fun to display ingenuity in such conjectural arguments that many editors of nineteenth-century writers continued to play the same game, even though the survival of the author's own drafts, fair-copy manuscripts, and marked proofsheets, as well as editions that the author had seen through the press, might have weighed against such freedom. Those such as Fleay who had been trained at Oxford, Cambridge, and other strongholds of the classical tradition were especially vulnerable to this temptation.

Luckily, A. E. Housman, one of the greatest of classical editors and textual critics, was also a significant poet and felt an author's outrage when such tinkering affected the texts of *his* poems. Housman's letters, laconic as they are, express his feelings on this topic better than do his formal lectures or publications on editorial theory and practice. His letters to Grant Richards, publisher of his poems, are filled with very specific instructions regarding the printing and presentation that are clearly designed to forestall textual changes due either to inadvertence or to editorial tinkering. On 11 December 1898, for example, he wrote to Richards: "I rather like the notion of a pocket edition. Large paper and illustrations are things I have not much affection for. In any case I should like to correct the proofs and to have them printed as I correct them. Last time someone played games with the punctuation."[15] And on 12 October 1902 he wrote: "When the next edition of the *Shropshire Lad* is being prepared, it would save trouble to the compositor as well as me if he were told that the third edition is almost exactly correct, and that he had better not put in commas

---

15. *The Letters of A. E. Housman*, ed. Henry Maas (Cambridge, Mass.: Harvard University Press, 1971), p. 49.

and notes of exclamation for me to strike out of the proof, as was the case last time" (*Letters*, p. 61). In his classical studies, Housman conjectured corrections for Manilius, Juvenal, Lucan, and other Latin poets in his area of specialization, and he also supplied Gilbert Murray with conjectures on the plays of Euripides to aid Murray with his translations. But he used much greater care in his treatment of modern poets. His respect for the texts of the Romantics appears in his refusal to publish his Cambridge Inaugural Lecture of 1911 because he "was unable to verify a statement which it contained as to the text of Shelley's *Lament* of 1821." (Later research has confirmed his point.)[16] It appears also in his single application of the methods of conjectural emendation (as practiced with classical authors) to Keats. In the *Times Literary Supplement* for 8 May 1924, he published a letter on "Keats, The Fall of Hyperion, I.97," in which he argues that a reading in one of the Woodhouse transcript books, "When in mid-way," emended by Milnes to "When in midday," should be "When in mid-May," arguing from the sense of the passage (including botanical accuracy) as well as from Keats's use of the phrase "in mid-May" in "Ode to a Nightingale."[17] Housman's crowning argument came from I.103 of the poem itself: "Sending from *Maian* incense." Housman's reading is accepted by Stillinger and other modern editors, but the more significant fact is that Housman begins his discussion of the crux with a clear understanding of the textual evidence available on the point: "This poem was not printed in Keats's lifetime, and his manuscript has been lost; but in the copy made under the direction of Woodhouse lines 97–101 of the first canto run as follows . . . ." And he goes on to show that Lord Houghton had already emended the text to "in mid-day." In short, Housman acted only within the province of his competence: there was no extant authorial version and the two chief authorities, the Woodhouse transcript book and the first printing by Lord Houghton, were in conflict. In such a case, he permitted himself to examine the internal evidence and propose an emendation.

Though Housman's judicious distinction between the canons of editing classical texts and those of editing modern texts was not shared or emulated by all of his colleagues in British and American universities, the next advances in editing the British Romantics came out of Oxford, in the work of Ernest de Selincourt (1870–1943), who began his editorial work with an edition of Keats's *Poems* (1905) and whose 1926 edition of *The Prelude*, pre-

---

16. See A. E. Housman, *The Confines of Criticism*, with notes by John Carter (Cambridge: Cambridge University Press, 1969), pp. 9–12, and John Carter and John Sparrow, "Shelley, Swinburne and Housman," *TLS*, 21 November 1968, pp. 1318–19.

17. See Housman, *Letters*, pp. 219–20.

senting versions of 1805 and 1850 on facing pages with accompanying notes and variants drawn from other manuscripts, set new standards for the presentation of heavily revised texts of modern literature. A decade later, H(eathcote) W(illiam) Garrod (1878–1960), who had begun à la Housman as a poet and as editor, commentator, and translator of Statius, Manilius, and other Latin poets,[18] reached the zenith of his career as a serious scholar in his Oxford English Texts edition of *The Poetical Works of John Keats* (1939; 2nd ed., 1958). Most students of Romantic texts consider Garrod's edition a milestone in the thoroughness of its editing, and Garrod even felt the need to defend himself in the Introduction for the thoroughness of his work from those who were affected by an "ethical scruple . . . when it is proposed to go behind the printed text and to scrutinize its sometimes inglorious origins by recording variants from the drafts as well as from printed authorities and fair-copy manuscripts" (p. xxiii). Yet Garrod himself in his 1939 Preface credited Forman with having set *his* standards:

A principal part of my work has consisted in collating MSS., or the facsimiles of MSS., collated before me by the late Harry Buxton Forman. In one of his prefaces, he professes to be, in respect of accuracy, only mortal. But of mortal frailty I have found, scrutinizing his work as rigorously as I was able, singularly few traces. . . . I have had the advantage of using a good many MSS. not known to him; and I should account myself fortunate if some one using them after me found my record of them comparable to his in accuracy.[19]

Garrod's hope was to be fulfilled in not quite the manner he would have intended, for Jack Stillinger criticizes him for his undue reliance on Forman's texts, especially in lending his name to an imperfectly revised reissue of Forman's error-ridden Oxford Standard Authors edition of 1906. Stillinger finds in the OET Keats that, treating only substantive matters, "Garrod has what I consider clear mistakes and inconsistencies—the latter most often the mixing of two or more discrete states of texts—in . . . fifty-seven poems" and after specifying his disagreements, he concludes: "Texts aside, Garrod's arrangement of the poems makes no sense, his introduction and headnotes are considerably out of date, and his cumbersome and error-filled apparatus does as much harm as good."[20] He goes on to analyze as "a large fault of Garrod's apparatus," his "treatment of all

18. Housman thought little of Garrod's work on Manilius II, as he made clear in his preface to Manilius V (1930); see Housman, *Letters*, p. 121, n. 1.
19. *The Poetical Works of John Keats*, ed. H. W. Garrod, 2nd ed. (Oxford: Clarendon Press, 1958), p. [ix].
20. *The Texts of Keats's Poems* (Cambridge, Mass.: Harvard University Press, 1974), pp. 277, 283.

MS and printed texts as having equal authority" (p. 285). Stillinger in *The Texts of Keats's Poems* for the first time analyzed the transmission of the manuscripts and printed texts of a modern poet with the same care that paleographers, dialecticians, and textual critics of biblical, classical, and medieval texts had applied to the surviving authorities in their fields, with the added advantage that surviving letters and journals by Keats and his associates often supplement the evidence of the manuscripts and printings themselves. Garrod and, to a certain extent, de Selincourt and Helen Darbishire in their editions of Wordsworth were both victims and perpetuators of the condescension toward the study of nineteenth- and twentieth-century English literature at such institutions as Oxford. They felt a greater need to defend expending their efforts on "modern" authors than to convince publishers of the need to present all that the editors' textual training had prepared them to undertake. Their editions, however much they surpassed those of the casual Silver Age by returning to primary authorities, did not always choose the correct copy-texts or present substantive variants fully and clearly. These editors almost inevitably revised such features as orthography and punctuation on the grounds either of consistency or the need for easier comprehension by their readers. And, as Stillinger's criticism of Garrod's eclecticism indicates, they too often selected their base texts without completing the biographical and bibliographical research and collation that, once a larger number of manuscripts were available for study, could (as Stillinger demonstrates) have established which ones are more, which ones less, authoritative.

III

If such classically trained editors as de Selincourt and Garrod were in danger of applying "scientific" principles too sparingly to Romantic texts, a far more rigorous school was developing concurrently in the textual criticism of Renaissance drama that brought the Brazen Age to full flower. Its milestones began, perhaps, with Ronald B. McKerrow's edition of *The Works of Thomas Nashe* (1904–1910) and include such diverse recent and continuing works as Charlton Hinman's Norton Facsimile of *The First Folio of Shakespeare* (1968) and *The Writings of Herman Melville* now emanating from the Newberry Library and Northwestern University Press. Equally impressive is the theoretical tradition that grew up in connection with these editorial labors. Contemporary with "Note on the Treatment of the Text . . ." (1:xi–xvi) and "Preface" (5:v–ix) to the Nashe edition, in which McKerrow (1872–1940) briefly discussed his editorial procedures both before and after the fact, was the bibliographical study of *Shakespeare Folios and Quartos* (1909) by his senior, Alfred W. Pollard (1859-1944) of the British Museum. Pollard and McKerrow exerted great influence through their work in the Bibliographical Society, as editors of scholarly journals, within university circles, and, especially, through McKerrow's *An Introduction to Bibliography for Literary Students* (based on "Notes" first published by the Bibliographical Society in 1913).[21] Their efforts were actively aided and supplemented by their close friend Walter Wilson Greg (1875-1959), who, as heir to *The Economist* of London, was able to devote his entire life to bibliographical research, reviewing more than two hundred scholarly studies and superintending the publications of the Malone Society, of which he served as general editor (1906-1939) and president (1939-1959). Later landmark publications on the theory of editing by this circle include McKerrow's *Prolegomena for the Oxford Shakespeare* (1939) and, especially, Greg's "The Rationale of Copy-Text."[22] Other names associated with this British bibliographical tradition that have more direct relevance to nineteenth-century studies are R. W. Chapman (1881-1960), editor of Jane Austen's novels (1923) and other writings of Austen and Samuel Johnson, as well as secretary to the delegates of the Clarendon Press (1920-1942), and Michael T. H. Sadleir (1888-1957), the most noted collector and bibliographer of nineteenth-century fiction, as well as an active and influential member of the publishing firm of Constable from 1920 onwards.

By the 1940s, the spark of enthusiasm for this rigorous tradition of bibliography and editing had jumped across the Atlantic and was marked by the founding of *Studies in Bibliography* in 1948 and the publication of Fredson Bowers's *Principles of Bibliographical Description* (1949), which is dedicated to Greg. Both events reflected and stimulated new interest in North America in the broader discipline that Bowers usually refers to simply as "textual criticism." Bowers viewed literary criticism "as directly dependent upon expert textual criticism"; that expertise he applied to four basic situations: (1) analysis of an extant manuscript; (2) hypothetical "recovery of the lost manuscript" that served as press copy for a printed text; (3)

---

21. Oxford: Clarendon Press, 1927. Pollard was honorary secretary of the Bibliographical Society, 1893-1934; co-editor of *The Library*, 1904-1920, and sole editor, 1920-1934; and honorary professor of bibliography at London University, 1919-1932. McKerrow was joint honorary secretary of the Bibliographical Society, 1912-1940, and founder and editor of *Review of English Studies*. In the *DNB*, 1931-1940, W. W. Greg writes of McKerrow: "he probably did more than any man to place the editing of English literature upon a scientific basis" (p. 580).

22. *SB* 3 (1950-1951): 19-36; reprinted in *Collected Papers of W. W. Greg*, ed. J. C. Maxwell (Oxford: Clarendon Press, 1966), pp. 374-91.

study of the transmission of a printed text; and (4) "the presentation of the established and edited text."[23] Having by the late 1950s convinced or coerced students of Renaissance drama into paying serious attention to textual problems, the school emanating from Pollard, McKerrow, Greg, and Bowers—and now spearheaded by the energy and enthusiasm of Bowers himself—attempted to apply the principles derived primarily from the study of Renaissance plays to all areas of textual criticism and editing.

I denominate this school of textual scholars the Brazen Age of editing because of the too-sanguine hopes they, at least for a time, entertained about the results obtainable through systematic application of fixed principles to a wide variety of literary texts. The keynote of Bowers's *Principles of Bibliographical Description* is "system." His Foreword makes clear that he has begun by considering "the whole subject in the round" and has ended by "codifying the results of this analysis" (p. vii). It is, he continues, "my purpose to present an organized bibliographical system which is based on what I consider to be the best current practices in scholarly works."[24] In the interest of arriving at such a system, Bowers argues, "since this volume does not purport to be an account of specific books . . . , the principles themselves are not affected if stray illustrations prove incomplete or faulty" (p. x). He thus begins his first chapter by characterizing "descriptive bibliography" as "one of the kinds of scholarship that may be defined as 'pure' scholarship, and consequently very exacting standards are applied to it" (p. 1), and he goes on to differentiate it from the mere making of library catalogues, author or subject checklists, bibliographical descriptions of a few copies of a title in a single collection, and other limited, unscientific enterprises.

Had Bowers been content to remain at this level of abstraction and to work out ideal principles, based on a truly philosophical comprehension of the various theoretical possibilities that present themselves (as has G. Thomas Tanselle, his more cogent successor in theoretical bibliographical analysis and description), Bowers would be worthy of even greater honor than he has deservedly received. But he (and some of his less circumspect disciples) soon began to use such words as "scientific" to describe both the principles and the practices of the McKerrow-Greg-Bowers tradition or school. In 1969, James Thorpe called attention to this tendency, its concomitant limitations, and its accompanying abuses in a paper entitled

23. *Textual and Literary Criticism* (Cambridge: Cambridge University Press, 1959), pp. vii-viii.
24. *Principles of Bibliographical Description* (Princeton: Princeton University Press, 1949), p. ix.

"The Ideal of Textual Criticism."[25] Bowers, by temperament a proselytizer, also chose to move beyond work in Renaissance drama and sought wider influence primarily in editions of American authors. After working on Whitman's manuscripts and serving as textual editor for the Centenary Edition of Hawthorne's works undertaken at Ohio State in the 1960s, Bowers and those in agreement with his principles, aided by grants from the National Endowment for the Humanities to the Center for Editions of American Authors (CEAA), set out both to produce texts of classic American authors edited according to the best theoretical principles and to inculcate and enforce in other areas of literary studies the (undoubtedly higher) standards of textual criticism and editorial procedures that had evolved from the great tradition studying English Renaissance drama—the principles of Pollard, McKerrow, Greg, and Bowers.[26]

Here I shall mention only a couple of the inevitable excesses of this militant program and a few of the equally inevitable reactions. Bowers, who had naturally enough drawn his examples of textual problems in authors and periods with which he was not personally familiar from scholars whose work sounded plausible to him, began to systematize his theories in areas where not only was there too little evidence available, but where some of the evidence upon which he generalized was simply wrong. For example, impressed by Charles H. Taylor's solid work on the transmission of Shelley's texts in *The Early Collected Editions of Shelley's Poetry*, Bowers argued that "modern editors have contented themselves with reprinting the presumed authoritative text of 1839 . . . and in so doing they have perpetuated a number of errors by their negligence."[27] In fact, as specialists in Shelley's texts soon noted, though Rossetti and a few others had followed Mary Shelley's editions, Forman's reliance on the first editions and manuscripts had eliminated from modern texts most of the variants that (as Taylor demonstrated) had entered Mary Shelley's later editions through her use of error-filled piracies as press copy. By making unsubstantiated claims for the importance of Taylor's work to the modern editor, Bowers opened the way for Neville Rogers and others unfamiliar with

---

25. First printed in *The Task of the Editor: Papers Read at a Clark Library Seminar, February 8, 1969* by James Thorpe and Claude M. Simpson, Jr. (Los Angeles: William Andrews Clark Memorial Library, 1969). Thorpe included a revised version of his lecture as the second chapter of his *Principles of Textual Criticism* (San Marino, Cal.: Huntington Library, 1972), pp. 50-79.
26. In Thorpe's words, "Bowers has been eager, it would seem, to insure that abuses are stripped and whipped" (*Principles of Textual Criticism*, p. 64).
27. *Textual and Literary Criticism*, p. 25. See also Bowers's review of Taylor's book in *Keats-Shelley Journal* 9 (1960): 35-38.

recent bibliographical and editorial methods to ignore the relevance of the entire discipline to their work.

Again, Bowers in his own editorial practice—especially in the Virginia Edition of *The Works of Stephen Crane*—carried to an excess the imposition of his own "system" and uniformity on works Crane had written at various times, for different purposes, and surviving in a variety of "authorities." David J. Nordloh, in a detailed review article,[28] wrote of Bowers's edition of Crane:

> The new texts are not simply reprintings of documents already available; they are the result of analysis of the materials which were part of the original process of Crane's creation, and of examination of correspondence and historical information bearing on that process. But such detailed research—and the detailed results which face the reader of this new edition—have yielded not definitive forms of Stephen Crane's various writings but muddles of editorial synthesis and intervention. . . . The texts based on these materials combine an insensitivity to what Crane was doing with an unwillingness to leave Crane as he was. . . . All the texts are battered by the intrusion of editorial conformity. . . . they bear no identifiable relationship to the Stephen Crane documents which supposedly constitute their basis. (pp. 103-4)

Nordloh himself began as a graduate student in the CEAA works at Indiana and rose to become general editor of *A Selected Edition of William Dean Howells*, as well as chairman of the MLA's Committee on Scholarly Editions (CSE)—the successor to CEAA. As a student of Ronald Gottesman, he was insulated from Bowers and some of his more fanatic disciples; and, though he accepted the goals they espoused, his understanding of the means to be employed was tempered by his own experience in the nitty-gritty work of collating Howells's fiction, by Tanselle's careful discussions of theory and practice (and the distinctions between them), and by the reactions to CEAA-prototype publications on Emerson and Hawthorne of such gadfly critics as Lewis Mumford and Edmund Wilson and—with much greater authority—Morse Peckham.

In the first volume of *Proof: The Yearbook of American Bibliographical and Textual Studies* (1971), Peckham contributed important "Reflections on the Foundations of Modern Textual Editing" that may mark the beginning of the end of the conjuring power of the names Pollard, McKerrow, and Greg in fields outside Renaissance drama. Drawing upon his experience as an editor of Charles Darwin and Browning (as well as an author's experience

28. "On Crane Now Edited: The University of Virginia Edition of *The Works of Stephen Crane*," *Studies in the Novel* 10 (1978): 103-19.

with publishers), Peckham—while dismissing as trivial the criticisms of Bowers by Edmund Wilson and James D. Thorpe—found some basic problems in Bowers's presuppositions. Peckham's critique begins, characteristically, with a fear of ossification: "the principles developed over the past thirty years (since Greg's *The Editorial Problem in Shakespeare*) are proving to be less satisfactory than they seemed to be ten years ago. Part of the difficulty lies in rhetoric, but much of it is the general truth that a great innovator's followers inevitably simplify and rigidify and sanctify their master's ideas." Centering on what he regards as the arbitrary differences between "substantives" and "accidentals," Peckham first cites Greg's precise and sensible distinction and then goes on to show how Greg's narrow and practical application had been reified. After instancing a number of cases (including some in the Centenary Hawthorne) in which the distinction has been overapplied, he concludes:

the lesson of this is that what to do about punctuation is an empirical matter, not a theoretical matter, not a matter of editorial principles or rules, as Greg pretentiously called them in *The Editorial Problem in Shakespeare*.
The textual editor should do away with this theological terminology of accidentals and substantives, and talk simply and clearly about words, punctuation, spelling, capitalization, and whatever else he needs to talk about. These things are there, before our eyes; accidence and substance are not. (pp. 125-26)

If Peckham's essay signals the first serious reaction to the Greg-Bowers tradition in those circles, Philip Gaskell's *A New Introduction to Bibliography* (1972), designed to replace McKerrow's *Introduction*, is based on a broader body of bibliographical evidence from later periods than had been available to McKerrow. Gaskell, therefore, is less inclined in that volume to generalize on the basis of problems peculiar to a single field than were earlier bibliographers. Again, reviews and essays by a variety of scholars and editors who had encountered in their studies exceptions to Bowers's theories led to a constant reexamination of the orthodoxies of that school. Gaskell followed this well-received volume with a more controversial one entitled *From Writer to Reader: Studies in Editorial Method*.[29] After a brief analysis of some areas and problems to be considered by the editor, Gaskell stresses "not only that every textual situation is unique and should be approached without editorial preconceptions, but also that there is seldom only one right way of editing a work of literature" (p. 10). He then proceeds

---

29. Oxford: Clarendon Press, 1978; *A New Introduction to Bibliography* was also published by the Clarendon Press.

to examine twelve texts, ranging from Harington's translation of *Orlando Furioso* (1591) to Tom Stoppard's *Travesties* (1974), discussing the available evidence and concluding in each case that the principles of Greg and Bowers are inadequate to the situation.

The most cogent recent defenses of what we may, for the sake of brevity, call simply the "Greg tradition" have come from G. Thomas Tanselle. He refutes Gaskell's criticisms of and departures from the Greg tradition in a review of *From Writer to Reader*.[30] Earlier, in his magisterial essay entitled "Greg's Theory of Copy-Text and the Editing of American Literature,"[31] Tanselle had discussed historically, in far greater depth, the significance of Greg's "The Rationale of Copy-Text" (pp. 170–82) and important additions to the theory in Fredson Bowers's "Multiple Authority: New Problems and Concepts of Copy-Texts" (pp. 182–84).[32] In "Greg's Theory of Copy-Text . . . ," Tanselle enumerates Bowers's general contributions to the dissemination of the Greg tradition through both his "general discussions of editing" and his "actual editions based on Greg's rationale" (p. 184), leading therefrom into an analysis of the principles employed by CEAA and promulgated in its *Statement of Editorial Principles: A Working Manual for Editing Nineteenth-Century American Texts* (1967). He also answers in detail a series of criticisms of the CEAA editions by Edmund Wilson, Paul Baender, Donald Pizer, John Freehafer, and Morse Peckham in the essay to which I have alluded.[33] While granting Peckham's essay higher status than the others as "a thoughtfully developed analysis of the nature of human communication" (p. 211), Tanselle is at pains to refute what he regards as Peckham's two principal arguments against Greg's theory: (1) Peckham's denial "that substantives and accidentals can be meaningfully segregated" and (2) "that the reconstruction of a text representing the author's intention is a meaningful (or attainable) goal" (p. 212).

Though Tanselle cogently refutes these objections or argues that their main points were implicit in Greg's theory, his summary of Peckham's argument does not fully reflect the message that Peckham's essay conveys to me. For I conceive Peckham's principal point as being that textual analysis is a branch of history, not a subdivision of philosophy. For all his own

---

30. *The Library*, 6th ser., 2 (1980): 337–50; contrast with this the favorable review by Jack Stillinger, *JEGP* 78 (1979): 422–24.
31. *SB* 28 (1975): 167–229.
32. Bowers's essay appeared in *The Library*, 5th ser., 27 (1972): 81–115.
33. The essays by Pizer and Freehafer, and critical responses to them, appeared in *Bulletin of the New York Public Library* under the editorship of David V. Erdman. I treat Erdman's editorial work and principles, along with those of other major editors of the British Romantics, in a companion essay to this entitled "Romantic Bards and Historical Editors" [the next item in this volume].

philosophical terminology, Peckham's thesis in this and other writings is that situational behavior—specific actions of human beings under very special (often unique) conditions—produces whatever we at any time choose to call works of art or literary texts. That Peckham's own theoretical propositions in the hands of the irresponsible *can* lead to an extreme relativism troubles me as much as it does Tanselle, but Peckham clearly does not think so himself, as should be clear from his praise of "analytical bibliography" and its "magnificent" "achievements in the past thirty years" and his further assertion: "Anyone who forces the noses of humanists onto the grindstone of hard, immutable fact has a genuinely redemptive function."[34] Peckham seems clearly to believe in the absoluteness of *facts*—"immutable" evidence resulting from behavior, past or present—but he has a relativistic position about *theories* developed to explain those facts. He wants the textual editor to present facts—to record variants accurately, for example—but to be very circumspect about developing theories on exactly how these variants came into existence, and even more so about what went on in the author's mind at the time. Peckham writes:

The "human factor" is not something that occasionally enters into the bibliographer's thinking when he finds himself in a spot; it is almost exclusively all that he is concerned with. The analytical bibliographer is a historian, and he should not forget it for a moment. The object of his inquiry is not printed artifacts as physical objects but human behavior in the past, human behavior that no longer exists and cannot now be examined. (p. 131)

Knowing Tanselle's opinions both from his writings and from numerous conversations with him on these matters, I judge that he would agree in principle that the function of the analytical bibliographer is historical rather than philosophical. But Tanselle argues that the exceptions noted by any number of reviewers of Bowers's editions—including those by Nordloh—do not invalidate Greg's *principles* but simply illustrate ineffective specific applications of them. That may be so, but if Bowers, the leading exponent of those principles for his generation, was unable to make effective use of them in his own editing of Hawthorne and Stephen Crane, the usefulness of the principles themselves inevitably comes into question.

Watson Branch's recent review of the editorial practice of David Nordloh in the Howells edition suggests that for certain adherents to the Greg tradition, rules, laws, and principles have become a trap rather than a path toward greater knowledge.[35] Whether an editor is being true to the "prin-

---

34. "Reflections on the Foundations of Modern Textual Editing," *Proof* 1 (1971): 129–30.
35. "Two Recent Volumes of *A Selected Edition of W. D. Howells*," *MP* 78 (1980): 59–72.

ciples" of Greg, Bowers, or Tanselle seems to have greater significance for Branch than whether or not the editor has accurately presented the surviving evidence from which all theories must derive. Doctrinal purity takes precedence over accuracy of transcription or collation. While acknowledging that Nordloh and his colleagues have described clearly and accurately the relevant textual materials and their editorial procedures, Branch writes, for example: "the editors are applying W. W. Greg's theory of copy-text. Unfortunately they have not applied it very well . . ." (p. 60). "The choices [of copy-text] are quite right, but a statement immediately following indicates a basic misconception regarding Greg's theory . . ." (p. 61). Branch glosses his statement of Gregian orthodoxy with citations to Greg's "The Rationale of Copy-Text" and to Bowers's "Remarks on Eclectic Texts" (*Proof* 4 [1975]). He then asserts that, though his own collations uncovered no "nonauthorial *Century* readings" in the portions of *A Modern Instance* where the manuscript was the copy-text but corrected photocopies of the *Century* installments served as press copy (i.e., was the version from which compositors set the text), he regrets Nordloh's use of this technical expedient because of its potentiality for error; he admits that by "careful proofreading" the Howells editors succeeded in frustrating Branch in his search for errors in the text, if not in the apparatus (pp. 62, 71). Branch, who studied under Hershel Parker, one of the editors of Melville, charges the Howells editors with heresy on a number of points where they deviate from Greg (p. 67), and on their practice of regularizing he quotes against them "the editors of the Melville edition" (p. 70).

This kind of petulant attack upon the CEAA-originated editions from within and without has finally led G. Thomas Tanselle to question the wisdom of invoking W. W. Greg's "Rationale" and Bowers's revisions and extensions of it as privileged texts. He believes that the *central principles* evolving from their writings (and his) will stand on their own feet, without the need to invoke authorities. In "Recent Editorial Discussion and the Central Questions of Editing,"[36] Tanselle first reviews the chief "editorial literature" discussing the CEAA since he wrote "Greg's Theory of Copy-Text and the Editing of American Literature" (1975) and, though he argues that many of the charges against CEAA editorial theory and practice are either uninformed or simplistic, he grants that reliance on certain terms has sometimes confused rather than clarified the issues. When in a succinct concluding section Tanselle delineates the three groups of "central questions of editing," he accepts the strictures of Peckham and Tom Davis

---

36. *SB* 34 (1981): 23–65.

by eschewing the use of "substantive," "accidental," and "definitive" and by carefully defining each term he introduces. In the "first set of questions," Tanselle distinguishes between "historical" editions—those that either reproduce "a particular text from the past" or attempt to reconstruct "what the author intended"—and "those in which the editor's own personal preferences" (rather than his judgment of what the *author* preferred) provide the basis of choice. "Historical" editions are the only "scholarly editions"; those in which the editor reproduces a single historical version of the text, from a manuscript or printing, without emendation are "noncritical" editions;[37] those in which "editorial judgment" determines "when, and whether, emendations are to be made in the text" are "critical" editions. Both regularizing and modernizing, writes Tanselle, "are ahistorical in orientation and therefore, have no place in . . . scholarly editions" (pp. 60–61). He underlines and supports this judgment by declaring that the author's "punctuation and spelling are integral parts of a text, affecting its meaning and impact" and thus must not be revised in a scholarly edition, "except possibly for some of the earliest works in a language, which might be said to require 'translation,' rather then simply 'modernization,' for the general reader" (p. 61 and n. 73).

Secondly, Tanselle faces the question of authorial intention. He writes: "the aim is to emend the selected text [i.e., the copy-text] so that it conforms to the author's intention; one can never fully attain such a goal (or know that one has attained it)," but the editor moves "toward it by applying informed judgment to the available evidence" (p. 62). On the question of when an author's revisions "indicate a new conception of a work" rather than "the process of perfecting the expression of the same conception," Tanselle argues that this "difficult decision . . . is central to critical editing." (Here he upholds the central thesis in Greg's "Rationale.") Moreover, the critical editor must attempt to unravel the author's positive "intention"—what he or she *preferred*—from textual changes imposed on or acquiesced to by the author because of the physical, legal, or practical considerations of publishing at that time. In evaluating each individual situation, however, "one must be extremely cautious about attributing authorial intention or preference to alternatives simply because they were passed, in one fashion or another, by the author" (pp. 62–63).

Finally, Tanselle confronts the sticky question of the "copy-text," which

37. The term *noncritical* seems to me to carry pejorative connotations. In Tanselle's essay "Textual Scholarship" in *Introduction to Scholarship in Modern Languages and Literatures*, ed. Joseph Gibaldi (New York: Modern Language Association, 1981), he uses as a synonym the good paleographic term *diplomatic* for a text that the editor does not feel free to alter in any way (p. 34).

the editor follows in cases of "indifferent variants" (i.e., those variants about which the application of the critical editor's knowledge and judgment to the extant evidence cannot determine which is more likely authorial). Tanselle points out that, if there are no "indifferent variants," "[i]t is not necessary to have a copy-text at all," but since, as a matter of fact, such variants "seem to occur, one needs a principle for favoring one text over another": "a copy-text is simply the text most likely to provide an authorial reading . . . where one cannot otherwise reach a decision" (p. 64).

Tanselle's answers to these three central issues of editing—his definition of a critical scholarly edition as an (always imperfect) *attempt* to present the author's intention; his defense of the need, toward that end, to construct an eclectic text on the basis of whatever surviving evidence can be assembled; and his reminder of the practical need to choose a basic text to follow when critical examination of all the evidence fails to reveal the authorial preference—all seem to me to be beyond reproach and to vindicate the central validity of Greg's "Rationale" against its critics. But they do more. By admitting the historical nature of the problems with individual texts, they also reiterate Peckham's main point that "system" and "principles" must always give way to the facts of the case, and they therefore take us from the Brazen Age, when all problems were to be solved by the systematic application of invariable principles (as many lesser followers of Bowers thought), to the Age of Iron, in which the rugged individuality of each text takes precedence over the theoretically "normal" or "accepted" patterns of punctuation and orthography that the "scientific" or, rather, doctrinaire editor once tried to impose on the recalcitrant vagaries of human behavior in authors and other editors alike.

IV

Karl Kroeber writes in his important essay "Experience as History: Shelley's Venice, Turner's Carthage,"[38] "'Romantic' sensibility . . . is alien to 'modern' sensibility, because the Romantic identifies individual experience with historical process, whereas to the modern, 'experience' and history are antithetical" (p. 321). Kroeber sees that for the Modernist poet, as for the Classic writer, history is a repetitive winding and unwinding of spools or gyres, expanding and contracting like a pulsating universe. Therefore, for the Modernist, the meaningful patterns of life are supplied by myths and archetypes. Taking Kroeber's distinction farther, we may

---

38. *ELH* 41 (1974): 321–39.

say: for the Romantic (and many students of Romantic writers), history is linear and, at least sporadically, progressive. For the Classic or Modernist critic, the fitting analogies for human experience are the cycles of day and night and the four seasons. For the Romantic, who inherits the Judeo-Christian conception of man, the appropriate image is that of a journey toward a distant earthly (no longer a heavenly) destination. For the editor following a Classic or Modernist philosophy, the pattern or principle stands at the center of editing. For the Romantic or historical editor—Peckham, or (at this point) Tanselle—the individual case is unique and ought not to be subsumed or erased to fit a generalized archetypal pattern.

To ignore the historicist milieu of Romantic poetry in order to make it more "modern" and "relevant" is akin to trying to read Dante without reference to Thomist theology, or to read Milton in ignorance of both the new science and the theological disputes of the seventeenth century. If textual theorists wish to argue that all Elizabethan texts should be edited on a single set of principles appropriate to the hierarchical ideal invoked by Church and State in the latter half of the sixteenth century, I am not in a position to challenge them. If they wish to regularize the texts of Pope, Swift, and Addison on the theory that these Augustan authors intended to follow Right Reason and the Common Sense of mankind, who am I to argue? But I know that I am on solid ground in saying that subtle peculiarities in orthography and punctuation are not only *characteristic* of the writings, but even *vital* to the meaning of Blake, Lamb, Shelley, and Keats—all authors who struggled hard to maintain their individuality amid an age of ever-encroaching uniformity. Though I am, therefore, willing to be convinced that a uniform application of principles evolved during the Brazen Age *may* be appropriate for the authors of other times and places, I am quite convinced that the Romantics should be edited according to the historicist conceptions of the Age of Iron.

To call the fourth age of editing the Iron Age is to suggest, first, a period of relatively rough and unpolished texts, allowed to reflect the vagaries of authorial behavior, rather than a regularized, polished redaction to fit an idealized conception of an author's intention. Beyond these qualities, the serviceable (rather than beautiful) texts of the Iron Age are expected to rust in time, as later generations of scholars discover flaws in the knowledge or understanding of the merely mortal historian-editors, or as newly discovered authoritative documents or analytical techniques corrode the cutting edge of these scholarly tools. For the editor of the Iron Age, editing is more nearly a practical craft than a science, and an edition is recognized as an attempt to serve the needs of a specified audience for a particular time, rather than to reach an immutable standard of perfection. The Romantic editor looks upon the turning cycle of sublunar mutability and (at least in moments of equanimity) accepts, as Shelley, Keats, and Yeats did, that the works of his mind and hands, like all products of creativity, are subject to the ravishment of "Fate, Time, Occasion, Chance, and Change." He also believes that, if his work has been done with proper care and attention, though it may ultimately decay as a standard (never a "definitive") edition, it will provide a *more accurate* representation of the creations of great writers for the readers of its time. It will, moreover, transmit to future generations of scholars an example of diligent and responsible devotion to the great writers of the past, to their literary creations, and to new readers whose lives may be changed by encountering these records "of the best and happiest moments of the happiest and best minds."

7

Romantic Bards
and Historical Editors

For *the background of how this paper came to be written in conjunction with "The Four Ages of Editing and the English Romantics," see the headnote to that essay (6). The most significant other fact about its approach and tone involves its occasion as part of a tribute to David V. Erdman. It is difficult to honor a senior colleague in one's own field of specialization without either implying that the honoree has done extraordinary work that has outdistanced the capabilities of the writer, or else focusing on the flaws in his or her achievements that leave room for younger scholar-critics to accomplish something new. Most would agree that scholarship, unlike the creation of* belles lettres *or even the critical understanding of earlier writings, is a cumulative and progressive endeavor. Scholars who are able to master the work of all their predecessors who wrote on the same topic should be able to build on that body of knowledge and, through the use of primary evidence unavailable to (or overlooked by) the earlier scholars, they ought to be able to push the frontiers of knowledge ahead, to whatever extent their individual capacities permit. (After all, the average college student of physics understands many things about the universe that Sir Isaac Newton never comprehended.)*

Harold Bloom's theory of "the anxiety of influence," whatever its merits may be as a description of the interactions of creative writers, ought not, therefore, apply to scholar-critics. But as commentators on Bloom's writings have pointed out, his own early enthusiasm for the ideas of M. H. Abrams, Northrop Frye, and Walter Jackson Bate and his subsequent rejections of them—like similar reactions to Bloom's work by his contemporaries, colleagues, and students—suggest that his theory may derive from, and apply even more directly to, the reactions of academics, rather than poets, to their senior contemporaries.

It isn't for me to decide whether I escaped this difficulty, but in assessing Erdman's virtues and limitations, I tried both to avoid condescension and to eschew hagiography, instead applying to his scholarly achievements tests that I would be pleased if eventually someone thought it worthwhile to apply to mine:

Can the flaws be attributed to the natural limitations of the human condition, in which the perspective of each individual is affected by particular experiences and environments, rather than to ideological biases or a failure to grapple with the evidence? Are the virtues of the work so much more pervasive than its limitations that scholarly understanding was advanced when the work first appeared and, after its advances have been absorbed by later scholar-critics, does it remain valuable for its inquiring spirit and as a record of Man thinking? Has the scholar, better than the majority of his or her contemporaries, maintained high intellectual and ethical standards that others should emulate? Under these criteria, David V. Erdman ranks very high in the annals of modern contextual literary scholarship. His writings on Blake, Byron, and Coleridge speak for themselves. He has also contributed in many more general ways to the sense of community among Romantics scholars in North America and Europe. As Stuart Curran said, in presenting David V. Erdman with the Keats-Shelley Association's Distinguished Scholar Award in 1982:

One has the impression that David has been everywhere that strenuous thinking has been going on in our time; or perhaps it is enough to say that for forty-five years, wherever he has been, strenuous thinking has been going on. There is a paradox here that tells us something essential about David: by necessity a scholar-gypsy for many years, his life and work dogged by an isolating force of circumstances, he has continually forged scholarly communities that transcend local departments or schools of criticism or specialized disciplines. . . . Few scholars have shown such an exemplary commitment to our profession as a collective and cumulative endeavor. The example has influenced all his academic associates—and there must by now be hundreds of them—as much as his great learning and his insistence on an exact grounding in history. (Keats-Shelley Journal 32 [1983]: 12)

For students of the Age of Johnson, I can perhaps characterize David Erdman's place in Romantics studies no better than to say that, though David has been far more productive as a scholar, he is also our James Clifford. In honoring him as he approached his seventieth birthday (though not his retirement), his contemporary peers and younger colleagues alike overcame much of the human frailty that tends toward one-upmanship (a failing occasionally indulged even by David Erdman) and honored him at once for being a superb scholar, a beloved friend, and a model of the Happy Warrior as academic.

In a recent paper addressed to an audience of editors, analytical bibliographers, and textual critics, I outlined (in the semi-detached tone of

Thomas Love Peacock) the Four Ages of Editing.[1] I can briefly recapitulate that argument as follows. The Golden Age of Innocence encompassed the years in which, after the death of each Romantic writer, his widow, children, friends, publishers, and disciples published (rather uncritically) as much as they could of the writings of the beloved departed, trying to win him a wider audience. This was followed by a Silver Age of superficial polish, in which editors (W. M. Rossetti and Thomas Hutchinson, for example) served as the factotums of publishers to smooth out, to polish, and, when necessary, to bowdlerize the texts of the Romantics so that their editions would capture as large as possible a share of the expanding commercial market. This age was, in turn, accompanied and followed by the development of a Brazen Age of editing, in which scholarly bibliographers and textual critics attempted to systematize principles of editing applicable to all writings of all periods, but derived largely from the study of Renaissance drama. Finally, I spoke of the emergence of a new Iron Age of editing in which—true to the historicist principles held by the major writers of the early nineteenth century—the editor of the Romantics is content to present "relatively rough and unpolished texts" that "reflect the vagaries of authorial behavior, rather than a regularized, polished redaction" reflecting "an editor's idealized conception of an author's intention." Whereas the Brazen Age tried to make textual criticism into an exact science and to develop editorial principles that exhibit *philosophical* Truth, the Iron Age attempts to display the *historical* reality of the author's text as it developed and was presented to its early readers.

In surveying the current state of editing the writers of the late eighteenth and early nineteenth centuries, I hope to develop from this admittedly overschematic paradigm a more detailed and truer picture of what has gone on recently and what is presently happening in the editing of the Romantics. I shall also attempt to extrapolate from the evidence of current editorial practice what we can expect to see during the next decade.

I

Though in "The Four Ages of Editing and the English Romantics" I cited Harry Buxton Forman as the earliest editor of the Brazen Age, in this closer look at editions of the Romantics, I must qualify that designation by saying that Forman, fighting the influence of William Michael Rossetti and other polishers and "improvers" of Shelley's texts, was—by all standards—

---

1. "The Four Ages of Editing and the English Romantics," *TEXT: Transactions of the Society for Textual Scholarship* 1 (1982), forthcoming. [Item 6.]

truer to the best authorities for the text of Shelley and Keats than were most contemporary and later editors. The emendations that he intentionally made on the basis of one of his theories (such as his contention that Shelley distinguished the spelling *desart* for the noun from *desert*, the adjective)[2] were always made in full view of the reader. Forman's conjectural verbal emendations were also clearly designated as such and accompanied by his evidence and reasoning. Even his theories of spelling evolved as a reaction to the efforts of Rossetti and his bad angel Frederick Gard Fleay to clean up Shelley's unusual orthography, polish his metrics, and "correct" his "errors" of diction. Forman developed his theories about Shelley's spelling while looking for evidence to vindicate the orthography he found in Shelley's manuscripts and first editions. Thus from the start of the Brazen Age of editing the Romantics, the tendency was to oppose the wholesale emendation of primary authorities that the training in editing classical texts tended to foster.

Forman, not a university man, was a bibliophile and a self-taught editor and bibliographer who derived his editorial principles from persistent examination of editions and manuscripts of British poetry of the nineteenth century. His mistakes were his own, not those of others whose textual principles evolved in their work on texts of other periods. In many ways, the activity during the past century of British nonacademic bibliophiles, such as R. W. Chapman and Sir Geoffrey Keynes, and of Americans not trained primarily in editing classical texts fostered the inductive, historical tradition of editing the Romantics.

The "Harvard School" of academic editors and bibliographers who have, directly or indirectly, trained the majority of recent editors of the Romantics was initiated by Hyder Edward Rollins, who was born in Abilene, Texas, in 1889, when it must have been still practically a frontier town. After graduating from Southwestern University (Georgetown, Texas) in 1910, Rollins took an M.A. at the University of Texas in 1912 and taught there (1912–1914). He then studied at Johns Hopkins (1914–1915), before ultimately finding his way to Harvard, where he took another M.A. (1916) and his Ph.D. (1917). After holding a traveling fellowship and teach-

---

2. In each volume of *The Poetical Works of Percy Bysshe Shelley* (4 vols., London: Reeves and Turner, 1876–1877), Forman appended a section entitled "On certain words used by Shelley in the Poems printed in the Present Volume" (1:401–13; 2:434–38; 3:471–76; 4:553–57). Forman first proposed that Shelley may have adopted "the *a* for *desart* (noun) to distinguish it from *desert* (adjective)" in 1:175, n. 2. Though in the appendixes to volumes 1, 2, and 3 he was fairly convinced that this interpretation was correct, by the time he wrote that in volume 4, he was finding more evidence against this hypothesis than for it. By that time he had begun to regularize both noun and adjective to *desert*.

ing at New York University, he returned to Harvard in 1926, succeeded George Lyman Kittredge, his mentor, as Gurney Professor of English Literature in 1939, and remained active there after his retirement in 1956 until his death in 1958, editing and directing dissertations in both Elizabethan and English Romantic literature. Rollins's editions of Shakespeare and of Elizabethan miscellanies and broadsides, like his editions of Keats and his circle (listed in the obituary memoir of him in *Keats-Shelley Journal*),[3] show him to have been primarily a historical researcher whose interest in bibliographical details and questions of textual authority was secondary to his efforts to place the lives and careers of authors within their historical and social milieus.

In his standard edition of *Tottel's Miscellany*,[4] Rollins divides the contents on the basis of authorship as well as textual source and not only retains all the old-spelling features of the original that can be transferred from the black-letter original to roman type (including ampersands, reversal of modern practice in occurrence of u and v, i and j), but also the original's variant spellings.[5] Rollins includes a Glossarial Index (2:333–85) that defines words where necessary and gives the locations of unusual forms. In his long Introduction (2:3–124), he shows himself much more interested in the historical and literary situation out of which *Tottel's Miscellany* grew than in textual criticism in the abstract; though he carefully describes each printing, he mentions his choice of copy-text only, as it were, in passing, as an appositive amid an argument on the priority of two other printings (*B* and *C*).[6] Many issues of textual theory that now, after years of debate, seem problematical, were to him obvious; he clearly valued the original source in its strangeness over uniformity or consistency. And in his "Notes" (2:127–330), he mixes his collations with historical information, quotation of probable sources, bibliographical information, and data on others' suggestions for emendation. He always lists the sources of all his information and quotations, most of which he has checked independently. Taken as a whole, Rollins's editing of *Tottel's Miscellany* shows a strong preponderance of—and preference for—factual research over theorizing.

Over the years, both John Livingston Lowes and Rollins set their Har-

---

3. *K-SJ* 7, part 1 (1959): 1–3.
4. 2 vols. Cambridge: Harvard University Press, 1928.
5. For example, the first four poems in the collection begin with the same word, twice spelled *Descripcion* (1 and 3) and twice, *Description* (2 and 4).
6. "All the editions after *A* conclude with a 'Table,' or index of first lines, which it would have been useless for me to reprint because it does not index the text of *A*, the basis of my own edition" (2:15).

vard students onto seminar papers and dissertation topics that emphasized the collection of new information from primary sources over the interpretation of facts gathered by others. Many of their students in nineteenth-century literature used manuscript sources to write dissertations on secondary or minor figures: Willard Bissell Pope (1932) on Benjamin Robert Haydon and John Hamilton Reynolds; Richard W. Armour (1933) on "Barry Cornwall"; Bradford Booth (1935) on John Galt; Ralph M. Wardle (1940) on "William Maginn and *Blackwood's Magazine*"; Carl Woodring (1949) on William and Mary Howitt and their circle; Cecil Y. Lang (1949) on Pre-Raphaelitism; David Bonnell Green (1953) on Thomas Hill and Edward Du Bois; Stephen M. Parrish (1954) on Fred Holland Day, Louise Imogen Guiney, and their circle; and Jack Stillinger (1958) on Charles Armitage Brown. Rollins also influenced the editorial procedures of his colleagues and of Harvard graduate students who did *not* write under him. Though Rollins was known as a dry, factual teacher, he impressed upon his students the need to verify all factual statements because he checked each such statement in their seminar papers. Chester L. Shaver (1937), Gwynne Blakemore Evans (1940), William H. Bond (1941), and other students who wrote dissertations under Rollins dealing with authors of the sixteenth and seventeenth centuries may have studied analytical bibliography and textual criticism, as developed by Alfred W. Pollard, Ronald B. McKerrow, and Walter W. Greg, but most of the editors of nineteenth-century materials who came out of the "Harvard School" began by training in historical or biographical research through documents and archives. Even though the younger members of the group also studied with William A. Jackson, only later in their careers did they turn their attention to bibliography (in some cases, enumerative to start with).[7] Rollins's students also played a leading role in editing scholarly journals in the field. Bradford Booth founded *Nineteenth-Century Fiction* and edited it for twenty years; Mabel A. E. Steele was the editor of *Keats-Shelley Journal* from its founding in 1952 until her death in 1964; David Bonnell Green was founding editor of *Studies in Romanticism*; and Jack Stillinger, succeeding Gwynne Blakemore Evans as executive editor, made *JEGP* a leading publisher of textual studies on Wordsworth and Keats in the 1960s and 1970s.

But the "Harvard School" formed by Rollins's students and *their* students has had even greater influence through its editions of letters, jour-

---

7. Lang, Woodring, Green, and Edwin Graves Wilson (another student of Rollins) served as bibliographers for the *Keats-Shelley Journal* from 1952 through 1969; recently Carl Woodring's students Robert A. Hartley, Robert M. Ryan, and Clement Dunbar have been among those who assumed that responsibility.

nals, and poetry of the nineteenth century. Rollins's own editions of *The Keats Circle* (1948), *More Letters and Poems of the Keats Circle* (1955), and *The Letters of John Keats* (1958) were followed by a series of significant scholarly and teaching editions of the Romantics and Victorians—Cecil Lang's Swinburne letters (6 vols., 1959–1962); W. B. Pope's *Diary of Benjamin Robert Haydon* (5 vols., 1960–1963); Carl Woodring's Riverside Edition of *Prose of the Romantic Period* (1961);[8] Jack Stillinger's Riverside Edition of Wordsworth's *Selected Poems and Prefaces* (1965), editions of John Stuart Mill's *Autobiography* and other writings (1961, 1969, 1981), *Letters of Charles Armitage Brown* (1966), and, ultimately, *The Poems of John Keats* (1979); and Leonidas Jones's *Letters of John Hamilton Reynolds* (1973). Stephen M. Parrish, after setting up Cornell's program of computer-generated concordances to major poets, became general editor of the Cornell Wordsworth.[9] Woodring and Walter Jackson Bate are among the editors of the Bollingen Collected Coleridge. Chester Shaver revised the first volume of the Wordsworth letters (1967), and Ralph Wardle edited letters between Godwin and Mary Wollstonecraft (1966) and the collected letters of Wollstonecraft (1979). As for the second generation, Lang, while teaching at Syracuse, helped shape the editorial principles of Edwin W. Marrs, Jr., an editor of Carlyle's letters and now of the Lambs' letters, and of Jerome J. McGann, editor of the new Oxford English Text Edition of Byron's *Complete Poetical Works*. Editorial work by Woodring's students includes John Clubbe's *Selected Poems of Thomas Hood* (1970) and his work as assistant editor of volumes 1–7 of *The Collected Letters of Thomas and Jane Welsh Carlyle* (1970–1977), Nancy Bogen's edition of *The Book of Thel* by Blake (1971), Thomas L. Ashton's edition of Byron's *Hebrew Melodies* (1972), John O. Hayden's Penguin Edition of Wordsworth's *Poems* (2 vols., 1977), and E. B. Murray's work as coeditor of the forthcoming Oxford edition of Shelley's prose. Many students of Parrish and Abrams have become editors of volumes in the Cornell Wordsworth. And though I worked at Illinois under Royal A. Gettmann (who himself knows the value of good editing), Gwynne Evans and Jack Stillinger encouraged me to study the manuscript and the transmission of the text of Shelley's "The Triumph of Life"; that work, in turn, qualified me to edit later volumes of *Shelley and his Circle* (1973–) and to undertake the Norton Critical Edition of *Shelley's Poetry and Prose* (1977). A number of the

8. Gordon N. Ray, a student at Harvard during Rollins's heyday, was general editor of Houghton Mifflin's Riverside Editions at the time when they were the most highly regarded literary texts for college students. Naturally, many of the editors he chose for that series had studied at Harvard—most under Rollins.

9. Parrish is also playing an advisory role for a projected Cornell edition of Yeats's poetic manuscripts.

scholarly editions mentioned above were published by Harvard University Press—many while Rollins still served as one of its primary advisers. Even the first two volumes of *Shelley and his Circle* (1961), edited by Kenneth Neill Cameron, were surveyed on behalf of the press by Rollins just before his death.

The mention of Cameron brings us to those leading editors of Romantic texts who were not students of Rollins or of Rollins's students. Cameron, a Rhodes scholar from McGill, had as his Oxford tutor H. F. B. Brett-Smith, coeditor of the Halliford Edition of *The Works of Thomas Love Peacock*. He absorbed the classical British tradition of editing also represented at Oxford in his time there by Ernest de Selincourt, Helen Darbishire, and H. W. Garrod. A Marxist, Cameron began his work on Shelley with a primary interest in the poet's historical milieu, an interest reflected in his early essays, in *The Young Shelley: Genesis of a Radical* (1950), and in *Shelley: The Golden Years* (1974). On the basis of his careful historical scholarship, Cameron was selected by the late Carl H. Pforzheimer to edit *Shelley and his Circle*.[10]

Kathleen Coburn, who early in her career became Coleridge's editor sans peer, began at Victoria College, University of Toronto, and later at Oxford continued to study Coleridge's philosophical ideas and debts.[11] Leslie A. Marchand, who began his career by publishing his historical study of *The Athenæum* (1941) and then edited some letters of Thomas Hood (1945), studied all aspects of Byron's life before turning again to editing in *Byron's Letters and Journals* (11 vols., 1973–1981).[12] Other editors of Byron, including Willis W. Pratt, Truman Guy Steffan, and Ernest J. Lovell at Texas, similarly began their editorial work as an adjunct to their studies of Byron's life, writings, and reputation. Their colleague David Lee Clark, who edited Shelley's *Prose* (1954), was really concerned with Shelley's ideas, as was James Notopoulos, editor of Shelley's translations from Plato in his massive study *The Platonism of Shelley* (1949). Lawrence John Zillman first studied the English sonnet tradition before attempting (twice) to edit *Prometheus Unbound* (1959, 1968). Among others of the senior generation of editors of the Romantics, the late Frederick L. Jones was, I believe, the only one whose editions—*The Letters of Mary W. Shelley* (2 vols., 1944), *Mary Shelley's Journal* (1947), the journals and letters of the Gisbornes and

10. See my account of Cameron's career, "Profile of a Contemporary: Kenneth Neill Cameron," *WC* 8 (1977): 253–57.

11. See her memoir *In Pursuit of Coleridge* (Toronto: Bodley Head, 1977). Her B. Litt. thesis director at Oxford was also H. B. F. Brett-Smith (see pp. 23–24).

12. See Jerome J. McGann, "Profile of a Contemporary: Leslie A. Marchand," *WC* 10 (1979): 290–91.

Edward E. Williams (1951), and P. B. Shelley's *Letters* (2 vols., 1963)—were his primary research interests.[13] In this hasty survey of American and Canadian editors of the Romantics, I have neglected the many British editors of the Romantics during the past thirty years (though I treat de Selincourt and Garrod in "The Four Ages of Editing and the English Romantics"). By way of apology, I invoke the best possible excuse for this omission: almost total ignorance of the backgrounds of most of the leading editors trained in British universities.

II

On a topic as broad as this one, it is imperative to move beyond name-dropping generalities into at least one detailed case history, and one American exemplifies better than any other the historical predispositions of the editors of English Romantic poetry. David V. Erdman, Geoffrey Keynes, and G. E. Bentley, Jr., form a triangle (*not* a triumvirate) of rival editors of Blake's writings, and Erdman has graced Coleridge studies as a most assiduous and cooperative discoverer and editor of Coleridge's political journalism. Anyone who knows David well is aware of both his breadth of interests and the enthusiasm and persistence with which he will pursue to its lair the answer to any kind of question that piques his susceptible curiosity. But as should be clear even to casual readers of his scholarship, David Erdman's *primary* interests are not bibliographical or theoretical, but biographical and historical.[14]

Having written his dissertation at Princeton on "Byron's Poetic Technique" (1936), Erdman turned almost immediately to analysis of Byron's political thinking. His first publication, "Byron's Stage Fright" (*ELH*, 1939), bridged the gaps between theater history, biography, and study of an author's writings. His next three papers—"Lord Byron and the Genteel Reformers" (*PMLA*, 1941), "Lord Byron as Rinaldo" (*PMLA*, 1942), and "Byron and Revolt in England" (first delivered as a paper at the MLA con-

13. Jones, like some of his contemporaries, paid a price for not having begun under the tutelage of someone as thorough and demanding as Rollins. For limitations in his editing (as well as that of Zillman, Neville Rogers, and some others), see Donald H. Reiman, "Editing Shelley," in *Editing Texts of the Romantic Period*, ed. John D. Baird (Toronto: A. M. Hakkert, 1972; more recently issued, New York: Garland Publishing, Inc.), pp. 27–45. [Item 1.]

14. The following outline of the career of David V. Erdman is based chiefly on published sources, such as various editions of the *Directory of American Scholars*, publications of The John Simon Guggenheim Memorial Foundation, and the usual scholarly bibliographical aids; in addition, David V. Erdman kindly provided me with an updated copy of his bibliography. The tone and various factual bits and pieces come from long personal knowledge and from conversations with David, his wife Virginia, and his friends, colleagues, and students over a period of eighteen years. See also Florence Sandler, "Profile of a Contemporary: David V. Erdman," *WC* 3 (1976): 212–16.

vention in 1943 and published in *Science and Society,* 1947)—together constitute the most important research ever done on Byron's involvement in British politics and the reform movement. By the time of the last of these papers, Erdman's own leftward political perspective was becoming clear to his academic colleagues, and that awareness did not contribute to his well-being during the 1940s and 1950s, when fear of communism, the Cold War with the Soviets, and the Korean War dominated the thinking of middle America. David himself—born in Omaha, Nebraska, and B.A. from Carleton College in Northfield, Minnesota (the alma mater of Thorstein Veblen)—was a middle American in the progressive tradition. His first employment after completing his Ph.D. had been a Depression expedient as professor and chairman of the English Department at the State Agricultural and Mechanical College of Arkansas. After one year there (1936–1937), he taught for four years as an instructor at the University of Wisconsin (Madison, of course, in those days), but he didn't stick, and after one-year appointments at Olivet College in Michigan and at The Citadel (Charleston, South Carolina), he spent three years in Detroit as managing editor for the publications of the United Auto Workers–CIO, the last year (1946) also teaching as a "special instructor" at Wayne State University.

In 1947, David Erdman received a Guggenheim Fellowship to work on the topic that best expresses his interests: "A Study of Social Change in England, 1789–1806, as it influenced and was influenced by the writers of the time," and by 1948 his bibliography began to reflect his new focus on William Blake.[15] He became assistant professor at the University of Minnesota from 1948 till the spring of 1954, though he was away for the year 1952–1953 teaching at Duke and at Michigan State. Again he failed to find a tenured appointment.

In 1954 there also appeared from Princeton University Press the book that marked one pole of Blake studies, Erdman's *Blake: Prophet Against Empire. A Poet's Interpretation of the History of His Own Times.* Here were the first fruits of the ambitious proposal for the 1947 Guggenheim, and he received a renewed Guggenheim year in 1954 to pursue the same topic. Having outlined his approach in 1950 at the English Institute with his influential paper entitled "Blake: The Historical Approach,"[16] Erdman became for the next twenty years the leading spokesman on this side of the Atlantic for the priority of history and biography, rather than philosophy,

15. Beginning with a three-page note on "Blake, Flaxman, and the £100" (*PQ,* 1948), Erdman published eleven articles, lectures, and notes on Blake before the end of 1954, as well as numerous reviews and notes on other subjects.
16. Published in *English Institute Essays, 1950* (New York: Columbia University Press, 1951), pp. 197–223, and reprinted in 1961 and 1963 in collections of criticism.

myths, and archetypes, to solve puzzles in Blake's writings. Partly because of the clear choice between methodologies posed by Northrop Frye's work and his and partly because of the sudden acceleration of interest in Blake, Erdman gained more attention for this effort than he had for his equally good research on Byron. But in 1955 he was living at Princeton, with Virginia (his wife) and their two daughters, trying to find a niche for himself in the scholarly world.

In 1956 David Erdman became editor of library publications at the New York Public Library. Aside from his editorial efforts with the United Auto Workers, where he had edited a periodical called *Ammunition*, this was the first time that Erdman's name was associated with "editing." He used his position as editor of the *Bulletin of the New York Public Library* (then a monthly publication) to publish more historical and biographical papers on the Romantics—his own and others'. The very nature and function of the *Bulletin*, however, soon encouraged him to publish texts of newly discovered works and manuscripts. In 1956, *BNYPL* carried Erdman's long two-part study entitled "Coleridge, Wordsworth, and the Wedgwood Fund." But in 1957 appeared (in a special issue devoted to George Washington), Erdman's "Coleridge on George Washington: Newly Discovered Essays of 1800,"[17] which—though not differing in kind from his quotation of documents in, for example, *Blake: Prophet Against Empire*—marks the first time that the texts of the documents themselves, rather than a point of literary, intellectual, or political history or biography, had been at the heart of one of his publications. Even here Erdman's introductions, footnotes, and conclusion discussing the background and significance of the articles from the *Morning Post* and the *Courier* occupy far more space than the texts quoted. Erdman does not indicate his textual principles, but he does footnote verbal variants between the texts as printed in the *Morning Post* and reprinted in the *Courier.* Collation of these texts in *BNYPL* with his own later publication of them in *Essays on His Times* (1978) in The Collected Coleridge suggests that Erdman provided in 1957 a literal transcription of his primary source; in both printings he leaves in his collations readings he knows to be corrections from the *Courier* of errors in the *Morning Post* text. In short, he presented a diplomatic reprint with collations and notes, rather than a "critical edition," as that term is used in the field of textual theory by W. W. Greg, Fredson Bowers, and G. Thomas Tanselle.[18]

17. *BNYPL* 61 (1957): 81–97; reprinted in *Evidence for Authorship: Essays on Problems of Attribution*, ed. Erdman and Ephim G. Fogel (Ithaca: Cornell University Press, 1966).
18. For the latest authoritative discussion of these issues, see G. Thomas Tanselle, "Recent Editorial Discussion and the Central Questions of Editing," *SB* 34 (1981): 23–65, especially p. 62; see also Tanselle's essay on the fundamentals of "Textual Scholarship" in *Introduction to Scholarship in Modern Languages and Literatures*, ed. Joseph Gibaldi (New

Rather than focusing on questions of copy-text, emendation, and like theoretical matters, David V. Erdman became one of the primary authorities on evidence for authorship of anonymous publications—particularly articles, reviews, and poems published in newspapers and periodicals. His article on Coleridge's writings about George Washington was the first of a number of contributions by Erdman and others later collected in *Evidence for Authorship* (see n. 17 above). Most of Erdman's contributions to these debates centered on Coleridge. But he was also, during the early 1960s, working with a team of younger scholars on a *Concordance* to Blake's writings in the computerized Cornell series headed by Stephen M. Parrish.[19] As he examined problems in Blake's text for the *Concordance* (to which he added an "appendix of corrected readings"), Erdman saw the need for a new edition of Blake. And while Harold Bloom, who had a contract with Doubleday to reedit Blake, contented himself with writing critical notes, Erdman produced the first major edition of Blake since Geoffrey Keynes's Nonesuch Edition of 1925.[20] What had happened to Erdman—as it had earlier to Coburn and Cameron—was that his interest in biographical, historical, and intellectual matters made him realize how inadequate were the basic tools available for his work. This need then kept drawing him farther into the basic priorities—from the historical and intellectual contexts of the Romantics into work on "The Romantic Movement: A Selective and Critical Bibliography," which provides a basic appraisal of scholarship in the whole field of English and European Romanticism (Erdman became general editor after 1961),[21] and from Blake's historical background to a concordance to, and thence to editions of, Blake's writings. As one critic of recent trends in American scholarship has suggested, many scholars are content to make one brick at a time and lay it in the brickyard, in the hope that someone will use it; but Erdman, after drawing up plans for the building of historical scholarship on the Romantics, has been designing and building machine tools, producing and erecting gir-

---

York: Modern Language Association, 1981), where he uses the nonpejorative word *diplomatic* as a synonym for certain kinds of what he otherwise terms *noncritical* editions (p. 34).

19. *A Concordance to the Poetry and Prose of William Blake,* ed. David V. Erdman, with the assistance of John E. Thiesmeyer and Richard J. Wolfe [et al.], 2 vols. (Ithaca: Cornell University Press, 1967).

20. *The Poetry and Prose of William Blake,* ed. David V. Erdman, with commentary by Harold Bloom (New York: Doubleday, 1965; 3rd [revised] printing, 1968; 4th [further revised] printing, 1969).

21. This bibliography first appeared in *ELH* (1937-1949, covering research published during 1936-1948); it next moved to *PQ* (1950-1964, covering 1949-1963), thence to *ELN* (1965-1979, covering 1964-1978), and finally became a separate annual volume issued by Garland Publishing, Inc., of New York. The first thirty-five bibliographies have been reprinted in photofacsimile and indexed: *The Romantic Movement Bibliographies, 1936-1970,* ed. A. C. Elkins, Jr., and L. J. Forstner, with a Foreword by David V. Erdman, 7 vols. (Ann Arbor, Mich.: The Pierian Press, in association with the R. R. Bowker Co., 1973).

ders, and exercising quality control on the bricks and girders produced by others. Only a person of unusual intelligence, intellectual curiosity, and energy would be able to produce as much of lasting value as he has—and perhaps only a person with a need to prove something to his peers would feel the *need* to do so.

Again and again, Erdman has redirected his aim from an obvious target and moved into the intellectual underbrush to flush out hitherto unknown quarry. In his Guggenheim pursuit of "social change in England, 1789–1806, as it influenced and was influenced by the writers of the time," he not only studied Blake, but engaged in massive research on the newspapers, magazines, and reviews of the period that had very little to do directly with Blake, but revealed many uncollected articles and reviews by Coleridge and one by Byron. From this work, he moved back into the theoretical questions of attribution on the basis of internal evidence. We have seen how he laid new foundations for Blake scholarship. In his most recent enterprise, Erdman has undertaken to write a historical-biographical study of Wordsworth, but while working out the background of *The Borderers*, he became so intrigued by the fascinating story of Colonel John Oswald, a British Jacobin who was the original behind the character of Oswald in *The Borderers*, that he has spent two or three years researching and drafting a life of Oswald and collecting Oswald's works for republication.[22] If life and good health were, as they ought to be, infinite, David V. Erdman would without question complete the study he proposed in 1946 to the John Simon Guggenheim Memorial Foundation—and more besides.

The "more besides," be it noted, includes all of Erdman's gargantuan labors on matters editorial, bibliographical, attributional, and concordancial. Besides those publications already noted, these include his editorial work on *The Poems of William Blake* in the Longman/Norton edition of 1971–1972; *The Notebook of William Blake* (Oxford: Clarendon Press, 1973; revised edition, New York: Readex, 1977); *The Illuminated Blake* (New York: Doubleday, 1974); the three volumes of Coleridge's *Essays on His Times*;[23] and his part in the extraordinary "complete edition" of *William Blake's Designs for Edward Young's Night Thoughts* (Oxford: Clarendon Press, 1980). It includes his numerous articles and reviews on textual matters, especially on Blake and Coleridge, as well as his editorial work on Byron in

22. A tip of this iceberg appears in Erdman's "The Man Who Was Not Napoleon," WC 12 (1981): 92–96, where research on Oswald has led Erdman back into speculations on a crux of Wordsworth's biography. [The full study has now appeared as *Commerce des Lumières: John Oswald and the British in Paris, 1790–1793* (Columbia: University of Missouri Press, 1986).]

23. This is the third title in *The Collected Works of Samuel Taylor Coleridge*, Bollingen Series LXXV (Princeton: Princeton University Press; London: Routledge & Kegan Paul, 1978).

the first six volumes of *Shelley and his Circle*. It also includes his guidance of would-be textual scholars in his work as editor at the New York Public Library and of *BNYPL* (more recently become *Bulletin of Research in the Humanities [BRH]*), as guest editor of *Keats-Shelley Journal* (1966), and as a reader and consultant for other journals and publishers. Finally, it includes his generous advising and counselling of other scholars on editorial and bibliographical matters. What many scholars consider the fair work of a busy career has been but one of the by-products of Erdman's *prolific* career. And if some are *devourers* enough to question whether he might not have done this or that a little differently, we must also recognize that he was also the first scholar in my experience to set a pattern for openly correcting errors he finds in his own work, not only in revised printings and new editions, but also by advertising and sending out errata lists for his texts.

My personal admiration and affection for David Erdman go beyond anything suggested by my analytical prose. He surpasses, I believe, all other textual scholars in our field in a way that cannot be seen from his publications and lectures: he is the quickest person I have ever seen in understanding and evaluating the evidence of a manuscript when he looks at it for the first time. I recall that, on two occasions when he brought his graduate seminars from SUNY at Stony Brook to the Pforzheimer Library to look at some manuscripts of Shelley and Byron, he asked me to project on the wall our microfilms of certain pages of the Bodleian Shelley manuscripts so that the class could see the evidence on certain cruxes in *Prometheus Unbound* and "Mont Blanc." Though I was more familiar with these materials than most scholars, having worked with both the originals and the microfilms, he left me far behind in his facility in reading Shelley's tortured drafts and in seeing the significance of the various false starts and revisions in those manuscripts. Whether we wish to attribute this unusual facility to his long experience in analyzing the manuscripts of a variety of writers, to exceptional eyesight and intelligence, or to his intense intellectual enthusiasm and concentration in trying to solve a puzzle, his performance on each occasion was truly remarkable.

III

Granting all Erdman's virtues, there are yet some textual critics and editorial theorists who might say—without questioning his skill in reconstructing the history of a text, his high level of accuracy in transcription and proofreading, or his generosity in presenting evidence and his unusual selflessness in publicly correcting his own errors—that his earlier labors were hindered by "the want of a true theory" of editing. They would point to his failure at times to emend his copy-text when evidence of the author's intention suggests that it should be so emended and to provide more complete collations of variants, including orthography and punctuation, instead of—as in the edition of Coleridge's *Essays on His Times*—emending some things silently.[24] And if such textual theorists would take a close look at other editions of the Romantics, they would find a number of other weaknesses in the practice of editing as it has grown up among the generality of such editors. They need not stop to criticize the aberrations in editorial method apparent in Lawrence John Zillman's two unsuccessful attempts to edit *Prometheus Unbound* or in Neville Rogers's disastrous two volumes of the Oxford English Texts edition of *The Complete Poetical Works of Percy Bysshe Shelley*, for other Romanticists have already exposed these shortcomings.[25] Nor need they concern themselves about mere human failures of imagination, diligence, or perceptiveness that lead to numerous errors in texts, collations, and the facts of annotation and make many editions more imperfect than they should be. Such poor scholars and lazy editors are always with us, and no amount of theorizing is going to extirpate them. But the editorial theorists of the Greg-Bowers-Tanselle tradition have a number of important things to teach most editors of the Romantics, among them these: (1) the need to assemble and examine all textual evidence (including the collation of all primary editions) and to work out the interrelations of all principal authorities *before* choosing a copy-text; (2) the value, when treating published texts, of probing the relations among author, publisher (or bookseller), and printer and—if possi-

---

24. "The texts reprinted from the *Morning Post* and *Courier* preserve the original spelling and even the punctuation, except when the punctuation (which may be the compositor's) obscures meaning and except for the correction of obvious printer's errors. But liberties have been taken with the paragraphing and in the invention of titles, since most newspaper 'paragraphs' lack them altogether—and in the addition of subtitles when they serve to indicate that the successive paragraphs of a given Paragraph . . . deal with separate subjects and were perhaps intended to be thought of as independent Paragraphs. . . . The newspaper practice, irregularly observed, of printing proper names in italics or small capitals has been ignored . . ." ("Editorial Practice, Symbols, and Abbreviations," *Essays on His Times*, 1:xxxiii). Erdman was once something of a gadfly to the Center for Editions of American Authors (CEAA) and its successor, the Center for Scholarly Editions (CSE), but has recently made his peace with them. He tells me that CSE has recently awarded its emblem of approval to Louise De Salvo's edition of Virginia Woolf's *Melymbrosia* that is being published by the New York Public Library under David's supervision, as well as to David's own "Newly Revised Edition" of *The Complete Poetry & Prose of William Blake* (Doubleday, 1981).

25. On the first volume of Rogers's Oxford English Texts edition of Shelley, see especially the following reviews: *TLS*, 2 March 1973, p. 246; Kenneth Neill Cameron in *SiR* 12 (1973): 693-99; Stuart Curran, *ELN* 11, supplement (1973): 59-60; Donald H. Reiman, *JEGP* 73 (1974): 250-60. On Zillman's editions, see especially reviews by Carl R. Woodring, *JEGP* 59 (1960): 304-6; Donald H. Reiman, *JEGP* 68 (1969): 539-43; and E. B. Murray, *K-SJ* 19 (1970): 119-25.

ble—learning something about characteristic practices in the relevant printshops, as well as the characteristic or preferred orthography and punctuation of the author, before deciding to what extent and where to emend a printed copy-text; (3) the necessity of recording all emendations of the copy-text, however trivial; (4) the usefulness (to the accuracy of the edition, as well as to the user of it) of recording in an appendix all variants found in selected authorities; (5) the possibility of establishing one text as the author's approved version of his work and presenting a clear-reading text of that version that is as accurate as the author might have done, had he or she enjoyed as much time to collate other versions and proofread the material as modern academic editors and publishers enjoy.[26]

There has, of course, been some commerce between editors of the English Romantics and the many teachers of Renaissance literature and American literature who have been trained in (or at least been exposed to) the textual principles of the Greg-Bowers-Tanselle tradition. But most teacher-scholars follow the models found in their own areas of specialization. Because most of the Romantics failed to achieve great popularity in their lifetimes, their works were not, in general, published in numerous contemporary editions. There is no work by an author issued simultaneously in two cities or countries, few first issued in unauthorized printings, and few rushed into print so rapidly that the authors lacked nominal control over their publications, and even few reprinted by an author's publisher during his lifetime under conditions that leave it uncertain whether the author approved the text. Lord Byron, the most popular poet, either left his record of revision and approval in letters and proofsheets in the John Murray archives, or else clearly indicated in his letters the lack of such consultation while he was abroad. For most of the other writers, the holograph evidence shows clearly if, when, and how much they revised from one infrequent republication to the next. Such textual problems as remain—for example, the punctuation and some of the words of *Prometheus Unbound*—are insoluble by bibliographical analysis, because both the authoritative press-copy manuscripts and the proofsheets are lost, probably forever, and there were no further authorial editions. Though there have been a few studies in the transmission of texts through transcripts and printed editions,[27] the failure of many edi-

---

26. Some of the editions of the Romantics in the historical tradition are open to the strictures that Tanselle directs at historians in "The Editing of Historical Documents," *SB* 31 (1978): 1–56. This effort to proselytize across disciplinary boundaries resulted in the formation of the Association for Documentary Editing (ADE), which brings together American historical and literary editors, the latter being chiefly from the CEAA and CSE, but also including David V. Erdman.

27. The two most notable examples are Charles H. Taylor, Jr., *The Early Collected Editions of Shelley's Poems: A Study in the History and Transmission of the Printed Text* (New Haven: Yale

tors of the Romantics to distinguish among different kinds of surviving holograph manuscripts and authorized transcripts (press copies, "safekeeping" copies, and rough drafts) has distorted the textual studies of some poets more than most scholars realize or will admit. This failure has placed undue authority on early manuscript versions that were never authorized for publication or, in some cases, were explicitly discarded when the author soon afterward revised his work to give it a more appropriate public form. Coleridge's "Dejection: An Ode" and Wordsworth's *The Prelude* are merely two such works.

The historical tradition in editing the Romantics is slowly but surely driving away those editors who condescended to their subjects by revising, correcting, or modernizing the texts of these writers. But it has introduced a concomitant problem. Those who come to edit a text with a paramount interest in the writer's biography, political influence, or religious thought are apt to develop a pattern, if not a *theory*, of editing that produces editions and textual studies designed to illustrate and emphasize the purest period of Wordsworth's altruism, or the development of Coleridge's Christian orthodoxy, or Shelley's moments of loneliness and despair, rather than the texts that the authors themselves finally selected and approved for publication. The editors of the Romantics least susceptible to this distortion seem to me to be those who, like Barbara Rooke and Jack Stillinger, began by writing dissertations that valued the editorial process over contextual historical research. The very fact of starting out with an editorial commitment encourages the acquisition of some knowledge of what the editors of classical texts, Renaissance texts, and (more recently) American literary texts have learned. It also inculcates an attitude in which modern scholars see themselves as servants and students of the author being edited. As historical scholars we may know more than Wordsworth and Coleridge about how various socio-political events, religious movements, or personal decisions were to turn out, but we certainly cannot know better than they what words they intended for the ideal texts of their poems and prose. The historical researcher almost inevitably suffers from the vanity of superior hindsight. Textual scholars, devoted to trying to recapture the author's intention, *ought* to be tolerably humble because of their patently abysmal ignorance of what actually happened during various stages in the transmission of the text from author's draft to the final authorized printing.

As students of history, biography, and the developmental creative pro-

---

University Press, 1958), and Jack Stillinger, *The Texts of Keats's Poems* (Cambridge: Harvard University Press, 1974).

cess, we would all enjoy and profit from seeing facsimiles and transcriptions of every holograph scrap, every proofsheet, and the records of every conversation that reveals the author's struggle to fulfill the artistic conception. As scholarly editors, intent upon recovering and presenting the author's works according to his or her intention, we should attempt to evaluate all the evidence in order to arrive at a text of the work that represents the final authorial intention—whether or not we personally prefer a rough-draft version or an earlier published text. We may include two or more discrete texts of a work in our editions, but we will not set up our judgment as to what constitutes *the* text of Wordsworth's poems against Wordsworth's own clear intention. When we teach Wordsworth, we will teach *his* poem—not ours. In doing so, we may discover that Wordsworth was a better artist than his modern critics—that he knew what he was doing, for example, when he cut and revised the thirteen-book *Prelude* into fourteen books.

IV

Among recent developments in editing the Romantics, I believe that the most important has been the increased attention given to textual integrity by the publishers of classroom textbooks. Earlier I mentioned that, under the general editorship of Gordon N. Ray, Houghton Mifflin's Riverside Editions set new standards for classroom texts of the Romantics in the late 1950s and 1960s. These editions included Leslie A. Marchand's edition of Byron's *Don Juan* (1958), Douglas Bush's *Selected Poems and Letters* of Keats (1959), and Carl Woodring's *Prose of the Romantic Period* (1961), all of which used the best standard texts and added scholarly annotation of a high order. Perhaps the most advanced of these editions was Jack Stillinger's *William Wordsworth: Selected Poems and Prefaces* (1965), which corrected the text of *The Prelude* on the basis of manuscript readings taken from de Selincourt's collations and notes.[28] By the time the Riverside Editions had gained a reputation for distinction among classroom texts, W. W. Norton launched a series of casebooks that provided both texts and gatherings of critical comments and explicatory essays. The name of the series, "Norton

---

28. None of the Riverside Editions of the Romantics seems to have been based on serious analysis of the authoritative manuscripts and early editions. On the problems of Neville Rogers's *Percy Bysshe Shelley: Selected Poetry* (1968) see my review in *ELN* 7, supplement (September 1969): 42-43. Though Oxford University Press in London also issued Rogers's badly edited volume, they had earlier issued as one of the best of their New Oxford English Series volumes (under the general editorship of A. Norman Jeffares) *Shelley: Selected Poems and Prose*, ed. G. M. Matthews (London: Oxford University Press, 1964). More recently, the Everyman Edition, *Percy Bysshe Shelley: Selected Poems*, ed. Timothy Webb (London: J. M. Dent & Sons; Totowa, N.J.: Rowman and Littlefield, 1977), has provided another excellently edited students' text.

Critical Editions," was intended to refer to the accompanying criticism—not to the critical editing of the literary texts. But when various teacher-scholars, unaware of this distinction, began to send Norton proposals that offered texts critically reedited, as well as selective criticism, John Benedict at Norton and M. H. Abrams, Norton's adviser on literary texts and editor of the fine *Norton Anthology of English Literature* (first edition, 1962), encouraged this expansion of features.[29] Several of the older Rinehart Editions, which had once set the standards in the field, were improved textually as they were revised and reissued to meet the competition in the expanding market of the 1960s. In Great Britain two series of editions designed for students and general readers also undertook to raise the textual quality of paperback editions. F. W. Bateson, one of the most knowledgeable of British Romanticists in both historical and textual scholarship, became general editor of a series published by the Longman group under the rubric of "Annotated English Poets"—a series marketed in the United States by Norton.[30] About the same time, Penguin Books began to issue a high-quality series entitled Penguin English Poets, with Christopher Ricks as general editor.[31]

Both the financial competition among publishers for a share of the market and the spirit of emulation among scholars within the same series, as well as the rivalries of those editing the same author in competing editions, led to at least two significant developments. First, the editors of textbooks of all kinds—period anthologies as well as texts of individual works and authors—learned perforce to keep up with developments in textual scholarship and to draw upon the latest textual advances by specialist editors. This awareness, reflected in textual introductions and in advertisements for the various series, in turn began to spread to classroom teachers hitherto unaware that there were such things as more and less authoritative texts and, from them, ultimately to new generations of graduate students. Secondly, the publishers of the better series showed an increasing willingness to allow, or even encourage, their editors to revise at least the better-selling

29. John Benedict discussed this evolution at a special session on "Editing the Romantics" at the MLA convention in Houston, 30 December 1980.

30. After F. W. Bateson's death in 1978, he was succeeded as general editor of the Longman/Norton Annotated English Poets by Professor John Barnard of the University of Leeds. Thus far the two editions of Romantic poets that have appeared in the series are *The Poems of John Keats*, ed. Miriam Allott (1970; Norton Edition, 1972) and *Blake: The Complete Poems*, ed. W. H. Stevenson, text by David V. Erdman (1971; Norton Edition, 1972).

31. The relevant editions in Penguin English Poets, under general editor Christopher Ricks, are to date: *William Blake: The Complete Poems*, ed. Alicia Ostriker (1977); *Lord Byron: Don Juan*, ed. T. G. Steffan, E. Steffan, and W. W. Pratt (1973); *John Keats: The Complete Poems*, ed. John Barnard (1973; 2nd ed., 1977); *William Wordsworth: The Prelude (A Parallel Text)*, ed. J. C. Maxwell (1971; 1977); *William Wordsworth: The Poems*, ed. John O. Hayden, 2 vols. (1977).

textbooks. The combination of having better-qualified specialist scholars editing the texts, a more alert group of teachers ordering them, and more enlightened publishers willing to improve their textbooks has led to some textbooks becoming primary scholarly editions. This situation seems to be good for scholarship in general, because it makes the most widely distributed texts of some poets the best texts to be quoted by scholars and to be explicated and judged by critics. Only a few antediluvian critics and recent theorists who believe in principle that they, rather than the authors, determine the poetic text have remained unaffected by this salutary change.

Unfortunately, a few publishers who once possessed a large share in the market of college textbooks and editions for the general reader have failed utterly to adjust to the new times. Houghton Mifflin, which at the turn of the century provided generally excellent editions of major British and American poets in their Cambridge Editions, hired scholars to write new matter for these volumes to gain new copyrights, but did not allow them to change the basic features of the texts, which were reproduced from old plates or by photofacsimile from the earlier printings. The results were at best inadequate and at worst disastrous.[32] At the same time, a new hierarchy at Houghton Mifflin determined to drop those Riverside Editions that did not meet certain sales criteria, thus weakening their coverage of our area by allowing Woodring's *Prose of the Romantic Period* and William Marshall's *Lord Byron: Selected Poetry and Letters* to go out of print. In a similar spirit, Oxford University Press, which once dominated the field of textbooks and popular editions with the Oxford Standard Authors Editions (OSA), tried various stop-gap measures to stem the erosion of its position. But instead of commissioning new editions, Oxford hired scholars to correct a few of the worst errors that could be eliminated without repaginating, while supporting massive reediting projects in Clarendon's Oxford English Text Editions. One of these was Neville Rogers's ill-fated effort at *The Complete Poetical Works of Percy Bysshe Shelley*; the others, the Blake edition by G. E. Bentley, Jr., and the first volume of Jerome J. McGann's Byron, are reviewed in these pages. But all the OSA volumes on the Romantics remain archaic.

New sophistication in textual matters thus caused some old leaders in the field of textbooks to fall behind the pack, but some American university presses began to emulate the progressive commercial publishers in making use of the textual revolution to recoup on major texts some of the

---

32. On the revised Cambridge Editions of Byron, Shelley, and Keats, see my review in *K-SJ* 25 (1976): 187–88.

losses they sustain in other areas of publishing. When Houghton Mifflin let some of its valuable Riverside Editions go out of print, New York University Press agreed with the holders of authorial copyrights to reissue them in its Gotham Library. Harvard University Press, after marketing the hard-cover version of Stillinger's *The Poems of John Keats* through bookclubs, is preparing to issue its own annotated students' edition. And Yale University Press is now marketing the Penguin editions under Yale's imprint. This is a far cry from the situation in the late 1960s, when the University of Illinois Press—glad to lose money and to share its losses with its authors—gave two editors of anthologies permission to reprint my text of Shelley's "The Triumph of Life" without fee and without even mentioning the requests to me.

Intelligent publishers of all kinds are now beginning to realize that the reading public and, especially, the college textbook market demand more from editions than clever introductions and a few hasty footnotes. Serious editions can be updated and kept in print long enough to return far more than the initial investment—and in an era when the costs of composition, paper, and printing are too great to permit gambling on the editorial quality of the textbook, more and more publishers will be seeking to issue the best possible texts and paying the relatively minor costs to revise them in subsequent printings in order to remain competitive. The time is thus arriving when the publishers of texts issued in paperback, whether Harvard University Press, Doubleday, W. W. Norton, Longmans, or Penguin Books, will see to it that any reader of Blake, Wordsworth, Coleridge, Byron, Shelley, or Keats can afford to own a text that approximates the author's intention. Under these conditions, the Romantic poets may finally reach with their most serious works the larger reading public that all but Byron failed to find during their lifetimes.

8

The Cornell Wordsworth and the Norton Prelude

In the spring of 1977, the first two volumes of The Cornell Wordsworth were submitted to the newly organized Center for Scholarly Editions of the Modern Language Association of America to be appraised for possible awarding of the CSE's "Approved Edition" emblem. I was asked late in April to inspect Stephen Gill's edition of The Salisbury Plain Poems of William Wordsworth (1975) and Stephen Parrish's edition of The Prelude, 1798–1799 (1977) after the fact; there was no way in which anything I said could alter the two volumes under review (unless they went into second, revised printings). It seemed, therefore, my first responsibility to make any general suggestions that I could about the theoretical assumptions and general editorial policies underlying the Cornell Wordsworth edition, insofar as these could be determined from the two volumes at hand; additionally, I felt it necessary to mediate between the ideals set forth in the "Introductory Statement" of CSE that was sent to guide my analysis—a statement reflecting particularly the ideas of G. Thomas Tanselle and other pioneers in the Center for Editions of American Authors (CEAA), from which the CSE had evolved—and the editorial traditions and standards then current in the field of English Romantic poetry.

On 13 June 1977, I submitted my report on the two Wordsworth volumes. I had been told by the administration at CSE that not only would my report and the response to it by Stephen Parrish determine whether or not the CSE would award the two Wordsworth volumes the "Approved Edition" emblem, but also whether Cornell University Press would submit further volumes of The Cornell Wordsworth to the CSE for inspection. So I knew that I had made two readers happy when, on 8 July 1977, CSE asked me to inspect on their behalf the third volume in the Cornell Wordsworth series, Beth Darlington's edition of Home at Grasmere (1977), which was then in corrected page proofs. Though obviously there had been little opportunity to implement the suggestions of my first report, I noted as a sign of immediate response insertion in the proofs of some page numbers that had originally been omitted. In appraising the Darlington volume (which, though following the guidelines and example of the previous two, was in many respects better executed than either), I was able to write less and concentrate on issues that were of general interest to editors of eighteenth- and nineteenth-century poetry, but which were not covered at all in the guiding questions prepared by those whose chief editorial experience had been with fiction rather than poetry.

Finally, while organizing the section on Romantic texts for the Erdman Festschrift *issue of* Studies in Romanticism *(see Item 7), I had secured the promise of a Wordsworth specialist who was not connected with the Cornell edition to review two volumes of that series—James Butler's edition of* The Ruined Cottage *and Paul F. Betz's edition of* Benjamin the Waggoner—*as well as the Norton Critical Edition of* The Prelude. *Personal problems caused that person to return the books to me, after a year had passed. As I wrote to Stephen Parrish on 20 November 1981,*

> I was then faced with a decision: since I would not trust anyone else to write a review by my deadline [i.e., the deadline by which my part of the Festschrift *issue of* SiR *was to go to Morris Eaves, the editor of the special issue], I could either ignore* The Cornell Wordsworth *or review some of it myself. I took the latter course, reviewing* Benjamin *as the later—and simpler—of the two on hand, as well as the Norton* Prelude, *which I used in my teaching last summer at Washington (Seattle).*

Later I wrote to Paul Betz: "I find that most scholars tend to ignore common reference books. Newman Ivey White and Frederick L. Jones left as great mysteries acquaintances of Shelley who appear in the DNB." *Though it may have been unfair to single out Betz's work publicly for a problem that occurs in some other early volumes of the series, I had learned in 1978 that my critiques of the first three volumes had been circulated to all the editors of* The Cornell Wordsworth, *and I reasoned, therefore, that forewarned ought to have made the editors of later volumes forearmed. After the review of* Benjamin the Waggoner *appeared in* SiR, *Stephen Parrish kindly sent me a copy of the response he had sent to CSE after reading my inspection report on the first two volumes of* The Cornell Wordsworth. *There he quite understandably objected to my characterizations of some problems I saw in those volumes. Parrish's vigorous defense of the original policies and procedures of the series doubtless reassured some of his colleagues that there was no need for them to reassess their own work then in progress in the light of my suggestions (or similar suggestions in early reviews). Equally understandably, I took the occasion of the review to go public with ideas that I still believe to be worthy of consideration.*

Report to Center for Scholarly Editions
May–June 1977
on Two Volumes of the Cornell Wordsworth

1. *The Salisbury Plain Poems of William Wordsworth,* edited by Stephen Gill. Ithaca: Cornell University Press, 1975.
2. *The Prelude, 1798–1799, by William Wordsworth,* edited by Stephen Parrish. Ithaca: Cornell University Press, 1977.

I

The Cornell Wordsworth project is so intrinsically valuable and so well conceived and executed in most of its substantive features that I can conceive of no possible reason why it should not receive the seal of approval of the Center for Scholarly Editions. In presenting some of Wordsworth's most significant longer works not only in carefully edited "Reading Texts" but also in facing-page facsimiles and transcriptions of the primary manuscripts that mark early and late stages of their evolution, the Cornell Wordsworth moves beyond any scholarly edition of a nineteenth-century English writer of which I am aware in providing materials for the scholar-critic to study Wordsworth's poetic development. Only Whitman's *Leaves of Grass* has, so far as I know, received comparable treatment for (some of) its stages of development. For these and other reasons, to deny the work the formal approbation of CSE would tend either to discredit the acumen of CSE itself (and the validity of *its* recognition) rather than the Cornell Wordsworth, or else scholars, university presses, and funding agencies (if they accepted the validity of CSE's negative judgment) would simply refuse to invest the requisite efforts and funds in such projects in the future, thereby setting back textual scholarship in the whole field of English and American literature.

Having said this, I must now add that the editors of the Cornell Wordsworth are (like the rest of us) mortal men who have overlooked a few things that would, in my judgment, have made their transcriptions a trifle more faithful, their descriptions a bit more precise, and their presentation a little clearer and more useful to readers—especially those readers who will not study entire volumes systematically but who may wish merely to consult a particular passage at various stages of its evolution for evidence on a critical crux.

II

But before I begin recording these blemishes (or *possible* blemishes—for I am at least equally liable to be wrong, checking against photocopies rather than original manuscripts), I want to comment on some very important things that are well-conceived and well-executed in these two volumes.

First (though it may seem an unlikely part of an edition and textual study to deserve praise), the contents page of each volume is exceptionally well conceived—particularly that in Parrish's volume. The detail in Parrish's contents page (for example, the fact that he breaks down the material in the "Letter to Coleridge, December 1798" into "Skating Scene" and "Boat-Stealing Scene") enables the reader to locate easily some of the evidence on particular passages he may be seeking. This facility is fostered by the several tables in the Introduction describing the material to be found in different manuscript sources and its arrangement within the different stages of the poem's evolution.

The Introduction by Parrish, "The Growth of the Two-Part *Prelude*," building on the research of several other Wordsworth scholars, is a model of clarity and precision, leaving no relevant method of analysis unemployed and no stage in the growth of the two-part *Prelude* unexplored. Any questions or disagreements I may have with Parrish's arguments and conclusions derive from his slight imprecision in describing the manuscripts as physical objects (see below) rather than as literary documents. I wish to record my special admiration for the careful observations and reasoning behind the analysis (pp. 9–16) of which lines of the *Prelude* drafts occupied several pages once present in Dove Cottage MS. 15 (the "*Christabel* Notebook") that now exist only as stubs, as well as for Parrish's lucid presentation of that argument. This analysis will be a model for studying similar problems facing the students of other nineteenth-century writers who composed in pocket notebooks.

Second, the tables of abbreviations in the two volumes are both generally excellent and especially so in view of the quite different books, periodicals, and individuals treated in the two lists. *It will be important for the general editor to be sure that the same abbreviations are never used to signify two different things during the course of the edition*, lest that oversight confuse readers turning from one volume to another. (The only imperfections I noted in the two lists of abbreviations are in Gill's volume, where he fails to note—or perhaps to utilize—the revised versions of volumes 1, 2, and 4 of *Poetical Works* [PW], and where he does not make clear that the text of the 1805 *Prelude* that he uses is the one also included in the de Selincourt–Darbishire edition of 1959.) The editors seem aware of the effects of ongoing progress in Wordsworth scholarship in their choice of abbreviations: though Gill was forced to use Grosart's imperfect edition of the prose, the only one available to him when he did his work, the abbreviation given it (Grosart) avoids confusion with the later scholarly edition of Wordsworth's prose by Owen and Symser used by Parrish (*Prose*). The editors might also have used an abbreviation like LY (E. de S.) to distinguish de Selincourt's now obsolescent edition of the letters of Wordsworth's (WW's) "Later Years" from the edition now in progress that will doubtless be used in later volumes of the edition. Finally, the appendixes in Gill's volume (especially the last two) will immeasurably aid the scholar in comprehending the process (if not the motivations) of WW's transformation of "Salisbury Plain" into "Guilt and Sorrow" through the several intervening steps.

III

Parrish clearly states the three purposes of the Cornell Wordsworth on the final page (p. xiii) of his Foreword to Gill's edition of *The Salisbury Plain Poems of William Wordsworth* (hereafter cited in this report as *SPP*); he does *not* repeat this information in his own edition of *The Prelude, 1798–1799* (hereafter cited in this report as *Prel.*). Since the volumes are not numbered and since—at least until the edition is further along—librarians are apt to catalogue and shelve individual volumes by title in scattered places among Wordsworth's writings, it may prove difficult for the student or teacher going to the library stacks to consult a problem on WW's *Prelude* to know, when he picks up *Prel.*, what kind of series it is part of and how this text relates to the 1805 and 1850 versions of *The Prelude* (not yet reproduced in the Cornell Wordsworth). I strongly urge, therefore, that at least a brief précis of Parrish's Foreword to *SPP* be included in each subsequent volume of the series, together with mention of *SPP* as the volume in which the longer Foreword appears.

Parrish's Foreword in *SPP* makes clear that the three purposes of the edition are: (1) to reveal the *earliest* complete versions of a number of WW's long poems, published as clean reading texts; (2) to follow the changes in the texts through the authorized versions published during WW's lifetime (1850) or authorized by him for posthumous publication; and (3) to make possible the study of his art by presenting graphically the changes in his poems through manuscript facsimiles (as well as full transcription therefrom), complete records of variants (substantives and accidentals), and facing-page presentation of closely related versions of a poem. These texts do not, therefore, replace (or compete with) critical editions based on WW's final authorized revisions, and this edition will have as its audience primarily specialists in WW's poetry, or at least those who teach or study it in detail at the graduate seminar level. The editors, by producing clean "reading texts," have, however, provided versions that—when republished elsewhere, as Parrish's edition of the two-part *Prelude* has been in the

Norton Anthology of English Literature—can enter the curriculum of undergraduate students as well. There underlies both the full Cornell Wordsworth and the more accessible "Reading Texts" reprinted elsewhere a fundamentally ambiguous textual premise that the editors should recognize and discuss, so that their readers will also be aware of it: the early "Reading Texts" they are preparing for dissemination are likely to drive out of some textbooks (and, therefore, out of the awareness of large numbers of students) later versions that WW himself authorized and approved for publication. Based on a theory that the earlier inspiration of WW was greater (or at least more interesting) than his later judgment, the editors will, in effect, be giving William Wordsworth a poetic face-lift, taking him back from his more mature outlook to his period of youthful experimentation and exploration. To have these early texts available for the scholar and student is valuable; to have the two-part *Prelude* of 1789–1790 the only version of the *Prelude* available to students encountering WW for the first time seems to me less unambiguously so. Though Parrish and his colleagues cannot totally control the ultimate use of the material they are producing, they owe it to their readers at least to warn them about the textual-historical-moral dilemma of presenting students with a text that: (1) is found in no single source as a completed version; (2) was never published during the author's lifetime and, therefore, was not a poem that affected either his contemporaries or his followers until the 1960s or 1970s; (3) was rejected by the author as not reflecting his intention as a man and/or as an artist. All these questions are begged by Parrish in one sentence in his Foreword: "We are at the outset concerned *to rescue* the long poems that Wordsworth wrote during *his most interesting and brilliant years*, then left unpublished . . ." (*SPP*, p. xii, italics added).

In terms of CSE's "Guiding Questions," I would say that the Cornell Wordsworth should, in the future, make clearer its intended readership (II.A.3.) and that (paradoxically) the preparation for wider dissemination of the text (III.E.1) may be better than it really needs—or ought—to be.

The basic sources of the "Reading Texts" presented in the two volumes under review are clearly identified and fully described manuscripts, most of which are reproduced in photofacsimile (with facing-page literal transcriptions). The other reading text presented in the *SPP* volume—"Guilt and Sorrow"—is (like the transcriptions from manuscript) presented faithfully as it appeared in its first published version (1842), with variants found in later editions reviewed by WW. Thus, none of the texts presented is a fully realized critical edition derived from emending a copy-text according to stated principles of regularization. In "Guilt and Sorrow," for example, one occasionally finds in the published version the abbreviated forms "tho'" and "thro'" (e.g., lines 36, 135) that are characteristic of WW's manuscripts but that the printers usually expanded to "though" and "through" (e.g., lines 23, 145). The printers also lowercased many nouns that WW had clearly marked—even corrected in his manuscript—to begin with capitals (see, for example, lines 180, 186, 215, 266, 275, 276). Though it is helpful in this kind of publication to have the precise state of each stage of the text presented without correction, it would have been helpful if Gill had commented on these anomalies, either in notes keyed to instances thereof or in an introduction to the last two versions ("Incidents upon Salisbury Plain" and "Guilt and Sorrow"), in which he could have assisted students of WW (and of other poets of the period) by attempting to sort out which accidental features WW and his household crew of copyists and proofreaders seem to have thought it important to correct in proof and which they left to the discretion (or whim) of particular compositors. Gill might also have made the point that, in spite of the reluctance of WW and his family to insist upon these accidental features, the scholarly editor working from this evidence should restore WW's clear intention about them either from the latest manuscript that had WW's attention or from the preponderance of manuscript evidence during a particular phase of his career.

IV

From the above remarks, it will be seen that I believe that the chief desiderata under the CSE's "Guiding Questions" II.B. and II.C. have been adequately, though not immaculately, fulfilled. Referring to II.D. and II.F., my spot-checking of the collations of later printed texts (done from my own copies of various editions of "The Female Vagrant" and "Guilt and Sorrow") turned up no errors at all and persuaded me of the care with which these collations were done. "Guiding Question" II.E. does not apply to the methodology of this edition. The textual notes (II.G.) seem to me quite adequate and, in a few cases (e.g., the notes to line 192 on page 238 and to line 363 on page 250 in *SPP*), actually superfluous, given the detail of facsimile and typographic representation of the manuscripts. To "Guiding Question" II.H., I can say that neither volume contains ambiguities about section or verse-paragraph breaks.

"Guiding Question" II.J. represents an area not treated in the Cornell Wordsworth that I think should be. Most of the nontextual notes deal with verbal parallels in other poems (or other versions of the same poem) by Wordsworth or others. There is almost no effort to provide material on the biographical, historical, or geographical details of the very circumstantial accounts by WW of his own experiences related in these poems. Nobody using the volumes would know, for example, that the gibbet, which occupies a crucial place in both *SPP* and *Prel.*, was a singular manifestation of a short period in British history, being employed legally in England only from 1752 to 1834; it was an innovation within living memory in the 1790s and an obsolete terror (like the thumbscrew) by the time "Guilt and Sorrow" was published. It seems to me that—as the various texts show the poems changing through various historical and biographical developments during WW's career—the editor ought to supply a substantial number of biographical-historical notes to call attention to the possible implications of such changes in the texts. For example, in *SPP,* when page 243 is compared with page 29, the change in the reasons for the Father's ruin (from "cruel chance and wilful wrong" by "Oppression trampled" to the failure of "Fortune" to "put on a kinder look") not only changes the whole character of the tragedy, but also reflects WW's changed circumstances and attitudes between the dates of writing the two versions. Such changes should be highlighted briefly but precisely.

To turn, now, to details of execution within the principles I have discussed, I would say that one relative weakness in both volumes concerns the description of the manuscripts' paper and notebooks. Though the paper and chain-lines are very precisely measured and the watermarks and countermarks have been roughly described, the editors have made little or no attempt to connect these data with the standard reference books on papermaking or to key the descriptions of symbols employed in the watermark to reproductions of watermarks in reference books or other books on manuscripts in the period. For example Parrish's description (*Prel.*, p. 71) of "a design showing two warriors" is vague (what kind of "warriors"? Indians? Vikings? Golden State Warriors?) but there is probably a sketch or photo in W. A. Churchill's *Watermarks in Paper . . .* (Amsterdam, 1935) or in *Les Filigranes* that approximates whatever it is that Parrish is trying to describe and to which he could refer the interested scholar. In the same way, the motto "PRO PATRIA" in the same watermark might give a clue to the papermaker, who might be identified from Alfred H. Shorter's *Paper Mills and Paper Makers in England, 1495–1800* (Hilversum, Holland, 1957). Describing the paper more precisely would not necessarily lead to more accurate critical analysis, but describing it imprecisely is a waste of everyone's time. Ideally the clear watermarks should be reproduced in facsimile (as in *Shelley and his Circle*, 2, between 658 and 659; 6:752–53), but that, of course, would represent an extra expense that is, perhaps, unjustified here. Moreover, for the description of the paper of DC MS. 10 (*SPP*, page 6), the "image of Britannia in a circle surmounted with a crown" is probably the standard symbol, usually designated "Britannia in crowned oval," that is reproduced in *Shelley and his Circle*, 2, plate XXVIII (preceding p. 659), and could be merely cross-referenced.

In describing the notebooks, the editors are also inexact in treating free and pastedown endpapers. In bound books the two endpapers are conjugate leaves added to the original gatherings after these are stitched and bound. Some manufacturers make pocket notebooks this way, but others simply paste down the first leaf of the first gathering and the last leaf of the last gathering (having no endpapers per se); and still others leave them without any semblance of endpapers, the binding simply being glued, stapled, or stitched to the spine of the gatherings, either with or without the usual "hollow tube" to allow free movement in opening and closing. Again, looking at Parrish's description of MS JJ (*Prel.*, page 71), we find that he is inexact in describing the binding ("bound in boards"—paper boards? drab or gray paper boards? marbled paper boards? marbled paper over drab paper boards?) and may be wrong in the number of leaves missing from the notebook, because he has not specified whether or not there are separate endpapers. If there were originally six gatherings of ninety-six leaves, plus two free endpapers, then nine rather than seven leaves are now missing (unless the free endpapers were pasted to the first and last leaf, producing two leaves of double thickness). In any event, my point is that the descriptions of paper and notebooks by both Gill and Parrish (which inexplicably appear in different positions in their two volumes) do not fully take into account the complexities of the subject, and they should give the matter further thought and study before the publication of subsequent volumes of the edition.

Though the Cornell Press's book designer(s) has (have) created commendable designs for the two volumes, one item ought to be changed. There are often several consecutive pages on which no page number appears (e.g., *Prel.*, pp. 68–71, 218–21). There is no good reason to omit page numbers on pp. 71 and 221, where important text appears and which the reader will often need to consult.

Finally, I have some queries about details of transcription and other miscellaneous queries and citations of error, some mere anomalies and others representative of recurring problems.

I. 1. *SPP*, p. 17: the term *doubled-back lines* is new to me; *run-over lines* has been in use, and perhaps, if new or nonstandard terminology is introduced, it should be accompanied by a definition or synonym.

2. *SPP*, p. 23: the note on "bustard" (line 68) doesn't give me a picture of or feeling about the bird. How big? Bird of prey, scavenger, songbird? Color? Poetic associations? If the bird is obscure enough to require a note at all, the note should inform the reader of more than its Latin name.

3. *SPP*, p. 35: the note to lines 424–27 concerning WW's reading list on the Druids should be further identified or expanded. Most of the abbreviated authors and titles could be expanded for the use of students who might not know the abbreviations to classical texts or Drayton.

4. *SPP*, p. 41: though the first "Hard is the life when naked" is clearly written earlier than the second, it is treated as a later addition. WW obviously began to transcribe the line in such a large hand that it could not fit on the paper. (Perhaps he was having trouble with his eyes at the time?)

5. *SPP*, p. 43: the repetition of line 18 can be explained as an attempt to see how small the Alexandrine had to be written to get it to fit on a single line.

6. *SPP*, p. 43, line 20: the "y" in "deadly" is canceled and the interlineation is "iest"; the reading of line 20 on page 21 should be "deadliest weight."

7. *SPP*, p. 45, line 38: the interlined letter above "wearily" is "o" and belongs to "stormy" in line 37.

8. *SPP*, p. 47, line 45: isn't the interlineation "dreary cornfields . . . bound" also in pencil?

9. *SPP*, p. 49, lines 58–59: "watched" is misplaced, belonging with line 59 below as an alternative for "sought."

10. *SPP*, p. 51, below line 72: we need a footnote explaining these lines (again, at the bottom of p. 53).

11. *SPP*, pp. 121–22: nowhere in the abbreviations does Gill indicate that the sign "1800–" signifies the 1800 edition, plus all subsequent editions collated.

12. *SPP*, p. 230, note to line 91: the postmarks on the lettersheets used to write the lines indicated show *not* that WW was using "any scrap of paper" but that all these revisions were made in mid-October 1841, using the most recently arrived expendable letter-covers.

13. *SPP*, p. 251, collation of 363, 366: Gill uses the phrase *inverted commas* for what Parrish and American editors call *quotation marks*; the Press should normalize this inconsistency.

14. *SPP*, p. 256, lines 440–41: isn't something missing between these two lines—or, rather, above line 441?

15. *SPP*, p. 274, note to 607: here (and elsewhere in this volume) Gill notes things that are obvious from the typographic presentation of the transcription. Perhaps it had not been determined that cancellations would be rep-

resented graphically, but after they were, these notes should have been dropped.

II.   1. *Prel.*, pp. 6–7: Parrish might have noted and commented upon a parallel use of "Is it for this" in *Salisbury Plain,* line 465 (*SPP,* p. 36), written before Coleridge's "Frost at Midnight." WW echoes STC's echo of *Salisbury Plain.*

2. *Prel.*, p. 31, 6 lines from bottom: page numbers not filled in ("000–000").

3. *Prel.*, p. 37: the sentence explaining the significance of roman type and italic type should appear (or be repeated) on p. 38 in the table of symbols.

4. *Prel.*, p. 41: Parrish's sentence relating to the need to modernize punctuation seems to me misguided in view of the audience at whom even the "Reading Texts" of this edition are primarily directed. Rather than rewrite WW's poems to make them easier for graduate students and Romantics scholars, I believe that it is important to teach them how to read the poetry as WW and his contemporaries wrote it, including unusual diction and punctuation. (See my Shelley texts and rationale of the punctuation in the *Norton Anthology of English Literature,* 3rd edition.)

5. *Prel.*, p. 77: the final line of text seems to me to begin with a lowercase "of" and end with "taut" [for "taught"].

6. *Prel.*, p. 79: I disagree, in general, with the editors' decision to print above the line additions that actually appear on the same level as the main line (as in the case of "hold" in the first line of text here); the cancel line through "occupy" shows that "hold" was added later to replace this word.

7. *Prel.*, p. 81: the third main line of text ends "that tends" or "thus tends" (not "*the* tends"). A few lines below, "things-" should appear on the main line, after "[?thoughts]."

8. *Prel.*, p. 83: the "I" beginning the line that continues "Though rarely in my wanderings" is actually a false start of a capital "T" for "Though."

9. *Prel.*, p. 93: in the footnote, Parrish should refer to "folio" (or "leaf") U^r and U^v, etc. because there are manuscripts designated "U," and V," etc. at Dove Cottage and the possibilities for confusion are endless.

10. *Prel.*, p. 103: the paste-up crew (or page-proof reader) should, in a case like this, move the text of the transcription down to place it opposite the manuscript it transcribes.

11. *Prel.*, p. 105: near the bottom, read "Gentle powers" (plural instead of followed by comma; compare "beatings" on pp. 110–11, line 3).

I have other queries about MS JJ (the most difficult manuscript presented in either volume). In general—though I may be wrong on my specific readings—I feel that the general editor especially must seek help from another WW specialist (such as Mark Reed) to give his transcriptions the same detailed checking he obviously gave Gill's and will give the contributions of other editors. Some of these points are so tricky that, if after careful consideration one reading is preferred to another likely one, the editor should include a note giving the other possibility and the basis of the final decision.

In a few cases—particularly in the *Prel.* volume—the quality of the photoduplicates leaves much to be desired. See, for example, *Prel.* pp. 152 and 154 (from the Alfoxden Notebook), where not only is the photofacsimile dark on the edges but the photos show edges of other pages. Such confusing additional matter, also found on pp. 250, 252, and elsewhere, could have been eliminated either by placing a larger white background sheet under the page and another over the adjacent leaf during photographing or by careful trimming of the photo before printing. In other cases (e.g., *Prel.* pp. 94 and 96, MS JJ), the photo either never included the entire manuscript page or else has been badly cropped so that text is missing. *Prel.* pp. 304, 306, and 308 were photographed with corners of the leaves turned up, covering text. Though it may be expensive to have new and better photoduplicates made for reproduction, rather than relying on those taken earlier for other purposes, it seems necessary if the full evidence is to be at the disposal of readers.

V

Since these were the first volumes of a series embodying very complex textual presentation, it was inevitable that there would be at least a few technical flaws in the production. On the whole, in spite of my questioning of details in the execution, I found both volumes not only illuminating aids to the study of Wordsworth's poetic development, but also, in a more general way, excellent examples of imaginative presentation of a complex of manuscript materials underlying quite different poetic texts. (While examining these volumes, I kept wishing that Shelley's draft notebooks in the Bodleian could somehow be given the same kind of treatment, with the draft texts presented side by side with the published poems.) Not once did I feel—as I am apt to do with publication projects of this sort—that the editors had made some fundamentally wrong decision that vitiated the basic values of their efforts. I wish that the photofacsimiles were more *consistently* excellent (many of them are very fine indeed). I wish that the descriptions of paper and the makeup of the notebooks were more detailed and keyed to standard reference works (though I cannot think, at the moment, of any practical use to which other scholars might put this information). I feel that the edition would be more useful as a record of WW's growth and development had the editors included more notes highlighting biographical, historical, and geographical information, instead of literary parallels that seem to me less relevant to later changes in WW's poetry; but perhaps this information can be more intensively gathered and more coherently presented in biographical studies of particular periods of WW's career—studies that will be greatly aided by the full presentation of the textual evidence found in these editions by Gill and Parrish. In conclusion, I found the first two volumes of the Cornell Wordsworth to be imaginatively conceived, competently edited, and handsomely produced scholarly editions that without any question merit both the approval and the praise of the Center for Scholarly Editions.

*   *   *

Report to
The Center for Scholarly Editions
July–September 1977

William Wordsworth, *Home at Grasmere: Part First, Book First, of the Recluse,* edited by Beth Darlington. Volume 3 of The Cornell Wordsworth. Ithaca: Cornell University Press, forthcoming.
6 September 1977

I refer the committee of the Center for Scholarly Editions to my Report, dated 13 June 1977, on the first two volumes of The Cornell Wordsworth—*The Salisbury Plain Poems,* ed. Stephen Gill, and *The Prelude, 1798–1799,* ed. Stephen Parrish. In the present report, I shall cover certain general matters relating to the overall series by reference to that document.

I

My favorable judgment of the intrinsic value of methods employed in The Cornell Wordsworth series—outlined in the first paragraph and the final two pages of the Report of 13 June—remains unchanged, or rather is strengthened by the *Home at Grasmere* volume (hereafter cited as *Grasmere*). Beth Darlington's Introduction (pp. 3–32) is, indeed, the best piece of scholarly prose I have encountered in the series, weaving together numerous quotations from the letters of Coleridge and the Wordsworth family and from earlier scholars and critics with her own ideas and opinions into a smooth, unified essay. The virtue of her mosaic method is that much of the primary evidence for her argument appears in the text itself, rather than in footnotes (or outside the reader's reach in other books and dissertations), but the skill required to produce a flowing narrative and argument by such means will be evident to any scholar who has attempted to torture "th' unwilling dross" to his or her purposes. The Introduction, because of the place of *The Recluse* in Wordsworth's poetic career, is an important document in WW's biography, as well as a skillful unraveling of the probable order and dates of composition of the various extant fragments and versions of *Home at Grasmere*. Altogether, I would recommend Darlington's Introduction (along with Stephen Parrish's excellent discussion of an even more complex mass of manuscripts and biographical evidence) as a model for all future editors in this (or any similar) series.

As an addendum to this praise, I'll add my commendation of Darlington's Appendix I, "Publication and Reception of *Home at Grasmere*," a very useful, thoroughly researched exploration of the interactions of various scholars and publishers of the late nineteenth and the early twentieth centuries. Darlington's descriptions of the individual manuscripts (e.g., pp. 410–11) are also very clear and concise, though she—like the editors of earlier volumes—is inexact in her descriptions of the paper found in the MSS (see 13 June Report, pp. 9–10); Darlington fails (as Parrish and Gill did not) to record the size of the manuscript sheets and to measure the distance between chain-lines on laid paper, an inconsistency that should have been called to her attention by the general editor and corrected before her volume went to press.

I should note that this report is based on copies of original page proofs and for all but the preliminaries, revised page proofs containing numerous "author's alterations." Comparing these two sets of proofs, I note a few minor changes that may be attributable to attempts by the editors of The Cornell Wordsworth to carry out, even at this late stage of production, suggestions made in my report of 13 June. For example, page numbers have been inserted on *Grasmere*'s pp. 36, 111, 112, 113, 139, 410, etc. to eliminate the problem, noted in my June 13 Report, of the designer having left too many significant pages unnumbered. This action, slight though it may be, suggests that the Cornell Press and the Editorial Board are amenable to making improvements suggested by CSE and its reviewers.

II

The quality of transcriptions from the manuscripts in *Grasmere* is, though not flawless, generally high, and the quality of major editorial decisions and their execution (such as the choice of texts to be collated in the *apparatus criticus* and the accuracy of those collations) are also—beyond question, it seems to me—worthy of CSE acceptance and approval. I shall, therefore, concentrate my attention in this Report on a matter that, I believe, has received too little attention from most editors—even those long active in CEAA and CSE—and which therefore has not been brought to the attention of editors generally. It is an issue that finds no specific place on the list of "Guiding Questions," possibly because it is relevant primarily to the study of poetic texts of a limited period in the eighteenth and early nineteenth centuries. This matter is the practice of a number of writers—WW clearly being one—who indicate by their orthography whether or not certain syllables (notably the final syllable of weak past participles) are to be pronounced. To take a selection of evidence in miniature from *Grasmere*, lines 416–31 of MS. B. (found in facsimile on p. 314, diplomatic transcription, p. 315, and "Reading Text," p. 64): in the fair-copy manuscript (in the hands of Dorothy and Mary Wordsworth) those participles in which the final syllable was to be pronounced (and therefore counted in the scansion) are spelled out in full—"unruffled" (428), "Untainted" (429), and "wanted" (430), whereas those in which the final syllable was *not* pronounced are indicated by omission of the final "e"— "enlighten'd" (416), "reachd" (423), "pleas'd" (431). The appearance of this phenomenon in the transcriptions of Dorothy and Mary show that even *they* often—or usually—carried over this feature into their transcriptions of WW's poems. But it is even more pronounced in WW's own drafts and fair copies. For example, in MS. B., lines 135–64 (pp. 46, 288–89) in WW's hand, we find "pleas'd" (136), "Cluster'd" (141), as well as "where'er" (160) and " 'tis" (156, 161), contrasted with "separated" (144), "unexpected" (149), "chosen" (159), and "blended" (163).

That WW *consciously* modified his orthography to indicate pronunciation and that he intended his orthography to be followed in published texts can be seen from the orthography in texts published under his supervision. For example, "Expostulation and Reply," in the second edition of *Lyrical Ballads* (1800), contains "bequeath'd" (5) and "breath'd" (7), "where'er" (19). The same orthography of these words is found in the fourth edition of 1805, though in the latter "grey" (lines 1 and 31) has been transformed to "gray." Coleridge's "Love" in *Lyrical Ballads* (1800) even more consistently follows the convention—"Ruin'd" (4), "lean'd" (13), "listen'd" (15, 25), "ling'ring" (16), "whene'er" (19), "play'd" (21), as opposed to "blended" (10) and "fitted" (23)—suggesting perhaps that WW got this idea (like so many others) from STC and perhaps explaining why WW's early poems like "Lines, Left upon a seat in a YEW-TREE" are less consistent in this feature than those he wrote after meeting STC. In any case, many poets of the period attempted (with varying degrees of consistency) to represent through their orthography the number of syllables in certain words of optional pronunciation (e.g., "lightning" vs. "lightening"). In some cases, as in Shelley's *Adonais*, line 384, the orthography indicates actually the elision of vowel sounds: "Torturing th'unwilling dross that checks its flight." (Shelley's use of the apostrophe in past participles is, however, more sparing than that of WW, STC, or Byron.) The same principle applies to WW's use of such alternative spellings as "capt" for "capped" (MS. D., line 58, page 41), and Darlington errs in not employing this and the other indicative orthography, clearly preferred by WW (and, as a matter of fact, helpful to the general reader or occasional reader of WW's verse), in her "reading texts."

This oversight, which also occurred in the two earlier Cornell Wordsworth volumes, indicates some degree of disinterest in preserving and attempting to understand certain details of WW's poetic art. Since the orthography does (or may) affect pronunciation and since pronunciation affects the rhythm (and sometimes the assonance) of the verse, one would think that editors devoting years to a few hundred lines of poetry would be highly conscious of such details. But there is no suggestion in any of the three volumes that these details aroused the editors' interest. Their primary concerns seem to center on changes in WW's ideas and the history of his emotional life.

III

I point again to my general criticism in the 13 June Report, which has recently been paralleled and underscored by Bishop C. Hunt in an excellent review of Parrish's *Prelude* volume in *The Wordsworth Circle* (8 [1977]: 217–19). Hunt writes: "The truth is, the two-part *Prelude* contains a lot of bad writing. How fortunate that Wordsworth chose to revise such stuff as the following: [quotes lines 248–58, page 49]. Nothing in 1805 or 1850 is so dull as this . . . ." Hunt is right. Though Darlington's *Grasmere* volume doesn't really raise the issue as clearly as do those of Gill and Parrish, I take this opportunity again to urge the editors of The Cornell Wordsworth to reconsider and more carefully define the aims, audience, and limitations of the early versions of WW's poems they are presenting in "Reading Texts," citing their usefulness as documents for scholars and biographers, but also warning of their limitations as poems—both because the ideas in these early poems were (to one extent or another) rejected by WW and because the verse is often unformed and unpolished artistically.

My admonitions have nothing to do with the question of "one" or "two"

Wordsworths or with the powers of his great decade: they have to do with the function of the editor as differentiated from that of the poet. WW is the object of our interest and concern, not Gill, Parrish, or Darlington, and any editorial policy or presentation that tends to subordinate WW's artistic (or philosophical) decisions to those of the modern editor—whether changing WW's intended orthography or promoting as superior versions of poems that WW clearly considered passé or inferior—are abrogations or supererogations of editorial responsibility.

In using strong language on this subject, I do not mean to imply that the editors of The Cornell Wordsworth are more culpable than most modern editors. Indeed, the very format of their editions—presenting full transcriptions as well as numerous facsimiles of various manuscripts and collations of authoritative printings in addition to their reading texts—enables the volumes to be self-correcting in the hands of discerning readers. But the Cornell Wordsworth editorial team, involving as it does many of the most experienced students of WW's texts from both sides of the Atlantic, should provide not only raw evidence but a detailed examination of WW's methods and peculiarities as a writer (and, in fact, those of Dorothy, Mary, and Dora Wordsworth, and others as amanuenses). To do so will require a somewhat sharper eye for orthographical and syntactical details and far greater curiosity about them than are evidenced in these first three volumes.

For example, in *Grasmere*, MS. D., line 6 (p. 39), is "devious" an adjective used in its modern sense (and hence a moral reflection by WW on his younger self), an adjective used in Milton's sense of "remote, distant" (*PL*, 3.489), or a truncated adverb, describing the wandering course of his journey? We need a footnote giving the alternatives, with the editor's best judgment of the meaning. MS. D., line 58 (p. 41), includes two editorial errors (i.e., unnecessary changes from WW's clear intention)—"clapped" for "clapt" and "name" for "Name"—that should have been caught simply from the (correct) collation with *1888*. Since *1888* includes "clapt" and "Name" (and since that anonymous editor clearly did not go out of his way to introduce archaic spellings or capitalizations of common nouns, but, on the contrary, lowercased most of WW's capitals used for emphasis), Darlington should have checked her transcription again and noted that *1888* is correct on both points. In MS. B., line 70 (p. 42), Darlington should have noted an anomaly in "King and crown," checked the manuscript again, and noted that "Crown" is also capitalized. On the same page, her note to line 98 is patently inadequate, the word *occasionally* standing as a poor substitute for real research and for a brief but precise characterization of the period and the poems in which WW referred to Dorothy as "Emma or Emmeline." (And, perhaps, how they relate to poems in which Dorothy is referred to as "Lucy.") This lack of intellectual curiosity—of a need to seek the reasons behind details and anomalies—seems to me the most negative aspect of the editorial work on The Cornell Wordsworth to date.

IV

But the editor's lack of intellectual curiosity about unsolved (and, possibly, insoluble) problems of diction and orthography does not constitute grounds for withholding the CSE's seal of approval from *Home at Grasmere*. As with the previous volumes of The Cornell Wordsworth, though not flawless it represents a very useful contribution to scholarship and fulfills in all important respects the criteria suggested in the CSE's "Guiding Questions," insofar as those apply to these volumes (which embody various documents, with transcriptions and cleaned-up texts thereof, rather than eclectic texts). I continue to find these volumes extremely stimulating and useful for my own investigations both into the poetic conventions of the period and into specific aspects of Wordsworth's life, thought, and art. The questions raised by the material within *Grasmere* are, for the most part, answered by reference to other parts of the volume itself. I do not find it lacking in any substantive way except for the lack of some pages of MS. D. in photofacsimile—an omission that must have been necessitated by the high cost of producing the volume. If any photofacsimiles had to be omitted, these late ones, containing few corrections, were certainly the primary candidates.

I strongly recommend that Beth Darlington's edition of William Wordsworth's *Home at Grasmere* be granted the seal of approval of the Center for Scholarly Editions. I also urge that the CSE's "Guiding Questions" be revised to call attention to details of orthography as they might affect pronunciation—especially in the case of poetic texts—and suggest that editors be advised to try to determine—and follow—the author's preference in this, as in other details.

* * *

William Wordsworth. *Benjamin the Waggoner,* ed. Paul F. Betz. The Cornell Wordsworth. Ithaca, N.Y.: Cornell University Press, 1981.
William Wordsworth. *The Prelude 1799, 1805, 1850: A Norton Critical Edition,* ed. Jonathan Wordsworth, M. H. Abrams, and Stephen Gill. New York: W. W. Norton, 1979.

Though *Benjamin the Waggoner,* the fifth volume to appear in The Cornell Wordsworth, is not the strongest exemplar of that series, it remains a useful volume both to students of William Wordsworth and to the reviewer who seeks to gauge the obvious strengths and more subtle weaknesses of the project as a whole. Having carried on a semi-private conversation with the editors on behalf of the Center for Scholarly Editions, I wish to raise some issues before a larger public. The Cornell Wordsworth makes available various stages of Wordsworth's major poems, giving students and scholars a view of material of substantial value for Wordsworth's biographers and for critics interested (as I am) in the interplay between the poet's subliminal sources of creative inspiration and the conscious artistry with which he shaped these poetic upwellings into aesthetic artifacts. But, in my opinion, these two stages of the creative process do not constitute two William Wordsworths; the conscious artist must always be given his rights as author, whatever biographical or critical uses we may find for the fragmentary evidence of the preliminary imaginative processes.

Stephen M. Parrish, the general editor, states the common aims of The Cornell Wordsworth as two:

> The first is to bring the early Wordsworth into view. Wordsworth's practice of leaving his poems unpublished for years after their completion, and his lifelong habit of revision—Ernest de Selincourt called it "obsessive"—have obscured the original, often the best, versions of his work . . . . The second aim of the series is to provide, for the first time, a complete and accurate record of variant readings, from Wordsworth's earliest drafts down to the final lifetime (or first posthumous) publication. (p. v)

Nobody, I think, would quarrel with anything here except the premise underlying the second sentence, which is that Ernest de Selincourt and the editors of The Cornell Wordsworth are better able to judge which versions of Wordsworth's poetry are "the best" than was William Wordsworth himself. I object to this attitude for the same reason that I protest "misreadings" of literary classics. The authors of such classics teach us things that the average critic or editor either does not know or cannot express. As Wayne Booth once put it, before universal problematics covered all: "The author makes his readers. . . . if he makes them well [he] makes them see what they have never seen before, moves them into a new order of perception and experience altogether . . ." (*The Rhetoric of Fiction*, pp. 397–98).

Rightly used, without preempting the author's prerogative to determine his intended text, The Cornell Wordsworth will continue to advance our understanding of Wordsworth's thought and art. At the same time, Paul F. Betz's edition of *Benjamin the Waggoner* also illustrates clearly how Wordsworth's revisions improved rather than spoiled his early attempts and that his "obsessive" habit of revision derived from a striving for perfection. Just as Milton successfully recast *Paradise Lost* in twelve instead of its original ten books, WW revised and polished his original drafts of many poems—*The Waggoner* and *The Prelude* among them—to embody his conception as clearly and precisely as he was capable of doing.

In presenting this edition of *Benjamin the Waggoner*, Paul F. Betz treats the following textual authorities: (1) holograph drafts for a total of twenty-five lines (and six lines in Mary Wordsworth's transcript) that survive because they were drafted in blank parts of Dove Cottage MSS containing fair copies of other works; (2) two fair-copy MSS entitled *Benjamin the Waggoner* in the hand of Mary Wordsworth (*Benjamin* MS. 1 and MS. 2), both dating from January–March 1806, the second of which was extensively revised, December 1811–March 1812, to form the basis of: (3) *Benjamin* MS. 3, in the hand of Sara Hutchinson (March 1812); (4) six lines drafted by WW in another Dove Cottage manuscript (DC MS. 60) after the transcription of *Benjamin* MS. 3; (5) the printed text of the first edition of *The Waggoner* (1819), printed from a revised fair copy, now lost but putatively in the hand of Mary Wordsworth; (6) six later printed editions, three of which contained "substantial revisions" (p. 27)—namely, *The Miscellaneous Poems of William Wordsworth* (1820), the six-volume *Poetical Works* (1836–1837), and the one-volume *Poems of William Wordsworth* (1845).

Betz prints on facing pages as reading texts (1) a transcription of MS. 1 (1806), in which he follows its earliest recoverable readings, and (2) the first printed version of 1819. Collations at the foot of the recto pages (below the 1819 text) record the changes between 1819 and the last text printed during WW's life (1849–1850 edition). He then reproduces in photofacsimile (and transcribes) fragments from Dove Cottage (DC) MSS. 44, 28, 47, and 60 before presenting a full photofacsimile and transcription of MS. 2 of *Benjamin the Waggoner*, a full transcription (with photoreproductions of nine pages) of MS. 3, and photofacsimiles, with transcriptions, of manuscript revisions of the 1830s located at Cornell, Wellesley, and in an Edward Quillinan manuscript at Dove Cottage. Two appendixes reproduce and transcribe "Coleridge's Proposed Revisions to MS. 1" and discuss a possible twentieth-century addition to MS. 2 by T. J. Wise. The photofacsimiles vary in quality and are, inevitably, on occasion partially illegible (as on pages 148, 162, and 208, where a draft in pencil occurs on the same page as, or has been written over by, a text in ink); what may be a more correctable limitation occurs where the text seems to have been cropped at the top (p. 148) or bottom (p. 162).

As a representation of what Wordsworth wrote and published or intended to publish, I find Betz's reading texts exemplary. They—like the other transcriptions—faithfully follow, or record corrections of, the relevant textual authorities. His collations accurately record changes in the later editions, giving a clear view of how tirelessly Wordsworth worked to improve his poem. But one failing of Betz's scholarship accentuates a weakness in other volumes in the series: questions of fact not ascertainable from the Wordsworth manuscripts or from one of the standard authorities on Wordsworth are not vigorously pursued into other sources. For example, two important changes in the text of "Benjamin the Waggoner" between MS. 1 (1806) and the first edition of *The Waggoner* (1819) concern facts relating to Nelson and the Battle of the Nile. In "Canto Second," when the old lame sailor brings in his ship model, the 1806 text reads: "This," cries the Sailor, "a first rate is; . . . . This was the Flag Ship at the Nile, / The Vanguard . . ." (p. 74). As Betz notes, Wordsworth changes "first rate" to "third rate" in the 1819 text. Had Betz gone beyond the *OED*, he would have found that Nelson's flagship, "the 74-gun 'Vanguard'" ("Nelson," *Encyclopædia Britannica*, copyright 1973), was—in terms of reference works available to Wordsworth himself—a "third rate" warship, thereby justifying Wordsworth's revision.[1]

In the same vein, Betz's parallel reading texts record a change in the description of the Battle of the Nile. In 1806 Wordsworth has his sailor do "his utmost to display / The history of that wondrous *day*,"; in 1819, he "does his utmost to display / The dismal conflict, and the might / And terror of that wondrous *night*!" (pp. 76–77; italics added). Wordsworth had doubtless learned in the meantime that when the English fleet first sighted the French in Abu Qir Bay on 1 August 1798, though "there were but a few hours before nightfall . . . Nelson gave orders to attack at once. . . . The climax came about 10 p.m.," and the battle ended in the morning of 2 August, when two French ships of the line and two frigates escaped ("Nile, Battle of the," *Encyclopædia Britannica*, 1973). Such information aids those attempting to evaluate Wordsworth's method of composition, but

---

1. The article on "Ship" in the first edition of the *Encyclopædia Britannica* (1771) not only gives a picture showing and naming every mast, sail, and spar in a fully rigged ship, but also provides detailed definitions of the six "rates" of warships. "A common first-rate man of war has its gun-deck from 159 to 178 feet in length, and from 44 to 51 broad. It contains from 1313 to 2000 tons; has from 706 to 1000 men, and carries from 96 to 100 guns. . . . Third rates . . . carry from 389 to 476 men, and from 64 to 80 guns" (3:584).

does not support the view that the "original . . . versions of his work" are "often the best." In fact, a very strong case can be made that, as Henry Crabb Robinson suggested in 1849, *The Waggoner* is much improved as printed in its final version.

Betz handles other factual matters with equal nonchalance. On page 3, adding an adjective to material from de Selincourt's notes, he refers to the comments of "Coleridge's *young* nephew" in 1836, when John Taylor Coleridge was forty-six years old. Whereas de Selincourt (correctly) identified Southey's Keswick landlord, Jackson, as the wagon owner who fires Benjamin, Betz cites Carol Landon's suggestion that the owner may have been John I'Anson (p. 104); he might have looked up Southey's letter to Wade Browne of 15 June 1819, in which Southey specifically identifies the man as Jackson.

The intellectual curiosity that should have prompted Betz to check his facts might also have led him to wonder about the original of the old Sailor who plays so prominent a part in the poem. I have searched the published letters, notebooks, and journals of the Wordsworth circle without finding such a character, though the answer may be available among the manuscripts or in local histories. If not, then the genesis of the character may well lie in the Wordsworths' strong admiration for Nelson immediately after the Battle of Trafalgar on 21 October 1805, vividly recorded in Dorothy Wordsworth's letter to Lady Beaumont of 29 November 1805 (Wordsworth, *Letters: Early Years* [Oxford, 1967], pp. 649-50). If the old Sailor *was* wholly Wordsworth's imaginative creation, he could be seen as Wordsworth's device for paying tribute to his hero in a poem written less than two months after Nelson's victory and death. Thus the search for factual information might clarify Wordsworth's thematic concerns in the poem.

The Norton Critical Edition of *The Prelude*, like most of the volumes in that series that have benefited from the attentions of M. H. Abrams and John Benedict, does not overlook factual matters of importance to teachers or students. Though subject to the limitations of mortality, it is valuable not only for including texts of the three milestone stages of Wordsworth's greatest poem and for its highly accurate notes but also for useful study aids and a selection of criticism. Here I shall have room only to survey cursorily the texts themselves and the significance of their interrelationships.

The editors provide both a list of surviving "Manuscripts of *The Prelude*" (pp. 507-9) and a narrative entitled "The Texts: History and Presentation" (pp. 510-26), which treats the interrelationships among Wordsworth's various stages of composition, the text as printed by his executors in 1850, and the texts in the Norton Critical Edition. The first paragraph of this essay begins: "There can be no perfect edition of any of the three major states of *The Prelude*"; the same paragraph ends with this useful credo: "In the circumstances the editor's task must be to arrive at the most helpful criteria [for evaluating conflicting authorities] and state them with clarity, to stick by them firmly but not inflexibly, and to note scrupulously where and why he departs from them on particular occasions" (p. 510). Though my spot-checking and collating indicate that Jonathan Wordsworth, who is responsible for the overall editing (p. xiii), has fulfilled these aims, a few of the "criteria" are themselves questionable. For example, whereas for the 1799 text "the spelling of the manuscript has been retained throughout," for the 1805 text exceptions have been (silently) made "in a few cases of major confusion." If the student is expected to read the 1799 text with the aid of notes, why is it necessary to spruce up *1805* any more—especially when confusion can be allayed by comparing *1805* with the facing text of *1850*? Again, the editor has decided "to mark the occasional 'èd' that requires a stress" rather than "to preserve apostrophe 'd' for the many that don't." Here he confronts a basic issue in early nineteenth-century poetry and makes a false dichotomy. The issue is not simply whether or not the final syllables of weak preterits and past participles were pronounced (as, I take it, the word *stress* implies here), but *how* William Wordsworth pronounced them. Spelling conventions of the time that modern editors do not take it upon themselves to modify (such as the spelling *learnt*) show that the poet represented not only the syllables to be pronounced, but also whether the consonant was voiced or unvoiced. As Jerome J. McGann argues in his Editorial Introduction to the Oxford Byron, there are significant complexities in the spelling of weak preterits during the period that modern scholars do not yet fathom. Should an editor then destroy the evidence of William Wordsworth's preferred practice?

The Norton editor supplies most of the punctuation for both the 1799 and 1805 texts because "punctuation in the manuscripts is so spasmodic that its absence tells us nothing." (This fact alone should convince us that the 1805 text was not a finished version that has authority as a poem independent of the version toward which Wordsworth worked in his later years.) And he states the "Capitalization can be similarly misleading. . . . Initial capitals in *1799* and *1805* have been retained only for the terms 'God' and 'Nature,' and for personifications . . ." (p. 511). But as I have shown from contemporary writer's manuals (and have since verified by analyzing the practice of William Cowper in both his poems and letters, as well as the publications of many minor poets in *The Romantic Context: Poetry* series), many poets trained in the later eighteenth century used initial capital letters—as we use italics or words written in full capitals—to indicate metrics and tone by showing which words in a line or sentence were to be emphasized.

For the 1850 text, the editor accepts "the spelling and capitalization of the first edition" and its punctuation, except in "roughly sixty" cases "where manuscript evidence shows the printed text to be wrong" (p. 512). But what authority has the first edition in spelling or capitalization—or in anything else—where it differs from the text in manuscript E, which Wordsworth approved before his death? It is my understanding that the only criterion for judging a text authoritative is the author's final intention, and not the views of the author's next of kin or the compositors. Jonathan Wordsworth restores the manuscript text (in all but one place) where unauthoritative verbal alterations were introduced between manuscript E and the first edition, but he compromises on orthography and punctuation. The tendency to take one feature of the text from column A and two from column B, based on convenience, custom, or the editor's preference, means simply that modern scholars have not fully reconciled themselves to the fact that the author of *The Prelude* is *William* Wordsworth and that *his* preference, insofar as that can be determined, counts more than the judgments of all his executors, compositors, critics, and editors weighed together.

But in these respects, the Norton edition is no worse than the earlier parallel texts of *1805* and *1850*, and by including the Two-Book ur-*Prelude* of *1799*, the Norton edition provides the teacher-scholar with the main evidence necessary to prove that Wordsworth's finished version of 1850 is (though not perhaps as revealingly autobiographical) vastly superior as a poem to the 1805 text now quoted so extensively by critics. In this review, a few examples can merely suggest what I intend to demonstrate at greater length elsewhere.

When we compare the transformation of passages between *1799* and *1805*, we see that sometimes Wordsworth lost sight of his earlier intended meaning or muffled it through imprecise rewriting. For example, at *1799*, I.242 ff., he speaks of sending up a "kite"; for *1805* (I.520 ff.), he revised so ambiguously that the line does not make immediately clear whether "The kite, high up among the fleecy clouds," is a toy kite or the bird of prey. This flaw he corrects in *1850*: "The paper kite high among fleecy clouds" (I.494). In many cases, Wordsworth not only tightened the style between *1805* and *1850*, cutting out words that merely fill out the meter, but he also improved the diction, as in the final line of the stolen boat episode, where "huge and mighty forms . . . were the trouble of my dreams" (*1799*; *1805*, I.424–26) becomes "were a trouble to my dreams" (*1850*, I.400), or in the ice-skating episode, where the change from "shadow of a star" (*1799*) to "image of a star" (*1805*, I.477) becomes (with what the Norton editors note as "an indefinable rightness") "the reflex of a star" (*1850*, I.450). Wordsworth's final choice here may have awaited his reading of *Prometheus Unbound*, where the "Spirit of the Earth" lies within a fountain "like the reflex of the moon" (III.iv.63).

Through detailed analysis of various passages, I could show how Wordsworth in *1850* omitted irrelevant personal facts and repetitions that detracted from the dramatic effects of *1805*. For example, of his three texts of the boat-stealing episode (*1799*, I.81–129; *1805*, I.372–426; *1850*, I.357–400) *1850* is not only more economically effective than *1805*, returning to the central inspiration of *1799* (and omitting the irrelevancies of *1805*, I.376–81), but also sharpens the language at various points—as in line 385, where the boy turns the boat with "trembling oars" instead of "trembling hands" (*1799, 1805*). Beyond increasing clarity and precision, the changes between *1805* and *1850* also greatly improve the *poetry*. At the opening of "Book Second," Wordsworth revises to retrace "The simple ways in which my childhood walked;" (where *1805* had read: "My life through its first years," and had included the repetitive filler-phrase "and measured back / The way I travelled when I first began"). On the same pages (pp. 66–67), we see the revision of "A grey stone / Of native rock" to "A rude mass / Of native rock" and related revisions that provide the same information both more succinctly and less prosaically.

To those who, without a line-by-line analysis, refuse to abandon the recent fad that employs *1805* rather than *1850*, I will mention only one significant fact: though *1850* contains fourteen rather than thirteen books, the final text is shorter than *1805* by 589 lines—more than the average length of one of those fourteen books. I know no one—student, teacher, poet, or critic—who admits to thinking that either version of *The Prelude* is too short. And if, as I think can be demonstrated, William Wordsworth says everything of thematic significance in 7,898 lines that he earlier said in 8,487 lines, we and our students ought to be grateful that when he exorcized his dæmons and lost his inspiration to undertake new poems of the quality of those drafted during the Great Decade, he did not lose his aesthetic critical faculty or the sense of what he had purposed in those earlier creations.

The editors of the Cornell and Norton editions of Wordsworth can be justifiably proud of the new versions and readings that they have rescued from the complex manuscripts and proofsheets. But they should be prouder still of the craftsmanship of the great artist in whose service they labor. That William Wordsworth had the sensitivity to reject most of those texts and readings—that his earliest, rejected texts are *not* "the best . . . versions of his work"—is one sign that he was a poet worthy of their efforts.

9

The Oxford Byron

Jerome J. McGann first came into my ken when I was asked to review Fiery Dust, his first book on Byron, for Keats-Shelley Journal (1970). That study seemed to me a very solid one, and my favorable review initiated a correspondence between us. In 1971, we met in London, where he was on leave, studying the Byron manuscripts at John Murray's in preparation for his Oxford English Text edition. Leslie A. Marchand originally had a contract with Oxford University Press to edit Byron's poetry, but seeing that his work on Byron's Letters and Journals would occupy him for several years, Marchand, with his characteristic combination of generosity, modesty, and good sense, turned the contract over to McGann and secured John Murray's cooperation for the venture.

I found Jerry McGann even more impressive in person than he had seemed in his publications. We and our wives hit it off immediately, and Jerry and I spent an exciting evening sharing ideas on editorial procedures and information on bibliographical curiosities. We continued to exchange such information and ideas whenever we met during the next few years. For the MLA convention at Chicago in 1973, I organized a seminar on "Editing the Younger Romantics" at which Jack Stillinger, Jerry McGann, and I talked about problems in our editorial work on Keats, Byron, and Shelley respectively. In short, from the start, I recognized McGann as one of the most talented and interesting younger scholar-critics working on the English Romantics. In 1976, when The Carl H. Pforzheimer Library acquired the presscopy manuscript of Byron's Beppo (for a price that set a record for a postmedieval manuscript sold at Sotheby's up to that date), I obtained the consent of Carl H. Pforzheimer, Jr., to invite McGann to edit it for Shelley and his Circle, both to make it available to him for his work on the Oxford Byron and to provide Shelley and his Circle with detailed information on the textual history of the poem. After Doucet Devin Fischer and Ricki B. Herzfeld at the Library had made the initial (all but flawless) transcription of the Beppo manuscript, McGann supplied a very entertaining and informative essay on the poem (Shelley and his Circle, 7:234–57). By 1982, when volumes 7–8 began to go to press, Jerry McGann had moved on to his many other interests and responsibilities, and he had little time to devote to proofreading his galleys or otherwise shepherding what he had researched *and written so well toward publication. In the case of* Shelley and his Circle, *his confidence in our diligence may not have been misplaced, but his Byronic magnanimity about the means of production has not always worked to his advantage.*

In 1982, when Timothy Webb asked me to write a review-essay for Keats-Shelley Memorial Bulletin *on the first three volumes of the Oxford Byron, I had mixed feelings about doing so. McGann had sent me complimentary copies of volumes 1 and 2, and I had recently asked him to serve as area editor for Byron's manuscripts in* The Manuscripts of the Younger Romantics; *moreover, my preliminary checking of the first two volumes of the Oxford Byron had revealed some problems there. If I ignored these, the review would look like one of the many put-up jobs in academic reviewing; on the other hand, if I focused on the flaws of the edition, which obviously was not only much better than the one it replaced, but a task that most scholars could not have attempted to do alone, I would appear to be ungraciously critical. Finally I decided that, as one of the few of McGann's peers who had access to many of the primary authorities for the texts of Byron's poetry and who had given enough attention to them to write a knowledgeable review of the edition, I had to take the responsibility of evaluating it. Still, I hoped to deal with the theoretical and factual problems without offending a friendly colleague whom I knew to be justly proud of his achievement.*

In December 1982, over lunch at the Huntington Library, I talked with Jerry McGann about the issues—and even specific examples—that I intended to raise in the review, giving him a chance to state in advance his side of the case. In drafting the review, I focused on two matters: first, the difficulties that confronted the editor of Byron's poetry, as compared with those facing editors of other Romantic texts; second, the gap between McGann's great achievement, under those circumstances, and the ideal of textual criticism that was being claimed for the edition in the early publicity and in papers McGann had published before the first volumes appeared (as well as in the front matter and notes of the volumes themselves). As a courtesy, I sent Jerry a copy of the review in typescript before it went to press, and he soon let me know that he was not at all happy with it, though he recognized that a reviewer must be free to state his or her convictions without being unduly swayed by personal considerations. After some of my friends and colleagues read my review again in the light of his specific objections, I altered a few phrases. But these changes did not affect his basic objection, which was that my review made it sound as though Byron's poetry will have to be edited again reasonably soon.

Indeed, as regards the first three volumes, that is precisely the conclusion I reached. But, I should add, I believe that all of my work and everyone else's will also eventually *have to be replaced (though some a little faster than others). I am old-fashioned enough to believe in intellectual progress, not because of the increasing power of individual intellects, but because, as I pointed out in the headnote to*

"Romantic Bards and Historical Editors" (7), scholarship is (or can be) cumulative.

Since the publication of the review—and several other reviews that pointed to the same limitations of arrangement and other specific errors of execution—McGann and the Clarendon Press have taken steps to implement most of the general suggestions in my review. Volume 4 of the edition (1986), for example, contains its own Short Title List and has running heads that identify the principal poems (and the years covered by groups of shorter poems); in the Commentary section, each page is headed by cross-references to the pages being annotated. McGann has also enlisted Barry Weller, a younger editor specializing in the English drama, to edit Byron's plays, beginning with Marino Faliero. I have not yet had time to collate the texts of volumes 4 and 5 against the primary witnesses, but with an editor of McGann's abilities and pride, I should be very surprised if the later volumes of the series are not done with even more care and attention than that which enabled him to master so many editions and manuscripts in editing the first three volumes.

Authors and publishers save themselves from grief and save the world from a number of errors when they arrange for their manuscripts to be given the detailed attention *before* publication that conscientious reviewers devote to them afterwards. I have read for friends and publishers a number of standard editions and critical studies in this way (including, for example, Earl R. Wasserman's Shelley: A Critical Reading, 1971); more significantly, I have (as the notes to the pieces here reprinted testify) personally benefited from the counsel of friends and colleagues on every piece of my writing that has seen print. Such prepublication critiques are, I believe, the most valuable ones. They are especially useful in those cases where the readers are not asked to judge the publishability of a manuscript (for if the work is generally good, they hesitate to point out its flaws, lest their comments may elicit a negative decision from a press board—and the author or editor becomes, on the same grounds, defensive about any criticism) but when readers are invited to catch errors and suggest improvements in a manuscript already chosen for publication. I have, therefore, made it a policy in recent years, whenever I submit a positive report, recommending publication, to ask the press to invite the author to write me directly for my notes of corrections and suggestions for improvement.

With major editions, this plan would seem to be the most basic kind of safeguard. It may not save a Neville Rogers from himself, but it will help perfect the work of a Jerome J. McGann. Since, under the inspection program of the Committee for Scholarly Editions (CSE; formerly the Center for Scholarly Editions), publishers can, with an investment of three or four hundred dollars, engage an expert textual critic to examine the details and a panel of editors and scholarly publishers to review the plan of an edition, it seems penny-wise and pound-foolish for editors and publishers to avoid this step, whether or not they covet the CSE emblem of approval. Certainly, most of the problems in the Oxford Byron might have been identified in *advance—probably in the planning stages by McGann and the Clarendon Press itself, as they prepared for such an inspection.*

Lord Byron. *The Complete Poetical Works*. Edited by Jerome J. McGann. Volumes 1, 2, 3. Oxford: Clarendon Press, 1980 (1–2), 1981 (3).

Leslie A. Marchand's edition of *Byron's Letters and Journals* not only more than doubles the number of Byron's collected letters, but it also presents Byron's letters to a larger audience than has read them for a hundred and fifty years. Jerome J. McGann's edition of Byron's *Complete Poetical Works* is unlikely to alter to an equal degree the public's apprehension of Byron's poetry. But because Byron is (I believe) the greatest of the English Romantic poets, this expansion and major redaction of the entire corpus of his poetry, based on all the available evidence of earlier editions, manuscripts, and proofsheets, will eventually affect the understanding not only of Byron, but of British Romanticism.

As McGann suggests, the chief textual problem confronting the editor of Byron's poetry is the overwhelming wealth of material. The quantity of Byron's verse approximates that of Wordsworth's much longer career, and the number of editions issued both during the author's lifetime and during the nineteenth century was, of course, much greater. McGann quickly reduces this mass by means of excellent criteria for "textual relevance" (1:xxx); even so, for most of the longer poems, McGann must base his choices of copy-texts and of possible emendations on collation of multiple manuscripts, early separate printings, (often) proofsheets and individual corrections in letters and copies marked in Byron's hand, and no less than sixteen collected editions of Byron's poetry, from 1815 to Paul Elmer More's Cambridge Edition of 1905—besides John Hunt's and the Galignani's contemporary collective editions. Further research on individual poems may turn up additional evidence. But perhaps no previous editor of any poet has had available so much evidence on the texts or has worked as hard to sort out the implications of that evidence.

McGann's choices of copy-texts have been questioned by reviewers of the first and third volumes. Indeed, there are flaws in his stated editorial principles: for poems *not* published during Byron's lifetime, McGann often uses Thomas Moore's *Life* of Byron or one of the collective editions—Murray's editions of 1831, 1832, and 1837, or C, and C 1905 (i.e., E. H. Coleridge's editions of 1898–1904 and 1905)—as copy-text, rather than (in some cases) the manuscripts on which these first printings were based (1:xxxv). Though the number of texts involved is small and relatively insignificant, I find it mildly disquieting that McGann states as a principle his preference for some of E. H. Coleridge's transcriptions over Byron's manuscripts just two pages after he has said that "C is an unreliable guide to poems which he first printed from manuscript" because E. H. Coleridge "almost invariably miscopied" (1:xxxiii). Even if McGann himself has eliminated all mistranscriptions of *words* in these early printings, he still relies on punctuation and orthography that differ from Byron's own. G. Thomas Tanselle and other editorial theorists have dropped W. W. Greg's *theoretical* distinction between so-called "substantive" and "accidental" features of texts (see *SB* 34 [1981]: 23–65), and now is a good time for all editors to follow the principle that a critical text ought to seek to follow *all* aspects of the author's final intention. (This is especially true in the case of fragments and unpolished drafts, for the scanty punctuation and such abbreviations and careless spellings as they may contain suggest their unfinished character and may prevent naive or over-eager critics from treating such jottings as though they were fully finished poems.)

I have two other minor quarrels with McGann's editorial principles. Like so many editors of nineteenth-century poetry, he allows for a "finagle-factor" in the texts of *all* the poems by writing: "For punctuation and other accidentals, then, the copy text is adhered to *unless it is clearly inadequate to carry the sense of the verse*" (1:xxxvii; italics added). He also modernizes in some instances (e.g., in eliminating ligatures; 1:xxxviii) where Byron's original forms should puzzle neither Clarendon's typesetters nor modern readers. I fail to see *any* gains in such practices; what their losses are, we may not know until someone reedits Byron's poetry on different principles, because McGann does not systematically record those changes of "accidentals" that he does make in his copy-texts.

Other than these (all too) common—and perhaps venial—departures from the test of authorial intention, McGann's editorial principles are very sound indeed. With Byron's poetry, the editor must frequently emend the chosen copy-text to conform to verbal revisions ordered by Byron in letters, proofs, or marked copies. Thus the practice adopted by Jack Stillinger in his edition of Keats's *Poems* of following the one version found in his copy-text in all respects, except for the correction of slips of the pen or obvious typos, would be inadequate here. McGann does an excellent job of collecting all relevant textual evidence and sorting it out to choose the proper copy-text for the great majority of the poems and for an even more overwhelming proportion of the poetic *lines* involved. If the arrangement of the material and the execution of the texts, collations, and factual annotations were as uniformly high in quality as are the editorial principles, the collection and analysis of textual authorities, and the histories of the various poems, this edition of Byron's *Complete Poetical Works* might approach our ideal of a "definitive" edition. As it is, flaws in book design and editorial presentation, as well as typographical or other errors in these three volumes, make it seem something less. Reviews of these three individual volumes in *Keats-Shelley Journal, Studies in Romanticism,* and *The Wordsworth Circle* have emphasized McGann's advances over previous editions in the texts of and annotations to particular poems. Here I shall view the edition vis-à-vis an ideal of editing. Inasmuch as the volumes in this edition that will include most of Byron's greatest poetry remain to be published, I trust that McGann and the Clarendon Press will be able to profit from the early reviews to improve forthcoming volumes to the point where no new collected edition will be necessary within the foreseeable future.

To begin with the design and plan of presentation, there was a problem in attempting to establish a single list of "Short Titles," a detailed "Contents of Complete Works," and a single presentation of editorial principles for the entire multi-volume, multi-year project. Not only does this plan force readers to carry the first volume with them whenever they wish to consult any other volume (in order to know which editions and reference works are being referred to in the collation, notes, and commentaries), but the publication of new authorities dictates that a number of items in the "Short Titles" list will become obsolescent before the completion of this edition. McGann might better have followed the practice of Marchand's *Letters and Journals* by providing each volume with a summary of editorial principles and a list of Short Titles relevant to that volume. There should also be cross-references between the poems and their relevant notes, as well as running heads to the notes, giving the pages of poetic texts to which each page of notes refers. Finally, there should be some typographical manner (boldface type, perhaps) to distinguish Lord Byron's own notes from Professor McGann's. This problem is aggravated in volume 2, because Byron's notes are given separately following Cantos I-II and IV of *Childe Harold*, but those for Canto III are interspersed with McGann's notes, while the passage explaining this anomaly appears only in volume 1 (xliii-xliv). Several other problems could also be corrected through a slight expansion of the information given in the notes. We would be glad, for example, to have citations to the volume and pages where the same poems appear in *C* (E. H. Coleridge's seven-volume edition).

Turning from form to substance, we find occasional errors in the texts and collations of these volumes. One of the few questionable textual emendations I have noted occurs in the first line of Byron's earliest poem (1:1), where McGann emends "Swan Green" to "Swine Green"—not on the basis of textual evidence suggesting that Byron intended "Swine" but because of E. H. Coleridge's factual note (*Poetical Works*, 7:1) that the place near Byron's home in 1799 was named "Swine Green." On the basis of similar factual evidence, some would emend "stout Cortez" to "Balboa" in Keats's sonnet "On First Looking into Chapman's Homer" and would have a field day "correcting" the history of Shakespeare and the geography of Homer. After all, young Byron may have intended to disguise—or upgrade aesthetically—the place for the sake of his poem. Another erroneous editorial emendation occurs at 1:66, where McGann follows (without collation or comment) C's error in adding a semicolon to the end of line 6 of "To the Duke of D[orset]," thereby completely skewing Byron's clear meaning in *Poems, Original and Translated*, McGann's declared copy-text ("Thee" in line 7 is the direct object of "command"). Again, while McGann uses as copytext for *English Bards and Scotch Reviewers* the suppressed fifth edition, which is the longest version of Byron's *poem*, he also retains, as part of the text, the Preface and prose Postscript, which Byron had deleted before authorizing that edition. Here the best expedient might have been to reprint this prose (which Byron obviously considered obsolescent by 1811–1812) either in the notes or (better) after the text of the poem as "Prose Associated with *EBSR*," as McGann has handled certain important poetic passages eventually rejected by Byron.

The collations are fairly accurate in the case of the printings of the major poems, though a few variants are unrecorded (e.g., "rage" for "frown" for *The Bride of Abydos*, line 78; 3:110). But the edition exhibits greater limitations where manuscript evidence is involved. While at the British Library in August 1982, I transcribed some of the several holograph versions of Byron's "Address, Spoken at the opening of Drury-lane Theatre," and in comparing this (unusually complicated) manuscript evidence with McGann's collations (3:17–21), I found omissions and errors in the Oxford edition. For one thing, McGann seems sometimes to have transcribed only the *words* of the manuscripts (more or less accurately) and then, when quoting from these manuscripts, to have reconstructed the punctuation without consulting the originals. For example, in the seventeen lines quoted from manuscripts in the collations for line 55 (3:20), my transcriptions (which I think are *roughly* accurate) record three differences in words or word order (e.g., read "Sense & Shakespeare" rather than "Sheridan and Shakespeare") and no less than seven differences in punctuation at the ends of lines. (Such errors can result, of course, from relying on imperfect photocopies rather than on the original manuscripts.)

Still, considering the mass of material that McGann has undertaken to collate and sift, both the texts and record of variants in *The Complete Poetical Works (CPW)* seem to me to mark a *great improvement* over those of all previous editions in representing Byron's final intention and in charting the road thereto. The changes that will be required in future editions are, probably, superficial rather than radical, though nobody should attempt to base any elaborate critical theories on McGann's texts or collations (or anyone else's) without consulting the relevant primary authorities.

The weakest aspects of these three volumes, when viewed from a standard of *ideal* accuracy, seem to me to be the factual notes and commentaries. These flaws have nothing to do, needless to say, with either Jerome J. McGann's standards of scholarship or his powers as a critic, which he has demonstrated in two fine critical books on Byron and in numerous essays. And many of the commentaries and annotations in *CPW* are excellent. But "Art is long"—you know the rest. Limitations of time and, presumably, space have prevented McGann from annotating every factual matter and from giving full, detailed commentary on every significant interpretive crux. Anxious not to rely on C or any other single source, McGann has researched and written on matters that interested him—chiefly involving the longer poems (those that he has, no doubt, been teaching). But he has taken too little time to polish his writing in the Editorial Introduction, as well as in the Commentary, and to check the notes to make certain that his comments are clear, complete, and to the point. For example, in the notes to poem #132 (1:419), readers might prefer to have the captain of the Lisbon packet identified precisely and briefly, rather than to be teased into turning to Moore's 1832 *Life of . . . Byron*: "Kidd was the captain's name" (*Life*, 1:190–92n), especially when the phrase "*Gallant Kidd*" already appears in the line of the poem being annotated. Moreover, Byron's "Note Erratum" to this line—"For 'gallant' read 'gallows'"—contains an allusion to the piratical Captain William Kidd (1645–1701) that McGann's note completely overlooks.

Too many of McGann's notes are similarly circular, adding little to what Byron's text or note has already revealed. For example, after Byron's note has informed us that he refers to "Mossop, a contemporary of Garrick, famous for his performance of Zanga, in Young's tragedy of the Revenge," McGann adds: "Henry Mossop (1729–73) . . . Zanga and Alonzo are characters in Young's *The Revenge*" (1:379). Annotating the attack on Fitzgerald that opens *English Bards* and the additional attack in Byron's own footnote is this editorial addition: "William Thomas Fitzgerald (c. 1759–1829), one of B's favourite butts" (1:400). And, to Byron's note in *The Curse of Minerva* about Hadrian finishing the "temple of Jupiter Olympius, by some supposed the Pantheon," McGann's note adds only: "Hadrian, Roman emperor (117–38) was a patron of the arts. The temple of Olympian Zeus is only one of his many public works" (1:449).

Where the identifications *seem* precise, they often appear to have been put together without a system. After Byron's note to poem #94, line 6, McGann identifies two of the more obscure from Byron's list of military heroes: both are French, but one name and title is anglicized to "James of Armagnac, Duke of Nemours (1433–77)," while the other *almost* retains his national style: "Maurice, the Comte de Saxe (1696–1750)" (1:384). But even here, it is hardly without question that Byron refers to the ambitious Jacques d'Armagnac, duc de Nemours, who was three times charged and finally beheaded for treason against the French king; more famous as a warrior and hero was Jacques de Savoie, duc de Nemours (1531–1585), whom Brantôme (according to the *Encyclopædia Britannica*) calls "*the paragon of chivalry*," as Bayard (also in Byron's list) was known as "le Chevalier sans peur et sans reproche."

In some cases, McGann's notes are either misleading or simply wrong. Benjamin West, who spent the last fifty-seven of his eighty-two years in England and who served as president of the Royal Academy, is identified as an "American historical painter." Sometimes it appears that McGann or a research assistant looked for identifications to names or places without having at hand the passage in Byron's poems that required the annotation. When Byron writes in *Childe Harold*, IV.124, "Witness Troy's rival, Candia!" the note misses the point by telling us that "Candia . . . did not fall to the Turks until 1669" (2:321); the pertinent fact is that it held out for *twenty years before* surrendering. Sometimes the notes (unintentionally) contradict Byron's own moral judgments of people and actions, as when in annotating lines 55ff. of "Ode to Napoleon Buonaparte" McGann calls Lucius Sulla "the *great* Roman dictator" (3:457; italics added) or when he identifies *Julie* as "Rousseau's epistolary novel . . . which treats the *illicit love* of Julie and her tutor Saint-Preux" (2:309; italics added).

Jerome J. McGann, though far from being (as he overmodestly styles himself) "*minimus inter pares*" (1:vi), just hasn't the time to collect, collate, sort out, and describe the textual authorities; sift, select, and check the collations; and research and write original factual and interpretative notes for all of Byron's poetry. Nobody has. McGann ought to prepare at this time accurate texts, collations, textual histories, and textual notes and to leave the factual and critical notes for his—or someone else's—old age. This self-limitation would reduce not only the time expended on those volumes, but the printing costs as well and (we all hope) their price.

In an age when most collected editions of the poetry or prose of major nineteenth-century figures have, of necessity, become cooperative efforts, Jerome J. McGann has undertaken one of the most difficult tasks, so far as the wealth of bibliographical and editorial sources (and problems) is concerned, and he has done most of the work himself—enumerating and locating the textual authorities, collating them, sketching histories of over four hundred separate poems (ranging in length up to *Don Juan*), choosing and emending copy-texts, sorting out and presenting significant textual variants, and collecting or researching and writing factual notes on the poems, as well as adding critical commentary. Whether any one scholar is capable of doing all these things so well that they deserve to be embodied in an edition that is priced (if not produced) to defy replacement for a generation remains an unanswered and, perhaps, an unanswerable question. Jack Stillinger completed with distinction the (much simpler) task of presenting a definitive *text* and collations of Keats's *Poems*, but he did so in stages, first analyzing the authorities in *The Texts of Keats's Poems* (1974) and then perfecting this information on the basis of reviews and his own rechecking of original authorities before presenting his final texts and collations in *The Poems of John Keats* (1978). He (wisely, I think) added factual annotation only at a third stage, in a paperback students' edition (1982). We have as yet no complete edition of the *poetry* of any other English Romantic poet that matches Stillinger's achievement, though the cooperative Cornell Wordsworth and the poetry volume in the Bollingen-Princeton Collected Coleridge may eventually challenge it and though the fine editions of Blake by Geoffrey Keynes, David V. Erdman, and G. E. Bentley, Jr., deal with materials so different from straight literary texts that comparisons with them may, perhaps, be unfair. If the Clarendon Press and Jerome J. McGann make some basic changes in the form and scope of subsequent volumes, the Oxford Byron edition may be judged as being in the same class as these other major editions.

But if this edition of Byron's *Complete Poetical Works* has thus far been slightly less than an *unqualified* scholarly success, it remains a personal triumph. For like some scholarly giants of past eras—David Masson, H. Buxton Forman, and Ernest de Selincourt, for example—Jerome J. McGann has undertaken a task big enough for two or three energetic scholars, and besides completing several other publications during the same period, as well as teaching and lecturing frequently, he has, within about a decade of beginning his textual study, published three volumes of the edition in which all his work is done with credit and, in its most significant parts, with distinction. The Titans of the past need not be our models for us to admire their grandeur. They have given place to mere Olympians, or even to such smaller local powers as Oberon and Puck. But we can still, occasionally, be made less forlorn—our conception of the scholarly profession enhanced—when we see a colleague take up Hyperion's reins and guide the coursers of the Sun out for a long, spirited ride.

10

"Versioning": The Presentation of Multiple Texts

In using and analyzing scholarly editions over the years, I have become less and less confident that an eclectic critical edition is the best way to present textual information to scholars. All of us tend to generalize our personal experiences into universal laws, and my distrust of eclectic critical editions arises, no doubt, partly because my own textual scholarship has consisted largely of preparing "versions" rather than conflated texts. When I, as a critic, am faced with a textual crux, I have found difficulty in reconstructing the primary textual authorities from the notes and collations in even the most comprehensive and accurate critical editions. And on several occasions, when I compared the information in a critical edition with the authorities that it purported to incorporate, the text, collations, or both proved to be untrustworthy. These experiences have led me to depend, not upon modern editions, but upon the primary authorities in rare-book and manuscript libraries, as well as in my own collection of first and other early editions of major Romantic and Victorian poets, checking the readings in the first editions or facsimiles of the manuscripts whenever the precise form and substance of the textual details might make a difference to my interpretation of the work.

I began collecting first and other early editions with nickels and shillings that Mary W. Reiman and I saved out of our food and lodgings budgets during research trips and on travels around the eastern U. S. in a car with 110,000 miles on it. But I was lucky enough to begin buying those books before the big run-up in prices put such collecting out of the reach of all but the wealthiest academics. No young instructor or assistant professor could now build a similar "working library," filled with first editions of the major nineteenth-century poets. In fact, the high cost of printing has rendered it almost impossible for those teachers with family responsibilities to own even the standard scholarly editions and other secondary works. But this situation, though foreclosing the teacher-scholar's chance to own and handle at will the same editions that the poets and their contemporaries used, or to own and mark the errors in the modern collective editions, has a potential benefit that should not be overlooked: no longer should serious scholar-critics suffer from the *delusion that they can carry out all their research at home, using the paperbacks on their shelves, instead of heading for the nearest or most accessible first-class research library. Even some well-known professors at a major university in Connecticut may be tempted to wander into the Beinecke Library occasionally to see whether there might not be some information there that they do not happen to have already in their overfull minds. When research libraries are once again utilized by scholars, teachers, students, and even literary critics, there will be an even greater need for all libraries that support scholarship and criticism to have available accurate (i.e., photographic) facsimiles of manuscripts, first editions, and other textual authorities if they do not have the originals, and if they do own the originals, the fragility of these primary witnesses and the danger that heavy use may destroy them will render the availability of facsimiles all the more urgent.*

" 'Versioning': The Presentation of Multiple Texts" *began as a paper less than six typescript pages long for a ten-minute presentation at a session, sponsored by the Division on Methods of Research, that was held at the MLA Convention in Chicago on 30 December 1985. I sent this paper to the organizer, Peter L. Shillingsburg, on 30 November, asking him to read it for me, when I learned that a family health emergency would cause me to miss the MLA Convention for the first time in some twenty-five years. The title, apparently, proved intriguing, for requests for copies of the paper came both before and after the Convention. I usually answer such requests by explaining that a paper written as a talk is meant to be heard, not read. (Sometimes I add that it is costly, time-consuming, and inefficient for an author to reproduce and mail individual copies of his writings, but that, luckily, a clever fellow named Johann Gutenberg invented a machine that solves the problem.)*

Though this unpublished essay was not part of the manuscript for Romantic Texts and Contexts *as I originally submitted it to the University of Missouri Press in June 1986, I felt in retrospect that an expanded version of the paper would represent my latest and best contribution to the debates now in progress on editing and textual criticism and provide a suitable conclusion for Part One.*

G. Thomas Tanselle, in a study recently published in *Studies in Bibliography,* argues for a pluralism of approaches to editing, because he sees certain basic questions as being ultimately irresolvable:

The basic issues that confront textual critics and scholarly editors are unchanging . . . . There will be no end to debates over these issues, because they are genuinely debatable; and the process of debate is the way in which each generation of editors thinks through the questions for itself. . . . that different people hold different opinions about basic issues is not a sign of crisis; it points to a perennial situation in any challenging and lively field.[1]

Tom Tanselle and I have been moving toward similar ideas of ultimate indeterminacy in recent years—perhaps partly under the pressure of the Spirit of the Age and partly as a result of our frequent informal discussions of editorial issues. Shortly before the publication of Tanselle's essay, I lectured at the twenty-first Toronto Conference on Editorial Problems in November 1985 and, soon afterwards, wrote an abbreviated version of the present paper.[2] These papers both described successful past editorial projects and suggested new developments that might extend the benefits of those past achievements to other areas of editing. The final section of the Toronto paper called for the formation of a Library of English Literature, similar in scope and purpose to the Library of America, to give greater currency to the best available editions of the major English writers, both expanding the market for sound texts and providing students and general readers with alternatives to the unscholarly reprints of shoddy editions, on the one hand, or overpriced, pedantic critical editions, on the other.

The present paper emphasizes another aspect of the problem. I suggest that it may be possible to make available to the public enough different *primary* textual documents and states of major texts (not all of which may need to be critically edited) so that readers, teachers, and critics can compare for themselves two or more widely circulated basic versions of major texts. By doing so, they may discover the value of textual criticism, and society may be relieved from some portion of the cost of funding elaborate editorial projects, as less expensive editions are circulated more widely by commercial publishers who do not require special subsidies for publication. In those cases where the basic problem facing the scholar or reader involves two or more radically differing versions that exhibit quite distinct ideologies, aesthetic perspectives, or rhetorical strategies, the alternative to "editing," as conventionally understood, may be what I call "versioning."

I

When I advocate "versioning," as distinguished from "editing," I do not mean to imply that editing is obsolete. Textual critics and editors will continue to analyze and edit particular versions or stages in the development

---

1. *SB* 39 (1986): 45.
2. The talk at Toronto, entitled "Gentlemen Authors and Professional Writers: Notes on the History of Editing Texts of the 18th and 19th Centuries," will appear in a volume, edited by Richard Landon and published by AMS Press of New York, entitled *Editing and Editors: A Retrospect*.

of literary works, using proven methods to evaluate the authorities and to emend copy-texts with readings that, according to the best witnesses, conform to the author's intentions. Often, however, it is both more useful and more efficient to provide critics and students with complete texts of two or more different stages of a literary work, each of which can be read as an integral whole, than to chop all but one version into small pieces and then mix and sprinkle these dismembered fragments at the bottoms of pages, or shuffle them at the back of the book as tables of "variants" or "collations."

Long works by the English Romantics have been successfully "versioned" at least since 1926, when Ernest de Selincourt's Clarendon Press edition of Wordsworth's *The Prelude* presented two main reading texts—those of 1805–1806 and 1850—on facing pages. Recently, Jonathan Wordsworth, M. H. Abrams, and Stephen Gill have produced an even more complex "versioning" of *three* stages in the growth of that poet's poem in a Norton Critical Edition that contains the short "Two-Part *Prelude*" of 1799, as well as reedited texts of the 1805 and 1850 versions on facing pages, with notes alluding to other stages at which various elements first entered *The Prelude* but without formally collating these.[3] Simultaneously, The Cornell Wordsworth edition is now "versioning" all of Wordsworth's major poems, publishing each in early and late reading texts, with collations at the foot of the page of each version that show when variants and new sections entered the poem and when Wordsworth cut out unwanted passages between the stages represented in the two major reading texts.[4] At the same time, each volume contains a large number of photofacsimiles of important manuscripts, accompanied by complete transcriptions, thus providing a range of primary evidence against which readers can check the procedures and accuracy of the editors. The textual data—both raw and edited—is accompanied by introductions giving detailed histories of the textual development of each poem and by notes clarifying specific aspects of those histories. Critics who own or consult this standard series are now able to trace changes in aesthetic effects as Wordsworth revised his poems, as well as to chart the growth of his political, social, and religious ideas. Although these expensive editions do not enjoy a large circulation, paperback reprints of the paired early and late reading texts, with their collations, of other works besides *The Prelude* might well find wider markets. In any case, the massive work underway on Wordsworth's poetry

---

3. William Wordsworth, *The Prelude: 1799, 1805, 1850*, ed. Jonathan Wordsworth, M. H. Abrams, and Stephen Gill (New York: W. W. Norton, 1979). For my review, see Item 8 in this volume.

4. I discuss four volumes of this edition at length in Item 8.

shows that there is no *practical* impediment to "versioning" even the longest works, provided that a readership exists—in this case the teachers and critics of Wordsworth—for multiple versions of the author's writings. This market seems to arise whenever teachers and critics demonstrate enough intellectual curiosity to wish to analyze different versions of a major author's works—a desire usually produced by exposure to the primary evidence for one of them.[5]

Students of the English Romantics are especially interested in discovering what elements bind youth to age and what happens to a poem when a writer revises it after he leaves the chamber of maiden thought. To satisfy this curiosity (probably initiated by the Romantics' own interest in the maturation process), evidence about such revisions survives in abundance and has been presented even for their long prose works. In The Collected Coleridge, for example, Barbara Rooke's edition of *The Friend* provides, in two hefty volumes, the two major versions of Coleridge's periodical miscellany.[6] Volume 1 contains Coleridge's revised text, published in three volumes in 1818, while the second volume reprints and annotates the text of the twenty-eight numbers of the periodical as Coleridge originally ground them out in 1809–1810 for his long-suffering subscribers. The two volumes, with scholarly apparatus and an exhaustive index, total almost 1,400 heavily subsidized pages. The critic or student who wishes to assess the significance of Coleridge's revisions no longer has to substitute phrase after phrase from lists of variants into the clear text; it is now possible to open the two volumes to the same essays and read a paragraph or an essay first in the 1809 text and then in the 1818 revision. (One wonders whether

---

5. That The Cornell Wordsworth has been successful in terms of academic publishing is evidenced by the willingness of Cornell University Press to undertake a similar series of transcriptions, with facsimiles, of the surviving manuscripts and typescripts of the works of William Butler Yeats as The Cornell Yeats, beginning with *The Death of Cuchulain*, ed. Phillip L. Marcus (1982). Other major series of facsimiles of literary manuscripts of the later nineteenth and earlier twentieth centuries include four published by Garland: *The James Joyce Archive*, ed. Michael Groden et al. (1977–1979); *Bernard Shaw: Early Texts*, ed. Dan H. Laurence (1981); *The Thomas Hardy Archive*, ed. Kristan Brady, Michael Millgate, et al. (1986); and *The Tennyson Archive*, ed. Christopher Ricks and Aidan Day (first ten vols., 1987).

6. Samuel Taylor Coleridge, *The Friend*, ed. Barbara E. Rooke, 2 vols., no. 4 in *The Collected Works of Samuel Taylor Coleridge* (London: Routledge & Kegan Paul; Bollingen Series 75; Princeton: Princeton University Press, 1969). In volume 1, "the text follows that of the 1818 edition" in all details "except for obvious errors. The corrections in the list of errata prefaced to vol I of the 1818 edition have been silently incorporated into the text. 'Corrections' in Coleridge's annotated copies and letters are given in footnotes" (1:xvii). In the second volume, "Appendix A" reprints "the original periodical *Friend* published at 'weekly' intervals from 1 June 1809 to 15 March 1810. Only obvious errors have been corrected. . . . Except for minor alterations of punctuation, all other changes made in the revised numbers issued in book form in 1812 are given in footnotes" (2:[2]).

the same opportunities might not have been provided at less cost, had the two versions of *The Friend* simply been reprinted in photofacsimile, accompanied by introductions and textual notes by the editor.)

In 1894, Richard Le Gallienne and W. Carew Hazlitt provided one of the most interesting kinds of "versioning" in an edition of Hazlitt's *Liber Amoris* that included the texts of eleven of Hazlitt's original letters to Peter George Patmore, which Hazlitt revised and shaped to form the heart of his confessional work.[7] This edition can also be called a source study or genetic edition. As we recognize more clearly today than ever before, all narrations—letters and journals, like other forms of autobiographical prose—are similarly shaped, though their degree of candor may differ, depending on the writer's intended audience. Diplomatic versions of early manuscripts of John Stuart Mill's and Leigh Hunt's autobiographies have appeared in the past thirty years that now provide similar evidence of the levels of candor and art in the final, published versions and that are, therefore, important resources for the apparatus of new critical editions.[8] With smaller works—particularly poems—this kind of comparison has always been invaluable. Among the parallel texts that have been long available are the two versions of Keats's "La Belle Dame sans Merci" (in several students' editions of Keats) and the early and late texts of Coleridge's *The Rime of the Ancient Mariner* in Royal A. Gettmann's casebook, which juxtaposed facing texts of the 1798 and 1834 versions.[9] In most cases, two or more versions of long novels cannot be easily presented within a single edition, because of considerations of cost and convenience. But many such novels are available in competing alternative versions—sometimes in two or more paperback editions. Mary Shelley's *Frankenstein*, for example, has been republished several times in paperback in the past twenty years, with reprintings as well as critical editions based on both the first edition of 1818 and Bentley's Standard Novels edition of 1831.[10] In the absence of access to

---

7. William Hazlitt, *Liber Amoris; or, The New Pygmalion, With additional Matter Now Printed for the First Time from the Original Manuscripts*; with an Introduction by Richard Le Gallienne (n.p.: privately printed, 1894).

8. *Leigh Hunt's Autobiography: The Earliest Sketches*, ed. Stephen F. Fogle (Gainesville: University of Florida Press, 1959); *The Early Draft of John Stuart Mill's "Autobiography,"* ed. Jack Stillinger (Urbana: University of Illinois Press, 1961).

9. *"The Rime of the Ancient Mariner": A Handbook*, ed. Royal A. Gettmann (San Francisco: Wadsworth Publishing, 1961).

10. Of scholarly editions of *Frankenstein; or, The Modern Prometheus*, M. K. Joseph's Oxford English Novels edition (London: Oxford University Press, 1969) is based on Bentley's edition of 1831; "Some misprints and irregularities have been corrected (where possible, by reference to the first edition of 1818); but otherwise occasional idiosyncratic spellings and irregularities of punctuation or syntax have been allowed to remain unchanged, except that double quotation marks have been changed to single throughout" (doubtless to be sure that the edition would not look too American!). James Rieger's edition

the original printings of these two versions, a critic could learn more about the overall effects of Mary W. Shelley's revisions by comparing reprintings of the two discrete versions than by trying to unravel a conflated eclectic edition. One of the ideas behind the project I initiated for Garland Publishing that became *The Manuscripts of the Younger Romantics* and its collateral series *The Bodleian Shelley Manuscripts* was to make available the major extant manuscripts underlying the literary texts of Byron, Shelley, and Keats (together with other significant literary manuscripts of their contemporaries), not only to encourage more scholars to analyze the full range of textual evidence on the genesis of these poems and the validity of the standard editions of the authors, but also to enable a broader spectrum of critics, teachers, and students to familiarize themselves with basic issues and techniques of textual criticism.[11]

II

Students of the Romantics did not, of course, invent versioning. In Renaissance studies, the two distinct forms of Sir Philip Sidney's *Arcadia* have often been presented separately and sometimes together.[12] Most strikingly, Edward Arber in 1871 "arranged" *A Harmony of the Essays. etc. of Francis Bacon* on the analogy of earlier "harmonies" of the synoptic Gospels. In this imaginative edition, Arber first provided a table recording *which* essays and meditations appeared in *what order* in each major version of Bacon's prose, beginning with the first edition of ten essays in 1597 and listing the contents of the several published editions in English, as well as Harleian MS. 5106, early French and Italian translations, and Bacon's own Latin version (published posthumously in 1638). Arber then divided the works into seven groups, according to their dates of first publication, and arranged the principal versions of the texts in each category side by side. In the case of the first ten essays of 1597, he arranged four principal texts in parallel columns across two facing pages to show the precise words appearing, first, in the edition of 1597 (with the few differences of 1598 col-

---

of *Frankenstein; or, The Modern Prometheus (The 1818 Text)*, first published by Bobbs-Merrill of Indianapolis and New York (1974) and reissued in a corrected state by the University of Chicago Press as a Phoenix Edition in 1982, reprints the 1818 first edition exactly, "typographical errors and all," but records in footnotes the changes that Mary Shelley made in the copy she gave to Mrs. Thomas in Genoa in 1823; in appendixes, Rieger reprints Mary Shelley's Introduction to the 1831 edition and collates the texts of 1818 and 1831.

11. For information on these series, see the Introduction to the present volume, n. 3.

12. See, for example, *The Complete Works of Sir Philip Sidney*, ed. Albert Feuillerat, 4 vols. (Cambridge: Cambridge University Press, 1912–1926), which publishes the 1590 version, or "New Arcadia," in the first two volumes and adds the "original version" (the "Old Arcadia") in vol. 4.

lated at the foot of the column); second, in the Harleian manuscript version of 1607–1612; third, in the printed text of 1612; finally, in the printing of 1625. Significant differences of meaning in the Latin text of 1638 appear at the foot of the page, with both the variant Latin words and their English translations provided.[13] Recently, following the argument of Steven Urkowitz and others that the eclectic text of Shakespeare's *King Lear* that provided the standard basis for study and production for two centuries probably conflates two incompatible versions of the text, the folio version being Shakespeare's own revision of the early text, Michael Warren has prepared a students' edition that will present both the quarto and the folio versions of *King Lear*.[14]

Problems that require versioning reach far beyond literary texts. A dramatic example of early versioning is Origen's *Hexapla*, which reproduced in six parallel columns the Hebrew Old Testament, a transliteration thereof into Greek characters, and four Greek translations—the Septuagint and the versions of Aquila, Symmachus, and Theodotion. (For the Psalms, Origen added two additional Greek translations.) An interesting modern application of versioning involves a recent recension of the Vulgate Bible. In his early work on the Latin Bible, St. Jerome first revised an Old-Latin text of the Psalter to agree with readings in Origen's *Hexapla*; later, with access to more Hebrew manuscripts, Jerome translated anew from the Hebrew Psalms. When the Vulgate texts were revised in the time of Charlemagne, Alcuin replaced Jerome's later "Hebrew" Psalter with his earlier redaction of the Old-Latin text, because the latter was the form currently in use in France (hence, the "Gallican" version). Alcuin's manuscript tradition was so strong that it formed the basis of the "Paris Bible" in the thirteenth century and, ultimately, of the official Roman edition authorized by Pope Clement VIII in 1592.[15] In the two-volume critical Vulgate text edited under the auspices of the Benedictines and published at Stuttgart in

---

13. *A Harmony of the Essays. etc. of Francis Bacon*, "arranged by" Edward Arber, English Reprints ("London: 5 Queen Square, Bloomsbury, W.C., 1 July, 1871"). I own a copy of this edition or "versioning," and I can make it available at the New York Public Library to anyone who may have difficulty finding one to consult. For information on Arber (1836–1912), best known to students of English literature for his *Transcript of the Registers of the Company of Stationers of London, 1554–1640*, and who was also the general editor of the English Reprints series, see the *DNB* Supplements.

14. Warren's *The Complete "King Lear,"* as discussed at the 1985 Conference of the Society for Textual Scholarship, will present facsimiles of the texts found in the first and second quartos and the first folio, with introductory and explanatory materials. The University of California Press will publish it in 1988.

15. Shelley scholars should recall that Clement VIII, known in ecclesiastical history as a puritan reformer of the papacy, was the Pope at the time of the destruction of Beatrice Cenci

1969,[16] the Preface discusses this history and then concludes a paragraph on the Psalter thus: "Consequently, we have thought it advisable to print both 'Gallican' and 'Hebrew' Psalters side by side, on opposite pages—though we would not have it thought that by doing so we wish to question in any way the 'Gallican' Psalter's established place as 'the Vulgate Psalter'!" The Catholic biblical scholars, lacking authority to change the canon, instead provide the next generation of Catholics with two versions side by side—Jerome's earlier recension that has centuries of use by the Western Church, together with the version that Jerome translated directly from the Hebrew. By "versioning" as well as editing, they have made possible a new comparison of the two chief contenders for Vulgate canonicity—the version that they clearly believe has the better claim to faithful rendition of the Hebrew text and the version that most Catholics have read and quoted from the eighth century to the present.

In other areas of literary study, there are many publications that make available various primary versions of texts that both allow the reconsideration of canonically accepted texts and permit critics to study the development of the author's work. One such edition in American literature is Fredson Bowers's *Whitman's "Leaves of Grass" (1860): A Parallel Text*, the work that launched Bowers's career as an editor of American literature.[17] Another important edition in that field is the California edition of Mark Twain's *No. 44, The Mysterious Stranger.* Though its publisher has billed *No. 44* as "The Only Authentic Version," this text—based on Twain's latest manuscript—can be compared with all the extant manuscripts presented by William M. Gibson in 1969 and with the text of *The Mysterious Stranger* as first published posthumously in 1916, based on the earliest of Twain's surviving manuscript versions, but roughly revised and curtailed (censored) by his literary executor and the publisher—the only version that readers and critics saw before 1969.[18]

---

and her family, as depicted in Shelley's play.

16. *Biblia Sacra: Iuxta Vulgatam Versionem*, adiuvantibus Bonifatio Fischer, OSB, Johanne Gribomont, OSB, H.F.D. Sparks, W. Thiele; recenuit et brevi apparatu instruxit Robertus Weber, OSB (Stuttgart: Württembergische Bibelanstalt, 1969).

17. Chicago: University of Chicago Press, 1955.

18. I quote the claim of *No. 44* as being "The Only Authentic Version" from the front cover of the paperback recension in the Mark Twain Library: *No. 44, The Mysterious Stranger: Being an Ancient Tale Found in a Jug, and Freely Translated from the Jug*, foreword and notes by John S. Tuckey, text established by William M. Gibson and the staff of the Twain Project (Berkeley: University of California Press, 1982). This edition is, in turn, based on *Mark Twain's Mysterious Stranger Manuscripts*, ed. William M. Gibson (Berkeley: University of California Press, 1969). Because of a television play based on the text of *No. 44*, this newly published version will rapidly become the best-known one.

III

Even though so much "versioning" has already taken place, there has recently been an emphasis on producing eclectic editions according to either the Anglo-American tradition centering on Greg's theory of copy-text, or the Franco-German theory of synoptic editing.[19] This emphasis on critical editions has led, in turn, to some prejudice against the "uncritical" presentation of primary manuscripts or early published versions. Thus, we find textual scholars criticizing publishers, not simply for introducing or perpetuating typographical errors in reprints, but for reproducing any earlier texts that have not been expertly emended by modern textual critics. One reason that those of us who spend at least part of our time editing may fail to encourage the republication of differing versions of novels, prose works, and plays that publishers would be willing to issue, either in facsimile or in carefully proofread texts of one stage in a work's development, is out of a fear that we may find ourselves out of work. That possibility (as Horace remarked on the relative duration of art and life) is the least of our worries.

Although not every version merits reissue, even in photofacsimile, let the publisher beware! We, as scholars and teachers, should not carp because a publisher has provided us (perhaps at a remainder price) with a facsimile of a version that we happen to think is only the second- or third-best one. Such a "mistake"—like an overgenerous raise in a colleague's salary—provides us with opportunities for remedial action. We can then issue the *best* text, with a relatively brief introduction saying why it is so and giving examples, but without having to proofread and publish an expensive and cumbersome textual apparatus. Instead, we need only refer readers to other, readily available versions. Ultimately, the availability of a wider range of texts will make it easier for us to illustrate—and for unsophisticated readers to grasp—the subtler points of our textual analyses. Few readers can comprehend why one eclectic text is inferior to the theoretical improvements suggested by reviewers. But when a good text and a bad one are both before the reader, textual critics with any powers of

---

19. The product of this school most familiar to students of English literature is probably James Joyce, *Ulysses: A Critical and Synoptic Edition*, ed. Hans Walter Gabler, with Wolfhard Steppe and Claus Melchior, 3 vols. (New York: Garland Publishing, 1984). Gabler and other leading practitioners of the tradition—Louis Hay, Jean-Louis Lebrave, and Klaus Hurlebusch—have published papers in English on their theoretical principles and editorial techniques in the first and third volumes of *TEXT: Transactions of the Society for Textual Scholarship* (1985 and 1987). Jean-Louis Lebrave's *Le traitement automatique des brouillons*, which occupies the entire third number of *Programmation et sciences de l'homme* (January 1984), provides more extended discussion of editing techniques using main-frame computers, with examples using drafts of the poems of Heinrich Heine.

persuasion ought to be able to demonstrate their points. And, should the judgment of a particular textual critic be flawed, or should the orthodox consensus of a generation of textual critics pass away, the two or more versions of the text will remain for the use of later textual critics in exploring and arguing different theses.

In a world where the normal result of the application of textual criticism was the production of various versions, rather than a single, academic "definitive" edition of each work, the role of the *editor* would obviously change in some respects. Editing might not always then require the detective skills to root out all the surviving evidence about the author's involvement—either in person or through his surviving documents or other people's memory of his or her verbal instructions—in a work throughout its entire textual history, and there might be less need for the major blocks of released time and for staffs of assistants to collate and proofread hundreds of pages in dozens of editions before a new edition could be produced. With separate presentation of each major document and edition of a work, there would be less need for the editor to hypothesize events and attitudes where the crucial evidence concerning the author's involvement in the text is lacking (as it is somewhere in the case of almost every text published before 1800 and many, many since then). There would be no need for the editor of a single state of the text—the press-copy manuscript or the first edition—to decide, in the absence of firm evidence, which differences between two such states resulted from the author's grateful acceptance of the publisher's or compositor's suggestions and corrections and which ones resulted from reluctant acquiescence in, or unawareness of, each particular change. Accordingly, there would be less scope for the textual critic to try to undo "unauthorized revisions" that had been part of the text since its initial publication. There would probably be fewer conflicts between those who accept the author's right to determine every detail in the text and those who believe that the social means of production, which initially provided the public with the text, ought to prevail over the isolated psyche of authors before they acceded to the careful scrutiny and good advice of friends, publisher, compositor, and (sometimes) the pointed observations of the representatives of church and state. The surviving pertinent materials would be before the reader and critic, the teacher and student, who could participate in the debate over issues that really matter until a new consensus emerged, rather than wait passively for a new canonical text to be imposed from "above."

The editor of a version need be responsible only for mastering the documents relevant to the composition and production of one particular manuscript or edition and to the later (re)printings that are clearly part of the same version of the text. If holograph manuscripts or authoritative transcriptions of the work survive in sufficiently distinctive states, they themselves ought to be published as versions (as we have seen in the case of Wordsworth's *The Prelude*). An editor will show the requisite qualities of good editing through care and faithfulness in treating the single authority (which must still be examined in multiple copies and collated with other states of the same version, both in order to select the best copy of the version for reproduction and to correct any typographical errors); but editors may not require great inventiveness, or the preternatural power to divine the unstated moods or preferences of dead authors. The copy-text will, in each case, be a version that has already received its systematic (or nonsystematic) pointing and orthography, which will not be emended in any wholesale way, lest what results is some version *other than* the one being advertised. Each of the relatively few emendations can be clearly listed at the foot of the page on which it occurs, for none should exceed a few words. The editor's textual introduction would outline the history of the particular version and its relationship to other versions, either published or potentially publishable, together with whatever remarks the editor may add to point up the critical implications of the several variant versions. The literary work (or historical, philosophical, or scientific work) itself thus could take center stage and provide the reader with its own justification for being.

Though the editor's efforts would be less demanding (and, perhaps, less creative), they would be more likely, in general, to achieve a satisfactory result. Other editors and reviewers would find it harder to reject a text that kept as close as possible to a primary authority, so long as the editor was careful in the presentation of that authority. In this age of photo-offset printing, one way to prevent the introduction of new errors is to reproduce the copy-text photographically and then emend typographical errors by printing corrected texts of a few words or lines in a compatible typeface and pasting these in place on the mechanicals, over the portions of the copy-text to be emended. (Palpable miswritings or other errors of an author's manuscript or typescript would, of course, be left in place when such a document was reproduced, but would be called to the reader's attention by means of textual notes that would also act as a check on the thoroughness and accuracy of the editor.)

There have, in fact, been some editions produced in exactly this way—though with apologies by the editors, who feel like second-class citizens because they have not been funded sufficiently to reset all the type of long first editions. These include editions of Mary Wollstonecraft's *A Vindication of the Rights of Woman* and Thomas Carlyle's *Latter-Day Pamphlets*.[20] Instead, these editors should take pride in having demonstrated a simple way for editors to avoid spending three or four years proofreading the careless typesetting of many of today's part-time, work-at-home word processors.

IV

To sum up this argument: there are good reasons to redirect our energies away from the attempt to produce "definitive" or "ideal" critical editions and, instead, to encourage the production of editions of discrete versions of works. First, such efforts take less time and are less costly both to prepare and to publish. The editor of a particular version—whether that be an early draft, a press-copy manuscript, or a published version with authorial sanction—usually avoids the most difficult theoretical and practical decisions and problems of presentation that face editors of eclectic texts.

Second, not only is the presentation of a single version simpler to plan and easier to execute than an elaborate eclectic text and apparatus (and, consequently, more likely to be completed successfully and published economically), but the version will likely be useful in all seasons; whatever theoretical program is in vogue, an accurate text—especially one providing photofacsimiles—of an original manuscript or an authoritative or historically important edition will retain its value as primary evidence for the development of a major work. By comparing the author's press-copy manuscript with the first edition, for example, readers and critics can judge for themselves what changes the work underwent during the process of publication and to what extent these changes affected the work's meaning. To this primary evidence can then be added (in the introductions or notes, if possible, but even in later publications, as new textual documents or letters come to light) evidence of the author's attitude toward those changes during the publication process. The first published version will show modern scholar-critics what the readers and reviewers of the author's time were reacting to, while the prepublication versions will show how the work evolved, what the publisher saw, and, perhaps, why the work was rejected by one publisher or modified by another.

Third, the presentation of versions produced by the author (either alone or in conjunction with amanuenses, compositors, and censors) focuses

---

20. Ulrich H. Hardt, *A Critical Edition of Mary Wollstonecraft's "A Vindication of the Rights of Woman: With Strictures on Political and Moral Subjects"* (Troy, N.Y.: The Whitston Publishing Company, 1982); *Carlyle's Latter-Day Pamphlets*, ed. M. K. Goldberg and J. P. Seigel (Ottawa: Canadian Federation for the Humanities, 1983).

the central interest of editing once again on the creative artists and their imaginative works of literature, to which we editors are ostensibly devoting our efforts, rather than on our achievements or the theoretical process of "restoration."

In my view, theories about editing are like other meta-studies—i.e., theories that focus, not on the main material to be studied (in this case, poems, dramas, and works of fiction), but on the methods of those who study them. After the theoretical issues have been raised and discussed for a time, the best theory is that which drives all meta-scientists out of business and back into *doing* what they have hitherto been *talking about*. Insofar as a theory about editing or literary criticism produces more and better texts and better understanding of them among a larger body of students or nonprofessional readers of the literary works, it is a good theory; insofar as it directs attention to itself and its practitioners, narrows the audience for the discipline it analyzes, or results only in a theory of theories, rather than in solid work in the primary discipline itself—here textual analysis and editing—it is pernicious.

Like meta-criticism, meta-editing should exist like the rare, unstable isotope of some elements and disintegrate back into the stable isotope after a short half-life. Its radioactivity may furnish energy, but so long as it remains eccentric to the norm, it cannot provide safe foundations for permanent structures. English departments need critics—and teachers of the history of criticism—but do not need meta-critical theorists. Literary studies also need textual critics—everyone who uses a text should learn to analyze its history and authority—and they need editors who, from their awareness of a broad range of editorial methodologies, understand how to apply those appropriately to the textual situations of the works they edit. But however much you and I may enjoy writing about techniques of textual criticism or methods of editing, to erect the theory of these questions into a separate discipline is vain and self-serving.

Part Two

Romantic Contexts

11

Poetry of Familiarity:
Wordsworth, Dorothy, and Mary Hutchinson

The *text and footnotes of this paper provide the reader with the proximate cause of my entry into the exploration of Wordsworth's sexuality, as that may be evidenced in his poetry. Though there was a certain amount of open hostility in* TLS *and* New York Review *to my letters to* TLS *that initially raised these questions, since the publication of this full treatment of it, the subject seems no longer to be a forbidden one. In May 1975, I delivered a short form of my argument as the DeCoursey Fales Memorial Lecture at New York University and then gave an expanded version, containing the discussion of "Laodamia," in July 1975 at the Wordsworth-Coleridge Conference at Ambleside, England, under the title "Wordsworth, Dorothy, and Mary Hutchinson: The Evidence of the Imagination." Members of both audiences—the second of which included several leading Wordsworthians—countered with alternative readings of the evidence, but because I was taking Wordsworth seriously as a poet and a human being struggling with issues that relate him to central concerns of other human beings, rather than pursuing a prurient interest in his sex life, others were able to consider the argument without extreme prejudice. It may have been important to Lord Clark or to Mary Moorman whether or not Wordsworth and his sister misbehaved, or were tempted to misbehave; at least each made a moral judgment upon what each seemed to consider a matter that had been factually established. I was—and am—agnostic about the specific expressions of feeling by the poet and his family, except as the feelings are embodied in poems exhibiting an exceptional emotional power that helped to reopen the wells of feeling in English society in the early nineteenth century. "Poetry of Familiarity" is, in fact, a companion study to my earlier "Shelley's 'The Triumph of Life': The Biographical Problem" (Item 16), in which I use similar biographical and textual evidence to refute an equally strong assertion that Shelley's final poem resulted simply from* his *sexually oriented feelings and actions. In both papers, I try to undercut biographical simplifications and dogmatisms that are unwarranted by the available evidence and to redirect the discussion to larger issues of the poet's psychological orientation and values and to the interplay between the original emo-*

tional poetic impulse and the traditional and technical constraints of the literary form, thereby suggesting some of the complexities of that interrelationship.

Great poetry results when the seams that mark the poet's struggle for self-expression within the constraints of language, genre, and versification do not show at all to the casual observer, but are turned under the fabric, to be inferred only by other "tailors" (poets) or by those who find the pattern and scraps in an old bin (the scholars who look through the drafts and various published revisions and who study the surviving biographical evidence). Almost axiomatically then, there can be no certainty about the genetics of a great poem, unless the evidence of the various stages of its creation is unusually complete. In Wordsworth's case, the evidence, though voluminous, is still incomplete. My explorations are, therefore, meant to suggest possibilities and to stimulate thinking on the part of others who bring to the questions different experiences and knowledge. The very attempt to follow these winding paths within the labyrinthine human psyche should help to banish the dogmatic air that oversimplifiers bring to their biographical analyses. As I answered a critic who accused me of holding a simpleminded view of Wordsworth's Lucy poems, the truly simpleminded biographical view of them is this: "Wordsworth loved a maiden who lived beside the springs of Dove; she died, and it made a great difference to him."

Though Wordsworth, I believe, so successfully infused power into the Lucy poems and "Laodamia" that for most readers their origins are immaterial, those origins must be of concern to scholars, critics, and other poets, because recognition of the springs of such great poetry will help all three groups better comprehend the operations of the poetic imagination. In Wordsworth's case, such comprehension may help us avoid oversimplifying his life and career to the point where he is said to have been a revolutionary Bohemian and great poet who married and simmered down into a conventional bore. On the contrary, Wordsworth's effort to bend his emotional attachments and sexual energies into socially acceptable forms was a heroic one that generated much of his most moving poetry precisely because he had to struggle so hard against some of his own deepest feelings—though, of course, he engaged in the struggle and succeeded in becoming a paterfamilias because that action fulfilled other deep needs within him. I treat some of those other needs in two other papers in this collection—"The Beauty of Buttermere as Fact and Romantic Symbol" (12) and "Wordsworth, Shelley, and the Romantic Inheritance" (19). In another paper now in progress, I explore Wordsworth's attachment to his daughters, and I treat Wordsworth's feelings for Annette Vallon in the chapter on the poet in Intervals of Inspiration: The Skeptical Tradition and the Psychology of Romanticism (Greenwood, Fla.: Penkevill Publishing, 1988).

"Poetry of Familiarity" was published in The Evidence of the Imagination: Studies of Interactions between Life and Art in English Romantic Literature *(New York: New York University Press, 1978; pp. 142–77), the Festschrift for Kenneth Neill Cameron, of which (with the extensive help of Doucet Devin Fischer, Ricki B. Herzfeld, and other members of the staff at the Pforzheimer Library) I was the principal editor, aided by Cameron's students Michael C. Jaye and Betty T. Bennett. Having donated the original subtitle of my lecture to serve as the title of that collection, I renamed my essay "Poetry of Familiarity" to point to its primary emphasis, which is—like that of Bateson's book—on the creative process and the resulting variations in the emotional qualities of different poems by Wordsworth, rather than on the biographical interactions per se.*

Since then, the publication of the full texts of The Love Letters of William and Mary Wordsworth, *edited by Beth Darlington (Ithaca: Cornell University Press, 1981), brought into public view important new evidence on the relations between William and Mary Wordsworth. Though when I published "Poetry of Familiarity" I was aware of the existence and tone of this correspondence through excerpts quoted in the Sotheby's auction catalogue (see note 27 below), those excerpts seemed to me and my friends to suggest a forced insincerity on William Wordsworth's part. The letters in their full panoply proved to be more impressive, though they clearly represented a new phase of the relations between William and Mary Wordsworth. Had I discussed the years in which those letters were written, I should have to revise a number of my inferences and conclusions. As it is, after giving due consideration to the new evidence and relating some of it to my original argument, pointing in note 25 of my paper on "The Beauty of Buttermere" (12) to new support for my thesis in Wordsworth's 1842 comments to Henry Crabb Robinson about the poems he had written to his wife, I still hold to my basic view of the psychological sources of the poems of 1798–1802, 1804, and 1813–1815, as I delineate them in "Poetry of Familiarity."*

Few subsequent studies have engaged my paper on its primary ground. In Dorothy Wordsworth *(Oxford: Clarendon Press, 1985), Robert Gittings and Jo Manton dodge the whole issue of the nature of Dorothy's and William's feelings for each other almost as naively—or repressively—as did Mary Moorman (see pp. 57–59, 91–99, and 104–6). Jean H. Hagstrum, in his Hodges Lectures, published under the title* The Romantic Body: Love and Sexuality in Keats, Wordsworth, and Blake *(Nashville: University of Tennessee Press, 1985), accepts my general conclusions about the Lucy poems (p. 98) but finds my suggestions about the circumstances surrounding the composition of "Laodamia" "brilliantly ingenious" but "unproven and, indeed, unprovable" (p. 88). At the 1984 MLA convention in Washington, Norman Fruman alluded to my argument while asserting that Wordsworth's real problem was that he was too prudish to discuss his sexuality in his poetry, thereby weakening his impact as a psychological poet. I do not find Wordsworth at all prudish by the standards of his time. Our candor in these mat-*

ters, though probably beneficial in our lives, seems not to have generated any poetry of such great emotional power as arose when such feelings and the expression of them had to be displaced into less graphic language. Part of my point in exploring the unprovable was to suggest how rich and strange this reincarnation of sexually allied feelings might be in situations—and cultures—where an artist was not as free as were Hemingway, Henry Miller, and Auden to describe in letters to friends or in creative writings every aspect of sexual desire or the emotional life as soon as it developed.

In 1954 F. W. Bateson created a minor scandal in the then-staid precincts of Wordsworth scholarship by declaring in *Wordsworth: A Re-Interpretation* that much of Wordsworth's best poetry arose directly from the *Sturm und Drang* not only of his love affair with Annette Vallon in 1792 (as well as the guilt consequent on their separation) but also of his unacknowledged love for his sister Dorothy.[1] Bateson's thesis is, in fact, much broader. In his opening chapter, "The Two Voices," and in his conclusion, "The Critical Verdict," he tries to explain all of Wordsworth's poetry by examining the conflict between the poet's stated motive of providing "his readers with moral instruction," which, Bateson believed, underlay the poems in Wordsworth's "Augustan Voice," and the unconscious motivation behind his writing of such poems as "Tintern Abbey," the Lucy poems, and *The Prelude*, which exhibit Wordsworth's "Romantic Voice."

Bateson's basic approach to Wordsworth—using the poetry as well as biographical evidence to pinpoint problem areas in the poet's psyche and then reexamining individual poems with these conflicts in mind—has gained wide acceptance.[2] But—though many earlier statements by Ernest de Selincourt in his notes to the Oxford English Text Edition and by Mary Moorman in her later two-volume *William Wordsworth: A Biography* provide factual material tending to corroborate Bateson's view of the poet—there has been a militant resistance on the part of some Wordsworthians, particularly in Great Britain, to accepting two possibilities: first, that William Wordsworth felt a stronger emotional tie to his sister Dorothy during their

---

1. I have used the 1963 impression of the second edition (London: Longmans, 1956), hereafter cited as "Bateson." In this edition, while maintaining his thesis, Bateson softened the language in various places. (See his "Preface to the Second Edition.") For a sidelight on Bateson's early differences with the Dove Cottage Trustees, see his letter to *TLS*, 9 April 1976, p. 430.

2. The most ambitious attempts thus far to interpret Wordsworth's poetry in relation to his psychology are Wallace W. Douglas's *Wordsworth: The Construction of a Personality* (Kent, Ohio: Kent State University Press, 1968) and Richard J. Onorato's *The Character of the Poet: Wordsworth in "The Prelude"* (Princeton: Princeton University Press, 1971). Though I have consulted both books, I have related my argument to the latter, hereafter cited as "Onorato."

years of living together at Windy Brow, Racedown, Alfoxden, Germany, and Grasmere (1794–1802) than he did to Mary Hutchinson, whom he married in 1802; and, second, that the Lucy poems and several other poems owe their inception to the conflict deep within Wordsworth between his strong feelings for his sister and his fear of the possibly dangerous consequences of their mutual love.

The strength of this resistance, which some of us believed to be dying out, was illustrated in 1970 in Mary Moorman's lecture to the Royal Society of Literature in which, by simplistic paraphrasing, she reduced Bateson's complex argument to this conception: "All the poems addressed to Dorothy, directly or indirectly, are considered to be out-and-out love poems, and on this evidence, and this alone—for there is no other—he based his 'reinterpretation' of Wordsworth."[3] Mary Moorman, provoked by Kenneth Clark's equally simplistic account of Wordsworth and Dorothy in his lectures on *Civilisation*, attempted to discredit what she termed "crude and insensitive writing about" William and Dorothy (p. 93). In her lecture she brings together much useful information about the history of Wordsworth's relationship with his sister, providing for example (as Helen Darbishire had earlier in the fine edition of *Journals of Dorothy Wordsworth* that bears both scholars' names)[4] a clear account of the history of Dorothy's later physical and mental deterioration. But she overlooks the tone of the many poems Wordsworth wrote to or about Dorothy (and Mary Hutchinson). Sometimes—even in the generally judicious account of Dorothy's health—she identifies superficial causes for reactions that, from the tone of both Dorothy's letters and journals and William's poetry, may well have had deeper psychological roots. For example, she mentions the many "headaches and internal upsets" that Dorothy and William suffered during their years of living alone and then attributes the "great improvement in her health" after William's marriage partly to the fact that "the care of her brother was now shared with Mary" (pp. 92–93). But the psychosomatic effects of conflicts between sexual desire and social taboos had been recognized at least as early as the biblical account of Amnon, who "was so tormented that he made himself ill because of his sister Tamar" (2 Samuel 13:2). Dorothy's minor illnesses and her later improvement in health cannot be definitely related to William's marriage, but Moorman's explanation of the possible relation is patently inadequate.

3. "William and Dorothy Wordsworth," in *Essays by Divers Hands, Being the Transactions of the Royal Society of Literature*, n.s., 55 (1972): 75–97.
4. *Journals of Dorothy Wordsworth*, ed. Mary Moorman, with an Introduction by Helen Darbishire (London: Oxford University Press, 1971; corrected 1973, 1974), hereafter cited as *Journals*.

During a subsequent exchange in the letters column of *TLS*, initiated by Alethea Hayter's contention that Moorman's lecture should have "refuted once for all" the "allegation of incest against William and Dorothy Wordsworth," I maintained the position that, while we could never know what exactly went on between William and Dorothy Wordsworth during their years together, several of Wordsworth's poems seem to reflect an emotional struggle to define his feelings toward Dorothy within a socially acceptable context.[5]

While I acknowledge my debt to *Wordsworth: A Re-Interpretation*, it will be clear that I reject a number of Bateson's detailed conclusions.[6] I believe that Wordsworth's great original contribution to English poetry lies in those poems that grew out of his own various psychological turmoils (which I do not regard, however, as ending with his marriage) and that his decline as a poet can be traced directly to the resolution, one by one, of the conflicts within him—one of the strongest of which arose from the mixed feelings of fraternal affection, passion, and guilt toward his sister Dorothy. Thus, though the following pages concentrate on some of the less frequently examined poetry relating to Wordsworth's feelings for his sister and his wife, the discussion should be seen as part of a larger view of Wordsworth's art relevant to all of his poems that evidently resulted from the series of internal conflicts that began to surface soon after his return to England from France in 1792. I do not attempt to trace the origins of these conflicts to possible deeper roots in Wordsworth's childhood, though I think that some suggestions made by Bateson and Onorato are probably relevant here.[7] My central focus, at present, is on the poetry arising directly out of the interactions of William, Dorothy, and Mary Wordsworth.

I

On 4 October 1802, Mary Hutchinson married William Wordsworth. The

---

5. The correspondence, most of it published under the heading "Brothers and Sisters," appeared in *TLS* in 1974 on 9 August (p. 859), 23 August (p. 906), 13 September (pp. 979–80), 4 October (pp. 1078–79), 1 November (p. 1231), 8 November (p. 1261), 15 November (p. 1288), 22 November (p. 1317), and 27 December (p. 1464). My contributions appeared on 13 September, 1 November, and 27 December.

6. Among them, his contention that "after the Lucy poems, . . . there was no place for [Dorothy] in the organs of Wordsworth's poetic imagination, and she was cut out like so much decayed tissue" (Bateson, p. 202). As will become clear, I believe that William's feelings for Dorothy remained a vital force in his poetry up to the very day of his wedding (see pp. 204–5) and beyond.

7. Both Bateson (pp. 41–56) and Onorato (pp. 24–25 et passim) rightly emphasize, for example, the effect upon the Wordsworth siblings of the early deaths of their mother and father and their unhappy childhood among unloving kinsmen. Onorato sees Wordsworth's repression of his sorrow at his early bereavement as determinative for his later attitude toward Nature.

emotional relationships among Mary, William, and his sister Dorothy during the months leading up to that union are adequately documented only by Dorothy, who in her *Journals* recorded her feelings about the event in great detail—too great to include here in full. After recounting with warmth and affection her last weeks alone together with William at Dove Cottage, Grasmere, and their departure from it on 9 July 1802, Dorothy describes their journey to see the Hutchinsons at Gallow Hill, where they arrived on Thursday evening, 15 July. Within this account of the week in transit, we find Dorothy and William, who were riding atop the coach, protecting themselves from the rain: "we buttoned ourselves up, both together in the Guard's coat and we liked the hills and the Rain the better for bringing [us] so close to one another—I never rode more snugly."[8] After a brief stay with the Hutchinsons at Gallow Hill, William and Dorothy traveled to London (where they arrived on 29 July) and thence via Dover to Calais (1 August) where they met Annette Vallon and William's natural daughter Caroline. They spent exactly four weeks at Calais, living in lodgings and seeing Annette and Caroline, or Caroline alone, daily. The Wordsworths returned to England on 30 August, having settled financial arrangements with Annette and having had an opportunity to become well acquainted with William's daughter.[9] After remaining in London from 31 August till 22 September, Dorothy and William returned to Gallow Hill on 24 September. Dorothy's account of the wedding day (even those crucial sentences omitted from earlier printed texts) is too well known to quote in full. Dorothy did not attend her brother's wedding, though she had worn the wedding ring the night before it; she lay on her bed in emotional shock during the time the wedding party was gone and pulled herself together to greet the groom (and bride) only at the insistence of Sara Hutchinson; Dorothy writes at the end of her account, perhaps projecting her feelings into Mary Hutchinson Wordsworth: "Poor Mary was much agitated when she parted from her Brothers and Sisters and her home."[10]

William Wordsworth's marriage, no matter how much Dorothy liked Mary Hutchinson, was a turning point in Dorothy's life, leaving her ever after half an outsider in the household that she and William had kept together for seven years. Dorothy's feelings are more than explicable: they are inescapable. William selected a mate who, as one of Dorothy's closest friends, would accept her as a continuing member of the family (begin-

---

8. *Journals*, pp. 147–48.
9. William and Dorothy had carried on a regular correspondence with Annette and Caroline that has disappeared. See *The Letters of William and Dorothy Wordsworth*, ed. Ernest de Selincourt, vol. 1, *The Early Years: 1787–1805*, 2nd ed., revised by Chester L. Shaver (Oxford: Clarendon Press, 1967), p. 282 (hereafter cited as *Early Letters*).
10. *Journals*, p. 154.

ning with their honeymoon), but even though his choice was itself an act of kindness and love, Dorothy was displaced as William's closest companion.

It was natural that at age thirty-two, seeing ahead the means to meet the responsibility of supporting a wife and children, William Wordsworth—a virile man of exceptional sexual magnetism, if we are to trust Coleridge[11]—should desire to marry. It was natural also that he should want to do so in a way compatible not only with his own needs, but also with those of Dorothy, whom he repeatedly acknowledged to be the person dearest to him throughout the years since his return from France. In those few allusions to Mary Hutchinson in William's surviving early letters there is, on the contrary, no evidence of warmth, passion, or love that was more than brotherly. Perhaps the most striking allusion occurs in a letter Wordsworth wrote to Coleridge from Grasmere on Christmas Eve 1799, five days after he and Dorothy had moved into Dove Cottage. After he and Coleridge had visited Grasmere to select the house, Coleridge had preceded him to Sockburn, Yorkshire, where Dorothy was staying with Mary and Sara Hutchinson and *their* brother Tom. William writes: "I arrived at Sockburn the day after you quitted it . . . . I was sadly disappointed in not finding Dorothy; Mary was a solitary housekeeper and overjoyed to see me. D[orothy] is now sitting beside me racked with the tooth-ache" (*Early Letters*, p. 274). William's disappointment at finding himself alone with Mary Hutchinson may be either genuine or feigned (Dorothy is sitting at his side). In neither case is it the sentiment a lover would express to his closest friend. The most charitable interpretation, and the one that fits best with the other evidence, is that William had no deep romantic feelings for Mary at this date, that Mary was (as the other surviving correspondence suggests) a closer friend of Dorothy's than of William's.

When William and Dorothy settled at Dove Cottage, Grasmere, neither of them apparently thought of marrying or of ever changing their household. For example, on 8 November 1799, a few weeks before the letter I have quoted, Wordsworth and Coleridge wrote a joint letter from Keswick in which William remarks to Dorothy: "C[oleridge] was much struck with

11. See, for example, Coleridge's frequent references to his jealousy of Wordsworth in relation to Sara Hutchinson. In *The Notebooks of Samuel Taylor Coleridge*, ed. Kathleen Coburn, vol. 2 (New York: Pantheon Books, 1961), entries 2001n, 2055n, 2975n, 2998 and n, 3148 and n (and others) show that Coleridge imagined that on Saturday, 26 December 1806, in the Queen's Head Inn, Stringston, Wordsworth had gone to bed with Sara Hutchinson, his sister-in-law and Coleridge's beloved. (Coleridge later accused his imagination of playing tricks on him in this instance.) Bateson (p. 44) quotes Thomas De Quincey, who wrote (in part): "Wordsworth's intellectual passions were fervent and strong: but they rested upon a basis of preternatural animal sensibility diffused through *all* the animal passions (or appetites) . . . ."

Grasmere and its neighbourhood and I have much to say to you, you will think my plan a mad one, but I have thought of building a house there by the Lake side." He goes on to discuss the cost and financing, mentioning that "a Devonshire gentleman has built a Cottage there which cost a £130 which would exactly suit us every way, but the size of the bedrooms we shall talk of this." He closes his part of the letter by mentioning Dove Cottage as an alternative: "There is a small house at Grasmere empty which perhaps we may take, and purchase furniture but of this we will speak. But I shall write again when I know more on this subject" (*Early Letters*, p. 272). In suggesting they borrow money to buy land and build a cottage suitable to the needs of the two of them, Wordsworth at the end of 1799 envisioned their joint household to be a permanent arrangement. Early in 1799 Dorothy had complained in letters from Goslar, Germany, that they could not afford to enter into German society: "a man travelling alone may do very well, but, if his wife or sister goes with him, he must give entertainments," for "*a man and woman*" were there "considered as a sort of family" (*Early Letters*, pp. 247, 244). Clearly throughout their time of living together since September 1795—first at Racedown with Basil Montagu's young son, then at Alfoxden, then in Germany—Dorothy and William had considered themselves a viable family.

Dorothy's own attitude toward spending a lifetime keeping house for her brother is mirrored interestingly in her letter from Sockburn in April 1795 to her childhood friend Jane Pollard. Dorothy writes:

You must recollect my friends the Hutchinsons, my sole companions at Penrith, . . . whose company in the absence of my brothers was the only agreeable Variety which Penrith afforded. They are settled at Sockburn—six miles from Darlington *perfectly to their satisfaction*, they are quite independent and *have not a wish ungratified*, very different indeed is their present situation from what it was formerly when we compared grievances and lamented the misfortune of losing our parents at an early age and being thrown upon the mercy of ill-natured and illiberal relations. Their brother has a farm, of about 200 £ a year, and they keep his house; *he is* a very amiable young man, *uncommonly fond of his sisters*, and in short, *every thing that they can desire*. (*Early Letters*, pp. 141–42, italics added)

In the pre-Freudian culture, Dorothy's emphasis on how the Hutchinson sisters' life with their brother *satisfied* their every *desire* did not, of course, carry the nuances that the same language would bear today. Rather, it suggested the limits of Dorothy's aspirations for her own life. She does not speak about either marriage (and children) or a separate life with some personal career as a situation more desirable than that of keeping house for one's brother.

Presumably, even in a pre-Freudian culture young women experienced sexual longings and needs, but their psychic and social censors must have been more militant, often preventing them from viewing consciously their needs in this direction. Ellen Moers, in a perceptive article in *The New York Review of Books*, after pointing to certain Gothic elements in the imaginations of Emily Brontë and Christina Rossetti, writes:

> both women grew up in a family of four siblings, male and female, bound together in a closed circle by affection and by imaginative genius, as well as by remoteness from the social norm. . . . Quentin Bell's recent biography of Virginia Stephen, a girl in another family of like-minded sisters and brothers, allows us at least to speculate openly on the sexual drama of tke Victorian nursery. (Though Mr. Bell does not . . . settle the question of the fantasy component in Virginia Woolf's memories of fraternal incest, to the reality of the incest fantasy he brings important evidence, if evidence is needed.) . . . to Victorian women the sister-brother relationship seems to have had . . . perhaps greater significance—especially to those women, so commonplace in the intellectual middle class, who in a sexual sense never grew to full maturity. The rough-and-tumble sexuality of the nursery loomed large for sisters: it was the *only* heterosexual world the Victorian literary spinsters were ever freely and physically to explore.[12]

Without speculating as to the specific nature of Dorothy Wordsworth's sexual development, it seems quite clear that her affection for her brothers—especially William and John—satisfied her and that she usually demanded no more sexually fulfilling relationship.[13]

II

As one would expect from a poet, William Wordsworth recorded his emotions during the months just before his marriage chiefly in his verse, embodying them in a group of poems he wrote at Grasmere in a prolific burst of inspiration from mid-March 1802 until the very day of his wedding, 4 October of the same year. Some of these poems center on the expe-

---

12. "Female Gothic: Monsters, Goblins, Freaks," *New York Review of Books* 21 (14 April 1974): 36–37.
13. Many have surmised Dorothy's interest in Coleridge from 1797, and John E. Jordan presents some evidence to support Malcolm Elwin's speculation that Dorothy at age thirty-eight may have been infatuated with young Thomas De Quincey during his early years in the Lake District. See *De Quincey to Wordsworth: A Biography of a Relationship* (Berkeley: University of California Press, 1962), pp. 228–30. I should add, also, in fairness to Dorothy and her modern admirers who would object to a description of her as a case of arrested sexual development, that a number of readers of the evidence are more willing than I to suggest the occurrence of actual physical incest between William and Dorothy. See, for example, Rachel Mayer Brownstein's excellent essay "The Private Life: Dorothy Wordsworth's Journals," *MLQ* 34 (1973): 48–63, especially 51–52.

rience of others and many draw upon the past, exemplifying the doctrine of the 1800 Preface by taking their "origin from emotion recollected in tranquillity" that generates "an emotion, kindred to" it and spontaneously overflows into expressions of "powerful feelings." Such are four poems of 11–17 March: "The Sailor's Mother," "Alice Fell; or Poverty," "Beggars," and "The Emigrant Mother."[14] But a large number of the poems of March through May of this year treat specifically and with great warmth and affection incidents in the long relationship between William and Dorothy Wordsworth. On 14 March he wrote "To a Butterfly" ("Stay near me—do not take thy flight!"), a poem recalling,

> Oh! pleasant, pleasant were the days,
> The time, when, in our childish plays,
> My sister Emmeline and I
> Together chased the butterfly!
>   (*PW*, 1:226)[15]

On 12 April, William wrote the poem later called "The Glow-worm," beginning,

> Among all lovely things my Love had been;
> Had noted well the stars, all flowers that grew
> About her home; but she had never seen
> A Glow-worm, never one, and this I knew.

The twenty-line poem ends: "I led my Lucy to the spot, 'Look here!' / Oh! joy it was for her, and joy for me!" (*PW*, 2:466). Mary E. Burton mentions a transcription by Sara Hutchinson "with the name of Mary where the printed versions use 'Lucy' and 'Emma.'"[16] That must have seemed right to the Hutchinson sisters when Dorothy transcribed the poem in a letter to Mary Hutchinson on 16 April 1802: who else could be addressed as "my

---

14. Unless otherwise indicated, Wordsworth's poems and their titles are quoted from *The Poetical Works of William Wordsworth*, ed. Ernest de Selincourt and Helen Darbishire, Oxford English Text Edition, 5 vols. (Oxford: Clarendon Press, 1940–1954), vols. 1–3 being the second editions (hereafter cited as *PW*). The reader will often have to consult the notes and variant readings to reconstruct the earliest texts.

15. Additional information may eventually be forthcoming from a previously unknown manuscript, sold at Sotheby's in London (6 July 1977, lot 405), which contains nine lines apparently intended as an addition to this poem, copied by Dorothy Wordsworth. This addition can be dated (from the contents of a fragmentary letter by Dorothy on the verso) before June 1802. This and other new letters and manuscripts by Wordsworth, Coleridge, and their circle, sold at the same time, are now in the Dove Cottage Library.

16. *The Letters of Mary Wordsworth, 1800–1855* (Oxford: Clarendon Press, 1958), p. xxiv.

Love" by William on that date? But as Wordsworth explained to Coleridge, in his letter of the same day where he transcribed the same poem (using "Emma" instead of "Lucy" for his beloved's name), "The incident of this Poem took place about seven years ago between Dorothy and me" (*Early Letters*, p. 348). Dorothy, not Mary, is the "Emma" or "Lucy" of the poem, which like "To a Butterfly" describes the siblings' appreciation of the minor elements of nature.[17] On 20 April, he wrote another poem "To a Butterfly" (beginning, "I've watched you now a full half-hour, / Self-poised upon that yellow flower"). The second stanza of this poem is significant for our theme:

> This plot of orchard-ground is ours;
> My trees they are, my Sister's flowers;
> *   *   *   *   *
> Sit near us on the bough!
> We'll talk of sunshine and of song,
> And summer days, when we were young;
> Sweet childish days, that were as long
> As twenty days are now.   (*PW*, 2:22–23)

The interaction between the Grasmere family—"we"—Dorothy and William—continues in the poems that follow, as Mary Moorman's edition of Dorothy's journal of the period, containing the texts of the appropriate poems, makes clear. The poems written early in 1802 about the smaller living forms of nature—the daisy, the cuckoo, the green linnet, the robin, the skylark, and the sparrow's nest—derived their imaginative force, as Wordsworth himself tells us in *The Prelude* (XIV.232–66), from his associations with Dorothy.[18] The chief emotional catalyst to Wordsworth's imagination during the unusual poetic activity early in 1802 was not Coleridge nor pleasurable excitement about his forthcoming marriage to Mary Hutchinson: rather, that imaginative stimulus was his struggle to take the step that would inevitably create an irrevocable psychic barrier between himself and his

---

17. In *William Wordsworth: A Biography*, Mary Moorman, always scrupulous both in handling facts and in acknowledging the force of William's affection for Dorothy, writes of "The Glow-worm": "It was written in the spring of 1802, when William was riding back to Dorothy after a visit to Mary Hutchinson, with whom he had just completed the arrangements for their wedding. His first and immediate thought even in that hour was for Dorothy, and [Mrs. Moorman adds by way of interpreting these facts] he speaks as if to reassure her that the communion between them could never be changed" (vol. 1 [Oxford: Clarendon Press, 1957; corrected 1967], pp. 319–20).

18. See, for example, Dorothy's account of the composition of "Children Gathering Flowers" ("Foresight") (*Journals*, pp. 116–17) and her allusion on 15 April to the flower that, two weeks later, Wordsworth immortalized in two poems "To the Small Celandine" (pp. 109, 118–19).

beloved sister. Wordsworth's regrets about breaking up his happy "Home at Grasmere"[19] are epitomized in a poem that Dorothy, in her journals, called "his poem on Going for Mary,"[20] which exhibits in almost painful detail the emotional struggle William faced. Though I cannot quote the entire poem here, three of its eight stanzas should illustrate my point:

> Farewell, thou little Nook of mountain-ground,
> Thou rocky corner of the lowest stair
> Of that magnificent temple which doth bound
> One side of our whole vale with grandeur rare;
> Sweet garden-orchard, eminently fair,
> The loveliest spot that man hath ever found,
> Farewell!—we leave thee to Heaven's peaceful care,
> Thee, and the Cottage which thou dost surround.
>   *   *   *   *   *   *
> We go for One to whom ye will be dear;
> And she will prize this Bower, this Indian shed,
> Our own contrivance, Building without peer!
> —A gentle Maid, whose heart is lowly bred,
> Whose pleasures are in wild fields gatherèd,
> With joyousness, and with a thoughtful cheer,
> Will come to you; to you herself will wed;
> And love the blessed life that we lead here.
>   *   *   *   *   *
> Help us to tell Her tales of years gone by,
> And this sweet spring, the best beloved and best;
> Joy will be flown in its mortality;
> Something must stay to tell us of the rest.
> Here, thronged with primroses, the steep rock's breast
> Glittered at evening like a starry sky;
> And in this bush our sparrow built her nest,
> Of which I sang one song that will not die.

19. William's exceptionally blissful reaction to the residence that he and Dorothy chose at Town End, Grasmere (the cottage now known as Dove Cottage), has been widely, if not universally, acknowledged. See, for example, Karl Kroeber, "'Home at Grasmere': Ecological Holiness," *PMLA* 89 (1974): 132–41. For a reading of "Home at Grasmere" involving Wordsworth's possible ambiguous feelings in the period, see Kenneth R. Johnston, "'Home at Grasmere': Reclusive Song," *SiR* 14 (1975): 1–28. Johnston and those who see underlying tensions in all parts of "Home at Grasmere" emphasize the poet's recognition that the idyllic situation is necessarily mortal and, therefore, temporary. One necessary cause of the transitory nature of the poet's bliss was, I submit, the instability of the situation involving the cohabitation of a brother and sister who could never fulfill each other's sexual longings without guilt. For the dating of various portions of this poem and Wordsworth's revisions, which gradually removed most of the references to Dorothy and cast the poem into a far less personal form, see Beth Darlington's edition of *Home at Grasmere: Part First, Book First of "The Recluse"* in the Cornell Wordsworth Series (Ithaca: Cornell University Press, 1978).

20. In the Appendix to *Journals* the poem is titled "Our Departure" (p. 217); when published in 1815 it was titled "A Farewell" (*PW*, 2:23–24).

William and Dorothy are the "we" into whose garden Mary, the "gentle Maid" with "lowly bred" heart, will come and "wed" the garden as she learns its history. He and Dorothy will tell her tales of "this sweet spring, the best beloved and best," though "Joy" will have "flown" with the "mortality" of the season. This poem is, in part surely, a poem about the mortality of the moment, about "Joy, whose hand is ever at his lips, / Bidding adieu," but it is something more. It is more than merely a poem of solidarity with Dorothy, assuring her that her brother will always love and value her and that the home they have loved together will always be theirs, no matter who else enters its magic garden. The poem is a farewell to an Eden that, as the tone clearly indicates, can never be recaptured, no matter how wide the world of choice that lies before them.

III

As we have seen, from March through May 1802, while he and Dorothy at Grasmere contemplated the end of their private Eden, many of Wordsworth's poems deal with the relationship of childhood experiences to the poet's adult attitudes. In the first poem "To a Butterfly," the poet says that the creature brings "a solemn image to my heart, / My father's family! . . . The time, when, in our childish plays, / My sister Emmeline and I / Together chased the butterfly!" When he listens "To the Cuckoo," Wordsworth can recall his "schoolboy days"—"till I do beget / That golden time again" (*PW*, 2:207-8). There is no question that the famous poem beginning "My heart leaps up when I behold / A rainbow in the sky," written on 26 March 1802, in the midst of these poems associated with Dorothy, also derives from the same inspiration. Wordsworth's greatest earlier assertion of the continuity of past and present, "Lines composed a Few Miles above Tintern Abbey," had also been written (1798) with Dorothy present, and it contains an address to her in the final lines.[21] The same is true of another poem in which the poet moves from an experience in his boyhood and relates it to his present state of mind—this on a theme of crucial importance to my argument.

In "Nutting," written in Germany late in 1798 when William and Dorothy were living alone at Goslar, Wordsworth recounts how, while he was a boy at Hawkshead School, he went out one day with his "nutting-crook in

---

21. Stephen Parrish reveals in his Cornell Wordsworth edition of *The Prelude, 1798-1799* (Ithaca: Cornell University Press, 1977) that in "the earliest state of *The Prelude*," found in MS JJ, "where a listener is identified at the close, it seems, as in *Tintern Abbey*, to be the poet's sister" (p. 8).

Poetry of Familiarity

hand": "O'er path-less rocks, / Through... tangled thickets, / Forcing my way, I came to one dear nook / Unvisited, where . . . hazels rose / Tall and erect, with tempting clusters hung, / A virgin scene!—" The poet recalls his reaction thus:

> A little while I stood,
> Breathing with such suppression of the heart
> As joy delights in; and with wise restraint
> Voluptuous, fearless of a rival, eyed
> The banquet;—or beneath the trees I sate
> Among the flowers, and with the flowers I played;
> A temper known to those who, after long
> And weary expectation, have been blest
> With sudden happiness beyond all hope.
> *   *   *   *   *
> . . . Then up I rose,
> And dragged to earth both branch and bough, with crash
> And merciless ravage: and the shady nook
> Of hazels, and the green and mossy bower,
> Deformed and sullied, patiently gave up
> Their quiet being: and, unless I now
> Confound my present feelings with the past,
> Ere from the mutilated bower I turned
> Exulting, rich beyond the wealth of kings,
> I felt a sense of pain when I beheld
> The silent trees, and saw the intruding sky.—

The version of the poem Wordsworth published in 1800 concludes with three lines addressed to Dorothy, urging her, in the manner of the conclusion to "Tintern Abbey," to learn the same lesson William believed he had learned from his earlier experience:

> Then, dearest Maiden, move along these shades
> In gentleness of heart; with gentle hand
> Touch—for there is a spirit in the woods.
> (PW, 2:211–12)

But in a long manuscript fragment published by de Selincourt in *Poetical Works* (2:504–6) there is another, much longer conclusion, which begins:

> Ah! what a crash was that! with gentle hand
> Touch these fair hazels—My beloved Friend!
> Though 'tis a sight invisible to thee
> From such rude intercourse the woods all shrink

> As at the blowing of Astolpho's horn.
> Thou, Lucy, art a maiden "inland bred"
> And thou hast known "some nurture"; but in truth
> If I had met thee here with that keen look
> Half cruel in its eagerness, those cheeks
> Thus [ ] flushed with a tempestuous bloom,
> I might have almost deem'd that I had pass'd
> A houseless being in a human shape,
> An enemy of nature, hither sent
> From regions far beyond the Indian hills—

Here William chides Dorothy for her almost unnatural "half cruel . . . eagerness" to ravage the hazel trees of a more recent day. And he calls Dorothy "Lucy," as he later referred to her in the manuscript of "The Glow-worm."

"Nutting," as has been recognized by recent critics, is filled with language of sexual ravishment. It describes, in fact, the rape of "a virgin scene" of Nature. The boy "voluptuous, fearless of a rival," toys with and fondles the secluded nook and then lets himself go in an act of "merciless ravage," leaving the "mossy bower, / Deformed and sullied." In the published poem, William cautions the "dearest Maiden" against making his mistake; in the manuscript version, he accuses her of having done so. All is expressed in terms of two hazel groves, one of the distant past and the other in the present.

Soon after William addressed these lines to Dorothy as "Lucy," asking her not to exhibit so much "tempestuous bloom" of the kind that he recalled as his own "voluptuous" state of being, he wrote the first versions of two of the five poems now called the "Lucy poems." Two of these poems, now identified by their first lines as "She dwelt among the untrodden ways" and "Strange fits of passion have I known," have their first surviving texts in a letter that William and Dorothy wrote to Coleridge on 14 or 21 December 1798 (*Early Letters*, pp. 236-38).

> 1
> My hope was one, from cities far,
>   Nursed on a lonesome heath;
> Her lips were red as roses are,
>   Her hair a woodbine wreath.
>
> 2
> She lived among the untrodden ways
>   Beside the springs of Dove,
> A maid whom there were none to praise,
>   And very few to love;

> 3
> A violet by a mossy stone
>   Half-hidden from the eye!
> Fair as a star when only one
>   Is shining in the sky!
>
> 4
> And she was graceful as the broom
>   That flowers by Carron's side;
> But slow distemper checked her bloom,
>   And on the Heath she died.
>
> 5
> Long time before her head lay low
>   Dead to the world was she:
> But now she's in the grave, and Oh!
>   The difference to me!

Wordsworth later revised the poem essentially by compression, eliminating its original first and fourth stanzas and rephrasing the first two lines of the final stanza (*PW*, 2:30). But the discarded stanzas cast considerable light on the poem, if only in the reference to "Carron's side": Carron is the name of a river and a lake in Ross and Cromarty County in the Highlands of Scotland, an area that Wordsworth had not visited by this date. Like "the bonny braes of Yarrow," it apparently came to him through his reading of eighteenth-century ballads (in this case "Owen of Carron" by John Langhorne). Since Wordsworth is attempting a ballad of an idealized sort, the equally arbitrary "springs of Dove" allusion cannot be used to identify—or eliminate—the personal origins or thematic content of the lyric. As de Selincourt observes, "Wordsworth knew a river Dove in Derbyshire, in Yorkshire, and in Westmorland; and it is impossible to say of which he was thinking" (*PW*, 2:472).

The early text of "Strange fits of passion" begins and ends quite differently than does the later, more familiar one:

> 1
> Once, when my love was strong and gay,
>   And like a rose in June,
> I to her cottage bent my way,
>   Beneath the evening Moon.
>   *   *   *   *
>
> 6
> Strange are the fancies that will slide
>   Into a lover's head.

>   "O mercy" to myself I cried
>   "If Lucy should be dead!"
>
>   7
>   I told her this; her laughter light
>   Is ringing in my ears;
>   And when I think upon that night
>   My eyes are dim with tears.

This poem—"a favorite of mine," Dorothy writes to Coleridge before copying it—certainly refers to Dorothy as Lucy, as de Selincourt observes. And, as he notes in connection with "She dwelt among the untrodden ways," "If Coleridge is right in saying that 'A slumber did my spirit seal' was written to suggest what W[ordsworth] would have felt on the death of his sister, this poem had probably a similar source."[22] From the last stanza of the version in the letter to Coleridge, we see not only the origin of the poem in Wordsworth's fearful premonition of Dorothy's death, but Dorothy's own reaction of "laughter light." There can be no doubt, I believe, that the five so-called "Lucy poems" were written about the same imagined death of Dorothy, as Wordsworth writes of his own imagined death in "There was a boy."[23] As I have argued elsewhere, another poem beginning "'Tis said that some have died for love" (written at Grasmere in 1800) is also about Dorothy's imagined death and William's imagined reaction to it.[24]

Most of the poems I have named as being inspired by William's affection for Dorothy are among his best, and the five "Lucy poems" are among the best short lyrics in English. "Tintern Abbey," whatever its structural difficulties, contains some of Wordsworth's finest language as well as his most elevated thoughts. Many of the lyrics on birds and flowers written at Grasmere are among Wordsworth's most characteristic and successful shorter poems. And one quality they convey is shared with Dorothy Wordsworth's journals: deep, spontaneous emotional commitment. The emotional force of the seven-quatrain lyric about Dorothy's death was undoubtedly what moved William to add the stanza that gives it both its name and its categorization as a love poem:

>   Strange fits of passion have I known:
>   And I will dare to tell,

---

22. *PW*, 2:472. See, in confirmation of this judgment, Moorman, *William Wordsworth*, 1:318–19.

23. The confirming evidence of the origin of this poem is found in MS JJ, where "my" appears in the place of "his" (see Onorato, p. 196).

24. *TLS*, 13 September 1974, pp. 979–80.

> But in the Lover's ear alone
> What once to me befell.
>
> (*PW*, 2:29)

Only a lover, says Wordsworth, can really appreciate this poem. Why? Because it is essentially a *passionate poem* about *true love*—not necessarily about passionate love, but about deeply felt, romantic love.

There has been considerable discussion about the question of Lucy's age. In one of the poems she is represented as dying very young, soon after "her virgin bosom" began to "swell."[25] But this aspect of the poems—a mystery if they are thought to have been associated with an actual lover of Wordsworth—becomes clear in the light of William's recurring emotional association of Dorothy with his own childhood and growth. The ambiguity of tone remains in the poems (though the text itself can be shown to speak in terms of a mature woman rather than a child) because Wordsworth loved "Lucy" as his sister from childhood as well as the helpmate of his adult years. William continually alludes to his childhood associations with Dorothy. William and Dorothy, though siblings, had been separated upon the death of their mother in 1778, when William was nine and Dorothy seven years old. There is no evidence that they so much as saw each other again until 1787, when William was seventeen and Dorothy fifteen years old. For sociological, if not genealogical purposes, they were (like Byron and his half-sister Augusta) not siblings but a boy and a girl of similar backgrounds and sympathetic aspirations meeting at a highly impressionable stage in their maturation.[26] The only surviving evidence[27]

---

25. "Three years she grew in sun and shower" (*PW*, 2:214–16). Some commentators have (mistakenly) interpreted the poem as referring to the death of a three-year-old child; but see lines 31–33. Frances C. Ferguson, whose essay "The Lucy Poems: Wordsworth's Quest for a Poetic Object" (*ELH* 40 [1973]: 532–48) takes rigidly anti-biographical analysis of the poems about as far as it can go, argues that "through the course of these poems, Lucy is repeatedly and ever more decisively traced out of existence," and she goes on to assert that "the chief difficulty in talking about these poems lies in our uncertainty about what the name 'Lucy' refers to" (p. 533). Many of the difficulties that Professor Ferguson explores disappear, however, if one recognizes that "Lucy" derives from Wordsworth's conflicting feelings about his sister Dorothy and that the ambiguities in "Lucy's" nature (as well as her eventual disappearance) evolve naturally from Wordsworth's symbolic, externalized resolution of his psychic dilemma.

26. Dorothy's first surviving letter, to Jane Pollard in July 1787, describes her brothers—especially William and John—with deep affection, but conveys no hint of romantic attachment. She clearly looked to her brothers to provide her the stable home that she had lacked since the death of their mother (*Early Letters*, pp. 4–5).

27. One of the nagging difficulties that haunts Wordsworth studies is the absence or mutilation of crucial manuscripts that might have cast light on some of the questions raised here. Dorothy's Alfoxden Journal has disappeared since 1897, and there are erasures and cancellations in the surviving journals by someone other than Dorothy (see Moorman in *Journals*, p. viii). What must have been numerous letters exchanged by the Wordsworths

of William's feelings for his newly found sister emerges from his poems, in which he repeatedly ties his adult relationship with her to their childish play as siblings. Perhaps he needed constantly to reinforce this sense of kinship with Dorothy, reminding himself (probably subconsciously) that Dorothy was an unacceptable object for a romantic or sexual attachment.

If I am correct in discerning this tendency in the pattern of William's poems, then the origin—not of the writing of the "Lucy poems" themselves, but of the dream or premonition of Dorothy's death that provided their emotional impact—may lie in William's subconscious struggle to avoid focusing his obviously strong sexual drive on the sister he lived with for seven years.[28] It would also suggest why, in such poems as "Strange fits of passion" and "The Glow-worm," Wordsworth would shift his imaginative stance from brother to lover. Because he had, for the most part, successfully repressed his desire for Dorothy in his dreams—which end in her death rather than in their forbidden union—he was free at the conscious level to revise them, fully utilizing their emotional energy by casting them as love poems.

IV

Having surveyed the emotional interaction between Dorothy and William, let us glance briefly at the much smaller body of poems William wrote to and about Mary Hutchinson. Here one crucial document is, obviously, "She was a phantom of delight," a poem written in 1804 that is usually pointed to as embodying Wordsworth's strong love for his wife. The poem begins, ostensibly, with an impression of Mary as she appeared to William on their first encounter:

> She was a Phantom of delight
> When first she gleamed upon my sight;
> A lovely Apparition, sent
> To be a moment's ornament. . . .
> (*PW*, 2:213)

---

and Annette Vallon are not to be found, and we know that some references to Annette and Caroline in surviving letters were destroyed by Gordon Graham Wordsworth (see *Early Letters*, p. 282 and n). No letters at all of Mary Hutchinson Wordsworth or Sara Hutchinson survive from the crucial years 1801–1804, and we have none of their letters to each other until 1811. In short, many important questions that may once have been answered in manuscripts that survived the principals cannot be answered, perhaps because the evidence has been destroyed or mutilated by those responsible for safeguarding the manuscripts for posterity. The emergence of previously unknown letters between Wordsworth, Mary, and Dorothy at the Sotheby sale of 6 July 1977 not only provides new evidence for the questions explored in this essay, but also offers some hope that further documents may ultimately come to light.

28. Here are relevant, I suggest, the headaches and tensions that Dorothy's journals record as afflicting William and her during the years of their life together (see p. 187 above).

But in his talks with Isabella Fenwick, Wordsworth explained the origin of these lines and of the poem: "The germ of this poem was four lines composed as a part of the verses on the Highland Girl. Though beginning in this way, it was written from my heart, as is sufficiently obvious" (*PW*, 2:506). If the first four lines were inspired by an unknown Highland girl seen on the six-week Scottish tour that William, Dorothy, and Coleridge took in 1803 (while Mary remained behind, caring for her first child), we must eliminate the first stanza from serious consideration as being about Mary—for the subsequent lines of that stanza merely elaborate the first four. The third stanza is of little help also, filled as it is with philosophical abstractions in which Mary is called a "machine" and "A Being breathing thoughtful breath, / A Traveller between life and death." The remaining stanza reads:

> I saw her upon nearer view,
> A Spirit, yet a Woman too!
> Her household motions light and free,
> And steps of virgin-liberty;
> A countenance in which did meet
> Sweet records, promises as sweet;
> A Creature not too bright or good
> For human nature's daily food;
> For transient sorrows, simple wiles,
> Praise, blame, love, kisses, tears, and smiles.

Here, I submit, is the true measure of William's feelings for Mary, articulated about two years after their wedding but referring to the feelings that determined his decision to marry her. He was attracted by her "household motions," her "virgin-liberty," a countenance combining "sweet records" with "promises as sweet," and he was glad that she was a "Woman" "not too bright or good / For human nature's daily food." The "daily food" image is fundamental to William's conception of Mary, as is evident from his poem "To M.H.," written late in December 1799, soon after he and Dorothy had taken up their residence at Dove Cottage.

> Our walk was far among the ancient trees:
> There was no road, nor any woodman's path;
> But a thick umbrage . . .
>   . . . of itself had made
> A track, that brought us to a slip of lawn,
> And a small bed of water in the woods.
> *   *   *   *

> The spot was made by Nature for herself;
> The travellers know it not, and 'twill remain
> Unknown to them; but it is beautiful;
> And if a man should plant his cottage near,
> Should sleep beneath the shelter of its trees,
> And blend its waters with his daily meal,
> He would so love it, that in his death-hour
> Its image would survive among his thoughts:
> And therefore, my sweet MARY, this still Nook,
> With all its beeches, we have named for You!
>
> (*PW*, 2:118)

It should be obvious that William here uses the place as a metaphor for Mary and that he is the "man" who may "plant his cottage" in this "still Nook" and "blend its waters with his *daily meal*," just as in "A Farewell" he speaks of Mary as "A gentle maid" who will come to the "little Nook of mountain-ground" at Dove Cottage and to it "herself will wed" (*PW*, 2:23–24). And, for those to whom these two "nooks" recall that other isolated, "virgin bower" in "Nutting," it may be equally clear that I shall suggest that all this "blending" and "daily food" are metaphors for sexual union. If, in "Nutting," Wordsworth recalled with regret his ravage of "one dear nook . . . a virgin scene" to convey to Dorothy during their dangerous isolated proximity at Goslar the perils of excessive passionate license, it is equally clear that Mary provided the proper and acceptable substitute object for those strong passions that were chained within William. She was acceptable to William as a "virgin" at "liberty," with graceful "household motions" and the promise of sweet "daily food" (*PW*, 2:213).

One of the most striking corroborations of this judgment is to be found in two sonnets, the first composed by Wordsworth on the day of his marriage as he, Mary, and Dorothy traveled toward Grasmere. At sunset among the clouds and light "in the western sky, we saw shapes of Castles, Ruins among groves, . . . a minster with its tower unusually distinct, minarets in another quarter, and a round Grecian Temple also" (*Journals*, p. 156). The sonnet, beginning "Dark and more dark the shades of evening fell," describes the scene faithfully as Dorothy records it before concluding: "but we felt the while / We should forget them; they are of the sky, / And from our earthly memory fade away" (*PW*, 3:25–26). The second sonnet, written sometime before March 1804, carries further the message that the poet must (regretfully) renounce the sky-castles in favor of the more mundane pleasures:

> Those words were uttered as in pensive mood
> We turned, departing from that solemn sight:
> A contrast and reproach to *gross delight*,
> And life's unspiritual pleasures *daily wooed!*
> But now upon this thought I cannot brood;
> It is unstable as a dream of night;
> Nor will I praise a cloud, however bright,
> Disparaging Man's gifts, and *proper food*.
> * * * * *
> The immortal Mind craves objects that endure:
> These cleave to it; from these it cannot roam,
> Nor they from it: their fellowship is secure.
> (*PW*, 3:26; italics added)

"Wordsworth is by nature incapable of being in Love," wrote Coleridge to Henry Crabb Robinson in 1811, "tho' no man more tenderly attached— hence he ridicules the existence of any other passion, than a compound of Lust with Esteem & Friendship, confined to one Object, first by accidents of Association, and permanently, by the force of Habit & a sense of Duty. Now this will do very well—it will suffice to make a good Husband— . . . but still it is not *Love*."[29] So, at least, Wordsworth's feelings for Mary, several years after marriage, appeared to Coleridge (whose own romantic attachment had much greater proportions of both fantasy and impossibility). And however much one discredits Coleridge, there remain Wordsworth's poems written to and about Mary that invariably stress the habitual and the practical, the "compound of Lust with Esteem & Friendship," and there remains the clear tone of his "poem on going for Mary" and the two sonnets written about the day he got her, saying he had knowingly sacrificed a romantic joy to cleave to "secure fellowship" and Man's "proper food."

Aside from the ambiguity of his own feelings, there was only one obstacle to William's union with Mary, and this was the known—and perhaps declared—affection of his brother John for her. We must assume that Mary had made clear to the younger brother her preference for William, but John's farewell letter, written "when he has returned from a voyage to

---

29. *Collected Letters of Samuel Taylor Coleridge*, ed. Earl Leslie Griggs, vol. 3 (Oxford: Clarendon Press, 1959), p. 305. It may be significant that Wordsworth composed "Yarrow Unvisited," which celebrates the free play of the visionary imagination, as a result of his Scottish tour with Coleridge and Dorothy in 1803, whereas he wrote "Yarrow Visited," a derivative poem that tells how the poet's loss of his "waking dream" was mitigated by a fine (though inferior) reality, in September 1814 while touring with Mary and Sara Hutchinson (*PW*, 3:83–85, 106–8).

receive her announcement of her plan to marry shows," the editor of Mary's letters writes, "much deeper emotion": "I have been reading your letter over and over again, My dearest Mary, till tears have come into my eyes and I know not how to express myself—Thou art a kind and dear Creature.—But whatever fate Befal me I shall love thee to the last, and bear thy memory with me to the grave."[30] "John, (who is to be the sailor,) has a most excellent heart," Dorothy had written to Jane Pollard in July 1787, and of the Wordsworth children's inheritance, she added: "John poor fellow! says that . . . two hundred pounds will be enough to fit him out, and he should wish Wm to have the rest for his education . . ." (*Early Letters*, pp. 3–4). Thus William, who began by sharing part of John's inheritance for his education, ended by appropriating John's beloved for his "daily food." And, though I do not intend to pursue this topic, William's resultant naggings of guilt had important consequences for another group of his greatest poems.[31]

V

Another subject there is no space to pursue here in detail is the large group of Wordsworth's early poems centering on the theme of "Guilt and Sorrow" (which is the ultimate title of one of them). Aside from the ballads and lyrics that derive from his feelings for Dorothy and for Mary Hutchinson, poems on this theme constitute almost all the poems about romantic love written before 1807. Included are such excellent works as "The Ruined Cottage" (later incorporated into the first book of *The Excursion*), "The Thorn," and "Ruth." In each of these poems, a loving, trusting woman marries or is seduced by a weak or thoughtless or undisciplined young man and is then abandoned with a child or two that she is unable to care for. These poems—which relate thematically to Wordsworth's many early poems and passages on such topics as poor, vagrant women or the abandoned Indian woman—clearly embody Wordsworth's feelings of guilt and sorrow for his own abandonment of Annette Vallon. All these are, in their published versions, rather long narratives, usually filtered through the consciousness of an objective observer (such as the Pedlar in *The Excursion*, or the curious retired sea captain in "The Thorn") whose presence is

---

30. *The Letters of Mary Wordsworth*, p. xxiii. The full text of this letter is to be found in *The Letters of John Wordsworth*, ed. Carl H. Ketcham (Ithaca: Cornell University Press, 1969), pp. 125–26.

31. I have not presumed to encroach upon the area of the relations between William and John Wordsworth in 1802 because Irene Taylor has stated the case so well in "By Peculiar Grace: Wordsworth in 1802," in *The Evidence of the Imagination*, pp. 119–41.

clearly intended to mitigate the pain generated by the tale itself.[32] After William and Dorothy visited Annette and Caroline at Calais in 1802, the only further poem on this theme is "Vaudracour and Julia," at one time destined for *The Prelude*. That retrospective, official account of the romance seems finally to have exorcized the demon of guilt and sorrow that had driven Wordsworth to so much of his best early poetry.

Likewise, after William's marriage to Mary in October 1802, there are no more passionate lyrics like the "Lucy poems." Instead, in 1802, Wordsworth, who had earlier written few sonnets that he thought worth preserving,[33] suddenly composed eighteen sonnets—some good, some excellent—most of them during his trip to see Annette and Caroline. As Carl Woodring observes, "His sonnet-writing began, then, in a period of great agitation. He probably had this private agitation much in mind when he wrote the sonnet beginning, 'Nuns fret not at their convent's narrow room.'"[34] The emotional force of his visits with Caroline on the beach at Calais and of his love for England in its confrontation with France is shaped into fourteen-line jewels. After this date Wordsworth never published a new volume of poetry without including one or more sonnets.[35]

---

32. A variant of this theme appears in "Michael," which—though partially based on the objective story associated with the sheepfold in Green-head Ghyll—generates much of its emotional force from the failure of Luke to vindicate his tutelage by Nature and the trust placed in him by his parents. Like the other poems on the "guilt and sorrow" theme, the story of Michael and Luke is told by a narrator who centers on the reactions of the betrayed party. Like the Youth who seduces Ruth and like the wayward husband in "The Ruined Cottage," Luke seeks "a hiding-place beyond the seas." The emotional power of this poem derives, I suggest, from Wordsworth's own passionate feelings about his failure to carry out his responsibility toward Annette Vallon, though by 1800 he was able to give his feelings further aesthetic distance through the story of Michael's devotion to his fathers' land and through the poet-narrator's own quest for a different kind of permanence—his desire for the immortality of poetry through which to relate the homely history "For the delight of a few natural hearts / And . . . for the sake / Of *youthful Poets, who* among these hills / *Will be my second self when I am gone*" (PW, 2:81; italics added).

33. The sonnet "Written in Very Early Youth" ("Calm is all nature as a resting wheel"; PW, 1:3), which de Selincourt dates in its present form ca. 1795-1797, but which Wordsworth retrieved and first published in the *Morning Post* on 13 February 1802, is one. On the questionable "Sonnet on Seeing Miss Helen Maria Williams Weep at a Tale of Distress," see Carl Woodring, *Politics in English Romantic Poetry* (Cambridge: Harvard University Press, 1970), p. 339n. Mark Reed, in *Wordsworth: The Chronology of the Early Years, 1770-1799* (Cambridge: Harvard University Press, 1967), lists also "Sonnet Written by Mr. —— Immediately after the Death of His Wife" (p. 19) and two unpublished sonnets preserved in manuscripts (pp. 22, 23).

34. *Wordsworth*, corrected ed. (Cambridge: Harvard University Press, 1968), p. 157.

35. I base this assertion on my personal conviction, held since 1963 and expressed at a number of conferences but not yet argued in print, that Wordsworth restructured *The Prelude* from thirteen to fourteen books to give it the form of the Italian sonnet, with the books now forming natural groupings of four/four/three/three, with the strongest break occurring between the first eight books and the last six.

The control that the sonnet form provided for his intense emotions of 1802 was later supplanted by the support it gave to his flagging imagination in such sequences as *The River Duddon, Ecclesiastical Sketches,* and "Sonnets on the Punishment of Death." This complete reversal of the needs of both his psyche and his poetry is epitomized in one of the few important poems that is not a sonnet and that he began after 1808. "Laodamia," Wordsworth told Isabella Fenwick, "cost me more trouble than almost anything of equal length I have ever written" (*PW,* 2:519). Why this should be so provides the focus of my final speculative look into the workings of Wordsworth's imagination.

"Laodamia" is based on a classical legend treated by Euripides, Virgil, and Ovid. Laodamia was the wife of Protesilaus, the first Greek to be killed by the Trojans. In her bereavement, as Wordsworth relates the tale, Laodamia prays to Jove to restore her husband to her. When the god grants her request and the shade of Protesilaus joins her for a three-hour visit, she is delighted and suggests that they go to bed:

> "No Spectre greets me,—no vain Shadow this;
> Come, blooming Hero, place thee by my side!
> Give, on this well-known couch, one nuptial kiss
> To me, this day, a second time thy bride!"

But at this proposal, "Jove frowned in heaven" and her husband admonished Laodamia for her light and irreverent thoughts:

> ". . . Earth destroys
> Those raptures duly—Erebus disdains:
> Calm pleasures there abide—majestic pains.
>
> "Be taught, O faithful Consort, to control
> Rebellious passion: for the Gods approve
> The depth, and not the tumult of the soul;
> A fervent, not ungovernable, love."
>   (*PW,* 2:269; lines 70–76)

> "And Thou, though strong in love, art all too weak
> In reason, in self-government too slow;
> *   *   *   *   *
> Learn, by a mortal yearning, to ascend—
> Seeking a higher object. Love was given,
> Encouraged, sanctioned, chiefly for that end; . . . ."
>   (*PW,* 2:271; lines 139–40, 145–47)

Laodamia, however, refuses to accept her husband's advice, and when "Hermes reappears" to carry off the shade of Protesilaus, she shrieks, and—anticipating the ending of Keats's *Lamia*—"on the palace-floor a lifeless corse She lay."

The poem's final regular six-line stanza, in which the poet passes judgment on Laodamia, was repeatedly revised during Wordsworth's lifetime, with the severity of the judgment increased dramatically. The first version, published in 1815 and 1820, reads:

> Ah, judge her gently who so deeply loved!
> Her, who, in reason's spite, yet without crime,
> Was in a trance of passion thus removed;
> Delivered from the galling yoke of time
> And these frail elements—to gather flowers
> Of blissful quiet 'mid unfading bowers.

But the final version (1845) is much harsher:

> Thus, all in vain exhorted and reproved,
> She perished; and, as for a wilful crime,
> By the just Gods whom no weak pity moved,
> Was doomed to wear out her appointed time,
> Apart from happy Ghosts, that gather flowers
> Of blissful quiet 'mid unfading bowers.
> (lines 158–63)

The poem concludes with eleven irregularly rhymed lines that, Wordsworth said, had provided the germ of his poem. They describe "a knot of spiry trees" which grew "for ages" along the Hellespont; whenever they grew tall enough to see the walls of Troy, "the trees' tall summits withered at the sight; / A constant interchange of growth and blight!"

If Wordsworth wrote the poem simply, as he told Isabella Fenwick, because "the incident of the trees growing and withering put the subject into my thoughts, and I wrote with the hope of giving it a loftier tone than . . . has been given it by any of the Ancients" (*PW*, 2:518), then his numerous revisions of the poem between manuscript and print, in proof in 1815, and during the next thirty years may simply indicate how slowly and intermittently his stream of inspiration flowed after the great years 1797–1808. But close examination of the text of the poem, as it evolved in proofs in 1815 and as Wordsworth revised it, suggests other possible reasons for his having written a moving poem on the theme of withering treetops and the need for a woman to control her passions.

Two of Wordsworth's children died in 1812, four-year-old Catharine in June and six-year-old Thomas late in November. Wordsworth tried to bear the deaths with Christian stoicism. Mary reacted more openly, especially to the death of Catharine. William wrote to his brother Christopher: "I have but a poor account to give of Mary. . . . she is yet little recovered from the deplorable dejection in which I found her. Her health has suffered: but I clearly see that neither thought nor religion nor the endeavours of friends, can at once quiet a heart that has been disturbed by such an affliction."[36] When Thomas died, however, Wordsworth depicted Mary as stronger in meeting their common suffering:

My Wife bears the loss of her Child with striking fortitude. . . . Miss Hutchinson also supports her sorrow as ought to be done. For myself dear Southey I dare not say in what state of mind I am; I loved the Boy with the utmost love of which my soul is capable, and he is taken from me—yet in the agony of my spirit in surrendering such a treasure I feel a thousand times richer than if I had never possessed it. God comfort and save you and all our friends and us all from a repetition of such trials—O Southey feel for me! (2 December 1818; *MY,* 2:51)

In January 1813 William began drafting additional lines for Book II and Book III of *The Excursion,* adding to the story of the Solitary, as the chief cause of that man's disillusionment, the deaths of a young son and daughter and the consequent alienation and (ultimately) the death of his beloved wife. De Selincourt was convinced by these additions that Wordsworth "was led to imagine personal bereavement as a leading contributory cause of his [the Solitary's] despondency by his own passionate grief at the loss of his two children" (*PW,* 5:419), but no one has, I believe, commented upon the significance of lines like these about the Solitary's marriage to his "Anna" (which again support the theme of the earlier sections of this paper):

"To my heart's wish, my tender Mate became
The thankful captive of maternal bonds;

---

36. *The Letters of William and Dorothy Wordsworth,* ed. Ernest de Selincourt, *The Middle Years,* revised by Mary Moorman and Alan G. Hill, 2 vols. (Oxford: Clarendon Press, 1969–1970), Part II, 26. Though there may be some confusion (since Parts I and II of *The Middle Years* are also numbered as volumes 2 and 3 of *The Letters*), I shall follow the established practice of Wordsworthians in citing these two volumes as *MY* 1 and *MY* 2 (plus the page references).

Poetry of Familiarity 211

> * * * * *
> Her whose submissive spirit was to me
> Rule and restraint—my guardian—shall I say
> That earthly Providence, whose guiding love
> Within a port of rest had lodged me safe;
> Safe from temptation . . . ."
> (Book III.554-55, 563-67; *PW*, 5:94)

Or these lines, about the aftermath of the bereavement of the Solitary and his wife:

> "Calm as a frozen lake when ruthless winds
> Blow fiercely, agitating earth and sky,
> The Mother now remained. . . .
> * * * *
> This second visitation had no power
> To shake; but only to bind up and seal;
> And to establish thankfulness of heart
> In Heaven's determinations, ever just.
> The eminence whereon her spirit stood,
> Mine was unable to attain. Immense
> The space that severed us! . . ."
> (Book III.650ff.; *PW*, 5:98-99)

From Dorothy's letter to Catherine Clarkson in January 1813, we learn how the family could not separate their sadness from their locale in the Rectory, Grasmere:

> in spite of all we could do, the very air of the place—the stillness—the occasional sounds, and above all the view of that school, our darling's pride and joy—that church-yard his playground—all oppressed us and do continue to oppress us with unutterable sadness— (*MY*, 2:60)

And in this letter Dorothy tells of their determination to move to Rydal Mount. On 1 May the family removed to their new home. In a letter to Francis Wrangham on 28 August 1813, Wordsworth speaks briefly of his children's deaths as a subject almost too painful to face. On 28 April 1814, he writes to Thomas Poole of the "heavy affliction" of the deaths and suggests that he has been unable to compose poetry. Later, in November 1814, Wordsworth writes to his brother Christopher that William, his second surviving son, is very ill. Between these two dates Wordsworth wrote his poem about the need to control passions, deriving it from a myth about how the very trees withered when they viewed the place that had been the cause of two lovers' deaths.

The story of Laodamia centers on a grief of bereavement, but Protesilaus's admonition is directed against misuse of the sexual passion. Is Wordsworth here using a metaphor to strengthen himself and his family in their Christian stoicism? Just as we have seen him use food as a metaphor for sex, we have seen him employ a sexual metaphor for a psychic problem of another nature in "Nutting" and we have seen him turn his fears about his sister's death back into love poems. But, as we have also seen, the conscious use of the sexual metaphor seems, in Wordsworth's case, to have released in a disguised form something otherwise trapped below his consciousness. Thus, when in the first published version of "Laodamia" he uses a highly charged sexual word in an unusual way and then entirely revises the line in the next edition, we can speculate on two possible reasons for the original choice and the revision. In 1815, the lines finally designated 74-76 read:

> Be taught, O faithful Consort, to control
> Rebellious passion: for the Gods approve
> The depth, and not the tumult of the soul;
> The fervour—not the impotence of love.[37]

In 1820, he revised the fourth line of the stanza to read: "A fervent, not ungovernable, love." Wordsworth's use of "impotence" conforms with *OED* definition 3, "Lack of self-restraint, violent passion." This usage, now obsolete, finds its latest *OED* examples in Milton's *Paradise Lost* (II.156) and Pope's translation of *The Iliad* (XXIV.53).[38] With such precedents, Wordsworth may well have included the word for its archaic precision. In this case, his revision is explicable as an attempt to make the line more immediately comprehensible and to avoid suggesting irrelevant meanings, such as *impotence* in its most usual modern meaning: *OED* 2b, "Complete absence of sexual power; usually said of the male." To a student of Shelley, however, who has traced from the letters of Shelley and *his* Mary through the complexities of the maniac's speeches in *Julian and Maddalo* the

---

37. Wordsworth's *Poems, including Lyrical Ballads and the Miscellaneous Pieces of the Author, . . . in Two Volumes* (London: Longman, Hurst, Rees, Orme, and Brown, 1815), 1:228.

38. The words *impotence* and *impotent* occur eight times in the texts analyzed in Lane Cooper's *Concordance to the Poems of William Wordsworth* (London: Smith, Elder, 1911). In every instance, the context shows that the meaning intended is either *OED* 1 ("utter inability or weakness; helplessness") or 2a ("Want of physical power; feebleness") for the noun and either 1 ("powerless, helpless; ineffective") or 2a ("Physically weak;...decrepit") for the adjective.

effect of the deaths of two children within one year into the dim world of *their* marriage bed,[39] it seems more than possible that the unusual diction in line 76 of "Laodamia" may point to another kind of withering in the wake of the Wordsworths' bereavement.

In her January 1813 letter to Catherine Clarkson, Dorothy had described Mary Wordsworth as being "as thin as it is possible to be except when the body is worn out by slow disease" (*MY*, 2:60), suggesting the state of Mary's health to be such as William in *The Excursion* pictures the Solitary's wife Anna, who "fell / Into a gulf obscure of silent grief," and, wasting away in his arms, "left me, on this earth, disconsolate!" (*PW*, 5:99). Sara Hutchinson's letters throughout 1813, even after the move to Rydal Mount, give evidence that, though life in the household had returned to normal at the surface, Mary's spirits remained precarious. On 23 June she wrote to Thomas Monkhouse: "We have had abundance of other visitors; I think we have scarcely been one day unengaged for the last month."[40] In the next surviving letter to Mary Monkhouse Hutchinson, Sara writes of her sister Mary: "Her spirits have I think been better—at least in company—and except when in bed she has never been out of it [i.e., company] for many weeks" (SH, *Letters*, p. 58). Forced to keep up her spirits in public because of the stream of summer visitors to Rydal Mount, Mary Wordsworth may well have had only one place to vent her true emotions—when she retired to bed. And if the emotional distance that Wordsworth describes coming between the Solitary and his wife after their children's deaths reflects, in part, an emotional distancing in Wordsworth's own marriage (a relationship Coleridge had described in 1811 as "a compound of Lust with Esteem & Friendship"), one element may have passed out of Wordsworth's feelings for Mary, never to return.

A year later, on 18 July 1814, William, Mary, and Sara Hutchinson set out on a tour of Scotland. By 3 August 1814, Sara could write to Mrs. Thomas Hutchinson: "dearest Mary is much improved by her journey; she truly enjoys herself; & William is happy that the journey has accomplished this his chief aim" (SH, *Letters*, p. 77). By October 1814, Mary Wordsworth had, by all the available evidence, resumed her accustomed equanimity. At the same time,[41] Wordsworth was composing "Laodamia," suggested by a

---

39. See Donald H. Reiman, *Shelley and his Circle*, vol. 6 (Cambridge: Harvard University Press, 1973), pp. 857-65.

40. *The Letters of Sara Hutchinson from 1800 to 1835*, ed. Kathleen Coburn (London: Routledge & Kegan Paul, 1954), pp. 55-56 (hereafter cited as SH, *Letters*).

41. Mark L. Reed in *Wordsworth: The Chronology of the Middle Years, 1800-1815* (Cambridge: Harvard University Press, 1975) dates the composition of the 130-line original version of "Laodamia" as ca. mid-October to 27 October (pp. 53, 580) and that of lines 115-20 ca. early February, "certainly by 5 Feb" (pp. 589, 590).

story of trees that repeatedly wither when confronted by a scene of former anguish, and including both an unusual use of the phrase "impotence of love" and stern admonitions to a woman to control her passions in the presence of a bodily lover who was yet only the ghost of his former self.

The possible inference is complicated further when we read in one of Mary Wordsworth's letters to Dorothy on 29 October 1814: "Poor William's right hand is crippled—the speck which he was examining thru the microscope last Saturday has proved another plaguy boil. It is situated between the thumb and forefinger of his right hand and carries the inflammation in a red line all the way to the arm-pit. I hope it may not be so tedious as his last was . . . but for this he meant to have written to you . . . ."[42] Here we have impotence of yet another kind and definition, a series of boils that incapacitate Wordsworth from writing. Is there a causal relationship among these phenomena that seem to coalesce in the various meanings of a single word? Does the progressively harsher judgment on Laodamia in late editions of the poem suggest that Wordsworth felt increasingly threatened by both conjugal and literary expectations that he was incapable of fulfilling?

These hints and complexities do not yield themselves to certainties. But I hope that my agnostic speculations about some of the possible motive forces behind "Laodamia," added to the somewhat more complete evidence surrounding the poems of 1797–1808, will contribute to the understanding of the kinds of circumstances that drove Wordsworth to produce great poetry. Like most artists, he seems to have had psychic wounds—feelings of guilt and isolation; hidden fears of incestuous passion and equally hidden guilt for dreaming Dorothy's death; guilt concerning his brother's sacrifices; sorrow at the deaths of loved ones; and, quite possibly, resentment toward his wife for his own feelings of sexual and creative inadequacy. And when these wounds are seen as the source of Wordsworth's poems that we all acknowledge to be great, the most obvious answer to those who ponder the later decline of Wordsworth's powers is that, one by one, the ghosts that haunted the poet's psyche were exorcized either by the march of events or by the transmutation of emotion into poetry.

Wordsworth's greatest poems—those nuggets of gold washed down the stream of time—derive from a massif that on its surface stonily resisted the winds of guilt, self-doubt, and despair. Whereas Coleridge was like a tree whipped, buffeted, and twisted by his fears, doubts, guilt, and sense of

---

42. *The Letters of Mary Wordsworth*, pp. 22-23. Mark L. Reed suggests that Mary began this letter on 27 October.

isolation, William Wordsworth flung back each blast of life's emotional storm in "an echo and a light unto eternity." Here again, his sister Dorothy knew him best, and he himself became her voice, speaking to us of William's sublime egoism, poetically triumphant over circumstance:

> There is an Eminence,—of these our hills
> The last that parleys with the setting sun;
> *   *   *   *   *
> . . . this Peak, so high
> Above us, and so distant in its height,
> Is visible; and often seems to send
> Its own deep quiet to restore our hearts.
> *   *   *   *   *
> . . . 'Tis in truth
> The loneliest place we have among the clouds.
> And She who dwells with me, whom I have loved
> With such communion, that no place on earth
> Can ever be a solitude to me,
> Hath to this lonely Summit given my Name.[43]

43. "Poems on the Naming of Places," III (*PW*, 2:115), written and published in 1800.

12

The Beauty of Buttermere as Fact and Romantic Symbol

This *paper, like much scholarly writing, grew almost by chance after I serendipitously ran across a fact (while reading for another purpose) that seemed likely to be useful to other scholars. While looking through volumes of the* Annual Register *for information on the death of someone mentioned in* Shelley and his Circle, *I found the obituary notice of Mary Harrison, "the Beauty of Buttermere" (whom I knew, of course, from* The Prelude).

Shortly afterwards, when I read the notes on Mary Robinson and John Hatfield in David Erdman's edition of Coleridge's Essays on His Times, *which I was then reviewing (see Item 5), I called David, told him that I'd found the information on Mary Robinson's death, and asked whether he wanted to do anything with it. He said that he was through with his work on that subject, but that he had a number of notes on it from contemporary newspapers that he'd be glad to send to me if I wished to pursue it further. Thus my attempt at generosity was topped by David's; I always felt that the paper (except for my reading of* The Prelude *as a sonnet in section V) was written on behalf of both David Erdman and me.*

From the start, I tried to approach the subject from the same socio-political perspective that I had found so appealing in a number of Erdman's best essays, including his studies of Byron's political orientation, his work on Coleridge's careers as parliamentary reporter and political journalist, and his fine essay entitled "Wordsworth as Heartsworth" in The Evidence of the Imagination. *The chief difference between my essay and those studies of his is that I concentrate on various writers' reactions to a single event (of more nearly sensational than national or international historical interest), rather than on one writer's reactions to a series of major historical or political events. I use the event as a touchstone both to measure the attitudes of several contemporaries toward people of lower social class, seeing how involved they became in the quite different tragedies of the two protagonists, and to compare those reactions to some modern responses. The focus of this essay is, then, less psychological than sociological; it relates most closely, perhaps, to "Shelley as Agrarian Reactionary."*

Though I did not center on any particular writer or work, the major literary treatment of the Beauty of Buttermere is, clearly, in Book VII of The Prelude. *For a number of years, I had been talking at conferences—as well as to students in my classes—about the idea that Wordsworth had revised* The Prelude *from thirteen to fourteen (shorter) books in order to put it into the sonnet form. This idea originated when I was preparing to teach the poem to my first group of graduate students at the University of Illinois during the summer of 1963. I first brought it up for public discussion after R. A. Foakes's paper at the Rydal Mount Wordsworth Summer School in 1971. Not discouraged by Foakes's response (he pronounced the idea "rubbish"), I raised it again during a discussion "On Teaching* The Prelude*" sponsored by the Wordsworth-Coleridge Association at the MLA convention in 1975 and mentioned it in print in 1978 in note 35 of "Poetry of Familiarity" (Item 11). To this point, I had not found the time to write up the supporting evidence.*

That effort became possible during the summer of 1981, when I taught a graduate seminar at the University of Washington (for the first time using the Norton Critical Edition of The Prelude*). That summer I was also reading manuscripts for Don H. Bialostosky and, especially, Raimonda Modiano (who had earlier read an outline of my ideas on the structure of both* Biographia Literaria *and* The Prelude*). With them, I discussed Wordsworth and Coleridge for hours. My analysis of the 1850* Prelude *as Italian sonnet was finally put on paper after Jared Curtis invited me that summer to give two lectures at Simon Fraser University; the second I entitled "The Prelude as Macrosonnet."*

In the summer of 1982, I mentioned the structure of The Prelude *when I spoke on "The Beauty of Buttermere" at the Dove Cottage Wordsworth Conference. A few months later, learning that someone who had attended that conference was proposing a paper on the subject of* The Prelude *as macrosonnet, I decided that it was time for me to publish a version of the analysis. So in revising "The Beauty of Buttermere" paper for publication in* Criticism *(26 [Spring 1984]: 139–70), I expanded the material in this section. A more detailed argument appears in Chapter 4 of* Intervals of Inspiration *as part of a full exposition of Wordsworth's development as a poet.*

Besides the help of the friends already mentioned—and, as always in the past dozen years, Hélène Dworzan (Reiman)—I had the benefit of a number of useful reactions from Romanticists at the meetings where I explored my ideas. There were also specific suggestions in conversations with Carl Woodring, William Ruddick, and Mary Wedd and, later, from Michael Scrivener and Clifford Siskin at Criticism. *Since the publication of "The Beauty of Buttermere," Lawrence Kramer, in a paper at MLA in December 1984, provided a psychological reading of Book VII of* The Prelude *that dovetails very well with my sociological perspective on Mary Robinson's significance for Wordsworth.*

Readers of *The Prelude* have long been charmed and impressed by Wordsworth's depiction, in Book Seventh of that poem, of Mary, "Maiden of Buttermere." Other, similarly impressive passages—such as the Discharged Soldier, the Drowned Man of Esthwaite, and the Penrith Beacon—have received extensive critical analyses, and their symbolic meanings to William Wordsworth (and to various readers) have been adduced again and again. But in the twentieth century, relatively little has been written about the significance, either within the symbolic structure of *The Prelude* or to Wordsworth the human being and his contemporaries, of Mary Robinson, from whose potentially tragic true story Wordsworth drew what were clearly for him important emotional resonances.

The factual materials needed to begin exploring the symbolic significance of Mary, the Beauty of Buttermere, have long been available in the notes to the de Selincourt–Darbishire edition of *The Prelude*. But bare facts, sans the emotional and attitudinal reactions that those facts elicited from Wordsworth and his contemporaries, cannot recreate in the reader—or, apparently, in most critics—the interest that the same recital of facts would have held for the Romantics. Not only William Wordsworth, but Dorothy Wordsworth, Samuel Taylor Coleridge, the Lambs, and Thomas De Quincey all left records of their interest and involvement in the story of the Beauty of Buttermere. When analysis of these documents is combined with a brief glance at the attitudes of the British public generally, it will be easier for us to understand why the seduction of Mary Robinson in 1802 caused a public reaction comparable to the kidnapping in 1932 of the infant son of Charles A. Lindbergh, the popular hero of American aviation, or the assassination in 1980 of John Lennon, the Beatle. Because of a prior identification by at least a segment of the public with the victims of these three events, each of these crimes produced a greater impact on the popular imagination than did any other seduction, kidnapping, or murder during the particular years in which these crimes occurred. To know what the seduction of the Beauty of Buttermere signified to Wordsworth and his contemporaries—especially to those who came from or who chose to make their homes in the Lake Country—we must begin with an outsider's discovery of this flower who, though born to blush unseen, was held up for public viewing during the rise of tourist literature about the Lakes at the end of the eighteenth century.

I

The Beauty of Buttermere first impinged upon the consciousness of the British public in travel writings by Joseph Budworth (later Joseph Palmer;

1756–1815),[1] a miscellaneous writer and frequent contributor to *The Gentleman's Magazine*. In 1792, Budworth, in a superficial and sentimental travel book entitled *A Fortnight's Ramble to the Lakes*, wrote of staying at the Fish Inn on Buttermere and encountering the landlord's daughter, whom he pictured in the conventional language of the day:

She brought in part of our dinner, and seemed to be about fifteen. Her hair was thick and long, of a dark brown, and, though unadorned with ringlets, did not seem to want them; her face was a fine oval, with full eyes, and lips as red as vermilion; her cheeks had more of the lily than the rose; and although she had never been out of the village (and I hope will have no ambition to wish it), she has a manner about her which seemed better calculated to set off dress than to dress *her*. She was a very Lavinia,

Seeming, when unadorn'd, adorn'd the most!

When we first saw her at her distaff, after she had got the better of her first fears, she looked an angel; and I doubt not but she is the reigning lily of the valley.

Ye travellers of the Lakes, if you visit this obscure spot, such you will find the fair SALLY OF BUTTERMERE.[2]

Captain Budworth's book soon became a companion for gentlemen touring in the Lake Country, and though Budworth had disguised (or misremembered) Mary Robinson's name, the Fish Inn at Buttermere was a location that could not be mistaken. According to Norman Nicholson, "Mary Robinson found herself the object of much curiosity both from tourists and from the local people . . . . and the walls of the Fish Inn were scrawled with compliments to her beauty." Returning to the site in 1798, Captain Budworth saw the effects of giving a simple country girl national publicity, and he tried, in his condescending way, to reduce the damage that his former encomium might have caused. In *The Gentleman's Magazine* for January 1800, he wrote:

Mary Robinson has really a heavenly countenance, yet is she far from a perfect beauty; and in a few years she may even grow too large ever to be thought what she now is. She is nineteen, and very tall; her voice is sweetly modulated; and in every point of manners she appeared such as might be fitted,

Or, to shine in Courts with unaffected ease, &c. . . . taking the opportunity of our being alone, I told her I knew the author of "A Fortnight's Ramble," and as such had something to say to her. She curtsied respectfully; and taking her by the hand I began:

---

1. For Budworth, see *Dictionary of National Biography* (*DNB*) under "Palmer."
2. Quoted from *The Lake District: An Anthology,* ed. Norman Nicholson (Harmondsworth, Middlesex: Penguin Books, 1982), pp. 290–91.

"Mary, I wrote it; and rejoice in having had such an opportunity of minutely observing the propriety of your behaviour. You may remember, I advised you, in that Book, never to leave your native valley. Your age and situation require the utmost care. Strangers WILL come, and have come, purposely to see you; and some of them with very bad intentions. We hope you will never suffer from them; but never cease to be upon your guard. You really are not so handsome as you promised to be; and I have long wished, by conversation like this, to do away what mischief the flattering character I gave of you may expose you to. Be merry and wise."

She told me she sincerely thanked me; and said, "I hope, Sir, I ever have, and trust I always shall take care of myself."[3]

II

Unfortunately, Budworth's article in *The Gentleman's Magazine* may have struck some of its readers as a challenge to be met, and within three years, Samuel Taylor Coleridge had to bring the public less happy news of Mary Robinson. From October through December 1802, Coleridge told her later story in a series of (unsigned) articles he wrote for *The Morning Post*, the very titles of which outline its tragic development.[4] In "Romantic Marriage" (11 October 1802), Coleridge tells how "a young woman, celebrated by the tourists under the name of *The Beauty of Buttermere*," "the daughter of an old couple, named Robinson, who kept a poor little pot-house at the foot of the small lake of Buttermere," had married "a Gentleman, calling himself Alexander Augustus Hope," member of Parliament for Linlithgowshire "and brother to the Earl of Hopetown." In the course of this account, Coleridge writes that, though Mary Robinson, "now about thirty," is "rather gap-toothed, and somewhat pock-fretten," she "has long attracted the notice of every visitor by her exquisite elegance," "her beautiful long hair," and her "fine Italian hand-writing"; he also adds: "she has ever maintained an irreproachable character, is a good daughter, and a modest, sensible, and observant woman." Even in delivering the news of Mary Robinson's good fortune, however, Coleridge adds a note of concerned doubt: "the good people of Keswick," he writes, take an interest in "the welfare of the beauty of Buttermere, . . . and they await with anxiety the moment when they shall receive decisive proofs that the bridegroom is the real person whom he describes himself to be" (1:357–58).

The publication of Coleridge's article of 11 October elicited two letters from Charles Hope, which appeared in the *Morning Post* on 14 and 19 October. They revealed that "The person who has been travelling . . .

3. Ibid., pp. 291–92.
4. Coleridge, *Essays on His Times*, ed. David V. Erdman (London: Routledge & Kegan Paul; Princeton: Princeton University Press, 1978), 1:357–58, 374–76, 390–91, and 403–16. Subsequent references to these articles appear in the text.

under the name of *The Hon. Alexander Augustus Hope*, and who, in that character, married a woman at Buttermere, is a notorious swindler and impostor.—Col. Alexander Hope has been in Germany for six months past."[5] Even before Coleridge had time to see these letters, he had written a second article (datelined "Keswick, Oct. 15") that appeared in the *Morning Post* on 22 October 1802, also under the title "Romantic Marriage," in which he describes further "particulars of the novel of real life, the scene of which has unfortunately been laid among our Mountains" (1:374). On the return of the newly married couple to Buttermere "in a coach and four," a servant of Judge Harding, an old acquaintance of the supposed bridegroom, "on seeing the man, instantly said, 'Here is some mistake—this is not Colonel Hope.'" The impostor then braved out the situation long enough to plan and execute his escape. Coleridge, besides recording "the sincere concern, which every inhabitant of the country takes in the misfortune of poor Mary, of Buttermere," goes on to testify: "I knew her well; and I can truly say, that she would have been an ornament to any rank of life." Then he supports his praise by repeating gossip about Mary Robinson's paternity: "It seems, that there are some circumstances attending her birth and true parentage, which would account for her striking superiority in mind, and manners, in a way extremely flattering to the prejudices of rank and birth" (1:375-76).

In the *Morning Post* for 5 November 1802 appeared Coleridge's article entitled "The Fraudulent Marriage" (datelined "Keswick, Oct. 30"), which announced the discovery by "poor Mary of Buttermere" that her "husband" already had a wife and children. "This atrocious villain is therefore a bigamist" as well as a felonious forger for franking letters under a false name. After mentioning "her mother, and nominal father," Coleridge concludes: "Poor Mary is the object of universal concern." By this time, while the absconded forger-bigamist was the object of a nationwide manhunt, Mary of Buttermere herself was being celebrated in a print by James Gilray, published on 15 November from a sketch "from life, July, 1800."[6] Coleridge concluded his published account of the seduction with a long "Narrative of What Is at Present Known at Keswick of the Keswick Impostor," which was announced in the *Morning Post* on 11 November (having been written, Erdman suggests, during STC's short visit to London that began on 8 November). Daniel Stuart, editor and publisher of the *Morning Post*, held this article, publishing the first half of it on 20 November and the conclusion on 31 December—both parts headed "Keswick Impostor."

    5. See ibid., 1:358-59, notes.
    6. For a copy of this portrait and one of her seducer, see plates 6 and 5 in ibid., facing 1:406 and 1:404, respectively.

By the time the second part of Coleridge's recapitulation appeared, his account had assumed the character of a retrospective history of the events in the Lake Country. For on Tuesday, 7 December 1802, an article (not by STC) in the *Morning Post* announced that Mary's seducer, one John Hatfield, "was brought to town from Brecnock, in Wales, by . . . one of the Bow-street Officers," and charged, on "a warrant from Sir Fletcher Vane, Bart., a magistrate for the County of Cumberland" with the (capital) crime of franking letters by forging Hope's signature.[7] The article concluded with descriptions of Hatfield's manner and dress and a list of the noblemen and gentlemen who were present at the examination, the most notable being the Duke of Cumberland, fifth son of King George III. A week later, the *Morning Post* for Tuesday, 14 December, under the daily listing "PUBLIC OFFICE, BOW-STREET," contained a report of Hatfield's second examination. The "Office was crowded long before he entered, and some hundreds besieged the door in vain." The evidence produced included a forged note for £30 and "a copy of the register of the prisoner's marriage, in the name of Alexander Augustus Hope, with Mary Robinson (the Beauty of Buttermere)." The magistrate promised to write to Mary Robinson "that she may come and prefer the charge against him. . . . Some Gentlemen have proposed to set on foot a subscription, for the purpose of defraying the expences of the Beauty of Buttermere to town, in order to appear against Hatfield." Besides the magistrates and commissioners of the Bow-Street Office, whose duties required them to be present, "the Duke of Roxburgh, Lord Grenville, Earl of Aylesbury, Earl of Ormond, Sir T. Molyneux, Sir E. Pellew, Sir E. Nagle, and a number of Gentlemen, attended out of curiosity."

On 18 December the *Morning Post* noted that "A Paper of Tuesday . . . says—'It is with much sorrow and sympathy we mention, that poor MARY of Buttermere is with child.'" The paper reported on 21 December, under "PUBLIC-OFFICE, BOW-STREET," on Hatfield's third examination, in which "Mr. Hume, inspector of franks at the General Post-office, swore" that a signature franking a letter in the name of Col. A. Hope, directed to Dr. Fell, "was, to the best of his knowledge and belief, not in the handwriting of the said Col. A. Hope." Meanwhile the magistrates had received a warrant from "W. Wilson, Esq. a magistrate for the county of Cumberland, against the prisoner, for having forged and uttered a bill of exchange . . . ." This notice concludes with the observation that Hatfield

---

7. For transcripts of this and the following non-Coleridgean articles and comments on Hatfield and Mary of Buttermere from the *Morning Post*, I am indebted to the characteristic generosity of David V. Erdman.

at this examination looked better; his hair was powdered and he was better dressed. Finally, on 24 December 1802, the following notice concluded the substantive news of the case so far as it was conducted in London:

A letter has been received by Sir Richard Ford [the chief Bow-Street magistrate], from a Gentleman at Keswick, by which it appears, that Mary Robinson of Buttermere, declines prosecuting Hatfield for the Bigamy, as she is now very advanced in her pregnancy, although she expresses the greatest detestation of his actions. She says, she certainly married him, under an idea of his being Colonel Hope, brother to the Earl of Hopetoun, with a view of bettering herself; and, that she has been injured by him in every way, as he left a very considerable bill for board, lodging, &c. at her father's house, unpaid, when he went off. *Hatfield* wishes the public to believe he was *seduced* in this affair!

On 27 December, Hatfield underwent a fourth examination in Bow Street, and on 3 January 1803 the *Morning Post* announced that Hatfield would "be tried at Carlisle for forging franks," a capital felony.

III

As it happened, John Hatfield's arraignment and examinations in London may have coincided with a period in which Charles Lamb renewed his contributions of humorous epigrams or fillers to the *Morning Post*.[8] David V. Erdman has transcribed from that newspaper, among other allusions to Hatfield and Mary of Buttermere, several brief comments belonging to the genre that Lamb described himself as producing for Stuart and that, whether or not he was the author, reflect his attitudes. The following can

8. See Lamb's Elian essay, "Newspapers Thirty-five Years Ago." Though Lamb wrote to Rickman in a letter assigned the date February 1802 that he was "no longer a Paragraph spinner" for the *Morning Post* because Stuart's warmth for Lamb's work seemed to cool with Stuart's growing dissatisfaction with Coleridge's contributions (see Lamb, *Letters*, ed. Edwin W. Marrs, Jr., vol. 2 [Ithaca: Cornell University Press, 1976], pp. 51–52), there is further evidence in the same volume that Lamb tried to keep contributing to the *Morning Post* and that he and Coleridge were even thinking of submitting work under STC's name that Lamb would write and for which he would receive the payment because he needed the money. David V. Erdman has identified some paragraphs dealing with Hatfield as probably the work of Lamb, and in spite of the dearth of supporting external evidence, I find the attributions plausible. There is every reason to think that Lamb would and could have submitted such paragraphs under another name, even if he was not openly contributing to the *Morning Post* at this time. But even if the external evidence against Charles Lamb being the author seems too strong to warrant admitting these minor pieces to the canon of Lamb's writings, they reflect clearly the attitudes and values that Lamb later exhibited in his essays by "Elia." We can, therefore, use them as exemplars of the attitudes of educated men of the London middle classes toward the values of the idle aristocracy and their "gentlemanly" imitators in the capital. Let it be clear, then, that in calling these epigrams the work of "Lamb," I am not absolutely asserting his authorship, but rather using them to show how one who held his values expressed his view of the moral implications of the response to Hatfield by upper-class Londoners.

stand as representative examples: "A great crowd of *men of fashion* went to see Hatfield examined at Bow-street yesterday, desirous, no doubt, of receiving a lesson from the *accomplished seducer*" (21 December). "*Hatfield* complains bitterly of the calumnies of the public prints. Indeed, they use him cruelly, considering that Sir Richard Ford has evidence of his having been an invariable swindler for *no more* than thirty years" (29 December). "HATFIELD'S panegyrists allege in his defence, that he seems addicted to *no one kind of vice in particular*." And "The Bond street loungers already dress *a la Hatfield*, with large black eye-brows, rolling eyes, a ruddy complexion, and even a hitch in the walk" (both 1 January 1803). "HATFIELD is to be tried at Carlisle for forging franks. As *Skirmish* says in *The Deserter*, 'this comes of your learning *to write*'" (3 January 1803).[9]

The bitterness of the humor in these "fillers" seems appropriate to the way that Charles Lamb, whose best work to that date was probably *Rosamund Gray*, would have regarded any London gentry and bourgeoisie who accepted John Hatfield as a model. If these or other, similar fillers were written by Lamb, their tone of moral indignation is directed equally at Hatfield and at a London reading public whose values Lamb could not basically respect. When, on the other hand, Mary Lamb addressed Dorothy Wordsworth on 9 July 1803, she felt no need to state the moral issues, knowing that the Wordsworths would share the Lambs' indignation toward Hatfield and their sympathy for Mary of Buttermere. Instead, she dwelt on the incongruous human comedy witnessed during a visit by John Rickman and his sister, Southey, and the Lambs to "the lowest and most London-like of all our London amusements," the theatricals at Sadler's Wells:

. . . the entertainments were Goody Two Shoes, Jack the Giant-Killer, and *Mary of Buttermere*! poor Mary was very happily married at the end of the piece, to a sailor her former sweetheart—we had a prodigious fine view of her fathers house in the vale of Buttermere—mountains very like large haycocks, and a lake like nothing at all: if you had been with us, would you have laughed the whole time like Charles & Miss Rickman or gone to sleep as Southey and Rickman did.[10]

At this point, the chronological narrative has unfolded enough of the story of Mary Robinson and John Hatfield to permit us to analyze the basic

9. For these and other fillers tentatively suggested as possible contributions by Lamb, I am again grateful to David V. Erdman, who collected them during his research on the *Morning Post*.
10. Lamb, *Letters*, ed. Marrs, 2:117. The theatrical piece has been identified as *Edward and Susan; or, The Beauty of Buttermere* by Charles Dibdin, the Younger.

elements in their tragic interaction that evolved into a Romantic (rather than merely "romantic") symbolism. The two poles of location are the small rural community in the isolated vale of Buttermere, a living pastoral Arcadia, and metropolitan London, where idly curious "Gentlemen" throng the police hearing room to observe Hatfield and where "Bond street loungers" imitate his dress and his very walk, while the middle classes at Sadler's Wells gawk at a shabby representation of Mary of Buttermere's story that is given an artificial, "Hollywood" ending, miraculously free of human suffering. Mary Robinson belongs to the former, pastoral scene, whereas John Hatfield, the cool, callous, fashionably dressed felon, belongs to the latter social milieu. These two contrasting environments provided Wordsworth, Coleridge, and De Quincey with a moral antithesis that each used in his own way to explore issues fundamental not only to his individual social perspective, but also to his personal psychological associations.

IV

There are no references in Dorothy Wordsworth's Grasmere journal or in William and Dorothy Wordsworth's letters in 1802 to the marriage of Mary Robinson to "Alexander Augustus Hope"—a quite natural omission in view of the fact that the fraudulent Scottish marriage took place within a week of the wedding of William and Mary Hutchinson Wordsworth, 4 October 1802, on the other side of England.[11] But there is strong evidence of the Wordsworths' interest in the story and of Coleridge's continuing concern with it in Dorothy Wordsworth's *Recollections of a Tour Made in Scotland, A.D. 1803*.[12] Dorothy and William set out on this Scottish excursion on 14 August 1803. (Mary Wordsworth and the infant John, her first child [born 18 June 1803], remained behind at Grasmere under the care of Joanna Hutchinson.)[13] Coleridge joined the Wordsworths at Keswick on 15 August for the early part of the tour (he left them on 29 August), and William and Dorothy finally returned to Dove Cottage on 25 September.

On 16 August, their second day on the road, Dorothy writes:

11. For details of the Wordsworths' activities during this period, see *Journals of Dorothy Wordsworth*, ed. Mary Moorman (London: Oxford University Press, 1971), and Mark L. Reed, *Wordsworth: The Chronology of the Middle Years, 1800–1815* (Cambridge: Harvard University Press, 1975).
12. Edited by J. C. Shairp (3rd ed.; Edinburgh: David Douglas, 1894).
13. See Reed, *Wordsworth: Chronology of the Middle Years*. For some possible implications of the scheduling of this tour, see Donald H. Reiman, "Poetry of Familiarity: Wordsworth, Dorothy, and Mary Hutchinson," in *The Evidence of the Imagination: Studies of Interactions between Life and Art in English Romantic Literature*, ed. D. H. Reiman, M. C. Jaye, and B. T. Bennett (New York: New York University Press, 1978), pp. 142–77. [Item 11, above.]

Dined at Carlisle; the town in a bustle with the assizes; so many strange faces known in former times and recognised, that it half seemed as if I ought to know them all, and, together with the noise, the fine ladies, etc., they put me into confusion. This day Hatfield was condemned. I stood at the door of the gaoler's house, where he was; William entered the house, and Coleridge saw him; . . . a debtor . . . told me in a dry way that he [Hatfield] was "far over-learned," and another man observed to William that we might learn from Hatfield's fate "not to meddle with pen and ink." . . . Walked upon the city walls, which are broken down in places and crumbling away, and most disgusting from filth. The city and neighbourhood of Carlisle disappointed me; the banks of the river quite flat, and . . . there is not much beauty in the vale from the want of trees— . . . to me the holms had not a natural look; there was something townish in their appearance, a dulness in their strong deep green. . . . Reached Longtown after sunset, a town of brick houses belonging chiefly to the Graham family. . . . Slept at the Graham's Arms, a large inn. Here, as everywhere else, the people seemed utterly insensible of the enormity of Hatfield's offenses; the ostler told William that he was quite a gentleman, paid every one genteelly, etc. etc. He and "Mary" had walked together to Gretna Green; a heavy rain came on when they were there; a returned chaise happened to pass, and the driver would have taken them up; but "Mr. Hope's" carriage was to be sent for; he did not choose to accept the chaise-driver's offer.[14]

On the next two days, the Wordsworths and Coleridge visited Dumfries, and there they encountered again the contrast between the superficial gentility of money and social station and the nobility of inner character, the discrepancy between social appearance and moral reality. In the churchyard where Robert Burns is buried, they were struck by the fact that "there is no stone to mark the spot" of Scotland's greatest poet, whereas their guide, a local bookseller, said, "pointing to a pompous monument, 'there lies Mr. Such-a-one'—I have forgotten his name,—'a remarkably clever man; he was an attorney, and hardly ever lost a cause he undertook. Burns made many a lampoon upon him, and there they rest, as you see.' We looked at the grave with melancholy and painful reflections, repeating to each other his own verses."[15] The verses of Burns that they repeated were from "A Bard's Epitaph," which Wordsworth (in opposition to Francis Jeffrey and other Scottish admirers of Burns) assumed had been intended by Burns to refer to

14. *Recollections of a Tour*, pp. 2–3. According to the *DNB* account of Hatfield, his trial took place at Carlisle on "15 August 1803. . . . He was sentenced to be hanged, and met his death with the utmost coolness on Saturday, 13 Sept." The "Appendix to the Chronicle" of the *Annual Register for 1803* (pp. 422, 428) gives the date of Hatfield's execution as 3 September 1803, but the *DNB*, which cites as sources two detailed published records of Hatfield's trial, should be more accurate. This would mean that the trial of Hatfield took place on 15 August and that the sentence of death was pronounced on 16 August, when the Wordsworths and Coleridge were present.

15. *Recollections of a Tour*, pp. 5–6.

himself.[16] And the sentiments in these lines about a man who can teach others, "Yet runs himself life's mad career / Wild as the wave" so that "thoughtless follies laid him low, / And stain'd his name," clearly apply not only to Burns, but even more pointedly to John Hatfield, then under of sentence of death at Carlisle.

V

For William Wordsworth, ruminating the story of the Beauty of Buttermere until he wrote the thirteen-book *Prelude* in 1805–1806, Mary Robinson's tale became a moral and emotional touchstone of his sense of his own roots in the Lake Country and his return to them in 1800. Wordsworth introduces Mary of Buttermere anachronistically into the poem about the growth of his mind while describing his "Residence in London," before his "Residence in France" provided the determinative encounter with the intellectual and moral issues raised by his commitment to the ideals of the French Revolution and his desire to live with Annette Vallon as a citizen of the world. Although there is not time here for a full exposition of my somewhat unorthodox ideas on the structure of *The Prelude*, a brief outline of that argument may clarify what follows.[17] When Wordsworth revised the thirteen-book *Prelude* of 1805–1806 into the fourteen books eventually published (with some changes and omissions) after his death in 1850, he reduced its length by 589 lines, more than the average length (564 lines) of the poetic books in the fourteen-book text. The change to a larger number of books, while the total number of lines is reduced, raises the question of what Wordsworth's formal model was, for if (as many think) Wordsworth's intentions were epic, the deletion of text equal to one of the thirteen original books could have validated a change to the epic number, twelve books. Instead, Wordsworth went to fourteen, the number associated with his favorite formal structure, the sonnet. And a careful analysis of *The Prelude*,

---

16. See Wordsworth's *Letter to a Friend of Robert Burns* (London: Longman, Hurst, Rees, Orme, and Brown, 1816), pp. 27–29; and his poem entitled "At the Grave of Burns, 1803" in Wordsworth, *Poetical Works*, ed. Ernest de Selincourt and Helen Darbishire (Oxford: Clarendon Press, 1940–1949), 3:65–67. In lines 61–72, Wordsworth speaks of Burns's dead infant son, buried with him, and declares this a source of "Some sad delight": "For *he* is safe, a quiet bed / Hath early found among the dead, / Harboured where none can be misled, / Wronged, or distrest; / And surely here it may be said / That such are blest." Compare these sentiments with Wordsworth's lines in *The Prelude* on Mary Robinson's dead infant. See also *The Works of Robert Burns*, ed. Allan Cunningham (London: Cochrane and McCrone, 1834), 2:331–33.

17. All quotations from and references to *The Prelude* follow the Norton Critical Edition: *The Prelude, 1799, 1805, 1850*, ed. Jonathan Wordsworth, M. H. Abrams, and Stephen Gill (New York and London: W. W. Norton, 1979).

as Wordsworth shaped its final text, shows that he consciously structured it as an Italian sonnet. The macrosonnet begins with an octave in which he describes his intellectual and moral development before his watershed encounter with the French Revolution. The first tercet of the sestet consists of three books (IX-XI), all entitled "Residence in France," that recount his revolutionary enthusiasm for, and subsequent disillusionment with, the course of events in France. The final three books discuss his revulsion against the calculating, utilitarian perspective that underlay the dominant revolutionary philosophies both in France and in England and then his return to reliance upon more fundamental human emotions arising from the influences of his early, formative years.

Book XI of *The Prelude* ends with Wordsworth's crucial imaginative vision of his friend Coleridge, absent in Sicily, climbing Mount Etna. In this passage (XI.369-469), the power of the poet's imagination not only unites him with a friend separated from him by distance, but also links both men with great spirits of the past associated with eastern Sicily—Empedocles, Archimedes, and Theocritus—and even with such fictional or mythic beings as Comates and Arethusa. Amid this vision and demonstration of the power of the human mind—the activity or faculty known as the Imagination—to transcend time, place, and even categories of existence, Wordsworth declares his new faith. Unable to sustain the posture of a rationalistic "citizen of the world" and equally unwilling to ally himself with the narrow pragmatic nationalism of the reactionary British "war hawks," he declares that men and women of moral insight and imagination create their own ideal society that stretches beyond physical limitations: "There is / One great society alone on earth: / The noble Living and the noble Dead." These words form the thematic center of *The Prelude*. They explain how Wordsworth was able to rebuild his personal society through the love and support of a living community that included such friends as his sister Dorothy, his brother John, Samuel Taylor Coleridge, the Hutchinsons, and the Calverts and through his communion with the noble Dead from Theocritus to Milton. The ascent of Mount Snowdon in Book XIV parallels—completes the "rhyme" of—the imagined ascent of Etna in Book XI, emphasizing the parallel functions of the final books in the two "tercets" of the sestet. Those mountain-top experiences (Mounts of the Transfiguration, in the eyes of some modern critics), also parallel, or rhyme with, another mountain-top experience at the beginning of Book VIII, the final book of the octave, where the poet imagines himself on—or even assumes the consciousness of—Helvellyn, as the mountain looks down upon a village fair in Wordsworth's native Lake Country. And

Wordsworth's use of the Beauty of Buttermere in Book VII, in contrasting her and her child with a child and mother seen in a London theater, leads up to the declarations of commitment to his native ground that conclude both the octave and the sestet of the poem. For if human beings, by purifying and employing their imaginations, can become citizens of a great society that transcends time and space, and even the metaphysical conditions of life, death, and fictionality, then they can best commit themselves to the scenes that most purify and stimulate their imaginations—especially when, as in Wordsworth's (though not in Coleridge's) case, such scenes happen also to be the very scenes of his childhood and youthful maturation.

Much critical confusion about the repetitions and apparent backtracking in the first eight books—the octave—of *The Prelude* disappears when this section is recognized to be divided thematically into two sections. The first quatrain, Books I-IV, recounts the growth of Wordsworth's imagination through his encounters with Nature, while Books V-VIII trace the positive influences of human society and its artifacts, beginning with the dream of the Arab with his stone and shell (a heavily symbolic passage probably not part of Wordsworth's experience at all, but imported into his "autobiographical" poem from an anecdote about Descartes that Coleridge or Beaupuy may have told to him).[18] The dream foreshadows the main theme of Books V-VIII: how human culture provides a momentary stay against Nature's eternal cycles, which inexorably destroy the fruits of the human imagination. And Book VII, in which the Beauty of Buttermere makes her appearance, plays a key role in Wordsworth's identification of the human culture that will characterize his "one great society."

In Book VII, Wordsworth tells how, after having encountered the cultures of the Continent during the walking tour on the long vacation of 1790 (Book VI)—especially after first encountering a serious disappointment with Nature as he crossed the Alps—he left Cambridge for London, "Well pleased to pitch a vagrant tent among / The unfenced regions of society" (VII.56-57). The image of London as being "unfenced" (compared with the university) not only suggests the amorphous and undifferentiated quality of life in London society that Wordsworth develops throughout Book VII, culminating in his portrayal of the city as one huge

---

18. Jane Worthington Smyser, who pointed out the parallels between the dreams of Descartes and Wordsworth in "Wordsworth's Dream of Poetry and Science: *The Prelude* V," *PMLA* 71 (March 1956): 269-75, thought that Michel Beaupuy probably told Wordsworth about the dream recorded by Descartes. Coleridge also knew Descartes's works and could have called Wordsworth's attention to the story. But during his years at Cambridge and in France, Wordsworth was certainly capable of turning to Descartes himself.

Bartholomew Fair (VII.675–730), but also carries the underlying pastoral metaphor in which the youthful Wordsworth is like a lost sheep wandering over the unfenced pasturage of the Lake Country in his search for the qualities of an ideal society.

Through his early interactions with Nature (Books I-IV) and with books (Book V), Wordsworth had developed his imagination, acquired basic moral and political ideals, and formed close relationships with a number of individuals and schoolboy groups. At Cambridge (Book III), in order to turn his back on less pleasant social realities, he sought sustenance in the calmer forms of Nature in East Anglia (III.91–127) or through identifying himself with the spirits of Cambridge's noble dead, such as Newton (III.57–63). But after his historical imagination and his political idealism had been stimulated by an encounter with the first flush of the French Revolution on the Continent, Wordsworth returned to seek his place within contemporary British society, as epitomized in its metropolis. The whole of Book VII shows why he did not feel at home there, and then Book VIII opens with the description of the country fair in the shadow of Mount Helvellyn that contrasts with the picture of London as a promiscuous and impersonal Bartholomew Fair concluding Book VII. Whereas Wordsworth experienced London as an "unfenced" region where he pitched his "vagrant tent," the rural society of his home region offers a personal context of social ties and caring, where wandering sheep are sought and found by faithful shepherds. He calls the villagers and rural folk gathered at the country fair "a little family of men," with "here and there a stranger interspersed" (VIII.7–10): even the outsider avoids the impersonality of London's amorphous world by acquiring an identity as "a stranger." As Book VIII develops its stated subject—"Love of Nature Leading to Love of Man"—we see that the image of Mary of Buttermere that Wordsworth had evoked (quite out of chronological sequence) in Book VII had foreshadowed the unfolding of this argument: in the Lake Country, human beings, dwarfed by the great forms of Nature, feel keenly their vulnerability and ultimate helplessness. Tutored by Nature in both fear and awe, they band together to protect one another and to share the harshness as well as the beauties and sublimities of the natural world. "Man free, man working for himself" is "by his wants, / His comforts, native occupations, cares, / Cheerfully led to individual ends / Or social" (VIII.104–8).

Mary of Buttermere first appears in *The Prelude*, amid the account of London in Book VII, in the ludicrous version of her story that Mary Lamb had depicted in her letter to Dorothy Wordsworth after seeing the play at Sadler's Wells in July 1803. After describing the various sights of London—

"spectacles within doors,—birds and beasts / Of every nature, and strange plants convened / From every clime; and, next those sights that ape / The absolute presence of reality," such as the painted and molded panoramas representing St. Peter's in Rome, "the Falls / Of Tivoli," and the like (VII.229-63), Wordsworth turns to "Half-rural Sadler's Wells," with its "giants and dwarfs, / Clowns, conjurors, posture-makers, harlequins," as well as its representations of:

> . . . recent things yet warm with life; a sea-fight,
> Shipwreck, or some domestic incident
> Divulged by Truth and magnified by Fame,
> Such as the daring brotherhood of late
> Set forth, too serious theme for that light place—
> I mean, O distant Friend! a story drawn
> From our own ground,—the Maid of Buttermere,—
> (VII.291-97)

In the account that follows, both in the published text of 1850 and in the earlier versions, Wordsworth notes that he and Coleridge (his "distant Friend," abroad in Malta and Sicily) had seen and admired Mary of Buttermere. Both "Ere the broad world rang with the maiden's name" and "since that time," she behaved with "discretion," "delicate reserve," "patience, and humility of mind" (though she was unafraid to express "Her just opinions").[19] Wordsworth concludes that she has been "Unspoiled by commendation and the excess / Of public notice—an offensive light / To a meek spirit suffering inwardly" (VII.313-15).[20]

In this passage, Wordsworth reiterates one of the central emphases of *The Prelude*. In London—whether in Parliament, the churches, the public displays, the playhouses, or even on the streets, in which Wordsworth was "pleased to note . . . all specimens of man"—Italian, Jew, Turk, Swede, Russian, Frenchman, Spaniard, "Hunter-Indian; Moors, / Malays, Lascars, the Tartar, the Chinese, / And Negro Ladies in white muslin

---

19. VII.298-381 (1850); VII.323-412 (1805). Regarding the perennial debate as to whether or not Wordsworth's later revisions rendered *The Prelude* more pious but less humanistic, I should point out that, whereas in the earlier version the seducer is said to have been "unfaithful" "To God . . . , children, wife, and home," in the later revision Wordsworth deletes God, the abstract "home," and the children (of whose feelings he had no knowledge) to center on the abandoned wife, whose pathetic letters remained: "unfaithful to a virtuous wife / Deserted and deceived, the spoiler came . . . ."

20. None of the Romantics mentions Budworth's earlier celebrations of the Beauty of Buttermere. Did they know his mentions of her? If so, did they avoid commenting on his harmful invasion of her privacy because their own writings also explored the lives and experiences of real people?

gowns" (VII.211-28)—everything was turned into an outward show, even the private tragedy of Mary Robinson, or that which (he imagined) awaited a young child he had seen there and whose putative fate he contrasts with that of the dead child of the unwed Beauty of Buttermere.

Between two passages on Mary of Buttermere and her infant (VII.296-333, 379-81), Wordsworth describes "a lovely Boy, / A sportive infant, who, for six months' space / . . . had been of age to deal about / Articulate prattle" (VII.336-39), who though apparently originally meant to be "a cottage-child" had been placed by his painted mother amid "a throng / Of chance spectators, chiefly dissolute men / And shameless women" by whom he was pampered and caressed (VII.356-61). This declamation against excessive notoriety, or praise bestowed by people of limited understanding or corrupted taste, articulates one of Wordsworth's central canons. The same sentiment seems self-serving, in the spirit of the fox speaking of the unattainable grapes, when he writes in his "Essay, Supplementary to the Preface" (1815): "Grand thoughts, (and Shakespeare must often have sighed over this truth) as they are most naturally and most fitly conceived in solitude, so can they not be brought forth in the midst of plaudits without some violation of their sanctity."[21] But through the example of Mary of Buttermere, as Wordsworth draws her in *The Prelude*, "wooed . . . and wedded . . . in cruel mockery" by "the Spoiler . . . 'a bold bad Man'" (text of 1805-1806; VII.322-25), we can accept the moral distinction between the shows of London and her secluded home village, where the child of her seduction lies in a country churchyard:

> . . . She lives in peace
> Upon the spot where she was born and reared;
> Without contamination doth she live
> In quietness, without anxiety:
> Beside the mountain chapel, sleeps in earth
> Her new-born infant, fearless as a lamb
> That, thither driven from some unsheltered place,
> Rests underneath the little rock-like pile
> When storms are raging. Happy are they both—
> Mother and child!
> (VII.320-29 [1850])

In the text of 1805-1806, however, Wordsworth seems to turn the message of this passage into another claim for himself and the virtue of his own

21. Wordsworth, *Poems: Including Lyrical Ballads . . . in Two Volumes* (London: Longman, Hurst, Rees, Orme, and Brown, 1815), 1:373.

upbringing:

> This memorial Verse
> Comes from the poet's heart, and is her due;
> For we were nursed—as almost might be said—
> On the same mountains, children at one time,
> Must haply often on the self-same day
> Have from our several dwellings gone abroad
> To gather daffodils on Coker's Stream.
> (VII.340-46)

By the time he revised (and cut) *The Prelude* to the 1850 text, Wordsworth must have recognized that his special pleading and the awkwardly self-conscious echo of Milton's *Lycidas* marred the passage, for he deleted both from the final text.[22]

The tale of Mary of Buttermere in *The Prelude* does not depend for its relevance upon Wordsworth's personal knowledge of her or even upon their shared background. She stands as a far more universal example of the power of true innocence, with the support of a familial social nexus, to resist the corruptions and depredations of the larger society, in which an aristocratic name could blind an entire community to a stranger's true character. The story of Mary Robinson, "the Maid of Buttermere," thus exemplifies the moral and egalitarian social ideals that first attracted Wordsworth to revolutionary France both during his summer itinerary of 1790 and during his early days at Orleans and Blois in 1791-1792. Wordsworth makes the thematic link clear in a passage in Book IX in which he describes how, "born in a poor district, . . . / It was my fortune scarcely to have seen, / . . . The face of one, who . . . / Was vested with attention or respect / Through claims of wealth or blood" (IX.215-22).[23] Because of this alleged background (he could hardly have been actually unaware of the power that "wealth or blood" gave the Lowthers, his father's employers) and his subsequent idealization of "academic institutes" (i.e., both Hawkshead School and St. John's College) that "held something up to

---

22. VII.340-46 (1805). Besides the echo of *Lycidas*, line 23, pointed out by the Norton editors, the last lines contain a submerged echo of the myth of Persephone going forth in innocence alone to gather flowers, only to be seized and carried off by the force of darkness. Like many young intellectual poets, Wordsworth at first tended to overload every rift with ore to show his knowledge and only later sifted out the less relevant allusions.

23. Michael H. Friedman explores the psychological needs behind Wordsworth's idealization of the community in the Lake Country and the political implications of that idealization in *The Making of a Tory Humanist: Wordsworth and the Idea of Community* (New York: Columbia University Press, 1979).

view / Of a Republic, where all stood thus far / Upon equal ground; that we were brothers all / In honour, as in one community, / Scholars and gentlemen" (IX.225-29), Wordsworth was fully predisposed to accept the ideals of "Liberty, Equality, and Fraternity." For him, however, the slogans could not remain abstractions, but were epitomized in particular human beings—Michael Beaupuy and a "hunger-bitten girl" of whom Beaupuy "In agitation said, ''Tis against *that* / That we are fighting'" (IX.516-18).

Immediately after Wordsworth's account of Beaupuy, their friendship, his influence, and his death (IX.288-552), *The Prelude*, in the text of 1805-1806, launches into the tale of "Vaudracour and Julia," a section that Wordsworth decided to publish as a separate poem in 1820 and to which he alludes only briefly in the 1850 text. David V. Erdman has shown how the republican ideal of Books IX and X of *The Prelude* and the unhappy love story of "Vaudracour and Julia" interrelate not only with Wordsworth's actual romance with Annette Vallon (whose family and associates were not only French but royalists), but also with the poet's dramatization of conflicting loyalties in *The Borderers*.[24] Here I wish to point out two further implications of Erdman's demonstration. First, Wordsworth's sudden identification of himself during 1802 with Milton as sonnet-writer and English patriot obviously had personal (psychological) as well as literary and historical sources. Wordsworth had courted, as Milton had married, a woman whose family's royalist sympathies drove them apart (and led Milton to write his explorations of divorce). Thus Wordsworth's identification of himself with Milton just at the time that he had decided to marry Mary Hutchinson (thereby foreclosing the possibility of a future rapprochement with Annette Vallon) played a part in his self-justification: to fulfill his patriotic duty he must divorce himself from his country's enemy, France, which was once again turning monarchical under Napoleon Buonaparte. Moreover, Mary Robinson, "the Maid of Buttermere," who was seduced and abandoned almost at the time of his marriage to Mary Hutchinson, became both the public symbol of his wisdom in choosing as his wife and helpmate another Mary who was also his own age (b. 1770), who had been raised in his native hills, and who exhibited the same innocent and graceful household virtues that characterized her less fortunate namesake of Buttermere.[25]

24. "Wordsworth as Heartsworth; or, Was Regicide the Prophetic Ground of those 'Moral Questions'?" in *The Evidence of the Imagination*, ed. Reiman, Jaye, and Bennett, pp. 12-41.

25. I have explored Wordsworth's motives for marrying Mary Hutchinson in "Poetry of Familiarity," also in *The Evidence of the Imagination*, pp. 142-77 [item 11, above]. The subsequent publication of the full text of *The Love Letters of William and Mary Wordsworth*, ed. Beth

The virtues of Wordsworth's Lake Country home, exemplified in Book VII of *The Prelude* by Mary of Buttermere, become in the later Books associated with the true ideals of republican France, as well as with "the good old cause" of the English Commonwealth. They are contrasted with the false values and specious shows of London, where the poet himself had found no place or function and where dissolute crowds gawked admiringly at both innocence (which, in the person of the pampered young child, they were likely to corrupt) and guilt (by which, in the person of John Hatfield, their morals were even further corrupted). Those homespun virtues also contrast with the equally specious shows of Paris, as Wordsworth describes that city in Book X, where the Assembly, combined with the volatile mob, elevated Robespierre over his more humane rivals.[26] William Wordsworth's passage on "the Maid of Buttermere" and its larger ramifications in *The Prelude* thus parallel Dorothy Wordsworth's descriptions of the confusion and obliviousness to deeper values that her brother, Coleridge, and she had found in Carlisle and Longtown on the day of Hatfield's conviction and in the churchyard at Dumfries on the same walking tour in 1803. The Wordsworths associated the "confusion" in cities (London, Paris, Carlisle) with the corruptions represented by John Hatfield. Yet they must have known by 1803 that Hatfield himself had been born and raised at Mottram in Longendale, in eastern Cheshire, which (though now not far from the suburbs of greater Manchester) was in those days closely identified with the area now encompassed by the Peak District

---

Darlington (Ithaca: Cornell University Press, 1981), demonstrates beyond question that William developed a passionate love for Mary by 1810 (a passion that she finds novel in his letters of that year) and that he expressed the same feelings in 1812. But the five poems that William named to Henry Crabb Robinson on 12 May 1842 as "exhibiting the different phases of his affection for his wife" contain none that expresses a passion approaching that of the "love letters." Those five poems are: "Our walk was far among the ancient trees" ("To M. H.," written December 1799), "She was a phantom of delight" (written 1804; I discuss these two early poems in "Poetry of Familiarity"), "Let other bards of angels sing" ("To ——," composed 1824), and two sonnets, entitled "To a Painter" and "On the Same Subject" and beginning "All praise the Likeness by thy skill portrayed" and "Though I beheld at first with blank surprise / This Work" (both 1840; see *Henry Crabb Robinson on Books and Their Writers*, ed. Edith J. Morley [London: J. M. Dent and Sons, 1938], 2:616). These poems all express deep devotion and admiration for her virtues. The late sonnets are particularly moving, as the husband at first refuses to accept the painter's likeness of his seventy-year-old wife (whose unfaded bloom stills holds "sovereign empire in a faithful heart"), but then, admitting the likeness, declares that "the old day was as welcome as the young, / As welcome, and as beautiful . . . ." For the texts of the three later poems, see Wordsworth, *Poetical Works*, 2:35, 3:54–55.

26. Wordsworth portrays the corruption in Paris at war with his ideals in Book Tenth, particularly lines 48–221 (1850). One technique that he uses to convey the disparity appears in the passage on Louvet's denunciation of Robespierre (X.94–120), where Wordsworth echoes Milton's portrayal of Abdiel's confrontation with Satan in the council in Heaven just at the time of Satan's rebellion (*Paradise Lost* V.803ff.).

National Park—an area of isolated natural beauty exceeded only by the Lake Country itself.[27] And even Robert Burns, from their point of view, had not remained unsullied in spite of his genius and his rural nurture. The distinction, it seems, must not have been between the country and the city, but between abandoning one's roots for a false sophistication or cosmopolitanism, or remaining true to the values of the nurturing home country. Mary, the Beauty of Buttermere, had made the terrible mistake of trying to pull free of her native habitat, but when confronted by her error, she had the virtuous good sense not to go to London to become a public display in person, as her story became at Sadler's Wells. Instead, she reclaimed her native virtue and blotted out her shame by staying among those who cared for her amid her native hills—just as Annette Vallon maintained her integrity, after the birth of her natural child, by remaining in France among her understanding friends and family.

VI

Whereas for Wordsworth the tragedy of the Beauty of Buttermere occurred because both she and Hatfield refused to remain in their rightful places in the social order, Coleridge, as we have seen (page 221 above), hinted that Mary Robinson had an air of noble illegitimacy about her. Coleridge was always deferential to the claims of old wealth and birth, whereas Wordsworth strongly believed, with Burns,

> A king can mak a belted knight,
> A marquis, duke, and a' that;
> * * * *
> The pith o' sense, and pride o' worth,
> Are higher ranks than a' that.[28]

But the differences between Wordsworth and Coleridge about the significance of the events at Buttermere in 1802 do not end there. As is clear from the account in *The Prelude*, Wordsworth's concern centered on the fate of Mary Robinson; whereas references in Coleridge's notebooks and Thomas De Quincey's account of Mary of Buttermere in his recollections of "Samuel Taylor Coleridge" show that STC was more profoundly affected by the

---

27. On the "High Peak," see John Aiken, *England Described, Being a Concise Delineation of Every County in England and Wales* . . . (London: Baldwin, Cradock and Joy, 1818), pp. 96, 109, 116–17. In 1801, in spite of considerable industrial growth in the region since Hatfield's childhood, the parish of "Mottram in Longden Dale" had only 948 residents. See Nicholas Carlisle, *A Topographical Dictionary of England* (London: Longman, Hurst, Rees, and Orme, 1808), vol. 2 [alphabetically arranged, but unpaginated].
28. "Is There, For Honest Poverty," stanza 4; Burns, *Works*, ed. Allan Cunningham

moral degeneration of John Hatfield. Although Coleridge's essays for the *Morning Post* exhibit sympathy for Mary Robinson, even in those initial accounts his interest centered on the man who had seduced and abandoned her and others. The very title given (by Coleridge or Stuart) to the two articles—"Keswick Impostor"—betrays STC's focus in the two-part study, which shows a markedly greater interest in the psychology of vice than of innocence. For Coleridge describes at length not only Hatfield's concurrent attempts to seduce "a young lady of family and fortune, and of great personal attractions" (identified by Erdman as a Miss D'arcy),[29] but also Hatfield's interactions with "a Mr. Crump, of Liverpool," who was "then sojourning" in the "simple and lovely vale" of Grasmere and had "long threatened, alas! to build a fine house there."[30] In Coleridge's published notebooks, the only possible reference to Mary of Buttermere herself is found in the note, drawn from Kathleen Coburn's encyclopedic knowledge, to Coleridge's cryptic jotting of the isolated phrase "Gap-tooth'd": Coburn writes: "'The Beauty of Buttermere' like the Wife of Bath, and the chaise-driver of [notebook entry] 1084 f43 was also 'rather gap-toothed.'"[31] Coleridge's reaction to John Hatfield and his depredations, on the other hand, was both intense and sustained.

In about April 1803, Coleridge jotted a laconic reference to "Hatfield—Cruickshanks—[in Greek characters] Penelope/ characters in my novel" (1, #1395). Though Coburn in her note identifies Cruickshanks and Penelope as, possibly, a friend of Thomas Poole and Poole's cousin and beloved Penelope Poole, Erdman may be nearer the mark in believing that "Penelope" refers to Hatfield's "faithful wife, Michilli Nation" (*Essays on His Times*, 1:416). "Cruickshanks," then, would be STC's nickname for Hatfield, whom Coleridge describes as having "a little hitch in bringing up one leg. This was occasioned (as it should seem) by an old wound" (1:404). Here we see Coleridge's interest in Hatfield as a kind of Richard III villain, interesting enough to adorn a tale as well as to point a moral. Another

---

(London: Cochrane and McCrone, 1834), 5:259.
29. Coleridge, *Essays on His Times*, 1:408 and n. 10. It is tempting to imagine that Jane Austen may have drawn on the gossip as well as the published accounts of the Beauty of Buttermere when she revised her early manuscript entitled *First Impressions* in 1802–1803 and in 1811, before it was published as *Pride and Prejudice* in 1813 (see Donald J. Gray's edition of that novel [New York: W. W. Norton, 1966], p. vii). If so, the subplot involving Wickham's attempt to elope with Miss Darcy might owe something to Hatfield's similar proposal to Miss D'arcy at Keswick.
30. Coleridge, *Essays on His Times*, 1:405. Wordsworth also deplored the proposed building of this house but, as Erdman notes, he became its first tenant when "Allan Bank" was completed.
31. *The Notebooks of Samuel Taylor Coleridge*, ed. Kathleen Coburn, vol. 1 (New York: Pantheon Books, 1957), note for entry 1177 (i.e., #1177n). Neither text nor notes are paginated, but are located by entry number.

entry in the notebooks (for 16 August 1803) parallels Dorothy Wordsworth's *Recollections*, but with quite different emphases:

> At Carlisle I alarmed the whole Court, Judges, Counsellors, Tipstaves, Jurymen, Witnesses, & Spectators by hallooing to Wordsworth who was in a window at the other side of the hall—Dinner!
> Walked on the wall—the divine pearly Whiteness of those rich fleecy Clouds, so deliciously shaded toward the top of their component fleecy parts—Think of this often
> Then visited Hatfield, impelled by Miss Wordsworth—vain, a hypocrite/ It is not by mere Thought, I can understand this man/[32]

In Coleridge's consciousness, the revulsion toward Hatfield's unfathomable vice, vanity, and hypocrisy became associated with STC's sense of the meanness and shortsightedness of contemporary ("modern") life, as in his association of Hatfield with Mr. Crump, the Liverpool merchant of great wealth but questionable taste. In Malta, Coleridge wrote in a notebook on 20 August 1805:

> I doubt, if it be not one of the "Signs of the Times" that the Theses of the Universities of Oxford & Cambridge are so generally drawn from events of the Day/ Stimuli of passing interests/ Dr Dodds, Jane Gibbses, Hatfields, Bonapartes, Pitts, &c &c &c &c, whereas the great end of that [i.e., university studies] ought to be tranquil time [,] should be to give a living Interest for the Permanent, the Generic, for that which is independent of the Times, in short for that which the Self-conceit of the Ephemerides has christened Common-place.[33]

Here Coleridge lumps Hatfield with Dr. William Dodd, a clergyman-forger (executed in spite of Dr. Johnson's efforts on his behalf), and Jane Gibbs, an ugly streetwalker ("who, if her power to attract attention failed, . . . used to charge with assault and battery those she had engaged in conversation"),[34] as well as with two of STC's least favorite public figures— William Pitt and Napoleon. Here the personal derelictions of John Hatfield have merged with a broader social issue, as in the social and political concerns that Wordsworth personified in the tragedy of Mary of Buttermere. Whereas Wordsworth dealt with the effects of a stable and supportive social environment upon the development of the individual, Coleridge deals with much the same question in terms of the permanent and timeless concerns that study of the past can identify versus the transitory and

32. Ibid., 1, #1432.
33. Ibid., vol. 2 (New York: Pantheon Books, 1961), #2651.
34. Ibid., 2, #2651n.

the sensational. Wordsworth articulated their complementary concerns in his Preface to *Lyrical Ballads,* where he wrote that "the encreasing accumulation of men in cities" produced "a craving for extraordinary incident," a "degrading thirst after outrageous stimulation," that wars with the "inherent and indestructible qualities of the human mind" and "certain powers in the great and permanent objects that act upon it which are equally inherent and indestructible . . . ."[35]

Coleridge recalls Hatfield again in a notebook entry of March 1810, where he writes: "It is a mark of a noble nature to be more shocked with the unjust condemnation of a bad man than of a virtuous one—as the sentence of the E[arl] of Strafford, of Hatfield, &c.—For in such cases the love of justice & hatred of the contrary is felt more nakedly, and is a strong passion per se, not only unaided by but even in conquest of the softer self-repaying Sympathies."[36] Finally, in June or July 1810, while reading and commenting on the life and works of St. Teresa, Coleridge observes: "An excellent remark, that the Devil can serve his Turn even of the Virtues which we have—at least, of those amiable or useful qualities, which have a natural tendency to unite themselves with virtue, & are its appropriate companions—Hatfield."[37] These notebook entries demonstrate that, though Thomas De Quincey errs in some factual particulars about Wordsworth's and Coleridge's reactions to Hatfield and Mary of Buttermere, his recollection that Coleridge had examined the letters of Hatfield's earlier wife and sweethearts is probably accurate:

Great was the emotion of Coleridge when he recurred to his remembrance of these letters, and bitter, almost vindictive—was the indignation with which he spoke of Hatfield. . . . Coleridge said often, in looking back upon that frightful exposure of human guilt and misery, that the man who, when pursued by these heartrending apostrophes, and with this litany of anguish sounding in his ears, from despairing women and from famishing children, could yet find it possible to enjoy the calm pleasures of a Lake tourist, and deliberately to hunt the picturesque, must have been a fiend of that order which fortunately does not often emerge amongst men.[38]

35. *Lyrical Ballads, with Other Poems,* 2nd ed. (London: T. N. Longman and O. Rees, 1800), pp. xviii-xx.
36. Coleridge, *Notebooks,* vol. 3 (London: Routledge & Kegan Paul, 1973), #3741. Coleridge evidently believed, like many of his contemporaries, that to prescribe capital punishment for such crimes as forgery was unjust.
37. Ibid., 3, #3926.
38. De Quincey, *Recollections of the Lakes and the Lake Poets, Coleridge, Wordsworth and Southey,* in *De Quincey's Works* (Edinburgh: Adam and Charles Black, 1872 [reprinted 1881]), 2:87. This edition is hereafter cited as De Quincey, *Works.* (Those using David Masson's edition will find the account of the Beauty of Buttermere at 2:177-84.)

Wordsworth hearkened to the eloquent silence of Mary Robinson's homely dignity and the mute testimony of her child's small grave, but Coleridge was moved by the "litany of anguish" in the letters of other betrayed women and children that pursued Hatfield to the Lakes. Wordsworth tried to understand the secret strength of wronged virtue, while Coleridge probed for the motive springs of unregenerate villainy and measured its effects on the psychology of others potentially as corrupt.

VII

Thomas De Quincey himself had taken cognizance of the story of Mary of Buttermere long before he met Coleridge or Wordsworth and settled in the Lake Country. Among expenses recorded at the back of his diary for 1803 appears the sum of ten shillings sixpence for "Mary of Butter," which Horace A. Eaton identified as William Mudford's fictionalized account, *Augustus and Mary, or the Maid of Buttermere: A Domestic Tale* (London, 1803).[39] De Quincey's interest in the individuals continued strong at least until 1834–1835, when he published his reminiscences of Samuel Taylor Coleridge in *Tait's Edinburgh Magazine*.[40] His account, though marred by numerous factual errors and sentimental exaggerations, takes Mary Robinson out of the realm of myth and symbol by restoring her to her gap-toothed, pock-fretten reality. Yet De Quincey, ever the romancer of real human experience, from drug dependence to travel by mail coach, tells the story of Mary Robinson from the perspective of one whose romantic preconceptions were reinforced rather than shattered by the limitations that he encountered. He writes:

One day in the Lake season, there drove up to the Royal Oak, the principal inn at Keswick, a handsome and well-appointed travelling carriage containing one handsome gentleman of somewhat dashing exterior. . . . The stranger['s] . . . visiting cards designated him as "The Hon. Augustus Hope." Under this name, he gave himself out for a brother of Lord Hopetoun's. Some persons had discernment enough to doubt of this; for the man's breeding and deportment, though showy, had an under tone of vulgarity about it; and Coleridge assured me, that he was grossly ungrammatical in his ordinary conversation. . . . It could be no blame to a shepherd girl, bred in the sternest solitude which England has to show, that she should fall into a snare which many of her betters had not escaped. Nine miles from Keswick, by the nearest bridle-road through Newlands, but fourteen or fifteen by any route which the honourable gentleman's travelling-carriage could traverse, lies the Lake of Buttermere. . . . At the foot of this lake (that is, at the end

---

39. *A Diary of Thomas De Quincey, 1803*, ed. Horace A. Eaton (London: Noel Douglas, n.d.), pp. 201 and 245, note 124.
40. *Tait's Edinburgh Magazine*, n.s., 1 (1834): 509–20, 588–96, 685–90; n.s., 2 (1835): 2–10.

where its waters issue), lie a few unornamented fields, through which rolls a little brook-like river, connecting it with the larger lake of Crummock; and at the edge of this miniature domain . . . stands a cluster of cottages, so small and few, that, in the richer tracts of England, they would scarcely be complimented with the name of hamlet. One of these, and I believe the principal, belonged to an independent proprietor, called, in the local dialect, a *"Statesman"*; and more, perhaps, for the sake of attracting a little society, than with much view to pecuniary profit at that era, this cottage offered the accommodations of an inn to the traveller and his horse.[41]

De Quincey goes on to tell how "the cruel spoiler" traveled to Buttermere "to witness or to share in the char-fishing," for the char breed only in such deep lakes as Crummock and Buttermere. There Hatfield saw "the daughter of the house, a fine young woman of eighteen . . . ."[42] Gone from De Quincey's account are not only the facts to be found in Coleridge's contemporary reports (e.g., the inn at which Hatfield stayed in Keswick was the Queen's Head, not the Royal Oak) but also the sense of evil intent and premeditation of all the actions of Hatfield (who, according to Coleridge's summary report, had "made eager and repeated attempts to debauch one beautiful girl" at Grasmere and at Keswick had "made a promise of marriage to Burkitt's daughter; and . . . something very like a promise of marriage to one of the maid servants at the Queen's Head" lest he "take leave of any place disturbed by the novelty of a peaceful conscience").[43] Instead, De Quincey centers on the pathetic and sentimental elements of the story, adding those for which he can claim no authority. Instead of learning that the couple traveled to Gretna Green to be married, he speculates on

whether the marriage was, or could have been, celebrated in the little mountain chapel of Buttermere. If it were, I persuade myself that the most hardened villain must have felt a pang on violating the altar of such a chapel; so touchingly does it express, by its miniature dimensions, the almost helpless humility of that little pastoral community . . . . It is not only the very smallest chapel by many degrees in all England, but is so mere a toy in outward appearance, that . . . the little chapel looks not so much a mimic chapel in a drop-scene from the Opera House, as a miniature copy from such a scene . . . .[44]

41. De Quincey, *Works*, 2:82–84.
42. Ibid., 2:84. De Quincey's declaration that Mary Robinson was eighteen years old in 1802 accords neither with Coleridge's and Wordsworth's statements that she was then twenty-eight to thirty, nor with the two dates that I have seen given as the year of her birth—1772 and 1778. Presumably the age of eighteen, if not the product of De Quincey's imagination, derived from his memory of early encounters with romanticized versions of Mary's story in novels, ballads, or plays performed at Sadler's Wells.
43. Coleridge, *Essays on His Times*, 1:407.
44. De Quincey, *Works*, 2:85.

In De Quincey's narration (written, obviously, from memory and from the depths of his own need to attenuate and sentimentalize everything), the important positive contribution is his clear sense of the attitudes of the local people—Coleridge, Wordsworth, Southey, and Mary Robinson herself. The corroborating evidence of Coleridge's notebook entries, in particular, suggests that De Quincey was here, as elsewhere, a more reliable historian of feelings than of facts. He reports that when Wordsworth and Coleridge visited Carlisle "on the day of" Hatfield's condemnation, they "endeavoured to obtain an interview with him. Wordsworth succeeded; but for some unknown reason, the prisoner steadily refused to see Coleridge; a caprice which could not be penetrated" (2:86). As we have seen from Dorothy Wordsworth's and Coleridge's accounts, nearly the opposite was true, just as De Quincey attributes Hatfield's earlier reluctance to associate with Coleridge to the (erroneous) recollection that Hatfield "was of a Devonshire family, and naturally feared the eye . . . of one who bore a name immemorially associated with the southern part of that county" (2:86).[45]

Earlier I quoted from De Quincey's account his record of the intense detestation with which Coleridge viewed Hatfield, and this squares with what we know from STC's own writings. De Quincey goes on to confirm Wordsworth's picture of Mary's acceptance by her community: "It was fortunate for a person in her distressing situation, that her home was not in a town: the few and simple neighbours, . . . having little knowledge of worldly feelings, never for an instant connected with her disappointment any sense of the ludicrous, or spoke of it as a calamity to which her vanity might have co-operated. They treated it as unmixed injury, reflecting shame upon nobody but the wicked perpetrator." De Quincey goes on to describe her personal appearance from his own diminutive perspective:

She was none of your evanescent, wasp-waisted beauties; on the contrary, she was rather large in every way; tallish, and proportionably broad. . . . except in her arms, which had something of a statuesque beauty, and in her carriage, which expressed a womanly grace, together with some degree of dignity and self-possession, I confess that I looked in vain for any positive qualities of any sort or degree. Beautiful in any emphatic sense, she was not. . . . the expression of her counte-

45. Hatfield, as we have observed, was born in a part of Cheshire near Derbyshire, and he had lived his early life in the North of England. But after marrying his second wife, Michilli Nation, in September 1800, Hatfield and she had lived for a short period at Dulverton, Somersetshire, and it was from Somerset that she had written Hatfield the pathetic letters recalled by De Quincey, whose dim recollections thus placed Hatfield as coming from the Southwest and embroidered the story with Hatfield's supposed fear of Coleridge's knowledge of the region.

nance could be disagreeable. This arose out of her situation; connected as it was with defective sensibility and a misdirected pride. . . . Yet, once at least, I must have seen her under the most favourable circumstances: for, on my first visit to Buttermere, I had the pleasure of Mr. Southey's company, who was incapable of wounding anybody's feelings, and to Mary, in particular, was well known by kind attentions, and I believe by some services. . . . She waited upon us at dinner, and talked to us freely. "This is a respectable young woman," I said to myself; but nothing of that enthusiasm could I feel, which beauty, such as I have beheld at the Lakes, would have been apt to raise under a similar misfortune. (2:90–91)

In his essay on Coleridge, De Quincey seems to introduce Hatfield, the cold-blooded seducer, as a symbol of evil to stand as the diametrical opposite of STC's ethical sensitivity. When the section that follows his account of Hatfield and the Beauty of Buttermere enumerates several of Coleridge's less admirable acts and traits—including his use of opium as a stimulant rather than as an anodyne (2:93–96), we are led to consider the larger structural function that the memoir of the Beauty of Buttermere may have been intended to perform in the essay on Coleridge. In any case, De Quincey's testimony reinforces Coleridge's picture in the *Morning Post* of Mary Robinson's gap-toothed, pock-fretten reality and the impression that Coleridge reacted more strongly to the issue of Hatfield's guilt than to that of Mary Robinson's innocence, which was the focus of Wordsworth's passage in Book VII of *The Prelude*.[46]

VIII

The English Romantic writers whose reactions to Mary Robinson we have examined responded in individual ways that, if not strictly predictable, are at least comfortably consistent with our understanding of the general tenor of their thought and art. Wordsworth's imagination tended to exorcize his personal feelings of inadequacy and guilt and to find a compensation or mitigation for all human suffering. For him, Hatfield is merely a natural hazard and "the Maid of Buttermere" was untouched by her misjudgment; she became a symbol of communal solidarity and security, rather than the protagonist in a tragedy. Coleridge, as has been universally acknowledged, tended to focus upon the shortcomings, or guilty sinfulness, not only in his own character but in others as well. He brooded on John Hatfield as one of the petty demi-villains of the modern world. Charles Lamb's moral indignation usually took an ironic or humorous turn in his publications, dwelling most often on the heartlessness or ethical

---

46. De Quincey added Wordsworth's lines on Mary of Buttermere in a footnote to his essay on Coleridge when it was reprinted in 1854, after *The Prelude* had appeared.

blindness of the social mores as they contrasted with the moral sensitivities of the individual. The quips on Hatfield attributed to him, as well as his sister's reaction to the portrayal of the Sadler's Wells production about Mary of Buttermere, reflect Lamb's usual penchant for laughing so that he may not have to weep. Thomas De Quincey, who frequently sentimentalized the past, his own experience, and especially the feelings and reactions of Coleridge, Wordsworth, and Southey, with whom (in that order) he tended to identify his own feelings, projected his judgment into a highly colored and greatly distorted picture of Mary Robinson and John Hatfield, as seen through their interactions with his great contemporaries.

Where, then, are we to look for the real Mary Robinson? Was she the saintly stoic of Wordsworth's imagination? the betrayed illegitimate daughter of a passing gentleman that Coleridge wrote of in his early newspaper accounts and then lost sight of in the dazzling darkness of John Hatfield's fate? the Lambs' occasion to resent the ignorant and heartless displays by "Bond-street loungers" and the most London-like of amusements—dramatizing the private lives of the unfortunate at Sadler's Wells? or Thomas De Quincey's innocent pastoral maid, Perdita, led to the altar in childish innocence by "a wicked perpetrator" whose action destroyed her good nature and, with it, her pretensions to beauty? Or was Joseph Budworth, the slightly lubricious "Rambler," closer to the mark than any of his literary betters when he advised "Sally" not to think so highly of her beauty and to use her God-given common sense to watch out for roués on the picturesque tour?

If we transpose the tale into a modern setting, we shall, I think, be better able to appreciate the issues. Imagine that a young woman who works at her father's restaurant in Buttermere (or in a village near Aspen, Colorado) is courted by someone claiming to be the younger brother of Robert Redford or Michael Caine. He proves, at last, to be a forger and a bigamist. Granted that the consequences of such a discovery would be far less serious to both principals now than in 1802, there would certainly be concern about the betrayed confidence of an innocent girl. But some observers would, doubtless, conclude that she—like most people who are swindled—had contributed to her fate because she was blinded and led on partly by her own vanity, greed, or ambition. That no such sentiments seem to have been voiced in the public reactions of 1802–1803 and that their absence is specifically noted by De Quincey in his retrospective view thirty-five years later suggest the vast differences between the social norms of Wordsworth's day and our own. Ambition to marry a person of higher social sphere—or even to be disclosed as the illegitimate child of such a person—was deemed to be the proper attitude. Though in *Shamela*, Henry Fielding might object to Richardson's portrayal of Pamela's motives as disinterested virtue, he and everyone down to Pip in *Great Expectations* believed that the proper way to rise in the world was to be lifted up by someone above, whose birth and station entitled him or her to elevate inferiors; it was not proper to climb the ladder through one's own native abilities and hard work. A complex history transformed this static view of social class, governed by what we might term an established apostolic succession, into our present fluid order, led by a de facto aristocracy made up of *nouveaux riches* technocrats, rock music stars, and TV newscasters. The suggestion by the Romantic writers that Mary Robinson's natural grace and innocence might actually render her of superior worthiness to any mere lounging "gentleman" of birth and wealth helped to make possible such a social revolution. But the Romantics themselves did not necessarily advocate such a change in society. And Mary Robinson did not live long enough to take advantage of it. The real reason that people in her social circle could not condemn her was that she acted exactly as was expected of her; John Hatfield was the one who had transgressed the social boundaries—who had declared himself a gentleman in the only way then open to a man who was not born one and whom no legitimate gentleperson invited to join the higher caste.

Thus, Mary Robinson's story, even after this false start, ended much as had the dramatization of it that the Lambs, Rickmans, and Southey had laughed at or slept through at Sadler's Wells in 1803. For in the lists of deaths in the "Appendix to the Chronicle" of the *Annual Register for 1837*, under the date 22 February 1837, appears this obituary:

Lately.—At Caldbeck, Cumberland, Mary, wife of Mr. Richard Harrison, of that Place. This amiable individual was formerly the far-famed, and much talked of "Mary of Buttermere," or as she was more commonly termed, "the Buttermere Beauty."

Richard Harrison, students of the region tell us, was "a local farmer."[47] As such, he certainly knew the history of her earlier betrayal, and the notice in the *Annual Register* shows that he was not averse to having his wife's past recalled to the world after her death. Caldbeck, just below Derwent, was a parish that in 1801 numbered just 1,171 souls.[48] News of Mary Harrison's

47. *The Prelude* (Norton Critical Edition), p. 244, n. 8.
48. See Nicholas Carlisle, *A Topographical Dictionary of England*, vol. 1 [alphabetically arranged].

death and the recollection of her past could hardly have reached the London publication without the consent and cooperation of her family and friends.

Perhaps the news of her death, combined with De Quincey's retrospective account in his essay on Coleridge, served to revive interest in the story of the Beauty of Buttermere, because in 1841 a novel was published by Henry Colburn under the title (either slightly askew or slightly disguised) of *James Hatfield and the Beauty of Buttermere: A Story of Modern Times*. A copy of the work was in Wordsworth's library, "bearing witness," as Ernest de Selincourt says, "to Wordsworth's continued interest in the story."[49] But the best evidence of Wordsworth's continued interest appears in his careful revision and polishing of the text of the passage between the version of 1805–1806 and the text he left to be published after his death. In the text that he finally approved, we can see his care in preserving the essential features of his earliest inspiration, while sharpening his thematic focus by removing eight extraneous lines that relate, not to his judgment of London's impersonality, but to other aspects of his own life. He also toned down the diction, as when he revises his first assertion that Mary's story was "too holy theme for such a place" as Sadler's Wells, terming it, instead, "too serious theme for that light place" (1805, VII.318; 1850, VII.295). Finally, as their respective focuses suggest, Wordsworth's account of Mary of Buttermere in *The Prelude* not only preserves her memory but lends a vital social significance to what was, even in the hands of Coleridge and De Quincey, merely a sensational incident of private misfortune. Whereas Coleridge's attempts to yoke John Hatfield with Pitt and Napoleon partake of the mental bombast with which he charged Wordsworth, that poet's contrasting portraits of two unwed mothers and their innocent young children, one seen as a stranger amid an anonymous, dissolute crowd in a London theater and the other sheltered in her small village by a loving family and supportive neighbors, provide not only a practical lesson in moral tolerance but also a profound socio-psychological insight that underlies at least one current in British Romanticism: in a generation of rapid technological change and profound social upheaval, a person's roots amid a nurturing human community were even more important than they had been in the past, and family ties, local attachments, and familiar traditions that in other situations might have stifled or restricted individual

---

49. Wordsworth, *The Prelude, or The Growth of a Poet's Mind*, ed. Ernest de Selincourt, 2nd ed. revised by Helen Darbishire (Oxford: Clarendon Press, 1959), p. 564. The anonymous novel was written by Edward Carrington, with illustrations by Robert Cruikshank.

development were then essential for both psychic stability and imaginative growth.

13

Thematic Unity in Lamb's Familiar Essays

As *a critic of the Romantics (as distinguished from my work as a textual and historical scholar), my two complementary roles have been to champion underdogs and to point out exceptions to the generalizations of other critics. The brief essay on Lamb's essays illustrates both these activities.*

The paper grew out of my first opportunity to teach a course on the English Romantics during my third and final year on the campus at Duke University in 1962–1963. During my first two years there, my teaching of the sophomore survey of major British writers had resulted in publishable essays on Shakespeare ("Appearance, Reality, and Moral Order in Richard II," MLQ 25 [1964]: 34–45) *and Chaucer ("The Real Clerk's Tale; or, Patient Griselda Exposed,"* TSLL 5 [1963]: 356–73). *During those years, I also wrote two* PMLA *essays on Shelley— "Structure, Symbol, and Theme in 'Lines written among the Euganean Hills'" (developed from a lecture on Shelley that I was asked to give to a class in comparative Romanticism) and "Shelley's 'The Triumph of Life': The Biographical Problem" (Item 16). In addition, I mined my grad-school term papers and the research ancillary to my dissertation for six other articles and notes on subjects ranging from* Beowulf *and* The Spanish Tragedy *to James's "The Author of Beltraffio" and Salinger's* The Catcher in the Rye, *and I wrote "Research Revisited" (College English, 1961; see Introduction), reviews for* JEGP, SAQ, *and* CE, *and two lectures—"Rhetorical Techniques in the Shorter Fiction of Henry James" and one that eventually became "Wordsworth, Shelley, and the Romantic Inheritance" (Item 19).*

What kept me so busy? No instructor in English at Duke had won tenure and promotion to associate professor since Grover Smith had done so several years earlier. Joseph N. Riddel and I were both running scared and, in fact, scaring each other. Every week or two each of us mailed out a piece to a scholarly journal, and every month or two one of us ran to the chairman with a letter of acceptance. We were insufferable, but perhaps excusable in the context of Duke's Department of English, then one of the stodgiest in academe. It not only had the reputation of never letting anyone teach a course unless he had first taught it somewhere else, but it was encrusted with a parvenue pseudo-gentility in which, as Grover Smith used to tell us, one book was worth a hundred articles and one good cocktail party was worth a dozen books. Joe and I both received help and encouragement from a number of colleagues, especially the younger faculty, and in my case also from Lionel Stevenson, Merle and Helen Bevington, Charles Richard Sanders, Benjamin Boyce, and Florence F. Brinkley. Most of the senior professors were, individually, decent and congenial people; but the department had been for so many years marked by the oppression of the young and by dissension at the senior levels that it was almost impossible for younger faculty to emerge unscarred. Many of the best younger people left, and even those of us who won promotion and tenure and who loved the university and Piedmont Carolina felt cheated when the suspicious, anti-intellectual atmosphere in the department forced us to look elsewhere for proper recognition.

To return to the main subject, my (unusual) chance to teach a full-year course in my specialty while still a non-tenured assistant professor provided me with an opportunity to use the same method for writing in my own field that I had learned to utilize in other areas. While preparing each class, I read standard secondary books and essays with a view to ascertaining the normal or orthodox position with regard to the author and works under discussion; then I studied the primary texts to see to what extent that generalized overview actually described those particular poems, essays, or novels. At Illinois I had studied the thinking of the New Critics under Royal Gettmann and had written a term paper on the thought of I. A. Richards in a seminar on aesthetics taught by D. W. Gotshalk (whose Art and the Social Order *remains the most complete and least eccentric system for arriving at aesthetic judgments that I have ever seen). But Illinois, when I studied there, was not much under the influence of the New Criticism. The chief theoretician in the department then was Murray Krieger, who had spindled the New Critics in* The New Apologists for Poetry *(1956). At Duke, however, several of the younger faculty from Ivy League grad schools who were passing through and even Joe Riddel—who had learned the New Criticism at Wisconsin without quite believing in it—persuaded me to take the New Critics more seriously. One callow Yalie assured me that there was hope for me, because even "old Fred Pottle" had managed "to learn new tricks" and avoid total obsolescence by hearkening to Brooks and Wimsatt.*

Though I resisted, I had earlier been converted by my grad-school friends Howard Waskow and James L. Scoggins to Earl R. Wasserman's broader version of close reading in The Finer Tone, *and I soon learned enough "new tricks" to explicate from the text alone and to find organic unity everywhere I looked. Since I took up the technique with an attitude of skepticism rather than discipleship, the training provided a useful supplement to my other methods of research and analysis rather than a doctrinal straitjacket. The chief difference between my approach to the formal analysis of literary works and that of the New Criticism's "true believers" of the time, so many of whom (Geoffrey Hartman and Stanley Fish among them) have since denigrated the method as harmful to their work, is that I have always considered it a technical means, never a philosophical end. To find the unity that any good writer inevitably imposes on a serious work and to show how the imagery and the subtleties of diction reinforce that thematic center seem to me basic first concessions to the author's right to a fair hearing. Then the scholar-critic should go on to analyze the appropriateness of the author's formal response to the existential situation out of which it grew, as well as its value for readers of another time and place. As a teaching tool, close verbal and thematic explication is extremely valuable, for it is the easiest way to force students to come to terms with the poem and the poet's thought, rather than wallow in their own limited prior knowledge and awareness.*

The greatest fault of the New Critics of the Vanderbilt-LSU-Yale axis was not (as I now view them) their pretended separation of the author's and the reader's existential concerns from the literary artifact: neither Richards, T. S. Eliot, Leavis, nor the Fugitive and Southern Agrarian movements that preceded the New Critical phases of Ransom, Warren, Cleanth Brooks, or Tate, nor the Johnsonian moralism of Wimsatt would lead anyone to believe that they ever relied on such artifactism (see, especially, Alexander Karanikas, Tillers of a Myth: Southern Agrarians as Social and Literary Critics *[Madison: University of Wisconsin Press, 1966]). Their greatest shortcoming was, on the contrary, that they chose in advance, on doctrinal grounds, the authors whose works they decided should exhibit the organic unity that they proclaimed to be a sine qua non of good poetry, as well as those who would fail to pass the test. They were, therefore, dishonest in applying their chosen tests of greatness. Shelley had been the victim of some of their most ruthless hatchet jobs, but by 1963 I had no reason to doubt that Shelley would be easy enough to vindicate under their own criteria for complex ordering of disparate materials into a higher imaginative unity. Earl R. Wasserman had already demonstrated this unity in some of Shelley's poems in* The Subtler Language, *and I had done so for "Lines written among the Euganean Hills" in* PMLA *and for "The Triumph of Life" in the book I was then completing.*

While teaching the six major Romantic poets, novels by Scott and Austen, and selections from Carl Woodring's Riverside Edition of Prose of the Romantic Period, *I chose Lamb's essays as a test case for the application of the principle of organic unity to Romantic literature as a whole, because Lamb's "whimsical" essays were generally conceded to lack any such thing. I worked out organic readings of the essays while preparing to teach two classes on Lamb on 12 and 14 December 1962, drafted the essay during the spring of 1963, and revised it and added footnotes during the following summer, while teaching as a visiting lecturer in the Graduate School at the University of Illinois. There I showed it to Jack Stillinger, who on 24 August 1963 accepted it for publication in* JEGP. *Unfortunately, in the rush of trying to keep ahead of two summer-school classes on the Romantics—one of graduate students and the other of advanced undergrads—I failed to cover all the recent literature as I should have done, entirely overlooking during my writing Richard D. Haven's fine essay "The Romantic Art of Charles Lamb"* (ELH, 1963). *By the time my paper appeared in the July 1965 issue of* JEGP (64: 470–78), *I mentioned Haven in a footnote, as I did Daniel J. Mulcahy's essay in the autumn 1963 issue of* SEL *(which appeared, of course, after my essay had been completed). Had I earlier read Haven's piece, which also explicates "Old China," I might have been tempted, for variety's sake, to omit my discussion of that essay and explicate another, for I had originally treated just three essays simply as a convenient number from which to demonstrate that Lamb's essays* are *serious and thematically unified, rather than disjointed and whimsical.*

Since publishing this paper, I have written an explication of "Social and Political Satire in 'A Dissertation upon Roast Pig'" (CLB, n.s., 15 [July 1976]), *studied Lamb's life and writings in conjunction with Hazlitt's in Chapter 2 of* Intervals of Inspiration, *and begun to edit the manuscript Lamb sent to the* London Magazine *of his Elian essay later known as "Imperfect Sympathies" for volume 10 of* Shelley and his Circle, *as well as to write an essay on the interactions among the Lambs and the Shelley circle. The understanding of Lamb has grown very slowly, partly because many of the best books, such as Fred V. Randel's* The World of Elia *(Port Washington, N.Y.: Kennikat Press, 1975) and Robert D. Frank's* Don't Call Me Gentle Charles! *(Corvallis: Oregon State University Press, 1976)—and even the monthly* Charles Lamb Bulletin—*have not been as widely circulated as they deserve. (When I taught at the University of Washington, I regretted that none of these publications was in the library there—the best in the Northwest.) Cornell University Press has published three volumes of Edwin W. Marrs's magnificent edition of* The Letters of Charles and Mary Anne Lamb *(1975–); New York University Press has issued Winifred F. Courtney's valuable* Young Charles Lamb, 1775–1802 *(1982); Duke University Press has published Gerald Monsman's fine* Confessions of a Prosaic Dreamer: Charles Lamb's Art of Autobiography *(1984); and the University of Missouri Press has issued John R. Nabholtz's* "My Reader My Fellow-Labourer": A Study of English Romantic Prose *(1986). With important work on Lamb by such scholars as Thomas McFarland and Ralph M. Wardle also in press or in progress, Lamb may yet receive his rightful recognition as a major Romantic artist.*

Even since 1957, when Stuart M. Tave pointed up the limitations of the writings on Charles Lamb,[1] most studies of Lamb have tended to avoid explication of his works in favor of remarks biographical, appreciative, or bibliographical. Recently there have appeared two excellent studies devoted to elucidating the artistic method that Lamb used in the Elia essays and to measuring its effectiveness. These critical essays—both essential to anyone with sufficient interest in the subject to read the present essay—are "The Romantic Art of Charles Lamb" by Richard Haven and "Charles Lamb: The Antithetical Manner and the Two Planes" by the late Daniel J. Mulcahy.[2] The present paper, written independently, also attempts to help fill the gap noted by Tave and to refute the arguments advanced in the past both by admirers of Lamb who delighted in what they took to be the disorder and unbridled whimsicality of the Elia essays and by those who admired Charles Lamb as a conversationalist and letter-writer but sensed a markedly inferior intellect and strength of character in his productions as Elia. I propose to argue that Elia did not fall short of Lamb. Through examining three of his best-known familiar essays, I hope to show that in the Elia essays Lamb strove for artistic excellence and, because his judgment was equal to his genius, he succeeded in molding disparate and apparently trivial subjects and ideas into artistic unities of thematic significance—that, in short, the essays of Elia are successful works of art in all that the term would have meant to the writer of "Sanity of True Genius" and the best friend of the fountainhead of modern English literary criticism.

As I hope to show by analyzing systematically "Mrs. Battle's Opinions on Whist," "The Two Races of Men," and "Old China," the essays attributed to Elia achieve their thematic and artistic integrity by exploring everyday events and trivial opinions that suggest, analogically, larger philosophical issues. Focusing his ideas around an unpretentious symbol, Lamb could remain nondogmatic and skeptical through the light tone appropriate to this ostensible subject and, by ironically understating his conclusions, could avoid all trace of the "mental bombast" that, according to Coleridge, occasionally marred Wordsworth's poems of high seriousness. Lamb himself provides the rationale of his method in "Imperfect Sympathies," where he thus characterizes those who share his mental habits:

The owners of the sort of faculties I allude to, have minds rather suggestive than

---

1. "Charles Lamb: Criticism," in *The English Romantic Poets and Essayists: A Review of Research and Criticism*, ed. Carolyn W. Houtchens and L. H. Houtchens (New York: MLA, 1957), pp. 52–71.
2. Haven's essay was published in *ELH* 30 (1963): 137–46; Mulcahy's in *SEL* 3 (1963): 517–42.

comprehensive. . . . They are content with fragments and scattered pieces of Truth. She presents no full front to them—a feature or side-face at the most. Hints and glimpses, germs and crude essays at a system, is the utmost they pretend to. . . . They seldom wait to mature a proposition but e'en bring it to market in the green ear. They delight to impart their defective discoveries as they arise, without waiting for their full developement. They are no systematizers, and would but err more by attempting it.[3]

I

Though Mrs. Battle did not take whist at all lightly, Elia seems to treat his old companion and her favorite game with some detachment. At the end of the essay, however, Elia confesses himself so dedicated to cards that he wishes his game of piquet with Bridget could go on forever. Is this mere whimsy? Or do the card games in this essay assume significance beyond innocent amusement? One should note in the opening paragraph that old Sarah Battle, "now with God," "loved" one thing better than "a good game at whist": "her devotions." This pairing does not seem to be simply an ironic juxtaposition of the cosmic and the trivial in the values of an eccentric old woman: the author tells us nothing to indicate that Mrs. Battle's religion was shallow or sentimental; on the contrary, the sole reference to the result of her piety—"now with God"—suggests the opposite conclusion, that there was some defensible relation between Mrs. Battle's devotions and her whist-playing, the two most important things in her life.

Mrs. Battle, indeed, considered that playing whist "was her business, her duty, the thing she came into the world to do,—and she did it" (par. 3). It was "her noble occupation, to which she wound up her faculties." Whist was, in other words, Mrs. Battle's "vocation," that to which she had been called, that in the proper performance of which she could win salvation. Not that Elia or Mrs. Battle would care to translate the analogy as I have just done—assert rather than suggest—but this unmistakable suggestion governs the entire essay.

The first three paragraphs of the essay tell how important whist was in Mrs. Battle's life. The fourth paragraph, on Pope's *The Rape of the Lock*, forms a transition between the importance of a card game (as compared, for example, with books) and the following paragraphs, which advance reasons for whist's superiority over all other card games. Though Mrs. Battle liked Pope's account of the game of ombre, she found that kind of game itself (illustrated in ombre's near-relation quadrille) "showy and

---

3. *The Works of Charles and Mary Lamb*, ed. E. V. Lucas (London: Methuen, 1912), vol. 2, *Elia and The Last Essays of Elia*, p. 68. All quotations from Lamb's essays are taken from this volume.

specious, and likely to allure young persons." She pronounced, for example, "the dazzling supremacy and regal investiture of Spadille—absurd," preferring the more regular "pure aristocracy of whist." Indeed, "a grave simplicity was what she chiefly admired in her favourite game" (pars. 5, 6). Mrs. Battle was, in fact, a Puritan at the card table. Elia, a lover of beauty, appealed to the aesthetic dimension of religion "in Roman Catholic countries, where the music and the paintings draw in many to worship, whom your quaker spirit of unsensualizing would have kept out," to remind her that the "*beauty* of cards" contributed something to the value of the game: "Stripped of all that is imaginative in them, they must degenerate into mere gambling" (pars. 7, 8). Mrs. Battle, who "with a smile, confessed the soundness of [Elia's] logic," later bequeathed him "a curious cribbage board, made of the finest Sienna marble," as well as "a trifle of five hundred pounds."

The portrait of Elia receives another character line in his reaction to the bequest; he keeps the cribbage board "with religious care," whereas Mrs. Battle, "to confess a truth, was never greatly taken with cribbage. It was an essentially vulgar game, I have heard her say." If, as Elia insists, "Sarah Battle was a gentlewoman born," then the author himself must have seemed just a trifle vulgar to Mrs. Battle. The two viewpoints appear without a judgment between them—that remains the reader's prerogative—but the ninth and tenth paragraphs prepare the reader for the conclusion of the essay by sharpening his awareness of the differences between Mrs. Battle's character and that of the persona who treats her ideas so lightly.

As the name "Mrs. Battle" itself suggests, and as Elia repeatedly emphasizes, the old lady considered card games to be a kind of warfare: "She loved a thorough-paced partner, a determined enemy. . . . She fought a good fight: cut and thrust." "The skirmishes of quadrille, she would say, reminded her of the petty ephemeral embroilments of the little Italian states . . . but the wars of whist were comparable to the long, steady, deep-rooted, rational, antipathies of the great French and English nations." In paragraph 11, however, she qualifies this analogy by saying that "cards are war, in disguise of a sport . . . ." She therefore disliked card games for two players ("when single adversaries encounter, the ends proposed are too palpable") and for three players ("a mere naked war of every man against every man"). In whist the game could go on seriously, but with two partners to share in the joys of victory and two to console one another in defeat. She always played for a small stake, and she did not believe in games without an element of luck, for "games of pure skill . . . played for a stake . . . were a mere system of over-reaching" (par. 12).

In short, Mrs. Battle believed that "man is a gaming animal" and that "this passion can scarcely be more safely expended than upon a game at cards" in which, "during the illusion, we *are* as mightily concerned as those whose stake is crowns and kingdoms." Whist is "quite as diverting, and a great deal more innoxious, than many of those more serious *games* of life, which men play, without esteeming them to be such" (par. 13). Mrs. Battle thus makes explicit the larger analogy and the ramifications of her vocation. To one skeptical of the objective value of religious, philosophical, political, or even aesthetic dogmas and slogans, to one for whom every endeavor seemed a commitment to an illusion, complete dedication to the game of whist might serve to develop one's character and purify the soul as surely as would devotion to any other cause or creed.

In the concluding paragraphs Elia, having already established the differences between his character and that of Mrs. Battle, remarks that he sometimes finds card games stimulating even if there is no stake, no reward to be won. Sometimes, when he is "in sickness, or not in the best spirits," he plays "a game at piquet *for love*[4] with my cousin Bridget—Bridget Elia." Though he breaks all of Mrs. Battle's stern injunctions, he yet manages to enjoy the game: "I wished it might have lasted for ever, though we gained nothing, and lost nothing, though it was a mere shade of play: I would be content to go on in that idle folly for ever." For Elia the aesthetic enjoyment of the game is its own reward. He need not vanquish his "enemy" nor anticipate a reward. The game of life has value in the present moment quite apart from subsequent developments, which might, indeed, prove as painful as "the gentle lenitive to my foot, which Bridget was doomed to apply after the game was over . . . ."[5]

Lamb in this essay and Hazlitt in his famous eulogy for John Cavanagh, the fives player,[6] developed the rationale for the elevation of sports and

4. See "New Year's Eve": "I am naturally, beforehand, shy of novelties; new books, new faces, new years. . . . I plunge into foregone visions and conclusions. I encounter pell-mell with past disappointments. I am armour-proof against old discouragements. I forgive, or overcome in fancy, old adversaries. I play over again *for love*, as the gamesters phrase it, games, for which I once paid so dear" (p. 32).

5. "I am not content to pass away 'like a weaver's shuttle.' Those metaphors solace me not, nor sweeten the unpalatable draught of mortality. I care not to be carried with the tide, that smoothly bears human life to eternity; and reluct at the inevitable course of destiny. I am in love with this green earth; the face of town and country; the unspeakable rural solitudes, and the sweet security of streets. I would set up my tabernacle here" ("New Year's Eve," p. 34).

6. William Hazlitt, "Death of John Cavanagh," *Examiner*, 7 February 1819; reprinted as the conclusion to "The Indian Jugglers" in *Table-Talk* (1821). Hazlitt wrote, in part: "He was a fine, sensible, manly player, who did what he could, but that was more than any one else could even affect to do. His blows were not undecided and ineffectual—lumbering like Mr. Wordsworth's epic poetry, nor wavering like Mr. Coleridge's lyric prose, nor short of the mark like Mr. Brougham's speeches, nor wide of it like Mr. Canning's wit, nor foul like the *Quarterly*, nor *let* balls like the *Edinburgh Review*. Cobbett and Junius together would have made a Cavanagh" (*Complete Works*, ed. P. P. Howe, vol. 8 [London: J. M. Dent, 1931], p. 87).

games as symbols or parables of human life's serious occupations, and Hemingway's billiard players, fishermen, and bullfighters are distant relations of Mrs. Battle.

II

"The Two Races of Men"[7] exhibits a subtler, more ambitious interweaving of theme and subject. The ostensible topic under discussion is the classification of "the human species" into "two distinct races, *the men who borrow,* and *the men who lend.*" After setting forth the thesis in two introductory paragraphs, Lamb explores it through two subsequent divisions of the essay: six paragraphs ironically chronicle the activities of those members of "the *great race*" who, like Ralph Bigod, Esq., specialize in borrowing money, and the remaining six paragraphs center on that "class of alienators more formidable" ("to one like Elia")—"your *borrowers of books.*" Chief among these scavengers is "Comberbatch" (Coleridge), "matchless in his depredations."

Elia, one sees immediately, distinguishes between these two classes of borrowers almost as sharply as he does between borrowers and lenders. He who "borrows" from his purse steals, not trash (Elia's refutation of the popular fallacy "That Enough Is as Good as a Feast" forbids this interpretation), but something that, once gone, is unlikely ever to return. Ralph Bigod, the Great Borrower of Money, "contrived to keep his treasury always empty. . . . A good part he drank away . . . , some he gave away, the rest he threw away, literally tossing and hurling it violently from him . . . into ponds, or ditches, or deep holes . . ." (par. 7). Elia's hyperbolic irony about the greatness of this Alexander, setting forth "borrowing and to borrow," who, in his "triumphant progress throughout this island," reportedly "laid a tythe part of the inhabitants under contribution," assures the reader that nobody, neither borrower nor lender, gained from the exchange.

With Comberbatch's borrowing of books it was otherwise. Though he occasionally borrowed Elia's books without returning them, three things comfort their owner: first, if Comberbatch "sometimes, like the sea sweeps away a treasure, at another time, sea-like, he throws up as rich an equivalent to match it" (par. 12); second, "to lose a volume to C. carries some sense and meaning in it" because "you are sure that he will make one hearty meal on your viands, if he can give no account of the platter after it"

---

[7]. *Elia,* pp. 26–31. This essay, published in the *London Magazine* in December 1820, preceded "Mrs. Battle's Opinions on Whist" by two months (with "New Year's Eve" intervening, January 1821).

(par. 13); and, finally, if one lends his books "to such a one as S. T. C.—he will return them (generally anticipating the time appointed) with usury; enriched with annotations, tripling their value" (par. 14).

Not all book-borrowers are like S. T. C. Some, like "spiteful K[enney]" and his wife, "part-French, better-part Englishwoman," borrow not to read but in "the mere spirit of contradiction, and childish love of getting the better of [their] friend." Borrowers like K. belong with Ralph Bigod and other borrowers of material possessions, which cannot be shared but only dissipated. Ideas, on the other hand, can multiply; Elia introduced S. T. C. to Sir Thomas Browne, and S. T. C.'s annotations have called Elia's attention to the beauties of Samuel Daniel.[8]

The real theme of "The Two Races of Men" is, then, that there is indeed a Great Race of borrowers, men exemplified by Alcibiades, Falstaff, Sir Richard Steele, and Richard Brinsley Sheridan (par. 2)—and by Coleridge; these borrowers, in their turn, contribute much to the world's welfare—not, perhaps, in a material way, with money or physical books, but through intellectual contributions to mankind in general and to their friends and companions in particular. Such men are those to whom Elia and all wishing to avoid combining the "penalties of Lazarus and of Dives" (par. 3) (poverty and parsimony) should open their hearts and their libraries and receive the rewards of their magnanimity from truly great-minded men.

III

The theme of "Old China" seems obvious enough, except for the apparent irrelevance of the remarks on old china with which the essay begins and concludes. The main body of the essay consists of Cousin Bridget's elegy on the passing of the good old days of poverty and Elia's unsentimental, hard-headed reply: "It is true we were happier when we were poorer, but we were also younger, my cousin. . . . Competence to age is supplementary youth; a sorry supplement indeed, but I fear the best that is to be had" (par. 16). Both Elia and Bridget regret the loss of their youth and its humble adventures, but whereas Bridget tries to externalize the problem by blam-

---

8. "The slight vacuum in the left-hand case . . . was whilom the commodious resting-place of Brown on Urn Burial. C. will hardly allege that he knows more about that treatise than I do, who introduced it to him, and was indeed the first (of the moderns) to discover its beauties . . ." (p. 29).

"I found two other volumes (you had three), the 'Arcadia,' and 'Daniel,' enriched with manuscript notes. I wish every book I have were so noted. They have thoroughly converted me to relish Daniel, or to say I relish him, for, after all, I believe I did relish him" (Lamb to Coleridge, 7 June 1809, *Letters of Charles and Mary Lamb*, ed. E. V. Lucas [New Haven: Yale University Press, 1935], 2:75).

ing the loss of past joys on the accumulation of wealth, Elia more realistically recognizes that the difficulty lies within himself and Bridget, subject to the gentle ravages of Fate, Time, Occasion, Chance, and Change.

Elia's love for old china is one of those tastes "of too ancient a date to admit of our remembering distinctly that it was an acquired one. I can call to mind the first play, and the first exhibition, that I was taken to; but I am not conscious of a time when china jars and saucers were introduced into my imagination" (par. 1). In the symbolic world of this essay, then, Time governs the plays and pictures that Bridget mentions in her lament for lost happiness and that thereby become symbols of the decay of human faculties (much as do beauties of nature, seen but no longer felt, in Coleridge's "Dejection: An Ode"). Because the love of old china is not, however, associated with any particular moment in the past, this attachment participates in a timeless world that mutability cannot affect.

Not only are the emotions that Elia attaches to old china free from time, but the painted figures on the china itself are free from the trammels of space: "those little, lawless, azure-tinctured grotesques . . . float about, uncircumscribed by any element, in that world before perspective—a china tea-cup" (par. 2). Elia likes to see his "old friends—whom distance cannot diminish—figuring up in the air (so they appear to our optics), yet on *terra firma* still" (par. 3). Though in describing the activities of these painted, imaginative figures Elia estimates distances between them, he doubts "if far or near can be predicated of their world": distance, like time, resides in the subject, not the object, and is an illusion of "our optics." Indeed, not only do time and space disappear within the imaginary-ideal world of the tea-cup, but even more basic antinomies are there reconciled: the men have women's faces, though the women, "if possible," have "still more womanish expressions." And, "seen through the lucid atmosphere of fine Cathay," one can see "a cow and rabbit couchant, and co-extensive" or, symbolically, without extension at all in the Cartesian sense, simply coexistent in a realm of Ideas.

Bridget bemoans the loss of human youth and novelty and joy against the backdrop of a world where Beauty *can* keep her lustrous eyes and where youth does *not* grow pale, and specter-thin, and die. Like Keats's Grecian urn, Yeats's lapis lazuli sculpture, or T. S. Eliot's Chinese jar, Elia's china tea-cups present a still point amid a world of flux and, at the same time, a stimulus for the human imagination both of him who creates and him who contemplates them. Elia turns back to the china, therefore, at the end of the essay, in order to retain his hold on the values of a summer world that he feels slipping away from him:

". . . could those days return—could you and I once more walk our thirty miles a-day—could Bannister and Mrs. Bland again be young, and you and I be young to see them—could the good old one shilling gallery days return . . . I know not the fathom line that ever touched a descent so deep as I would be willing to bury more wealth in than Crœsus had, or the great Jew R[othschild] is supposed to have, to purchase it. And now do just look at that merry little Chinese waiter holding an umbrella, big enough for a bed-tester, over the head of that pretty insipid half-Madona-ish chit of a lady in that very blue summer-house."

Could the world of human affairs, even the great world of Crœsus and the Rothschilds, retain its values, man might find his ultimate meaning in worldly activity—in the affairs of the East India Company, for example. But because Elia feels this to be impossible, he turns instead to a world of fragile art that proves to be a never-fading source of delight—as we, for example, turn to the essays of Elia.

IV

Lamb, as I have said, intentionally avoided the kind of overt moralizing that I have explicated from his hints and analogies. Once the thematic unity of an essay becomes clear, however, one can return to Lamb's writings with a new appreciation of the perfectly balanced tone that suggests deeper meanings without committing Lamb or his reader to the logical analyses or marshaled facts that must have accompanied a discursive development of the thesis. Lamb, the humane skeptic, preferred not to dogmatize—or even to speculate systematically—on the nature of the state of being that must inevitably follow "that last game" of piquet he played with his "sweet cousin," but he was not unwilling to set forth his opinions on the game of life and the stakes for which a man ought willingly to play. He therefore created a symbol-world through which he could explore universal human problems in a truly imaginative way; like the pastoral world of Robert Frost's best poetry, the trivial universe of Elia and Bridget, of whist games, borrowed books, and frail china tea-cups, provided a language for one who truly desired both to teach and to delight.

14

Shelley as Agrarian Reactionary

"*Shelley as Agrarian Reactionary*" *arose out of research I was doing for* Shelley and his Circle *in the late 1970s (especially for the essay "Shelley and the Upholsterers of Bath," vol. 8 [1986], pp. 827–42), the review-article that I was writing on Coleridge's* Essays on His Times *(Item 5), and the Marxist ideas of Kenneth Neill Cameron, my predecessor as editor of* Shelley and his Circle.

Though Ken Cameron and I respect one each other's scholarship, we have never been personally close. We first met to any purpose when Ken was on the same MLA-sponsored charter flight that Mary W. Reiman and I took to England in the summer of 1961. While departure of the flight was delayed, we struck up a conversation that included discussions of our work on Shelley (the Pforzheimer Library had ordered my dissertation from University Microfilms and Ken had looked at it) and our respective plans for the summer. A month later, I met Ken Cameron in the Upper Reading Room of the Bodleian Library during his brief visit to Oxford, and he invited Mary and me to dine with him and his wife and daughter at the Mitre, the Oxford hotel where they were staying. Later in the summer, we met the Camerons, again quite by chance, on Princes Street in Edinburgh, where we were spending three days (during a two-week trip from Oxford to Edinburgh and thence to Cambridge) and where the Camerons had just arrived, following a visit to Russia. It was at this time that I first became aware of Cameron's admiration for the Soviet Union, but not until much later did I learn how fully absorbed his thinking was by orthodox Marxist doctrines.

Four years later, when with Ken Cameron's recommendation I was appointed to succeed him as editor of Shelley and his Circle and we saw one another regularly in New York, we became much better acquainted. But not until he was no longer around the Library did I learn from other colleagues that he had been much more committed to the Communist movement than he had given me any notion of. His silence was clearly intentional, for my political perspective, largely shaped by my family, was quite different from his. Henry W. Reiman, my father, was an idealistic history teacher who hated social injustice so much that he could hardly believe in its existence. My parents, their parents (both farm families), and most of their friends were fundamentally Willkie Republicans, and I, who have always prided *myself on fighting for the underdog, saw Republicans as the most overwhelmed of underdogs in our working-class Italian neighborhood in Erie, Pennsylvania, during the tenure of Franklin D. Roosevelt. (I finally became a Democrat in reaction to the Goldwater campaign of 1964.) Moreover, I was a believing and active Presbyterian churchman, while both Ken Cameron and his wife Bess sprang from generations of atheists.*

Thus, though Ken Cameron and I share certain ideals of scholarly responsibility and ethical behavior, we are temperamental and ideological opposites. What he means by Shelley's radicalism and what I mean by it are two entirely different things. For Ken, to be a radical is to be in the ideological tradition of Marx and Engels; for me, to be radical means to oppose abuses of power by those in control of society, whatever ideology they may espouse. All Shelley's actions that were offensive to middle-class values once seemed to me to be aberrations from the justice he said he was fighting for, while Ken Cameron just found them amusing. Some of our differences may be reflected in the tone of my "Profile of a Contemporary: Kenneth Neill Cameron" that Paul Magnuson asked me to write for The Wordsworth Circle *(8 [1977]: 253–57).*

As student radicalism of the late sixties and early seventies helped me to understand better why Shelley dissented from middle-class values, I also learned through my historical reading how his rebellion differed both from that of the babyboom children of America's suburbs and from the radicalism of some of his contemporaries. I found it first strange and then significant, for example, that Shelley never protested against the Corn Laws, the bêtes noires of so many other English radicals in the nineteenth century. I saw differences between the programs promoted by Robert Owen (an ancestor of Bess Cameron) and Shelley's ideas, and other differences between Shelley's politics and those of Henry Brougham (on whom I was writing for Shelley and his Circle, *vol. 7), who kept moving back and forth between the Holland House Whigs and the Westminster "Philosophical Radicals" such as Jeremy Bentham and Francis Place. When reading Coleridge's (and some of Southey's) political prose, I realized that their "conservative" programs resembled the "liberal" panaceas of the mid-twentieth century, while most of the radicals of that era stood for laissez faire, as Shelley did not. He, it seemed, shared more than literary interests with Coleridge and even with Southey.*

Shortly before this, I had read Cameron's Humanity and Society: A World History *(see note 15), a Marxist overview of human social relations on all continents from the emergence of mankind to the French Revolution. One point he made there impressed me as particularly relevant to Shelley's development: the mind-set of landed aristocrats differed from that of the urban commercial classes, even in such basic ways as the distinctions between the characteristic modes of thought of Plato (a landed aristocrat) and Aristotle (the scion of a colonial commercial family).*

Clearly, Shelley fit into the former category, both in social origins and in perspective. While I worked on "Shelley as Agrarian Reactionary," I was reading both Terry Eagleton's little book on Marxism and Literary Criticism *and the much more profound study by the Nigerian scholar-critic Michael J. C. Echeruo entitled* The Conditioned Imagination from Shakespeare to Conrad *(New York: Holmes & Meier, 1978). Eagleton explains why a reactionary critic of society often emerges with a more deeply radical analysis of the ills of a society than does a conventional liberal, while Echeruo shows that the works of the greatest writers have embodied rather than evaded the prejudices of their own social heritage. (Echeruo, with his wide knowledge of early European literature about Africans, is especially enlightening on Shakespeare's evocation in* Othello *of the popular conceptions of "blackamoors" in Tudor England.) From these writers, I gained the framework for a new understanding of Shelley's radicalism that could take into account the Marxist understanding of the effects of social and economic forces on an author without stereotyping and judging the variations of his or her thought on the basis of predetermined tests for doctrinal purity. I looked at Shelley's political ideas in terms of his personal heritage to show how his background had helped to shape his thought in ways quite different from that of the urban and middle-class reformers of the day. I cite Cameron and Eagleton in my notes; I intended to cite Echeruo, too, but his argument ultimately seemed too complex to characterize briefly, while explaining how Shelley fit into it.*

Timothy Webb, then the new editor of the Keats-Shelley Memorial Bulletin, *had asked me to submit an essay to help get that journal back into full swing after a few years of drifting. When I first sent this paper to him, he found it lacking in specificity, and so I added the analysis of* The Mask of Anarchy. *The paper appeared in KSMB 30 (1979): 5–15. Since its appearance, even younger scholars previously committed to a Marxist view of Shelley as a radical have been able to integrate my observations into a larger view of Shelley as an anarchist and utopian thinker, as Michael Henry Scrivener does in* Radical Shelley *(Princeton: Princeton University Press, 1982). Kenneth Neill Cameron, however, then at work on his defense of Josef Stalin (*Stalin: Man of Contradiction, *1987) and others of his culture heroes, was not impressed, as can be seen in his "Shelley as Philosophical and Social Thinker: Some Modern Evaluations" (SiR 21 [1982]: 357–66).*

Leigh Hunt noted that "the family connexions of Mr. Shelley belonged to a small party in the House of Commons, itself belonging to another party. They were Whig Aristocrats. . . ."[1] Though (as Hunt goes on to point out) Shelley was offended by the moral and political hypocrisy and the anti-

---

1. *Lord Byron and Some of His Contemporaries* (London: Henry Colburn, 1828), p. 178.

intellectualism of the country gentry as he knew them in his youth, he never lost some perspectives that developed with his character from the very fact that he was brought up as the heir to large landed estates in Sussex in an area of prosperous grain and foodstuff farming. As Hunt (with benign humor) and Peacock (with general sympathy) also noted, Shelley never quite outgrew his predisposition to think of social, economic, and moral questions from the viewpoint of a landed aristocrat.

In transcribing and commenting on Shelley's ideas and even his imagery in *A Philosophical View of Reform*,[2] I became aware of some of the implications of Shelley's background for his political and social ideas; since then, I have had a greater opportunity to study the lives and politics of landed Whig aristocrats and the transformation of Whig and Tory politics from the mid-eighteenth century to the agitation for repeal of the Corn Acts in the 1830s and 1840s that tore both parties asunder and gave entirely new meanings in British politics to the terms *liberal* and *conservative* (with or without capital letters).[3] The conclusion I have reached is that it may be a historical error to call Shelley simply a "radical" in terms of the larger sweep of British social and political development during this period. Rather, when Shelley's political and social program is measured by the massive changes in British economic, social, and political activity and institutions, many of his ideas must be judged "reactionary" by virtue of their emphasis on forms characteristic of and beneficial to the agricultural estate system of the eighteenth century and earlier. Like Wordsworth, Coleridge, and William Cobbett (to name only three contemporaries whose thinking to some degree parallels his), Shelley generally opposed laws and programs that favored monetary, commercial, and industrial expansion. He ignored the Corn Laws, which maintained artificially high prices for grain and thereby increased the profits of farmers while squeez-

---

2. *Shelley and his Circle*, vol. 6 (Cambridge: Harvard University Press, 1973), pp. 945–1066.
3. Among secondary sources (besides the *DNB*, *Annual Registers*, peerages, and encyclopedias), I have found the following useful in studying the political background: F. O'Gorman, *The Whig Party and the French Revolution* (London: Macmillan, 1967); Michael Roberts, *The Whig Party, 1807–1812* (London: Frank Cass, 1965); A. S. Turberville, *The House of Lords in the Age of Reform, 1784–1837* (London: Faber and Faber, 1958); G. E. Mingay, *English Landed Society in the Eighteenth Century* (London: Routledge and Kegan Paul, 1963); F. M. L. Thompson, *English Landed Society in the Nineteenth Century* (London: Routledge and Kegan Paul, 1963); E. P. Thompson, *The Making of the English Working Class* (London: Victor Gollancz, 1963); Douglas Hay et al., *Albion's Fatal Tree: Crime and Society in Eighteenth-Century England* (New York: Pantheon, 1975); J. P. D. Dunbabin, *Rural Discontent in Nineteenth-Century Britain* (New York: Holmes & Meier, 1974); Norman McCord, *The Anti-Corn Law League, 1838–1846* (London: George Allen & Unwin, 1958); Travis L. Crosby, *English Farmers and the Politics of Protection, 1815–1852* (Hassocks, Sussex: Harvester Press, 1977).

ing the growing urban population (whose prosperity depended upon foreign trade) between high food prices and low wages or—when foreign competition increased in the 1830s and 1840s—chronic unemployment. Shelley did not oppose—and in his dealings with tradesmen and moneylenders personally took advantage of—laws that prohibited the confiscation and sale of hereditary landed estates to pay the owner's debts.[4] In 1807 Sir Samuel Romilly (the leading barrister who later acted in important legal battles involving Shelley and Byron) was serving as solicitor general and introduced in the House of Commons legislation designed to correct this legal vestige of the feudal system. William Lamb (later Lord Melbourne) wrote in his journal on the occasion:

> The third reading of the Solicitor-General's (Sir S. Romilly's) Bill for making the freehold estates of persons dying insolvent assets for the payment of their simple contract debts. The landed interest were much alarmed, and all the old topics of the danger of innovation, the value of country gentlemen, the sanctity of family settlements, the antiquity of the present law, were very strongly insisted upon. . . . The Bill was rejected—sixty-nine to forty-seven—the majority having in it many landed proprietors, either in possession or expectancy; a most disgraceful division, and one which really hurt and mortified me deeply, as I could see no plausible argument *ab inconvenienti* . . . that . . . ought to prevail against the glaring injustice of the law as it at present stands.[5]

As social and political historians have noted, the members of the House of Lords effectively controlled the House of Commons at least until the passage of the first reform bill of 1832. But as F. M. L. Thompson also observes, the nobility had such great power during most of the period between 1660 and 1832 that they were divided by private interests and personal rivalries. Though I have not all the facts at hand to sketch the interactions of the various factions that called themselves "Whigs" and "Tories" during the late eighteenth century, I will observe (and this is far from a truism among the social and political historians of England that I have read) that the heart of the "Whig Connexion"—the great magnates such as the Howard dukes of Norfolk and the Russell dukes of Bedford—had their chief estates in the east or south of England and derived the bulk of their income from the rents of tenant farmers with long-term leases who raised

4. Some instances of this penchant have been discussed by Kenneth Neill Cameron and Donald H. Reiman in *Shelley and his Circle*; see, for example, "Shelley's Chariot" (vol. 3 [1970], pp. 153–78), SC 262, Commentary (vol. 3, pp. 333–39), SC 454, Commentary (vol. 5 [1973], pp. 478–84), and "Shelley and the Upholsterers of Bath" and related commentaries forthcoming in vol. 8.

5. *Lord Melbourne's Papers*, ed. L. C. Sanders (London: Longmans, Green, 1889), pp. 32–33.

cereal grains ("corn") and other foodstuffs.⁶ The Tory lords, on the other hand, included a much larger number who derived their chief income—or, at least, whose family fortunes had been recently established—from activities other than rents from corn farming: for example, the Lowther earls of Lonsdale derived a large part of their income from coal mines at Whitehaven and from the development of the port there. Many of the peers whose estates were in Ireland, Wales, the Border and Highlands of Scotland, and the west of England drew their chief income from raising sheep to supply the textile industry or from land development of the new industrial cities and towns that were springing up in the Midlands, Lancashire, the West Riding of Yorkshire, and the Scottish Lowlands. The family of Lord Grosvenor (patron of William Gifford) had built its chief fortune from subdividing and developing one rather small manor (acquired through marriage in 1677) into what is now the part of London surrounding Grosvenor Square (in Shelley's time the most fashionable address in London).⁷ The wealth of Robert Banks Jenkinson, Earl of Liverpool and long-time Tory prime minister, came in the first instance from his father's and his own lucrative government positions and sinecures and from involvement in foreign (particularly East Indian) trade. Other leading Tories drew their wealth from West Indian plantations or from supplying goods and services to the British army and navy. (The same owners of forested lands in the west of England, Wales, Scotland, or the colonies profited, for example, from the sale of timber for shipbuilding and repairs.) These Tories, with deep personal interests in foreign trade, the colonial empire, and open markets throughout the world, and in expanding the amount of money that passed through their hands as government officials and contractors, naturally tended to identify British national

6. F. M. L. Thompson's *English Landed Society in the Nineteenth Century* includes a map (p. xiii) reproducing a line of demarcation between "the predominantly corn counties of the east from the grazing counties of the west . . . from J. Caird, *English Agriculture in 1850–51.*" In addition to major seats at Arundel Castle in Sussex and Worksop Manor, Nottinghamshire, the Duke of Norfolk had a northern seat at Greystoke (or Graystock) Castle, near Penrith, Cumberland, where Shelley, Harriet Shelley, and Eliza Westbrook were his guests from 1 December to 8 or 9 December 1811. Though this estate falls on the "grazing" side of Caird's line, I recall from a brief visit to Greystoke in 1971 that the area surrounding it is relatively level rather than hilly and was at the time of my visit devoted to raising grain rather than sheep. Kenneth Neill Cameron's assertion in *The Young Shelley: Genesis of a Radical* (New York: Macmillan, 1950) that Sir Bysshe Shelley and the Duke of Norfolk, because they were Whigs, supported the mercantile interests and drew a great part of their wealth from sheep farming and timber (pp. 37–38) was based on insufficient information about the Shelley estates and the agricultural situation in the southern and eastern parts of England, as well as on generalizations made about the dominant Whigs of the seventeenth and eighteenth centuries that were not valid for the Foxite Whigs of the 1790s. Walpole was a mercantilist; Bedford and Norfolk certainly were not.

7. See A. I. Dasant, *A History of Grosvenor Square* (London: Macmillan, 1935).

interest with defeating French expansion, controlling the seas, and seizing new colonies and overseas markets. The agrarian Whig magnates, on the other hand, saw the French Wars only as an excuse to increase their taxes, draw off their labor force for the military, and add to the wealth of the capitalists, industrialists, and overseas slaveowners who were their rivals for political control of the country. (Some of the Whigs would have favored the increase in the bureaucracy, government spending, and peculations of officialdom if they had been the "ins" instead of the "outs.") In short, the "radicalism" of such Whig magnates as Francis, Duke of Bedford (whose attacks on the Pitt administration's aggressive policies of containing the French Revolution elicited Burke's *Letter to a Noble Lord*), and Charles, Duke of Norfolk (who was the political ally and sponsor of Sir Bysshe Shelley and Timothy Shelley, M.P.), was essentially an attack by the older landed aristocracy on government policies designed to enrich the capitalist-commercial interests. These so-called "radical" Whigs of the 1790s hoped to rally a coalition of the food-farming interests in the populous agricultural areas of the south and east of England, small merchants, craftsmen, and professional men, and ideological humanitarians who opposed slavery and the bloodshed of war (some of whom also favored broadening the franchise, particularly in the growing towns and cities). France when ruled by the old aristocracy had competed with the British agricultural interests, whereas France ruled by the bourgeoisie would compete with British capital, manufacturing, and commercial interests. Why shouldn't Bedford and Norfolk favor the French Revolution? But should a modern historian call Bedford and Norfolk radicals or reactionaries?

According to G. E. Mingay, in 1790 "there were some 400 families [in all Great Britain] who could be described as great landlords" with incomes of at least £5,000 to £10,000 per year.[8] Certainly Sir Bysshe Shelley fell into that category, for after his death—when his estates were divided between his two principal heirs (Sir Timothy Shelley, his eldest son by his first wife, and Sir John Shelley Sidney of Penshurst, his eldest son by his second wife) and after all the younger siblings of each had been provided for (as well as Sir Bysshe's mistress Eleanor Nicholls of Canterbury and his four children by her)—the rent-rolls of the lands in trust for Sir Timothy Shelley's estates totaled about £4,500 per year and the trustees held at least £15,000 in unencumbered mortgages and accounts receivable for Sir Timothy and his heirs.[9] (Sir Bysshe had also directed that the residue of his

---

8. *English Landed Society in the Eighteenth Century,* pp. 19–20.
9. These facts are drawn from two legal documents in The Carl H. Pforzheimer Library: (1) "Analysis of the Will and Codicils of Sir Bysshe Shelley Bart. deceased" (Shelleyana

personal property be used to purchase additional land in England.) Thus Bysshe Shelley's heirs in Sussex and Kent grew up in the knowledge that Bysshe was one of the small number of very wealthy landowners in Britain, and yet—when the estates were divided—found themselves on the lower edge of this elite class. As time passed and great fortunes were made in trade, manufacturing, and government appointments (with their vast opportunities for speculation and peculation added to the acknowledged emoluments), all the landed families sank in relation to these *nouveaux riches*.[10] On the growth of this new class of wealthy men, Shelley (like Peacock, for example, in his genealogical account of "Ebenezer Mac Crotchet, Esquire" in *Crotchet Castle* [1831]) expressed himself very negatively in *A Philosophical View of Reform* (1819–1820):

Instead of one aristocracy, the condition which in the present state of human affairs, the friends of justice and liberty are willing to subscribe as to an inevitable evil, they have supplied us with two aristocracies: The one, consisting [of] the great land proprietors and wealthy merchants, receive and interchange the produce of this country with the produce of other countries; in this because all other great communities have as yet acquiesced in it we acquiesce. . . . [But there] is an aristocracy of attorneys and excisemen and directors and government pensioners, usurers, stock jobbers, country bankers with their dependents and descendants. These are a set of pelting wretches in whose employment there is nothing to exercise, even to their distortion, the more majestic faculties of the soul. Though at the bottom it is all trick, there is something magnificent in the chivalrous disdain of infamy connected with a gentleman. . . . But in the habits and lives of this new aristocracy created out of an increase [in] the public calamities, and whose existence must be determined by their termination, there is nothing to qualify our disapprobation. They eat and drink and sleep, and in the interval of those [actions] being performed with the most ridiculous ceremony and accompaniments, they cringe and lie.[11]

Shelley goes on to pillory the *nouveaux riches* in several equally stinging sentences, and he writes that, because "the merchant and the country gentleman," the "instruments of the fraud," are "as usual" the people first deceived, they "may be excused for believing" that the existence of this

---

170B) and (2) a list of "Property & Estates under the Settlement of 1782[,] Settlement of 1791 & Will of John Shelley Esq." (Shelleyana 173). This second document, dated 20 January 1815 for delivery to Shelley's solicitor P. W. Longdill, contains a full list of landed properties under the settlements, together with the names of tenants and the lengths and terms of leases. These documents are cited by permission of The Carl and Lily Pforzheimer Foundation, Inc.

10. Mingay, *English Landed Society in the Eighteenth Century*, p. 4; details on the decline are given in F. M. L. Thompson's companion volume, *English Landed Society in the Nineteenth Century*.

11. Edited from the literal transcription published in *Shelley and his Circle*, 6:1016–17.

second aristocracy "is connected with the permanence of the best practicable forms of the social order."[12] In short, Shelley believes that custom, tradition, and the higher nature of their character and utility sanction the landed and older merchant aristocracy, but denies the value of those whose wealth was newly created by the need to fund the national debt, the issuing of paper money and credit, and the expansion of governmental bureaucracy during the American and French wars, 1775–1815. Shelley does not, at this point, mention wealth created by industrialists. In another part of *A Philosophical View of Reform*, he presents "two descriptions of property"—a legitimate one deriving from "labour, industry, economy, skill, genius, or any similar power honourably and innocently exerted" and another that was procured "by fraudulent and violent means" or "has its foundation in usurpation or violence, without which, by the nature of things, immense aggregations of possessions of gold or land could never have been accumulated." Here, we see, he lumps all substantial gains from capital investments, rather than from "skill" or "genius," as illegitimate property of the second kind.

Shelley then proceeds to state that the second kind of property "being transmitted from father to son, acquires, as property of the more legitimate kind loses, force and sanction, but in a more limited manner." And he suggests that all such property, in excess of the needs of common life, might be liable to expropriation by the nation to pay off the "national debt"—but at a discount, since that debt is not truly national, but "is a debt contracted by the whole of a particular class in the nation towards a portion of that class."[13]

As radical as this solution seems to be, it would merely, as he said earlier, "determine" (i.e., "to put an end to," *OED* I.1) the entire race of "pelting wretches" in the second aristocracy. Once the national debt, paper money, and other "fraudulent . . . means" had been abolished, thought Shelley, these drones would be forced to earn their livings by their "labour, industry, . . . skill, genius." That would, we note, leave only the older landed and commercial aristocracy, though reduced in wealth by the nation's expropriation of the gross excess acquired by their ancestors by "grants from feudal sovereigns, . . . lands of the antient Catholic clergy, . . . or the products of patents and monopolies" (*Shelley and his Circle*, 6:1035).

It would be interesting to know the full history of Sir Bysshe Shelley's acquisition of land and money. The supposition is that his original lands came chiefly from directly inheriting small holdings that had been in the family for generations and from marrying two heiresses of estates—in the

12. Edited from ibid., 6:1017.
13. Edited from ibid., 6:1033–37.

case of Shelley's own grandmother, Mary Catherine Michell, the sixteen-year-old orphan daughter of Rev. Theobald Michell of Horsham, perhaps herself the heiress of a series of small holdings inherited by her father from various relatives. The Michells and Shelleys had earlier intermarried, and Field Place itself had belonged to the Michells through the sixteenth and seventeenth centuries.[14] If these inferences are true, then it just happens that the bulk of landed wealth held in trust by the terms of Sir Bysshe Shelley's will for his son Sir Timothy, grandson Percy Bysshe, and *his* eldest surviving son, might be of that class of property—according to Shelley's arguments in *A Philosophical View of Reform* (an unfinished draft, to be sure)—that would be exempt from national confiscation.

Shelley, I suggest—benevolent and generous though he was and possessing a highly sensitive social conscience though he did—was not himself exempt from being unconsciously swayed in his social, economic, and political theories by inbred class prejudices.[15] He might agree (with Burke) that the Russell dukes of Bedford, whose lands were gifts of Henry VIII for service in the suppression of the Roman Catholic church, or the Howard dukes of Norfolk, whose lands descended from the feudal titles of the Norman barons who followed William the Conqueror, should have their patrimony reduced or entirely confiscated, but his arguments led toward the conclusion that, in the name of justice, *his* ox should not be gored. These observations are not meant to discredit Shelley's social thought, which is, in many respects, altruistic and far ahead of both his time and ours. They merely point to a few limitations of perspective that even the best persons exhibit because of their interests or experience.[16]

14. See Roger Ingpen, *Shelley in England* (London: Kegan Paul, Trench, Trubner, 1917), pp. 7-8. According to J. and J. A. Venn's *Alumni Cantabrigiensis*, Theobald Michell, son of Walsingham Michell of Horsham, Sussex, matriculated at Cambridge from Wadham College, Oxford, at the age of seventeen on 2 December 1706. He received his B.A. from Oxford in 1710 and took his M.A. at Jesus College, Cambridge, in 1725. He became rector of South Heighton, Sussex, in 1720 and rector of West Tarring (or West Terring, a mile and a quarter from Warnham, Sussex) in 1721. He was buried at Horsham, 23 March 1737.

15. Kenneth Neill Cameron has noted in *Humanity and Society: A World History* (Bloomington: Indiana University Press, 1973) how Plato's ideas were influenced by his connection with "the landowning aristocracy of Athens" and how Aristotle's ideal of the "middle path" reflects "the views of his own class, the professional class, which occupied a middle position in society," as well as the fact that, because he "came from Stageira . . . a Greek colony," he could "view Athenian society and thought with critical objectivity" (pp. 216-18).

16. David V. Erdman has noted an ambivalence similar to Shelley's in Byron's attitude toward "the economic and social and especially the political conditions of his heritage" (see *Shelley and his Circle*, 3:283ff.). Recently I observed in an account of Tadeuz Kosciuszko that, though he fought bravely, honorably, and well for the freedom of the American colonies and of Poland and though, when he was released from a Russian prison in 1796 and returned to America, he used the money awarded him by Congress to buy the freedom of Negro slaves, he (like Thomas Jefferson) did not free the serfs on his own Polish estates until near the time of his death.

Shelley's political ideas sound, at the theoretical level, extremely radical. From his *Proposals for an Association* and *Declaration of Rights* (both 1812) to *A Proposal for Putting Reform to the Vote* (1817) and *A Philosophical View of Reform* (1819–1820), Shelley continually holds up as his ideal a free, classless society in which there would be unlimited freedom of speech and interposition of government only to stop one person from infringing the rights of another. Like Jefferson, he believed that the less government, the better, and thus his social thought parallels Godwin's brand of philosophical anarchism. But at the practical level, Shelley believed compromise and an orderly, step-by-step progression to be necessary. In his note to *Queen Mab* on "and statesmen boast / Of wealth" (V.94), Shelley observes: "I will not insult common sense by insisting on the doctrine of the natural equality of man. The question is not concerning its desirableness, but its practicability: so far as it is practicable, it is desirable." At the end of *A Proposal for Putting Reform to the Vote,* Shelley also enunciates his ideals as "Universal Suffrage" and "a pure republic," and yet temporizes by arguing that, because of the "imprepared state of public knowledge and feeling," "I think that none but those who register their names as paying a certain small sum in *direct taxes* ought, at present, to send Members to Parliament" (direct taxes in 1817 being chiefly real estate taxes) and that "nothing can less consist with reason . . . than the plan which should abolish the regal and the aristocratical branches of our constitution, before the public mind, through many gradations of improvement, shall have arrived at the maturity which can disregard these symbols of its childhood."[17]

Even in *The Mask of Anarchy,* Shelley's most radical major poem, his agrarian and aristocratic biases are apparent. The identifiable social institutions that he attacks as evil are the slave trade (line 8; see footnote glosses to "bloodhounds"); the Court of Chancery (lines 14–21); the church hierarchy, lawyers, the House of Lords, and the use of spies and *agents provocateurs* (line 29); the standing army (lines 42–49); royal prerogatives (lines 78–81); the Bank of England, Tower of London (another symbol of royal power), and the corrupt, unreformed Parliament (lines 82–85); the practice of hiring (industrial) workers by the day at subsistence wages (lines 160ff.); paper currency (lines 176–83); and the thirst for revenge. All these had been from time immemorial enemies to the untitled landed gentry.

And what positive goals does Shelley put before the wretched populace in *The Mask of Anarchy*? Fundamentally, enough "clothes, and fire, and food" in "a neat and happy home" (lines 217–25; "happy" here means free

---

17. Shelley, *Works* (Julian Edition), ed. R. E. Ingpen and Walter E. Peck, 6:68.

from want). Beyond those basics, the people must possess enough boldness to redress excessive wrongs by the rich (lines 226-29); they must enjoy equal protection under the law, freedom from religious superstition (lines 230-33), and peace—especially from such liberticide wars as those against France (lines 239-41). Finally, Shelley praises "Love" that leads some of the rich (such as Shelley) to "give their substance" or even "turn their wealth to arms" in a war against "wealth, and war, and fraud" and "power" (lines 246-53). He goes on to set his ideal for the common people:

> "Science, Poetry, and Thought
> Are thy [Freedom's] lamps; they make the lot
> Of the dwellers in a cot
> So serene, they curse it not."
>
> (lines 254-57)

Did Shelley actually believe that a knowledge of science and poetry would make the poor content in their relative poverty, even if they possessed an adequate supply of food, fuel, and clothing "in a neat and happy home," or was this assurance mere rhetoric to calm the fears of the upper classes? In neither interpretation are his words exactly the sentiments of an egalitarian leveler, arousing farm laborers and the urban proletariat to claim full legal and economic equality.

Shelley in his lifetime certainly gave ample evidence of his benevolent disposition to help those less fortunate than himself, from giving sheets, blankets, and medicines to the poor weavers of the Marlow area to funding the follies of Godwin, Hunt, and Henry Reveley. But he also found it difficult to avoid sounding patronizing, as he and Mary Shelley learned to their sorrow in their dealings with William Thomas Baxter and his family (see *Shelley and his Circle*, 5:333-92, 505-8). Thomas Love Peacock, apparently, also resented the situation in which, for a few years, Shelley maintained his services as a factotum for an annual stipend of £100 to £125. Not only did Peacock suppress all evidence of this arrangement after Shelley's death by destroying letters of his own and letters from Shelley to him in which this annuity was mentioned, but at the time he even made out the quarterly checks (at least four of which survive) to his friends Thomas Hookham and Robert Madocks or Maddocks, as though in payment of Shelley's debts to them.[18] Yet Peacock seems to have understood and

---

18. For some of the checks, see Walter E. Peck, *Shelley: His Life and Work* (Boston: Houghton Mifflin, 1927), 2:392-93. We know from Peacock's surviving correspondence that Shelley's debts to Hookham and Maddocks were never paid. From the evidence of others, summarized in *Shelley and his Circle*, 4:590-92, we know that Peacock for an undetermined period received financial help from Shelley.

appreciated Shelley's need to patronize others, for he depicts it very sympathetically in his characterizations of Shelley both as Sylvan Forester in *Melincourt* (1817), where (as David Garnett has observed) Peacock's tone and ideas most nearly coincide with Shelley's, and as Algernon Falconer in *Gryll Grange* (1860), where Peacock idealizes the young Shelley as he never did during Shelley's lifetime. Both Forester and Falconer are aristocrats in the best sense of that term—wealthy, cultured, well-educated, and strongly motivated by *noblesse oblige*. Falconer protects (as his servants) seven orphaned sisters, whom he determines never to abandon, even at the cost of his own happiness. When it is explained that they, like him, wish to marry, he gives each a generous dowry. Sylvan Forester in *Melincourt* is more identifiably a country squire—what Shelley might have become had he inherited his patrimony in 1816–1817, when he was disposed toward a life of retirement as the "hermit" of Bishopsgate or Marlow. Besides sponsoring his friend Oran Haut-ton (an orangutan who becomes both a baronet and a member of Parliament), Forester is benevolent to individuals and encourages such direct social action as refusing to use sugar or other products of slave plantations (see especially Chapter 5). But in a number of speeches (as well as in his general behavior), Forester refuses to renounce fully the class distinctions of the day. In answer to a criticism of his radicalism by Mr. Fax, Forester replies:

I am no revolutionist. I am no advocate for violent and arbitrary changes in the state of society. I care not in what proportions property is divided (though I think there are certain limits which it ought never to pass, and approve the wisdom of the American laws in restricting the fortune of a private citizen to twenty thousand a year), provided the rich can be made to know that they are but the stewards of the poor, that they are not to be the monopolizers of solitary spoil, but the distributors of general possession; that they are responsible for that distribution to every principle of general justice, to every tie of moral obligation, to every feeling of human sympathy: that they are bound to cultivate simple habits in themselves, and to encourage most such arts of industry and peace, as are most compatible with the health and liberty of others.[19]

This chapter of *Melincourt* and Chapter 26, "The Cottagers" show more clearly than any of Shelley's own theoretical pronouncements how he might have carried out his social philosophy, had he inherited the life-interest in the estates entailed to him. And if the picture of the life of Forester's estate—"the neatness and comfort of the dwellings, the exquisite

19. Peacock, *The Complete Novels*, ed. David Garnett (London: Rupert Hart-Davis, 1963), 1:243–44.

order of the gardens, the ingenuous air of happiness and liberty that characterized the simple inhabitants, and the health and beauty of the little rosy children that were sporting in the fields"—owes something to Peacock's own ideals, as well as to eighteenth-century nostalgic or utopian scenes from Squire Allworthy's estate to "sweet Auburn" to Rasselas's Happy Valley, we can be sure from Shelley's own publications and letters that it accords with his ideals as well. Peacock, as a semi-objective observer of his friend and patron, knew what Shelley often refused to admit, even to himself—the importance to Shelley of an appropriate response to his generosity:

Mr. Forester had been recognised from a distance. The cottagers ran out in all directions to welcome him: the valley and the hills seemed starting into life, as men, women, and children poured down, as with one impulse, on the path of his approach, while some hastened to the residence of Miss Evergreen, ambitious of being the first to announce to her the arrival of her nephew. Miss Evergreen came forward to meet the party, surrounded by a rustic crowd of both sexes and of every age, from the old man leaning on his stick, to the little child that could just run alone, but had already learnt to attach something magical to the sound of the name of Forester. (Peacock, *Complete Novels*, 1:251)

If this idyll and others like it, expressed or implied, in Shelley's own works and those of his close friends writing about him strike us as being excessively paternalistic—even dangerously close to "Massa's in de cold, cold ground"—we must remember that such more recent ideals as that which sees the poor but rugged individualist who maintains his independence by always triumphing over adversity and that which imagines the abolition of poverty and dependence through an equitable state system of social welfare are also conditioned by particular times, backgrounds, and experiences and that each of these also may strike other people with different ideals as either naive or immoral. Shelley's social ideals were, like ours, limited by his perspective within the human condition. To recognize that fact helps us understand certain patterns of behavior that might otherwise seem inexplicable.[20] But it does not invalidate his claim to our attention. As Morse Peckham has pointed out more cogently than any other theorist

20. For example, Peacock relates that as "we were walking . . . through a village where there was a good vicarage house, with a nice garden," Shelley, impressed by the quiet beauty of the scene, "suddenly said to me,—'I feel strongly inclined to enter the church'" ("Memoirs of Percy Bysshe Shelley" in Peacock, *Works*, ed. H. F. B. Brett-Smith and C. E. Jones [London: Constable, 1934], 8:76). Peacock calls this "the most singular" of Shelley's many schemes of life, but, viewed from his delight in magnanimously patronizing and teaching others, it is no stranger than his later desire for a position in the East India Company.

that I know, "complete historical interpretation" not only takes into account the historical context being analyzed, with a view to seeing the circumstances and limitations of those persons and works being studied, but also recognizes that the historian is himself a limited human being caught within the partial blindness of his own historical perspective.[21] Recognizing this truth, we can come to terms with Shelley's inevitable limitations without condescending to him. We can acknowledge of him—as he acknowledged of Keats (whose limitations Shelley keenly recognized)—that though he like us was once caught within the unwilling dross that checks the Spirit's flight, his poetry and the general tendency of his life and thought rank him, along with a few others of his age (a minority even more select than the rich landed gentry of England), as one of the splendors of the firmament of time.

21. Peckham outlines his important theory in "On the Historical Interpretation of Literature," reprinted in Peckham's *The Triumph of Romanticism: Collected Essays* (Columbia: University of South Carolina Press, 1970), especially pp. 449-50. Another useful theoretical position relevant to this paper is outlined by Terry Eagleton in *Marxism and Literary Criticism* (Berkeley: University of California Press, 1976). Eagleton, unlike less perceptive Marxist critics, recognizes that great works such as Conrad's *Nostromo* or Eliot's *The Waste Land* can be written by political conservatives or even reactionaries: "in the absence of genuinely revolutionary art, only a radical conservatism, hostile like Marxism to the withered values of liberal bourgeois society, could produce the most significant literature" (p. 8).

15

Roman Scenes in Prometheus Unbound *III.iv*

In *the spring of 1963, the American Council of Learned Societies awarded me one of their first Study Fellowships, to enable me to study the Italian background of Shelley and the other younger Romantic poets. Mary W. Reiman and I first went to Urbana, Illinois, where I had my initial chance to teach the Romantics at the graduate level. That summer, I finished my paper on Lamb's essays (Item 13), came up with the idea on* The Prelude *as a macrosonnet that finally appeared in "The Beauty of Buttermere" essay (Item 12), and wrote reams of notes on the Romantics that have served me for ready reference ever since. Mary Reiman spent much of her time working with a portable microfilm reader, compiling detailed lists of the contents of several reels of Duke's microfilms of Lord Abinger's papers.*

In August we returned to our parents' homes in Ohio, before proceeding to Middletown, Connecticut, where three other ACLS Study Fellows and I were to be Junior Fellows at Wesleyan's Center for Advanced Studies. The senior Fellows at the Center that term included Lewis Mumford, Hans Kohn (the great historian of middle Europe), Ernest J. Simmons (the biographer of Russian literary figures), Carl Schorske, Frank Kermode, Aage Petersen (a Danish physicist), Douglas Cater, Congressman Richard E. Bolling (when he could manage it), and the inimitable director of the Center, Paul Horgan, effete novelist of the old West. We four Junior Fellows spent the term having our egos battered by the Wesleyan faculty's penchant for lionizing the visiting senior Fellows, while ignoring the illustrious obscure that they considered us to be. Exceptions to this generalization included Alexander Cowie, Richard Ohmann, Richard Wilbur, and Edward Williamson, with whom Mary Reiman and I studied Italian; but during our four months there, the only faculty home that we saw from the inside was that of Edward Taylor of the physics department, whose mother was a friend of Mary W(arner) Reiman's mother in Oberlin, Ohio. Our location in Connecticut enabled us to see friends who lived in New England and to visit the Yale Library (where I encountered René Wellek) and to have dinner at the E. D. Hirsches'. A trip to New York enabled us to see our first Broadway play—Who's Afraid of Virginia Woolf?—and for me to visit The Carl H. Pforzheimer Library.

Though I accomplished almost nothing concrete that semester except grounding myself in Italian, the time at the Wesleyan Center was one of the most valuable in my career, because it gave me a chance both to read widely in areas I had been too busy to master (I read War and Peace, *for example) and to measure myself against a selection of certified intellectual giants. I emerged with my hopes and dreams intact and better prepared for the larger academic world. Frank Kermode and Carl Schorske, two of the younger Fellows, could not have been kinder to us Junior Fellows; sensitive both to our situation and to the peculiarities of some of the other senior Fellows, they took time to listen and discuss with us the inchoate ideas we were trying to work out. Hans Kohn was one of the wisest and most sympathetic of human beings (as can be seen from his autobiographical book,* Living in a World Revolution: My Encounters with History, 1964*). Lewis Mumford, who was at the Center to write his autobiography, spoke like an automaton fitted with recorded selections from his recent books; he had no interest in listening to anyone else and never seemed to doubt that all the wisdom of the world was to be found either in something he had written or something he was about to write. Ernest J. Simmons, an insufferable snob, seemed bitterly jealous of any attention given to Mumford or Kohn.*

In December 1963, at MLA in Chicago, I was offered an associate professorship at the newly developing campus of the University of Wisconsin at Milwaukee. I was even more pleased by the offer of a chance to teach graduate courses in both the Romantics and the Victorians than by the quick jumps in rank and salary. Duke, true to its form at that time, offered me tenure (which meant nothing in those days of a teacher shortage) but promised no teaching above the sophomore level. Joe and Ginny Riddel, our closest friends at Duke, were planning to move to California the next year. In New York, on 17 January 1964, the night before we sailed for Italy, Mary and I dined with Professor and Mrs. Allan H. Gilbert, in whose stately home in Durham we had lived during our three years at Duke. Allan and Mary Moss Gilbert then lived in New York during the academic year so that he could continue teaching after Duke had forced him into retirement against his will. His dissatisfactions with the school reinforced mine. Against Mary Reiman's wishes, I called to accept the new position at Milwaukee a few hours before we sailed for Naples on the Leonardo da Vinci.

On the ship, after passing through midwinter storms and seasickness, we met Arthur Freeman, then known as a poet and member of Harvard's Society of Fellows (more recently a Renaissance scholar and expert in printed books at Bernard Quaritch, Ltd., the leading London antiquarian bookshop). Arthur, who had been on his way to Rhodes to write poetry, instead stayed at our hotel in Naples, and I accompanied him on a couple of excursions to antiquarian book dealers on behalf of himself and Stephen Weissman, his partner in Ximenes: Rare Books. Through this chance meeting, we became acquainted with literary rare bookmen who would become leaders in that field in Boston, New York, and London.

Mary and I soon went on to Rome, where we lived in pension for nearly three months in the Casa Fersen on the Piazza Cucchi, Monteverdi Nuovo, not far from the American Academy in Rome. This pensione, recommended by the American Academy, was run by the Countess Olga Fersen, the elderly youngest survivor of a family of Russian emigrés who had lived in Rome since the early 1920s. Among the permanent pensioners were Countess Fersen's elderly aunt (a Russian princess who had lived a migratory life as a farm owner in Austria and a language teacher in Argentina before returning in her old age to live with her niece in Rome); a White Russian colonel who was also the retired librarian of the American Academy; and the Countess Leonora Lichnowsky, of the distinguished Prussian diplomatic family, who had fled Hitler, worked in China, and ended up in Rome as an agricultural economist in the East Asian section of the UN's Food and Agricultural Organization. Also on hand through most of the winter was Fred Carey, emeritus professor of classics from UCLA, who had spent several seasons at the Casa Fersen while doing research in Rome. At this stage, he was just enjoying the city and took time to be helpful to us in our research. With the help of these urbane and kindly people, Vera Cacciatore of the Keats-Shelley Memorial in the Piazza di Spagna, and my Italian tutor, Signora Lina Marchi (who taught Italian to the staff at the American Embassy), we spent four most profitable and enjoyable months in Rome, seeing every corner of the city and—since I was also reviewing F. L. Jones's edition of Shelley's Letters for SAQ—checking out every aspect of the Shelleys' experience there.

During our first visit to the Sala della Biga at the Vatican Museum, I recognized it as the source of one passage in Act III, Scene iv, of Prometheus Unbound. As I then read through the play again, the origins of other passages also seemed to become evident. When, however, I drafted the article—trying to keep it within the fifteen to twenty-five double-spaced typescript pages that was then the norm for papers published in the major scholarly quarterlies other than PMLA—I confined myself to writing on the background of just two passages in a single scene, convinced that I had made the point strongly enough that Shelley (pace Leavis) did have his eye on the actual so that other critics would not assume, when Shelley described something that they had never seen, that he was the one who "did not know enough." Unfortunately, Philological Quarterly had a big backlog at the time, and by January 1967, when the essay finally appeared (PQ 46: 69–78), the annual Romantics bibliography, which when I submitted the essay had made PQ a place where specialized papers on the Romantics reached their proper audience, had moved to ELN. *This one additional paper on* Prometheus Unbound *thus received minimal attention.*

"Roman Scenes" remains one of my favorite publications, not only for the memories it evokes of our days of solitary sightseeing and study, followed by spirited dinner-table and evening conversation and debate at the "Cucchi Academy," but also because, I believe, its genesis shows how certain scholarly problems that yield neither to close reading nor to library research can be solved by attentive and informed traveling in the steps of the poets, trying to respond as they did to the sense of a place. This is certainly true for much of Wordsworth's poetry. Recently, Shelley studies have been enriched by Richard Holmes's Shelley: The Pursuit (1974), though Holmes failed to pursue library research with the dedication he showed in following Shelley's travels, thus rendering his biography of Shelley less accurate than those by Dowden and White, and even those by Peck and Blunden. The Romantics scholar who, I believe, has best combined the necessary research in books with emulation of his subject's wanderlust is Leslie A. Marchand (one of Richard D. Altick's Scholar Adventurers), whose Byron: A Biography and its updated condensations brilliantly combine these complementary aspects of biographical research.

Sometimes, for the literary explicator and critic, even when travel is not necessary to unlock the meaning of a text, a visit to the site of the poet's experience can revivify his poetry. In June 1963, while Mary Reiman and I drove north to Venice, we spent a night in the town of Este, where in the late summer of 1818 Shelley had begun to write Prometheus Unbound. That evening, we dined at a restaurant perched on the upper slopes of Monte Rua', highest peak in the Euganean Hills; below us lay the scene that Shelley describes in his immortal "Lines written among the Euganean Hills," which we read aloud as the light changed and eventually faded, first over Venice and then over Padua. In such moments, scholar-critics can add to their appreciation of the music and sentiments of the verse a special understanding of the entire nexus of the poet's experience at the time he composed the poem, together with the joy of knowing that they are beholding the same scene that inspired it. That evening we silently grieved with the bereaved and lonely poet, while thanking God and all the fates that Shelley had been empowered to capture so much beauty and truth in such simple words for us to reexperience from the same vantage point 146 years later.

I

Mary Shelley, near the end of her note to *Prometheus Unbound,* writes of Shelley:

The charm of the Roman climate helped to clothe his thoughts in greater beauty than they had ever worn before. And, as he wandered among the ruins made one with Nature in their decay, or gazed on the Praxitelean shapes that throng the Vatican, the Capitol, and the palaces of Rome, his soul imbibed forms of loveliness which became a portion of itself. There are many passages in the *Prometheus* which show the intense delight he received from such studies, and gave back the impression with a beauty of poetical description peculiarly his own.[1]

Among the passages of *Prometheus* that were inspired by the artistic sights of Rome are two in Act III, Scene iv, that have hitherto been less than satisfactorily glossed, perhaps because, to one unacquainted with the scenes that evoked them, the lines may seem fanciful and entirely unrelated to anything in nature. Both passages, however, describe Roman scenes that have been shaped to reinforce the symbolic function of the lines in the poem.

The last speech in Act III (the concluding speech of the drama as Shelley originally conceived it and drafted it at Rome in the spring of 1819) is delivered by the Spirit of the Hour who in II.iv and v and III.iii charioted Asia and Panthea to their reunion with Prometheus. At his release Prometheus had told this Spirit of the Hour to sound a "curvèd shell," proclaiming the fall of Jupiter's tyranny and the advent of a new age of love. At the end of the Third Act, the Spirit of the Hour returns to describe what she has done and seen. According to the mythology of the Hours suggested in II.iv and v, each chariot-hour should naturally run its course and then disappear. In III.iv.106–10, however, the Spirit of the Hour drifts down to earth, while the steeds that drew her chariot—that is, the energy that propelled the course of time—return to "their birthplace in the sun." The Spirit announces to Prometheus:

> my moonlike car will stand within
> A temple, gazed upon by Phidian forms
> Of thee, and Asia, and the Earth, and me,
> And you fair nymphs, looking the love we feel;
> In memory of the tidings it has borne;
> Beneath a dome fretted with graven flowers,
> Poised on twelve columns of resplendent stone,
> And open to the bright and liquid sky.
> Yoked to it by an amphisbænic snake
> The likeness of those wingèd steeds will mock
> The flight from which they find repose.[2]

---

1. *The Complete Poetical Works of Percy Bysshe Shelley*, ed. Thomas Hutchinson (London: Oxford University Press, 1960), p. 274.
2. III.iv.111–21. All quotations from *Prometheus Unbound* are from *The Poems of Percy Bysshe Shelley*, ed. C. D. Locock, 2 vols. (London: Methuen, 1911). (This edition is based on a study of the fair-copy manuscripts.)

The scene in Shelley's mind when he wrote these lines was, almost beyond question, "La Sala della Biga" in the Vatican Museum, and from that exhibit, as it was in 1819 and as it is today, Shelley took the leading elements in the imagery of the passage.[3]

The room of the Biga (two-horse chariot) would have been a more important attraction in the smaller Vatican Museum of Shelley's time than it is today. The Biga itself, though still regarded as a spirited piece of sculpture, is less highly valued than many other sculptures in the Vatican Museum because it is so largely restored, so little original. The chassis of the chariot and part of one horse are alone antique, the chariot having been preserved for centuries as the episcopal seat in the church of San Marco. F. A. Franzoni restored the group in 1788, and a special room was constructed for the Biga during the Pontificate of Pius VI (1775–1799). An early print in Feoli, *Il Museo Pio-Clementino* (n.d. but ca. 1800),[4] shows the circular room in virtually the same physical state that it is today. The interior of the room is roughly circular, about ten meters in diameter. At ninety-degree angles to one another are four arched recesses; one contains the doorway and the other three contain large windows. Between each two of these arches are two pillars with Corinthian capitals, and between each pair of pillars, in turn, is a niche within which stands a large statue. In the center of the room is the Biga, mounted on a rectangular pedestal that is, in turn, on a low circular platform. Around this platform the floor is decorated with four circular tile inlays representing the four winds (one in front of the door and each window), and between each two winds is a tile marker pointing to the eight principal points of the compass. The ceiling is domed and coffered; every second one of the coffers contains an eight-pointed figure resembling the compass-point design on the floor and seeming, at a distance, to represent either a star or a flower.

The Biga itself is a marble sculpture consisting of a chariot drawn by two horses of great energy whose hind legs rest on the pedestal but whose forelegs are raised, pawing the air. (The weight of the marble rests upon a decorated support under the middle of each horse's belly.) The reins are

3. Lawrence John Zillman in *Shelley's Prometheus Unbound: A Variorum Edition* (Seattle: University of Washington Press, 1959) notes that III.iv.111–24 "are, in effect, in draft state" (p. 252), and Locock wrote that "these fourteen lines were also [like III.iv.86–96] an afterthought" (1:620). Although it is beyond the scope of this paper to reexamine the dating of Acts II and III, one might come to some conclusions about the date at which the Bodleian fair-copy manuscript was completed in its original form by comparing Shelley's, Mary's, and Claire Clairmont's accounts of visits to Roman museums with such late additions to the manuscript.

4. I am grateful for a reproduction of this plate to the Countess Leonora Lichnowsky and to Dr. H. Speier of the Library of the Vatican Museum. I wish to take this opportunity to thank also the American Council of Learned Societies for a Study Fellowship, 1963–1964, during which the initial research for this article was done at Rome.

tied to the chariot, and the horses are yoked together by a marble representation of a serpent with a head at each end—an "amphisbænic snake."[5] This scene, clearly, helped to inspire III.iv.111-21; the Biga, described in Shelley's poem as a static representation of the Chariot of the Hour, is a "moonlike car" (111) because traditionally the chariot of the moon is a *biga*, as opposed to the chariot of the sun, which is a *quadriga* or four-horse chariot.[6]

The "moonlike car" in Shelley's description stands "within / A temple, gazed upon by Phidian forms / Of thee [Prometheus], and Asia, and the Earth, and me [Spirit of the Hour], / And you fair nymphs . . ." (III.iv.111-14). The Biga was in Shelley's day, as today, surrounded by statues; though I am unable to ascertain exactly which sculptures were in the Sala della Biga in 1819 when Shelley saw them, several of those pictured in the early print in Feoli are still in the room. These include two discus throwers, one at rest and a marble copy of Myron's famous *discobolus*; an Apollo with a lyre; a gladiator with one foot on a helmet; an elderly Roman robed to make sacrifice; Bacchus *effeminate*; and a victorious charioteer. Of these figures, the last might well have been thought of by Shelley as representing the Spirit of the Hour, victorious in having during her career freed Prometheus and introduced a new era on earth. The Apollo with a lyre might have suggested Prometheus, for as the Sun is Shelley's recurring symbol of the Supreme Being, so he uses Apollo, the anthropomorphic embodiment of such divinity, as the symbol of human imagination and the source of poetic inspiration—the best side of the human mind, and thus roughly equivalent to Prometheus.[7] There were, perhaps, no figures that

---

5. Shelley would have been familiar with the amphisbæna from the chief classical source of commentary, Pliny's *Natural History* (five references), which he translated in part when he was a schoolboy. See Newman I. White, *Shelley* (London: Secker & Warburg, 1947), 1:50, 576. For a full list of classical references to the amphisbæna, I am grateful to Frederick Carey, professor emeritus of classics at UCLA.

6. The *biga* is mentioned as the chariot of the moon in Lucan's *Pharsalia* I.78 (see Lucan, *The Civil War*, trans. J. W. Duff, Loeb Classical Library [London: Heinemann, 1928], p. 8). The *quadriga* appears as sun-chariot in such works of art in Rome as the Rospigliosi ceiling fresco of "Aurora," which was the masterpiece of Guido Reni, one of Shelley's favorite painters, and which (according to Claire Clairmont's journal) Shelley's party saw on 20 March 1819.

7. In another connection, Carlos Baker points out that among the identifications recognized by John Frank Newton and other syncretic mythologists of the late eighteenth and early nineteenth centuries, one was the identification (from the Dendera Zodiac) of Jupiter with Seva the Destroyer of Hindu thought and of Apollo with Krishna the Restorer. These two occupy the lower hemisphere of the Zodiac, which half is under the rule of Ahrimanes, the Zoroastrian principle of evil (*Shelley's Major Poetry* [Princeton: Princeton University Press, 1948], p. 67). From the relevant works of Peacock, Byron, and Shelley one can see how Shelley might transmute the myth into one in which Prometheus, the free spirit of man, replaces Apollo, the ultimate source of that imaginative freedom, as Jupiter's direct antagonist in a phenomenal world subject to Necessity. The scene between Apollo and Ocean (III.ii) thereby takes on greater thematic significance.

strongly suggest Asia and her sister oceanides.

In other details, as well, the passage of *Prometheus* moves away from systematic representation of the Sala della Biga. The interior of the dome is, as I have suggested, "fretted with graven flowers," but the room (on the upper level of the museum) is not, of course, a temple; it is "open to the bright and liquid sky"[8] only so far as three large windows can make it so; and it has eight columns rather than Shelley's twelve. At least two of these three departures from the scene of the Sala della Biga may be attributed to Shelley's coalescing the chief features of that room with certain aspects of the Pantheon, as described by Shelley in a letter to Peacock of 23 March 1819 (which, as we shall see below, is relevant to another passage in the same speech). After comparing the Pantheon favorably with St. Peter's, Shelley writes:

It is open to the sky, & its wide dome is lighted by the ever changing illumination of the air. The clouds of noon fly over it and at night the keen stars are seen thro the azure darkness hanging immoveably, or driving after the driving moon among the clouds. I visited it by moonlight. It is supported by sixteen columns, fluted & Corinthian, of a certain rare & beautiful yellow marble exquisitely polished called here *Giallo antico*. Above these are niches for the statues of the 12 Gods. This is the only defect of this sublime temple; there ought to have been no interval between the commencement of the dome & the cornice supported by the columns. (*Letters*, 2:87-88)

The Pantheon was a temple, "open to the bright and liquid sky," and, if it had been built according to Shelley's conception, it might have had twelve columns, rather than twelve niches in a section that, according to Shelley, was a "diversion from the magnificent simplicity of its form." The number twelve has many and varied symbolic functions in Western religious and mythological systems; in the context, I should think, the twelve columns should be associated, not with the twelve gods of whom the chief was Jupiter, but with the functions of the number twelve in symbolizing periods of time—for example, twelve months or twelve signs of the Zodiac.

8. See Shelley to Thomas Love Peacock, 23-24 January 1819, writing about a visit to Pompeii: "I now understand why the Greeks were such great Poets, & above all I can account, it seems to me, for the harmony the unity the perfection the uniform excellence of all their works of art. They lived in a perpetual commerce with external nature and nourished themselves upon the spirit of its forms. Their theatres were all open to the mountains & the sky. Their columns that ideal type of a sacred forest with its roof of interwoven tracery admitted the light & wind, the odour & the freshness of the country penetrated the cities. Their temples were mostly upaithric; & the flying clouds the stars or the deep sky were seen above" (*The Letters of Percy Bysshe Shelley*, ed. F. L. Jones [Oxford: Clarendon Press, 1964], 2:74-75; hereafter cited as *Letters*).

Surely a temple commemorating the release of Prometheus and mankind from Necessity, or the laws of temporal cause and effect, should not only image the speeding Chariot of the Hour that brought such redemption but should also represent the entire cycle of "Fate, Time, Occasion, Chance, and Change" that has been overthrown in the victory of "love and reason" over "the despot's rage, the slave's revenge."

Undergirding the symbolism of *Prometheus* III.iv.111-21 is an accuracy of description characteristic in Shelley's poetry but all too often overlooked. The coherence and consistency of Shelley's symbolism arose from his systematic mind and his consistent attitude toward the underlying moral significance of his physical, cultural, and social environment, and he frequently drew the elements that he wove into his symbolic patterns directly from that "actual" world.

II

In the last half of the same speech, the Spirit of the Hour says that, in the millennium introduced by Jupiter's fall,

> Thrones, altars, judgment-seats, and prisons . . .
> *   *   *   *   *   *
> Were like those monstrous and barbaric shapes,
> The ghosts of a no more remembered fame,
> Which, from their unworn obelisks, look forth
> In triumph o'er the palaces and tombs
> Of those who were their conquerors, mouldering round.
> These imaged, to the pride of kings and priests,
> A dark yet mighty faith, a power as wide
> As is the world it wasted, and are now
> But an astonishment; even so the tools
> And emblems of its last captivity,
> Amid the dwellings of the peopled earth,
> Stand, not o'erthrown, but unregarded now.
> (III.iv.164-79)

The meaning of these lines was thoroughly discussed in the 1860s and 1870s when Swinburne argued the need for a new text of Shelley's poems, and William Michael Rossetti and Harry Buxton Forman were reediting Shelley's poetry, for the punctuation and syntax of this passage were subjects of dispute. But since C. D. Locock's edition (1911), in which the punctuation was corrected on the basis of an examination of the Bodleian faircopy holograph, published comments on these lines have been, I believe, less relevant to their fundamental meaning. Without going into all the ramifications of the textual dispute, one can epitomize the interpretations of the passage that were proposed in conjunction with the discussion of the text by quoting Rossetti's paraphrase of the passage:

Thrones, altars, judgment-seats, and prisons, were like those monstrous and barbaric shapes sculptured by the ancient Egyptians on still unworn obelisks, and recording matters once famous, now forgotten,—which shapes yet look forth in triumph over the palaces and tombs of their Saracenic or other conquerors, now mouldering around them. Those shapes did, at the time when their meaning was understood, image forth, unto the pride of kings and priests of that remote age, a dark yet mighty faith, a supernatural and desolating power coextensive with the world: now, being no longer understood, those shapes are mere objects of astonishment. And even so the thrones, altars, judgment-seats, and prisons, remain as yet unruined, and, whereas they used once to have a practical meaning, they now have none such.[9]

In all subsequent commentaries on the passage that I have read, I have found nothing that brings one closer to understanding the passage except Locock's suggestion "that Shelley is referring to one particular group of shapes in some definite locality known to him."[10]

Shelley is in fact once again describing scenes in Rome and using the description symbolically much as he uses particular scenes in his letter to Peacock of 23 March 1819. In that letter, after briefly describing the course of the journey from Naples to Rome, Shelley writes: "And what shall I say to you of Rome? If I speak first of the inanimate ruins, the rude stones piled upon stones which are the sepulchres of the fame of those who once arrayed them with the beauty which had faded will you not believe me insensible to the vital, the almost breathing creations of genius yet subsisting in their perfection?" (*Letters*, 2:84). He then proceeds to discuss the Colosseum (described at length in an earlier letter to Peacock), the Baths of Caracalla, the Forum and the Palatine, the triumphal arches of Septimius Severus and Constantine, and the statues of Castor and Pollux taming the horses on the steps of the Capitol. Next he turns to living Rome: "What shall I say of the modern City? Rome is yet the Capital of the World. It is a city of palaces & temples more glorious than those which any other city contains, & of ruins more glorious than they" (2:87).

In the course of describing some of the wonders of Renaissance Rome, especially St. Peter's and some of the fountains, Shelley mentions three of the many Egyptian obelisks that appear in the leading piazzas of the city—

9. *The Poetical Works of Percy Bysshe Shelley* (London: E. Moxon, 1870), 1:499.
10. *Poems*, 1:622.

those in Piazza San Pietro, Piazza Navona, and Piazza Quirinale. Shelley's letter itself exhibits an artistic shaping of materials to fulfill his palpable intention of contrasting classical with baroque art to the advantage of the former. Of St. Peter's he begins, "Externally, it is inferior in architectural beauty to St. Pauls, though not wholly devoid of it: internally it exhibits littleness on a large scale, & is in every respect opposed to antique taste," and he concludes his description by declaring: "The effect of the Pantheon is totally the reverse of that of St. Peters. Though not a fourth part of the size, it is as it were the visible image of the universe; in the perfection of its proportions, as when you regard the unmeasured dome of Heaven, the idea of magnitude is swallowed up & lost" (2:87). In the next paragraph, he writes (italics mine):

The fountains in Rome are in themselves magnificent *combinations of art* such as alone it were worth coming to see. That in the Piazza Navona, a large square is composed of enormous fragments of rock piled on each other, & penetrated as by caverns. This mass supports an Egyptian obelisk of immense height. On the four corners of the rock recline in different attitudes colossal figures representing the four divisions of the globe. . . . They are sculptured with great spirit; one impatiently tearing a veil from his eyes, another with his hands stretched upwards, &c. The Fontana di Trevi is the most celebrated, & is rather a waterfall than a fountain, gushing out from masses of rock, with a gigantic figure of Neptune, & below are two river Gods, checking two winged horses struggling up from among the rocks & waters. The whole is not ill conceived or executed—but you know not how delicate the imagination becomes by dieting with antiquity day after day. (2:88)

As becomes clear when one analyzes this letter in terms of the classical-baroque opposition that Shelley has carefully developed, the relative failure of the later art was its overelaboration; not wanting energy or skillful execution, the baroque sacrificed simplicity to a multiplicity of details. The best of Rome's fountains, according to Shelley, is among the simplest and one that is associated with classical sculptures.

The fountain on the Quirinal, or rather the group formed by the statues the obelisk, & the fountain is however the most admirable of all. . . . On a pedestal of white marble rises an obelisk of red granite piercing the blue sky. Before it is a vast basin of porphyry in the midst of which rises [a] column of the purest water which collects into itself all the overhanging colours of the sky, & breaks them into a thousand prismatic hues & graduated shadows. . . . On each side on elevated pedestals stand the statues of Castor & Pollux, each in the act of taming his horse. . . . These figures combine the irresistible energy with the sublime & perfect loveliness supposed to have belonged to the divine nature. The reins no longer exist, but the position of their hands & the sustained & calm command of their regard seem to require no mechanical aid to enforce obedience. (2:88–89)

Shelley associates the three Egyptian obelisks with baroque Rome of Pope Sixtus V and his successors, who had, in fact, placed the ancient monuments in their present locations and used them as members of architectural and sculptural groupings such as Shelley describes. The hieroglyphics on the Egyptian obelisks in Rome provided Shelley with a perfect analogue for the lost significance of "Thrones, altars, judgment-seats, and prisons" postulated in III.iv.164–79. With the loss of a reading knowledge of hieroglyphics,[11] the inscriptions had degenerated from memorials of specific victories and achievements of Egyptian rulers into "monstrous and barbaric shapes"; "These [mysterious shapes]," Shelley suggests, "imaged, to the pride of kings and priests [the Holy Roman emperors and the popes], / A dark yet mighty faith": that is, the very mystery and incomprehensibility of the hieroglyphic shapes became an image of the dark religious Tree of Mystery (to use Blake's term) that Shelley saw as characteristic of the Christian "faith" (a word that in Shelley's poetry always has pejorative connotations). After Jupiter has fallen, thrones and altars—"tools / And emblems of its [the world's] last captivity"—will be unregarded. The hieroglyphic language, which originally had significance as a historical record and then in its very mysteriousness symbolized obscurantist hierarchies of church and state, *now* (that is, as the Spirit of the Hour is speaking) becomes a source of astonishment—a mystery in a new culture in which mysteries have no significance beyond themselves (or, perhaps, beyond the scientific curiosity they may arouse).

The stages of the obelisks' significance are important to Shelley's thought in a subtle way. The ordinary lesson taught by the ruins of past civilizations throughout the eighteenth century was that suggested by Shelley in "Ozymandias" and articulated by Peacock in *Palmyra* (1808):

> The noblest works of human pow'r
> In vain resist the fate-fraught hour;
> The marble hall, the rock-built tow'r,
>   Alike submit to destiny:
> OBLIVION'S awful storms resound;

11. Although the famed Rosetta Stone had been found in 1799, not until 1818 did Young begin to show that at least some of the characters were alphabetic, and not till 1822 did Champollion, using for comparison an inscription found on an obelisk at Philae, prove the purely alphabetic nature of the signs by reading a number of proper names. In the 1830s Champollion's method was accepted, and understanding of Egyptian hieroglyphics advanced extensively.

> The massy columns fall around;
> The fabric totters to the ground,
> And darkness veils its memory!
>   (stanza I)

But this is the lesson to men in their fallen condition, who fear death and who ordinarily take comfort in religion's hopes for immortality. Even Peacock, so well known as a religious skeptic, ends his early poem on the vanity of human achievements with a dramatic speech that contains an admonition to seek the Lord while He may be found:

> "Bow then to Him, for He is Good,
>   And loves the works His hands have made;
>   *   *   *   *   *
> Bow then to Him, for He is Just,
>   Though mortals scan His ways in vain;
>   *   *   *   *   *
> Bow then to Him, for He is Great,
> And was, ere Nature, Time, and Fate,
>   Began their mystic flight;
> And still shall be, when consummating flame
>   Shall plunge this universal frame
>   In everlasting night."
>   (XXV)

For Shelley's picture of a society redeemed from such a fear of death and from such an escapist faith, the artifacts of men—even those dedicated to unworthy purposes—have great value as products of the human imagination:

The Divina Commedia and Paradise Lost have conferred upon modern mythology a systematic form; and when change and time shall have added one more superstition to the mass of those which have arisen and decayed upon the earth, commentators will be learnedly employed in elucidating the religion of ancestral Europe, only not utterly forgotten because it will have been stamped with the eternity of genius.

. . . it exceeds all imagination to conceive what would have been the moral condition of the world if neither Dante, Petrarch, Boccaccio, Chaucer, Shakspeare, Calderon, Lord Bacon, nor Milton, had ever existed; if Raphael and Michael Angelo had never been born; if the Hebrew poetry had never been translated; if a revival of the study of Greek literature had never taken place; if no monuments of antient sculpture had been handed down to us; and *if the poetry of the religion of the antient world had been extinguished together with its belief.*[12]

12. *A Defence of Poetry,* in *Prose of the Romantic Period,* ed. Carl R. Woodring (Boston: Houghton Mifflin, 1961), pp. 505, 507–8 (italics mine).

Therefore the temples (like St. Peter's) with their "thrones" (Bernini's chair of St. Peter) and "altars" (under Bernini's baldachin), and the palaces with their "judgment-seats, and prisons"[13] will remain unregarded so far as their original functions are concerned, but they should be available to stir the imaginations of men. This stimulation of the imagination takes the form neither of the second stage in the history of the obelisks, when they stimulated a blind faith in mystery during the age of tyrannies, nor that of the third stage during the Age of Enlightenment, when they simply showed the vanity of human achievements and thereby either stifled human aspirations or directed them toward some other-worldly fulfillment. Shelley in the letter to Peacock showed himself too much a product of the Enlightenment, for he was unable to appreciate the aesthetic excellence of the Roman triumphal arches because they reminded him too painfully of the tyranny they were raised to commemorate. He realized, therefore, in writing *Prometheus Unbound* that the monuments associated with the age of priests and kings should be "unregarded" at first, arousing neither veneration nor hatred; as time passed, however, regenerated man would be able to wander among the ruins made one with Nature in their decay, or gaze on the Praxitelean shapes that throng the Vatican, the Capitol, and the palaces of Rome, and from these his soul would imbibe only forms of loveliness which would become a portion of itself.

13. Relevant to this phrase are Shelley's remarks about the Doge's palace in Venice in his letter to Peacock of 8 October 1818 (*Letters*, 2:42–43).

16

Shelley's "The Triumph of Life": The Biographical Problem

Back in 1960, when I was friendly with Neville Rogers, he wrote to tell me that G. M. Matthews (Rogers's enemy ever since having written a devastating review of Shelley at Work for Essays in Criticism) had an essay forthcoming in Review of English Studies claiming that "The Triumph of Life" related to an affair between Shelley and Jane Williams. Thus forewarned, I had begun to gather evidence on the issue even before I saw Matthews's "Shelley and Jane Williams" early in 1961. When Mary W. Reiman and I spent the summer of 1961 working on the Bodleian manuscript of "The Triumph of Life," we devoted a good deal of time to examining the basis of Matthews's assertions and found that we disagreed with both his selection of the evidence and his conclusions. Near the end of that summer, Geoffrey and Daphne Matthews came down to Oxford from Leeds, and Mary and I found that we liked them very much. I told Geoffrey not only my doubts about his interpretation, but my conviction that the crucial interlineation on folio 52 verso reads, not "Alas I kiss you Jane," but "Alas I kiss you Julie." This suggestion took Geoffrey back a bit—not the less because he had just finished writing a critical study of "The Triumph of Life" that centered on Rousseau's impact on Shelley ("On Shelley's 'The Triumph of Life,'" Studia Neophilologica 34 [1962]: 104–34).

In 1962, Mary Reiman and I spent the summer in Durham, North Carolina, checking the text and collations of Neville Rogers's version of The Esdaile Poems (see the headnotes to Items 1 and 3 above) and completing the research for "Shelley's 'The Triumph of Life': The Biographical Problem." Because Matthews was, by virtue of his four major articles based on the manuscript, the world's recognized authority on "The Triumph of Life," I felt it necessary to establish my own credentials vis-à-vis his before publishing my book on that poem. Shelley scholarship and criticism were then extremely polemical, Matthews's review of Rogers's Shelley at Work being one of the recent prize exhibits, and I was not one to back away from a controversy. Yet Mary and I liked Geoffrey and Daphne Matthews so much better than we liked Neville Rogers (with whom I was fighting that summer over our different views of editorial responsibility) that I made up my mind to deal with my *differences from Geoffrey in an article and then try to leave the biographical speculations behind me so far as my book was concerned; for I hoped that it would remain a useful reference source long after such controversies were forgotten.*

The response of other scholars to "The Biographical Problem" (as I refer to this essay) was dramatic. Read for PMLA *by Kenneth Neill Cameron, Frederick L. Jones, and Robert Gorham Davis, it appeared in* PMLA *for December 1963 (78: 536–50), while I was at the Wesleyan Center for Advanced Studies. I received letters of encouragement and congratulation from a number of scholars and teachers whom I had never met—most notably Carl Woodring, who recommended me for the Romantics position at the University of Wisconsin–Milwaukee. (Even people in English at Wesleyan began to notice me.) Later, a number of scholars told me that the command of Shelleyan sources, both printed and manuscript, displayed in the essay gave them an impression of a scholar far more advanced in years and experience than I was then. The essay almost certainly paved the way for scholarly acceptance of* Shelley's "The Triumph of Life": A Critical Study, Based on a Text Newly Edited from the Bodleian Manuscript *(Urbana: University of Illinois Press, 1965).*

On the other hand, several younger critics used the essay to discredit all of Matthews's views on Shelley's last poem, and I was surprised to note how the polemical tone gained the piece more readers than my equally good (I think) earlier essay in PMLA *entitled "Structure, Symbol, and Theme in 'Lines written among the Euganean Hills'" (September 1962). I now have ambivalent feelings about this essay: though I regard it as both a solid piece of scholarship and a successful rhetorical argument, showing how intensive biographical research can refute sensationalized biographical speculation, I feel some guilt from knowing that its publication not only aided my career, but also hurt that of Geoffrey Matthews, who was (as I have written elsewhere) "one of the finest gentlemen who ever added scholar to that title." Unfortunately, many American scholars who accepted my disagreements with Matthews's essay on "Shelley and Jane Williams" did not take equally seriously my sincere (though also, I suppose, rhetorically effective) characterization of him as "a thorough scholar, a cogent reasoner, and a persuasive writer" and thus failed to accept his other work as among the best criticism of Shelley ever done in England. (The best American Shelleyans, including Wasserman, Woodring, Cameron, and Stuart Curran, continued to admire and appreciate Matthews's work.) Because Geoffrey Matthews has many loyal friends and students in England, where he was recognized as the dean of Shelleyan critics and textual scholars until the recent emergence of Timothy Webb, my polemical article generated bad feelings toward me by a number of British Romanticists. Geoffrey himself, however, refused to let our disagreements cloud either our mutually respectful professional dealings—as exemplified in his reviews of my books, his participation in the* Festschrift *for Cameron that I coedited, and our exchanges of both our own publications and also of hard-to-find Shelley texts and criticism—or our friendly personal relations, in later meetings in Italy (June 1964, when we drove together on a pilgrimage to Shelleyan sites from Pisa to Bagni di Lucca and Monte San Pellegrino), at his home in England (the summers of 1971 and 1975), and at the Gregynog Shelley Conference in Wales in August 1982.*

My observations of what was memorable in literary criticism eventually taught me that a dramatic conflict between one critic and another adds human interest to a dry, factual topic and gains the attention of readers who might otherwise not persevere to the end of a long argument that lacked such a conflict. On this point, Shelley writes in A Defence of Poetry: *"from an inexplicable defect of harmony in the constitution of human nature, the pain of the inferior is frequently connected with the pleasures of the superior portions of our being. . . . Our sympathy in tragic fiction depends on this principle; tragedy delights by affording a shadow of the pleasure that exists in pain." In 1965, I commented on this effect, as it had influenced my perceptions, in a review for* College English *of René Wellek's* Confrontations: Studies in the Intellectual and Literary Relations between Germany, England, and the United States during the Nineteenth Century:

> *Wellek's "positive" articles, in which he explores literary relationships, will save those who use them from numerous errors. The equally detailed third and fourth essays, refutations of the mistaken scholarship of others, are even more interesting for the drama of the pursuit. Did not Professor Wellek's humanity and intellectual integrity forbid such a course, one would be tempted to suggest that his erudition might make an even greater impression were he habitually to lie in wait for the mistakes of his parochial colleagues, rather than setting forth, in logical order and with full documentation, studies in which he has quite successfully tried "to keep the totality of Western thought in mind."*

Many a beginning scholar or critic trying to take advantage of this flaw in human nature has attempted to make a quick reputation by gunning down some well-known rival. But I have seen such attempts backfire more often than they succeed. The mere show of aggression is not a bit nobler among literary scholars than among stags at rutting time—and far less picturesque. Such attempts succeed only when they are based on reasoned aesthetic or ethical principles that the aggressor is willing to apply to his or her own work, as well as the work being criticized. Above all, any attack on the work of another scholar must be based on the truth of the factual situation, insofar as the facts can be known. (It is always safer to concede that there may be other facts that could change the case, should they surface.) Finally, the degree and the tone of criticism should be proportionate to the nature of the offense. In Matthews's case, I thought "Shelley and Jane Williams" to be mistaken on both factual and theoretical grounds, but I respected his other work and did not doubt that he had uncovered important material, even if he had not made the best possible use of it in this particular essay. In the cases of the work by Rogers and Zillman that I treat in Items 1, 2, and 3, I did not feel that much useful thought and work remained after the critical errors had been exposed, and I employed a much harsher tone. In two or three instances since then—in reviews or responses to papers at MLA—I have overstated the negative case in ways that have hurt not only the objects of my rebukes but myself, through the negative reactions of those whom I respect most in the profession. Though I have tried to atone for these offenses in other ways, it is easier to inflict a damaging judgment than to compensate for its effects on another occasion.

Those who wish to examine for themselves the MS evidence in dispute here can consult the facsimile of Bodleian MS Shelley adds. c. 4, folios 18–58, in the first volume of The Bodleian Shelley Manuscripts, *ed. D. H. Reiman (New York: Garland Publishing, 1986).*

In two articles based on his study of the Bodleian manuscript of Shelley's "The Triumph of Life," G. M. Matthews has presented evidence which proves, he suggests, that during the weeks immediately preceding Shelley's trip to Leghorn with Edward Williams and their subsequent drowning, Shelley and Jane Williams engaged in "a love-affair, passionate on Shelley's part and at least complaisant on Jane's, cutting across the pattern of marriages within the confined little community of Casa Magni"[1] and that much of the somber tone of "The Triumph of Life" can be attributed to this domestic crisis.

The alliance with Mary represented the edifice on which his life had been built: the reform of the world, the achievement of fame, his entire moral and political commitment. The alliance was also his justification for the past: the desertion of Harriet, and his claim on the Lord Chancellor for her children. All this would fall by the wayside. Yet he must have asked himself: is it worth the pain of holding out any longer? To give his love to Jane Williams meant to abandon his principles, for the first time consciously and deliberately; but it meant a transient happiness, "a mitigated pain", which he desperately needed as a man. Hence the profound personal despair of "The Triumph of Life" . . . .[2]

Because Mr. Matthews is a thorough scholar, a cogent reasoner, and a

1. "Shelley and Jane Williams," *RES,* n.s., 12 (February 1961): 46. Hereafter cited as "S and JW."
2. "On Shelley's 'The Triumph of Life,'" *Studia Neophilologica* 34 (1962): 133. Hereafter cited as "On Shelley's TL."

persuasive writer, his argument is likely to gain wide acceptance among those who have not examined in detail the evidence upon which his theories rest.[3] Although I am reluctant to increase the volume of polemicism in Shelley studies, as I have had occasion recently to study the manuscript of "The Triumph of Life" and the materials relating to Shelley's last years, I feel it incumbent upon me to register publicly my disagreement with Mr. Matthews's arguments. In the first two sections of this paper I shall attempt to show that not only is there insufficient evidence that Shelley loved Jane Williams in the way Matthews contends, but that hitherto unpublished passages in the letters and journals of Shelley's circle, joined with other testimony by those contemporaries best able to evaluate the situation, suggest that although Shelley may have been unhappier with Mary than has been generally acknowledged, if he did commit some indiscretion of word or deed (as Newman Ivey White conjectured), it is likely that he was rebuffed by Jane. In the last section I shall point out some previously unnoted parallels between the character of "Rousseau" as he appears in "The Triumph of Life" and the life and writings of the real J. J. Rousseau, and I shall then attempt to suggest what Shelley's use of Rousseau in "The Triumph" and some cryptic remarks in Shelley's late letters may reveal about his state of mind in 1822.

I

In "Shelley and Jane Williams" Matthews wrote that "W. E. Peck claimed to have found" direct evidence of an affair between Shelley and Jane "and may well have done so";[4] in his later article he bases his dating of the consummation of the alleged affair on Peck's reference to a letter from Shelley to Byron implying that Shelley and Jane had experienced an "actual fulfillment of passion, one evening, after an Italian *festa* which they together had attended."[5] Peck's evidence had been dismissed not only, as Matthews declares, because "this letter is not available" but more because of Peck's unsatisfactory answers to Newman Ivey White when White personally questioned him about the letter[6] and, most of all, because of the extreme unlikelihood that Shelley, having hardly rid himself of the embarrassment

---

3. That such an intelligent critic of Shelley as Peter Butter accepts the theory as fact is clear evidence of this likelihood ("Sun and Shape in Shelley's *The Triumph of Life*," RES, n.s., 13 [February 1962]: 50).
4. "S and JW," p. 46.
5. *Shelley: His Life and Work* (Boston: Houghton Mifflin, 1927), 2:199. Discussed in "On Shelley's TL," pp. 130–31.
6. *Shelley* (New York: Knopf, 1940), 2:626–28. White's discussion of Peck's allegation is a model of judicious and responsible biographical analysis.

of the "Hoppner Scandal" (and whatever its nature, it was decidedly troublesome), would have confided such a matter to Byron. Shelley is even less likely to have told Byron if the "fulfillment of passion" transpired on or near 24 June 1822, the date Matthews suggests ("On Shelley's TL," p. 131), than if it had occurred earlier at Pisa, as Peck's ambiguous statement seems to imply.[7] On 18 June 1822 Shelley wrote to John Gisborne: "I shall see little of Lord Byron, nor shall I permit Hunt to form the intermediate link between him and me. I detest all society—almost all, at least—and Lord Byron is the nucleus of all that is hateful and tiresome in it."[8]

One cannot, however, dismiss Mr. Matthews's allegations as easily as Peck's, for Matthews bases his contention chiefly on evidence derived from the Bodleian manuscript of "The Triumph of Life," which includes the holograph of "Lines written in the Bay of Lerici." Mr. Matthews, who interprets these "Lines" as a near-literal autobiographical record of a particular night, assures us that "a short name at line 28 of the full text, heavily and decoratively obliterated except for its initial, 'J', confirms what most readers have already agreed, that the poem is about Jane Williams."[9] Matthews may be correct; but after examining folio 35 verso of the manuscript frequently and carefully, I cannot agree that the initial, unobliterated letter is, beyond question, a capital "J" or that the canceled word is "Jane". First, the cancellation that follows the single, uncanceled letter is far too long to be simply the word "Jane"; if "Jane" does appear, there follows another word of at least equal length that was canceled at the same time. Secondly, the unobliterated initial letter appears to me more likely to be a capital "G", which Shelley made with a long downstroke like an elongated lower-case "g".[10] The context does not particularly demand a proper name, inasmuch as the word just before the cancellation is followed by a period.

---

7. The setting for Peck's statement concerns the Pisan circle; he mentions that the Williamses lived "in the same house with the Shelleys, though on another floor" as they did at Pisa (see Trelawny's *Recollections*, Chapter 3) but not at Lerici (see Mary Shelley's descriptions of Casa Magni to Maria Gisborne, 15 August 1822, in *The Letters of Mary W. Shelley*, ed. Frederick L. Jones [Norman: University of Oklahoma Press, 1944], 1:180; hereafter cited as *Letters*).
8. *The Complete Works of Percy Bysshe Shelley*, ed. Roger Ingpen and Walter E. Peck (London: Ernest Benn; New York: Scribner's, 1926–1930), 10:402 (hereafter cited as "Julian"). See also Shelley's letter to Hunt, 2 March 1822 (ibid., 10:361).
9. "S and JW," p. 40.
10. All quotations from "The Triumph of Life" and from "Lines written in the Bay of Lerici" are based on Shelley's holographs in Bodleian MS Shelley adds. c. 4 and are printed with the kind permission of the Delegates of the Clarendon Press. Those who are interested in consulting the manuscript can compare this doubtful cancellation (f. 35v) with indisputable occurrences of capital "J's" and "G's" in the same manuscript: "God" (canceled), f. 27v; "God" and "Good", f. 30r; "Gregory", f. 37v; "June", f. 22r; "Janus", f. 23r; "Jane", f. 56r (in a draft of the opening of "To Jane: 'The keen stars were twinkling'").

As Mr. Matthews says, however, "most readers have already agreed, that the poem is about Jane Williams." This has been concluded from the date of its composition and its thematic relationship to others of the Jane poems (e.g., "The Magnetic Lady to her Patient"). Yet, though I believe firmly even without accepting Matthews's evidence that "Lines written in the Bay of Lerici" concerns Shelley and Jane, I do not see how either the uncanceled lines of the poem or the canceled line-fragments in the manuscript lend the slightest support to the theory that Shelley's relations with Jane were anything but platonic. Let us examine, for example, the full context of the manuscript at the point in question (canceled words in italics):

[f. 35v] That even fancy dares to claim.—
    And I was happy.? G or J [?] [?]
    Thus I was happy, *if the name*
    Of happiness
        The wildest thoughts
    Her presence
    Within her presence
    Charmed by her presence, meek & tame
        The demon of my spirit lay

    Her presence had made weak & tame
        All passions, and
    Desire & fear.—I was thought no more
        I lived alone,
    Of pleasures lost or sorrows
        is
    In the time which *was* our own:
    The past & future were forgot
        had been, & would be, not.—
    As they *would be &*
    But now I desired,—I dare not
    But soon, the guardian Angel gone
    The demon reassumed his throne

[f.36r]   faint
    In my *weak* heart . . I dare not *tell* speak
    The My thoughts; but thus disturbed & weak
    I sate and watched the vessels glide
    Along the Ocean bright & wide

These are lines in which Mr. Matthews apparently finds evidence that "Shelley's desire for [Jane] at this time was not exactly that of the moth for the star."[11] As the subsequent uncanceled lines tell us clearly, the desire

11. "S and JW," p. 46. See also Matthews's notes on the text of lines 25-26, 29, 33 of the poem (p. 43).

and fear that Shelley refers to in the cancellation are desire and fear for the future and regret for the sorrows of the past, and it is when the guardian Angel (or Magnetic Lady) leaves Shelley that these hopes and fears return. In the presence of Jane, Shelley's passions were "made weak & tame"; only in her absence did whatever "sweet & bitter pain" was troubling him return to master his spirit. That Shelley found more comfort in Jane's sunny nature than in Mary's neurotic melancholy during this period there can be no doubt; as he affirms in "To Edward Williams," the very happiness enjoyed by Edward and Jane brought to his senses doubly strong the bleakness of his own "cold home." But in the "Lines written in the Bay of Lerici" Shelley tells us that he did not find it difficult to control his feelings in her presence.

On the text of the poem itself there is only one point where I would disagree with Matthews, but this is a crux upon which his reading of the poem leans heavily. He reads the final line: "Seeking Life alone <u>not peace</u>." In a note he records Garnett's reading ("Destroying life alone, not peace!") and adds this explanation:

> *Destroying* is firmly cancelled in MS., with a space before the next word, and probably had no connexion with the rest of the line as it stands: "destroying" would go with "regret" and the fisher, "seeking" goes with "pleasure" and the fish. I take the primary meaning to be: "They are enviably happy who, in exchanging more placid existence ('peace') for active sensuous enjoyment ('Life'), can remain blind to the price they must pay for it (the spear)."
>
> ("S and JW," pp. 43-44)

After examining the last lines of the poem, I am unable to agree that Shelley intended "Seeking" to replace "Destroying". It is true that the first seven letters of "Destroying" are firmly canceled, but I find the space between this word and "life" no more significant than the even larger space found two lines above between "Extinguishes" and "all" or the generous spacing characteristic of other uncanceled lines on the same page (f. 36v). "Seeking" is written a good distance below "Destroying" and in a large hand, although there is sufficient room above the line to have written in a substitute word for "Destroying" on the same level that Shelley wrote "alone", a late addition to the line. There is no doubt in my mind that Shelley, at one moment at least, intended this line to read "Destroying life alone not peace:"; whether he was about to cancel this line and replace it with one that began "Seeking" or whether "Seeking" was simply the first word of an entirely new line is conjectural. The point is that the final couplet that we have is incomplete (as the absence of a concluding rhyme-word in the penultimate line, "of the regret that pleasure", amply testifies), and that there is a colon after "peace" (not a period, as Matthews has it) indicates that, even were this couplet complete, the poem must still be regarded as fragmentary, making it dangerous to explicate it as a self-contained unit.

Moreover, even if one accepts Matthews's reading "Seeking" for "Destroying", the basic implications of the figure are not drastically altered and certainly do not support the implications that Matthews finds in them. The earlier lines of the poem tell that with "the guardian Angel gone / The demon reassumed his throne" in the Poet's heart, bringing once again the hopes and fears, desires and sorrows of the future and the past. The Poet then gazes about him and contrasts his human state, subject to these hopes and fears, to two other metaphysical possibilities: first, the vessels that seemed to glide "like spirit winged chariots" sailing to "some Elysian star"; if the Poet were, like these imaginative boats, raised above the limitations of mortality, he would find an immortal "drink to medecine / Such sweet & bitter pain". Or, if he were like the dumb animals such as the fish that, like lambs led to slaughter, cannot foresee the devastating end of their pursuit of pleasure, he, too, might be able "to worship the delusive flame". But the Poet, neither a spirit nor an animal but a man, cannot, as they do, seek pleasure without counting the cost.

Mr. Matthews rests his case for a love affair between Shelley and Jane most heavily, however, on "certain remarkable interlineations in Shelley's hand on the draft of *The Triumph of Life*, amounting to a private gloss on the poem, which seem to put the matter beyond doubt" ("S and JW," p. 46). These interlineations prove, according to Matthews, that "the love-affair with Jane Williams must have a crucial bearing on the interpretation of the poem, whether as illustration or as cause: Shelley has practically told us so himself; and the relationship will have to be accepted in the end for what it certainly was, the most profoundly disturbing personal experience of Shelley's whole maturity" ("S and JW," p. 48). One naturally expects that the textual evidence on which this strong statement is based will be conclusive beyond all possible doubt. Unfortunately, this is not the case.

In a note to line 451 of "The Triumph of Life" Matthews writes: "The top of f. 47r above this line carries, after a few calculations, the first eight or nine words of a letter, heavily overwritten, of which I can be sure only of the first five:

Dear Roberts
Williams and I [?& ?Jane ?are].[12]

Folio 47 is conjugate with folio 48, on the verso of which was begun, *reverso*, this letter to Captain Dan Roberts:

Dear Roberts
I have just received a letter from Hunt which makes me anxious to see him before he leaves Genoa—How would you like a trip there & back with me & Williams

Close examination of the fragment on f. 47r, which is obviously another attempt to begin the same letter,[13] reveals that Shelley, perhaps unsure exactly what he wanted to say, has superimposed some words upon an earlier draft of the same words: "Dear Roberts" is superimposed on "Dear Roberts"; "Williams and I are" seems to be superimposed on, though taking rather more space than, "Williams and I sail"; I find no indication that "Jane" appears at all, though one might perhaps see "Jane" at one occurrence of the first-person pronoun. Because Mr. Matthews has not, however, considered this possible appearance of "Jane" strong enough to mention in "Shelley and Jane Williams," it is on his three identifications of the word in that article that his case must stand or fall.

At the top of f. 52r, according to Matthews, "adjoining line 524 is the single word, 'Jane'." The word that Matthews identifies as "Jane" ("S and JW," p. 46) is, apparently, a faint word to the left of and slightly below "shone"; this word, which was begun with an almost dry quill, seems to me to be an earlier attempt to write "shone", the ink being exhausted before Shelley had completed more than the first three letters.[14]

12. " 'The Triumph of Life': A New Text," *Studia Neophilologica* 32, no. 2 (1960): 303 (hereafter cited as "New Text").
13. Matthews dates this letter 19 June 1822 ("S and JW," p. 48n and "New Text," p. 304), but it was probably written 24 June. Hunt wrote to Shelley from "on board the *David Walter*, Genoa / 15th June, 1822," (*Correspondence*, ed. Thornton Hunt [London: Smith, Elder, 1862], 1:181–82), the letter reaching Shelley on 19 June; Shelley replied the same day (Julian, 10:406–7) describing the situation at Casa Magni, telling of Mary's miscarriage, and welcoming Hunt to Italy. Hunt responded on receipt of this letter (21 June, *Correspondence*, 1:182–83); Thornton Hunt has apparently edited out the conclusion of this letter, but from Shelley's reply on 24 June it is reasonably clear that Hunt was in some kind of financial difficulty and had written an alarmed appeal. After telling Hunt what steps he has taken to solve the problem, Shelley assures Hunt that "This morning, on the receipt of your letter, I was on the point of setting sail to Genoa . . . and Williams had already gone on board to weigh anchor, when poor Mary suffered a relapse, which . . . was sufficient to warn me of the necessity of remaining with her for the present" (Julian, 10:408).
14. That Matthews does not mention this alleged appearance of "Jane" in "On Shelley's TL" suggests that he might have felt this one to be less certain than the other two.

The second instance that Mr. Matthews advances is on f. 26v. After quoting lines 153–54 and 161–64 of "The Triumph," he writes: "Ink gives place to pencil between the words 'Oceans wrath', and a few corrections have been made in pencil in this and other recent passages. Also in pencil, written into the space between the tercets shown immediately above, are what appear to be the words: 'Jane & I'" (p. 47). Matthews's caution in this reading is, I think, quite justified, for the penciled additions, originally not especially large or clear, are badly smeared.[15] The second word of the three doubtful ones (below "*rainbows* after" and to the left of "Oceans" and "roar") appears to be an ampersand, the "lowercase" ampersand that, although often used by Shelley in his earlier MSS, does not appear elsewhere in the MS of "The Triumph of Life"; the third word may be "I"; but I find myself unable to imagine any way in which the first word of the trio can be read "Jane". Although I am not satisfied that my reading makes enough sense to be taken seriously, until a more plausible one is suggested, I shall have to read the mysterious words "Sun & I", the proximity of "rainbows" forming the only thread by which I can relate the phrase to the context. Nevertheless, this reading takes into account the shapes of the letters to be deciphered and, on the other hand, has the negative virtue of not carrying one far from the text.

"The last example, and the clearest," writes Mr. Matthews, is on the final leaf of the *Triumph*, where Rousseau is made to say:

> f. 52v And some grew weary of the ghastly dance   540
> And fell, as I have fallen by the way side

Just below this last line, and partly enclosed by it, Shelley has written in ink in a minute hand:

> Alas I kiss you Jane

The phrasing, and the sombre intensity of the context, leave little doubt that these words are a wry but unrepenting acknowledgement of his own fall from earlier principles of conduct—a recognition that, as the "Lines written in the Bay of Lerici" had expressed it, Life was what he had sought with Jane Williams, not peace. ("S and JW," p. 47)

Once again Matthews's assertion has outrun the manuscript evidence, though again it is difficult to prove him categorically wrong, for the words

---

15. In "New Text" (p. 285n) he wrote, "From 164–175 the draft continues in scrawled pencil," and in "On Shelley's TL" (p. 131), "at this point in the draft (unless I am misreading it) the words 'Jane & I' are inserted in pencil . . . ."

to which he refers are indeed minute and he has transcribed the clearly legible words accurately: the phrase "Alas I kiss you" does appear immediately below "have fallen by" and to the left of "way side" on f. 52v. But although the final word may begin with a capital "J", the remaining marks do not seem to be "ane", but, more likely, "ulie". And far from the context supporting Matthews's thesis and leaving "little doubt that these words are a wry but unrepenting acknowledgement of his own fall," the context gives one a quite different impression. If Shelley had fallen from his "earlier principles of conduct," the phrase "Alas I kiss you Jane", included with the tale of the decayed and tattered ruin of "what was once Rousseau," a shape so horrible to the poet that upon his first realization that it was not a tree root but a man, he cried out, "O Heaven have mercy on such wretchedness!" (line 181), can hardly be judged "a wry but unrepenting acknowledgement" of error. Shelley's fall, if indeed one took place, was certainly not taken lightly or unrepentently by the author of "The Triumph of Life," a poem in which, as in Dante's *Inferno*, each crime provokes its own appropriate punishment. Nor would Shelley's alleged "fall" relate directly to the "fallen" of the context, for Rousseau tells of those who "grew weary of the ghastly dance / And fell, as I have fallen by the way side": they had left the train of those captive to the car of Life or those who voluntarily flew before or followed the triumph. Rousseau's words, placed in their context, explain how some who had plunged into a sea of sensual experience eventually freed themselves from its grasp, and, scarred by their earlier excesses, nevertheless put that life behind them. If Shelley intended by his interlineation to relate his own experience directly to that of Rousseau in the poem, the effect of his words is almost the opposite of that which Matthews finds in them.

Thus, in no one of the five places in the Bodleian MSS Shelley adds. c. 4 that Mr. Matthews finds "Jane" or what appears to be "Jane" can I corroborate his findings. As I have indicated, in some of the places I give more credence to his readings than in others, but in every case he has elaborated his claims to a point at which I must object. Mr. Matthews must assume at the outset of "Shelley and Jane Williams" what he ostensibly has set out to prove. He concedes in a footnote that Mary Shelley seems not to have noticed these "remarkable interlineations" during her painstaking transcription of "The Triumph of Life" and preparation for its publication in 1824 ("S and JW," p. 47), and if another editor, examining the manuscript in the light of Matthews's suggestions, cannot detect the name "Jane" at any point, the evidence is, perhaps, insufficient to support an elaborate biographical and critical theory.

II

Mr. Matthews attempts to establish circumstantially the passionate liaison between Shelley and Jane Williams by reinterpreting the events of Shelley's last days. Because, aside from the alleged mentions of Jane in the MS of "The Triumph," Matthews has not provided any new evidence not examined by White, perhaps the most useful way to evaluate his conclusions is to reexamine briefly the old material and to shed some new light from unpublished portions of Mary Shelley's journals and from unpublished letters of the Shelley circle in the Abinger Collection.[16]

Matthews and White have described Mary Shelley's dislike of Casa Magni as "too extreme and irrational" and "intense, almost morbid,"[17] Matthews drawing from this judgment the implication that Mary was jealous of Shelley's attentions to Jane. But a reappraisal of the primary evidence leads me to reject both the judgment and the implication. In her 15 August 1822 letter to Maria Gisborne, Mary—in the deepest throes of grief over the death of Shelley, whose body had been cremated the previous day—expresses an aversion to Casa Magni and its environs but also enumerates reasons for her feelings:

I wrote to you either at the end of May or the beginning of June. I described to you the place we were living in:—our desolate house, the beauty yet strangeness of the scenery and the delight Shelley took in all this—he never was in better health or spirits than during this time. I was not well in body or mind. My nerves were wound up to the utmost irritation, and the sense of misfortune hung over my spirits. No words can tell you how I hated our house & the country about it. Shelley reproached me for this—his health was good & the place was quite after his own heart—What could I answer—that the people were wild & hateful, that though the country was beautiful yet I liked a more *countryfied* place, that there was great difficulty in living-that all our Tuscans would leave us, & that the very jargon of these *Genovese* was disgusting—This was all I had to say but no words could describe my feelings— (*Letters*, 1:179)

To one who has read the letters Mary Shelley wrote during the first year of her bereavement—those published by Jones but even more those unpublished ones to Jane in the Abinger Collection—Mary's tone here is

---

16. Since 1952 the bulk of Lord Abinger's collection has been available on microfilms made for Duke University, copies of which are in the Bodleian and other centers of Shelley studies. See Lewis Patton, "The Shelley-Godwin Collection of Lord Abinger," *Library Notes* (Duke University), no. 27 (April 1953): 11–17. Quotations from the Abinger Collection are printed here with the kind permission of Professor Patton, who supervises the use of these microfilms.

17. "On Shelley's TL," p. 129; *Shelley*, 2:361.

moderate, almost matter-of-fact, by comparison. A fairer basis of judging Mary's reaction to Casa Magni is her letter to Mrs. Gisborne, 2 June 1822, in which, not oppressed by Shelley's death, she made light of her problems. Her complaints about Casa Magni at that time were, specifically, these:

> . . . but one house was to be found for us all . . . . The poverty of the people is beyond anything, . . . while we find it hard work to purvey miles around for a few eatables. We were in wretched discomfort at first, but now are in a kind of disorderly order, living from day to day as we can. . . . As only one house was to be found habitable in this gulf, the Williams' have taken up their abode with us, and their servants and mine quarrel like cats and dogs; and besides, you may imagine how ill a large family agrees with my laziness, when accounts and domestic concerns come to be talked of. *Ma pazienza.* After all the place does not suit me; the people are *rozzi*, and speak a detestable dialect, and yet it is better than any other Italian seashore north of Naples. (*Letters*, 1:170–71)

On the other hand, Mary said several favorable things about their summer home: "it is beautifully situated on the sea-shore, under the woody hills . . . . Our colony is much smaller than we expected, which we consider a benefit. . . . The air is excellent, and you may guess how much better we like it than Leghorn, when [where], besides, we should have been involved in English society—a thing we longed to get rid of at Pisa"; and she enumerated several problems quite unconnected with the domestic arrangements at Casa Magni: the effect on Claire Clairmont of the news of Allegra's death ("You may judge of what was her first burst of grief and despair"), her own health ("I have been very unwell for some time past, but am better now"), and William Godwin's financial crisis ("the lawsuit went against my Father. This was the summit and crown of our spring misfortunes . . .") (*Letters*, 1:170–72).

Shelley's letters and Edward Williams's journal corroborate each of Mary's complaints: to Byron, Shelley wrote, "*You* will be delighted with Spezia, although the accommodations are as wretched as the scenery is divine" (Julian, 10:386), and to Roberts, "I hope . . . soon to see you here, and although I cannot boast very capital accommodation, that you will put up with such quarters as we can afford . . ." (Julian, 10:389); he wrote to Mary Jane Godwin on 29 May that "in Mary's present state of health and spirits" he was unwilling to show her Godwin's last letter, which conveyed "a supposition that she could do more than she does . . ." (Julian, 10:393–94).

Writing twice to Claire during her absence, Shelley remarked on 29 May that though "Williams seems happy and content . . . Jane is by no means acquiescent in the system of things, and she pines after her own house and saucepans to which no one can have a claim except herself," and a day or two later, "Jane the other day was very much discontented with her situation here, on account of some of our servants having taken something of hers . . . Mary, though ill, is good. . . . I wish you could mark down some good cook for us . . ." (Julian, 10:396–97). Among numerous petty frustrations recorded in Williams's journal, he wrote on 3 May, "Went to Lerici with S[helley] being obliged to market there, the servant having returned from Sarzana without being able to procure anything" and on 21 May, "Beta & Domenico leave Mary's service."[18] When the journals and letters of Mary, Shelley, and Edward are carefully compared, there is virtually no discrepancy among their respective evaluations of their summer home at Casa Magni. Shelley enjoyed himself because of the scenery and the boating and because he was in exceptionally good health; Mary was miserable because the housekeeping difficulties fell heavily upon her and because she was too ill to enjoy the only recreations afforded by the place.

Mary later expressed her only cause for dissatisfaction with Casa Magni that did not seem to be shared by others, while recalling her feelings as she awaited the return of the *Don Juan* from Leghorn:

When Jane & Claire took their evening walk I used to patrole the terrace, oppressed with wretchedness, yet gazing on the most beautiful scene in the world . . . . did not my William die? & did I hold my Percy by a firmer tenure?—Yet I thought when he, when my Shelley returns I shall be happy—he will comfort me, if my boy be ill he will restore him & encourage me. (*Letters*, 1:181)

When one recalls that in another beautiful but isolated setting, during a similar absence by Shelley, their daughter Clara became ill and died before she could receive adequate medical attention, that William Shelley had died suddenly in Rome during one of the happiest and most creative periods of Shelley's Italian sojourn, that during Mary's previous pregnancy the Shelleys had gone to Florence especially to put her under the care of "Mr. Bell, a famous Scotch surgeon," that news of the death of Claire's Allegra had come just a week before the Shelleys took Casa Magni, that Mary, first threatened by a miscarriage on 9 June, was saved from death during its occurrence on 16 June only by decisive action on the part of Shelley before

---

18. *Maria Gisborne & Edward E. Williams, Shelley's Friends: Their Journals and Letters*, ed. Frederick L. Jones (Norman: University of Oklahoma Press, 1951), pp. 146, 150 (hereafter cited as *Shelley's Friends*). "Beta" or "Betta" was the cook for whom Shelley asked Claire to find a replacement.

a doctor could arrive,[19] and that, in effect, Mary's only surviving child was hostage to chance in their isolated residence, one will perhaps conclude that Mary's aversion to their home was neither "too extreme" nor "irrational."

Newman Ivey White, discussing a possible "indiscretion" involving Shelley and Jane, cites as one of the most important problems in ascertaining the nature of that indiscretion the extent of Jane's gossip in 1827 about Shelley and Mary. "It would appear," says White, "that Jane asserted that Shelley was actually in love with her at San Terenzo."[20] White, using *Shelley and Mary,* did not have available to him the full text of Mary Shelley's journals after Shelley's death. The unexpurgated version of the entry for 13 July 1827 makes it appear extremely doubtful that Jane's gossip had anything to do with Jane and Shelley at all:

Jane My friend has proved false & treacherous! Miserable discovery—for four years I was devoted to her—& I earned only ingratitude

Not for worlds would I attempt to transfer the deathly blackness of my meditations to these pages—let no trace remain—save the deep-bleeding, hidden wound of my lost heart—of such a tale of horror & despair

Writing—study—quiet—such remedies I must seek—woe the while—I thought fresh hopes were to be mine—but who can sustain the mortal sadness which such a discovery must produce

Am I not a fool! What deadly cold flows through my veins—my head weighed down—my limbs sink under me—I start at every sound as the messenger of fresh misery—& despair invests my soul with trembling horror

> What hast thou done?
>   Nothing! I cannot charge
> My memory with much—save sorrow; but
> I have been so beyond the common lot
> Chastened & visited that I must needs think
> That I was wicked
>   (Abinger Collection, Duke Microfilms, Reel 11)

Mary seems here less angered at Jane's actions than defensive because Jane

---

19. *Shelley,* 2:36–39; 2:91–96; Julian, 10:87; *Shelley,* 2:354–56; 2:367–68; Julian, 10:401; *Letters,* 1:179–80.

20. *Shelley,* 2:628. White dates Mary's discovery of Jane's talk "1828" instead of 1827. Mary discovered that her friend was "false & treacherous" about 13 July 1827 and, on the advice of Tom Moore, disclosed her discovery to Jane on 12 February 1828 (*Mary Shelley's Journal,* ed. Frederick L. Jones [Norman: University of Oklahoma Press, 1947], pp. 198–200; hereafter cited as *Journal*). Between these dates Mary increased her correspondence with Jane (writing at least ten times between 27 July and October), praising Jane very highly, perhaps in an attempt to prick her conscience (Abinger Collection, Duke Microfilms, Reel 14).

has charged her with some fault; she is shocked and hurt that her closest friend should have criticized her behind her back.

The entire "Journal of Sorrow" (so titled on the inside cover of the notebook) can be seen as Mary's guilt-ridden attempt to redeem herself, through excessive worship of Shelley's memory, for the pain her despondency caused him during his lifetime. Mixed with its self-pity are certain strong remarks of self-reproach for her conduct toward Shelley: for example, in an unpublished passage in the first entry of the "Journal of Sorrow," 2 October 1822, after exclaiming, "What a change! O my beloved Shelley!" (*Journal*, p. 181), Mary continues: "It is not true that this heart was cold to thee. Tell me, for now you know all things—did I not in the deepest solitude of thought repeat to myself my goodfortune in possessing you?" (Reel 11). Perhaps in the deepest solitude of thought Mary had loved Shelley, but as this entry shows, she was aware that to others and to Shelley himself in his merely mortal state her love was not always clearly evident. Again on 3 June 1823 she wrote: "My Shelley—But for one instant of Sympathy!—ah, my beloved one!—didst thou when leaving me for ever—think of me—did you think of the faults, the coldness & weaknesses of your unhappy Mary—or did you think of the tears she shed during her parting embrace, of the love that deeply dwelt in her heart—of her sufferings—her anguish—?" (Reel 11).

Jane had told Leigh Hunt on his arrival in Italy—what she assumed he already knew—that "the intercourse between Shelley & Mary was not as happy as it should have been" (*Shelley's Friends*, p. 166), and Hunt wrote to his sister-in-law, Bessie Kent, in England that Jane had set him against Mary. Jane may also have confided her feelings about Mary to Thomas Jefferson Hogg. But the tone of Mary's letter introducing Jane to Hogg indicates that in 1822 Mary had no doubts about either the innocence of Jane's relations with Shelley or the sincerity of Jane's friendship for her:

My dear Hogg

This letter will be delivered to you by Mrs Williams, the widow of the dear friend who was lost with mine own Shelley. You will find in her the friend whom he saw daily for nearly two years, to whom he was affectionately attached, & who more than any person can describe to you the last actions & thoughts of your incomparable friend. If you still retain the affection you once had for him, and think of him with that kindness which he always felt for you, her company will be invaluable to you—although you can in part repay her by talking of the former years of the life of one whom she loved, esteemed & admired beyond all her other friends.

You did not know Edward, & cannot tell what she has lost in losing him. They were enthusiastically attached to each other, and he by his talents, angelic disposition, his gentle, brave & generous nature fully merited all the tenderness which she, the model of all gentleness, and grace, bore him. If my own unhappiness had not penetrated my heart so entirely I could never have endured to see her divided from one she loved so well; and you who used to be a fervent admirer of that devotion which distinguishes the sentiment of love in a woman, will appreciate her virtues, although they are repaid, as all earthly virtue is, by desolation & misery.

I would say do all in your power to be of use to her, but to know her is sufficient to make the desire of serving her arise in an unselfish mind. Do what little you can to amuse her.

By the time you receive this you will probably have heard from me by the post, so I say nothing of such a nullity as I now am.—Adieu

Truly yours
Mary W. Shelley

Pisa. Sept[r] 9th 1822

(Abinger Collection, Duke Microfilms, Reel 10)

This letter marked the beginning of the rapidly developing intimacy and friendship between Hogg and Jane that eventually resulted in their living together as man and wife.[21]

But Hogg and Jane apparently felt reservations about Mary Shelley of which Mary must have been aware even though she seldom allowed herself to admit it.[22] When Jane learned that Mary was definitely returning to England (contrary to the advice of Hogg and of Jane, who hated England and longed to return to Italy), Jane communicated this news to Hogg, who replied from Stockton, 17 August 1823:

I fear indeed that nothing is left for Mary's friends, but to hope, that her return will

21. Matthews writes that Jane "was certainly no strict moralist: married at sixteen and deserted, she lived unmarried first with Edward Williams, and then with Hogg—apparently not far from her real husband" ("On Shelley's TL," p. 128). Such an argument is unconvincing on two counts: first, the stringent divorce laws of the time made it virtually impossible for many worthy people to achieve legal release from their marriages. (Jane's letters to Mary of 13 November 1822 and 27 March 1823 reveal that her "legal tyrant" was a fraudulent adventurer who, when exposed, hired an assassin to kill the man who exposed him [Abinger Collection, Duke Microfilms, Reel 10].) There is, moreover, no evidence that Jane Williams's fidelity first to Edward Williams and, later, to Hogg was ever seriously questioned by anyone who knew her (any more than was George Eliot's fidelity to George Henry Lewes during his lifetime). In 1870 W. M. Rossetti recorded in his diary after a visit to Trelawny: "I am to dine with T[relawny] next Tuesday, and may perhaps meet Mrs Hogg: she never professed to be in love with Hogg, but to have been passionately in love with Williams, and incapable of loving any one else. 'I have kissed the shirt off his back'" (*Rossetti Papers: 1862–1870* [London: Sands, 1903], p. 501).

22. On 18 January 1824 Mary wrote in her journal: "I love Jane [Williams] better than any other human being, but I am pressed upon by the knowledge that she but slightly returns this affection" (*Journal*, p. 192).

be more auspicious than they can venture to augur—I tremble because of her want of tact (to borrow her favorite expression), & because of those wretches, the G[odwin]s, who wo^d sink a much better vessel with a much better pilot—they have a talent for failing & for failing disgracefully.—Her conversation will be painful, just as her letters are, because, to those, who saw behind the scenes, the subject of it is a mere fable; our loss is real, your's, dearest girl, I acknowledge, in spite of my hopes, irreparable, mine bad enough, but her's, however painful, is in fact imaginary for to suppose that matters co^d have continued as they were, wo^d have been the vanity of vanities, & any other termination wo^d have been for her, except as to money-matters, infinitely worse.— (Abinger Collection, Duke Microfilms, Reel 14)

Hogg definitely implies that Shelley, had he lived, would have left Mary. It is possible—even likely—that Hogg first learned of Shelley's dissatisfaction with Mary from John and Maria Gisborne, with whom he began to be intimate soon after their arrival in England in June 1820.[23] As early as 19 July 1820 Shelley had written to Maria Gisborne (in a postscript to one of Mary's letters): "Mary who, you know, is always wise, has been lately very good. I wish she were as wise now as she will be at 45, or as misfortune has made me. She would then live on very good terms with Clare—"[24] To John Gisborne he wrote on 18 June 1822:

As to me, Italy is more and more delightful . . . . I only feel the want of those who can feel, and understand me. Whether from proximity and the continuity of domestic intercourse, Mary does not. The necessity of concealing from her thoughts that would pain her, necessitates this, perhaps. It is the curse of Tantalus, that a person possessing such excellent powers and so pure a mind as hers, should not excite the sympathy indispensable to their application to domestic life. (Julian, 10:402–3)

The Gisbornes, who clearly had understood for some time that "the intercourse between Shelley & Mary was not as happy as it should have been," probably discussed the situation with Shelley's oldest friend, Hogg (of whom Shelley speaks highly in this same letter to John Gisborne), just as Jane had discussed the estrangement with Hunt. It is reasonably clear that all of Shelley's friends in England (with the possible exception of Peacock, who always remained Harriet's partisan) knew of Shelley's disaffection from Mary, or at least of Mary's coldness to him.

After Hogg and Jane began their union in 1827, Isabel Robinson told

---

23. See the Gisbornes' letters and journal in *Shelley's Friends*.
24. At the end of this note Shelley adds: "Of course you will not suppose that Mary has seen . . . this transverse writing—so take no notice of it in any letter intended for her inspection" (Frederick L. Jones, "Mary Shelley to Maria Gisborne: New Letters, 1818–1822," *SP* 52 [January 1955]: 66–67).

Mary of some things that Jane had let slip about Mary's petulance before Shelley's death and about Jane's own "inadequate affection for Mary."[25] That the report to Mary of Jane's gossip probably did not go beyond remarks on Mary's bad temper and coldness to Shelley is evident from an expurgated portion of Mary's journal entry for 21 October 1838; while evaluating her own strengths and weaknesses, Mary writes:

My early friends chose the position of enemies. I had faults—instead of exposing these to a candid mind & tender conscience I was villified behind my back. I discovered this—I discovered the sad influence exercised there when the grave permitted no appeal—& the sense of my own faults redoubled (erroneously perhaps) the bitter curse of unjust treatment. When I first discovered that a trusted friend had acted thus by me, I was nearly destroyed—my health was shaken. I remember thinking of Guatamotzin's bed of torture & with a burst of agonizing tears exclaiming I would prefer that to the unutterable anguish a friend's falsehood engendered!—I cannot forget that—it is wrong. She has many virtues I have no right still to feel sad—but in vain I try to cicatrize the wound—there is no resentment—but the world can never be to me what it was before— (Abinger Collection, Duke Microfilms, Reel 11)

Mary's early friends wronged her, then, by discussing her faults behind her back; there is no hint of a deeper betrayal.

One can, of course, argue that if Jane had an affair with Shelley in 1822 she would have been discreet enough to keep it to herself, and mere absence of her testimony does not prove that no affair took place; but perhaps English and American scholars should follow common law to the extent that the burden of proof does not fall on the accused. Other contemporary witnesses, though their testimony may be prejudiced for one reason or another, deserve consideration. Thomas Medwin, who was responsible for introducing the Williamses to Shelley and who observed their interaction in Pisa, wrote: "a purer being than Mrs. Williams cannot exist. Not a breath of scandal could possibly attach to her fame. The verses addressed to her always passed through the hands of Williams himself, and who had too much confidence in the virtue of one devotedly his, to harbour for a moment any jealousy of an attachment the most innocent and disinterested."[26] Trelawny in *Records of Shelley, Byron and the Author* (1878) adds a story that Shelley, when he had taken Jane and her two children out in a small boat, suddenly "exclaimed joyfully 'Now let us

---

25. Winifred Scott, *Jefferson Hogg* (London: Jonathan Cape, 1951), p. 195. See Mary to Jane, 14 February 1828, *Letters*, 1:369–71.
26. *Life of Percy Bysshe Shelley . . . Amended and Extended by the Author*, ed. H. Buxton Forman (London: Oxford University Press, 1913), pp. 318–19.

together solve the great mystery'." This incident, if authentic, must have taken place between 13 June and 18 June 1822 during the brief visit of the *Bolivar* on its way to Leghorn. Trelawny reports Jane's words when she reached the shore: "'Oh, I have escaped the most dreadful fate; never will I put my foot in that horrid coffin. Solve the great mystery? Why, he is the greatest of all mysteries. . . . He is seeking after what we all avoid, death. I wish we were away, I shall always be in terror. . . . You won't catch me in a boat with Shelley alone' said Jane."[27] If we can believe even the spirit of Trelawny's anecdote, Jane hardly thought of Shelley in a way likely to produce complaisance in a love affair within the week. In 1870 Trelawny told Rossetti flatly that "he is certain there was no intrigue between Shelley and Mrs Williams—'he might as well have wanted the Virgin Mary'" (*Rossetti Papers*, p. 502).

Nor did Edward himself have the slightest doubt of the fidelity of his wife or of his closest friend. His last letter from Leghorn, 6 July 1822, shows both his deep love for Jane and his unclouded trust in Shelley's regard for her:

A letter from Mary of the most gloomy kind reached S[helley] yesterday and this mood of hers aggravates my uneasiness to see you; for I am proud, dear girl, beyond words to express in the conviction that *wherever* we may be together you would be cheerful and contented. . . .

I am tired to death of waiting. This is our longest separation, and seems a year to me—absence alone is enough to make me anxious, and, indeed, unhappy. . . . Poor S[helley] desires that I should return to you, but I know secretly wishes me not to leave him in the lurch. He, too, by his manner, is as anxious to see *you* almost as I could be . . . .[28]

Though the journals, letters, and writings of all contemporaries who were close to the situation agree that Shelley was unhappy with Mary, none even suggests a romance between Shelley and Jane. This does not mean, of course, that there could not have been, at some moment known only to the two principals, a scene in which Shelley declared his love for Jane, but such an admission merely vindicates the judgment of White: "The only authentic record of the high-water mark of Shelley's attraction to Jane Williams is Shelley's own poems" (*Shelley,* 2:627).

The more we learn about Shelley's creative method, his symbolic lan-

27. Chapter 10 (London: George Routledge & Sons, n.d.), pp. 91–92.
28. *Shelley's Friends,* p. 162. Note Trelawny's remark in *Recollections of the Last Days of Shelley and Byron*: "I . . . found Shelley in ecstasy with his boat, and Williams as touchy about her reputation as if she had been his wife" (*The Life of Percy Bysshe Shelley . . .* , ed. Humbert Wolfe [London: Dent, 1933], 2:209).

guage, the purpose and the ideas of his poetry, the less likely we are to be led into the mistake of regarding any poem by Shelley as simply an autobiographical record. Personal experiences are used in Shelley's poetry, as they are in the work of any great artist, but Shelley, drawing like his masters Dante and Milton upon a wide and profound intellectual heritage, transmuted the dross of phenomenal experience into the golden reality of art. Even if undeniable evidence of an affair between Shelley and Jane Williams were forthcoming, "The Triumph of Life" is based upon ideas and attitudes that had been Shelley's for so long that any biographical developments during the last months of his life must be regarded as subsidiary, though not irrelevant, to the understanding of the poem.[29]

III

If the word after "Alas I kiss you" on the final page of "The Triumph" MS is "Julie" (a point upon which I have no desire to dogmatize), the phrase would correlate very appropriately with Shelley's representation of Rousseau's life history ("The Triumph of Life," lines 308–543). The common assumption has been that, to discover the source of Shelley's knowledge concerning the life of Rousseau, one should turn to the *Confessions*, but, perhaps because Shelley's single recorded judgment of the *Confessions* is that "they are either a disgrace to the confessor or a string of falsehoods . . . probably the latter,"[30] those comparing "The Triumph" with Rousseau's autobiographical writings have produced very few close parallels between them. Many critics have, therefore, concluded that the account of "Rousseau" in "The Triumph" merely repeats Shelley's idealized accounts of his own experience. This judgment renders virtually arbitrary, however, Shelley's choice of Rousseau, rather than another, as the Poet's guide in "The Triumph." The truth seems to be that Shelley took his conception of Rousseau for his poem from *Julie, ou la Nouvelle Héloïse*, Rousseau's own idealized account of his search for love and a work for which Shelley had nothing but praise. Writing to Hogg against marriage, he exclaims, "can

---

29. In "New Text" (p. 272) Matthews points out that an earlier version of lines 389–90 of "The Triumph" is to be found in Bodleian MS Shelley adds. e. 8, f. 130r *reverso*; on internal evidence Shelley's use of this notebook can be dated from late 1819 through early 1821; there are in other Bodleian Shelley notebooks fragments that relate very closely in theme and imagery to the early lines of "The Triumph," particularly to the rejected openings printed by Matthews in *TLS* (5 August 1960). This suggests that, although the actual draft of "The Triumph" in MS Shelley adds. c. 4 probably postdates the removal to Lerici, Shelley's mind had been grappling with some of the ideas and even words of "The Triumph of Life" for at least several months.

30. Shelley to Hogg, 14 May 1811, quoted from the corrected text of this letter edited by Kenneth Neill Cameron, *Shelley and his Circle: 1773–1822*, vol. 2 (Cambridge: Harvard University Press, 1961), p. 785.

you compare Eloisa & a ruffian . . . Eloisa who sacrifised all *self* for another, McHeath who sacrifised every other for himself."[31] Shelley's long letter to Peacock of 12 July 1816 (one of two letters of the period that Shelley believed significant enough to publish, along with "Mont Blanc," in Mary Shelley's *History of a Six Weeks Tour* . . . [1817]) is little more than an extended tribute to "the divine beauty of Rousseau's imagination, as it exhibits itself in 'Julie'."[32] And on 10 April 1822, about the time Shelley must have begun "The Triumph of Life," he wrote to John Gisborne of a passage in *Faust*, "Do you remember the 54th letter of the 1st part of the Nouvelle Héloïse? Göthe, in a subsequent scene evidently has that letter in his mind . . . ."[33] Although Shelley knew Rousseau's philosophical and political writings— perhaps all his works—there seems little question but that *Julie* had made the greatest impression upon him.[34]

In the *Confessions* (Book IX) Rousseau tells that during his stay at the Hermitage,

ne voyant rien d'existant qui fût digne de mon délire, je le nourris dans un monde idéal, que mon imagination créatrice eut bientôt peuplé d'êtres selon mon cœur. . . .

Je me figurai l'amour, l'amitié, les deux idoles de mon cœur, sous les plus ravissantes images. . . . J'imaginai deux amies. . . . Je donnai à l'une des deux un amant dont l'autre fut la tendre amie. . . Épris de mes deux charmants modèles, je m'identifiois avec l'amant et l'ami le plus qu'il m'étoit possible; mais je le fis aimable et jeune, lui donnant au surplus les vertus et les défauts que je me sentois.[35]

Such a statement would have been more than enough to provide Shelley with the conception that the experience of Saint-Preux, Julie's lover,

31. 9 May 1811, *Shelley and his Circle*, 2:781. This letter is misdated in both Hogg's *Life* (9 August 1811) and the Julian Edition (?13 May 1811). The eighteenth-century English translation of *Julie* was entitled *Eloisa* and the name of the heroine altered throughout (*Eloisa: Or, A Series of Original Letters*. Collected and published by J. J. Rousseau. Translated from the French. 3rd edition. 4 vols. London: Printed for T. Becket and P. A. De Hondt, 1764). This reference to "Eloisa" may indicate that Shelley first read *Julie* in translation.
32. Julian, 9:167. (This letter continues through 9:177.)
33. Julian, 10:372. Such an exact reference suggests that either Shelley knew *Julie* almost by heart or else that he had recently reread it; Shelley's remark on Goethe's use of a particular passage of Rousseau's novel suggests that use of such conscious correlatives to other well-known works was not foreign to his own artistic method. See Julian, 10:371: "*Cypriano* evidently furnished the germ of Faust, as Faust may furnish the germ of other poems; although it is different from it in structure and plan, as the acorn from the oak."
34. In "On Shelley's TL" Matthews, who says that "Rousseau . . . stands, ideologically speaking, at the centre of the 'Triumph'" (p. 105), provides the most complete discussion of parallels between Rousseau's works and "The Triumph" that has hitherto appeared, though he makes only one passing allusion to *La Nouvelle Héloïse* (p. 126).
35. *Œuvres complètes de J. J. Rousseau* . . . , 2nd ed. (Paris: Baudouin Frères, 1826), 16:263, 268.

formed an idealized picture of Rousseau's interior experience such as Shelley had himself recently depicted in *Epipsychidion*.[36] It is not surprising, therefore, that in "The Triumph" Shelley portrayed Rousseau's history in terms of the experience of Saint-Preux. When one reads the *Nouvelle Héloïse* with "The Triumph of Life" in mind, it becomes clear that Shelley regarded Julie herself as Rousseau's vision of the Ideal, a Spirit of Intellectual Beauty.[37] Shelley allegorizes Saint-Preux's love of Julie into Rousseau's pursuit of Ideal Love. In a sense, Shelley simply reversed the creative process that gave birth to *La Nouvelle Héloïse* by abstracting the seminal encounter between Rousseau and his vision of the Ideal.

When the Poet in "The Triumph of Life" first hears the shout, "Life," he discovers that what he thought was an old root, hung with white grass, is really the decayed remains of a man (lines 180–88). Writing to Julie from his exile in Meillerie, the languishing Saint-Preux declares:

Dans les violents transports qui m'agitent, . . . je parcours à grands pas tous les environs, et trouve partout dans les objets la même horreur qui règne au dedans de moi. On n'aperçoit plus de verdure, l'herbe est jaune et flétrie, les arbres sont dépouillés . . . et toute la nature est morte à mes yeux, comme l'espérance au fond de mon cœur. (Part I, Letter 26; *Œuvres*, 8:154)[38]

Illuminating parallels between *Julie* and "The Triumph of Life," both in figurative language and in larger expression of ideas, enrich the meaning of "The Triumph" throughout a great part of its 548 lines. Shelley, writing within a cultural context in which *Julie* was read by all educated people, could assume that the highly restricted audience of his poetry would be thoroughly familiar with Rousseau's novel and would perhaps have formed its conception of Rousseau largely from it. An enumeration of the many parallels between the two works and of the implications of these parallels for "The Triumph of Life" belongs more properly to the explication of "The Triumph" than to this discussion of the biographical back-

36. "The 'Epipsychidion' I cannot look at . . . . If you are anxious, however, to hear what I am and have been, it will tell you something thereof. It is an idealized history of my life and feelings." To John Gisborne, 18 June 1822 (Julian, 10:401).

37. Shelley's interpretation is authorized by Rousseau's statement that the two beings he created (Julie and Claire) were embodiments of "the two idols" of his heart, "love and friendship." That Rousseau, like Shelley, adorned his ideal "de tous les charmes du sexe que j'avois toujours adoré" (*Œuvres*, 16:268), provides one more instance of the inherent tendency observed by Jung and others for each person to envision his antitypical ideal as one of the opposite sex. See S. K. Heninger, Jr., "A Jungian Reading of 'Kubla Khan,'" *JAAC* 18 (March 1960): 358–67.

38. All quotations from *Julie* are from *Œuvres complètes* . . ., 2nd ed. (Paris, 1826), vols. 8–10.

ground. Here let me simply lay down the general outlines of the relationship between *Julie* and "The Triumph" and then suggest what this relationship can tell us about Shelley's state of mind during the final weeks of his life.

As Shelley has equated Rousseau in "The Triumph" with Saint-Preux, so he has identified the "shape all light" with Julie, Saint-Preux's beloved. The awakening of "Rousseau" in the "oblivious valley" (TL, lines 303-39) has no exact parallel in *La Nouvelle Héloïse,* for the novel begins with Saint-Preux's passion for Julie. Shelley has, however, drawn certain features of the initial encounter between "Rousseau" and the "shape all light" from later parts of *La Nouvelle Héloïse.* For instance, the description of the "oblivious valley" with its "gentle rivulet" echoes features of Julie's garden at Clarens called "Elysium" (Part IV, Letter 11).

En entrant dans ce prétendu verger, je fus frappé d'une agréable sensation de fraîcheur que d'obscurs ombrages, une verdure animée et vive, des fleurs éparses de tous côtés, un gazouillement d'eau courante et le chant de mille oiseaux portèrent à mon imagination du moins autant qu'à mes sens; . . . et il me sembloit d'être le premier mortel qui jamais eût pénétré dans ce désert.

Toutes ces petites routes étoient bordées et traversées d'une eau limpide et claire. . . . On voyoit des sources bouillonner et sortir de la terre, et quelquefois des canaux plus profonds dans lesquels l'eau calme et paisible réfléchissoit à l'œil les objets.

Nous descendîmes par mille détours au bas du verger, où je trouvai toute l'eau réunie en un joli ruisseau, coulant doucement entre deux rangs de vieux saules . . . . (*Œuvres,* 9:275, 280, 282)

As the approach of the "shape all light" is compared in a simile to "Day upon the threshold of the east" treading out the stars, so Saint-Preux writes to Julie, "Ne te vis-je pas briller entre ces jeunes beautés comme le soleil entre les astres qu'il éclipse?" (Part I, Letter 34; *Œuvres,* 8:182).

The key incident in Saint-Preux's irresistible passion for Julie is their first kiss, which Julie grants him in the grove at Clarens (opposite the spot where Julie later builds her "Elysium"). Immediately afterwards Saint-Preux writes: "Qu'as-tu fait, ah! qu'as-tu fait, ma Julie? tu voulois me récompenser, et tu m'as perdu. Je suis ivre, ou plutôt insensé. Mes sens sont altérés, toutes mes facultés sont troublées par ce baiser mortel" (Part I, Letter 14; *Œuvres,* 8:111). Again and again throughout the novel Saint-Preux alludes to the fatal effects of this kiss for which he had longed so eagerly. "Ce premier, cet unique amour qui fit le destin de ma vie, et que rien n'a pu vaincre que lui-même, étoit né sans que je m'en fusse aperçu; il m' entraînoit que je l'ignorois encore: je me perdis sans croire m'ètre égaré" (Part VI, Letter 7; *Œuvres*, 10:258). Julie herself also felt the adverse influence of that kiss: "J'appris dans le bosquet de Clarens que j'avois trop compté sur moi. . . . Un instant, un seul instant embrasa les miens d'un feu que rien ne put éteindre; et si ma volonté résistoit encore, dès-lors mon cœur fut corrompu" (Part III, Letter 18; *Œuvres*, 9:61). Thus the phrase "Alas I kiss you Julie" would be a natural exclamation for "Rousseau" when he recalled the ruin that his inordinate passion had inflicted upon him.[39]

The relationship between Saint-Preux and "Rousseau" of "The Triumph" receives an added dimension of complexity because the situation when Saint-Preux joins Julie and Wolmar, her husband, at Clarens is an idealization of Rousseau's own love for Madame d'Houdetot and his friendship for her lover Saint-Lambert. Though Rousseau maintains in his *Confessions* (IX) that his passion for Madame d'Houdetot remained chaste, it was no less violent and tormenting for him. He says of his growing affection, "j'avalois à longs traits la coupe empoisonnée, dont je ne sentois encore que la douceur. . . . Hélas! . . . ce fut bien cruellement brûler d'une passion non moins vive que malheureuse pour une femme dont le cœur étoit plein d'un autre amour! . . . je ne m'aperçus pas d'abord de ce qui m'étoit arrivé: ce ne fut qu'après son départ que, voulant penser à Julie, je fus frappé de ne pouvoir plus penser qu'à madame d'Houdetot" (*Œuvres*, 16:286–87). The poisoned cup alluded to in the *Confessions* could well be one origin of the cup presented to "Rousseau" by the "shape all light" (though many of the details of the "crystal glass / Mantling with bright Nepenthe" are to be found in Milton's *Comus*). Surely here one finds cross-references between Shelley's life and Rousseau's life, Saint-Preux's experience and

---

39. Here are other selected verbal or thematic parallels between "The Triumph" and *Julie* (TL = "The Triumph"; *NH* = *Nouvelle Héloïse*, listed by Part [Roman numeral] and Letter [Arabic]): TL, 155–57; "quelques heures agréables s'éclipsent comme un éclair et ne sont plus" (*NH*, I, 39); TL, 201–2, 206–7: "c'est . . . du premier transport de mon cœur, que s'alluma dans lui cette flamme éternelle que rien ne peut plus éteindre" (*NH*, II, 13); TL, 228–29: "n'as-tu point plutôt consulté ton désir que ton pouvoir?" (*NH*, VI, 2); TL, 305–8: "Je trouve aussi que c'est une folie de vouloir étudier le monde en simple spectateur. . . . On ne voit agir les autres qu'autant qu'on agit soi-même: . . . il faut commencer par pratiquer ce qu'on veut apprendre" (*NH*, II, 17); TL, 382–90: "c'est de te chérir quoique tu m'éclipses. . . . tu me subjugues, tu m'atterres, ton génie écrase le mien, et je ne suis rien devant toi" (*NH*, IV, 2); TL, 434–50: "J'entre avec une secrète horreur dans ce vaste désert du monde" (*NH*, II, 14); TL, 465–68: "Enfin me voilà tout-à-fait dans le torrent" (*NH*, II, 17); TL, 480–538: "En attendant, juge si j'ai raison d'appeler cette foule un désert . . . où je ne trouve qu'une vaine apparence de sentiments et de vérité, qui change à chaque instant et se détruit elle-même, où je n'aperçois que larves et fantômes qui frappent l'œil un moment et disparoissent aussitôt qu'on les veut saisir. Jusqu'ici j'ai vu beaucoup de masques; quand verrai-je des visages d'hommes?" (*NH*, II, 14).

"Rousseau's" experience. When Shelley wrote "The Triumph" his situation may have been similar to that of Rousseau when he wrote *Julie*: attached to a woman with whom he had little communication, Shelley may have been enamored of a woman (Jane) who loved one of his dearest friends. Thus, forced both by the laws of friendship and by the necessity of his beloved's prior attachment to restrain his own passion, Shelley may have found himself learning through the suffering of love to "rule the empire of himself," at the same time sublimating his passion into the beautiful lyrics to Jane[40] as Rousseau sublimated his into the tenderest scenes of *Julie*.

The main theme of *Julie* is the need to subject passion to duty, the triumph of Virtue over Love; the chief error of those greatest captives chained to the chariot in "The Triumph of Life" is their failure to rule over their own passions: Plato is enslaved because of his passion for the youth Aster (lines 254–59), and

> "The Wise,
>
> "The great, the unforgotten: they who wore
>   Mitres & helms & crowns, or wreathes of light,
> Signs of thought's empire over thought; their lore
>
>   "Taught them not this—to know themselves; their might
>   Could not repress the mutiny within . . . . ."
>   (lines 208–12)

When in 1822 Shelley, who was in his thirtieth year, reread *Julie*, he must have paused long and thoughtfully over the first letter of Part V, in which Lord Bomston chides Saint-Preux for his failure to overcome his passion:

Sors de l'enfance, ami, réveille-toi. Ne livre point ta vie entière au long sommeil de la raison. L'âge s'écoule, il ne t'en reste plus que pour être sage. A trente ans passés il est temps de songer à soi; commence donc à rentrer en toi-même, et sois homme une fois avant la mort.

Mon cher, votre cœur vous en a longtemps imposé sur vos lumières. Vous avez voulu philosopher avant d'en être capable; vous avez pris le sentiment pour de la

---

40. Besides the "Lines written in the Bay of Lerici" the following Shelley lyrics can reasonably be associated with Jane Williams: "To ——" ("One word is too often profaned"); "The Magnetic Lady to her Patient"; "To Jane: The Invitation" and "To Jane: The Recollection" (originally, "The Pine Forest of the Cascine near Pisa"); "With a Guitar, to Jane"; "To Jane: 'The keen stars were twinkling'"; "Lines: 'We meet not as we parted.'"

Irving Massey has shown that the two stanzas of the lyric known as "To ——: 'Music when soft voices die'" were reversed by Mary Shelley and that the poem is not about love at all but about immortality (*JEGP* 59 [July 1960]: 430–38; see also E. D. Hirsch, Jr., *JEGP* 60 [April 1961]: 296–98). "Lines: 'When the lamp is shattered,'" which Medwin says (p. 318) was "addressed to Mrs. Williams," is also demonstrably not a love poem but a metaphysical poem about the limitations of the human situation.

raison, et, content d'estimer les choses par l'impression qu'elles vous ont faite, vous avez toujours ignoré leur véritable prix. . . . C'est peu de connoître les passions humaines, si l'on n'en sait apprécier les objets . . . .
. . . Dans un espace de douze ans vous avez épuisé tous les sentiments qui peuvent être épars dans une longue vie, et vous avez acquis, jeune encore, l'expérience d'un vieillard. (*Œuvres*, 10:3-4)

It was twelve years since Shelley had published his first work, the Gothic novel *Zastrozzi*, and entered University College, Oxford. Looking back on the past, he had many acts and words to regret, for even as Trelawny knew him at Pisa, " 'Shelley was more self-willed than myself:' with exquisite gentleness of manner, he would always do, and do on the instant, what he resolved on" (*Rossetti Papers*, p. 501). But he seems to have been coming to full cognizance of what he had acknowledged with his mind from the beginning: that the measure of the mature soul lies not only in the intensity and sincerity of its passions but also in the virtue and appropriateness of their objects.

Late in March 1822 Shelley wrote to Claire Clairmont:

Some of yours and of my evils are in common, and I am therefore in a certain degree a judge. If you would take my advice, you would give up this idle pursuit after shadows, and temper yourself to the season, seek in the daily and affectionate intercourse of friends a respite from these perpetual and irritating projects. Live from day to day, attend to your health, cultivate literature and liberal ideas to a certain extent, and expect that from time and change which no exertion of your own can give you. (Julian, 10:365-66)

This advice he took to himself in the following weeks at San Terenzo, enjoying the moments as they came and putting behind him his own pursuit of shadows. To John Gisborne he declared, "I think one is always in love with something or other; the error, and I confess it is not easy for spirits cased in flesh and blood to avoid it, consists in seeking in a mortal image the likeness of what is perhaps eternal" (18 June 1822; Julian, 10:401).

In his last unfinished major work Shelley had taken up once again the problem of the dichotomy of "power" and "will" in the mortal world; those who possess power, military or legal, ecclesiastical or intellectual, all too often enslave their own wills to their passions, while "the good want power but to weep barren tears." This somber speculation was not a new thought to Shelley, but it presented itself to his mind more forcefully during his last months because of his feeling that his writings were unread and exerted no influence: again and again his late letters reflect this despair:

... pray tell me if Ollier has published *Hellas,* and what effect was produced by Adonais. My faculties are shaken to atoms, and torpid. I can write nothing; and if Adonais had no success, and excited no interest what incentive can I have to write? (To Leigh Hunt, 25 January 1822; Julian, 10:351)

Indeed, I have written nothing for this last two months . . . . What motives have I to write? I *had* motives, and I thank the God of my own heart that they were totally different from those of the other asses of humanity who make mouths in the glass of time. But what are *those* motives now? (To Hunt, 2 March 1822; Julian, 10:362)

I write little now. It is impossible to compose except under the strong excitement of an assurance of finding sympathy in what you write. Imagine Demosthenes reciting a Philippic to the waves of the Atlantic! (To John Gisborne, 18 June 1822; Julian, 10:403–4)[41]

It was, I believe, a sense of the futility of his literary career that motivated Shelley to write to Trelawny (also on 18 June 1822): "should you meet with any scientific person, capable of preparing the *Prussic Acid, or essential oil of bitter almonds,* I should regard it as a great kindness if you could procure me a small quantity" (Julian, 10:405). He added, however, "I need not tell you I have no intention of suicide at present . . . ." Trelawny insisted to W. M. Rossetti "that Shelley would have separated from Mary, but for the unhappy result to Harriet . . ." (*Rossetti Papers,* p. 500). Certainly one reason that Shelley had "no intention of suicide" in 1822 was the uncertain provision for his son and Mary should he die before Sir Timothy. In his 10 April letter Shelley tells Gisborne that he has determined "to make a new will, as changes have taken place which render such a measure necessary" and asks Gisborne's help in securing an aggressive lawyer who, on the death of Sir Timothy, could put Shelley's affairs in order without the necessity of his returning to England. "I have altered my determination about coming to England at my father's death. I *will not* come at any rate. Even in a pecuniary view I should lose more than I should gain, and with regard to my own feelings I should lose every thing. . . . The change in my determination about coming to England has sprung from considerations of more importance than any thing that regards money . . ." (Julian, 10:373–74).

Perhaps at one time Shelley had believed that by assuming his father's seat in Parliament he could exert an ameliorating influence in English politics, but in his last letter to Horace Smith, 29 June 1822, he wrote:

England appears to be in a desperate condition, Ireland still worse; and no class of

---

41. See also Julian, 10:353, 363, 370, 376, 377, 401.

those who subsist on the public labour will be persuaded that *their* claims on it must be diminished. . . . I once thought to study these affairs, and write or act in them—I am glad that my good genius said *refrain*—I see little public virtue, and I foresee that the contest will be one of blood and gold, two elements which however much to my taste in my pockets and my veins, I have an objection to out of them.—[42]

In his youth Shelley had gone to Ireland to act in "these affairs" and at Great Marlow he had drafted *A Proposal for Putting Reform to the Vote* in the hope that concerted action by liberal leaders might initiate parliamentary reform before the English political situation could further deteriorate. After the Peterloo Massacre, Shelley had turned his pen from efforts "simply to familiarise the highly refined imagination of the more select classes of poetical readers with beautiful idealisms of moral excellence" to poetry of direct political action designed to further the revolutionary forces at work. But *Swellfoot the Tyrant* was suppressed, *The Mask of Anarchy* was not published until 1832, several of the shorter political songs first appeared in 1839, and the great unfinished torso of his political theory, *A Philosophical View of Reform*, remained in MS until 1920. Neglected by his publisher as well as by the larger reading public and unaware that his poetry had made its impression on some of "the more select classes of poetical readers" for whom it was intended, he came quite understandably to consider himself "Demosthenes reciting a Philippic to the waves of the Atlantic!" Now his good genius told him to refrain from further attempts to reform the world.

Unwilling, however, to subdue himself to the element that surrounded him and thus contribute to the evils he lamented by his hypocrisy (see Julian, 10:410), Shelley determined to "see the truth, whatever that may be" and to set down in "The Triumph of Life" his latest vision of the human situation and the pitfalls into which so many of the world's wise, great, and unforgotten had fallen. In *Queen Mab* Shelley had written: "when the power of imparting joy / Is equal to the will, the human soul / Requires no other Heaven" (III.11–13). One question raised but not satisfactorily answered in "The Triumph"—at least in its fragmentary state—is whether or not "power" and "will" are indeed compatible in the mortal world: besides the few who "fled back like eagles to their native noon," the only men not captive to the car seem to be "those who put aside the diadem / Of earthly thrones," those who resisted the temptation to exercise earthly power, which corrupts the will. Shelley's realization of his own impo-

---

42. Julian, 10:410. It is, perhaps, noteworthy that Smith's letter of 5 June 1822 (Abinger Collection, Duke Microfilms, Reel 14), which Shelley is answering, deals exclusively with Godwin's financial crisis and does not mention English politics.

tence—of his incapacity to legislate to the political world of his time through his writings and of his failure to discover "in a mortal image the likeness of what is perhaps eternal"—gave rise, I believe, to his statement to Gisborne (in the same paragraph as the Demosthenes reference): "I stand, as it were, upon a precipice, which I have ascended with great, and cannot descend without *greater,* peril, and I am content if the heaven above me is calm for the passing moment" (Julian, 10:404).

"The Triumph of Life" demonstrates that Shelley recognized the dangers both of abandoning his ideals to conform to the values of the senseless, sensual crowd and of drinking too deeply of the cup of Ideal Love that betrays men into the pursuit of shadows. Tempering his desires to the season without losing sight of that vision of Intellectual Beauty, first seen in youth like the radiant star of morning, he hoped that, beyond the ken of his limited, human, cognitive powers, the vision still moved beside him and would at the end of mortal life reveal itself once more, this time as Hesperus, "the folding star." But even concerning the "great mystery" Shelley's tough-minded intellectual honesty could not be enslaved to his desires:

Let it not be supposed that I mean to dogmatise upon a subject, concerning which all men are equally ignorant . . . . That there is a true solution of the riddle, and that in our present state that solution is unattainable by us, are propositions which may be regarded as equally certain: meanwhile, as it is the province of the poet to attach himself to those ideas which exalt and ennoble humanity, let him be permitted to have conjectured the condition of that futurity towards which we are all impelled by an inextinguishable thirst for immortality. Until better arguments can be produced than sophisms which disgrace the cause, this desire itself must remain the strongest and only presumption that eternity is the inheritance of every thinking being.[43]

In "The Triumph" Shelley portrays vividly the limitations of the historical process, indeed, of the entire phenomenal realm, but by depicting melodious fountains and "grassy paths," commemorating those "sacred few who could not tame / Their spirits to the Conqueror," and distinguishing between those who, like Rousseau, created and those whose "power was given / But to destroy," Shelley attached himself "to those ideas which exalt and ennoble humanity." Had he lived to complete the poem—which gives every indication of having been clearly envisioned as a longer, well-ordered whole—he would, no doubt, have "conjectured the condition of

43. Note to *Hellas,* in *Poetical Works,* ed. Thomas Hutchinson (London, 1943), pp. 478–79.

that futurity" aspired to by all who see in this world the recurring triumph of evil over good.

"The Triumph of Life" is firmly in the tradition of Shelley's own earlier poetry and in a noble literary tradition of works by Dante and Petrarch, Milton and Rousseau. If any personal experience deeply colored the poem, it was Shelley's feeling that his literary efforts had failed. The companionship of Jane and Edward Williams, whose dispositions enabled them to enjoy the simplest pleasures of their immediate surroundings, encouraged Shelley's attempts to find in the present "one moment's good / After long pain,"[44] but his very desire to preserve his pleasure in Jane's singing and Edward's boating, to keep this joy from turning to gall in the future, probably encouraged him to refrain from idealizing yet another mortal woman into a goddess who would, in turn, become a piercing reed to the pursuing Pan.[45] In short, Shelley had reached a maturity comparable to that finally achieved by Saint-Preux in *Julie*, a state in which both love and duty, no longer in violent conflict, contributed their respective rewards, chaste love bringing him a sense of personal security, and duty, its modicum of peace and tranquillity.

For Shelley, however, a "nerve o'er which do creep / The else unfelt oppressions of this earth," mere personal tranquillity—even should he have achieved it—could never overcome his sense of the world's wrongs. Thus it was that he composed his darkest vision of the human predicament at a time when his own health and spirits were better than they had been for years. Because Shelley's poetry is the product of a *human* nature, a nature capable of benevolently espousing ideals and causes that in some measure transcend the self, only when critics of Shelley put behind them reductively biographical interpretations of his poems will they come to understand his art.

44. "To Jane: The Invitation," in ibid., p. 669.
45. "Hymn of Pan," in ibid., pp. 613-14.

17

Keats and the Humanistic Paradox: Mythological History in Lamia

Harold Bloom has been the most stimulating influence on academic criticism of the Romantic tradition during the past twenty-five years. Paradoxically, this influence arises, not because he is the most accurate or responsible reader of English Romantic poetry; rather, whatever subject he writes on, several readers invariably respond: "Yes, that's almost right. But he should have thought of such and so"; or, "But what about these other poems that don't fit his theory?" A really comprehensive scholar-critic who spends the requisite time in research and reflection, or who tries out his ideas on well-informed and level-minded students and colleagues and takes into account their queries and objections before publishing—an Earl R. Wasserman or an M. H. Abrams, for example—can never stimulate such immediate reactions from others. Though the scholarly criticism of Abrams or Wasserman also has its limitations, the reader discovers them only through long thought and study, retracing the many steps taken by the master scholar-critic. With Bloom, who from the time he published his dissertation has always shot from the hip, the errors are almost always gross and palpable to the informed reader. Bloom's criticism provides perfect straw-persons for every occasion and, hence, frequently sets the agenda for ensuing debates.

I was deep into my dissertation on "The Triumph of Life" when Bloom's *Shelley's Mythmaking* appeared. In my first publication on Shelley, I reviewed it for The Daily Illini, the student newspaper at Illinois. Though I don't have a copy of that review, I remember praising the book as a serious attempt to come to terms with Shelley's poetry, but also criticizing Bloom for at least two faults—first, for his harsh tone toward earlier critics of Shelley, commenting that he should rather have expressed gratitude to them for leaving him something new to say on the subject. In retrospect, we can see that his rancor toward most scholars and critics, like his early hero-worship of the trinity of Frye, Abrams, and Pottle, probably sprang from anxiety about his own possible lack of originality. This response on his part is easy enough to account for when one reads that he has a photographic memory and can actually recite Paradise Lost *and even* The Faerie Queene *upon request.*

Whereas most of us strive to recall a few pointed allusions to slip into our writing in order to show the breadth of our reading, nobody cursed with total recall could ever write a phrase without being aware that almost every word he wrote echoed somebody or other.

My second objection to Shelley's Mythmaking *was more serious: by importing Martin Buber's concept of I/Thou relationships into a study of Shelley, Bloom had turned the poet's whole philosophy on its head. Shelley's entire religious perspective, from his earliest days until he wrote "The Triumph of Life," demanded the abolition of anthropomorphism in religious thought. Shelley's "Essay on Christianity" (1817) proclaims, "It is important to observe that the author of the Christian system had a conception widely differing from the gross imaginations of the vulgar relatively to the ruling Power of the universe. He every where represents this power as something mysteriously and illimitably pervading the frame of things. [His doctrines] do not represent God . . . as a being subject to passion." Whereas Buber and Bloom (and I, in 1959) felt the need for a more personal God amid the abstractions of twentieth-century science, philosophy, and even theology, Shelley—amid the childish superstitions of his day—felt the need to wipe out all ideas that God could or would personally communicate with man, or fight on the side that prayed the loudest. Bloom, writing out of his own needs instead of Shelley's texts, not only reversed the impact of a number of Shelley's poems, but also invented a course of disillusionment for the poet in which, when Shelley came to imagine that he could not communicate directly with the supreme Power, he became suicidal; the uncompleted "The Triumph of Life" was cited as Bloom's primary evidence. In* Shelley's "The Triumph of Life" *I engaged in a running dialogue with Bloom's early writings on Shelley, showing that Shelley's imagery actually points to conclusions about the poet's values and beliefs quite different from those that Bloom attributes to him. I also show how correction of the corrupted text of the poem solves a number of interpretive cruxes that had troubled all earlier critics.*

In the headnote to Item 19, I discuss more of my reactions to Bloom's criticism (to which I have given rather more attention than I should have in reviews, lectures, and responses to articles in PMLA *and* TLS*). To my friends, I admit that my reaction to Bloom parallels, in some respects, Hazlitt's hostility toward Coleridge. I regard Bloom as the lost leader of my generation of critics. He is, without question, the most gifted critic of poetry of our time, with almost impeccable taste, a laudable passion for great literature, and respect for its impact on human lives. Bloom has seldom led me to poets who were not worth my attention (though I often find their writings quite different from his descriptions of them). He has also taught me a great deal about specific poetic images and passages. But he has, in my view, distorted almost every one of his contributions through his need to center his atten-*

tion on his own personal fears or wishes, rather than on the subject—whether poem or poet—that he is ostensibly discussing. In short, he exemplifies the critic who (as I said in the Introduction) attempts to force readers to believe that what he, as a modern reader, needs to get from Romantic poetry is exactly what the (quite different) Romantic poets of nearly two centuries ago needed to put into it.

"Keats and the Humanistic Paradox" responds to Bloom's stimulating essay "Keats and the Embarrassments of Poetic Tradition," which appeared in the Festschrift for Frederick A. Pottle entitled From Sensibility to Romanticism, edited by F. W. Hilles and Bloom (1965). I lavished praise on this collection in a series of short notices of it and its essays for David Erdman's Romantics bibliography in ELN (1966). But in my detailed marginal notes to Bloom's essay, I stuck on this sentence: "The Ode to a Nightingale is the first poem to know and declare, wholeheartedly, that death is the mother of beauty." Those familiar with Wasserman's once canonical (but now, I fear, neglected) essay on "Ode to a Nightingale" in The Finer Tone and those conversant with Greek and Latin poetry will realize why I winced at this careless sentence. Having tried to turn Shelley, an admirer of Spinoza and one who sought to abolish anthropomorphism, into a fellow-disciple of Martin Buber, Bloom now tried to portray Keats—who spent most of his career seeking personalized encounters with the Divine and who hoped for (though he could not fully believe in) personal immortality—as a naturalist who was content to fade into the landscape. At best, Bloom imported into "Ode to a Nightingale" a common (but, I believe, mistaken) interpretation of the ideas in "To Autumn." At worst, he denigrated the faith that Keats maintained through most of his life against overwhelming odds. The contrast between Bloom's views and the emotional realities can be seen by comparing any account of Keats's last bitter days in Rome with Shelley's positive portrayal of Keats being "made one with Nature" in Adonais.

I first wrote a paper that I delivered at the session of the English Romantics division at the MLA convention in Chicago in 1967 (Jack Stillinger presided, and the other speakers were Geoffrey Hartman and Edgar Johnson). In the summer of 1969, I reworked that talk for publication, clarifying the relationship of my ideas to Wasserman's work and the key ideas of other scholars on the basis of a reading of Lamia I had drafted during the summer of 1963, while teaching the Romantics at Illinois. On 29 July 1969, I submitted it to Studies in English Literature, and on 13 October 1969, Carroll Camden accepted it, with a handful of helpful corrections and constructive suggestions made by an anonymous reader who was, I later learned, Carl Woodring. The paper appeared in the autumn issue for 1971 (SEL 11: 659–69).

At least two suggestions in this paper have never been followed up. The first is the impact of the Pervigilium Veneris on the poetry of the period. As I have since *learned, the poem was a staple of the Latin school texts then in use; its overall pattern, in which a man finds himself unable to celebrate the joys of rejuvenation felt by the merely natural creatures around him in the spring of the year, is basic to dozens of poems by the Romantics and others down through Gerard Manley Hopkins, T. S. Eliot (who quotes the poem), and Allen Tate (who translated it). Second is the conception of a "humanistic paradox," in which values created by the human mind (or Imagination) become suspect and non-viable simply because people who believe in no outside, objective powers to support their values come to feel that those values they themselves have created cannot be sustained beyond the scope of their own mortal powers. This anxiety is a crucial issue in much Romantic, Victorian, Modernist, and Postmodernist literature. (Yeats raises the issue directly, for example, in such poems as "Mad as the Mist and Snow" and "The Circus Animals' Desertion.") But not even the several subsequent studies centering on Keats's ideological and religious thought have fully grappled with this issue (though Robert M. Ryan approaches it in* Keats: The Religious Sense, *1976).*

Some leading students of the Romantics—Thomas McFarland, Jerome J. McGann, and Peter L. Thorslev, among them—have written critically of what they regard as fallacies in the thought of the Romantics. In many instances, I believe, their criticisms are misdirected, applying more to the ideas of recent critics of Romanticism (including Bloom) than to the Romantics themselves. Of the six major poets, both Wordsworth and Coleridge avoided the humanistic paradox by returning to orthodox Christian views of God and of man's place in the universe; Byron and Shelley avoided the abyss by remaining Skeptical—intellectually neither affirming nor denying the existence of a Power that sustains the highest humane values, but living as though the ultimate value of such moral and imaginative achievements was assured. Blake also refused to accept disillusionment, sustaining his faith that the divine—whether within him or outside him—was still the Divine and had power to prevail over the dross of experience. Only Keats, the last of the line, took so seriously the age's claims for the power of the human Imagination that the frail frame he inhabited could not sustain them. But though Keats provides the clearest example of the dangers faced by his peers, after his disillusionment he can hardly be charged with being deluded by a Romantic ideology. Many twentieth-century writers whose beliefs suggest that they might come to share Keats's dilemma have, instead, learned from Kierkegaard or Sartre to become connoisseurs of chaos in ways that were impossible for Keats. Young poets today, thoroughly involved in the Romantic ideology, may imagine the immortality of their influence, such as Shelley suggested in Adonais, *as one possible comfort for the death of Keats. This comfort was, unfortunately, unavailable to Keats himself, who asked that his tombstone be marked, not by his name, but by the words: "Here lies one whose name was writ in water." For young John Keats, Death seemed the mother, not of Beauty, but of Oblivion.*

It has been suggested by an influential critic that Keats in his later poems moved toward a "naturalistic" poetic stance. According to Harold Bloom's reading, Keats in "To Autumn" rejected "the paradise of poets bequeathed . . . by tradition" and replaced it with "a tragic paradise of naturalistic completion and mortal acceptance. . . ." Keats becomes, in this reading, a forerunner of Wallace Stevens: "Ode to a Nightingale" is "the first poem to know and declare, wholeheartedly, that death is the mother of beauty." "The poet does not accept what is as good, and he does not exile desire for what is not. Yet, for him, what is possible replaces what is not. . . . [T]here is a time of all-but-final satisfaction, the fullness of lines 35 to 58 of this ode." Bloom declares that, because Keats avoids both the theophany of Milton and Wordsworth and the Orphism of Shelley, his is the most original poetic resolution of the human dilemma "since the Bible."[1]

Even if one accepted this interpretation of "Ode to a Nightingale," to claim such originality for the poem is to forget a literary tradition as old as Lucretius and including Stoic, Epicurean, and Skeptical writers who glorified natural law and accepted human limitations with at least as much grace as Keats can muster. But on this particular poem Earl R. Wasserman's interpretation, it seems to me, comes to grips with more of the problems and without violating its stanzaic divisions.[2] "Ode to a Nightingale," rather than recording an acceptance of death, explores the relationship between *natural* beauty and the human imagination. There Keats concludes that neither through wine (moderns, read "drugs"), nor poetry, nor death can man bridge the gulf between himself and nature; man must always encounter the sensation of natural beauty like exiled Ruth amid the *alien corn* of a nature, that, at its core, is "an eternal fierce destruction." Wine is incapable of sustaining the moment of mystic unity between man and nature with which the poem opens, because of the poet's recurring remembrance of human sufferings. Poesy is unable to do so permanently because Keats (unlike blind Homer of Keats's sonnet) feels that he has "no light" with which to sustain a vision beyond nature.[3] To accept death as a gateway to the good is, in "Ode to a Nightingale," to "become a sod,"

1. "Keats and the Embarrassments of Poetic Tradition," in *From Sensibility to Romanticism*, ed. F. W. Hilles and Harold Bloom (New York: Oxford University Press, 1965), pp. 513–26.
2. Earl R. Wasserman, *The Finer Tone: Keats' Major Poems* (Baltimore: Johns Hopkins Press, 1953), pp. 178–223.
3. Compare Keats's skeptical sonnet "Written upon the Top of Ben Nevis" (2 August 1818) with the earlier, more idealistic "To Homer" (?January–April 1818).

incapable of enjoying even the transitory pleasures of the bird's lovely song. Death, far from being "the mother of beauty," as Bloom claims, is the mother only of sods, insensitive to all beauty, natural or human. Death—or rather the premonition of death—has caused the great divorce between man and natural creatures "not born for death." The cry is as old as the *Pervigilium Veneris* and is the theme of more poems by the six great Romantic poets than one could name and characterize within the scope of this paper.

"Ode to a Nightingale," like most of Keats's other poems and his letters, shows him to be philosophically not a "naturalist" (one who derives the ultimate values or significance of human life from the laws and operations of external nature) but a "humanist"—one who believes that at least the knowable values governing human life are to be found in the human mind or imagination. In this orientation he is hardly unique among Western poets. Keats's originality in the English poetry of his day (and one should be hesitant about claiming absolute novelty) centers in his refusal to affirm what Bloom terms "the moral instrumentality of the imagination."[4] For Keats the imagination remains an inevitable and necessary faculty, but an ambiguous one. In *Endymion* and "The Eve of St. Agnes" Keats had allowed his desire to outrun his realistic appraisal of the human situation. It is a long journey from the both/and world of Milton's prelapsarian Eden recreated at the end of *Endymion* to the sharply divided world of Kierkegaard's "Either/Or" that one finds in Keats's odes. But the poetry of heaven in the "Ode" beginning "Bards of passion and of mirth" and the poetry of earth in "To Autumn" represent moods of a moment. Keats's odes, sonnets, and other lyrics are true to the traditional function of lyric poetry. None is intended to present a rounded world-view. The fullest expression of his later vision appears in *Lamia*. In this paper I intend to suggest how the thematic development of that poem weaves together strands found in others of Keats's late poems to form a commentary on human life that is as complete a record of a stage of thinking as *Endymion* had been for an earlier stage.

"Ode on a Grecian Urn" examined the role of *art* in transmitting and preserving the inspired moments of the human imagination beyond the ephemeral individual life, and here the poet found a modicum of comfort. Although he could not know what the destiny of the individual soul might be, long after he and his generation were dead and gone, this antique work of art—and, he hopes, his own poetry—would remain "in midst of

---

4. *From Sensibility to Romanticism*, pp. 520–21.

other woe / Than ours" to say to men: "Beauty is truth, truth beauty." In "Ode to Psyche" Keats declared his allegiance to a humanistic faith in which he would worship the emblem of the creative human mind:

> I see, and sing, by my own eyes inspired.
> (line 43)

> Yes, I will be thy priest, and build a fane
> In some untrodden region of my mind.
> (lines 50-51)

Man, not nature or any other known external power, is the creator of human values: "What the imagination seizes as Beauty must be truth—whether it existed before or not."[5] But Keats also shows in poems and letters his awareness that even the individual's own imagination is apt to change, so that what he values one day may seem, on the morrow, an empty dream. The humanist who says that "every mental pursuit takes its reality and worth from the ardour of the pursuer—being in itself a nothing"[6] knows that, sooner or later, ardor must cool. Unless both the pursued maiden and her lover exist only in a dead work of art, she must eventually escape or be enjoyed, and in either case, leave the "heart high-sorrowful and cloy'd, / A burning forehead, and a parching tongue" ("Ode on a Grecian Urn," lines 29-30). Without human desire, objects are dead, but human adoration is a transient rock upon which to build a palace for the soul.

Endymion had portrayed an aspiring idealist who created his divine ideal, pursued it, encountered the frustrations attendant on trying to live entirely within the realm of the imagination, and finally modified his ideal to conform to human sympathies and human limitations. In *Lamia* Keats mythologized this paradox of the gods' descent to human forms from the point of view, not of man, but of those gods of his creation, as he had also begun to do in the first *Hyperion*.

There has been considerable discussion of the relationship between the love of Hermes for the nymph early in *Lamia* and Lamia's love for Lycius that follows. According to one view, the love of the gods and demigods, who do not grow pale "as mortal lovers do," is an ideal unattainable by mere mortals such as Lycius and the woman Lamia.[7] This reading holds,

---

5. Keats to Bailey, 22 November 1817, in *The Letters of John Keats*, ed. Hyder Rollins (Cambridge: Harvard University Press, 1958), 1:184 (hereafter cited as *Letters*).
6. Keats to Bailey, 13 March 1818 (*Letters*, 1:242).
7. Newell F. Ford, *The Prefigurative Imagination of John Keats* (Stanford, Calif.: Stanford University Press, 1951), pp. 142-43; Wasserman, *The Finer Tone*, pp. 161-62.

in short, that Hermes's love is that of a realm of Being while the love of Lamia and Lycius exists in a realm of Becoming. The opening six lines of the poem, however, set the story of Hermes and the nymph into another perspective:

> Upon a time, before the faery broods
> Drove Nymph and Satyr from the prosperous woods,
> Before King Oberon's bright diadem,
> Sceptre, and mantle, clasp'd with dewy gem,
> Frighted away the Dryads and the Fauns
> From rushes green, and brakes, and cowslip'd lawns,
> The ever-smitten Hermes empty left
> His golden throne. . . .
> (I.1–8)

Keats clearly says here, as he does in *Hyperion*, that the world of gods and goddesses, dryads and fairies, is *not* a timeless world freed of all historical change. As products of the human imagination, the gods themselves are as subject to change as are ideals of human heroism, whose transformation Keats laments in his poem on Robin Hood.[8] This brief allusion in the opening lines of *Lamia* to the process of what, for want of a better name, we may call "mythological history" provides a context for the sequence of events that follows.

Hermes becomes enamored of the nymph not because of any intrinsic value she possesses, but because she has gained value from the ardor of other pursuers:

> Ah, what a world of love was at her feet!
> So Hermes thought, and a celestial heat
> Burnt from his winged heels to either ear. . . .
> (I.21–23)

Urged by this new challenge to conquest, Hermes rejects the good he already possesses; he did "not hear / The soft, lute-finger'd Muses chaunting clear, / Nor even Apollo when he sang alone . . ." (I.72–74). He is stimulated to the pursuit by "painful jealousies" just as the sensual desires of Lycius and Lamia are stimulated when Lamia plays "the cruel lady" to him

---

8. "Robin Hood: To a Friend," included with Keats's letter to Reynolds, 3 February 1818 (*Letters*, 1:225), and published in the 1820 volume, is an important parallel to the opening lines of *Lamia*. For Keats's ideas on the origin of religions, see the "Vale of Soulmaking" passage (21 April 1819) in his long journal-letter to George and Georgiana Keats (*Letters*, 2:100–104).

on their first meeting and later when "against his better self," Lycius "took delight / Luxurious in her sorrows" (II.73–74).

To Hermes and other gods, imaginary creatures of the fears, hopes, and desires of men, no obstacle can be permanent. For every spell that hides the nymph from view there must be an antidote. And when Hermes discovers that the serpent holds the key to unlock the spell, he can say both earnestly and lightly, "Possess whatever bliss thou canst devise" (I.85), for he can swear oaths without fear of their consequences. Existing in an entirely fictive realm, he is subject to none of the limitations of the real world so long as the human desires that produced *him* continue to find value in imagining his adventures. It is in this respect that the poet can say, once Hermes has discovered the nymph,

> It was no dream; or say a dream it was,
> Real are the dreams of Gods, and smoothly pass
> Their pleasures in a long immortal dream.
>   (I.126–28)

The dreams of the gods are of the same fictive stuff as their waking moments. The dreams of men are *not* of a piece with *their* existential reality, and men are thus subject to disillusionment.

In *Hyperion*, Oceanus had instructed the fallen Titans in the process of mythological history:

> as thou wast not the first of powers,
> So art thou not the last. . . .
> From Chaos and parental Darkness came
> Light. . . .
>   and Light, engendering
> Upon its own producer, forthwith touch'd
> The whole enormous matter into life.
> Upon that very hour, our parentage,
> The Heavens and the Earth, were manifest: . . .
> As Heaven and Earth are fairer, fairer far
> Than Chaos and blank Darkness, though once chiefs;
> And as we show beyond that Heaven and Earth. . . .
> So on our heels a fresh perfection treads,
> A power more strong in beauty, born of us
> And fated to excel us, as we pass
> In glory that old Darkness. . . .
>   for 'tis the eternal law
> That first in beauty should be first in might:

> Yea, by that law, another race may drive
> Our conquerors to mourn as we do now.[9]

Keats and his readers knew—though Oceanus could not—that several more revolutions were to take place in the mythological world—that the hierarchy of Olympus would fade (according to Milton's record on the morning of Christ's nativity) and that Nymph and Satyr would be driven from the prosperous woods, only to be replaced by new folk-myths of the fairy broods and King Oberon.

It is not surprising, then, to find that the so-called supernatural creatures in *Lamia* see no particular advantage in remaining at their respective levels in the scale of being, for all are ultimately creatures of human hopes, fears, loves, and hatreds.[10] The banquet hall of the major gods on Mount Olympus; the woods and waters of Crete, filled with nymphs, satyrs, tritons, and other demigods; and the human world, in this case epitomized at Corinth, are all shaped by the human imagination, which often posits a confrontation between the differing levels. In *Endymion* the poet had decreed that the confrontation be seen chiefly from the point of view of the human protagonist, but in *Lamia* the encounter is viewed from Hermes's side in his pursuit of the nymph and from Lamia's perspective in her conquest of Lycius. Bored by the unmoved serenity of Jove's Olympus and deaf to the singing of the Muses and Apollo, Hermes slips away to hunt the elusive nymph in a realm of the demigods. Unhappy in her second life as a serpent-magician on Crete, Lamia cries out, "When from this wreathed tomb shall I awake! . . . I was a woman, let me have once more / A woman's shape, and charming as before" (I.38, 117-18). If human beings in Keats's early poems envy the apparent permanence and immutability of the gods, his mind-created gods and goddesses, from Cynthia and Venus in *Endymion* to Hermes and Lamia, are much more interested in "life, / And love, and pleasure, and the ruddy strife / Of hearts and lips!" (I.39-41). This desire for the beautiful beyond the self that motivates all Keats's gods and men merely dramatizes the speculation about *eros* in the first book of *Endymion*:

> so may love . . .
> Produce more than our searching witnesseth:

---

9. *Hyperion* II.188-231 passim.
10. The idea that the gods are creatures of the human mind accounts for the difference between the Romantic conception of *eros* and the more traditional concept found in Renaissance literature. See Jerome J. McGann, *Fiery Dust: Byron's Poetic Development* (Chicago: University of Chicago Press, 1968), pp. 162-64.

> who, of men, can tell
> That flowers would bloom, or that green fruit would swell
> To melting pulp, that fish would have bright mail,
> The earth its dower of river, wood, and vale,
> The meadows runnels, runnels pebble-stones,
> The seed its harvest, or the lute its tones,
> Tones ravishment, or ravishment its sweet,
> If human souls did never kiss and greet?[11]

To desire the beautiful beyond the present moment, one must be able to imagine it, and this ability to see beyond her bourne is given to the mythic Lamia in abundance. She possesses, in fact, the "triple sight" of blind Homer in Keats's sonnet or of *Diana triformis* in *Endymion*, being able to see, from Crete, both Olympus and Corinth.[12] But as one experienced in the uses of the imagination, she knows that the same visionary power that stimulated her to pursue young Lycius may cause him to become dissatisfied with her love. Once he is enraptured by passion, she must shut the windows of his imagination, for power to see beyond one's bourne will spoil the pleasures of all sensations—even the singing of the nightingale.[13]

Lamia is in this (like Hermes) a devotee of Venus, rather than of Apollo (who is mentioned as an enemy of serpents).[14] She creates a palace of sensual delight, an urban bower of bliss, in which the present moment is all in all. Denying that she is from another realm, she accepts the human condition at its lowest, sensory level. When in the second part of the poem her

11. *Endymion* I.832–42.
12. Although Lamia, when the reader first encounters her, has the form of a serpent (sacred to Hermes, I.89), she exists in a world of potentiality. Among other characteristics, she is "freckled like a pard" (sacred to Bacchus), "eyed like a peacock" (sacred to Juno), "full of silver moons" (Phoebe-Cynthia), "sprinkled with stars, like Ariadne's tiar" (see I.47–65). When she chooses, and Hermes executes, her transformation into a woman and lover, she loses her wide range of potentialities (see I.146–70), becoming simply a devotee of Venus and Bacchus. See notes 14 and 15 below.
13. See Keats's "Epistle to John Hamilton Reynolds," lines 78–85.
14. Walter H. Evert's *Aesthetic and Myth in the Poetry of Keats* (Princeton: Princeton University Press, 1965) follows Keats's development of a mythological pattern emphasizing Apollo and Cynthia-Diana. My study of Keats's poems, both before and after reading Evert's study, has led me to ideas paralleling, but in some respects differing from, his. Briefly, I feel that Cynthia-Diana is the goddess of dreams and sleep, as opposed to imagination and poetry, whose god is Apollo. In his early poetry Keats emphasized the kinship of "Sleep and Poetry," seeing the twins of Latona as complementary; by the time he wrote *The Fall of Hyperion*, he had rejected the dreamer. See also Jack Stillinger, "The Hoodwinking of Madeline," *SP* 58 (July 1961): 533–55.
Opposed to, or independent of, Cynthia and Apollo are at least two other groups of Olympians: Jupiter and Juno were tutelary spirits of power and ambition, while Venus and Hermes (allied with Bacchus, an earth-god) championed pleasure and erotic love. In *Endymion* Keats tried to represent a synthesis of the realm of Venus with that of *Diana triformis* and Apollo. But later the three choices personified in "Ode on Indolence" as Love, Ambition, and Poesy appear in dramatic opposition under the guise of various Olympian gods.

world of love is threatened by the results of Lycius's moment of thought—which is "passion's passing bell"—she attempts to defend herself against the intruders from the "busy world" of Corinth by overpowering them with music and wine, the food and drink of love.

As the opening lines of Part I had dealt with the mutability of the demigods, so those of Part II concentrate on the limitations of love, whether in a hut or a palace. "Had Lycius liv'd," says the narrator, he might have clinched the aphorism that "Love in a palace is perhaps at last / More grevious torment than a hermit's fast" (II.3-4). But the "bliss" enjoyed by Lycius and Lamia was "too short . . . To breed distrust and hate" (II.9-10). The narrator suggests that, quite apart from the intrusion of Apollonius, their love could not have survived at its first level of ideal intensity, but it, too, would have faded in the light of very common day. Thus the opening lines of both parts of *Lamia* declare that no matter how potent in her motive powers may be Venus (whose idyllic mythological home was the prosperous woods of Crete), her realm is constantly in flux and has no permanence either as myth or as human reality.

The basic weakness of both love and of the palace into which Lycius and Lamia retreat is that they are of human construction. Although the walls of the palace had been raised by music like Amphion's, that music, like the myth of Amphion himself, had been a product of the human imagination. What though Lycius had worshipped Jove, who "heard his vows, and better'd his desire" (I.229)? What though Lamia as woman had faithfully worshipped the twelve Olympians and, in preparing for her marriage feast, had erected an altar to each of them? These deities were—as the poetic narrator of this story knew—merely the arbitrary creations of human desires and dreams. Thus the intrusion of the simple reality-principle in the person of Apollonius is enough to bring down the fragile dream-castle without providing any alternative. Apollonius (who is, like Oceanus, called a "sophist") can point out the circularity of Lycius's folly. When Lycius attempts to stop Apollonius by calling down on his teacher the curse "of all the Gods, whose dreadful images / Here represent their shadowy presences,"[15] Apollonius responds at first with the single word, "Fool!" For he knows that the gods, like love, the palace, and the magic of the rainbow, are merely constructs of the human imagination. When put

15. II.279-80. Viewed in a context in which Lycius has abandoned his earlier worship of Jove (I.223-29) to devote himself to love and pleasure, his appeal to the twelve Olympians is inexplicable, as is Apollonius's contemptuous retort to Lycius's appeal. But set within Keats's view of mythological history—the transience of gods created by men—Lycius's appeal is to the power of man's imaginative faculties and the sophist's reply does not support Minerva or Jove against Venus, but denies the stability of all creative aspirations.

to the test, "the fancy cannot cheat so well / As she is fam'd to do" ("Ode to a Nightingale," lines 73–74). Lamia, a creature conflating the myths of Eve and the serpent who led her into the sin of knowledge, cannot withstand the scrutiny of the inquiring, skeptical mind. She disappears, and the disillusioned Lycius dies—unable to live in a world stripped of its mythology.

Who is to blame? Not Lycius, whose world of myth and gods had been given him by his religious and literary heritage and whose natural human desires seemed to require a hope for a poet's paradise on earth, if not in heaven. Not Lamia, merely a mythic product of the human imagination. Not Apollonius, merely looking with an objective eye at the facts of the physical world and human experience. Indeed, the narrator of the poem takes the same analytical view of his story and understands the situation much in the way that Apollonius himself does. Keats could hardly condemn the viewpoint of Apollonius, for not only had he written an early sonnet in disgust of the "vulgar superstition" of Christianity, but in a late fragment on "modern love" he had twice called those who believed in love "Fools!"

The poem *Lamia* is a dramatic presentation of the dangers inherent in the "humanistic paradox." If Man knows that his gods are merely the creation of his own imagination, which is in itself changeable, how can he worship those myths or ideals? What is to keep him from the abysmal vision of a world without myths, without gods, without ideals, without values? The story from Burton's *Anatomy of Melancholy* became for Keats a parable exhibiting the situation of modern man confronted by the blankness of unbelief—a warning to young men not to expect too much from love, friendship, fame, or from any other idol that might attract them to its worship. At the same time, the poem of *Lamia* reaffirms the message both of "Ode to Psyche"—that the human imagination *is* the creator of all human values—and of "Ode on Melancholy"—that mutability prevents men from continuing to enjoy the same sensation and that the deepest source of melancholy is the transitoriness of all things human, including man's mind-created gods.

18

Don Juan *in Epic Context*

An easy trap for scholar-critics to fall into—one that I certainly have not avoided—is to focus so completely on particular questions before them that they dismiss as unimportant the study of other, equally significant writers, works, or issues. When a scholar-critic singles out a handful of poems to explicate in a book, the Introduction often suggests that any others works that might fall into the same category are somehow less important or less interesting. In most cases, it would be sufficient—and nearer the truth—for the scholar-critic to say that he or she lacked the time (and perhaps the knowledge) to explicate the other poems, or to explore the additional issues. (As the reader will have observed, the size and shape of most of the studies here republished was determined by factors other than the natural borders of the subjects under discussion—by, for example, the length of scholarly articles then being considered by a particular journal, or the amount of time I had to work up a topic.) Even if scholar-critics did have sufficient time and learning, publishers and readers would lack the money to produce and to purchase comprehensive studies of all possible ramifications of their favorite subjects. One person's expendable periphery thus inevitably becomes another's central issue, and readers who focus on one of those other matters will judge as inadequate, to some degree, any study that depreciates their topic.

My interest in Don Juan's place in the epic tradition grew out of my review of Brian Wilkie's fine Romantic Poets and Epic Tradition (JEGP 64 [1965]: 747–51). Wilkie's study so impressed me that I proposed him as my successor at the University of Wisconsin–Milwaukee, when I moved on to New York. But I felt that the one flaw in his book was that he had not sufficiently applied his own liberal standards for the renewal of the epic to Don Juan, which he seemed to feel had fallen short of the ideal. Having in my review explained (out of C. S. Lewis) how Don Juan *revived the "primary epic," I waited for Byron scholars to take up the idea. I had high hopes that Jerome J. McGann might have done so when "Don Juan" in Context appeared in 1976.

Now I know—and can pass on to others—a sad truth about reviewing: few readers of reviews (not even the authors of the books being discussed) try to learn anything substantive from them; reviews are read chiefly by those working in the same field to learn what the book contains (and thus, whether or not it impinges on their research-in-progress or teaching interests), or by those who know either the author or the reviewer and are curious about what overall judgment is to be saddled on the book and how cleverly the reviewer will be able to phrase it. Most readers of reviews skip, therefore, from the description of the book's contents to the punch-lines in the last paragraph, ignoring all the reviewer's careful qualifications and original discoveries that appear in between. Time and time again, I have reworked a review over a period of weeks, introducing subtle revisions designed to convey the exact nuances of tone that seemed appropriate to different parts of the book (as well as to my relationship with the author or with the subject); then I filled a paragraph or two with my freshest, best ideas on the subject so that, should I die too soon or work too slowly, another scholar-critic could take them up and develop them for the benefit of posterity. Ten years afterwards, I realize that nobody really read the blooming review clear through!

I don't blame Jerry McGann for not noticing my discovery on Don Juan as primary epic in a review published before I came into his consciousness by reviewing his first book on Byron. But I did believe that the ideas I had accumulated since writing that review—and had since taught in Romantics courses at CUNY, Columbia, and St. John's—were worth another airing. At MLA in December 1976, when I invited Jerry to become a Contributing Editor to Volumes 7–8 of Shelley and his Circle, I mentioned my dissatisfaction with his scanting of the question of genre in "Don Juan" in Context. He responded, with characteristic magnanimity, that George Ridenour had submitted to SiR a response to McGann's book and that David Wagenknecht was seeking further responses from others, to which McGann would then reply. Jerry suggested that I call David to see whether SiR's schedule would enable me to prepare a formal response. It did—and I did.

While I was preparing the paper, Thomas McFarland asked me to speak at a symposium on the Romantics that he was organizing at the CUNY Graduate Center in April 1977. I wrote a quite different, oral version of the paper (to avoid the common error through which speakers lose their audiences because their prose, meant for leisurely reading and study, is too dense for aural comprehension) and delivered it at the evening session on 1 April 1986. The published version appeared in the Fall 1977 issue of SiR (16: 587–94). Since its appearance, Hermione de Almeida has made good use of the ideas in Byron and Joyce through Homer: "Don Juan" and "Ulysses" (1981), her comprehensive, standard study of Don Juan's place in the epic tradition.

Jerome J. McGann at the outset of *"Don Juan" in Context,* his excellent study of the style, form, subject-matter, and perspective of Byron's poem, announces that he has eliminated a chapter on the epic nature of *Don Juan* "because the issue appeared to me, in the end, semantic and perhaps philosophical, but not scholarly." In the four paragraphs of the Preface that McGann devotes to *Don Juan*'s relationship to the tradition of the epic, he asserts that "the work is epic because Byron wanted it to be thought of as such, and because the consensus of history has agreed."[1]

I agree that *Don Juan* is epic, but I believe that the question of *Don Juan*'s epic stature is neither a pseudo-problem nor a semantic one and that there are scholarly criteria far more objective than Byron's desires or even the consensus of the mere century and a half since its publication (if such a consensus in fact exists—and the works I have read on the subject fail to reveal one). *Don Juan* is epic because it fulfills all the principal criteria for an epic poem enumerated in both the most perceptive studies of the genre and the best account of its fate among the English Romantic poets, Brian Wilkie's *Romantic Poets and Epic Tradition*.[2] More significantly, *Don Juan* fulfills the role of a *great* epic poem in the sense in which Shelley in *A Defence of Poetry* declared Dante's *Commedia* to be an epic: it is a "bridge thrown over the stream of time," and Byron is the fourth epic poet by the criteria Shelley used to name Homer, Dante, and Milton as the three earlier epic poets. The poetry of Byron, like their masterworks, "bore a defined and intelligible relation to the knowledge and sentiment and religion and political conditions of the age in which he lived, and of the ages which followed it: developing itself in correspondence with their development."

Shelley in *A Defence of Poetry* distinguished epic from drama, which he describes not as a *bridge* from the past age to the future, but as "a prismatic and many-sided *mirror*, which collects the brightest rays of human nature and divides and reproduces them from the simplicity of these elemental forms." Though he does not spell out the distinction at length, in his account of the history of literature he notes that "in periods of the decay of social life, the drama sympathises with that decay," whereas in just such transitional periods when the old order waned, giving place to new, the great epics were written. Shakespeare, for example, grew up and flourished at the culmination of Renaissance Christian-humanism, before its

1. Page xiii. George M. Ridenour writes similarly in his chapter entitled "My Poem's Epic," which argues for more serious consideration of Byron's "claims . . . for *Don Juan* as an epic": "The question, be it understood, is not whether *Don Juan* is or is not an epic, and in what sense. That is not a very interesting question. . . . [I]t is the metaphoric implications of the concept of epic with which we are primarily concerned" (*The Style of "Don Juan"* [New Haven: Yale University Press, 1960], p. 90).

2. Madison: University of Wisconsin Press, 1965. I refer specifically to Wilkie's excellent first chapter, "The Romantics and the Paradox of the Epic." It will be seen from this paper, as well as my review of Wilkie's book (*JEGP*, 1965), that I do not believe he has followed out the full implications of his own theory in his final chapter on "Byron and the Epic of Negation."

synthesis had begun to dissolve in a growing skepticism. Milton, on the other hand, lived in an intellectual doorway that led from the Renaissance exploration of ancient verities toward the Enlightenment spirit of rational inquiry; he utilized the epic form to synthesize a new world-view from recent modes of thought and older mythic structures. And, though Shelley was too close to *Don Juan* and too fully immersed in Byron's age to be aware of the fact, Byron also stood between two intellectual eras: having been raised in the Enlightenment (with its cocksureness about the powers of rational systems), he contributed in his early works to a renewed awareness of the irrational powers haunting the human psyche that would eventually find their expositors in Darwin, Marx, and Freud. Thus, by the time Byron wrote *Don Juan*, he was prepared to delineate the encounter between a rationally oriented human culture and the irrationalities of human experience.

As McGann demonstrates, the action of *Don Juan* is relentlessly unteleological and often fortuitous, the force of random circumstance interacting with—and often overpowering—imaginative ideals that served as focus for purely Romantic narratives, as well as the providential teleology that governs such epics as *The Aeneid*, *Jerusalem Delivered*, and *Paradise Lost*. What has not been said (unless my review of Wilkie counts) is that in *Don Juan* Byron reintroduces aspects of the mode of the "Primary Epic," as C. S. Lewis defines it in his *Preface to Paradise Lost*; specifically, *Don Juan*, like *The Iliad*, *The Odyssey*, and *Beowulf* (but unlike the epics of Virgil, Dante, Tasso, Milton, or Camoëns), is without "a heroic story and cares nothing about 'a great national subject.' . . . Heroism and tragedy there are in plenty, therefore good stories in plenty; but no 'large design that brings the world out of the good to ill.' The total effect is not a pattern but a kaleidoscope."[3] Unconsciously, perhaps, Lewis alludes to *Don Juan*, which as he may have known is often described by a word that Byron was the first to use in poetry—a "kaleidoscope." Lewis goes on to clarify his point in this striking example:

> In Homer, its [Primary Epic's] greatness lies in the human and personal tragedy built up against this background of meaningless flux. It is all the more tragic because there hangs over the heroic world a certain futility. "And here I sit in Troy," says Achilles to Priam, "afflicting you and your children." Not "protecting Greece," not even "winning glory," not called by any vocation to afflict Priam, but just doing it because that is the way things come about. . . . Perhaps this was in Goethe's mind when he said, "The lesson of the *Iliad* is that on this earth we must enact Hell." (p. 31)

3. Lewis, *A Preface to Paradise Lost* (1942; rpt. London: Oxford University Press, 1960), pp. 29–30.

If Goethe saw *The Iliad* in the terms Lewis describes, so might Byron or Shelley. Thus there is a distinct possibility that Byron's use of the subject-matter of the Primary Epic was not only precedented but calculated, even though he lacked the temerity to broach the comparison.

What of the other elements that Lewis identified as belonging to the Primary Epic—the language, the style, and the ritualistic conventions? Lewis describes the language of the Primary Epic as "a Poetic Diction; that is, a language which is familiar because it is used in every part of every poem, but unfamiliar because it is not used outside of poetry" (pp. 21-22). This combination was necessary, says Lewis, because the audience to whom the poetry was read aloud had to be able to grasp the meaning instantly but would expect the poet to rise above everyday speech. The language of *Don Juan*, of course, opposes this ideal in both respects, for Byron not only employs common, everyday language that is anything but specifically "poetic," but he also employs strange words from various languages, as well as English slang and neologisms.[4] It should be remembered, however, that the epic poetic diction had carried over directly from Primary Epic into the great Secondary Epics like *Paradise Lost* and that Byron (who wrote for print and not for an audience of hearers) had to distinguish the focus and vision of his epic from those of traditional epics by finding or creating a language as apparently chaotic and unpredictable as the moral nature of the treacherous world through which his hero navigates. What I have said of the language may be said also of the standard epic conventions—the address to the Muse, the opening of the story *in medias res*, the epic similes, the detailed descriptions (e.g., of the shield of Achilles), the catalogue(s), etc.—each of which Byron rejects or subverts. These conventions, like the poetic diction, were carried over from Primary to Secondary Epic without alteration and had become elements or accompaniments of the High Style; and one of Byron's means of justly distinguishing his epic purpose from that of Virgil or Milton was to disrupt or reverse the significance of their conventions in his work.

To understand fully the relationship of Byron's narrative method in *Don Juan* to that of the Homeric Primary Epics, we must turn from C. S. Lewis to another master scholar, Erich Auerbach. In "Odysseus' Scar," the first

---

4. It has not been sufficiently (if at all) emphasized that, though Byron thought that the example of Shakespeare and Elizabethan language had become debased in British drama, and he therefore eschewed them in *Marino Faliero* and his other dramas to revivify English dramatic writing through the use of Continental models, in *Don Juan* he employs far more echoes and direct quotations from Shakespeare than from any other writer. Obviously Shakespeare's vital, colloquial language aided Byron's efforts to break with the Latinate formality of British epic diction.

essay of *Mimesis,* Auerbach explains clearly and precisely that "Homer . . . knows no background. What he narrates is for the time being the only present, and fills both the stage and the reader's mind completely."⁵ Auerbach also, in discussing a correspondence between Goethe and Schiller in 1797 on the nature of "the retarding element" and the episodic structure of the Homeric poems, quotes Schiller as saying that Homer gives us "'simply the quiet existence and operation of things in accordance with their natures'; Homer's goal is 'already present in every point of his progress.'" When Auerbach concludes that "the true cause of the impression of 'retardation' appears to me to lie . . . in the need of the Homeric style to leave nothing which it mentions half in darkness and unexternalized" (p. 3), he delivers an oblique but recognizable account of Byron's narrative mode in *Don Juan.*

To take a cluster of examples almost at random from Byron's poem, let us look briefly at the opening of the second published unit (Cantos III-V). After his "Hail, Muse! *et cetera*" and a "digression" on the nature of love and marriage (III.ii-xii, in which, incidentally, Byron associates himself with his epic predecessors Dante and Milton even in his marital difficulties), Byron describes Lambro and his return in a passage (III.xiii-lxi) that contains a pointed allusion (III.xxiii) to the parallels and differences between his return and that of Odysseus to Ithaca. During this passage there is much detailed description of Lambro's character, emotions, and activities (recent and customary) that we may accept as germane to the subsequent action, but as Lambro begins to glimpse the signs of holiday on his island, Byron further retards his narrative to describe "a troop of Grecian girls" dancing, the feast, "children round a snow-white ram," "a dwarf buffoon," and several other people and things that never reappear or affect the subsequent action. After Lambro has queried the ignorant revellers concerning his own and his daughter's fates, he enters the house—only to have the action retarded once more by several stanzas that examine in greater detail Lambro's character and feelings—and when Lambro finally "stood within his hall," Byron again suspends the action for fully seventy-five stanzas (III.lxi-cxi, IV.i-xxxiv), besides the lyric on "The Isles of Greece," before Lambro confronts the lovers. Within this

5. *Mimesis: The Representation of Reality in Western Literature,* trans. Willard Trask (1953; rpt. New York: Anchor Books, 1957), pp. 2-3. Haskell M. Block has pointed out to me that many classical scholars have challenged Auerbach's analysis of Homer's style. Since, as Auerbach's use of Goethe and Schiller makes clear, the ideas were not unknown in Byron's day, I need answer only that Homer may well have been read by Byron as Goethe and Schiller read him and that Auerbach's descriptions are accurate for *Don Juan,* even if not for *The Odyssey.*

long "retardation" are passages that may be considered reflective and/or satirical (such as the detailed description of the trimming Poet Laureate), but other sections—especially the long account of the appearance and dress of Haidée and Juan, their table setting, and their food (III.lxi-lxxvii, a passage that many teachers of the poem may have difficulty remembering at all)—seem to serve no other function than to describe the physical details of one particular moment held in stasis before the narration resumes.

I suggest, then, that—whether or not Byron was aware of the effects in Homeric epic first adumbrated by Goethe and Schiller in 1797 or the reason for those effects since analyzed by Auerbach—he wrote in the mode of the Homeric, Primary Epic by keeping every (or almost every) character, object, place, and event that he mentions fully in the foreground, holding an importance (as long as it occupies the stage) equal to that of every other person, object, place, or event, existent or fictional. I could go on to argue—perhaps to demonstrate—that the state of such a blurring of the traditional hierarchies of "important" or "momentous" or "significant" people, places, and things is a natural outgrowth of the British empirical tradition in psychology and epistemology. If every human was, in effect, the prisoner of his own mind, then (Earl Wasserman points out in his analysis of *Tristram Shandy* in *The Subtler Language*) "meaning had become a function of each person's private, subjective concerns, which alone remained as an interpretive organization" (p. 170). For most of the Romantics (as for Uncle Toby), knowledge of this subjectivity challenged them to create private, personal hierarchies that distorted and accentuated priorities according to their own beliefs or experiences. They rode their own personal hobbyhorses that they might not be trampled by another man's. But Byron in writing *Don Juan* chose to cast himself as an author-god in whose mind every idea of his creation was equally present, equally real, and equally important—the real-life objects of his indifference and his scorn, as well as the ideals of his devotion.

Even those who find unconvincing my suggestions for the reasons behind Byron's style in *Don Juan* must confront the style itself. *Mimesis* shows us how Homer's narrative method corresponds to the capriciousness that C. S. Lewis sensed in the moral universe of *The Iliad* and *The Odyssey*; the poet brings all facts into the foreground, giving the shield of Achilles or the scar on Odysseus's knee a narrative interest equal to that accorded to the wrath of Achilles or the slaughter of Penelope's suitors. Employing a modern version of the same technique, Byron's digressive narrative weighs equally the fates of nations and the stylistic and moral peccadilloes of the Lake poets, and he describes and narrates in similar detail and with equal gusto an idyllic scene of young love, cannibalism among the survivors of a shipwreck, and the persons and history of a group of opera singers who appear only to disappear from the life of his hero.

The randomness of *Don Juan*—along with the failure of this epic to exhibit a traditional beginning, middle, or end—is only one among many features that link the poem with the thought and literature of the past fifty years, during which period the orthodox teleological systems deriving from German Romantic idealism (including the Marxist dialectic) have been taking hard knocks from the recalcitrant facts of history and personal experience, as well as from the anti-systems of thinkers from Kierkegaard to Wittgenstein. Byron's Skepticism, rooted in the thought of Voltaire, Hume, and others who demolished earlier Panglossian systems (only to rouse a new generation of system-builders from their dogmatic slumbers into equally categorical alertness), allows him to reflect or to anticipate all modes of thought from the Enlightenment to Existentialism. And for this reason *Don Juan* fulfills the role of Shelleyan epic in ways no one of Shelley's era could fully have known.

Byron's religious upbringing imposed on him an uncomfortable awareness of God, even when his own beliefs and behavior failed to conform to doctrinal Christianity. Byron more than Shelley—*Don Juan* more than *Prometheus Unbound*—connects the age of Pope with the age of Sartre, respecting the fruits in human society (as well as reflecting the mythic force) of the Christian doctrines of sin, grace, and redemption, while insisting upon the need for a humane personal ethic that cuts across doctrinal boundaries (and through religious cant). Thus Byron, with *Don Juan*, builds a bridge between the litigious religious temper of post-Reformation Europe and the restless, non-doctrinal individualized god-seeking in modern secular society. Byron, through *Don Juan*, takes seriously the material facts of human existence, including such elementary physiological drives as hunger and the sexual instincts, thereby subverting ideologies of the political and moral right and left that attempt to avoid or ignore these elements of mundane existence. At the same time, he shows Juan and other characters transcending merely animalistic behavior through the quirky strength of a reverent humanism that refuses to allow their ideals of conduct to be completely overridden by merely material considerations. Thus Byron, through *Don Juan*, explores the relationship of traditional, humanistic idealisms to analytical scientism.

As a scion of the old feudal aristocracy who personally held many of the ideals of the French Revolution, Byron in *Don Juan* bridges the gap between the hierarchical orders of all past societies (depicted and upheld with varying emphases by Homer, Dante, and Milton) and modern egalitarian ideals. Each character in *Don Juan* is judged on his moral characteristics alone, whether fate has cast him into the role of Lambro, a pirate, or the Czarina Catherine the Great; Daniel Boone, a private citizen, and George Washington, the head of state, carry equal weight—ideal inhabitants of a commonwealth. (This blend of aristocratic and egalitarian ideals, by the way, is the moral and thematic thread that makes so effective Byron's blend of the Horatian and Juvenalian styles in his satirical passages.)

One can, in like manner, go through the other ideals depicted in Byron's poem, and find that they bear "a defined and intelligible relation to the knowledge and sentiment" of the age out of which he grew and that which his poems both anticipated and helped create. The personal physical courage that Juan exhibits (during the shipwreck, at the siege of Ismail, and in the face of the armed highwaymen) combines, for example, with his tenderness both as a lover and as the protector of helpless innocents (and with his disgust at useless carnage) to link the macho knight-errantry of the past with the pacific ideals of loving, sacrificial heroism that have been voiced (if not widely exemplified) in our own time. As I wrote on another occasion,

> *Don Juan* incorporates all the central themes of later Western literature, and it does so more pertinently than does any other work written by one author under a single title. Goethe's *Faust* is at once too intellectual and too aristocratic in its perspective. . . . Tolstoy's *War and Peace* says nothing about human life that is not clearly stated in *Don Juan*. Browning's multiplicity of possible viewpoints, Eliot's vision of a spiritual *Waste Land*, Stevens's identification of the human imagination as the author of the Supreme Fiction, Henry James's exploitation of manners as signs of morals, and even Kierkegaard's outcry against smug conventionality in religious observance are all woven integrally into the texture of Byron's poem. Only the exclusive visions of extreme beatitude (as in *Epipsychidion* or *Four Quartets*) or unremitting horror (dozens of twentieth-century works) lie outside its boundaries.[6]

And Byron's refusal to opt for one extreme in *Don Juan* is, in itself, a sign of

---

6. Donald H. Reiman and Doucet Devin Fischer, *Byron on the Continent* (New York: New York Public Library, 1974), pp. 49–50. In my last rereading of *Don Juan*, I noted a number of other areas in which Byron has anticipated not only his generation but also their grandchildren: Byron says, referring to beauty in African women, that "black is fair" (XII.lx, lxi); he also predicts that technology deriving from the scientific discoveries of men like Newton will soon carry man to the moon (X.ii). As the notes in the Variorum *Don Juan* attest, these opinions were not idle speculations but convictions based on Byron's understanding of human nature.

the poem's epic inclusiveness, for to omit either the earthly beatitude of Juan's sojourn with Haidée or the horror of the fall of Ismail without acknowledging the presence of its opposite would have been untrue both to Byron's vision of the human condition and to the inclusive function of the epic.

For me, then, *Don Juan*—far more than any other literary work—seems to fulfill the conditions of modern epic. In that capacity, it not only recreates the nature of the epic itself (in ways demonstrated by Wilkie and suggested by McGann), but also—as great epics do—plays the part of an encyclopedic work that we moderns can use to point students back to the ideals and attitudes that have dissolved during the past one hundred and fifty years, as well as to epitomize those that have emerged. As the Greek writers of the fifth and fourth centuries quoted Homer, who connected the elder age of heroic barbarism with their own civilization, as the Enlightenment revered *Paradise Lost*, so we can find in *Don Juan* the clearest articulation of the stage of Western civilization in which we live and the roots from which it sprang. Such a judgment is neither subjective nor semantic; it resides within the nature of Byron's life and art and his relationship to history, just as it explains why the popularity that he enjoyed as a poet during his lifetime was both unprecedented and rationally inexplicable to his immediate contemporaries and to the Victorians. Only now, when the transformations implicit in Byron's masterpiece have become manifest in the society we inhabit, can a true estimate of his achievement begin.

19

Wordsworth, Shelley, and the Romantic Inheritance

This essay, one of the latest published pieces in the volume, can claim the longest gestation of any paper here. I wrote the first version of it in the late winter and spring of 1963, to read at the Erasmus Club at Duke University under the simple title "Wordsworth and Shelley." In that first incarnation, the lecture explored the writings of the two poets in the light of Morse Peckham's paper entitled "Toward a Theory of Romanticism: II. Reconsiderations," which I had heard Peckham read at MLA in New York in December 1960 and which Peckham published in the inaugural issue of Studies in Romanticism in the fall of 1961. (At that MLA session, I first encountered David V. Erdman, who was another speaker, and I first talked with Kenneth Neill Cameron immediately after that session.)

In 1971 Richard Wordsworth invited me to speak at his Rydal Mount Wordsworth Summer School, chiefly because I was then coordinating American fundraising efforts on behalf of the Wordsworth Rydal Mount Trust. (As part of that activity, I founded the Wordsworth-Coleridge Association as a support group for Rydal Mount.) Pressed for time, I reworked my old lecture on Wordsworth and Shelley in the light of new information on Shelley's development from the poems published in The Esdaile Notebook (1964), my growing knowledge of Modernist poetry, and the opening chapters of Harold Bloom's Yeats. The lecture now played off what seemed to me Bloom's misinterpretation of the evidence on the poetic affinities of Wordsworth and Shelley. I delivered that lecture ("Wordsworth, Shelley, and the Romantic Inheritance") both at Rydal Mount in August 1971 and at Boston University in January 1972 (where Helen Vendler loyally defended Bloom's work). In 1974, I again revised the lecture in the light of Bloom's further publications on literary influence, sharpening its polemical aspects and entitling it "On the Discrimination of Anxieties in Romantic and Modern Poetry." I gave this version in 1974 at both the University of Maryland and St. John's University and delivered it again in March 1977 at Adelphi University, having revised it for that occasion to embody my most recent reading and thinking on the issues.

Finally, when Stuart Peterfreund, editor of the newly transformed Milton and the Romantics, *asked those of us who served on the Advisory Board for contributions to assist the emergence of* Romanticism Past and Present, *I pulled out the paper that had served me so well, toned down the polemicism, and further updated and documented my argument. It appeared in the second issue of Volume 5 (December 1981) of* Romanticism Past and Present, *nineteen years after I had first begun to work on the original version.*

During the intervening years, I had explored the relationship of life to art and the psychological predispositions of various writers in several essays here republished, as well as in essays and extended commentaries in Shelley and his Circle. *I have had no formal training in psychology and have never been psychoanalyzed. Nor have I read informally in the field. I therefore know little about the terminology of psychology or psychiatry in any of their formal schools and sects. Whatever merit there may be in my appraisals of human motivations and temperamental predispositions in the poets derives simply from careful observation of my own behavior and motivations and from what I can garner through observation and the conversations of my friends and associates about theirs.*

In probing the actions and possible motivations of particular Romantic writers, I must, therefore, rely on the detailed research I have done with the primary documents for their biographies, in working through the developmental stages of their poems, in observing the characteristic—and individual—modes of feeling and response in the letters exchanged by members of the Shelley and Byron circles, and in reading the discussions and analyses of other scholar-critics of literature who have read and trained themselves through psychological analysis. My research has given me, perhaps, a surer grasp of the details of the lives and works of a wider range of the Romantic writers and their contemporaries than is customary for recent scholar-critics. Many of those who apply scientific categories to the experience of one writer at a time, taken in isolation, seem to find that the most meaningful interactions are those between the author under examination and the scholar-critic who is analyzing that writer's words, rather than among the author and that author's contemporaries.

For most Modernist and Postmodernist poets, I claim no such advantage; if my analyses of the temperamental affinities of Yeats and Eliot, of Stevens and Auden, are erroneous, I hope that those better versed in their lives and works will write papers that draw on my analyses of Wordsworth and Shelley, while illustrating the related affinities of Modernist and Postmodernist writers who do *share their psychological predispositions, either "Pastoral" or "Gothic."*

It has become (again) a critical commonplace that the Romantic poets introduced into English literature a Copernican revolution comparable to the philosophical reorientation that is usually fathered on Kant. In philosophy, after Sir Francis Bacon and his contemporaries had broken the stranglehold of the Aristotelian-Thomist orthodoxies and had opened the natural and moral worlds to reexamination, the basis of philosophical certainties and values swung rapidly from the nature and will of God to the nature and will of the human individual. The flagship names in the history of this reorientation are, we now agree, Descartes, Hume, Kant, and Kierkegaard.

In English letters, the withdrawal of the poet from the role of confident expositor of the universe to a tentative interpreter of his own experience followed a parallel course: Milton's attempt to "justify the ways of God to man" became Pope's "The proper study of mankind is man," then Wordsworth's "Here must thou be, O Man! / Power to thyself; no Helper hast thou here;" and finally Byron's "We live and die, / But which is best, *you* know no more than I." Byron's *Don Juan* is the epic of the new thought, dissolving the old verities within its seven types of irony and yet asserting the essential worth and dignity of Juan, the new Everyman, as he remains true to his private code of moral imperatives amid the flux of social and natural worlds that offer him no support at all.

Perhaps Byron will prove at last to be what almost all of his contemporaries (including Shelley and Goethe) considered him: the great representative poetic genius of his age. But if so, it was left to W. H. Auden and to us to rediscover this truth. Most of the Victorians and Modernists from Tennyson, Browning, and Arnold to Yeats, Eliot, Stevens, and Williams considered Wordsworth and Shelley the two poetic giants who struggled for, or divided, the empire of Romantic tradition.

There are a number of ways to analyze and distinguish the influence of Wordsworth and Shelley. One of these distinctions is at once epistemological and ontological: Wordsworth remained in the grip of a Cartesian dualism that tempered all his thought. All the happy interchanges between the mind and nature, between mind and mind, and—in Wordsworth's Christian revival—between man and God are predicated on a dualistic view of Being that, in turn, either presupposes or generates the Cartesian epistemological dilemma in which the Self and the Other struggle valiantly to touch across a logical chasm. Shelley, on the contrary, after writing *Queen Mab* (1812), rejected the dualism inherent in what he came to term "the popular philosophy" by accepting Sir William Drummond's version of Hume's Skepticism. To any human being there was only *one* knowable reality: the images apprehended by the mind. Some or all of these images or "ideas" might correspond to some outward reality (nature), as revealed through the senses; some or all might be generated by the mind itself; some or all might be impressed on the mind by some occult source of power—God, or a universal mind of which each human mind was only an aspect—perhaps through an intermediary Spirit of Intellectual Beauty. But man had no sure criterion or mechanism for ascertaining whether there was a single cause or a variety of causes, or what the cause or causes of these "ideas" might be; he could know them only as data. Such an epistemology (which Shelley—following Drummond—calls the "intellectual philosophy") enabled Shelley to assert the truth-for-him of central ideas on man, society, and the universe without declaring them true for all mankind. His doubts and the doubts his epistemology raised regarding all other doctrines left him with a firm basis for universal toleration and made "Freedom" and "Liberty" the touchstones of his intellectual, social, and ethical orientations.

We could, I suggest, distinguish between the thought and poetry of Wordsworth and Shelley and trace their influence through later writers by means of these intellectual considerations. But in this discussion, I intend to focus primarily on the nature of temperamental affinities between individual Romantic poets and particular Modernist poets, all of whom inherit collectively the ontological and epistemological problems and perspectives that faced the Romantics.

In his generally useful study of *Yeats*, Harold Bloom traces a particular line of poetic influencing that moves from Milton to Wordsworth to Shelley and then on to Browning and Yeats: "the single poem that most affected [Yeats's] life and art (and Browning's as well) is Shelley's *Alastor*, and the line leading to *Alastor* and its remorseless version of Romantic quest goes from *Il Penseroso* through Wordsworth's *Excursion*."[1] Bloom's grouping does not pay sufficient attention to the *tone* of the poems he lists. *Alastor*, as Earl Wasserman demonstrated in his last book, has at least two levels of meaning that play against one another in what Wasserman reads as a dramatic dialogue between the words and actions of the youthful, visionary poet, on the one hand, and the comments of the Wordsworthian narrator of the youth's adventures, on the other.[2] Bloom may be able to twist one of his six fabulous "ratios" of "misprision," or misreading, to account for how the *intellectual* level of Shelley's narrative poem depends on the analogous level in pastoral dialogue that is *The Excursion*. But Bloom does not address the more fundamental level from which *Il Penseroso*, *The Excursion*, and *Alastor* draw their emotional force. *Alastor* is, as Bloom, Wasserman, and I would agree, Shelley's most Wordsworthian poem; and yet it dwells in another country of the mind.

Shelley does not consciously echo Wordsworth's diction, rhythm, and

1. *Yeats* (New York: Oxford University Press, 1970), p. 8.
2. *Shelley: A Critical Reading* (Baltimore: Johns Hopkins University Press, 1971), pp. 11–41.

tone simply to "swerve" from Wordsworth's philosophical conclusions (though he certainly does have a different viewpoint). Rather, Shelley draws on Wordsworth (as Keats turns to Milton in *Hyperion*) to help him overcome a predilection for the pseudo-history and Gothic adventure-romances that constitute much of Shelley's early reading, including forgotten works and a few semi-memorable ones, such as Lewis's *The Monk*, Southey's *Thalaba the Destroyer*, and Scott's *Marmion*. Though he later developed a taste for the poetry of Coleridge and Byron, Shelley's affinity for these other works was far deeper and longer-lasting than was the merely "literary" influence that the verse of Mrs. Tighe, Beattie, and Leigh Hunt exerted on Keats's poetry. Besides many poems in the Esdaile Notebook, including the truncated romance "Zeinab and Kathema," the Gothic-romance tradition spawned Shelley's abortive poem "The Wandering Jew," two Gothic "novels," *Original Poetry* by "Victor and Cazire," and the serious prank entitled *Posthumous Fragments of Margaret Nicholson*. The same impulse in a more exalted mood lies behind both *Queen Mab* and *The Revolt of Islam* and can be clearly identified in a work as late as *Hellas*. And even in those poems of Shelley's early period that show none of the more outlandish trappings of Gothicism and have subjects like those that Wordsworth treats, Shelley's language displays a nervous tension and impassioned diction that remind one at times of Coleridge rather than of Wordsworth at his best or most characteristic. Here are lines from "A Tale of Society as it is, from facts, 1811," a poem that in subject parallels Wordsworth's *The Ruined Cottage*, but in overall tone suggests Coleridge more than Wordsworth:

> For seven years did this poor woman live
> In unparticipated solitude.
> Thou might'st have seen her in the desart rude
> Picking the scattered remnants of its wood;
> If human thou might'st then have learned to grieve.
> The gleanings of precarious charity
> Her scantiness of food did scarce supply;
> The proofs of an unspeaking sorrow dwelt
> Within her ghastly hollowness of eye.[3]

Even the most Wordsworthian poem in the Esdaile Notebook used to seem more Wordsworthian than it is because it was originally published without its opening lines. "The Retrospect. Cwm Elan, 1812" begins:

3. Edited from *Shelley and his Circle*, vol. 4, ed. Kenneth Neill Cameron (Cambridge: Harvard University Press, 1970), pp. 950ff.

> To trace Duration's lone career
> To check the chariot of the year,
> Whose burning wheels forever sweep
> The boundaries of oblivion's deep. . . .
> To snatch from Time, the monster's, jaw
> The children which she just had borne
> And, ere entombed within her maw,
> To drag them to the light of morn
> And mark each feature with an eye
> Of Cold and fearless scrutiny. . . .
> It asks a soul not formed to feel,
> An eye of glass, a hand of steel;
> Thoughts that have passed and thoughts that are
> With truth and feeling to compare;
> A scene which wildered fancy viewed
> In the soul's coldest solitude,
> With that same scene when peaceful love
> Flings rapture's colour o'er the grove,
> When mountain, meadow, wood and stream
> With unalloying glory gleam
> And to the spirit's ear and eye
> Are unison and harmony.[4]

In spite of the obvious echo of the "Immortality Ode" in the last lines I have quoted, it may stretch credulity to believe that "The Retrospect" is a consciously Wordsworthian poem, a Shelleyan version of "Tintern Abbey," with Harriet Shelley assuming the role played by Dorothy Wordsworth in the earlier poem. Actually, the form, language, and tone, as well as the structure and thought of "The Retrospect," remind one of Wordsworth chiefly by contrast. Shelley uses impassioned tetrameter couplets instead of Wordsworth's meditative blank verse, and Shelley's message is that only the joy of the present moment can redeem the scenes of his despairing past.

If Wordsworth can be said to be the poet of self-continuity in a world of cultural discontinuity, Shelley is a poet of self-*dis*continuity who eventually achieved a sense of cultural continuity that spans the entire Western tradition from Homer to Goethe. Wordsworth rejects, one by one, the influences of the Schoolmen and their Renaissance successors that he encountered at Cambridge, the Enlightenment cosmopolitanism that he lived in France and London, and the reforming Utilitarianism that was to be the (somewhat brackish) wave of the future in nineteenth-century En-

---

4. *Shelley's Poetry and Prose*, ed. Donald H. Reiman and Sharon B. Powers (New York: W. W. Norton, 1977), p. 8.

gland, returning instead to the bosom of his own family, in his own Lake Country, to write great poems about his own past. For Wordsworth the child is the father of the man; for Shelley, on the contrary, the inspired man recreates his past in mythic terms. To Wordsworth's mind, the great danger lies in being torn loose from one's mundane roots in home, family, friends, country, and local, traditional values; for Shelley, on the contrary, a greater threat lies in being bound in mundane, limited traditions and values so that one loses sight of the hope for improvement represented by what he calls in *A Defence of Poetry* the imaginative records of the best and happiest moments of the happiest and best minds.

There was another danger, of course, for each poet—one that gave him much less anxiety and to which he therefore succumbed. Wordsworth in the years of his greatest creativity identified himself very closely with his early heritage and with a limited circle of family and friends. In later years he accentuated the tendency to remain in such a circle, even to the point of repeating his father's mistake by selling his services to the Earl of Lonsdale (at both too low and too high a price). Shelley, rejecting family, church, country, and—one by one—most of his mentors and friends, cut himself off from the living community that could have and should have given him the support, encouragement, and counsel he needed both for temporal happiness and poetic popularity. But that the poetry of either Wordsworth or Shelley suffered because of his choice is, at best, disputable. The greatest poetry of each results, in fact, precisely from the tension between the two poles represented by their opposite choices. The chief concern of *The Prelude* is the struggle between the centrifugal forces exerted by the external world and the centripetal force of the poet's inward journey toward the central self, while the consequent loss of the visionary gleam is the central matter of Wordsworth's *Poems; in Two Volumes* (1807). Many, though not all, of Shelley's finest poems—*Alastor, Epipsychidion, Adonais,* "The Triumph of Life"—treat the struggle of the poet to free his soul from the mundane without entirely destroying his ties with the human community he desires to serve.

With such obviously different emphases in response to a central question such as the relationship between the mundane and the ideal (to say nothing of the difference in their poetic diction and styles), Wordsworth and Shelley may be seen as representing two opposite poles of temperament within the Romantic tradition. Shelley, as I have suggested, consciously imitates Wordsworth's style (most strongly in *Alastor*) as a counterweight to free himself from the weakness of the early Gothic style that he is too easily prone to. Neither Wordsworth nor Milton could have been Shelley's true precursor, because Shelley was not temperamentally akin to the thought or the style of either. The best sense of a poet's artistic affinities can be inferred from the thought and language of his most extemporaneous effusions, particularly his earliest work and those later poems that he never polished for publication. I have alluded briefly to the strain of Gothic adventure-romance that runs through Shelley's early writings, including the poems of the Esdaile Notebook. The same strain is found in many of Shelley's later, more or less extemporaneous lyrics or meditational fragments—such as "To Constantia," "Marianne's Dream," and "To William Shelley" of 1817; the "Invocation to Misery" and the Spenserian "Stanzas written in Dejection—December 1818, Near Naples"; the fragments on the death of William Shelley and "On the Medusa of Leonardo da Vinci in the Florentine Gallery" of 1819; "Death" ("Death is here and death is there") and "The Tower of Famine" of 1820; the many lyrics of 1821–1822 to Jane Williams and "To Time" ("Unfathomable Sea! whose waves are years, / Ocean of Time, whose waters of deep woe / Are brackish with the salt of human tears!"), or the lines beginning, "The flower that smiles today / Tomorrow dies."[5] None of these poems or fragments can be said to be Miltonic or Wordsworthian, either by direct descent or as the result of any imaginable sequence of Rube Goldberg "swerves," except in terms so broad as to empty them of meaning. Shelley's great achievements of the years in Italy—*Prometheus Unbound, The Cenci, Julian and Maddalo,* "The Witch of Atlas," *Epipsychidion, Adonais,* and "The Triumph of Life"— owe far more to Homer, Aeschylus, Plato, Dante, Shakespeare, Calderón, Goethe, and Byron than to Milton or Wordsworth, though Shelley does, of course, echo both these poets to set up ironic contrasts at the intellectual level so that his readers will be able to orient themselves to his thought by reference to easily accessible fixed points.

Shelley possessed a "Gothic sensibility," which may be opposed to the "pastoral sensibility" in its primal response to the moral dimensions of nature and society. Shelley's early fascination with "Tales of Wonder," to use the title of one of "Monk" Lewis's collections, indicates not merely an undeveloped literary taste, but a set of mind that caused him to see both the natural and the social worlds around him as essentially dangerous and hostile. With more developed taste, Shelley still preferred literary works in which the hero struggles—often vainly—against "Fate, Time, Occasion, Chance, and Change": Greek tragedy, *King Lear, The Iliad,* Byron's *Cain,* Goethe's *Faust,* in all of which the cosmic order is challenged by the individual. This preference helps to explain Shelley's sympathy for Satan in

---

5. Some of these poems are found in *Shelley's Poetry and Prose* (Norton); the rest can be seen (in uncorrected texts) in *Shelley's Poetical Works,* ed. Thomas Hutchinson, Oxford Standard Authors Edition (London: Oxford University Press, 1980 et seq.).

Paradise Lost. But the Gothic strain, as I have redefined it, is no more essentially "Romantic" than is the Wordsworthian "pastoral" mode, which governs the poetry of Emily Dickinson and Robert Frost as well as Wordsworth. The pastoral involves not simply rural settings, but a view of life in which men are guarded from danger by pastors—shepherds.[6] The individual is under the care and protection of a social community or beneficent spiritual forces. In pastoral, the chief threats come from the foolishness or evil within the individual. Jane Austen and Milton are pastoralists; Chapman and Webster are pre-Romantic Gothicists.

The typical Wordsworthian poem is Miltonic in that the world order is in the hands of an omnipotent, benevolent Power and the poet's chief concern is repeatedly to ask himself, "Doth God exact day-labor, light deny'd?": What is my function? Am I ready to begin fulfilling it? Has my experience prepared me for my mission? How will today's experiences sustain me tomorrow? The central Shelleyan poem asks, on the contrary, Why must the righteous suffer? Why won't the world listen? Why must the outer world always fail me? In those lyrics that Shelley probably purposely refrained from publishing, the note is unmistakable:

> Rarely, rarely, comest thou,
>   Spirit of Delight!
> Wherefore hast thou left me now
>   Many a day and night?
> Many a weary night and day
> 'Tis since thou art fled away.
>
> Virtue, how frail it is!—
>   Friendship, how rare!—
> Love, how it sells poor bliss
>   For proud despair!
> But these though soon they fall,
> Survive their joy, and all
> Which ours we call.—

---

6. My uses of the terms *pastoral* and *Gothic* to define temperamental affinities do not quite conform to accepted historical usages of those terms as explored, for example, by Renato Poggioli in *The Oaten Flute: Essays on Pastoral Poetry and the Pastoral Ideal* (Cambridge: Harvard University Press, 1975) and Patrick Cullen in *Spenser, Marvell, and Renaissance Pastoral* (Cambridge: Harvard University Press, 1970), or in various studies of the Gothic tradition. But, by defining and exemplifying my conception of the temperamental tendencies, I try to avoid confusing readers versed in these historical traditions. This note will warn readers that I have not attempted to treat *pastoral* or *Gothic* as historical or literary conventions and that my generalizations apply chiefly to Romantic and post-Romantic poetry. I do not believe in coining strange words from foreign languages to char-

> After the slumber of the year
> The woodland violets reappear;
> All things revive in field or grove
> And sky and sea, but two, which move
> And form all others—life and love.—[7]

Even in the published poetry, consciously and artistically aimed at instilling hope in the hearts of despairing idealists, the poet's own struggle with despair is a primary theme, whether portrayed dramatically, as in Prometheus's temptation by the Furies and in the dialogue between the poet and the phantom of Rousseau in "The Triumph of Life," or lyrically in lines like these:

> Oh! lift me as a wave, a leaf, a cloud!
> I fall upon the thorns of life! I bleed!
>
> A heavy weight of hours has chained and bowed
> One too like thee: tameless, and swift, and proud.[8]

II

In his influential paper "Toward a Theory of Romanticism: II. Reconsiderations," Morse Peckham defines three stages of Western culture and thought. The first of these is the Classical-Christian view, in which social values and the individual's identity are defined by a realm beyond Nature—in the Christian view by a creative God and in the Platonic scheme by a realm of perfect Forms. The second is the Enlightenment view, which seeks value and identity through a study of Nature and natural law—emphasizing that "whatever is, is right," and seeking to determine proper modes of conduct by means of straw polls and Kinsey reports. The third is the Romantic view, which holds that the Enlightenment view fails to provide either a standard for improving individual and social behavior or a satisfactory explanation for people's sense of sin and guilt. The Romantic, unable to return to a belief in a hierarchy of values descending from the clouds—or, in any other metaphor, from beyond the range of human experience—must turn instead to faith in the human values he finds within himself. In Peckham's words, "Value enters the world through the self, which is not supported by any perceptible social or cos-

---

acterize phenomena we all encounter and recognize daily.
7. *Shelley's Poetry and Prose*, pp. 370, 441, 442.
8. See *Shelley's Poetry and Prose*, pp. 145–55, 460, 463, 223.

mic order, and the self projects upon the world an order which serves to symbolize that self-generated value."9

Not accepting all the implications that Peckham derives from this thesis, I nevertheless accept his analysis of the relationship of Romanticism to the Classical-Christian and the Enlightenment world-views. But I would want to add—emphatically—that no Romantic thinker of any consequence in the English tradition asserted or practiced under the delusion that *whatever* the self might will would therefore be valuable. Each had seen and read about the errors of numerous people (of whom Catherine the Great, Robespierre, and Napoleon were merely egregious contemporary examples) who gave way completely to the tyranny of their unchecked self-wills and thereby destroyed others and themselves. And each poet realized that he himself was more alive to the higher values during a few inspired moments than during the ordinary, routine pattern of life. Wordsworth, who once believed in the essential goodness and benevolence of the natural world and of human beings, measured the moral quality of his uninspired hours against the moments in which his moral consciousness had been most fully stimulated.

In the poem titled "To My Sister" ("It is the first mild day of March"), Wordsworth invokes those inspired experiences and their uses; he declares that "in this moment there is life and food / For future years":

> One moment now may give us more
> Than years of toiling reason:
> Our minds shall drink at every pore
> The spirit of the season.
>
> Some silent laws our hearts will make
> Which they shall long obey:
> We for the year to come may take
> Our temper from to-day.
>
> And from the blessed power that rolls
> About, below, above,
> We'll frame the measure of our souls:
> They shall be tuned to love.10

The mind *absorbs* values from the pervasive "power that rolls / About,

---

9. Given first as a lecture at the 1960 Modern Language Association convention, this paper was published originally in *SiR* 1 (Autumn 1961): 1–8, and reprinted in Peckham's *The Triumph of Romanticism* (Columbia: University of South Carolina Press, 1970), pp. 27–35.

10. William Wordsworth, *Selected Poems and Prefaces*, ed. Jack Stillinger (Boston: Houghton Mifflin, 1965), p. 48.

below, above," during those intermittent encounters with that power. And then the heart makes its own silent laws that it endeavors to obey during the uninspired year.

In the decade from 1798 to 1807—the height of Wordsworth's "Romanticism"—he relied on "spots of time," many of them experiences remembered from his childhood, to illuminate the rest of his life. Perhaps feeling that the "burden of the mystery" weighed too heavily upon him after he had struggled with his ambiguous love for his sister Dorothy, witnessed Coleridge's personal disintegration, and endured the deaths of his brother John and two of his own children, Wordsworth gradually abandoned his attempt to rely solely upon his own inner resources.[11] Or perhaps, as Geoffrey Hartman's analysis of the language in "Ode to Duty" would suggest, Wordsworth's change was essentially one of trying to propound his private faith as a guide for other hearts as well as his own.[12] In either case, the poet about 1805 bid farewell to "the heart that lives alone, / Housed in a dream, at distance from the Kind!"

That Shelley never experienced the same loss of faith in the values he espoused may be partly attributable to his age at the time of his death. But, more profoundly, Shelley's assurance that he had a mission rested on two convictions: (1) the overwhelming power of his own conversion experience, and (2) his certainty that the social order was essentially corrupting. Wordsworth records the slow, almost imperceptibly growing awareness of his significant childhood experiences as he recollects them in tranquillity. But for Shelley, the revelation of his own mission had been sudden and overpowering. And, as Shelley's two most revealing poetic accounts of his conversion make clear, the experience was generated less by a sense of what he himself could become than by a revelation of the misery of the world and society as they existed. In "Hymn to Intellectual Beauty" he writes:

> When musing deeply on the lot
> Of life, at that sweet time when winds are wooing
> All vital things that wake to bring
> News of buds and blossoming,—
> Sudden, thy shadow fell on me;
> I shrieked, and clasped my hands in extacy!

11. On these questions, see studies by Irene Tayler and Donald H. Reiman in *The Evidence of the Imagination*, ed. D. H. Reiman, M. C. Jaye, and B. T. Bennett (New York: New York University Press, 1978), pp. 119–77.

12. See Hartman, *Wordsworth's Poetry, 1787–1814* (New Haven: Yale University Press, 1964), pp. 277–83.

> I vowed that I would dedicate my powers
> To thee and thine—have I not kept the vow?

In the "Dedication" to *The Revolt of Islam*, he is more explicit:

> Thoughts of great deeds were mine, dear Friend, when first
>   The clouds which wrap this world from youth did pass.
> I do remember well the hour which burst
>   My spirit's sleep: a fresh May-dawn it was,
>   When I walked forth upon the glittering grass,
> And wept, I knew not why; until there rose
>   From the near school-room, voices, that, alas!
> Were but one echo from a world of woes—
> The harsh and grating strife of tyrants and of foes.
>
> And then I clasped my hands and looked around—
>   —But none was near to mock my streaming eyes,
> Which poured their warm drops on the sunny ground—
>   So, without shame, I spake:—"I will be wise,
>   And just, and free, and mild, if in me lies
> Such power, for I grow weary to behold
>   The selfish and the strong still tyrannise
> Without reproach or check." I then controuled
> My tears, my heart grew calm, and I was meek and bold.
>
> And from that hour did I with earnest thought
>   Heap knowledge from forbidden mines of lore,
> Yet nothing that my tyrants knew or taught
>   I cared to learn, but from that secret store
>   Wrought linked armour for my soul, before
> It might walk forth to war among mankind;
>   Thus power and hope were strengthened more and more
> Within me, till there came upon my mind
> A sense of loneliness, a thirst with which I pined.[13]

Perhaps the most significant result of the poet's startled awakening is this renewed sense of loneliness, of isolation from those about him. He laments that "love should be a blight and snare / To those who seek all sympathies in one," but he is grateful for the love and understanding of Mary Shelley, to whom the "Dedication" is addressed. Four years later, when he wrote *Epipsychidion*, Shelley felt estranged from Mary and had decided that *no* human being could embody the ideal that he envisioned. The central idea of *Epipsychidion* derives very directly (as Shelley himself tells us) from Dante's *La Vita Nuova*, and that conception is to be found in

---

13. *Shelley's Poetry and Prose*, pp. 95–97.

Dante's exchange with "some ladies" who were friends of Beatrice.

Then I said to them: "Ladies, the end aim of my love formerly lay in the greeting of this lady . . . . But since it pleased her to deny it to me, my lord, Love, through his grace, has placed all my bliss in something that cannot fail me." . . . And after these ladies had spoken among themselves awhile, that lady who had first addressed me spoke to me again, saying: "We beg you to tell us wherein this bliss of yours now lies." And I answered her by saying: "In those words that praise my lady."[14]

Shelley had come to realize that, whereas he was, perhaps, seeking in a mortal form something that must, ultimately, remain eternal and whereas union with that Ideal was impossible, he could place all his happiness in something that was within his power—in his poems, those *words* that praise the Ideal.

For Wordsworth, values arose within the self over a period of time and were confirmed, supported, and sustained not only by a beneficent nature, but by a community of beloved friends. Wordsworth's poems are often openly addressed to a particular friend, as he addresses Coleridge in *The Prelude* and Dorothy in "Tintern Abbey." One recalls, among the shorter pieces, the "Matthew" poems in which an interchange is imagined between the poet and a composite figure embodying characteristics of his favorite teachers. In the great address to Coleridge that concludes Book XI of *The Prelude,* Wordsworth—imagining Coleridge wandering in Sicily amid scenes of classical grandeur and climbing Mt. Etna—exclaims, "There is / One great society alone on earth: / The noble Living and the noble Dead." For Wordsworth the important and meaningful members of that "one great society" were those living, such as Coleridge, Dorothy, and Mary Hutchinson, whom he knew and loved, and those dead whom he had known and still loved, such as William Taylor, his teacher at Hawkshead School, Michael Beaupuy, and Raisley Calvert. Shelley—who might well have defined the one great society in similar words—would not have considered the most important encounters with value to have been among living men and women but between living men and great works of art, the precious life-blood of master spirits treasured up for a life beyond life.

Shelley drew his inspiration from books and the creative arts, and his maturation as a man and as a poet parallels exactly the improvement in his literary and artistic taste. For Wordsworth, the growth of the value center

14. *La vita nuova* of Dante Alighieri, translated by Mark Musa (Bloomington: Indiana University Press, 1962), p. 30.

of the self is a long, slow process resulting from numerous small experiences and from years of reflection upon them. Moreover, for him the necessity of drawing upon those internal values did not come until the Enlightenment ideals were shattered by the degeneration of the hopeful dawn of the French Revolution into the September Massacres, the Reign of Terror, and the Subjugation of Switzerland. Wordsworth turned backward to his own childhood and inward to the circle of those upon whose love he could depend after the ideals of republican Rome and of the English Commonwealth men—the "good old cause" of British republicans—had been attempted, distorted, and destroyed in revolutionary France. As Wordsworth wrote in the fragment of *The Prelude* that he first published in *The Friend* in 1809 (and reprinted in 1815 under the title "French Revolution, as it appeared to Enthusiasts at its Commencement"), men of good will felt in that dawn that they could

> exercise their skill
> Not in Utopia, subterraneous Fields,
> Or some secreted Island, heaven knows where!
> But in the very world, which is the world
> Of all of us,—the place where in the end
> We find our happiness, or not at all![15]

Shelley, on the contrary, in his uncompleted "Essay on Christianity" declared that "According to Jesus Christ, and according to the indisputable facts of the case, some evil Spirit has dominion in this imperfect world."[16] He considered Wordsworth's lines on the home of happiness almost blasphemous; as he wrote to John Gisborne on 10 April 1822, just three months before his death:

I have been reading over & over again Faust, & always with sensations which no other composition excites. . . . the pleasure of sympathizing with emotions known only to few, although they derive their sole charm from despair & a scorn of the narrow good we can attain in our present state, seems more than to cure the pain which belongs to them.—Perhaps all discontent with the *less* (to use a Platonic sophism) supposes the sense of a just claim to the *greater,* & that we admirers of Faust are in the right road to Paradise.—Such a supposition is not more absurd, and is certainly less demoniacal than that of Wordsworth—where he says—

15. *Poems* by William Wordsworth (London: Longman, Hurst, Rees, Orme, and Brown, 1815), 2:71.
16. Shelley, *Works,* ed. Roger Ingpen and Walter E. Peck, Julian Edition (New York: Charles Scribner's Sons, 1929), 6:235.

> This earth,
> Which is the world of all of us, & where
> *We find our happiness or not at all.*

As if after sixty years of suffering here, we were to be roasted alive for sixty million more in Hell, or charitably annihilated by a coup de grace of the bungler, who brought us into existence at first.[17]

Thus, though Wordsworth and Shelley both typify the Romantic worldview in taking their values and achieving their identity by looking within rather than by accepting "given" values transmitted by the established social or religious institutions, their radically different views of the external world led the two poets to nearly opposite orientations. Having come to rely on memories of his childhood and on the support of a few close friends, Wordsworth interpreted the gap between his private values and the traditional values of his nation, his church, and his wife and friends as resulting from a weakness on his own part, and he turned more and more toward a message that reads like the moral of *The Wizard of Oz*, where Dorothy repeats over and over again: "There's *no* place like *home*." For Shelley, on the other hand, dreams of Utopia, the Elysian Fields, the Golden Age, Eden, the New Atlantis, or Plato's Republic were all preferable to quietistic acceptance of the myriad imperfections of the social, political, and religious establishments that he had encountered. Wordsworth preferred to bear those ills he had, rather than chance a flight to others he knew not of. Shelley, writing to Horace Smith less than two weeks before his death, states the opposite proposition in a defense of Byron's *Cain*:

It seems to me that things have now arrived at such a crisis as requires every man plainly to utter his sentiments on the inefficacy of the existing religious no less than political systems for restraining & guiding mankind.—Let us see the truth whatever that may be.—The destiny of man can scarcely be so degraded that he was born only to die—and if such be the case, delusions, especially the gross & preposterous ones of the existing religion, can scarcely be supposed to exalt it.—If every man said what he thought, it could not subsist a day. But all, more or less, subdue themselves to the element that surrounds them, & contribute to the evils they lament by the hypocrisy that springs from them.—[18]

III

The inheritance that Modernist poets received from the "high Romantics"

17. Shelley, *Letters*, ed. Frederick L. Jones (Oxford: Clarendon Press, 1964), 2:406–7.
18. Shelley, *Letters*, 2:442, with four corrections, one substantive ("religions" to "religious"), from the original manuscript, Keats-Shelley Memorial, Rome.

of the early nineteenth century consisted neither of a doctrinal "faith in the imagination" nor of any specific ideational content. For the whole Romantic experience declares that there is no single set of answers to life's deepest questions, but rather a pluralist plethora of questions and answers put forward at various times by the Romantics themselves, as well as a willingness to leave some questions ultimately unanswered.[19] But besides their ideological diversity, ranging from the intellectualized Academic Skepticism of Shelley and Byron's more natural Pyrrhonist Skepticism to the extreme faith in the power of human imagination advocated and celebrated at times by Keats, the Romantics also bequeathed temperamental disparities than can be traced among their Modernist heirs. Though ideologically T. S. Eliot and W. H. Auden would seem to be soul mates, each having found his way back into the fold of Christian orthodoxy, and though W. B. Yeats and Wallace Stevens exhibit affinities in their celebration of the human imagination and its power to transform natural chaos into meaningful art and order, these paired poets may be divided by their sensibilities into the "pastoral" vs. "Gothic" dichotomy that we have seen in the case of Wordsworth and Shelley. Auden accepts the limitations of the human condition:

> Lay your sleeping head, my love,
> Human on my faithless arm;
> . . . in my arms till break of day
> Let the living creature lie,
> Mortal, guilty, but to me
> The entirely beautiful.
> *   *   *
> Beauty, midnight, vision dies:
> Let the winds of dawn that blow
> Softly round your dreaming head
> Such a day of sweetness show
> Eye and knocking heart may bless,
> Find the mortal world enough . . . ,[20]

and he believes in the pastoral protection of universal powers:

> Make this night loveable
> Moon, and with eye single

19. L. J. Swingle and I explore the varieties of Skepticism during the period in *Romantic Inquiry,* a book now in its final stage of revision. [See Preface to Reiman, *Intervals of Inspiration* (1988).]

20. "Lullaby," in *Selected Poetry of W. H. Auden,* Chosen . . . by the Author (New York: Modern Library, 1958), pp. 27-28; Auden's poetry is quoted by permission of the publisher.

> Looking down from up there
> Bless me, One especial
> And friends everywhere.
>
> With a cloudless brightness
> Surround our absences;
> Innocent by our sleeps,
> Watched by great still spaces,
> White hills, glittering deeps.[21]

Eliot, on the other hand, is the poet of the unending quest, a magus who cannot be satisfied by earthly way-stations and whose heart is restless until it rests in the Absolute:

> This is the time of tension between dying and birth
> *   *   *   *   *   *
> Teach us to care and not to care
> Teach us to sit still
> Even among these rocks,
> Our peace in His will
> *   *   *
> Suffer me not to be separated
>
> And let my cry come unto Thee.[22]
>
> We returned to our places, these Kingdoms,
> But no longer at ease here, in the old dispensation,
> With an alien people clutching their gods.
> I should be glad of another death.[23]
>
> What we call the beginning is often the end
> And to make an end is to make a beginning
> The end is where we start from . . .
> *   *   *   *
> We shall not cease from exploration
> And the end of all our exploring
> Will be to arrive where we started
> And know the place for the first time.
> *   *   *   *
> And all shall be well and
> All manner of thing shall be well
> When the tongues of flame are in-folded

---

21. "Nocturne"; ibid., pp. 141–42.
22. "Ash Wednesday, 1930"; T. S. Eliot, *The Complete Poems and Plays, 1909–1950* (New York: Harcourt, Brace, 1958), pp. 66–67. Eliot's poetry is quoted by permission of the publisher.
23. "Journey of the Magi"; ibid., p. 69.

> Into the crowned knot of fire
> And the fire and the rose are one.[24]

William Butler Yeats's later poetry is so marked by his dissatisfaction with mortality, his outcry against "all the complexities of mire or blood,"[25] that to illustrate his Gothic sensibility might seem an act of supererogation. Yet, there are two kinds of Gothic sensibility—the optimistic and the pessimistic. One can feel that society and the forces of the universe are hostile and yet, like Byron's Manfred, defy them. An optimist of Gothic sensibility finds comfort in the strength of human powers and proclaims, with W. E. Henley's "Invictus," his "unconquerable soul." And Yeats, through most of his mature poetry, exhibits this brand of Gothic optimism. Whereas Eliot, whether representing J. Alfred Prufrock, displaying *The Waste Land* or "Journey of the Magi," or meditating in *Four Quartets*, always finds himself outside of the Promised Land, gazing across the Jordan, Yeats's poems suggest that he has answers to the dilemmas he faces. There *are* occasional shudders of doubt and suspicion that the power that created his "circus animals" might be gone and that he might be forced to "lie down where all the ladders start, / In the foul rag-and-bone shop of the heart."[26] But Yeats's overriding optimism emerges time and again from his late poems. If, in "The Second Coming," some "rough beast . . . / Slouches towards Bethlehem to be born," in a later poem, "The Gyres," he prophesies the return of a nobler order:

> Conduct and work grow coarse, and coarse the soul,
> What matter? Those that Rocky Face holds dear,
> Lovers of horses and of women, shall
> From marble of a broken sepulchre,
> Or dark betwixt the polecat and the owl,
> Or any rich, dark nothing disinter
> The workman, noble and saint, and all things run
> On that unfashionable gyre again.[27]

"Lapis Lazuli" celebrates the triumph of the indomitable human imagination, in spite of the fact that—or perhaps because—"all things fall," for "those that build them again are gay."[28]

24. "Little Gidding"; ibid., pp. 144–45.
25. "Byzantium"; *The Collected Poems of W. B. Yeats* (London: Macmillan, 1952), p. 281. Yeats's poetry is quoted by permission of the publisher.
26. Ibid., p. 392.
27. Ibid., pp. 210, 237.
28. Ibid., p. 339.

The Romantic Inheritance

Yeats is under no illusion that there are any pastors or shepherds in nature or society to help and guide the individual; on the contrary, he seems "to know / That everything outside us is / *Mad as the mist and snow*."[29] Wallace Stevens, in spite of the emphasis of his middle poems on the necessity of exercising the human imagination toward the creation of a supreme fiction, both began and ended his career with poems that leave no doubt that he differed from Yeats, not ideologically, but by virtue of his pastoral sensibility. In Stevens's first volume, *Harmonium* (1923), we find the Enlightenment view that man can accept the natural world and its laws as the basis of human value and identity. In the climax of "Sunday Morning," even death becomes a positive good because it is viewed as part of the natural cycle:

> Death is the mother of beauty, mystical,
> Within whose burning bosom we devise
> Our earthly mothers waiting, sleeplessly.
>
> Supple and turbulent, a ring of men
> Shall chant in orgy on a summer morn
> Their boisterous devotion to the sun,
> Not as a god, but as a god might be,
> Naked among them, like a savage source.
>   *   *   *   *   *
> They shall know well the heavenly fellowship
> Of men that perish and of summer morn.
> And whence they came and wither they shall go
> The dew upon their feet shall manifest.[30]

Other poems in *Harmonium* also seem to exhibit little genuine doubt or tension in the poet's attitude toward either the ideal or the mundane. In Auden's poems quoted above, the poet accepted the limited and mundane but viewed them as under the judgment of higher standards: "*Mortal, guilty, but to me / The entirely beautiful.*" But for Stevens in *Harmonium*, the *given* of "Sunday Morning" is the ideal:

> We live in an old chaos of the sun,

---

29. Ibid., p. 302.
30. "Sunday Morning"; *The Collected Poems of Wallace Stevens* (New York: Alfred A. Knopf, 1961), pp. 69-70. Though Stevens revised the collection entitled *Harmonium*, in later recensions adding and deleting poems, and though he once planned to give his *Collected Poems* the title *The Whole of Harmonium*, we can treat the poems in the section of *Collected Poems* (copyright 1954) entitled "Harmonium" as a unit reflecting the poet's final, revised text of the conception adumbrated in his first volume. Stevens's poetry is quoted by permission of the publisher.

> Or old dependency of day and night,
> Or island solitude, unsponsored, free,
> Of that wide water, inescapable.[31]

Or, as he says in "Peter Quince at the Clavier,"

> Beauty is momentary in the mind—
> The fitful tracing of a portal;
> But in the flesh it is immortal.
> The body dies; the body's beauty lives.
> So evenings die, in their green going,
> A wave, interminably flowing.
> So gardens die, their meek breath scenting
> The cowl of winter, done repenting.[32]

Nowhere in *Harmonium*, I believe, does the quest for unity with nature, identification with the *ding an sich* rather than Romantic symbolization of it, become more explicit than in the striking short poem entitled "Nuances of a Theme by Williams" in which Stevens, following a course set by William Carlos Williams, treats the morning star not as Lucifer, the Light Bringer—not as the soul of Adonais—but simply as the star, the thing itself.

> NUANCES OF A THEME BY WILLIAMS
> *It's a strange courage*
> *you give me, ancient star:*
>
> *Shine alone in the sunrise*
> *toward which you lend no part!*
>
> I
> Shine alone, shine nakedly, shine like bronze,
> that reflects neither my face nor any inner part
> of my being, shine like fire, that mirrors nothing.
>
> II
> Lend no part to any humanity that suffuses
> you in its own light.
> Be not chimera of morning,
> Half-man, half-star.
> Be not an intelligence,
> Like a widow's bird
> Or an old horse.[33]

31. Ibid., p. 70.
32. Ibid., pp. 91–92.
33. Ibid., p. 18. Note the rejections of specific Romantic poetic symbols: in line 3 ("fire, that mirrors nothing") of Shelley's *Adonais*, stanza 54; in line 7 ("Half-man, half-star") of *Adonais*, stanza 46; in line 9 ("widow's bird") of Shelley's lyric, "A widow bird sate mourning" (hitherto printed as part of "Charles the First"); and in line 10 ("an old horse") of Browning's "Childe Roland to the Dark Tower Came," stanzas 13–14.

Though Stevens in *Harmonium* demythologizes the world of the Romantics, he cannot, in the Modernist ideological milieu, see man as totally content with a world in which a star is just a star and a primrose is nothing more than a primrose. As he had half-stated, half-lamented in "Le Monocle de mon Oncle," "The honey of heaven may come or may not come, / But that of earth both comes and goes at once."[34] And in "Anatomy of Monotony" he had recognized that, even when the sun gives comfort and enlists the music of the spheres, natural man demands "still finer, more implacable chords" (as Keats looked forward to "a finer tone"). In *Ideas of Order*, Stevens strikes the fully Romantic note, and he himself articulates his new affinities. "Farewell to Florida" states the split between the harmonious natural world of the Florida Keys and the world of human society to which the poet must return and to which he *wills* to return. Stevens opposes a beautiful slavery to natural Necessity (symbolized in the snake that has once again shed its skin) to the jangle of human freedom, or at least the human *struggle* for freedom:

> To be free again, to return to the violent mind
> That is their mind, these men, and that will bind
> Me round, carry me, misty deck, carry me
> To the cold, go on, high ship, go on, plunge on.[35]

The discontinuity between what *is* and what *ought to be* reveals itself more and more sharply in successive poems of *Ideas of Order*, which sound a tone of skeptical *Weltschmertz* that seldom if ever intruded into *Harmonium*.

> Perhaps it's the lunch that we had
> Or the lunch that we should have had.
> But I am, in any case,
> A most inappropriate man
> In a most unpropitious place.[36]

In "Lions in Sweden" the poet questions whether to blame the human soul for requiring abstract values—"these lions, these majestic images"—or to blame man's dis-ease on the limited images themselves:

> If the fault is with the soul, the sovereigns
> Of the soul must likewise be at fault, and first.

34. Stevens, *Collected Poems*, p. 15.
35. Ibid., p. 118.
36. "Sailing after Lunch"; ibid., p. 120.

> If the fault is with the souvenirs, yet these
> Are the soul itself. And the whole of the soul, Swenson,
> As every man in Sweden will concede,
> Still hankers after lions, or, to shift,
> Still hankers after sovereign images.[37]

In "The Idea of Order at Key West," Stevens declares that the individual human imagination creates those ordered, sovereign images out of a nature that is not a naked god, walking among men in "heavenly fellowship," but a chaos of conflicting forces engaged in natural destruction that is ineluctably opposed to all human ideals and forms of order. Two realities are in conflict, but only one is relevant to human needs and human aspirations:

> The sea was not a mask. No more was she.
> *   *   *   *   *
> But it was she and not the sea we heard.
>
> For she was the maker of the song she sang.
> The ever-hooded, tragic-gestured sea
> Was merely a place by which she walked to sing.
> *   *   *   *   *   *
>   It was her voice that made
> The sky acutest at its vanishing.
> She measured to the hour its solitude.
> She was the single artificer of the world
> In which she sang.[38]

Stevens here articulates, in his highly individual voice, the extreme Romantic perspective that places the source of values and identity within the creative imagination rather than—as *Harmonium* asserts—within the sun or the maternal earth. But for Stevens, there is an ultimate reconciliation. And this willingness to be reconciled with the sun makes Stevens, in his old age, as he had been in *Harmonium*, a Wordsworthian rather than a Shelleyan poet. In "The Planet on the Table," Stevens writes:

> Ariel was glad he had written his poems.
> *   *   *   *   *
> His self and the sun were one
> And his poems, although makings of his self,
> Were no less makings of the sun.

37. Ibid., pp. 124–25.
38. Ibid., pp. 128–29.

> It was not important that they survive.
> What mattered was that they should bear
> Some lineament or character,
>
> Some affluence, if only half-perceived,
> In the poverty of their words,
> Of the planet of which they were part.[39]

In this and other very late poems such as "The River of Rivers in Connecticut" and "Not Ideas about the Thing but the Thing Itself," though Stevens no longer sees the sun as a god naked among men "like a savage source," he envisions man's imagination as a subordinate co-worker with the sun, the ultimate source of its creativity. Stevens in this and his other mature poems exemplifies the pastoral mode of Romantic sensibility in which both nature and society are fundamentally allied to the best workings of the human imagination. Though he sees a gap between the natural world and human ideals, he asserts that the imaginative goals that men add to the sum of natural creation derive support from such institutions as the Hartford Insurance Company and such natural processes as the seasonal cycle and death—factors that Shelley, Yeats, and Eliot saw as threatening the survival of humanistic values.

Long before a poet learns to reason or to intellectualize on such matters, long before he reads other poets and studies their works so that he can, if he chooses, "swerve" from the older poets' meanings, he has a positive or negative visceral reaction to the external world and his relationship with it. From these depths rise the "Gothic" and "pastoral" sensibilities that divide the realm of poetry—and life—between them.

39. "The Planet on the Table"; ibid., pp. 532-33.

Afterword

I

Common to the essays and reviews in this volume is a tendency to cut against the grain, to stand against the tide of majority opinion, to debunk current fads and fashions. Good fortune and the operation of this anti-establishment mind-set led me to study Percy Bysshe Shelley in 1958, when his stock was, perhaps, the lowest it has ever been in American academe. After having been battered earlier in the century by the New Humanists, by such leading writers as T. S. Eliot and Aldous Huxley, and by F. R. Leavis and his followers, Shelley's reputation had come under the direct fire of the academic New Critics in this country, newly installed in positions of national influence. Entire generations of students had gone from grammar school through graduate school without hearing a good word for Shelley or his poetry from any major critical voice (though many individual teachers and a few committed scholars—Frederick L. Pottle and Kenneth Neill Cameron among them—continued to make clear to others the central themes of Shelley's life and writings).

By the late 1950s, the academic establishment in a number of major universities had come so fully under the influence of those who considered Shelley a bad poet that, as Henri Peyre once told me, he (who had written and published his thesis on *Shelley et la France*) was warned not to mention Shelley's name when he came back to interview for a position at Yale. At the traditionalist College of Wooster, on the other hand, my teachers—especially Mary Rebecca Thayer, Frederick W. Moore, and Lowell W. Coolidge—represented a more balanced tradition of literary study that avoided such fashions and could accept Shelley (even though some of them remembered Walter E. Peck as the bad boy of their English department in the 1920s). At Illinois, Royal A. Gettmann's class in the Romantics was one of the four courses in which I was enrolled during the semester in which I took doctoral comprehensive examinations. After writing four four-hour exams on periods of our choice, we faced a two-hour oral exam, a half-hour of which was devoted to discussing a major work. At the time, I was planning to write under Royal Gettmann either on Keats and existentialism (an interest remaining from days as a Presbyterian pre-theological student and admirer of Kierkegaard), or on Conrad's fiction. Royal, a (critical) admirer of Leavis, with little respect for Shelley, knew that I tended to work dialectically, questioning the opinions of my teachers; so he gave me as my major work "The Triumph of Life," prepared to see whether I could convince him that Shelley's poetry was worth more attention than he had been giving it. I was amused, because the only reading assignment that I had failed to complete as an undergraduate at The College of Wooster was the reading of the last two acts of *Prometheus Unbound*. But once I began to dig into "The Triumph of Life," I found it filled with interest and challenges.

After the oral exam, I told Royal that I'd like to write my dissertation on "The Triumph." A few weeks later, Gwynne Blakemore Evans, another favorite teacher, asked if I had looked at the poem's textual situation; Neville Rogers then responded to my query that, though he knew of nothing in the manuscript of "The Triumph of Life" that would be helpful to me, nobody else had looked at it in detail, and I was welcome to study it. While I was engaged on the dissertation, Gwynne Evans asked me to review for *JEGP* Charles H. Taylor's Yale dissertation *The Early Collected Editions of Shelley's Poems,* work that taught me the evidential value of collation and forced me to learn more about the textual authorities of Shelley's poetry. In 1959 there appeared major books on Shelley by Zillman, Bloom, and Wasserman. I had, unbeknownst to me, begun riding a wave of interest in Shelley then gathering that has yet, I believe, to crest and break. By refusing to follow the established trend of my time, I found myself near the head of the next popular movement in academic scholarship and criticism.

The dissertation on Shelley's "The Triumph of Life" set out to make that final poem the focal point for a total understanding of Shelley's life, thought, and writings. I read not only every book and essay on Shelley in the Illinois Library, but also all additional ones in the bibliographies on Shelley that seemed likely to mention "The Triumph of Life" and that Interlibrary Loan could find for me, and I compiled for the dissertation (though later dropped from the book) a survey of the reputation of the poem and a variorum summary of the commentary on it, both scholarly and critical. Besides learning the rudiments of textual criticism by working through the textual authorities in an attempt to restore the poem's text to the state of Shelley's latest intention, I also tried to read all the major authors whom Shelley had read (especially those such as Rousseau, Dante, and Petrarch who were known to have influenced "The Triumph" directly). By limiting the scope of my dissertation, I was thus able to learn several different tools of the scholar's trade, while mastering the writings of one (relatively neglected) major English poet and part of the literary tradition he inherited.

In 1961, Cameron's first two volumes of *Shelley and his Circle* appeared, followed in 1964 by both Jones's edition of Shelley's *Letters* and Cameron's edition of *The Esdaile Notebook,* each making available new material—including a major cache of Shelley's juvenile poetry that revealed for the first time his slow development in the mastery of poetic techniques. These three publications also made something of a stir in the popular press—especially *The Esdaile Notebook,* published by Alfred A. Knopf. Shelley began to be talked about and read again by people outside the academy. This interest continued to develop with the student radicalism of the later 1960s and early 1970s.

As I studied the major books on Shelley, I realized that many of the best scholar-critics from the 1930s through the 1950s who had written a dissertation and, perhaps, one substantial book on Shelley had then moved on, many of them into American or Canadian literature: among these scholars were Floyd Stovall, Ellsworth Barnard, Carlos Baker, Richard Harter Fogle, Roy R. Male, C. E. Pulos, Milton Wilson, and Ross Woodman. For this reason, the writings of students of Shelley, rather than those of the poet himself, might justly be charged with immaturity. On the other hand, such scholar-critics as Kenneth Neill Cameron (who maintained his research on Shelley over an extended period of time) or Earl R. Wasserman (who turned to Shelley after mastering eighteenth-century poetry and Keats's works) were able to begin to comprehend and convey the essential complexity and sophistication of Shelley's thought and art. I vowed at the time I completed my dissertation to devote twenty years to the study of Shelley's life, thought, and art, in the hope of advancing the understanding of them beyond that achieved by those who worked on him just long enough to fulfill the requirements for the Ph.D. degree or for academic tenure.

It is questionable whether I could have completed as much useful work, or have enjoyed as successful an academic career, had I followed the trends of the times and written, instead, on Faulkner, Conrad, Keats, Donne, or G. M. Hopkins. Shelleyan studies of the early 1960s gave me access to something that I probably could not have enjoyed in working on any other major author in whom I was interested in 1958, even had I similarly mastered the available materials. The Bodleian Shelley manuscripts provided an unworked mass of notebooks and other drafts containing new information on most of Shelley's mature works. Once I had learned to find my way around in those manuscripts and in the microfilms of Lord Abinger's collection at Duke (where I had gone to teach partly because of the tradition in Shelleyan studies established there by Newman Ivey White), I became the logical person to succeed Cameron as editor of *Shelley and his Circle* at The Carl H. Pforzheimer Library, one of the two most ambitious programs of scholarly research and publication then underway on the English Romantic poets (the other being The Bollingen Coleridge, safely in the able hands of Kathleen Coburn).

It is not easy to translate my good fortune into a lesson for those now beginning careers in literary study, but I profited greatly from two pieces of advice given by teachers at Illinois about the choice of a dissertation topic: first, Robert W. Rogers told us to study a major author, both because there is far more opportunity for a novice scholar to publish on a major author than on a minor one and because work on minor figures takes more time to locate the basic materials—letters, biographical information, texts—that are usually already available for major figures. Second, Royal Gettmann warned us to limit our topics to a scope manageable within a reasonable time: to write on "Coleridge in the *Morning Post*," rather than "Coleridge in the Nineteenth Century"; that way, one might finish up a book for publication promptly without making it so superficial that it exposed one's limitations rather than showed off one's capabilities. My heart still goes out, years after I last saw him, to a colleague at the University of Wisconsin–Milwaukee, acknowledged by his peers to be one of the most brilliant and learned members of the English faculty there (and the one whom I joined in reading Dante's *Paradiso* in the original Italian during my year there), who failed to win a tenured appointment because he had not completed his dissertation (at Berkeley) on Milton's religious thought. I was also moved—though less with sorrow than irritation—when in 1984 and 1985 I reviewed dozens of dissertation-books on broadly defined theoretical topics that, to master fully, would have required deep knowledge and understanding of hundreds of literary works of different cultures and periods, only to find that a half-dozen novels or ten poems were about all that the novice scholars knew well enough to write on meaningfully. There is a proverb I find useful in life—"It is better to light one candle than to curse the darkness"; in reference to the launching of useful scholarly careers, this might be modified to a sentiment that Charles Lamb would approve: "It is better to light one candle than to set the house afire."

Having related the positive side of my experience, let me add a few words of caution to those who find themselves inclined to follow my example. The two things that did the most to insure my successful career were my choice of parents and the timing of my birth. Henry W. Reiman and Mildred A. Pearce Reiman not only provided me with the right genes (as my sister and daughter also testify), but they also prompted and fostered every intellectual interest I followed during my formative years. My first major research project was an attempt at home, when I was ten or eleven years old, to write a book entitled *The Lives of the World's Great Generals*. (I finished chapters, researched chiefly from my father's history textbooks, on Alexander the Great and Hannibal and was working on Julius Caesar when my attention wandered otherwise.) My year of birth, 1934, saw the lowest birthrate during the Great Depression; I finished my Ph.D. in 1960, when the children of the wartime baby boom began to reach the colleges. These facts of demography assured that there was always room for me in schools and a chance for rapid advancement in my chosen career. Such matters cannot be changed later in life. But one can avoid picking a career early in one's undergraduate years on the basis of its supposed chances for employment some five to ten years before the requisite training will be completed. Since the primary rewards of teaching and scholarship in the humanities are never monetary, nobody should enter the field who does not love the work and who is not willing to assume, that as with professional artists and performers, the majority will have to be content with their own personal pride in their work and occasional recognition from students and peers, rather than an appearance on "Lifestyles of the Rich and Famous."

II

In spite of the insecurities of the early stages of an academic career and the persistence of relatively low salaries for teacher-scholars in the humanities (especially in view of the long training and the superior intelligence required, if one is to make any mark in the field), I doubt that—once I had decided that I had no real vocation in the Presbyterian ministry—I could have done anything else. My upbringing had not prepared me either to say, "You're paying me well, so whatever you want me to do is fine," or to covet as the inscription on my gravestone, "He always drove a late-model Cadillac." The pedagogical urge is, in fact, so strong within me that I was moved to write this Afterword to demonstrate it; whatever this volume may fail to achieve, I have complete confidence in the success of this particular demonstration.

Harder to demonstrate, especially in a brief compass, is the fact that this pedagogical urge, as worked out through the practical, skeptical quality of the scholarly criticism that I advocate and practice, represents at the social level the strain of native American criticism that both Geoffrey Hartman and Harold Bloom have called for.[1] Like Bloom, I favor Emersonian roots

1. See Hartman, *Criticism in the Wilderness* (New Haven: Yale University Press, 1980), pp. 9–13, and Bloom's "Viewpoint" in *TLS* for 30 May 1980.

for a native American critical perspective, but I would also draw heavily on two of Emerson's disciples—Henry David Thoreau and Theodore Parker. Both these Yankees had Emerson's interest in first principles, to which each added a practical imperative; both demanded and demonstrated in their lives that ethereal knowledge and abstract principles should and can be embodied in practical action. Whereas Emerson called upon Americans to turn away from materialistic values and to support justice, Thoreau went to live in the woods and spent a night in Concord jail to actualize his similar principles. Theodore Parker, according to Henry Steele Commager, his biographer, went even farther in turning theory into action:

> Religion, philosophy and scholarship combined so harmoniously to require active participation in the affairs of society and of the nation that we may suspect it was not so much logic as temperament which led to a conclusion so inescapable. . . .
> In any event, Parker could no more keep out of the social and political battleground than he could the theological. He was by nature and temperament—and soon by habit—a controversialist, even a fighter; a champion of ideas and causes that were neglected and condemned, as of men and women who were neglected and condemned.[2]

In his oration entitled *The Position and Duties of the American Scholar* (1849), Parker defined the difference between American and European scholarship in terms of the relations between the scholar-teacher and the American audience:

> In America . . . there are no royal or patrician patrons, no plebian clients in literature, no immoveable aristocracy to withstand or even retard the new genius, talent, or skill of the scholar. There is no class organized, accredited, and confided in, to resist a new idea; only the unorganized inertia of mankind retards the circulation of thought and the march of mind. . . .
> Not much more is the scholar impeded by the ignorance of the people, not at all in respect to the substance of his thought. There is no danger that he will shoot over the heads of the people by thinking too high for the multitude. We have many authors below the market; scarce one above it. The people are continually looking for something better than our authors give. No American author has yet been too high for the comprehension of the people, and compelled to leave his writings "to posterity, after some centuries shall have passed by." *If he has thought with the thinkers, and has something to say, and can speak it in plain speech, he is sure to be widely understood.* There is no learned class to whom he may talk Latin or Sanscrit, and who will understand him if he write as ill as Immanuel Kant; . . . but there is an

---

2. *Theodore Parker: An Anthology*, ed. Henry Steele Commager (Boston: Beacon Press, 1960), pp. 4–5.

intelligent class of men who will hear a man if he has what is worth listening to, and says it plain. It will be understood and appreciated, and soon reduced to practice.[3]

Perhaps the chief objection that a large number of us have voiced to recent trends in literary theory is that the new lit. crit. does not respect or accept the level of comprehension of its chief and natural audience—students in America's (or Canada's or Britain's) colleges and universities. Instead, those importing Continental systems seemed to foster a narrow clique united through a capacity to "write as ill as Immanuel Kant"—as if to do so proved that they can *think* as well as Kant did. That correlation is by no means demonstrable. For those who suppose that it is, or who believe that clear writing in standard English somehow disqualifies the rest of us from their intellectual level, I can only accede in the words of Austen's Catherine Morland: "I cannot speak well enough to be unintelligible."

A vigorous home-grown American criticism does not, in my view, depend on creating an intelligentsia of the European variety or an elitist, self-proclaimed "interpretive community"; rather, it will derive its strength from a respect for the intelligence of the ordinary men and women who, first as boys and girls, come into the classrooms of English teachers in high schools, move on into colleges, and eventually form a literate public that, whether or not it rereads the classics in their original forms, will certainly encounter them and their derivations in films and in TV presentations of dramas, ballets, and operas that are now available to all American families in their living rooms.

Though some graduate professors in Ivy League schools may find this hard to believe, the brokers, medical technicians, and secretaries who ride the express bus with me from the Bronx to Manhattan each day read many good books and, when questioned about them, respond with interest and intelligence. I believe that if there were literary columns in weekly newsmagazines and major daily papers that discussed literary classics, just as there are reviews of current books, plays, and television programs, and if these were written at about the level to which the art and music critics for *Newsweek* and *Time* key their discussions of the classics in their fields, those columns would be widely read and would influence a far larger share of the population than is now reached by *New York Review* and the other periodicals aimed at an intellectual minority. John Ashbery (who as a poet has an audience just a fraction of the size of those who sought out the poems of

---

3. Ibid., pp. 185–86; italics added.

Pope, Byron, or Tennyson in their much smaller literate societies) communicated perfectly well with millions about equally difficult conceptions in his columns in *Newsweek* on painting exhibitions at major museums in the United States and Europe. There is no reason why, as the anniversaries of the births or deaths of major writers come along, or when major literary classics are republished, mass-circulation magazines and newspaper syndicates cannot enlist scholar-critics to write brief columns to help remind the public and update their information about the lives, thought, and art of the giants in their literary heritage. Each time a literary classic is revived as a drama on public television, the book is marketed successfully to thousands of new readers; why cannot the print media, which help promote movies and television through reviews, also promote good reading?

With an egalitarian faith in the ability of many (not *all*) Americans to read clearly written critical prose that does not depend upon a specialized technical vocabulary (read: jargon), we could begin to bring to literary criticism the kind of wide readership and vitality that it had in the work of Lionel Trilling, Edmund Wilson, and Lewis Mumford. Because such humanistic criticism concerns itself with vital questions of all kinds, as well as with vital language, it inevitably involves public issues as well as literary classics, as Edmund Wilson moved from the psychology of the governess in *The Turn of the Screw* to the significance of the Dead Sea Scrolls to the vagaries of the income tax to the accuracy of the language in a translation of Pushkin. The ideal American scholar lives both in the Ivory Tower (or in a remote cabin on Walden Pond) and in the practical world: she learns from the past and reflects on the great issues of the nature and future destiny of humankind; he takes to the streets as a participant in protest marches; or she writes letters to editors on social issues and knocks on doors on behalf of environmental concerns or political candidates.

American critics should not be amateurish in their attitudes toward their professional responsibilities, but they should avoid becoming a distinct, ingrown class of mandarins who talk only to one another and dissociate themselves from the flow of commerce, labor, politics, and science around them. Even those who believe that the essence of literature resides in language and signs, rather than in concepts and emotions, must heed the words of Emerson: "If it were only for a vocabulary, the scholar would be covetous of action. Life is our dictionary. . . . Colleges and books only copy the language which the field and the workyard made." Those of us nurtured on the ever-fresh touchstones of American democracy will wish to continue with Emerson's thought: "Character is higher than intellect. Thinking is the function. Living is the functionary."[4] To follow this dictum, American scholar-critics must both draw upon the life of the people around them (as did the great writers before them) and also bring into classrooms, town-meetings, juries, and all their human relationships, both personal and civic, the same kind of sympathy, probing curiosity, and questing for the truth-that-is-beyond-the-facts that they develop to achieve success in their specialized disciplines and professions. For the truth that we ultimately seek involves both beauty and goodness as well.

4. From "The American Scholar," in *Ralph Waldo Emerson: Essays and Lectures* (New York: The Library of America, 1983), pp. 61–62.

Index

This Index cites not only all significant references, from the Preface through the Afterword, to both earlier and modern people, places, publications, and institutions that are named or whose works are quoted, but also some more oblique allusions to, or echoes of, writers and works not identified in the text. The entry for each writer who receives substantial attention—Robert Browning (RB), Lord Byron (LB), Samuel Taylor Coleridge (STC), John Keats (JK), Charles Lamb (CL), Percy Bysshe Shelley (PBS), and William Wordsworth (WW)—is subdivided into entries on his life and ideas and his works, insofar as the book treats these substantively. The names of closely associated writers are abbreviated in some index entries as follows: Leigh Hunt (LH), Mary W. Shelley (MWS), and Robert Southey (RS). References to relationships between writers and their respective friends and relatives usually appear only once, under the heading with the smaller number of references. Thus interactions between Dorothy and William Wordsworth appear only in Dorothy's entry; relations between Hazlitt and Coleridge are indexed under "Hazlitt, and STC."

There is no section on "editing and editorial theory," a rubric that I consider too broad to be very useful. Instead, various special topics that might be considered subdivisions of that broad one (e.g., "authorial intention" and "copy-text"), along with related subjects, such as "manuscripts," are marked with asterisks to enable the reader interested in these topics to identify and locate easily the various headings under which they are indexed.

Abinger, James Richard Scarlett, 8th Baron: his MS collection, 175, 301, 304, 306, 307, 318, 370
Abrams, M(eyer) H., 11, 12, 109, 115, 127, 147, 151, 170, 227, 321
*"Accidentals" (orthography and punctuation), 25, 35, 37, 38, 39, 44, 60-64, 73-74, 96, 101, 105, 136, 178; poets adjust to signal pronunciation and prosody, 144-45; regularizing of, 61-62
Addington, Henry, 78
Addison, Joseph, 107
Adelphi University, 344
Aeschylus, 351
"Affective fallacy," 8
Ahrimanes, 281
Aiken, John, 236
Albee, Edward, 276
Alberoni, Giulio, 66
Alcibiades, 257
Alcuin, 174
Alexander the Great, 372
Alexander I, Czar, 75
Allott, Miriam, 127n
Altick, Richard D., 278
Alumni Cantabridgiensis, 269
American Council of Learned Societies (ACLS), 275
Ammons, A(rchie) R., 2, 11

*Annotation of facts, 27, 73, 136-37, 142, 150-51
Annual Register, 73, 216, 226, 245, 263
The Anti-Jacobin, 71, 78
Arber, Edward, 173-74 & n
Archimedes, 228
Ariosto, Ludovico, 102
Aristotle, Aristotelian, 66, 70, 261, 269, 346
Armour, Richard W., 114
Arnold, Matthew, 87, 346
Ascham, John, 50, 51
Ashbery, John, 374-75
Ashley Collection, British Lib., 45, 49
Ashton, Thomas L., 115
Association for Documentary Editing (ADE), 124n
The Athenæum, 116
*Attribution of anonymous writing, 71, 74
Auden, W. H., 186, 345, 346, 360, 361, 363; "In Memory of W. B. Yeats," 79; "Lullaby," 360; "Nocturne," 360-61
*Audiences for scholarly criticism, 20, 135, 169, 373-75
Auerbach, Erich, 338-39, 340
Austen, Jane, 33, 97, 237, 250, 352; *First Impressions*, 237; *Pride and Prejudice*, 237; *Northanger Abbey*, 374
*Authorial intention, 1, 25, 42-43, 44, 93, 105-6, 126, 135-37, 148, 170, 179-80; limits

editors' discretion, 146, 153
Aylesbury, T. B. Brudenell, Earl of, 222

Bacon, Sir Francis, 346; *Harmony of the Essays. etc. of,* 173–74 & n
Baender, Paul, 102
Baird, John D., 18
Baker, Carlos, 281, 370
Bannister, John (actor), 259
Barnard, Ellsworth, 370
Barnard, John, 127 & n
Bate, W(alter) Jackson, 11, 79–84, 109, 115
Bateson, F. W., 127 & n, 185–88, 190
Baum, L. Frank, 359
Baxter, William Thomas, 271
Beattie, James, 348
Beaumont, Sir George, 77; Lady B., 151
Beaupuy, Michel (Michael), 229, 234, 357
Bedford, Francis Russell, 5th Duke of, and forebears, 264, 265, 266, 269
Bell, Dr. John, 303
Bell, Quentin, 192
Benedict, John, 127 & n, 151
Bennett, Betty T., 10n, 185, 355
Bentham, Jeremy, 261
Bentley, G. E., Jr., 117, 128, 165
Bentley, Samuel & Richard, 30
Beowulf, 248, 337
Berkeley, George, Bishop of Cloyne, 79
Beta or Betta (PBS's servant), 303
Betz, Paul F., 131, 147–51
Bevington, Merle & Helen, 249
Bialostosky, Don H., 217
Bible, 174–75, 325; Old Testament, editions of, 174–75, 187, 325; Vulgate Psalms, history of, 174–75; New Testament, 2, 257
Bibliographical Society (U.K.), 97n
Bixby, W. K., 92
Blackwood's Edinburgh Magazine, 21, 77, 114
Blake, William, 24, 33, 35, 36n, 86, 90n, 107, 110, 118–19, 121, 165, 185; his religious faith, 324; Works: editions of, *Book of Thel,* 115; *Complete Poems of,* 123n, 127n, 129; *Notebook of,* 121n; poems, 117, 121n
Bland, Maria, 259
Block, Haskell M., 339
Bloom, Harold, 120, 321–23, 325–26, 344, 347, 369, 372; anxiety/influence, 109
Blunden, Edmund, 278
Bodleian Library, Oxford, 5, 47, 54, 260, 280, 283; Bodleian Shelley MSS, 122, 294n, 370 & *other entries under* PBS
The Bodleian Shelley Manuscripts, 4, 6 & n, 173, 292
Bogen, Nancy, 115
Bolles, Mr., 90
Bolling, Congressman Richard E., 275

Bond, William H., 114
Boone, Daniel, 342
Booth, Bradford, 114
Booth, Wayne C., 148
Boston University, 344
Bourne, Vincent, 46
Bowers, Fredson T., 17, 18, 26, 30, 35, 36, 38n, 59, 60, 85, 86, 97–104, 106, 119, 123, 124; and "scientific" "system," 98; defines textual criticism, 97–98; edits American authors, 99, 103, 175; his disciples, 106; on descriptive bibliography, 98; reactions to, 98–102
Boyce, Benjamin, 249
Brady, Kristan, 171n
Branch, Watson, 103–4
Brett-Smith, H. F. B., 116 & n
Brinkley, Florence F., 249
British Library (Museum), 45, 58, 162
Brontë, Emily, 192
Brooks, Cleanth, 249
Brooks, John, 50, 51
Brougham, Henry, 255, 261
Brown, Charles Armitage, 43, 114, 115
Browne, Sir Thomas, 257
Browne, Wade, Southey's letter to, 151
Browning, Elizabeth Barrett, 56
Browning, Robert (RB): 55–68, 342, 346, 347; and "accidentals," 60, 61–62, 63; editing of, 55–68, 100; his letters, 56, 60; "house styling" and, 62; marks proofs, 63–64; rewrites to correct pronunciation, 63; witnesses to his texts: first editions, 62; manuscripts, 55, 56, 57, 58, 62, 63; proofsheets, 55, 56, 58, 63; revised copies, 58, 59–60; RB's collective editions: 1849, 60, 63; 1863, 60, 63; 1868, 60, 63, 67; 1888–1889, 59–60, 64, RB corrects errors in, 59–60, 64; 1889, 59, 64;

textual witnesses sold, 56, 58; modern editions: Ohio Browning, 55–68; "accidentals" in, 55, 60–64; annotations, 64, 66; collations, 64, 66; copy-text, 55, 57, 59–61; emendation of copy-text, 60; gathering of materials for, 57; limitations of, 56, 57, 67; suggested improvements for, 63, 67;

Oxford English Texts, 56; Yale English Poets, 56

—**Works**: *Balaustion's Adventure,* 61; *Bells and Pomegranates,* 58; *A Blot in the 'Scutcheon,* 57n, 61; "A Dream of Arcady," 58; "Cavalier Tunes," 57; "Childe Roland to the Dark Tower Came," 364n; *Colombe's Birthday,* 57n, 58; "Count Gismond," 63; "Cristina and Monaldeschi," 63–64; *Dramatic Lyrics,* 57, 57n; *Dramatic Romances and Lyrics,* 57n; *Dramatis Personae,* 58;

Essay on Chatterton, 57n; *Ferishtah's Fancies*, 58; *Jocoseria*, 58, 61, 63-64; *King Victor and King Charles*, 57n, 62, 63, 65, 68; *La Saisiaz and The Two Poets of Croisic*, 58; *Luria*, 57n; *Men and Women*, 64; "A Miniature" (attribution), 58; *Paracelsus*, 58; *Pippa Passes*, 57n; *Red Cotton Night-Cap Country*, 58; *The Return of the Druses*, 57n, 61, 65; *Sordello*, 58, 64; "Stanzas," 58; *Strafford*, 58

Browning Institute Essays, 59
Brownstein, Rachel Mayer, 192
Brown University Library, corrected copy of RB's *Poetical Works*, 59-60
Bryan, William Jennings, 76
Buber, Martin, 322, 323
Budworth, Joseph (later Palmer), 218, 219, 220, 231, 244
Buell, Lawrence, 82
Bulletin of the New York Public Library (BNYPL), 119, 122; *later BRH*, 122
Burke, Edmund, 266, 269
Burney, Sarah Payne ("Mrs. Battle"), 252-56
Burns, Robert, 226, 227, 236
Burton, Mary E., 193, 206
Burton, Robert, 333
Bush, Douglas, 126
Butler, James, 131
Butter, Peter, 293
Byng, Admiral George, 66
Byron, Augusta (*later* Leigh, LB's half-sister), 201
Byron, [Clara] Allegra (LB's natural daughter), 302
Byron, George Gordon Byron, 6th Baron (LB), 11, 13, 19, 20, 89, 91, 110, 116, 122, 128, 145, 156-66, 264, 269, 335-43, 346, 351, 375; and Christianity, 341; and French Revolution, 342; and Lake poets, 341; and Pope, 341; and "primary" epic, 338; and PBS, 281, 294, 302, 348; and WW, 201; as fourth great epic poet, 336; as scion of feudal aristocracy, 341; editions of, 86, 91, 129; *Byron's Letters and Journals*, 91, 116, 156, 157, 161; *Complete Poetical Works* (OET), ed. McGann, 115, 152, 156-66, annotation in, 163-64; arrangement problems, 161; copy-texts, 159-60, 162; criteria for textual relevance, 159; difficulty of task, 159; editorial principles, 159-60; emendations, 160-62; gathering of evidence, 160-61; improvements in later volumes, 158; introduction, 163; orthography & punctuation, 160; price, 165; reviews of, 158, 161; text & collations, 161-62; use of photocopies for, 163; *Complete Works*, ed. E. H. Coleridge & R. E. Prothero, 72; *Don Juan* (2), 126, 127n; *Hebrew Melodies*, ed. Ashton, 115; *Manuscripts of the Younger Romantics*, 4, 6n, 173; *Variorum Don Juan*, 342; his literary preeminence, 159; his political views, 117-18, 216; his religious training, 341; his reverent humanism, 341; his ship, the *Bolivar*, 309; his Skepticism, 324, 341, 360; his use of sate, 36; review by, 121; textual evidence for his works, 124

—**Works, Letters and Prose**: letters & their expanded readership, 159

—**Works, Poetry**: "Address, Spoken at the opening of Drury-lane Theatre," 162; *Beppo*, 156; *Cain*, 351, 359; *Childe Harold's Pilgrimage*, 164; *The Curse of Minerva*, 164; *Don Juan*, 165, 334, 335, 337, 340-42; a bridge from Enlightenment to Existentialism, 341; as Skeptical epic, 346; language of, 338; narrative method in, 338-41; relation to "primary" and "secondary" epics, 334-38; retardation of action in, 340; Cantos III-V, 339; "The Isles of Greece," 339;
English Bards and Scotch Reviewers, 164, its Preface and Postscript, 162; *Manfred*, 362; *Marino Faliero*, 158, 338; *Ode to Napoleon Buonaparte*, 164; *Poems, Original and Translated*, 162; "To the Duke of D[orset]," 162
Byron's circle, 345

Cacciatore, Vera, 277
Cadell, Robert, 86
Caesar, Julius, 372
Caine, Michael, 244
Calderón de la Barca, Pedro, 311, 351
Calvert, Raisley, 228, 357
Camden, Carroll, 323
Cameron, Bess, 261
Cameron, Kenneth Neill, 11, 18, 19n, 20, 23, 41, 45, 52, 53, 116, 120, 123, 185, 260, 261, 262, 264, 265, 269, 290, 291, 310, 344, 348n, 368, 370, 371
Camoëns, Luis de, 337
Campbell, J. Dykes, 47, 59, 60
Canning, George, 75, 78, 255
Capital punishment, 239
Carey, Frederick, 277, 281n
Carlisle, Nicholas, 236
Carlyle, Thomas, 115; *Latter-Day Pamphlets*, edition of, 179 & n; & Jane W., 115
Carrington, Edward, 246
Carter, John, 91 & n, 94n
Cater, Douglas, 275
Catherine the Great, Empress, 342, 354
Cavanagh, John, 255
Censorship of texts, 177, 179

380 Index

Center for Editions of American Authors (CEAA), 62, 99, 100, 102, 104, 124n, 130, 144; *Statement of Editorial Principles*, 102, 123n
Center for Scholarly Editions (*later* MLA Committee on Scholarly Editions; CSE), 1, 100, 123n, 124n, 130-47, 148; "Guiding Questions," 135, 136, 144, 147; "Introductory Statement," 130; value of pre-publication review, 158
Chapman, George, 352
Chapman, R. W., 33, 97, 112
Character, higher than intellect, 376
Charlemagne, Emperor, 174
Charles Lamb Bulletin, 251
Chaucer, Geoffrey, 2, 248
Chernaik, Judith, 30
Chicago, University of, 17
Christensen, Jerome C., 82
Christian II, King of Denmark, 53
Christianity, 21, 107, 346, 353, 360
"Christiern." *See* Christian II
Christ's Hospital, 36n
Churchill, W. A., 137
City University of New York (CUNY), 335
Clairmont, (Mary Jane) Claire, 280, 302, 303, 307; her journals, 20, 281
Clare, John, 35, 36n
Clark, David Lee, 116
Clark, Kenneth, Lord, 183, 187
Clarkson, Catherine, 211, 213
Classical-Christian world view, 353-54
Clement VIII, Pope, 174 & n
Cleveland, John Wheeler, 24
Clifford, James, 110
Clubbe, John, 115
Cobbett, William, 71, 79, 255, 263
Coburn, Kathleen, 11, 19, 70, 72, 80, 116 & n, 120, 190, 237, 371
Colburn, Henry, 246
Coleridge, E(rnest) H(artley), 72, 159, 160, 161, 162
Coleridge, Henry Nelson (STC's nephew & son-in-law), 83, 86
Coleridge, John Taylor, 151
Coleridge, Samuel Taylor (STC), 13, 52, 125, 145, 149, 222, 225, 226, 228, 243, 261, 322, 341; and Beauty of Buttermere, 218, 220, 221, 231, 236, 237; and capital punishment, 239; and "clerisy," 77; and German thought, 81-82; and Hatfield, 220, 221, 226, 236-37, 238, 239, 240, 243, 246; and Sara Hutchinson, 190; and Sterne's *Tristram Shandy*, 79; and G. Washington, 119, 120; and Wedgwood Fund, 119; and Dorothy Wordsworth, 192, 200; and WW, 82, 119, 133, 144, 190, 203, 205, 213, 225, 228, 229, 231, 236, 356, their views on love, 205, touring together, 203, 205; as book-borrower, 257; as Grub-Street journalist, 76-77; as "Silas Tomkyn Comberbatch," 256; as "trimmer," 71, 76-78; at Carlisle, 242; at Keswick, 225; collaborative works, 71; editions of, 86, 110, 129; Bollingen Coleridge, 5, 69-84, 115, 119, 121, 165, 171 & n, 371; its sympathy for STC, 70, 81; editions by Henry N. & Sara C., 78, 83;

his ethical sensitivity, 243; his great achievements, 79; his orthography, 144-45; his plagiarisms, 81-82; his political opinions, 263; his psychological problems, 214; his prose style, 255; his religious views, 324; his search for a profession, 76-77; his view of love, 205; in Malta, 238; letters by, 72, 80, 142, to H. C. Robinson, 205; on economics & society, 74-76; on property & the vote, 75; on reviewers, 79-80; reviews by, 121; use of "sate" for "sat," 36
—**Works, Poetry**: *Christabel*, 133; "Dejection: An Ode," 125, 258; "Frost at Midnight," 140; *Kubla Khan*, 312; "Love," 144; *The Rime of the Ancient Mariner*, 172
—**Works, Prose**: *Biographia Literaria*, 217; ed. Engell & Bate, 70, 79-84, plagiarisms, 79, prose style, rhetoric, 79, 82, Shandean tone of, 70, 79, structure of, 217; *Courier*, contributions to, 71, 74, 78, 119, 123n; *Essays on His Times*, 69-79, 119, 121, 122, 216, 260; *The Friend*, 71, 171-72 & n, 358; lectures, 71; marginalia, 80; *Morning Post*, contributions to, 71, 74, 75, 119, 123n, 220-21, 237, as dissertation topic, 371; "The Fraudulent Marriage," 221; "Keswick Imposter," 221, 237; "Narrative of What Is at Present Known . . . ," 221; "Once a Jacobin Always a Jacobin," 75; "On the French Constitution," 75; "Romantic Marriage," 220, 221; *Notebooks*, 72, 80, 190, 237 & n, 238, 239
Coleridge, Sara (STC's daughter), 78, 86
Coley, Betty A., 56
*Collating texts, recording variants, 38, 44, 45, 83, 95, 113, 119, 122, 143, 165, 170, 177; sigla for, 139
College English, 7-8, 291
Collins, Rowland L., 55, 57
Collins, Thomas J., 55, 56
Colmer, John, 72, 74
Columbia University, 13, 26, 335
Comates, 228
Commager, Henry Steele, 373
*Compositors. *See* Printers
Conrad, Joseph, 274, 368, 370

Constant, Benjamin, 78
*"Contamination," critical & scholarly, 11; textual, 43, 125
Contextual scholarship, 7
Cook, Davidson, 47
Cooke, Michael G., 82
Coolidge, Lowell W., vii, 368
Copernicus, Nicholas, 3, 345
*Copy-text, theory of, 33, 35, 42, 96–106; practical applications, 31, 33, 39, 82–84, 113, 120; use of photofacsimiles as, 178
Cornell University Press, 130, 143, 171n; Cornell Wordsworth, 5, 115, 130–51, 165, 170, 171n; Introduction, 143; Cornell Yeats, 171n
Corn Laws, 261, 263
Courier, The. See STC, Works, Prose
Courtney, Winifred F., 251
Cowie, Alexander, 275
Cowper, William, 2, 152
Crane, Stephen, 100, 103
*Critical editions, 4, 39, 43, 60, 69–70, 105–6, 160; vs. diplomatic versions, 105, 119, 167, 169–80
Criticism, defined in relation to scholarship, 8–11
Croesus, 259
Crosby, Travis L., 263
Crump, John Gregory, 237, 238
Cullen, Patrick, 352n
Cumberland, Prince Ernest Augustus, Duke of, 222
Cunningham, Allan, 227
Curran, Stuart, 30, 110, 123n, 290
Curtis, Jared, 217

Daily Illini, 321
Daniel, Samuel, 257
Dante Alighieri, 107, 310, 320, 336, 339, 342, 351, 357n, 369; *Commedia*, 337; *Inferno*, 300; *Paradiso*, 371; *La Vita Nuova*, 356–57
Darbishire, Helen, 65, 96, 116, 133, 187, 193, 218
D'arcy, Miss, 237
Darlington, Beth, 130, 142–47, 185, 195n
Darwin, Charles, 337
Darwin, Erasmus, 52
Dasant, A. I., 265
*Dating letters, methods of, 21; postmarks, 20; post days, 20
Davis, Robert Gorham, 290
Davis, Tom, 104
Day, Aidan, 6n
Day, Fred Holland, 114
Dead Sea Scrolls, 375
De Almeida, Hermione, 335
De Beer, Sir Gavin, 19n

Deconstructionism, 12
"Definitive" editions, 65, 71–73, 105, 108, 152, 161, 165, 177, 179
Demosthenes, 317, 318, 319
De Quincey, Thomas, 190, 192, 225, 240, 242; and Beauty of Buttermere, 218, 236, 239, 240, 242, 243; and STC, 236–37, 239, 242–43, 244, 246; and Hatfield, 241–43; and Southey, 244; and WW, 239, 242, 244; his diary, 240
De Salvo, Louise, 123n
Descartes, René, 229, 346; Cartesian, 258, 346
De Selincourt, Ernest, 94, 96, 116, 117, 126, 133, 134, 148, 151, 165, 170, 186, 193, 197, 200, 207n, 210, 218, 246
Dickens, Charles, 245
Dickinson, Emily, 352
Dictionary of National Biography, 66, 131, 219, 226, 263
*Diplomatic texts, versions, 39, 105n, 120n, 172
Dodds, Dr. William, 238
Domenico (PBS's servant), 303
Donne, John, 370
Doubleday (publisher), 129
Douglas, Wallace W., 186n
Dove Cottage Library, 193
Dowden, Edward, 47, 52, 53, 90n, 278
Drayton, Michael, 139
Drummond, Sir William, 346
Dryden, John, 87
Du Bois, Edward, 114
Duke University, 17, 248–49, 275, 276, 344, 370
Dunbabin, J. P. D., 263
Dunbar, Clement, 114n
Dworzan (Reiman), Hélène, viii, 217

Eagleton, Terry, 262, 274
East India Company, 259, 273n
Eaton, Horace A., 240
Eaves, Morris, 85, 131
Echeruo, Michael J. C., 262
Eclectic Review, 23–24n
Edinburgh Review, 23n, 255
Editing. See Annotation; Authorial intention; Bibliographical analysis; Collations; Copy-text; Critical editions; "Definitive" editions; Diplomatic texts; Emendation; Manuscripts; Textual criticism; Versioning, etc.
*Editorial theory, 85; vs. practice, 180
*"Editors" vs. "transcribers," 46
Einstein, Albert, 3
"Eliot, George," 306
Eliot, T(homas) S(tearns), 324, 342, 345, 346, 360–62, 367; *Ash Wednesday*, 361; *Four Quar-*

tets, 342, "Burnt Norton," 258, "Little Gidding," 362; "Journey of the Magi," 361–62; *The Love Song of J. Alfred Prufrock*, 362; *The Waste Land*, 274, 342, 362
Elizabethan, Renaissance literature, editing of, 35, 96–97, 98, 107, 113, 114, 124, 173–74
Ellegard, Alvar, 74
Elwin, Malcolm, 192
*Emendation, 35, 38, 45, 48, 63, 87–89, 112, 123, 160, 161–62, 170, 178; conjectural, 50–51, 93–94, 112; silent, 123, 152
Emerson, Ralph Waldo, 100, 372–73, 375–76
Empedocles, 228
Encyclopaedia Britannica, 150 & n, 164
Engell, James, 79–84
Engels, Friedrich, 261
English Language Notes (*ELN*), 278
Enlightenment thought, 337, 341, 342, 349, 353, 354, 358, 363
Epics, primary & secondary, 337–38, 340
Epicureans, Epicureanism, 325
Epistemology, Romantic, 346
Erdman, David V., 11, 19, 35, 41, 85, 86, 102n, 109–10, 117–23, 124n, 127n, 131, 165, 216, 221, 222, 223, 224, 234, 237, 269, 323, 344; and anonymous journalism, 120–21; and editorial theory, 120, 122, 123n; edits & annotates STC's *Essays on His Times*, 69–84, 121; emends punctuation of, 73–74; establishes canon for, 73, 74; his annotation of, 74; his biographical & historical interests, 117, 118–19; his career & Cold War, 118; his expertise with MSS, 122; his intellectual curiosity, 121; his sense of scholarly community, 110; his work, on Blake, 117, 118–19, 120–21; on LB, 117–18, 121–22; on J. Oswald, 121 & n
Erdman, Virginia B., 117, 119
Errata lists, 43, 122
Eton, 36n
Euripides, 94, 208
Evans, Gwynne Blakemore, vii, 17, 114, 115, 369
The Examiner, 53, 255
Existentialism, 341
Explication & scholarship, 8, 10

*Facsimile reprints, 61n, 74, 141, 170, 176, 179
Faulkner, William, 370
Fell, Dr., 222
Fenwick, Isabella, 203, 208, 209
Feoli, 280, 281
Ferguson, Frances C., 201
Fersen, Countess Olga, & Casa Fersen ("Cucchi Academy"), 277
Feudal system, 264

Fielding, Henry, 273; *Shamela*, 245; *Les Filigranes*, 137
Fischer, Doucet Devin, viii, 19n, 156, 185, 342
Fish, Stanley E., 250, 374
Fitch, Raymond, 57n
Fitzgerald, William Thomas, 163–64
Flaxman, John, 118n
Fleay, Frederick Gard, and "schoolmaster editing," 18, 88–89 & n, 112; influence of classical studies on, 93
Flexner, Eleanor, 19n
Foakes, R. A., 217
Fogel, Ephim G., 119n
Fogle, Richard Harter, 370
Fogle, Stephen F., 172
Ford, Newell F., 327
Ford, Sir Richard, 222, 224
Formal analysis, 250
Forman, Harry Buxton, 37, 46, 48, 49, 50, 51, 53, 89, 91–93, 95, 99, 111–12, 165, 283, 308; forges rare books, 92; his book collections, 92 & n; HFB vs. W. M. Rossetti, 111–12
Foster, Stephen Collins, 273
*Four Ages of Editing, 86–108, 111; Golden Age (collecting & disseminating poetry), 86–87, 111; Silver Age (polishing & "improving" it), 87–91, 111; Brazen Age (scientific editing), 91–100, 103–4, 106, 107, 111; Iron Age (pragmatic editing), 100–103, 104–8, 111; Ages of Editing & Romantics, 107
Fox, Charles James, 75, 78; Foxite Whigs, 265, 266
Foxon, David F., 31n
France, French society, 266; French Revolution, 261, 266, 342, Reign of Terror, 358, September Massacres, 358; French Wars, 266
Frank, Robert D., 251
Franzoni, F. A., 280
Freehafer, John, 102
Freeman, Arthur, 276
Frere, John Hookham, 77, 78
Freud, Sigmund, Freudian thought, 3, 337
Friedman, Michael H., 233
Frost, Robert, 259, 352
Fruman, Norman, 185
Frye, Northrop, 109, 119, 321

Gabler, Hans Walter, 176n
Galignani brothers, 159
Gamaliel, 2
Garland Publishing, 6n, 173, 176n, 292
Garnett, David, 272
Garnett, Richard, 45, 47, 90n, 296
Garnett, R(obert) S., 47n, 90n

Index 383

Garrick, David, 163
Garrod, H. W., 95–96, 116, 117
Gaskell, Philip, 59, 101–2
Gay, John, 311
*Genetic edition vs. critical edition, 134
Gentleman's Magazine, 219, 220
George III, King of England, 222
German Romanticism, Idealism, 341
Gettmann, Royal A., vii, 11, 13, 17, 115, 172, 249, 368–69, 371
Gibaldi, Joseph, 119n
Gibbet, its use in England, 137
Gibbs, Jane (streetwalker), 238
Gibson, William M., 175 & n
Gifford, William, 78n, 265
Gilbert, Allan H. & Mary Moss, 276
Gilchrist, Anne, 86, 90n
Gilchrist, Herbert, 90
Gill, Stephen, 130, 132–40, 141–42, 143, 145, 146, 147, 170, 227
Gisborne, John, 116, 294, 307, 311, 312, 316, 317, 319, 358–59
Gisborne, Maria James Reveley, 24, 116, 294, 301, 302, 303, 307
Gittings, Robert, 185
Godwin, Mary Jane, 302, 307
Godwin, William, 19, 20, 52, 115, 271, 302, 307, 318; *Enquiry concerning Political Justice*, 52
Goethe, Johann Wolfgang von, 337, 338, 339, 340, 346, 349, 351; *Faust*, 311, 342, 351, 358
Goldberg, M. K., 179n
Goldsmith, Oliver, 273
Goldwater, Barry, 261
Gothic sensibility, 345, 352 & n, 367; defined, 351; two types, 362
Gotshalk, D. W., 249
Gottesman, Ronald, 100
Gray, Thomas, "Elegy . . . ," 218
Greek and Latin poetry, 323
Greek Anthology, 46
Greek tragedy, 351
Green, David Bonnell, 114
Greetham, David C., viii, 85, 86
Greg, Walter W., 17, 26, 33, 35, 85, 97–106, 114, 119, 123, 124, 160; on copy-text & emendation, 42, 102, 104–6, 176; on substantives & accidentals, 60, 101
Gregynog Shelley Conference, 291
Grenville, William Wyndham, Baron, 222
Griggs, Earl Leslie, 72
Grolier Club Library, 58
Grosart, A. B., 133
Grosvenor, Richard, 1st Earl, 265
Grylls, R. Glynn. *See* Mander, Rosalie
Guatamotzin (Aztec ruler), 308
Guggenheim Memorial Foundation, John Simon, 117n, 118, 121
Guiney, Louise I., 114
Gutenberg, Johann, 168

Hagstrum, Jean H., 185
Hannibal, 372
Hansard, Thomas C., 31n
Hardinge (Harding), Judge George, 221
Hardt, Ulrich H., 179n
Harington, James, 102
Harkness, Bruce, 17
Harrison, James, 31n
Harrison, Richard, 245
Harrow, 36n
Hartford Insurance Company, 367
Hartley, David, 78
Hartley, Robert A., 114n
Hartman, Geoffrey H., 250, 323, 355 & n, 372 & n
Harvard University: "Harvard School" of editing, 17, 26, 84, 112–16; Houghton Library, 5, 38; Harvard University Press, 116, 129
Hatfield, John, 216, 220–26, 235, 237–46
Haven, Richard D., 251, 252
Hawthorne, Nathaniel, 99, 100, 101, 103
Hay, Douglas, 263
Hay, Louis, 176n
Hayden, John O., 115, 127n
Haydon, Benjamin Robert, 53, 114, 115
Hayter, Alethea, 188
Hazen, Allen, 26
Hazlitt, W. Carew, 172
Hazlitt, William, 74, 79, 251, 255; and STC, 71, 78–79, 82, 255, 322; and WW, 255; letters to Patmore, 172; "Death of John Cavanagh," 255; "Indian Jugglers," 255; *Liber Amoris*, 172; "My First Acquaintance with Poets," 79; "On Going a Journey," 79; *The Spirit of the Age*, 78–79; *Table-Talk*, 255
Heine, Heinrich, 176
Hemingway, Ernest, 186, 256
Heninger, S. K., Jr., 17, 312
Henley, W. E., 362
Henry VIII, King of England, 269
Herzfeld, Ricki B., 185
Hexapla, 174
Hill, Thomas, 114
Hillis, F. W., 323
Hindu thought, 281
Hinman, Charlton, Hinman collator, 38n, 96
Hirsch, E. D(onald), 315; & Polly, 275
Historical studies, 21; vanity of hindsight in, 125
Hogg, Thomas Jefferson, 305, 306, 307, 310
Holland House Whigs, 261–65

Holmes, Richard, 278
Homer, 335, 336, 337, 339, 342-43, 349, 351; Homeric geography, 162; Homeric, "primary" epic, 337, 338, 340; *Iliad*, 8, 337, 338, 340, 351; *Odyssey*, 335, 337, 339, 340
Honan, Park, 57n, 66
Hood, Thomas, 115, 116
Hoon, A. J. (Miss), vii
Hope, Col. Alexander A., 220. See also John Hatfield
Hope, Charles, 220
Hopetoun ("Hopetown"), Charles Hope, 3rd Earl of, 220, 223, 240
Hopkins, Gerard Manley, 324, 370
Horace, 163, 176
Horgan, Paul, 275
Hotten, John Camden, 91
Houdetot, Elisabeth, Comtesse d', 314
Houghton, H. O. & Co., 90
Houghton Mifflin Co., 90, 128; Cambridge Editions, 90, 128 & n; Riverside Editions, 115n, 126, 128, 129
"House styling," 62
Housman, A(lfred) E., 18, 93-95; *A Shropshire Lad*, 93-94; Cambridge Inaugural Lecture, 94; conjectural emendations, 94; letters to G. Richards, 93-94
Howe, Ellic, 31
Howells, William Dean, 100, 103-4
Howitt, William & Mary, 114
Hudson, Ronald, 56
Hulsman, John, 57n
Humanism defined, 326; "humanistic paradox," 324
Hume, David, 341
Hume, Mr. (inspector of franks), 222
Hunt, Bishop C., Jr., 145
Hunt, Henry L. (LH's nephew), 52
Hunt, Leigh (LH), 2, 19, 20, 21, 22, 52-53, 305; and JK, 348; and PBS, 262-63, 271, 294, 317, to PBS, 295; as political journalist, 79; at Genoa, 298; *Autobiography*, 172 & n
Hunt, John (LH's brother), 159
Huntington Library, Henry E., 5, 45, 47, 157
Hurlebusch, Klaus, 176
Hutchinson, Joanna, 225
Hutchinson, Mary. See Wordsworth, Mary
Hutchinson, Mary Monkhouse, 213
Hutchinson, Sara, 189, 190, 191, 193, 202, 205, 210, 213, 228; amanuensis for WW, 149
Hutchinson, Thomas (brother of above), 189, 190, 191
Hutchinson, Thomas (editor), 29, 41, 42, 44-46, 48-51, 65, 90, 319, 279n, 351n; his reverent capitalization, 49, 91
Huxley, Aldous, 368

I'Anson, John, 151
Idealism, academic, 13
*"Ideal state" of text, 39. See also "Definitive" edition
Illinois, University of, 217, 249, 275, 368-69, 371; University of Illinois Press, 129
*"Improving" & revising texts, 87, 89, 96
Incest, incestuous feelings, 183-88, 191-92, 197-98, 201-2, 214; as literary subject, by LH & PBS, 21; legal status in Regency England, 21
Indexes as scholarly resources, 71, 113
Ingpen, Roger E., 269n, 294; and W. E. Peck, Julian Shelley, 72, 270, 294n et seq., 358n
"Intentional fallacy," 8

Jack, Ian, & Margaret Smith, 56
Jackson, William (RS's landlord), 151
Jackson, William A., 17, 26, 114
James, Henry, 248, 342, 375
James, Patricia, 75
Janus, *Bifrons* and *Quadrifrons*, 66
Jaye, Michael C., 10n, 185, 355
Jefferson, Thomas, 75, 269
Jeffrey, Francis, 23n, 226
JEGP (*Journal of English and Germanic Philology*), 114, 369
Jerome, St., 174-75
Jesus Christ, 358; confused with John Wheeler Cleveland, 24
Johnson, Edgar, 323
Johnson, John (printer), 31n, 37
Johnson, Dr. Samuel, 97, 110, 238, 250, 273
Johnston, Kenneth R., 195n
Jones, Frederick L., 19n, 45, 72, 116-17, 131, 277, 290, 294n, 301, 304n, 307n, 359n, 370; his editorial practices, 23-24
Jones, Leonidas M., 74, 115
Jordan, John E., 192
Joseph, M. K., 172n
Joyce, James, *Ulysses*, 336; synoptic edition of, 176n
Judeo-Christian concept of man, 107
Julian Edition. See Ingpen, and Peck
Jung, Karl, 312
Junius, 74, 255
Juvenal, 94

Kant, Immanuel, 345, 346, 373-74
Karanikas, Alexander, 250
Keach, William, viii
Keats, John (JK), 9, 20, 107, 108, 209, 274, 323-33, 365, 370; and existentialism, 368; and the "humanistic paradox," 324, 333; and Milton, 348; and "mythological his-

tory," 332; and Naturalism, 325; and *Pervigilium Veneris*, 323–24; and PBS, 274, 323; and WW, 209; as Humanist, 327; editions, of his letters, 24, 86, 113; editions of his poems, 72, 86, 89, 90, 91, 92, 94, 95–96, 112, 115, 126, 127n, 129, 156, 160, 165; his diction, 36n; his epitaph, 324; his illness and death, 323, 324–25; his mythmaking, 328–29; adapts Greek myths, 330–32 & n; his originality, 326; his religious thinking, 324; his sexuality, 185; manuscripts of, 6n, 173, 192; on eros, 330–31; on "vale of Soul-making," 328; "sophists" in his poems, 332

—**Works, Letters**: 327, to Bailey, 327, to George & Georgiana Keats, 328, to Reynolds, 328

—**Works, Poems**: *Endymion*, 90, 326, 327, 330–31, Diana *triformis* in, 331, Preface to, 287; "The Eve of St. Agnes," 326; *The Fall of Hyperion*, 94; *Hyperion: A Fragment*, 327, 328, 329–30, 348; "La Belle Dame sans Merci," 172; *Lamia*, 208, 323, 326–33, Hermes loves nymph in, 327, Lamia's love for Lycius, 327, mythological history in, 328; "Ode: 'Bards of passion . . . ,'" 326; "Ode on a Grecian Urn," 258, 326; "Ode on Melancholy," 196, 333; "Ode to a Nightingale," 94, 323, 325, 326, 333; "Ode to Psyche," 327, 333; "On First Looking into Chapman's Homer," 162; "Robin Hood," 328; "To Autumn," 323, 326; "To Homer," 325, 331; "Written upon the Top of Ben Nevis," 325

Keats-Shelley Assoc. of America, 54, 110
Keats-Shelley Journal, 113, 114 & n, 122, 156, 161
Keats-Shelley Memorial Assoc., 54
Keats-Shelley Memorial Bulletin, 157, 262
The Keepsake (annual gift book), 47
Kelley, Philip, 56, 59–60, 67
Kenney, James, & Louisa Mercier, 257
Kent, Elizabeth (Bessie), 305
Kermode, Frank, 275, 276
Keynes, Sir Geoffrey, 35, 112, 117, 120, 165
Kidd, Captain William, 163
Kierkegaard, Søren, 324, 341, 342, 346, 368; *Either/Or*, 326
King, Roma A., Jr., 55, 57 & n, 58, 64
Kittredge, George Lyman, 113
Knopf, Alfred A., 370
Kohn, Hans, 275, 276
Kosciuszko, Tadeuz, 269
Kramer, Lawrence, 217
Krieger, Murray, 249
Kroeber, Karl, 106, 195n

Lachmann, Karl, his textual analysis, 6
Laise, Janet Ruth Reiman, ix
Laise, William Harold, ix
"Lake Poets," 341
Lamb, Charles (CL), 79, 107, 218, 275, 371; and Beauty of Buttermere, 218, 245; and STC, 252, 256, 257; and Hatfield, 223–24, 243–44; and Mary Lamb, letters, 115; and Shelley circle, 251; and WW, 252; as humane Skeptic, 252, 259; Elia as CL's persona, 223, 252, 253, 254, 257, 259; his diction, 36n; his style, rhetoric, 252, 258–59; his pastoral mode, 258–59; letters, 72, 223, to STC, 257

—**Works**, 250, 252, 259, 275; "A Dissertation . . . Roast Pig," 251; "Imperfect Sympathies," 251, 252, 253; "Mrs. Battle's Opinions on Whist," 252, 253–56; "Newspapers Thirty-Five Years Ago," 223; "New Year's Eve," 255, 256; "Old China," 251, 252, 257–59; *Rosamund Gray*, 224; "Sanity of True Genius," 252; "That Enough Is as Good as a Feast," 256; "The Two Races of Men," 252, 256–57

Lamb, Mary Anne ("Bridget Elia"), 115, 253, 257, 258, 259; and Beauty of Buttermere, 218, 224, 230, 244
Lamb, William (*later* Lord Melbourne), 264
Landon, Carol, 151
Landon, Richard G., 169
Lang, Cecil Y., 11, 114, 115
Langhorne, John, 199
Leavis, F(rank) R., 250, 277, 368, 369
Lebrave, Jean-Louis, 176n
Lefebvre, Georges, 78
Le Gallienne, Richard, 172
Lempriere's *Classical Dictionary*, 66
Lennon, John, 218
Lewis, C(live) S., 326, 334, 340; on primary & secondary epics, 337–38
Lewis, George H., 306
Lewis, Matthew G. ("Monk"), 348, 351
The Library, 97
Library of America, 169
Library of English Literature (proposed), 169
Lichnowsky, Countess Leonora, 277, 280
Lindbergh, Charles A., 218
Linguistic evidence, 22
Liverpool, Robert Banks Jenkinson, 2nd Earl of, 265
Lockhart, John Gibson, 77, 86
Locock, C(harles) D(ealtry), 48, 50, 51, 93, 279, 280, 283
London Magazine (Baldwin's), 256
London Review of Books, 56

Longdill, P(ynson) W(ilmot), 267
Longfellow, Henry Wadsworth, 89,
Longinus, 34
Longman/Norton Annotated English Poets, 127 & n, 129
Lonsdale, William Lowther, 1st Earl of, 233, 265, 350
Lovell, Ernest J., 116
Lowell, James Russell, 90
Lowes, John Livingston, 113
Lucan, 94, 281
Lucas, E. V., 72
Lucretius, 50, 325

Mac-Carthy, Denis Florence, 46
Machiavelli, Niccoló, 82
Macmillan & Co., 90
Maddocks (Madocks), Robert, 271
Maginn, William, 114
Magnuson, Paul, viii, 261
Male, Roy R., 370
Malone, Edmond, 48
Malone Society, 99
Malthus, Thomas Robert, 75
Mander, Rosalie, Lady (R. Glynn Grylls), 19n
Manilius, 94, 95 & n
Manton, Jo, 185
*Manuscripts, collections of, 2, 5, 19, 56, 57, 58, 124, 132-55 passim, 289-309 passim; description of, 19-21, 133, 137-38, 141, 143; editing of, 6, 19, 25; evidence for dating, 22, 139; facsimiles of, 4, 6 & n, 141, 149-50, 171n, 173, 292; features of interest: recopying to make text fit, 139, use of short forms, 61, 136; notebooks, analysis of, 138; relative authority of, 43; types of: holograph (in author's hand), 25, 27, 144, transcripts, authorized, 43, 61, 144, scholarly, 132-47;
states of: draft, 25, 34-35; fair-copy, 43; press-copy, printer's copy, 22, 25, 26, 38-39, 43, 60, 61, 62, 179; intermediate, safe-keeping copies, 22, 25, 26, 35, 39, 43
Manuscripts of the Younger Romantics, 4, 6n, 157, 173
Marchand, Leslie A., 11, 91, 116 & n, 126, 156, 159, 161, 278
Marchant, William (printer), 31, 38
Marchi, Lina, 277
Marrs, Edwin W., Jr., 115, 223, 251
Marx, Karl, 3, 261; Marxism, 75, 78, 260, 262
Maryland, University of, 344
Masi, Glauco, 30
Massey, Irving, 30, 315n
Masson, David, 165
Matthews, G(eoffrey) M., 29-30, 48, 126n, 289, 290, 291-301, 306n, 310n, 311n; & Daphne, 289
Maxwell, J. C., 127
McCord, Norman, 263
McFarland, Thomas, 79, 81, 251
McGann, Jerome J., 5, 10, 11, 86, 115, 116n, 128, 152, 156-66
McKerrow, R(onald) B., 26, 33, 35, 60, 96-97 & n, 98-99, 100, 101, 114
Medwin, Thomas, 53, 308, 315n
Melbourne, Wm. Lamb, 2nd Viscount, 264
Melchior, Claus, 176n
Melville, Herman, 96, 104
Meta-studies, 180
Michell, Theobald (PBS ancestor), 269
Mill, John Stuart, 115; *Autobiography*, versions of, 172 & n
Miller, Henry, 186
Milnes, Richard Monckton (*later* 1st Baron Houghton), 86, 94
Milton, John, 107, 146, 228, 234, 310, 320, 347, 348, 350, 351, 352; his religious thought, 371; Works: *Comus*, 314; *Il Penseroso*, 347; *L'Allegro*, 87; *Lycidas*, 233; *Paradise Lost*, 146, 149, 196, 212, 235, 346, 352
Mingay, G. E., 263, 266, 267
Modernist poets, 345, 346, 347, 359, 360; and Postmodernists, 345
*Modernizing, normalizing, regularizing texts, 36, 105, 140
Modern Language Association of America (MLA), Book Club, 26; conventions, 1, 25, 127, 156, 168, 185, 217, 260, 276, 292
Modiano, Raimonda, 69, 217
Moers, Ellen, 192
Molyneux, Sir T., 222
Monkhouse, Thomas & Mary, 113
Monsman, Gerald, 251
Montagu, Basil, 83; Sr. & Jr., 191
Monte Rua', 278
Moore, Frederick Wall, 368
Moore, Thomas, 21, 24, 159, 163, 304n
Moorman, Mary, 183, 185, 186, 187, 188, 194, 200, 201, 225
More, Paul Elmer, 159
Morgan, John James, 81, 84
Pierpont Morgan Library, 5, 38
Morley, Edith J., 235n
Morning Post, 71, 74, 75, 76, 78, 119, 123n, 207n, 220, 221, 222, 223, 243
Mossop, Henry, 163
Moxon, Edward, 50
Moxon & Co., 86, 87; Moxon's Popular Poets, 89-90
Mudford, William, 240
Mulcahy, Daniel J., 251, 252
Mumford, Lewis, 100, 275, 276, 375

Murray, E(ugene) B., viii, 115, 123n
Murray, Gilbert, 94
Murray, John II (1778-1843), 26, 77, 86, 159
Murray, John IV (1851-1928), 91
Murray, Sir John V (18??-196?), 26
Murray, John (Grey) VI (19??-), 91, 124, 156
Myron, 281

Nabholtz, John R., 251
Nagle, Sir E., 222
Napoleon I, Bonaparte (Buonaparte), 75, 78, 234, 238, 246, 354
Nashe, Thomas, 96
Nation, Michelli, 237, 242
National Endowment for the Humanities (NEH), 99
Nelson, Horatio, Viscount, 150-51
New Critics, New Criticism, 7, 249, 250, 368
New Humanists, 368
Newsweek, 374-75
Newton, Sir Isaac, 3, 230
Newton, John Frank, 281
New York Public Library, 4, 5, 119, 122, 174n
New York Review of Books, 374
New York University Press, 129
Nicholes, Eleanor L., 19n
Nicholls, Eleanor, 266
Nicholson, Norman, 219
Nineteenth-Century Fiction, 114
Nordloh, David, 86, 100, 103, 104
Norfolk, Charles Howard, 11th Duke of, 266; & his forebears, 264, 265, 269
Norman, Sylva, 19
Norton Co., W. W., 126-27 & n, 129; *Norton Anthology of English Literature*, 127, 140; Norton Critical Editions, 5, 126-27, 131, 147, 151-54, 170-71
Notes and Queries, 87
Notopoulos, James, 116

O'Gorman, F., 263
Ohio University, 55; Ohio University Press, 56, 57, 67
Ohmann, Richard, 275
Ollier, Charles, 20, 21, 31, 37, 317
Ollier, James, 21
O'Neill, Eliza, 29
Onorato, Richard J., 186n, 188
Ontology, Romantic, 346
Origen (Origenes Adamantius), 174
Originality (in scholarly criticism), 3
Ormond, Walter Butler, Earl of, 222
Ostriker, Alicia, 127n
Oswald, Col. John, 121 & n
Ovid, 208
Owen, Robert, 261

Owen, W. J. B., 18-19, 133
Oxford English Dictionary (OED), 22, 23, 48, 51, 212, 268
Oxford University, 54
Oxford University and City Herald, 46
Oxford University Press, 54, 128, 156; Clarendon Press, 24, 51, 54, 97, 158, 159, 165, 294n; Oxford English Texts, 28, 33, 34, 41-42, 44, 54, 55, 65, 90, 91, 95, 156-66, 170; Oxford Standard Authors, 65, 90, 91, 95, 128

Padua, 278
Paley, Morton D., 91n
Palmer, Joseph. *See* J. Budworth
Palmyra, 52
Pantisocracy, 75, 76
Papers, analysis of. *See* Manuscripts
Parker, Hershel, 104
Parker, Theodore, 373-74
Parrish, Stephen M., 114, 115 & n, 120, 130-38, 140-42, 143, 145, 146, 196
Pastoral, 345, 352n; pastoral sensibility, 351, 360, 367; defined, 352
Patmore, Peter George, 172
Patton, Lewis, 301n
Payne, J. Bertrand, 87-88, 89
Peacock, Thomas Love, 20, 111, 116, 271, 307; and PBS, 263, 271, 272, 273, 281, 311; his correspondence, 271; his Skepticism, 287; Works: *Crotchet Castle*, 267; "The Four Ages of Poetry," 86; *Gryll Grange*, 272; *Melincourt*, 272, 273; *Palmyra*, 286-87
Peck, Walter E., 270, 271, 278, 293-94, 358n, 368. *See also* Ingpen, Roger, & Peck
Peckham, Morse, 11, 56, 57n, 62-63, 64-68, 100-104, 106, 107, 344, 353, 354 & n; his letter, 56, 64; on "accidentals," 101; on bibliographers as historians, 103; on historical interpretation, 273-74
Pellew, Sir E., 222
Penguin English Poets, 127 & n, 129
Peterfreund, Stuart, 344
Petersen, Aage, 275
Peterson, William S., 59-60
Petrarch (Petrarca), Francesco, 315, 320, 369
Pettigrew, John, 55, 56
Peyre, Henri, 368
Pforzheimer, Carl H(oward) (1879-1957), 20, 92, 116
Pforzheimer, Carl H., Jr. (1907-), 156
Pforzheimer Foundation, Carl & Lily, 267
Pforzheimer Library, The Carl H. (now The Carl H. Pforzheimer Shelley and His Circle Collection, New York Public Library), 2, 4, 21, 49, 51, 55, 56, 57, 63, 69, 88n, 89, 90n, 92n, 122, 156, 185, 260, 266, 276, 371

Philological Quarterly, 277
Photoduplicates, hazards of relying on, 141, 162–63
Pitt, William, the Younger, 71, 75, 78, 238, 246, 266
Pius VI, Pope, 280
Pizer, Donald, 102
Place, Francis, 261
Plato, 261, 269, 315, 351, 358; *Republic*, 359; Platonic, 353; Platonism, 52
Pliny, the Elder, 281
PMLA, 2, 290
Poggioli, Renato, 352n
Pollard, A(lfred) W., 26, 35, 97 & n, 98, 99, 100, 114
Pollard, Jane, 191, 201, 206
Poole, Penelope, 237
Poole, Thomas, 71, 211, 237
Pope, Alexander, 107; *The Dunciad*, 148; *An Essay on Man*, 346, 353; *The Rape of the Lock*, 253; translation of *Iliad*, 212
Pope, Willard B., 114, 115
Postmarks. *See* Manuscripts
Poststructuralist criticism, 2, 7
Pottle, Frederick A., 249, 368
Powers, Sharon B., viii, 2, 349n
Pratt, Willis W., 25, 116
*Primary vs. secondary evidence, 1, 4, 67, 69, 163, 167–68, 169, 178
Princeton University Press, 118. *See also* Collected Coleridge
*Printers, 62; compositors, 62, 179; composing-room readers, 62
*Proofreading, proofsheets, 43, 55, 58, 63–64, 159
Prothero, Rowland E., 91. *See also* LB, editions, *Complete Works*
*Provenance, scholarly use of, 45, 47
Psychological study of literature, 1, 345; subtexts, in scholarship & criticism, 12
Pulos, C(ristos) E., 370
Pushkin, Aleksandr Sergeevich, 375
Pythagoras, Pythagoreans, 53

Quadriga (4-horse chariot), 281
Quaritch, Bernard, Ltd., 276
Quarterly Review, 53, 77, 255
Quillinan, Edward, 86, 149

Raben, Joseph, 30
Radicalism, 261
Randel, Fred V., 251
Ratchford, Fannie E., 92n
Ray, Gordon N., 115n, 126
Redford, Robert, 244
Reed, Mark L., 207n, 225, 141
*Regularizing. *See* Modernizing

Reiman, Donald H., 7, 10n, 55, 183, 225, 260, 264, 275, 334, 342; and H. Bloom, 321–23, 344; and Cameron, 116n, 260–62; and Erdman, 69, 109–10, 216; and Matthews, 289–92; and McGann, 156–57; and Parrish, 131; and N. Rogers, 17–18, 41, 70, 117n, 123, 289, 292, 369; and Tanselle, 103, 169; and Zillman, 33; as book collector, 69, 167; as reader for publishers, 158; education of, vii, 17, 249–50, 368–69; professional credo, 7–10; publications not reprinted herein, 2, 3–4, 6n, 12, 25n, 41, 72, 78n, 89n, 126n, 128n, 129, 152, 156, 157, 248, 290, 292, 321–22, 334–35, 336n, 349n, 355n, 360n
Reiman, Hélène Dworzan. *See* Dworzan
Reiman, Henry W., vii, 260, 371–72
Reiman, Laurel E., viii
Reiman, Mary Warner, viii, 17, 18, 167, 260, 275, 276, 289
Reiman, Mildred A., vii, 260, 371–72
Renaissance Christian humanism, 336, 349
Reni, Guido, 281
Reveley, Henry, 271
*Revise (as noun & verb), 37
Rewards of teaching & scholarship, 372
Reynell, C(arew) H(enry), 30–31, 38
Reynolds, John Hamilton, 74, 114, 115
Richards, Grant, 93
Richards, I. A., 250
Richardson, Samuel, 245
Rickman, John, & Mary, 223, 224, 245
Ricks, Christopher, 6n, 127 & n
Riddel, Joseph N., 248, 249, & Ginny, 276
Ridenour, George, 335, 336
Rieger, James, 172n–73n
Rinehart Editions, 127
Roberts, Capt. Daniel, 298, 302
Roberts, Michael, 263
Robespierre, Maximilien de, 235, 354
Robinson, Eric, 35
Robinson, Henry Crabb, 151, 205, 235
Robinson, Isabel, 307–8
Robinson, Mary (later Harrison; Beauty of Buttermere), 216–47; and Mary Wordsworth, 234; her age, 241; her death, 245–46; her marriage, 245; her paternity, 221, 236; her pregnancy, 222; her virtue, 236; refuses to prosecute Hatfield, 223
Rogers, Neville, 5, 17, 41–54, 55, 65, 72, 117, 158, 292, 369; and Matthews, 289; and Reimans, 289, 369; his contributions to Shelley studies, 54; his editorial theories, 18, 34, 41, 42, 43; his practice, 17, 28–29, 41, 43, 99–100, 123 & n, 126n, 128; on punctuation, 17–18; on "starting text," 44, 49, 65
Rogers, Robert W., viii, 13, 371
Rollins, Hyder E., 17, 26, 39, 84, 112–16, 117n,

327; his career, 112–13; his training of editors, 113–15
Romantic historicism vs. Classical & Modernist cyclical patterns, 106–8
Romanticism Past and Present, 80, 345
"Romantic ideology," 324
The Romantic Movement Bibliographies, 120 & n
Romantics & Romanticism, 243, 245, 246, 347, 353, 354, 359, 360
Rome, 277, 278–82, 284–86, 288; Egyptian obelisks, 284, 285, 286, 288; fountains, 285; Pantheon, 282, 285; piazzas, 285; Rospigliosi Palace, 281; St. Peter's, 284–85, 288; Vatican Museum, 277, 280–82
Romilly, Sir Samuel, 264
Rooke, Barbara E., 125, 171 & n
Roosevelt, Franklin D., vii, 261
Rossetti, Christina, 192
Rossetti, Dante Gabriel, 24
Rossetti, William Michael, 46, 47, 48, 50, 51, 86, 87–90, 91n, 92, 99, 111–12, 283, 284, 306, 309, 316, 317
Rothschild, Nathan Mayer, 259
Rousseau, Jean-Jacques, his impact on PBS, 289, 293, 310–20, 353; Works: *Confessions*, 310–12; *Julie*, 28–29, 164, 310–20, translated as *Eloisa*, 311n
Roxburgh, William Ker, 4th Duke of, 222
Ruddick, William, 217
Russia oil, 21
Ryan, Robert M., 114, 324

Sadler's Wells Theatre, 224, 225, 230, 231, 236, 241, 244, 245, 246
Sadlier, Michael T. H., 97
Saint-Lambert, Jean-Francois de, 314
St. John's University (New York), 335, 344
Salinger, J. D., 248
Sanders, Charles Richard, 249
Sandler, Florence, 117
Sartre, Jean-Paul, 324, 341
Savage, William, 31n
Schiller, Johann Christoph F. von, 339, 340
"Scholarship" defined, relations with "criticism," 8–10
Schoolmen, The, 349
Schorske, Carl, 275, 276
Schulz, Max F., 72
Scoggins, James L., 249
Scott, Sir Walter, 86, 89, 250, 348
Scott, Winifred, 308n
Scrivener, Michael H., 217, 262
Seigel, J. P., 179n
Septuagint, translation of Hebrew Bible, 174
Shackleton, Robert, 53

Shakespeare, William, 2, 96, 162, 336; and his age, 87; and history, 162; editorial problems, 101; editors of, 24, 31, 33, 113, 174 & n; language, 338; Works: *As You Like It*, 198; *Hamlet*, 359; *Henry IV*, 257; *King Lear*, 174 & n, 351; *Othello*, 256, 262; *Richard II*, 248; *Richard III*, 237; *The Tempest*, 48; *A Winter's Tale*, 244
Shaver, Chester L., 114, 115
Shelley, Sir Bysshe (PBS's grandfather), 266, 267, 268, 269
Shelley, Clara (PBS's child), 212, 303
Shelley, Elizabeth Sidney, 266
Shelley, Harriet (PBS's wife), 28, 52, 53, 265, 292, 307, 349
Shelley, John (will of), 267
Shelley, Mary C. Michell (PBS's grandmother), 266, 269
Shelley, Mary W. (MWS), 20, 21, 52, 53, 212, 271, 292, 293, 294n, 296, 356; amanuensis for PBS, 25, 39, 43; and PBS, 303, 305, 307–9, 317; and E. E. & J. Williams, 304–8; and Naples, 302; dislikes "Casa" (Villa) Magni, 301–4; edits PBS's writings, 34, 35, 44, 50, 51, 86, 89, 99, 300, her notes on his poems, 278–79, 288; her miscarriage, 298n, 303–4
—**Works**: *Frankenstein*, editions of, 172–73 & n; *History of a Six Weeks' Tour*, 311; Journals, 116, 280n, 301, 304, 306n, 308; "Journal of Sorrow," 305; letters, 116, 301, 302, 303, 304n, 305–6, 307, 308n
Shelley, Percy Bysshe (PBS), 11, 12, 13, 20, 21, 33–40, 86, 89, 94, 107, 108, 212, 249, 260–74, 275–88, 289–320, 325, 344–53, 355–57, 358–59, 360, 366; against hypocrisy, 262; an agrarian aristocrat, 263, 270, 271–73; and LB, 294; and God, 347; and Godwin, 271, 302; and Gothic literature, 348; and Hoppner Scandal, 294; and Ireland, 318; and JK, 323; and Peterloo, 318; and politics, 270, 318; and the poor at Marlow, 271; and MWS, *see her entry*; and Spinoza, 323; and suicide, 317; and J. Williams, 289, 292–301, 303–5, 308–10, 315, 320, poems to her, 294–97, 315n; and WW, 344–59; and Yale, 368; as eldest son & heir, 269; as "Falconer" & "Forester," 272; as "Hermit" of Marlow & Bishopsgate, 272; as poet of liberty, 342, 350; as poet of self-discontinuity, 349–50; as transcriber of his own writings, 25; attacks foes of landed gentry, 270; diction, word usage, 27, 36, 48, 51; editions of his works, 17, 18, 25, 26, 28–30, 33–40, 86, 88–92, 94, 99, 111, 115–17, 122–24, 129, 156, 358n, 359n; family lands in Sussex, 263, 266–67n, 267, acquired by

marriages, 268-69; his benevolence, 271; his boat, the *Don Juan,* 303; his circle, 131, 345; his conversion experience, 355-56; his death, 358; his debts, 271; his "Gothic" sensibility, 345, 351-53; his ideas and beliefs: Academic Skepticism, 324, 346-47, its debt to Drummond, 346, 347; "atheism," 52; on "blood and gold," 318; on classical, baroque art, 284-86; on epic vs. drama, 336; on hieroglyphics, 283, 286-88; on love & personal fulfillment, 271; on the national debt, 268; on "new aristocracy" (capitalists), 267; on poetry as source of happiness, 356-57; on "power" and "will," 316, 318-19; on property rights, 268; on religion, 322; on Rome, 284-86; on society as corrupting, 355; on slavery, 270; on vegetarianism, 52-53; his language, diction, 348; his mythmaking, 321-22, 350; his need to patronize, 272; his orthography & punctuation, 37, 45-46, 48, 49, 50, 144-45; his poetry, plan for editing it, 30-31; his presumed patience with sloppy editors, 44; his radicalism, 262, 263, 270; his reactionary goals, 263; his reputation in 20th century, 368-70; his residences: Bagni di Lucca, 291; Este, 278; "Casa" (i.e., Villa) Magni, Lerici, 292-304, 310, 316; Field Place, 269; Marlow (Great), 52, 272, 318; Oxford, University College, 316; Pisa, 291, 294, 302, 308, 316; Rome, 278-80, 282, 284-86 (*see also under Prometheus Unbound*); Venice, 106;
his social ideals, 270-72, limited by his perspective, 269, 273; his symbolic language, 310; inspiration of books and arts, 357; journey from Naples to Rome, 284; "Memoir" of, 88; manuscripts of, 19-21, 27, 30, 37-38, 39, 69, 122, 124, 141, 294n; draft notebooks (Bodley, Huntington, etc.), 34, 39, 122, 141; Esdaile Notebook, 28, 39; Harvard Notebook, 39; lost MSS, 37, 39; *Prometheus* copybooks, 39; "Triumph" MS, 293-300, 310;
New Critics and, 250; polemicism in scholarship on, 289, 291; press-copy, his preparation of, 37; seeks post in East India Co., 273n; thinks of becoming clergyman, 273n; visits Greystoke Castle, 265
—**Works: Letters, Notebooks**: 92, 277, 282, 283, 293, 359n, 370; to LB, 302, (alleged) 293-94; to Clairmont, 303, 316; to Gisbornes, 307, 312n, 316, 317, 358-59; to Hogg, 310, 311; to Hunt, 294n, 317; to Peacock, 282, 284-86, 288, 311; to H. Smith, 317-18, 359
—**Works: Poetry**: *Adonais,* 38, 143, 145, 214, 274, 317, 323-24, 350, 351, 364; *Alastor,* 30, 347, 350; "Athanase: A Fragment," 89n; "A widow bird sate mourning," 364n; *The Cenci,* 30, 38, 174n, 351, printer of, 30; "Charles the First," 27, 30, 364n; "The Daemon of the World," 49-50; "Death: 'Death is here and death is there,'" 351; *The Esdaile Notebook (Esdaile Poems),* 45-46, 289, 344, 348, 348, 351, 370; "The Retrospect. Cwm Elan," 348-49; "A Tale of Society as It Is," 348; "To Harriet," 46; "Zeinab and Kathema," 46, 348;
Epipsychidion, 30, 312n, 341, 350, 351, 356; *Hellas,* 30, 317, 319, 348; *History . . . Six Weeks' Tour,* 30; "Hymn [i.e., Song] of Pan," 320n; "Hymn to Intellectual Beauty," 319, 347, 355-56; "Invocation to Misery," 351; *Julian and Maddalo,* 29, 38, 92, 212, 320, 351; "A Lament," 94; *Laon and Cythna* (later *The Revolt of Islam*), 37, 38, 53, 88, 348, Dedication to, 356; "Lines . . . Bay of Lerici," 294-97, 315n; "Lines . . . Euganean Hills," 28, 248, 250, 278, 283, 290; "Lines: 'We meet not as we parted,'" 315n; "Lines: 'When the lamp is shattered,'" 315n; lyrics to Jane Williams, 351; "The Magnetic Lady . . . ," 295, 296, 315n; "Marianne's Dream," 351; *The Mask of Anarchy,* 38, 262, 270-71, 318; "Mont Blanc," 89n, 311; "Mutability: 'The flower that smiles today,'" 351, 352; *Œdipus Tyrannus, see Swellfoot;* "Ode to Liberty," 28; "Ode to Naples," 28; "Ode to the West Wind," 353; "On the Medusa of Leonardo," 351; *Original Poetry* "by Victor and Cazire," 44-45, 348; *Ozymandias,* 286; *Posthumous Fragments of Margaret Nicholson,* 44-46, 348; posthumous lyrics, 28; *Posthumous Poems,* 28, 30-31, 38, 89; *Prometheus Unbound,* 88, 92, 108, 258, 277-78, 280-82, 288, 341, 351, 369; Bodleian MS, 38, 280n, 283; editions of, 33-40, 279n, 280n, 283-84; press copy missing, 37, 38; printer of, 31, 38; Rome in Act III.iv: 288, mythology of the Hours, 279, 283, obelisks & fountains, 284-86, the Pantheon, 282-83, Sala della Biga, 279-82, symbolism of, 281-83, 286, 288;
Queen Mab, 38, 47-53, 91, 270, 318, 346, 348; *The Revolt of Islam, see Laon and Cythna; Rosalind and Helen,* 30, 89n; "Song of Pan," *see* "Hymn of Pan"; "Song: 'Rarely, rarely, comest thou,'" 352; "Sonnet: Political Greatness," 315; "Stanzas written in Dejection," 351; *Swellfoot the Tyrant*

(*Œdipus Tyrannus*), 318; "To Constantia," 351; "To Edward Williams," 296; "To Jane: The Invitation," 315n, 320n; "To Jane: 'The keen stars,'" 295n, 315n; "To Jane: The Recollection," 315n; "To ——: 'Music when soft voices die,'" 315n; "To ——: 'One word is too often profaned,'" 315n; "To Time: 'Unfathomable Sea!,'" 351; "The Tower of Famine," 351; "To William Shelley," 351; translations, 28; "The Triumph of Life," 27, 29, 33, 66, 89n, 248, 250, 289–90, 292–301, 310–20, 321, 322, 350, 351, 353, 369; MS of, 289, 292–95, 297–301, Rousseau and, 293, 310–16; *The Wandering Jew*, 348; "When Passion's Trance Is Overpast," 353; "The Witch of Atlas," 351; "With a Guitar, to Jane," 315n
—*Dubia* (unproved attributions): "Ode: To the Death of Summer," 46; "Sadak the Wanderer," 46–47; translations from V. Bourne, 46–47; translations of Greek epigrams, 46
—**Works (Prose)**: *Declaration of Rights*, 270; *A Defence of Poetry*, 108, 287, 291, 336, 341, 350; "Essay on Christianity," 322, 358; "On Life," 53; *A Philosophical View of Reform*, 53, 263, 267–68, 269, 270, 318; *A Proposal for Putting Reform to the Vote*, 270, 318; *Proposals for an Association*, 270; *St. Irvyne*, 348; *Zastrozzi*, 316, 348
Shelley, Percy Florence (PBS's son), 303, 304, 317
Shelley, Sir Timothy (PBS's father), 266, 269, 317
Shelley, William (PBS's son), 28, 212, 303, 351
Shelley and his Circle, 19–23, 37, 49, 51, 72, 89n, 115, 116, 122, 137–38, 156–57, 212n, 216, 251, 260–61, 263, 267–69, 271, 310, 311n, 335, 345, 348n, 370, 371; accepts & addresses authorial readings, 22–23; raises questions, 22
Shelley-Sidney, Sir John, 266
Shepherd, Richard Herne, 50
Sherburn, George, 13
Sheridan, Richard Brinsley, 162, 257
Shillingsburg, Peter L., 168
Shorter, Alfred H., 31, 137
Sidney, Sir Philip, 257; *Arcadia*, versions of, 173 & n
Simon Fraser University, 217
Simmons, Ernest J., 275, 276
"Simpleminded" criticism, 184
Simpson, Claude M., 99
Siskin, Clifford, 217
Skeptics, Skepticism, 325; Academic, 360; Pyrrhonist, 360
Smalley, Donald, 57n

Smiles, Samuel, 77
Smith, Adam, 52
Smith, Grover, 248, 249
Smith, Horace (Horatio), 317, 318n, 359
Smyser, Jane Worthington, 133, 229
Society for Textual Scholarship, 85, 174n
Sotheby, William, 77
Sotheby's (auction house), 156, 185, 193
Southern Agrarian movement, 250
Southey, Robert (RS), 77, 82, 151, 242–43, 244, 261, 341; and Beauty of Buttermere, 224, 245; and CL, 2; and WW, 210; "On the Rise of . . . Popular Disaffection," 77; *Thalaba the Destroyer*, 348
Soviet Union (USSR), 260
The Spanish Tragedy, 248
Sparrow, John, 94n
Speier, Dr. H., 280
Spenser, Edmund, 321
Spinoza, Benedictus (Baruch) de, 323
Staël, Germaine, Madame de, 78
Stalin, Josef, 262
Statius, 95
Steele, Mabel A. E., 114
Steele, Sir Richard, 257
Steffan, Truman Guy, 25–26, 116
Steppe, Wolfhard, 176n
*Stereotyping, use of flong molds in, 59
Sterne, Laurence, *Tristram Shandy*, 79, 340
Stevens, Wallace, 325, 326, 342, 345, 346, 360, 363 & n, 364, 366–67; and the *Ding an Sich*, 364; rejects Romantic symbolism, 364 & n; his romantic *Weltschmertz*, 365
—**Works**: "Anatomy of Monotony," 365; "Farewell to Florida," 365; *Harmonium*, 363 & n, 364, 365, 366; "The Idea of Order at Key West," 366; *Ideas of Order*, 365; "Le Monocle de mon Oncle," 365; "Lions in Sweden," 365–66; "Not Ideas about the Thing . . . ," 367; "Nuances of a Theme by Williams," 364; "Peter Quince at the Clavier," 364; "The Planet on the Table," 366–67; "The River of Rivers in Connecticut," 367; "Sailing after Lunch," 365; "Sunday Morning," 363–64, 367
Stevenson, Lionel, 249
Stillinger, Jack, viii, 6 & n, 11, 13, 17, 41, 65, 86, 94, 95–96, 102n, 114, 115, 125 & n, 126, 129, 156, 160, 323, 354n
Stocking, Marion Kingston, 19
Stoics, 325
Stoppard, Tom, 102
Stovall, Floyd H., 370
Stower, Caleb, 31n, 37
Strafford, Thomas Wentworth, 1st Earl of, 239
Stuart, Daniel, 71, 75, 77, 221, 223, 237

Studies in Bibliography, 97, 168–69
Studies in Browning and his Circle, 58, 64
Studies in Romanticism, 69, 70, 85, 114, 131, 161, 344
Sulla, Lucius Cornelius, 164
Summerfield, Geoffrey, 35–36
Swift, Jonathan, 107; *Gulliver's Travels*, 7
Swinburne, Algernon, 24, 87, 88, 94, 283
Swingle, L(arry) J., 360n
Switzerland, 358
*Synoptic editions, 176 & n

Tanselle, G. Thomas, 18, 42, 85, 86, 98, 100–107, 119, 123, 124, 130, 160, 168–69; defends Greg tradition, 102–3; on "central questions of editing," 104–6
Tasso, Torquato, 337
Tate, Allen, 250, 324
Tave, Stuart M., 251, 252
Tayler, Irene, 355n
Taylor, Charles H., Jr., 30, 50, 99, 124, 369
Taylor, Edward, 275
Taylor, William, 357
Tennyson, Alfred Tennyson, 1st Baron, 346, 375
Texas, University of, 26
TEXT, 85, 111n, 176n
Textbooks, improvement in textual quality, 126–28
*Textual criticism (study of authority of texts), 5; as history, 63; relativism in, 25, 31; standards of, 31–32; textual critics, their function, 10, 180, training of, 5–6
Textual notes, 19, 23, 39, 44, 178; need for, 141
Thayer, Mary Rebecca, 368
Thelwall, John, 82
Theocritus, 228
St. Theresa, 239
Thiesmeyer, John E., 120
Thomism, Thomists, 107, 346
Thompson, E(dward) P., 263
Thompson, F. M. L., 263, 264, 265, 267
Thomson, James, 89
Thoreau, Henry David, 373
Thorpe, James, 98–99 & n, 101
Thorslev, Peter L., 324
Tighe, (Mrs.) Mary, 348
Time Magazine, 374
Times Literary Supplement (*TLS*), 56, 94, 188
Timperley, Charles H., 31n, 37
The Tinker Library, ed. R. Metzdorf, 57
Todd, William B., 17, 26, 92n
Tolstoy, Leo, 276, 342
Tone in academic disputes, 18–19
Tories, Tory politics, 263, 264, 265
Toronto Conference on Editorial Problems, 18–19, 32, 40, 169

Tottel's Miscellany, 113
Trelawny, Edward John, 20, 294n, 306n, 308–9, 316, 317
Trilling, Lionel, 375
Tuberville, A. S., 263
Tuckey, John S., 175n
Turner, J. M. W., paints Carthage, 106
Turner, Robert K., Jr., 18
"Twain, Mark" (Samuel Clemens), *No. 44, The Mysterious Stranger*, 175 & n

Upas tree, 52
Urkowitz, Steven, 174
"Useful knowledge," and Society for the Diffusion of, 48–49
Utilitarians, utilitarian thought, 349

Vallon, Annette, 184, 186, 189, 202n, 206, 207, 227, 234, 236
Vane, Sir Fletcher, 222
*Variant readings, 35, 39, 40n, 44, 49. *See also* collations
Vatican Museum, 277, 278; Sala della Biga, 280–82
Veblen, Thorstein, 118
Vendler, Helen, 344
Venice, 106, 278
Victoria, Queen, 28
Victorian Poetry, 55
Victorian poets, 346
Virgil (Vergil), 208, 337, 338
Voltaire (François-Marie Arouet), 341

Wagenknecht, David, 69, 70, 85, 335
Walpole, Robert, 265
Wardle, Ralph M., 114, 115, 251
Warren, Robert Penn, 250
Washington, George, 119, 120, 342
Washington, University of, 131, 217, 251
Waskow, Howard, 249
Wasserman, Earl R., 158, 249, 250, 290, 323, 325, 327, 340, 347, 369, 370
Webb, Timothy, 30, 126n, 157, 262, 290
Webster, John, 352
Wedd, Mary R., 217
Weissman, Stephen, 277
Wellek, René, 275, 291
Weller, Barry, 158
Werkmeister, Lucyle, 72
Wesleyan University and Center for Advanced Studies, 275–76, 290
West, Benjamin, 164
Westbrook, Eliza, 265
Westminster Philosophical Radicals, 261
Whigs, radical, 266
White, Augusta, 20
White, Newman Ivey, 53, 131, 278, 281, 293 &

n, 301, 304, 309, 370
Whitman, Walt, 90n, 91n, 132
Wilbur, Richard, 275
Wilkie, Brian, 334, 336, 343
William the Conqueror, 269
Williams, Edward E., 30, 117, 292, 294, 296, 298, 302, 303, 305-6, 309 & n, 315, 320; his Journal, 302, 303; letter, 309
Williams, George Walton, 17
Williams, James (of Portsea), 21
Williams, Jane, 289, 292-310, 315 & n, 320, 351; her "legal tyrant," 306n
Williams, William Carlos, 346, 364
Williamson, Edward, 275
Willkie, Wendell, vii, 260
Wilson, Edmund, 100-101, 102, 375
Wilson, Edwin Graves, 114n
Wilson, Milton, 370
Wilson, W., Esq., 222
Wimsatt, W(illiam) K., 249, 250; and Monroe C. Beardsley, 8
Winer, Bart, 70n, 71, 72, 80
Wisconsin, University of, at Milwaukee, 249, 276, 290, 334, 371
Wise, T(homas) J(ames), 45, 92
Wittgenstein, Ludwig, 341
Wolfe, Richard J., 120
Wollstonecraft, Mary (*later* Godwin), 20, 115
Woodberry, George Edward, 50, 51
Woodhouse, Richard, 94
Woodings, Robert B., 30
Woodman, Ross G., 370
Woodring, Carl, 11, 34, 72, 74, 76, 86, 114 & n, 115, 123n, 126, 290, 207 & n, 217, 250, 323
Woolf, Virginia Stephen, 123, 192
Wooster, College of, 368, 369
Wordsworth, Caroline (WW's daughter), 189, 202, 207
Wordsworth, Catharine (WW's daughter), 184, 210, 355
Wordsworth, Christopher (WW's brother), 210, 211
Wordsworth, Christopher (WW's nephew), 86
Wordsworth, Dorothy (WW's sister), 183, 185-91, 193-96, 198, 200, 202-5, 207, 211-15, 226, 228, 230, 234, 235, 242, 349, 354-55, 357; and Beauty of B, 218, 224; and STC, 192, 200, 235; and Hatfield, 226, 235; and De Q, 192; and WW, 186-89, 191, 194-96, 200, 202, 203-4, 214-15, and "Nutting," 197-98; as amanuensis for WW, 43, 144, 146; as "Emma," 147, 193-94; as "Lucy," 147, 193-94, 198, 200-201; her health, 187, 202; her Journals, 187, 189, 194-95, 200, 202, 204, 225, Alfoxden Journal, 201; her letters, 151, 191, 192, 200, 202, 206, 211, 213; her sexuality, 192; on Carlisle and cities, 226, 235, 238; on Longtown and Dumfries, 226, 235; *Recollections of a Tour*, 225-26, 238
Wordsworth, Dorothy ("Dora," WW's child), 184; as amanuensis for WW, 146
Wordsworth family letters, 142
Wordsworth, Gordon Graham, 202
Wordsworth, John (WW's father), 233
Wordsworth, John (WW's brother), 192, 201, 205-6, 228, 355; letter, 206; shares inheritance with WW, 206
Wordsworth, John (WW's son), 203, 225
Wordsworth, Jonathan, 147, 151-55, 227
Wordsworth, Mary Hutchinson (WW's wife), 183-84, 187-91, 194-96, 202-5, 210, 213-14, 225, 228, 235, 357, 359; as amanuensis for WW, 144, 146, 149; as WW's "daily food," 203-6, 212; WW's "Love Letters" & poems to, 234n-35n
Wordsworth, Richard (actor, descendant of WW), 344
Wordsworth, Thomas (WW's son), 210, 355
Wordsworth, William (WW's son), 211
Wordsworth, William (WW), 11, 12, 13, 60, 71, 76, 119, 125, 126, 159, 183-215, 216-18, 225-36, 239, 240, 242, 243-47, 278, 325, 341, 344-59, 366; and Beaupuy, 229, 234; and Beauty of Buttermere (Mary Robinson), 216, 217, 225, 227, 229, 231, 238, 243; and books, 230; and Burns, 226-27; and Christianity, 210, 212; and STC, *see* STC, and WW; and France, French Revolution, Napoleon, 227, 230, 233, 234; and Hatfield, 226, 243; and Hazlitt, *see* Hazlitt, and WW; and Lake Country, 235, 350; and London, British society, 225, 235; and Milton, 234; and Nature, 229, 230; and Paris, 235; and psychosomatic illness, 187, 214; and Southey, 210; and touring, 203, 205, 229; and Annette Vallon, *see her entry*; as poet of self-continuity, 349; at Alfoxden, 187, 191; at Cambridge, 229, 230; at Carlisle, 242; at Gallow Hill, 189; at Grasmere, 187, 189, 191, 194-96, 200, 204, 211, Dove Cottage, 189, 190, 191, 195, 203, 217, 225; at Hawkshead and vacations, 196, 233, 357; at Racedown, 187, 191; at Rydal Mount, 211, 213, 217; at Sockburn, 191; at Windy Brow, 187; diction, rhythm, tone, 347-48; **editions**: letters, 134; poetry, 86, 90, 94, 96, 115; Cornell Wordsworth, 130-151, Foreword, 134-35, limitations of, 132, 135-37, 145-47, virtues of, 132, 141-42, 147, 148, queries on, 138-40, reading texts in, 135, separate volumes: *Benjamin the Waggoner*, 131, 147-51, *Home at Grasmere*, 130, 142-47,

The Prelude, 1798-1799, 130, 132-42; *The Ruined Cottage*, 131, *Salisbury Plain Poems*, 130, 132-40, 141-42; The Norton *Prelude*, 131, 151-55; Oxford English Texts editions, *see* Oxford University Press;
editions, prose, 133; his ambivalent feelings for Dorothy W, 186, 188, 192, 202, *see also her entry*; his feelings of guilt, isolation, 186, 188, 206, 214; his "Great Decade," 154, 355; his marriage, 187-89, 194, 204, 207, 225, 234; his orthography, punctuation, 144-46, 152-53; his pastoral sensibility, 351, 352, 354-55, 357; his political ideas, 263; his prudery (alleged), 185; his psychological orientation, 183; his religious thought, 324; his revisions of poetry, 134, 145-46, 148, 149, 150, 153-55, 199, 210, 227, 232-33; his search for roots, community, 228-29, 350, 356, 359; his sexuality (expressed & repressed), 183-85, 190, 198, 202-5, 212, 214; his "two voices," 186; in France, 233, 349; in Germany, 187, 191, 196, 204; in London, 349; **manuscripts**: 132-55; *Benjamin MSS. #1, #2, & #3*, 149; Cornell University MS, 149; Dove Cottage (DC) MSS: MS. #10, 138; DC MS. #14 (Alfoxden Notebook), 141; DC MS. #15 (*Christabel* Notebook), 133; DC MS. #28, MS. #44, MS. #47, & MS. #60, 149; DC MS. B., 144; DC MS. D., 145; DC MS. E., 153; DC MS. JJ., 138, 140; DC MSS. U. & V., 140; DC Quillinan MS., 149; Wellesley College MS, 149
—**Works, Letters**: 194, 202; editions, 186, 193; *Love Letters*, 184, 234; to STC, 190, 194, 198, 200; to Mary Hutchinson, 202; to Poole, 211; to Southey, 210; to Vallon, 201; to Christopher W, 210; to Wrangham, 211
—**Works, Poetry**: "A Farewell," 195, 204, 205; "Alice Fell," 193; *An Evening Walk*, 48; "At the Grave of Burns," 226-27; "Beggars," 193; *Benjamin the Waggoner*, see *The Waggoner*; *The Borderers*, 121, 234; *Ecclesiastical Sketches*, 208; "Elegiac Stanzas . . . Peele Castle," 355; "The Emigrant Mother," 193; *The Excursion*, 206, 210, 211, 213, 347, as pastoral dialogue, 347, Solitary in, 213, Pedlar in, 206; "Expostulation and Reply," 144; "The Female Vagrant," 136; "Foresight," 194; "The Fountain," 357; "French Revolution . . . at Its Commencement," 358-59; "The Glow-Worm," 193, 194, 198, 202; "Guilt and Sorrow," 135-36, 206; *Home at Grasmere*, 130, 142-47; "Incidents upon Salisbury Plain," 136; *Laodamia*, 183-85, 208-9, 212-14, textual changes in, 209; "Let other bards of angels sing," 235; "Lines composed . . . Tintern Abbey," 186, 196, 197, 200, 349, 355, 357; "Lines, Left upon a Seat in a YEW-TREE," 144; Lucy poems, 184-87, 198, 200-202, 207; *Lyrical Ballads* (1800), 144; "Michael," 207; *Miscellaneous Poems of WW*, 149; "Nutting," 196-98, 204, 212; "Ode: Intimations of Immortality," 349; "Ode to Duty," 355; "Our Departure," *see* "A Farewell"; *Peter Bell*, 365; *Poems* (1845), 149; *Poems; in Two Volumes* (1807), 350; "Poems on the Naming of Places," 203-4, 215; *Poetical Works* (1836-1837), 149; *The Prelude*, 86, 94, 125-27, 131, 147, 149, 151-54, 186, 194, 196, 200, 207, 216, 217, 227-36, 346, 350, 357, 358; 1798-99 version, 130-38, 140-42, 145, 152, 153; 1805 version, 133, 145, 152, 153-54, 232-33, 234, its biographical importance, 153; 1839 version (MS. E.), 153; 1850 version (1st ed.), 145, 152-54, as macrosonnet, 207n, 216, 217, 227-31, 233, 275, its artistic preeminence, 145, 153-54; spots of time, key passages: Arab, stone, and shell, 229; Ascent of Snowdon, 228; Beauty of Buttermere, 218, 229-36, 246; Boat-Stealing Scene, 133, 153-54; STC on Etna ("one great society"), 228-29, 357; Crossing the Alps, 229; Discharged Soldier, 218; Drowned Man of Esthwaite, 218; London, Bartholomew fair, 230, 231, 235; London theatre, 229, 232, 246; Penrith Beacon, 218; Skating Scene, 133, 154; View from Helvellyn, 228, 230;

"The Rainbow" ("My heart leaps up"), 196; *The River Duddon*, 208; "The Ruined Cottage," 206, 207, 348; "Ruth," 206, 207; "The Sailor's Mother," 193; *Salisbury Plain*, 140, *see also* WW, editions, *above*; "She dwelt among the untrodden ways," 198-200; "She Was a Phantom of Delight," 202-3, 235; sonnets, 207-8: "Calm is all nature . . . ," 207; "Composed After a Journey . . . ," 204-5; "Nuns fret not . . . ," 207; "Sonnet, . . . Helen Maria Williams," 207; "Sonnets on the Punishment of Death," 208; "Sonnet Written by Mr. ——," 207; "Sonnet Written in Very Early Youth," 207; "Those words were uttered," 204; "To a Painter" & "On the Same Subject," 325n; "Strange fits of passion," 198-202; "There Was a Boy," 200; "The Thorn," 206; "To ——," *see* "Let other bards"; "To

a Butterfly" (2 poems), 193, 194, 196; "To M. H.," 203-4, 235; "To My Sister," 354-55; "To the Cuckoo," 196; "To the Small Celandine," 194; "The Two April Mornings," 357; *Vaudracour and Julia*, 207, 234; *The Waggoner* (earlier *Benjamin the Waggoner*), 131, 147-51, Nelson & old Sailor in, 150-51; "Yarrow Visited," 205; "Yarrow Unvisited," 205
—**Works, Prose**: "Essay Supplementary to the Preface," 232; *Letter to a Friend of Robert Burns*, 227; "Preface" to *Lyrical Ballads*, 239

The Wordsworth Circle, 145, 161
Wordsworth-Coleridge Association, 344
Wordsworth-Coleridge Summer Conference, 183
Wordsworth Rydal Mount Trust, 344; Rydal Mount Summer School (1971), 344
Wrangham, Francis, 211

Ximenes Rare Books, 277

Yale University, 249; Beinecke Library, 5, 57; Yale University Press, 40, 129
Yeats, William Butler (WBY), 108, 115, 360, 362, 367; and optimistic Gothic mode, 345-46, 347, 362
—**Works**: "Byzantium," 362; "The Circus Animals' Desertion," 324, 362; "The Gyres," 362; "Lapis Lazuli," 258, 362; "Mad as the Mist and Snow," 324, 363; "The Second Coming," 362
Young, Edward, 121, 163

Zillman, Lawrence John, 5, 18, 25, 26, 28, 33-40, 116, 117, 123, 280, 292, 369; editorial principles, 35; edits *Prometheus Unbound*, 25, 26, 28, 33-40, 123 & n; *The Complete Known Drafts*, 34-35; *The Texts & the Drafts* (1968), 25n, 34-40; *A Variorum Edition* (1959), 25n, 33
Zodiac of Dendera, 281
Zoroaster, Zoroastrian, 281